NORTH CAROLINA HISTORY
TOLD BY CONTEMPORARIES

NORTH CAROLINA HISTORY

TOLD BY CONTEMPORARIES

EDITED BY

HUGH TALMAGE LEFLER

KENAN PROFESSOR OF HISTORY
THE UNIVERSITY OF NORTH CAROLINA

CHAPEL HILL

THE UNIVERSITY OF NORTH CAROLINA PRESS

To

My Wife

Ida Pinner Lefler

PREFACE

This volume, *North Carolina History Told by Contemporaries*, is designed to meet a practical need in the teaching and study of North Carolina history. It has been prepared in response to requests made by teachers and students for a source book in the history of the state. It may be used as a supplementary text for either high school or college courses.

The author has attempted to compile and edit a large number of contemporary accounts illustrating the political, social, and economic development of North Carolina from colonial beginnings to the present day. An effort has been made to show the relation of the state to United States history. In order to do this it has been deemed necessary to reproduce constitutions, laws, legislative documents, messages and speeches of governors, resolutions, reports, travel accounts, newspaper editorials, magazine articles, letters, diaries, and other historical sources. In controversial matters, such as the Mecklenburg Declaration and the Mecklenburg Resolves, both sides are presented.

Some documents have been reproduced in full; others have been condensed by the omission of unimportant provisions; and in some cases only a few pertinent extracts have been quoted. No changes have been made in the original spelling, capitalization, and punctuation of quotations. In the arrangement of chapters and sections the chronological method of organization has been followed. Teachers, pupils and general readers will find the Table of Contents, Select Bibliography, and Index helpful guides in using this volume.

My sincere thanks are extended to my colleagues, R. D. W. Connor, A. R. Newsome, and Fletcher M. Green for valuable suggestions; to the late W. K. Boyd of Duke University and the late John Livingstone of the North Carolina Supreme Court Library for helpful advice; to authors and publishers severally mentioned in the footnotes; to Charles Scribner's Sons, Yale University Press, Henry Holt and Company, The University of North Carolina Press, and *The Saturday Evening Post* for permission to use certain copyrighted materials.

In this, the fourth edition, I have extended the story to 1965 by the inclusion of additional selected documents relating to the economic, social, educational, political, and military history of North Carolina in recent years.

HUGH TALMAGE LEFLER

Chapel Hill, North Carolina
June, 1965

TABLE OF CONTENTS

III. TRANSITION FROM COLONY TO STATEHOOD

IV. The Independent State

V. Education in North Carolina to 1860

VI. Social and Economic Problems of Ante-Bellum Days

VII. ANTE-BELLUM ECONOMIC DEVELOPMENT

VIII. THE NEGRO IN NORTH CAROLINA PRIOR TO 1860

IX. Four Years of Strife: The Civil War

X. The Tragic Years of Reconstruction

XI. REBUILDING

XII. THE DAWN OF A NEW ERA

XIII. NORTH CAROLINA IN RECENT YEARS

I

THE FOUNDING OF NORTH CAROLINA

1. A Voyage Along the Atlantic Coast, 1524

One of the first Europeans to explore and describe the coast of what is now North Carolina was Iohn de Verrazzano, an Italian navigator in the service of France. In the spring of 1524 he made some explorations along the lower Cape Fear and on July 8 of that year sent to King Francis I "the earliest description known to exist of the shores of the United States." This report was published in Hakluyt's *Divers Voyages*, in 1582, and probably influenced Walter Raleigh in the formulation of his plans for the establishment of an English colony in the New World. France made no serious efforts to colonize the territory thus discovered, and it fell to England's lot to plant the first permanent colonies in that region.

THE 17. of Ianuary the yeere 1524 . . . we departed from the . . . isle of Madera, . . . with 50. men, with victuals, weapons, and other ship-munition very well prouided & furnished for 8. moneths : . . . and the 20. of Februarie we were ouertaken with as sharpe and terrible a tempest as euer any saylers suffered : . . . And in other 25. dayes we made aboue 400. leagues more, where we dis-couered a new land, neuer before seene of any man either ancient or moderne, and at the first sight it seemed somewhat low, but being within a quarter of a league of it, we perceiued by the great fires that we saw by the Sea coast, that it was inhabited : and saw that the land stretched to the Southwards. . . . At length being in despaire to finde any Port, wee cast anchor vpon the coast, and sent our Boate to shore, where we saw great store of people which came to the Sea side; and seeing vs approach, they fled away, and sometimes would stand still and looke backe, beholding vs with great admiration : but afterwards being animated and assured with signes that we made them, some of them came hard to the Sea side, seeming to reioyce very much at the sight of vs, and marueil-ing greatly at our apparel, shape and whitenesse, shewed vs by sundry signes where wee might most commodiously come aland with our Boat, offering vs also of their victuals to eate. . . . These people goe altogether naked, except only that they cover their priuie parts with certaine skins of beasts. . . . Some of them wear garlands of byrdes feathers. The people are of colour russet, . . . their hayre blacke, thicke and not very long, which they tye together in a knot behind and weare it like a little taile. They are well featured in their limbes, of meane stature, and commonly somewhat bigger than we : broad breasted, strong armed, their legs and other parts of their bodies well fashioned, and they are disfigured in nothing. . . . We could not learne of this people their maner of liuing, nor their particular customs, by reason of the short abode we made on the shore, . . . The shoare is all couered with small sand, and so ascendeth vpwards for the space of 15. foote, rising in forme of little hils about 50. paces broad. . . . And beyond this we saw the open Countrey rising in height aboue the sandie shore with many faire fields and plains, full of mightie great woods, some very thicke, and some thinne, replenished with diuers sorts of trees, as pleasant and delectable to behold, as is possible to imagine. . . . But they are full of Palme trees, Bay trees, and high Cypresse trees, and many other sortes of trees unknowen in Europe, . . . And the land is full of many beastes, as Stags, Deere and Hares, . . . with great plentie of Fowles, conuenient for all kind of pleasant game. This land is in latitude 34. degrees, with good and wholesome ayre, temperate, betweene hot and colde, no vehement windes do blowe in those Regions, . . . The Sea is calme, not boysterous, the waues gentle : and although all the shore be somewhat sholde and without harborough, yet it is not dangerous to the saylers . . .

Departing from hence, following the shore which trended somewhat toward the North, in 50. leagues space we came to another land which showed much more faire and ful of woods, . . . We found those folks to be more white then those that we found before, being clad with certaine leaues that hang on boughs of trees, which they sewe together with threads of wilde hempe. . . . We saw many of their boats made of one tree 20. foote long, and 4. foote broade, which are not made with yron or stone, or any other kind of metall . . . they helpe themselues with fire, burning so much of the tree as is sufficient for the hollownesse of the boat. . . .

We saw in this Countrey many Vines growing naturally, . . . which if by husbandmen they were dressed in good order, without all doubt they would yeeld excellent wines. . . .

We found also roses, violets, lilies, and many sorts of herbes, and sweete and odoriferous flowers different from ours. . . .

Hauing made our aboade three dayes in this country, and ryding on the coast for want of harboroughs, we concluded to depart from thence.—Iohn de Verrazzano, in Richard Hakluyt, *Collection of the Early Voyages, Travels, and Discoveries of the English Nation*, III, 357-60.

2. WALTER RALEGH'S PATENT, 1584

The first attempt to plant an English colony in what is now the United States was made by Walter Ralegh, better known as Sir Walter Raleigh. His efforts to establish a colony on the coast of North Carolina failed, but "the idea remained," and he may be justly called "the author of the English colonizing movement." Raleigh's first attempt to colonize was made in coöperation with his half-brother, Sir Humphrey Gilbert. Apparently Gilbert took the initiative. In 1577, Queen Elizabeth received an anonymous letter, supposedly written by Gilbert, asking for permission to lead an expedition to America. He said that if the queen would "resolve" to do this, he would destroy the Spanish fishing fleets, "take the West Indies from Spain," seize "the gold and silver mines" in the Spanish colonies, and make Elizabeth "monarch of the seas." In June, 1578, Gilbert received a patent, and in the fall of that year he and Raleigh sailed for America. They were forced back by Spanish ships, however. In 1583, Gilbert sailed without Raleigh. He never returned from this voyage.

On March 25, 1584, Gilbert's patent was renewed in the name of Walter Raleigh. He was given authority to establish colonies and to govern them. The settlers were to have "all the priviledges of free Denizens, and persons native of England." No laws could be passed repugnant to the laws of England.

ELIZABETH by the grace of God of England, ... Know ye that . . . we haue giuen and graunted, and . . . doe giue and graunt to our trusty and welbeloued seruant Walter Ralegh Esquire, and to his heires and assignes for euer, free liberty & licence from time to time, and at all times for euer hereafter, to discouer, search, finde out, and view such remote, heathen and barbarous lands, contreis, and territories, not actually possessed of any Christian prince, nor inhabited by Christian people, . . . and the same to haue, holde, occupy & enjoy to him, his heires and assignes for euer, with all prerogatiues, commodities, iurisdictiōs, royalties, priviledges, franchises and preeminences. . . .

And moreouer, we do . . . giue and grant licence to the said Walter Ralegh, . . . that he, and they, . . . shall and may . . . for his and their defence, encounter and expulse, repell and resist . . . all and euery such person and persons whatsouer, as without the especial liking and licence of the sayd Walter Ralegh, . . . shall attempt to inhabit within the sayde Countreys, or any of them, or within the space of two hundredth leagues neere to the place or places within such Countreys. . . . And wee do graunt to the sayd Walter Ralegh, his heires and assignes, and to all, and euery of them, . . . being of our allegiance, . . . that with the assent of the sayd Walter Ralegh, his heires or assignes, . . . that they, and euery or any of them, being eyther borne within our sayde Realmes of England or Ireland, or in any other place within our allegiance, . . . shall and may have all the priuiledges of free Denizens, and persons native of England, and within our allegiance in such like ample maner and forme, as if they were borne and personally resident within our said Realme of England, any law, custome, or vsage to the contrary notwithstanding. . . .

. . . wee . . . doe giue & grant to the said Walter Ralegh, his heires and assignes for euer, that he and they, . . . shall and may . . . have full and meere power and authoritie to correct, punish, pardone, gouerne, and rule by their and euery or any of their good discretions and policies, as well in causes capitall or criminal, as ciuil, . . . all such our subjects as shal from time to time aduenture themselves in the said iourneis . . . or that shall inhabite any such lands . . . within 200. leagues of any of the sayde place or places, where the sayd Walter Ralegh . . . shall inhabite. . . . — Richard Hakluyt, *Collection of the Early Voyages, Travels, and Discoveries of the English Nation*, III, 297-301.

3.   FIRST VOYAGE TO VIRGINIA, 1584

On March 25, 1584, Walter Raleigh was given "free liberty and license . . . to discover, search, finde out, and view such remote, heathen, and barbarous lands, contreis, and territories, not actually possessed of any Christian prince, nor inhabited by Christian people." Within a month he prepared an expedition, which was led by Philip Amadas and Arthur Barlowe. They were instructed to explore the country and to decide upon a site for future settlements. They touched the coast at Wocokon (Ocracoke) at the entrance of Pamlico Sound, and then landed on Roanoak Island. The following document is an account of "the first voyage made to the coasts of America, with two barks, wherein were Captaines M. Philip Amadas, and M. Arthur Barlowe, who discovered part of the country now called Virginia, Anno. 1584. Written by one of the said Captaines, and sent to Sir Walter Ralegh, knight, at whose charge and direction, the said voyage was set forth."

THE 27 day of Aprill, in the yeere of our redemption, 1584 we departed the West of England, with two barkes well furnished with men and victuals. . . .

The second of Iuly, we found shole water wher we smelt so sweet, and so strong a smel, as if we had bene in the midst of some delicate garden abounding with all kinde of odoriferous flowers, by which we were assured, that the land could not be farre distant : and keeping good watch, and bearing but slacke saile, the fourth of the same moneth we arriued vpon the coast, which we supposed to be a continent and firme lande, and we sayled along the same a hundred and twentie English miles before we could finde any entrance, or riuer issuing into the Sea. The first that appeared vnto vs, we entred, though not without some difficultie, & cast anker . . . and after thanks giuen to God for our safe arriual thither, we manned our boats, and went to view the land next adjoyning, and to take possession of the same, in the right of the Queenes most excellent Maiestie, as rightfull Queene, and Princesse of the same, . . . Which being performed, according to the ceremonies vsed in such enterprises, we viewed the land about vs, being, whereas, we first landed, very sandie and low towards the waters side, but so full of grapes, as the very beating and surge of the Sea ouerflowed them, . . .

This lande lay stretching it selfe to the West, which after wee found to bee but an Island of twentie miles long, and not aboue sixe miles broade. . . .

This Island had many goodly woodes full of Deere, Conies, Hares, and Fowle, euen in the middest of Summer in incredible abundance. The woodes are not such as you finde in Bohemia, Moscouia, or Hercynia, barren and fruitles, but the highest and reddest Cedars in the world, . . . Pynes, Cypres, Sassaphras, . . . and many other of excellent smell and qualitie. We remained by the side of this Island two whole days before we saw any people of the Countrey : the third day we espied one small boate rowing towardes vs, hauing in it three persons : this boat came to the Island side, four harquebuz-shot from our shippes, and there two of the people remaining, the third came along the shoreside towarde vs, and wee being then all within boord, he walked vp and down vpon the point of the land next vnto vs. . . .

The King [of the Indians] is greatly obeyed, and his brothers and children reuerenced. . . .

A day or two after this, we fell to trading with them, exchanging some things that we had, for Chamoys, Buffe, and Deere skinnes : when we shewed him all our packet of merchandize, of all things that he sawe, a bright tinne dish most pleased him, which hee presently tooke up and clapt it before his breast, and after made a hole in the

brimme thereof and hung it about his necke, making signs that it
would defend him against his enemies arrowes : . . . We exchanged
our tinne dish for twentie skinnes, . . . and a copper kettle for fifty
skinnes woorth fifty Crownes. . . .

Tneir boates are made of one tree, either of Pine, or of Pitch trees :
a wood not commonly knowen to our people, nor found growing
in England. They haue no edge-tooles to make them withall : if they
haue any they are very few, and those it seems they had twentie
yeres since, which, . . . was out of a wrake which happened vpon
their coast of some Christian ship, . . . The manner of making
their boates is thus : they burne downe some great tree, or take such
as are winde fallen, and putting gumme and rosen vpon one side
thereof, they set fire into it, and when it hath burnt it hollow, they
cut out the coale with their shels, and euer where they would burne
it deeper or wider they lay on gummes, which burne away the timber, and by this meanes they fashion very fine boates, and such as
will transport twentie men. Their oares are like scoopes, and many
times they set with long poles, as the depth serueth. . . .

The soile is the most plentiful, sweete, fruitfull and wholsome of
all the worlde : there are aboue fourteene seuerall sweete smelling
timber trees, and the most part of their vnderwoods are Bayes, and
such like : they haue those Okes that we haue, but farre greater and
better . . . and the euening following, wee came to an Island,
which they call Raonoak, distant from the harbor by which we entred, seuen leagues ; and at North end thereof was a village of nine
houses, built of Cedar, and fortified round about with sharpe trees,
to keepe out their enemies, and the entrance into it made like a
turne pike very artificially. . . .

Beyond this Island called Roanoak, are maine Islands very plentifull of fruits and other naturall increases together with many townes,
and villages, along the side of the continent. . . .

We brought home also two of the Sauages being lustie men,
whose names were Wanchese and Manteo.—Arthur Barlowe, in
Richard Hakluyt, *Collection of the Early Voyages, Travels, and Discoveries of the English Nation*, III, 301-6.

4. THE LOST COLONY

In April, 1587, Sir Walter Raleigh, "intending to persevere in the
planting of his Countrey of Virginia," sent out a colony headed by John
White, "whom he appointed Governor." By August of that year supplies
had begun to run low and "the whole company both of the Assistants
and planters came to the Governor, and with one voice requested him

to return himselfe into England, for the better and sooner obtaining of supplies, and other necessaries for them." White did not desire to leave the colony, but he was finally "constrayned to returne into England," and sailed from Roanoke Island about August 27, 1587. Due to the war with Spain, he was unable to return to America for several years. When he finally returned, in 1591, he was unable to locate the colony. Just before his departure for England they had told him of their intention to move some distance into the interior—probably about fifty miles.

The fate of the Lost Colony has been a favorite subject for speculation. Some writers have maintained that they mingled with the Indians, and that the so-called Croatans of Robeson County are their descendants. The early Virginia historians, Smith and Strachey, heard that the colonists of 1587 were still alive in 1607. John Lederer heard of them in 1670 and made note of their beards, which were not worn by full-blooded Indians. Rev. John Blair mentioned them in 1704. John Lawson met some Hatteras (Croatan?) Indians about 1709, who told him that "several of their ancestors were white people."

The Croatans of today claim descent from the Lost Colony. "Their names are in some cases the same as those of the original colonists, and their language is the English of three centuries ago. They do not have any Indian names or words. Their habits, disposition, and mental characteristics show traces both of savage and civilized ancestry."

Dr. John R. Swanton, ethnologist of the Smithsonian Institution, says that there is no reason to believe that the so-called Croatans have any connection with the Lost Colony. From a study based on early documents, maps, tribal connections, and language, he has concluded that they are closely related to the Cheraws, a Siouan tribe first encountered in South Carolina by De Soto in 1540. He also says that the "Croatans" were only one of many "lost races" scattered throughout the East and South, all predominantly of Indian origin, but with strong admixtures of other racial stocks.

EXTRACTS FROM JOHN WHITE'S NARRATIVE, 1591

THE 15 of August towards Euening we came to an anker at Hatorask, in 36 degr. and one third, in fiue fadom water, three leagues from the shore. At our first coming to anker on this shore we saw a great smoke rise in the Ile Raonoak neere the place where I left our Colony in the yeere 1587, which smoake put vs in good hope that some of the Colony were there expecting my returne out of England.

. . . Being thus wearied with this iourney, we returned to the harbour where we left our boates, who in our absence had brought their caske a shore for fresh water, so we deferred our going to Roanoak vntill the next morning, and caused some of those saylers to digge in those sandie hills for fresh water, whereof we found very sufficient. That night we returned aboord with our boates and our whole company in safety.

The next morning . . . our boates and company were prepared againe to goe vp to Roanoak, . . . The Admirals boat first passed the breach but not without some danger of sinking, . . . for at this time the winde blue at Northeast and direct into the harbour so great a gale, that the Sea brake extremely on the barre and the tide went very forcibly at the entrance. . . . There were a 11 in all, & 7 of the chiefest were drowned, . . . Our boates and all things fitted againe, we put off from Hatorask, being the number of 19 persons in both boates: but before we could get to the place where our planters were left, it was so exceeding darke that we ouershot the place a quarter of a mile: there we espied towards the North end of the Iland, ye light of a great fire thorow the woods, to the which we presently rowed: when we came right ouer against it, we let fall our Grapnel neere the shore, & sounded with a trumpet a Call, & afterwards many familiar English tunes of songs, and called to them friendly; but we had no answere, we therefore landed at day-breake, and coming to the fire, we found the grasse & sundry rotten trees burning about the place. From hence, we went thorow the woods to that part of the Island ouer against Dasamongwepeuk, & from thence we returned by the water side, round about the North point of the Iland vntil we came to the place where I left our Colony in the yeere 1586. In all this way we saw in the sand the print of Saluages feet of 2 or 3 sorts trodden ye night, and as we entered vpon the sandy banke vpon a tree, in the very browe thereof, were curiously carued these faire Romane letters CRO: which letters presently we knew to signifie the place, where I should find the planters seated, according to a secret token agreed vpon betweene them & me at my last departure frō them, which was, that in any wayes they should not faile to write or carue on the tree or posts of the dores the name of the place where they should be seated; for at my coming alway they were prepared to remoue from Roanoak 50 miles into the maine. Therefore at my departure from them in Ann. 1587 I willed them, that if they should happen to be distressed in any of those places, that then they should carue ouer the letters or name, a Crosse + in this forme, but we found no such signe of distresse. And hauing well considered of this, we passed toward the place where they were left in sundry houses, but we found the houses taken downe and the place very strongly enclosed, with a high palisado of great trees, with cortynes and flankers very Fort-like, and one of the chiefe trees or posts at the right side of the entrance had the barke taken off, and 5 foote from the ground in fayre Capitall letters was grauen CROATOAN without any crosse or signe of distresse; this done, we entered into the palisado, where we found many barres of Iron, two pigges of lead, foure yron fowlers; Iron sacker-shotte, and such like heauie things throwen here and there, almost ouergrowen with grasse and weedes. From thence, wee went along the water side, towards the poynt of the Creeke to see if we could find any of their botes or Pinnesse, but we could perceiue no signe of them nor any of the last Falkons and small Ordinance which were left with them at my departure from them. —John White, in Richard Hakluyt, *Collection of the Early Voyages, Travels, and Discoveries of the English Nation,* III, 353-55.

JOHN LAWSON'S ACCOUNT OF THE HATTERAS INDIANS, 1709

The firſt Diſcovery and Settlement of this Country was by the Procurement of Sir *Walter Raleigh,* in Conjunction with ſome publick-ſpirited Gentlemen of that Age, under the Protection of Queen *Elizabeth;* for which Reaſon it was then named *Virginia,* being begun on that Part called Ronoak-Iſland, where the Ruins of a Fort are to be ſeen at this day. . . .

A farther Confirmation of this we have from the *Hatteras Indians,* who either then lived on Ronoak-Iſland or much frequented it. Theſe tell us, that ſeveral of their Anceſtors were white People, and could talk in a Book, as we do; the Truth of which is confirm'd by gray Eyes being found frequently amongſt these *Indians,* and no others. They value themſelves extremely for their Affinity to the *English,* and are ready to do them all friendly Offices. It is probable, that this Settlement miſcarry'd for want of timely Supplies from *England;* or thro' the Treachery of the Natives, for we may reaſonably ſuppoſe that the *Engliſh* were forced to cohabit with them, for Relief and Conversation; and that in proceſs of Time, they conform'd themſelves to the Manners of their *Indian* relations.—*A New Voyage to Carolina,* p. 62.

5. GRANT OF CAROLINA TO SIR ROBERT HEATH, OCTOBER 30, 1629

The region which was later called Carolina was a part of the original Virginia grant of 1606. The Virginia colony, however, did not make any serious attempts to settle this section. So when Virginia became a royal

colony in 1624, the territory later known as Carolina became subject to
the Crown's disposal. As early as February, 1622, John Pory, "Secretarie
of Virginia trauelled to the South River Chawonock some sixtie miles
ouer land which he found to be a uery fruitful and pleasant Country
yielding two haruests in a yeere." Within a few years this section was
beginning to attract attention in England.

By a patent dated October 30, 1629, Charles I conveyed to his attorney-general, Sir Robert Heath, the region south of Virginia, between
31° and 36° north latitude, "To have exercise use & enjoy in like manner as any Bishop of Durham within the Bishopric or County palatine
of Durham in our kingdome of England ever heretofore had held used
or ehjoyed or of right ought or could have hold use or enjoy."

When the British government made a proprietary grant it was not in-
venting something new. It was simply using a form of government which
had been in existence in the English county of Durham for centuries.

CHARLES by the grace of God of England Scotland France & Ireland King Defender of the faith &c : To all to whom these present
l res shall come, greeting we have seen the inrolement of certaine
of our l res patents under our great seale of England made to Sr
Robert Heath Knight our Atturney Generall, bearing date at West-
minster the 30. day of October in the 5 yeare of our reigne & in-
rolled in our Court of Chancery, & remaining upon Record among
the Roles of the Said Court in these words : The king to all to whom
these present &c : greeting. Whereas our beloved and faithfull subject and servant Sr Robert Heath Knight our Atturney Generall,
kindled with a certaine laudable and pious desire as well of enlarging the Christian religion as our Empire & encreasing the Trade &
Commerce of this our kingdom : A certaine Region or Territory to
bee hereafter described, in our lands in the parts of America betwixt one & thirty & 36 degrees of northerne latitude inclusively
placed (yet hitherto untild, neither inhabited by ours or the subjects of any other Christian king, Prince or state But in some parts
of it inhabited by certaine Barbarous men who have not any knowledge of the Divine Dietye) He being about to lead thither a Colonye
of men large & plentifull, professing the true religion ; sedulously &
industriously applying themselves to the culture of the sayd lands &
to merchandising to be performed by industry & at his owne charges
& others by his example. And in this his purpose in this affayre for
our service and honour he hath given us full satisfaction, which
purpose of his beeing soe laudable & manifestly tending to our
honour, & the profitt of our kingdome of England Wee with a Royal
regard considering these things doe thinke meete to approve &

prosecute them, for which end the sayd Sr Robert Heath hath humbly supplicated that all that Region with the Isles thereunto belonging with certaine sorts of priveledges & jurisdictions for the wholesome government of his Colonye & Region aforesaid & for the estate of the appurtenances may be given granted and confirmed to him, his heires & Assignes by our Royall Highnesse.

Know therefore that we . . . doe give, grant & confirme all that River or Rivelett of St Matthew on the South side & all that River or Rivelett of the great passe on the North side, & all the lands Tenements & Hereditaments lying, beeing & extending within or between the sayd Rivers by that draught or Tract to the Ocean upon the east side & soe to the west & soe fare as the Continent extends itselfe with all & every their appurtenances & alsoe all those our Islands . . . which lye inclusively within the degrees of 31 & 36 of Northerne latitude; And all & singular the ports & stations of shippes & the Creeks of the sea belonging to the Rivers, Islands & lands aforesaid ; with the fishings of all sorts of fish, whales, sturgeons & of other Royaltyes in the sea or in the rivers moreover all veines, mines or pits either upon or conceald of Gold, Silver Jewells & precious stones & all other things whatsoever, whither of stones or metalls or any other thing or matter found or to be found in the Region Territory Isles or limits aforesaid. . . .

Know that we . . . doe erect & incorporate them into a province & name the same Carolina or the Province of Carolina . . . Furthermore know yee that we . . . doe give power to the said Sr Robert . . . to forme make & enact & publish . . . what lawes soever may concerne the publicke state of the said province or the private profitt of all according to the wholesome directions of & with the counsell assent & approbation of the Freeholders of the same Province. . . .

Furthermore least the way to Honours & Dignityes may seem to be shutt . . . doe for ourselves our heires & successors give full & free power to the foresayd Sr Robert Heath . . . to confere favours graces & honors upon those well deserveing citizens that inhabit within the foresayd province & the same with whatever Titles and dignityes (provided they be not the same as are now used in England) to adorne at his pleasure alsoe to erect villages into Borowes & Borowes into Cittyes for the meritts of the inhabitants and conveniency of the places. . . . —*Colonial Records of North Carolina*, I, 5-11.

91595

6. EXPLORATIONS OF CAROLINA FROM VIRGINIA: THE DISCOVERY OF NEW BRITTAINE, 1650

Sir Robert Heath did not attempt to settle his Carolina grant. Between 1629, the date of his patent, and 1663, a number of expeditions were made from Virginia into the Carolina country. Some of these explorers and fur traders left accounts of their observations. In 1651 an interesting pamphlet was published in London describing an expedition made into Carolina by Edward Bland and others.

Bland was a Virginia merchant interested in the Indian trade. He believed that the settlement of "Virginia's Confines" and the conversion of the Indians would be beneficial to the merchants of Virginia. Accordingly, he and his business friends asked the Virginia Assembly for permission to make settlements "to the southward." The petition was granted on condition that Bland and his associates would "secure themselves with a hundred able men sufficiently furnished with Armes and Munition." To promote the settlement of their grant they published a pamphlet describing "New Brittaine," as they called the country.

TO THE READER

Who ever thou art that desirest the Advancement of Gods glory by conversion of the Indians, the Augmentation of the English Common-wealth, in extending its liberties; I would advise thee to consider the present benefit and future profits that will arise in the wel setling Virginia's Confines, especially that happy Country of New Brittaine, in the Latitude of 35. and 37. degrees, of more temperate Clymate then that the English now inhabit, abounding with great Rivers of long extent, and encompassing a great part, or most of Virginia's Continent; a place so easie to be settled in, in regard that Horse and Cattle in foure or five dayes may be conveyed for the benefit of Undertakers, and all inconveniences avoyded which commonly attend New Plantations, being supplied with necessaries from the Neighbourhood of Virginia.

That the Assembly of Virginia (as may be seene by their Order since my returne hereto procured) have conceived a hundred to be a sufficient force and competence for the establishment of that Country in which Tobacco will grow larger and more in quantity. Sugar Canes are supposed naturally to be there, or at least if implanted will undoubtedly flourish: For we brought with us thence extraordinary Canes of twenty-five foot long and six inches round; there is also a great store of fish, and the Inhabitants relate that there is plenty of Salt made to the sunne without art; Tobacco Pipes have been seene among these Indians tipt with Silver, and they weare Copper Plates about their necks : They have two Crops of Indian Corne yearely, whereas Virginia hath but one. What I write is what I have proved ; I cordially wish some more then private Spirits would take it into their consideration, so may it prove most advantagious to particular and publick ends ; for which so prayeth,

Your faithfull servant,

EDWARD BLAND

OCTOBER 20, 1650. BY THE ASSEMBLY [OF VIRGINIA]

It is Ordered by the Grand Assembly, that according to the Petition of Mr. Edward Bland, Merchant, that he the sayd Bland, or any other be permitted to discover and seate to the Southward in any convenient place where they discover ; and that according to his petition for furthering his Designes hee bee permitted to have correspondence with the Indians, and also receive the benevolence of the well-affected, and use all lawfull meanes for affecting thereof, provided that they secure themselves in effecting the sayd Designe with a hundred able men sufficiently furnished with Armes and Munition.

JOHN CORKES, Clerk

—*Narratives of Early Carolina, 1650-1708* (edited by A. S. Salley), pp. 6-7.

7. FRANCIS YEARDLEY'S NARRATIVE OF EXCURSIONS INTO CAROLINA, MAY 8, 1654

Francis Yeardley, author of the following letter, was the son of Sir George Yeardley, who was governor of Virginia three times between 1616 and 1627. The letter was addressed to John Farrar. It gives the usual glowing account of the region which was later called North Carolina.

SIR,

. . . yet the honour I bear you, for your fervent affections to this my native country, commands me in some measure to give you an account of what the Lord hath in short time brought to light, by the means of so weak a minister as myself; namely, an ample discovery of South Virginia or Carolina, the which we find a most fertile, gallant, rich soil, flourishing in all the abundance of nature, especially in the rich mulberry and vine, a serene air, and temperate clime, and experimentally rich in precious minerals ; and lastly, I may say, parallel with any place for rich land, and stately timber of all sorts; a place indeed unacquainted with our Virginia's nipping frosts, no winter, or very little cold to be found there. . . .

In the interim, whilst the house was building for the great emperor of Rhoanoke, he undertook with some of his Indians, to bring some of our men to the emperor of the Tuskarorawes, and to that purpose sent embassadors before, and with two of our company set forth and travelled within two days journey of the place, where at a hunting quarter the Tuskarorawes emperor, with 250 of his men, met our company, and received them courteously; and after some days spent, desired them to go to his chief town, where he told them was one Spaniard residing, who had been seven years with them, a man very rich, having about thirty in family, seven whereof are negroes; . . . yet the Tuskarorawe proferred him, if he would go, he would in three days journey bring him to a great salt sea, and to places where they had copper out of the ground, the art of refining which they have perfectly; for our people saw much amongst them, and some plates of a foot square. There was one Indian had two beads of gold in his ears, big as rounceval peas; and they said, there was much of that not far off. . . . The Tuskarorawe told them, the way to the sea was a plain road, much travelled for salt and copper; the salt is made by the sea itself, and some of it brought in to me. . . .

Sir, if you think good to acquaint the states with what is done by two Virginians born, you will honour our country. . . . I am lastly, Sir, a suitor to you, for some silk-worm eggs, and materials for the making of silk, and what other good fruits, or roots, or plants, may be proper for such a country. Above all, my desire is to the olive, some trees of which could we procure, would rejoice me; for wine we cannot want with industry.—*Narratives of Early Carolina, 1650-1708* (edited by A. S. Salley), pp. 23-29.

8. THE OLDEST RECORDED LAND GRANT IN NORTH CAROLINA, 1662

The earliest land grant in North Carolina of which we have a record was made by King Kilcocanen of the Yeopim Indians to George Durant, dated March 1, 1661 (1662), for a tract of land then called Wecocomicke, which was located on the Perquimans River and "Roneoke Sound." The tract is now known as Durant's Neck. Grants had been made prior to this, however, for the deed records that Kilcocanen had formerly sold land to Samuel Pricklove.

KNOW All men by these presents that I, Kilcacenen, King of Yeo-pim have for a valeiable consideration of satisfaction received with the consent of my people sold, and made over and to George Durant a Parcell of land lying and being on Roneoke Sound and on a River called by the name of Perquimans which. Issueth out of the North Side of the aforesaid Sound which Land at present bears the name of Wecocomicke, begining at a marked Oak Tree, which divides this land from land I formily sold to Saml Pricklove and extending westerly up the said Sound to a Point of Turning of the aforesaid Perquimans River and so up the eastward side of the said River to a creek called by the name of Awoseake, to-wit;—All the Land be-twixt the aforesaid Bounds of Samuel Pricklove and the said Creek; thence to the Head thereof. And thence through the Woods to the first Bounds.

To have and to hold the quiet possession of the same to him and his heirs forever, with All Rights and Priviledges thereunto forever from me or any Person or Persons whatsoever. As witness my hand this first day of March 1661.—

Test: THOS. WEAMOUTH
    CALEB CALLEWAY.

The mark of
KILCOCANEN
or KISTOTANEN
—*Colonial Records of North Carolina*, I, 19.
—*Records of Perquimans County*, Book A, no. 374.

9. THE PROPRIETARY CHARTER OF CAROLINA, MARCH 24/APRIL 3, 1662/3

As we have already observed, the region south of Virginia between 31 and 36 degrees north latitude was granted to Sir Robert Heath in 1629. He made no serious efforts to settle his grant, however. Meanwhile traders and settlers continued to come from Virginia into the Carolina country, and by 1660 certain English courtiers were beginning to take notice of this movement. In that year, Charles II was "restôred" to the throne of England, and within a few years this "merrie monarch" granted Carolina to eight of the most prominent men in England. Soon after the proprietary grant was made, the Heath claimants protested, maintain-ing that they had the prior rights to this territory. The dispute was re-ferred to the Privy Council, which was dominated by certain of the Proprietors. Accordingly, an order in council of August 22, 1663, de-clared the Heath patent void for non-use. "Claims under it continued to be urged until 1768, when the descendants of Daniel Coxe, of New

Jersey, to whom the patent had been transferred in 1696, received from the Crown a grant of 100,000 acres of land in New York in satisfaction of their claim."

The names of most of the eight Proprietors have been preserved in the names of counties, towns, rivers, sounds, and otherwise.

CHARLES THE SECOND, &c. . .

1ST. WHEREAS our right trusty, and right well beloved cousins and counsellors, Edward, Earl of Clarendon, our high chancellor of England, and George, Duke of Albemarle, master of our horse and captain general of all our forces, our right trusty and well beloved William Lord Craven, John Lord Berkeley, our right trusty and well beloved counsellor, Anthony Lord Ashley, chancellor of our exchequer, Sir George Carteret, knight and baronet, vice chamberlain of our household, and our trusty and well beloved, Sir William Berkeley, knight, and Sir John Colleton, knight and baronet, being excited with a laudable and pious zeal for the propagation of the Christian faith, and the enlargement of our empire and dominions, have humbly besought leave of us, by their industry and charge, to transport and make an ample colony of our subjects, natives of our kingdom of England, and elsewhere within our dominions, unto a certain country hereafter described, in the parts of America not yet cultivated or planted, and only inhabited by some barbarous people, who have no knowledge of Almighty God.

2D. . . . Know ye, therefore, that we, favoring the pious and noble purpose of the said Edward Earl of Clarendon, . . . [and others] . . . by this our present charter, . . . do give, grant, and confirm . . . all that territory or tract of ground, scituate, lying and being within our dominions of America, extending from the north end of the island called Lucke island, which lieth in the southern Virginia seas, and within six and thirty degrees of the northern latitude, and to the west as far as the south seas, and so southerly as far as the river St. Matthias, which bordereth upon the coast of Florida, and within one and thirty degrees of northern latitude, and so west in a direct line as far as the south seas aforesaid ; . . .

4th. To have, use, exercise and enjoy, and in as ample manner as any bishop of Durham in our kingdom of England, ever heretofore have held, used or enjoyed, . . . we do by these presents, . . . make, create and constitute the true and absolute Lords Proprietors of the country aforesaid, and of all other the premises ; saving always the faith, allegiance and sovereign dominion due to us, . . .

for the same, and saving also the right, title and interest of all and every our subjects of the English nation, which are now planted within the limits and bounds aforesaid, (if any be). . . . yielding and paying yearly to us, our heirs and successors, for the same, the yearly rent of twenty marks of lawful money of England, at the feast of All Saints, yearly forever, . . . and also the fourth part of all gold or silver ore, which, within the limits aforesaid, shall from time to time happen to be found.

5th. . . . Know ye, that we . . . do, . . . erect, incorporate and ordain the same into a Province, and call it the province of Carolina, . . . that we, . . . do grant full and absolute power by virtue of these presents to them . . . for the good and happy government of the said province, to ordain, make, enact, and under their seals to publish any laws whatsoever, either appertaining to the publick state of the said province, or to the private utility of particular persons, according to their best discretion, of and with the advice, assent and approbation of the freemen of the said province, or of the greater part of them, or of their delegates or deputies, whom for enacting of the said laws, when and often as need shall require, we will that the said Edward, Earl of Clarendon, . . . [and other proprietors], . . . shall from time to time assemble in such manner and form as to them shall seem best, and the same laws duly to execute upon all people within the said province and limits thereof, . . .

6th. And because such assemblies of freeholders cannot be so conveniently called, as there may be occasion to require the same, we do, therefore, . . . give and grant unto the said [proprietors] . . . full power and authority, from time to time to make and ordain fit and wholesome orders and ordinances, within the province . . . to be kept and observed as well for the keeping of the peace, as for the better government of the people there abiding, and to publish the said to all to whom it may concern; which ordinances, we do streightly charge and command to be inviolably observed within the said province, under the penalties therein expressed, so as such ordinances be reasonable, and not repugnant or contrary, but as near as may be, agreeable to the laws and statutes of . . . England, and so as the same ordinances do not extend to the binding, charging, or taking away of the right or interest of any person or persons, in their freehold, goods or chattels whatsoever. . . .

9th. . . . We . . . do give and grant unto the said [proprietors] . . . full and free license, liberty and authority, . . . as well to import, and bring into any of our dominions from the said province

2

of Carolina, or any part thereof, the several goods and commodities, hereinafter mentioned, that is to say, silk, wines, currants, raisins, capers, wax, almonds, oyl, and olives, without paying or answering to us, . . . any custom, import, or other duty, for and in respect thereof; for and during the term and space of seven years, . . . as also to export and carry out of any of our dominions, into the said province of Carolina, custom free, all sorts of tools which shall be usefull or necessary for the planters there, in the accommodation and improvement of the premises, . . .

13th. And because many persons born, or inhabiting in the said province for their deserts and services, may expect and be capable of marks of honour and favour, . . . we do . . . give and grant . . . full power and authority, to give and confer, unto and upon, such of the inhabitants of the said province, . . . such marks of favour and titles of honour as they shall think fit, so as these titles of honour be not the same as are enjoyed by, or conferred upon any the subjects of this our kingdom of England. . . .

18th. And because it may happen that some of the people . . . of the said province, cannot in their private opinions, conform to the publick exercise of religion, according to the liturgy, form and ceremonies of the church of England, or take and subscribe the oaths and articles, made and established in that behalf, and for that the same, by reason of the remote distances of these places, will, we hope, be no breach of the uniformity established in this nation, our will and pleasure therefore is, and we do . . . give and grant unto the . . . [proprietors], . . . full and free license, liberty and authority, by such legal ways and means as they shall think fit, to give and grant unto such person or persons, . . . who really in their judgments, and for conscience sake, cannot or shall not conform to the said liturgy and ceremonies, and take and subscribe the oaths and articles aforesaid, . . . such indulgences and dispensations in that behalf, . . . as they in their discretion think fit and reasonable; . . . —*Colonial Records of North Carolina*, I, 20-33.

10. THE CAROLINA CHARTER OF 1665

The boundaries of Carolina under the 1663 charter were not extensive enough to satisfy the Proprietors, and at their "humble request" a second charter was issued in 1665, which extended the boundaries one-half degree to the north and two degrees to the south. This was done largely to settle a dispute which had arisen over the Heath grant of 1629, and in order definitely to place the Albemarle settlements within the limits of

Carolina. The extension of the boundary northward led to a prolonged boundary controversy with Virginia.

Now know ye, That we, . . . are graciously pleased to enlarge our said grant unto them, according to the bounds and limits hereafter specified, . . . all that province, territory, or tract of ground, scit-uate, lying and being within our dominions of America aforesaid, extending north and eastward as far as the north end of Currituck river, or inlet, upon a strait westerly line to Wyonoak Creek, which lies within or about the degrees of thirtysix and thirty min-utes northern latitude; and so west in a direct line as far as the south seas, and south and westward, as far as the degrees of twenty-nine, inclusive, of northern latitude; and so west in a direct line, as far as the south seas; together with all and singular the ports, harbours, bays, rivers, and inlets, belonging unto the province or territoiy aforesaid; . . .

And that the province or territory hereby granted and described, may be dignified with as large tythes and privileges, as any other parts of our dominions and territories in that region: Know ye, That we, . . . do, . . . annex and unite the same to the said province of Carolina.—*Colonial Records of North Carolina*, I, 102-14.

11. ADVICE ON GRANTING LANDS, 1665

The following suggestions relative to land grants in Carolina were made by Thomas Woodward, who was official surveyor for the Lords Proprietors. They show the small value of lands in a new country and indicate the eagerness of the Proprietors to promote settlement. William Drummond was the "first governor of Albemarle."

I UNDERSTAND by Mr. Drummond and Mr. Carterett that you and the rest of the Right Honorable the Lords Proprietors of the Prov-ince of Carolina have appointed me to be Surveyor for your Countie of Albemarle . . . And though I know it befitts not me to dispute your comands . . . I cannot omit to performe another part of my dutie (so I am though unworthy) one of the counsell here to give you my opinion concerning some passages of the Instructions your Honore sent us. First for the bounds of the Countie of Albe-marle fortie miles square will not comprehend the Inhabitants there already seated. . . .

Next the Proportione of Land you have alloted with the Rent, and conditione are by most People not well resented and the Rumor

of them dis-courages many who had intentions to have removed
from Virginia hether : Whilst my Lord Baltamore allowed to every
Persons imported but fiftie acres, Maryland for many years had
scarce fiftie families, though there Rent was rather easier then in
Virginia ; but when he alloted one hundred Acres for a Person, it
soone began to People. and when he found them begin to increase,
he brought it to fiftie a head againe So if your Lordships please to
give large Incouragement for some time till the country be more
fully Peopled, your Honore may contract for the future upon what
condition you please But for the Present, To thenke that any men
will remove from Virginia upon harder Conditione then they can
live there will prove (I feare) a vaine Imagination, It bein Land
only that they come for. . . .

And it is my Opinion, . . . that it will for some time conduce
more to your Lordshipe Profit to permit men to take up what tracts
of Land they please at an easie rate, then to stint them to small proportions at a great rent, Provided it be according to the custome of
Virginia which is fifty Pole by the river side, and one mile into the
woods for every hundred acres ; there being no man that will have
any great desire to pay Rent . . . for more land than he hopes to
gaine by. Rich men (which Albemarle stands in much need of)
may perhaps take up great Tracts ; but then they will endeavor to
procure Tenants to helpe towards the payment of their Rent, and
will at their owne charge build howseing . . . to invite them : Besides to have some men of greater possessions in Land then others,
will conduce more to the well being and good Government of the
Place than any Levelling Paritie To reduce Planters into Townes,
is here almost impossible ; when the Country is Peopled and com-
erce increased it may more easily be effected, by appoynting Ports
and Marketts whether not only Merchants but all Tradesmen and
Artificers will resort for habitation, and in short time lay the foundation to superstructures of Townes and Citties ; Always Provided
there be a course taken for procuring a coine with out which no
Towne nor Markitt can well subsist : And this can no way be effected
but by the ballance of Trade : And therefore I doe most highly ap-
plaude your Lordshipe designe of making Wine in this Country :
. . . —Thomas Woodward, in *Colonial Records of North Carolina*, I,
99-100.

12. A BRIEF DESCRIPTION OF THE PROVINCE OF CAROLINA, 1666

The following account of Carolina was one of many pamphlets issued for the purpose of attracting settlers to develop the Proprietors' grant. It is believed that Robert Horne wrote it, although there is no absolute proof of his authorship. It described the soil, climate, and resources of the province and showed the privileges to be obtained by settling in Carolina.

CAROLINA is a fair and spacious Province on the Continent of America: so called in honour of His Sacred Majesty that now is, Charles the Second, . . . This Province lying so neer Virginia, and yet more Southward, enjoys the fertility and advantages thereof: and yet is so far distant, as to be freed from the inconstancy of the Weather, which is a great cause of the unhealthfulness thereof. . . .

In the midst of this fertile Province, in the Latitude of 34 degrees, there is a Colony of English seated, who Landed there the 29 of May. *Anno* 1664. and are in all about 800 persons, who have overcome all the difficulties that attend the first attempts, and have cleered the way for those that come after, who will find good houses to be in whilst their own are in building. . . .

If therefore any industrious and ingenious persons shall be willing to pertake of the Felicites of this Country, let them imbrace the first opportunity, that they may obtain the greater advantages. . . .

The chief of the Privileges are as follows.

First, There is full and free Liberty of Conscience granted to all, so that no man is to be molested or called in question for matters of Religious Concern; but every one to be obedient to the Civil Government, worshipping God after their own way.

Secondly, There is freedom from Custom, for all Wine, Silk, Raisins, Currance, Oyl, Olives, and Almonds, that shall be raised in the Province for 7. years, after 4 ton of any of those commodities shall be imported in one Bottom.

Thirdly, Every Free-man and Free-woman that transport themselves and Servants by the 25 of March next, being 1667, shall have for Himself, Wife, Children, and Men-servants, for each 100 Acres of Land for him and his Heirs for ever and for every Woman-servant and Slave 50 Acres, paying at most ½d. per acre, *per annum*, in lieu of all demands, to the Lords Proprietors: Provided always, That every Man be armed with a good Musquet full bore, 10 l.

powder, and 20 l. of Bullet, and six Months Provision for all, to serve them whilst they raise Provision in that Countrey.

Fourthly,. Every Man-Servant at the expiration of their time, is to have of the Country a 100 Acres of Land to him and his heirs for ever, paying only ½d. per acre, *per annum,* and the Women 50. Acres of Land on the same conditions; their Masters also are to allow them two Suits of Apparrel and Tools such as he is best able to work with, according to the Custom of the Countrey.

Fifthly, They are to have a Governour and Council appointed from among themselves, to see the Laws of the Assembly put in due execution; but the Governour is to rule but 3 years, and then learn to obey; also he hath no power to lay any tax, or make or abrogate any Law, without the Consent of the Colony in their Assembly.

Sixthly, They are to choose annually from among themselves, a certain Number of Men, according to their divisions, which constitute the General Assembly with the Governour and his Council, and have the sole power of Making Laws, and Laying taxes for the common good when need shall require. . . .

Is there therefore any younger Brother who is born of Gentile blood, and whose Spirit is elevated above the common sort, and yet the hard usage of our Country hath not allowed suitable fortune; he will not surely be afraid to leave his Native Soil to advance his Fortunes equal to his Blood and Spirit, and so he will avoid those unlawful ways too many of our young Gentlemen take to maintain themselves according to their high education, having but small Estates; here, with a few Servants and a small Stock a great Estate may be raised. . . .

If any Maid or single Woman have a desire to go over, they will think themselves in the Golden Age, when Men paid a Dowry for their Wives; for if they be but Civil, and under 50 years of Age, some honest Man or other will purchase them for their Wives.— Robert Horne (?), in *Narratives of Early Carolina, 1650-1708* (edited by A. S. Salley), pp. 65-73.

13. THE GREAT DEED OF GRANT, 1668

The first General Assembly in Albemarle convened in 1665. Probably the most important matter to come before it dealt with the terms of landholding offered by the Lords Proprietors. The Assembly drew up a petition to the Proprietors, stating that they were paying, in specie, a quit rent of one-half penny per acre, while in Virginia the quit rent was only one farthing per acre, payable in produce. On May 1, 1668, the

Lords Proprietors granted that the inhabitants of Albemarle should hold their lands upon the same terms and conditions as the people of Virginia. This document was considered so significant that it was called the Great Deed of Grant.

. . . WHEREAS we have received a petition from the Grand Assembly of the County of Albemarle praying that the Inhabitants of the said County may hold their Lands upon the same terms, and conditions that the Inhabitants of Virginia hold theirs. And for as much as the said County doth border upon Virginia, and is much of the same nature; we are content, and do grant, that the Inhabitants of said County do hold their lands of us the Lords Proprietors upon the same terms and conditions that the Inhabitants of Virginia hold theirs. . . . We have appointed to such persons as shall come into our said County to plant, or inhabit; To be held of us, our heirs and assigns upon the same terms, and Conditions that land is at this present usually granted in Virginia; anything in our Instructions and Concessions aforesaid, to the Contrary not withstanding. —*Colonial Records of North Carolina*, I, 175-76.

14. LEGISLATIVE EFFORTS TO PROMOTE THE SETTLEMENT OF CAROLINA, 1669

The Assembly of 1669 passed a number of laws designed to encourage immigration. New settlers were to be tax exempt for one year, and they were to be protected from suits for debts contracted outside the colony for five years after their arrival. Three acts were passed in an effort to check land speculation which might be unfair to settlers. One of these prohibited the transfer of land rights until after two years' residence in the colony; another opened to reëntry any partially improved land that had been abandoned by its owner for as long a period as three months; while the third prohibited settlers from holding more than 660 acres in any one tract, without the special permission of the Proprietors. "Strangers from other parts" were excluded from the Indian trade, unless they became settlers of Albemarle.

The passage of these measures, particularly the stay law, caused much criticism in Virginia. In spite of these liberal legislative offers, settlers came into Albemarle at a slow rate for many years.

AN ACT PROHIBITING SUEING OF ANY PERSON WITHIN 5. YEARES.

WHEREAS ther hath not binn sufficient Encouragement hitherto granted to persons transporting themselves and Estates into this County to plant or inhabit. For remedy whereof be it enacted by the Pallatine and Lords Proprietors by and with the advice and consent of this present grand Assembly and the authority thereof that noe person transporting themselves into this County after the date hereof shall be lyable to be sued during the terme and space of five yeares after their Arrival for any debt contracted or cause of action given without the County. . . .

AN ACT EXEMPTING NEW COMMERS FROM PAYING LEVYS FOR ONE YEARE.

Be it enacted . . . that any person or persons transporting themselves and Families into this County to plant and here seat themselves shall be exempted from paying levys for one whole yeare after their arrivall. . . .

AN ACT CONCERNING TRANSFERRING OF RIGHTS

There being divers persons who resort into this County and perhaps in a short time leave it againe yett neverthelesse whilst they are here, they make sale of their Rights to land which thing may prove very prejudiciall to our Lords Proprietors and to the speedy setlement of this County be it therefore enacted. . . . That noe person or persons whatsoever shall make sale of their Right or Rights to land untill he hath binn two compleate years at least an inhabitant in the County.

AN ACT WHAT LAND MEN SHALL HOULD IN ONE DEVIDEND.

Whereas there are divers men that have right to great tracts of land, and not nigh people enough to manure and people the same, by which means the Country will great part thereof lye unseated and unpeopled. . . . For prevention whereof it is therefore enacted, . . . that noe person or persons whatsoever he be within this County under the degree of a Proprietor, Landgrave or Cassique shall have Liberty for the space of five yeares next ensueing to survey or ley out above six hundred and sixty acres of Land in one devidend that soe the County may be the speedier seated. . . .

AN ACT FOR THE SPEEDIER SEATING OF LAND.

Whereas there are severall of the Inhabitants within this County that formerly did cleare some small quantity of Land and build some houses thereon which now have forsaken it espetially on South Lanchester side of the west of Chowan and other parts of the County And in as much as the said Land lyes voyd and unplanted which proves a hindrance to the Setlement of the County Be it therefore enacted. . . . That if any person or persons that have bestowed

any Labour . . . on any Land within the County shall not repaire
to it and seat the same within sixe months . . . that then it shall
and may be lawfull for the Governor and Councell to lett it out to
any other person to doe it The party to whom it is soe lett out paying
to the first labourer so much as it shall be adjudged by fower honest
men to be worth.

AN ACT PROHIBITING STRANGERS TRADING WITH THE INDIANS.

For as much as there is often recourse of Strangers from other
parts into this County to truck and trade with the Indians which is
conceived may prove very prejudiciall Wherefore be it enacted . . .
that if any person or persons . . . shall presume to come into this
County to truck or trade with any of our neighbouring Indians . . .
it shall bee lawfull for any person or persons to apprehend any such
persons or Forreigners that shall be found amongst the Indians . . .
and him or them bring before the Governor or any one of the Councell who shall hereby have power to comitt them to prison there to
abide till they have paid tenn thousand pounds of tobacco and caske
otherwise to stand to the censure of the Vice Pallatine and Councell
And it is further declared that whatsoever Trade is found with the
person apprehended One halfe thereof and one halfe of the fine shall
belong to the Apprehendor and the other halfe to the Lords Proprietors.—*Colonial Records of North Carolina*, I, 183-87.

15. THE FUNDAMENTAL CONSTITUTIONS OF CAROLINA, 1669

There was much uncertainty and confusion in the government of
Carolina during the first fifty years of its existence. Soon after the
granting of the 1663 charter, Sir William Berkeley, then governor of
Virginia, was instructed to set up a government in Albemarle. Two
years later the Concessions of 1665 were drawn up as a general plan of
government. The Concessions were unsatisfactory, and the Lords Proprietors requested Lord Ashley to prepare a permanent constitution for
Carolina. In 1669 John Locke, who was Ashley's secretary, drew up the
Fundamental Constitutions, which were adopted and signed by the
Lords Proprietors July 21, 1669. The purpose of this instrument of government, or Grand Model, as it was called, was to provide "for the better
settlement of the government of the said place, and establishing the interest of the Lords Proprietors with equality, and without confusion; and
that the government of this Province may be most agreeable to the Monarchy under which we live, and of which this Province is a part; and
that we may avoid erecting a numerous democracy."

The Fundamental Constitutions set up a cumbersome and complex
system of government which might have worked in Europe during the

days of feudalism, but which was not adapted to conditions in the colony. In spite of the fact that they were declared to be unalterable, the Fundamental Constitutions went through no less than five editions before they were completely abandoned. The fifth and last edition bore date of April 11, 1698. As late as 1702 the Lords Proprietors were still endeavoring to enforce them, however. As a whole, the Fundamental Constitutions were impractical; yet they contained some very desirable provisions, such as the registration of births, marriages, and deaths; the registration of land titles; biennial parliaments; trial by jury; and religious toleration. Professor Bassett said, "Their reactionary features were hardly worse than their generation, and their liberal features were much better than their time."

OUR sovereign Lord the King, having . . . granted unto us the Province of Carolina . . . for the better settlement of the government of the said place, and establishing the interest of the Lords Proprietors with equality, and without confusion; and that the government of this Province may be made most agreeable to the Monarchy under which we live, and of which this Province is a part; and that we may avoid erecting a numerous democracy: We, the Lords and proprietors of the Province aforesaid, have agreed to the following form of government, to be perpetually established amongst us. . . .

1st. The eldest of the Lords Proprietors shall be Palatine; and upon the decease of the Palatine the eldest of the seven surviving proprietors shall always succeed him.

2d. There shall be seven other chief officers erected, viz. the Admirals, Chamberlains, Chancellors, Constables, Chief Justices, High Stewards and Treasurers; which places shall be enjoyed by none but the Lords Proprietors. . . .

3d. The whole Province shall be divided into Counties; each county shall consist of eight signories, eight baronies and four precincts; each precinct shall consist of six colonies.

4th. Each signory, barony, and colony, shall consist of twelve thousand acres, the eight signories being the share of the eight proprietors, and the eight baronies of the nobility; . . . leaving the colonies, being three fifths, amongst the people; . . .

16th. In every signiory, barony, and manor, the respective Lord shall have power in his own name to hold court leet there, for trying of all causes, both civil and criminal. . . .

17th. Every manor shall consist of not less than three thousand acres, and not above twelve thousand acres, in one intire piece and colony. . . .

28th. There shall be eight supreme Courts. The first called the palatine's court, consisting of the Palatine and the other seven Proprietors. The other seven courts, of the other seven great officers, shall consist each of them of a Proprietor, and six counsellors added to him. Under each of these latter seven courts, shall be a college of twelve assistants. . . .

33d. The Palatine's court . . . shall have power to call Parliaments, to pardon all offences, to make election of all officers in the Proprietor's dispose, and to nominate and appoint port townes. . . .

35th. The chancellor's court, consisting of one of the Proprietors, and his six counsellors . . . shall have the custody of the seal of the Palatine, under which charters of lands or otherwise, commissions and grants of the Palatine's court, shall pass. . . .

38th. The Chief Justice's Court consisting of one of the proprietors and six counsellors . . . shall judge all appeals in cases both civil and criminal, except all such cases as shall be under the jurisdiction . . . of any other of the Proprietor's courts. . . .

39th. The Constable's Court . . . shall order and determine of all military affairs by land. . . .

41st. The Admiral's Court . . . shall have the care and inspection over all ports, moles, and navigable rivers so far as the tide flows, and over all the public shipping of Carolina. . . .

43d. The treasurer's court . . . shall take care of all matters that concern the public revenue and treasury. . . .

44th. The high Steward's Court . . . shall have the care of all foreign and domestic trade, manufactures, public buildings, work houses, highways . . . and all things in order to the public commerce and health. . . .

45th. The Chamberlain's Court . . . shall have care of all ceremonies, precedency, heraldry, reception of public messengers, pedigrees, the registry of all births, burials and marriages, legitimation, and all cases concerning matrimony . . . and shall also have power to regulate all fashions, habits, badges, games and sports. . . .

50th. The grand council shall consist of the Palatine and seven Proprietors, and the fortytwo Counsellors of the several Proprietor's Courts, who shall have power to determine any controversy that may arise between any of the Proprietor's Courts, about their respective jurisdictions. . . .

51st. The grand council shall prepare all matters to be proposed in Parliament. . . .

61st. In every county, there shall be a court consisting of a sheriff, and four Justices of the county, for every precinct, one. The Sheriff shall . . . have at least five hundred acres freehold within the said county; and the justices shall . . . have each of them five hundred acres apiece. . . .

68th. In the Precinct court, no man shall be a Juryman, under fifty acres of freehold. In the County court . . . under three hundred acres. . . . In the Proprietor's courts . . . under five hundred acres. . . .

69th. Every jury shall consist of twelve men; and it shall not be necessary they should all agree, but the verdict shall be according to the consent of the majority.

70th. It shall be a base and vile thing, to plead for money or reward; nor shall any one, (except he be a near kinsman . . .) be permitted to plead another man's cause, till before the judge, in open court, he hath taken an oath that he doth not plead for money or reward. . . .

79th. To avoid multiplicity of laws, which by degrees always change the right foundations of the original government, all acts of Parliament whatsoever . . . shall at the end of a hundred years after their enacting, respectively cease. . . .

84th. There shall be a Registry . . . wherein shall be recorded all the births, marriages and deaths that shall happen. . . .

95th. No man shall be permitted to be a freeman of Carolina, or to have any estate or habitation within it, that doth not acknowledge a God, and that God is publicly and solemnly to be worshipped. . . .

109th. No person whatsoever shall disturb, molest, or persecute another, for his speculative opinions in religion, or his way of worship.

110th. Every freeman of Carolina, shall have absolute power and authority over his negro slaves. . . .

111th. No cause, whether civil or criminal, of any freeman, shall be tried in any court of judicature, without a jury of his peers.

120th. These fundamental constitutions, in number a hundred and twenty, and every part thereof, shall be and remain, the sacred and unalterable form and rule of government of Carolina forever.
—*Colonial Records of North Carolina*, I, 187-206.

16. AN ACCOUNT OF THE PROVINCE OF CAROLINA, 1682

Samuel Wilson, who was secretary to the Lords Proprietors, has given one of the earliest descriptions of Carolina. His account shows the importance which the Proprietors attached to the Ashley River settlements. It is interesting to note that he referred to Carolina as "part of Florida."

CAROLINA, is that part of Florida, which lies between *twenty nine* and *thirty six* degrees, and *thirty* minutes of Northern Latitude; On the East it is washed with the Atlantic Ocean, and is bounded on the West by Mare Pacificum (or the South Sea) [Pacific Ocean] and within these bounds is contained the most healthy Fertile and pleasant part of Florida, which is so much commended by the Spanish authors. . . .

. . . the Lords Proprietors have power with the consent of the Inhabitants to make By-Laws for the better Government of the said Province : So that no Money can be raised or Law made, without the consent of the Inhabitants or their Representatives. They have also power to appoint and impower Governours, and other Magistrates to Grant Liberty of Conscience, make Constitutions &c. . . . With many other great Priviledges, . . . And the said Lords Proprietors have there setled a Constitution of Government, whereby is granted Liberty of Conscience, and wherein all possible care is taken for the equal Administration of Justice, and for the lasting Security of the Inhabitants both in their Persons and Estates.

By the care and endeavours of the said Lords Proprietors, and at their very great charge, two Colonys have been setled in this Province, the one at Albemarle in the most Northerly part, the other at Ashly-River. . . . Albemarle bordering upon Virginia, and only exceeding it in Health, Fertility, and Mildness of the Winter, is in the Growths, Productions, and other things much of the same nature with it. . . .

Ashly-River was first setled in April 1670 . . . they [the settlers] have been for divers years past, and are arrived to a very great Degree of Plenty of all sorts of Provisions. Insomuch, that most sorts are already cheaper there, than in any other of the English Collonys, and they are plentifully enough supplied with all things from England or other Parts . . . about an hundred Houses are there built, and more are Building daily by the Persons of all sorts that come there to Inhabit, from the more Northern English Collonys, and the Sugar Islands, England, and Ireland ; and many Persons who went to Carolina Servants, being Industrious since they came out of their times with their Masters, at whose charge they were Transported, have gotten good Stocks of Cattle, and Servants of their own ; have here also Built Houses, and exercise their Trades : And many that went thither in that condition, are now worth several Hundreds of Pounds, and live in a very plentiful condition, and their Estates are still encreasing. And land is become of that value near the Town (Charles Town), that it is sold for twenty Shillings

per Acre, though pillaged of all its valuable Timber, and not cleared
of the rest, and Land that is clear'd and fitted for Planting, and
Fenced, is let for ten Shillings per annum the Acre, though twenty
miles distant from the Town. . . .

At this Town, in November 1680. There Rode at one time sixteen
Sail of Vessels (some of which were upwards of 200 Tuns) that came
from divers parts of the Kings Dominions to trade there, which
great concourse of shipping, will undoubtedly in a short time make
it a considerable Town.—Samuel Wilson, *An Account of the Province
of Carolina, in America* (London, 1682), in *Historical Collections of South
Carolina* (edited by R. B. Carroll), II, 22-24.

17. NORTH CAROLINA BECOMES A ROYAL COLONY, 1729

Proprietary rule in Carolina was not satisfactory to the British government or to the settlers. As early as 1686 an unsuccessful effort was made
to transfer the colony to the Crown. For the next forty years British officials and agents "carried on a propaganda against the proprietary colonies with the design of bringing them under the direct government of
the Crown."

Many accusations were brought against the proprietary government
of Carolina. It had failed to enforce the navigation laws, had passed
laws "contrary and repugnant to the Laws of England and directly prejudicial to Trade," had encouraged piracy and smuggling, had debased
the currency, had promoted manufactures, and had neglected their
defenses.

In January, 1728, some of the Lords Proprietors drew up a memorial
offering to surrender their interests. An agreement was reached and an
act of Parliament was passed to carry it into effect. By the agreement,
each of seven shares was to be purchased for £2,500, being £17,500 in
all. Lord Granville (Carteret) did not sell his share. The King also allowed the seven Proprietors a lump sum of £5,000 to satisfy their claims
for quit rents due them.

The purchase of Carolina by the Crown seemed to please many of the
North Carolinians. The Council wrote the King, "As it is with the great-
est Pleasure we receive the Notice of Your Majesty's having taken this
Government under Your Immediate direction."

AN ACT FOR ESTABLISHING AN AGREEMENT WITH SEVEN OF THE
LORDS PROPRIETORS OF CAROLINA, FOR THE SURRENDER OF
THEIR TITLE AND INTEREST IN THAT PROVINCE TO HIS
MAJESTY.

. . . AND whereas, the said Henry, now Duke of Beauford, William, Lord Craven, James Bertie, Henry Bertie, Sir John Colleton,

and Archibald Hutcheson, . . . being six of the present Lords Proprietors of the Province and territory aforesaid, have by their humble petition, to his Majesty in Council, offered and proposed to surrender to his Majesty, their said respective shares and interests, not only of and in the said Government, Franchises and Royalties, . . . but also all the right and property they have in and to the soil in the aforesaid Provinces or territories. . . . That in consideration of such surrender, his Majesty would be pleased to direct, and to cause to be paid to each of them, . . . the sum of two thousand five hundred pounds apiece, . . . that from and after the payment of the said sum of seventeen thousand five hundred pounds . . . his Majesty, his heirs and successors, shall have, hold and enjoy, all and singular the said seven eight parts or shares. . . .

And be it further enacted, . . . that seven eight parts, . . . of all and every the said arrears of quit rents, and other rents, sum and sums of money, debts, duties, accounts, claims and demands whatsoever, now due and owing to them . . . shall . . . be vested in the said Edward Bertie, Samuel Horsey, Henry Smith, Alexius Clayton, . . . upon trust, and to the intent that they . . . shall, upon payment by his Majesty . . . of the sum of five thousand pounds of lawful money of Great Britain . . . on or before the said twenty ninth day of September, in the said year, to the said Edward Bertie, Samuel Horsey, Henry Smith, and Alexius Clayton, . . . grant and assign to his Majesty . . . all and every the said seven eight parts or shares. . . .

Saving and reserving always to the said John, Lord Carteret, his heirs, executors, administrators and Assigns, all such estate, right, title, interest, property, claims and demands whatsoever, in, unto or out of, one eight part or share of the said Provinces or territories, with all and singular the rights, members and appurtenances thereof, and of, in and to one eight part or share of all arrears of quit rents, and other rents, sum and sums of money, debts, duties, accounts, reckonings, claims and demands whatsoever, now due and oweing to the present Lords Proprietors.—*Colonial Records of North Carolina*, III, 32-47.

18. INSTRUCTIONS TO GOVERNOR GEORGE BURRINGTON, DECEMBER 14, 1730

George Burrington was the first royal governor of North Carolina. He had been governor during the proprietary period, but had met with such disfavor that he was removed from that office in 1725. His appointment as royal governor, however, met with general approval in the province. It was not long before he became unpopular again, and his administration was one of confusion and disorder. Yet he did much for North Carolina. He made a close study of economic conditions, investigated the settlement of lands, laid out roads, built bridges, and tried to promote immigration. His growing unpopularity, however, caused him to be replaced by Gabriel Johnston in 1734.

Burrington was appointed and received his commissions and instructions in 1730, but did not formally take charge of the government until February 25, 1731. North Carolina had five royal governors, George Burrington, Gabriel Johnston, Arthur Dobbs, William Tryon, and Josiah Martin. All of these officials received instructions from the home government from time to time. These were sent out by the Board of Trade and Plantations. In 1730 Burrington received 117 instructions. A few of the most significant are given below.

---

12. You shall take care that the Members of the Assembly be elected only by freeholders as being more agreeable to the custom of this Kingdom to which you are as near as may be to conform yourself in all particulars.

13. In case you find the usual Salaries of pay of the Members of the Assembly too high you shall take care that they be reduced to such a moderate proportion as may be no grievance to the country wherein nevertheless you are to use your discretion so as no inconvenience may arise thereby. . . .

21. And whereas great mischiefs may arise by passing bills of an unusual and extraordinary nature & importance in the Plantations which Bills remain in force there from the time of enacting until our pleasure be signified to the contrary We do hereby will and require you not to pass or give your assent to any Bill or Bills in the Assembly of our said Province of unusual and extraordinary nature and importance wherein our prerogative or the property of our subjects may be prejudiced or the trade & shipping of this Kingdom be any ways affected until you shall first have transmitted unto us the draught of such a Bill or Bills and shall have received our Royal pleasure thereupon unless you take care in the passing of any Bill of such nature as aforementioned that there be likewise a clause inserted therein suspending & deferring the execution thereof until our pleasure shall be known concerning the same. . . .

26. And we do hereby particularly require and enjoyn you upon pain of our highest displeasure to take care that fair books of accounts of all receipts and payments of all public monies be duly kept and the truth thereof be attested upon oath and that all such

accounts be audited & attested by our Auditor General of our Plantations or his Deputy. . . .

27. And you are likewise to transmit authentic copies of all laws statutes and ordinances which at any time hereafter shall be made or enacted within our said Province. . . .

37. You are not to suffer any public money whatsoever to be issued or disposed of otherwise than by warrant under your hand by the advice and consent of our Council but the Assembly may nevertheless be permitted from time to time to view and examine all accounts of money or value of money disposed of by virtue of laws made by them which you are to signify to them as there shall be occasion. . . .

42. Whereas great inconveniences have arisen in many of our Colonies in America from the granting of excessive quantities of land to particular persons which they have never cultivated and have thereby prevented others more industrious from improving the same more particularly in North Carolina where several persons claim a right to many thousand acres. . . . It is our Will and Pleasure that you do not suffer any person to possess more acres of uncultivated land than are mentioned in their respective grants. . . .

44. You shall not displace any of the Judges Justices Sheriffs or other Officers or Ministers in our said Province without good and sufficient cause. . . .

56. And for the better prevention of long imprisonment You are to appoint two Courts of Oyer and Terminer to be held yearly. . . .

57. You are to take care that all prisoners in case of treason or felony have free liberty to petition in open Court for their tryals. . . .

62. You are to take care that no Man's Life Member Freehold or Goods be taken away or harmed in our said Province otherwise than by established and known laws not repugnant to but as near as may be agreeable to the Laws of this Kingdom And that no persons be sent prisoners to this Kingdom from our said Province without sufficient proof of their crimes and that proof transmitted along with the said prisoners. . . .

63. You shall endeavor to get a Law passed (if not already done) for the restraining of any inhuman severity which by ill masters or their overseers may be used toward their Christian servants and their slaves and that provision be made therein that the wilful killing of Indians & Negroes be punished with death and that a fit penalty be imposed for the maiming of them. . . .

74. You are to permit a liberty of conscience to all persons (ex-

8

cept papists) so as they be contented with a quiet and peaceable enjoyment of the same not giving offence or scandal to the Governt.

75. You shall take especial care that God Almighty be devoutly & duly served throughout your Governt the Book of Common Prayer as by law established read each Sunday & Holiday and the blessed Sacrament administered according to the rites of the Church of England.

76. You shall take care that the Churches already built there be well and orderly kept and that more be built as the Province shall by God's blessing be improved. . . .

82. And We do further direct that no Schoolmaster be henceforth permitted to come from this Kingdom and to keep school in that our said Province without the license of the Lord Bishop of London and that no other person now there or that shall come from other parts shall be permitted to keep school in North Carolina without your license first obtained. . . .

88. You shall also cause an exact account to be kept of all persons born christened & buried and send yearly fair abstracts thereof to us. . . .

89. You shall take care that all Planters Inhabitants and Christian Servants be well and fitly provided with arms and that they be listed under good officers and when and as often as thought fit mustered and trained whereby they may be in a better readiness for the defence of the said Province. . . .

90. You are to take especial care that neither the frequency nor unreasonableness of remote marches musterings & trainings be an unnecessary impediment to the affairs of the inhabitants. . . .

100. You shall cause a survey of all the considerable landing places and harbours in our said Province and with the advice of our Council there erect in any of them such fortifications as shall be necessary for the security and advantage of the said Province which shall be done at the public charge. . . .

105. You are to examine what rates and duties are charged & payable on any goods exported or imported within our said Province. . . . And you are to suppress the engrossing of Commodities as tending to the prejudice of that freedom which Trade and commerce ought to have and to use your best endeavors in improving the trade of those parts.

106. You are to give all due encouragement & invitation to Merchants & others who shall bring trade into our said Province or anywise contribute to the advantage and in particular to the

Royal African Company & others our Subjects trading to Africa And as we are willing to recommend unto the said Company & others our subjects that the said Province may have a constant & sufficient supply of Merchantable Negroes at moderate rates in money or commodities so you are to take special care that payment be duly made within a competent time according to their respective agreements. . . .

115. You are likewise from time to time to give unto us and to our Commrs for Trade and Plantations an account of the wants and defects of our said Province what are the chief products of what are the new improvements made therein by the industry of the inhabitants & planters and what further improvements you conceive may be made or advantages gained by trade and which way We may contribute thereunto.—*Colonial Records of North Carolina,* III, 90-118.

19. ROYAL GOVERNOR *Versus* COLONIAL LEGISLATURE

Throughout the colonial era there were controversies between the governor and the legislature. The governor was considered the representative of the Proprietors or of the King. The legislature was deemed the representative of the people, and the speaker of the house was looked upon as the champion of their rights. Many of the disputes were over major matters, such as taxation, quit rents, the selection of officials, and the enforcement of British laws, while many of the arguments were about the petty details of government. The royal governor was supposed to "serve two masters." He was appointed by the Crown, while his salary, if any, was voted by the legislature. In this way the North Carolina Assembly held the whip-hand over the governor. On one occasion the friction between Governor Burrington and the legislature became so intense that three sessions of that body failed to pass a single law. Gabriel Johnston, who succeeded Burrington, was a more efficient and more popular official. Yet he had constant difficulty with the Assembly over financial matters, and was forced to dissolve that body on certain occasions.

GOVERNOR GABRIEL JOHNSTON DISSOLVES THE NORTH CAROLINA
ASSEMBLY, 1737

I was obliged to prorogue last Assembly at Edenton which at first promised very fair to settle this Country by enacting some good Laws. But an Emissary from the late Governour who arrived here during their sitting did amuse them with so many representations that it was impossible to do business with them, according to the last prorogation I met them here on the first current and recommended to their consideration the present miserable case of the Province. But instead of mending that the first thing they attempted was to take the Officers who distrained for his Majesty's Quit Rents during the time of Collection into Custody upon which I dissolved them by the enclosed proclamation. I hope Sir you will be so good as to say before their Lordships what I have now wrote to you in a very great hurry, But as the affair is pressing I hope you will excuse any oversight.

GAB : JOHNSTON

Newbern March 11th 1736/7

North Carolina

By his Excellency Gabriel Johnston Esqre Capt Genl & Governr in Chief of the said Province.

A PROCLAMATION

Whereas the Lower House of Assembly instead of redressing the many Grievances the Country labour under for want of a sufficient maintenance being provided for the Clergy & proper additions to and amendments of the Laws in force which are at present so defective both which have been so often and so earnestly recommended to them, Have taken upon them in a very disorderly and undutiful manner to intimidate his Majesties officers in the execution of their duty by order of them into Custody, thereby to prevent the Collection of the Quit Rents so long due to his Majesty I do therefore by and with the advice and consent of his Majesty's Council, dissolve this Assembly, & this present Assembly is accordingly dissolved.

March 4th 1736/7—*Colonial Records of North Carolina*, IV, 243-44.

II

SOCIAL AND ECONOMIC CONDITIONS IN THE COLONY

20. EARLY TOBACCO TRADE OF NORTH CAROLINA, 1679

Tobacco was the "money crop" of the Albemarle section, which was the first part of North Carolina to be settled. On account of the dangerous coast, however, the Albemarle planters were largely dependent upon Virginia ports for the exportation of their products. In 1679 the Commissioners of the Customs in London made the following report relative to Carolina tobacco production and trade.

THE quantity of Tobacco that groweth in Carolina and those Parts is considerable & Increaseth every year but it will not appear by the Customhouse bookes what customes have been received in England for the same for that by reason by the Badnesse of the Harbours in those parts most of the Tobaccoes of the growth of those Countreyes have been and are Carryed from thence in Sloopes and small fetches to Virginia & New England & from thence shipped hither. So that the Entries here are as from Virginia & New England although the Tobacco be of the growth of Carolina & Albemarle.—*Colonial Records of North Carolina*, I, 242-43.

21. A PLEA FOR PROTECTIVE DUTIES, 1704

The following document illustrates the desire of English and Colonial industrialists for protective legislation. The "infant industry," in which they were particularly interested at that time, was naval stores. The arguments which they advanced are quite similar to those still used by protectionists.

CONSIDERATIONS HUMBLY OFFERED, WHY NAVAL STORES CANNOT BE BROUGHT IN GREAT QUANTITY'S FROM HER MAJESTY'S PLANTATIONS, UNLESS ASSISTANCE BE GIVEN BY THE GOVERNMENT.

1ST Planters, proprietors, or Trading people will not make it their business to provide such Goods, nor bring them in the usual way of

Trade unless they have a prospect, they shall have sales for them at such rates, as may afford them profit, their cost & Charges considered; if there be no such prospect then they will bring them only when they can be secure of Gaine by some particular contract with the Navy officers or other persons.

2nd This is verified by what has past in relation to Naval Stores from the plantations, Several have offer'd to bring them upon a Contract made, or Charter granted or other advantages, but few or none have been brought as other Commodities to be sold at a Common Markett Thō it was foreseen above 50 Yeares Since; that it would be dangerous to depend entirely upon the Northern Crownes, for Naval Stores, and was then taken into Consideration Now to be supplied from the Plantations, yet few have been brought, thō in those parts there is great plenty of Timber for building of Ships, and also to produce Pitch, Tarr & Rozin, and a Soil capable to afforde hempe.

3ly Upon which it may be concluded that no Methods can be effectual, for the bringing in, of great quantity's, but such as may give encouragement, to the Trading people, to bring them upon the same foundation, as they bring other Commodities from other parts vizt

Hopes of making a proffit, by trading & dealing in them which cannot be, unless these Comodities be eased of the great burthen, which lyes on them, by the great wages paid to labouring men on the Plantations, and the high freights given to Ship Masters, for Goods brought from those parts, which being farr above the rates which are paid for the same Sorts of Goods if they come from Norway or the Baltick, deprives the traders of making proffit by these Goods from the Plantations, and gives a priority to those from the North.

4ly The Northern Crownes are our Competitors in this Case, the advantages they have cannot be overcome, by a Charter, in which most of the proposalls that have been made do center, Corporations must have Governours, Directors, book keepers & Agents, the Charges will amount to at least ten per cent, which must be added to the Cost, and other necessary Charges, and give a Further advantage to our Competitors, by which they will be enabled to undersell our Traders in these Commodities, and yet Subsist & make profit, because they will be eased in these Several Charges & outgoings : Charters cannot remove, nor decrease the Cloggs that lye on this Trade, but rather increase them unless the Swedes & Danes and all others could be excluded from bringing those goods into England.

Therefore Unless these Comodities from the North can be Charged with a great Custome, and those from the Plantations be eased from all Custome: or her Majesty be graciously pleased to cause these goods to be brought freight free to the Planters or owners, or to give to them some recompense at a Certain rate per Tunn for what they may bring, as may equallize the Charge of freight.

The Naval Stores from the North will always hinder their being brought from the Plantations, as Comodities in the way of Trade, which only can cause a large importation of them for the use of our Navigation in General, hinder the Exportation of our Coyne to the North and prevent the inconveniences that may happen, by our dependence upon these Crownes.—*Colonial Records of North Carolina*, I, 598-99.

22. JOHN LAWSON'S ACCOUNT OF ECONOMIC AND SOCIAL CONDITIONS IN THE COLONY

John Lawson, explorer, surveyor, historian, and co-founder of New Bern, came to America in 1700. On December 28 of that year he set out on "a thousand mile travel" through the Indian country into North Carolina. A large part of his journey was along the "Catawba path." He probably followed this trail as far as the present town of Hillsboro. Then he turned to the southeast and followed the Neuse for more than a hundred miles, probably passing near the present site of Goldsboro. He crossed the Contentnea near Grifton and the Tar at Greenville, and then proceeded to the English settlement on the "Pampticough River." In September, 1711, he was captured by the Indians and burned at the stake at the Indian town of Catechna, near the present town of Snow Hill, in Greene county. De Graffenried, who had been taken captive at the same time, was freed by the Indians.

Lawson's *A New Voyage to Carolina*, published in London in 1709, consisted of three parts: (1) Journal of a thousand miles' travel; (2) Description of North Carolina; (3) An account of the Indians of North Carolina.

THE Chriſtian Natives of *Carolina* are a ſtraight, clean-limb'd People; the Children being ſeldom or never troubled with Rickets, or those other Diſtempers, that the *Europeans* are viſited withal. . . . The Vicinity of the Sun makes Impreſſion on the Men, who labour out of doors, or uſe the Water. As for thoſe Women, that do not expoſe themselves to the Weather, they are often very fair, and generally as well featur'd, as you ſhall ſee any where, and have very brisk charming Eyes, which ſets them off to Advantage. They marry very young; ſome at Thirteen or Fourteen; and She that ſtays till Twenty is reckon'd a ftale Maid; which is a very indifferent Character in that warm Country. The Women are very fruitful, moft Houses being full of Little Ones. It has been obferv'd that Women long marry'd, and without Children, in other Places, have remov'd to *Carolina* and become joyful Mothers . . . Many of the Women are very handy in Canoes, and will manage them with great Dexterity and Skill, which they become accuftomed to in this watry Country. They are ready to help their Husbands in any fervile Work, as Planting when the Seafon of the Weather requires Expedition; Pride feldom banifhing good Housewifry. The Girls are not bred up to the Wheel, and Sewing only; but the Dairy and the Affairs of the House they are very well acquainted withal; . . . The Children of both Sexes are very docile, and learn anything with a great deal of Eafe and Method . . . The young Men are commonly of a bafhful, fober Behaviour; few proving Prodigals, to confume what the Induftry of their Parents has left them, but commonly improve it. . . .

. . . And as for feveral Productions of other Countries, much in the fame Latitude, we may expect, with good Management, they will become familiar to us, as Wine, Oil, Fruit, Silk, and other profitable Commodities, such as Drugs, Dyes, &c. And at present, the Curious may have a large Field to fatisfy and divert themfelves in, as Collections of ftrange Beasts, Birds, Insects, Reptiles, Shells, Fifhes, Minerals, Herbs, Flowers, Plants, Shrubs, intricate Roots, Gums, Tears, Rozins, Dyes and Stones, with several other that yield Satisfaction and Profit to those whose Inclinations tend that Way. . . .

The Fishing-Trade in *Carolina* might be carried on to great Advantage confidering how many Sorts of excellent Fifh our Sound and Rivers afford, which cure very well with Salt, as has been experienced by fome fmall Quantities, which have been fent abroad and yielded a good Price. . . . Great Plenty is generally the Ruin of Industry. Thus our Merchants are not many, nor have thofe few there be, apply'd themselves to the *European* Trade. The Planter fits contented at home, whilft his Oxen thrive and grow fat, and his Stocks daily increase; the fatted Porkets and Poultry are easily raif'd to his Table, and his Orchard affords him Liquor, fo that he eats and drinks away the Cares of the world, and defires no greater Happinefs than that which he daily enjoys. Whereas, not only the *European*, but also the *Indian*-Trade, might be carried on to a great Profit, becaufe we lie as fairly for the Body of *Indians* as any fettlement in *English-America*; . . .

One great advantage of *North-Carolina* is, That we are not a

Frontier, and near the Enemy, which proves very chargeable and troublefome in time of War, to those Colonies that are fo feated. Another great Advantage comes from its being near *Virginia,* where we come often to a good Market.—John Lawson, *A New Voyage to Carolina,* pp. 84-88.

23. Indentured Servitude and Apprenticeship in North Carolina

Indentured servants constituted one of the chief sources of North Carolina's labor supply in its early years. It has been estimated that there were more indentured white servants than black slaves in the first half century of the colony's existence. Many of these servants were "redemptioners," that is, people who had voluntarily "bound" themselves to some master for a fixed number of years, in order to "redeem" their passage to this country. Some were political prisoners; some were convicts sold into bondage in lieu of jail service; while others were persons who had been kidnapped in English cities and sent to America. The period of service depended on the contract, usually being three or five years. At the expiration of this time, the servant usually received fifty acres of land from the colony, as well as some food, clothing, tools, and other supplies from the master. Many of the indentures provided that the servant should be taught a trade and to read and write. Laws were enacted to prevent cruel punishments of servants.

There is a striking similarity between the apprenticeship system of the eighteenth and nineteenth centuries and the indentures of the seventeenth century. Many of the contracts are almost identical. Children were apprenticed, with the consent of their parents; orphans and illegitimate children were frequently "bound out" by order of the court; while Negro children were often apprenticed to learn "plantation business." No less than thirty different trades have been noted in the apprenticeship records of North Carolina. Some of those most frequently mentioned are: mechanic, blacksmith, carpenter, cooper, cord winder, weaver, tailor. joiner, mariner, wheelwright, fisherman, silversmith, ditcher, and barber. Most of the indentures provided that the master should teach the apprentice to read and write. This provision was stricken out of some of the contracts which involved Negro children. Probably the best known apprenticeship in the history of North Carolina is that of Andrew Johnson. who was apprenticed to learn the trade of a tailor, in 1822.

INDENTURED SERVANT TO BE GIVEN LAND, CLOTHING, AND TOOLS,
1666

Every servant at the Expiration of their service (which is 4 yeares) are to have the same quantity of land for him or herselfe, that their mrs had for bringing over and on the same condition allso the mr is bound to give them two suits of apparell and a set of tools to work with when he is out of his time.

ORPHANS APPRENTICED TO LEARN A TRADE, 1703

Upon a petition of Gabriell Newby for two orphants left him by Mary Hancock the late wife of Thoms Hancocke and proveing the same by the oathes of Eliz. Steuward and her daughter the Court doe agree to bind them unto him he Ingaging & promising before the Courte to doe his endeavour to learne the boy the trade of a wheelwright and likewise give him at the expiration of his time one ear old heifer and to ye girle at her freedome one Cow and Calfe besides the Custome of the Country and has promised at ye next orphans Court to Signe Indentures for that effect.

SERVANTS DISCHARGED BECAUSE MASTER HAD NOT TAUGHT THEM TO READ AND WRITE, 1714

Upon Petition of George Bell setting forth that he had two servts bound to him by the precinct Court of Craven in ye month of July 17⅓ namely Charles Coggdaile and George Coggdaile as by Indenture may appeare. And further that ye Court afsd have pretended to sett ye said Servt at Liberty as he is informed by reason that they could not perfectly read and write when as the time of their servitude is not half expired. . . .

AN ACT CONCERNING SERVANTS & SLAVES, 1715

II. And It Is Hereby Enacted that all Christian Servants Imported or to be Imported into this Government above Sixteen Years of Age without Indentures shall serve Five Years. And all under the Age of Sixteen Years at the time of their Importation shall serve until they be Two & Twenty Years of Age. And the Age of such Servant or Servants to be adjudged by the Precinct Court where the Master or Mistress of such servant resides. . . .

III. And Be It Further Enacted by the Authority afors'd that every Christian Servant whether so by importattion or by Contract made in this Government that shall, at any time or times absent him or herself from his or her Master or Mistress' service without his or her License first had shall make satisfaction by serving after the time by Custom or Indenture or Contract for serving is expired, double the time of Service lost or neglected by such time or times of Absence & also such longer time as the Court shall see fit to adjudge in consideration of any further Charge or Damages accrueing to the Master or Mistress by such time or times of Absence as aforesaid. . . .

V. Be It Further Enacted that every Master or Mistress shall provide for their servants so Imported or Indented Competent Dyet, Clothing & Lodging. And shall not exceed the Bounds of moderation in correcting them beyond their Demerits. And that it shall & may be lawfull for any Servant having just Cause of Complaint to repair to the next Magistrate who is hereby impowered, required & directed to bind over such Master or Mistress to Appear & answer the Complaint the next precinct Court. . . .

VI. Be It Enacted that every Christian Servant shall be allowed by their Master or Mistress at the expiration of his or her time of service Three Barrells of Indyan Corn & two new Suits of Apparrell of the Value of Five pounds at least or in lieu of one suit of Apparrell of good well-fixed Gun, if he be a Manservant.

VII. And Be It Further Enacted by the Authority afors'd that if any person or persons shall entertain or Harbour any Runaway Servant or Slave above one Night he or they so offending shall for every Four & Twenty hours afterwards forfeit & pay the sum of Tenn Shillings to the Master or Mistress of such Servant or Slave together with all Costs, Losses & damages which the Master or Mistress shall sustain by means of such entertainment or Concealment to be recovered in any Court of Record within this Government. . . .

X. . . . Whosoever shall buy, sell, Trade, Truck, Borrow or Lend to or with any Servant or Servants or Slave or Slaves without the Licence or Consent in Writing under the Hand of his or her or their Master or Owners for any Condition whatever such person or persons so offending contrary to the true Intent & Meaning of this Act shall forfeit treble the Value of the thing Bought, sold, Traded or Trucked Borrowed or lent. . . .

ORPHAN TO BE TAUGHT TO READ, 1716

Upon the Peticon of John Swain praying that Elizabeth Swain his Sister an Orphane Girle bound by the Precinct Court of Chowan to John Worlet Esqr May in the time of her service be taught to read by her said Master

Orderd, that she be taught to read

CHILDREN OF VAGRANTS TO BE APPRENTICED, 1755

That Vagrants be restrained from Strolling and wandering about, And that Children whose parents are unaule or neglect to Educate and teach some usefull Business may be bound out to proper Trades. —*Colonial Records of North Carolina*, I, 155, 577; II, 172, 266; V, 299. *State Records of North Carolina*, XXIII, 62-66.

A CRAVEN COUNTY APPRENTICESHIP PAPER, 1748-1779

THIS INDENTURE,

Made the Seventh Day of January in the Year of our Lord One Thousand Seven Hundred and Sixty four Witnesseth, That John Williams Esqr. Residing Chairman of the Inferior Court of Craven County have put and placed Richard Daves—an Orphan, of Richard Daves—deceased, aged Nine Years an Apprentice to Joseph Jones—of the said County, Merchant with him to dwell, reside, and serve, until he the said Apprentice shall arrive at the Age of Twenty one Years, according to the Act of Assembly in that Case made and provided; during all which Time the said Apprentice his said Master shall faithfully serve in all lawful Business, and Orderly and obediently in all Things behave himself towards his said Master, for and during the said Term, as an Apprentice ought to do. And the said Joseph Jones—doth Covenant, promise and agree, to and with the said John Williams and his Successors, that he the said Joseph Jones—will provide and allow his said Apprentice Convenient and sufficient Meat, Drink, Lodging and Apparrel, and use his best Endeavours to instruct him in the Art and Mystery of a Mariner and also teach him to read and write before the Expiration of his Apprenticeship—*Craven County Apprenticeship Papers*, 1748-1779.

24. AN ACT TO PROHIBIT STRANGERS TRADING WITH INDIANS

The following act reveals the efforts of the colony of North Carolina to monopolize the Indian trade, which was quite profitable at that time.

I. FORASMUCH as there is often recourse of strangers from other parts into this Country to truck and trade with the Indians which is conceived may prove prejudicial, wherefore,
II. Be it Enacted by the Palatin & Lords Proprietors by & with the advice and consent of the present Grand Assembly & the Authority thereof, that if any person or persons of what Quality or Condition soever they be, shall presume to come into this Country to Truck & Trade with any of our Neighbour Indians belonging to the Country, or shall be found to have any Indian Trade purchased from them, or being found or appearing that they come to trade with any Indians as aforesaid whether in their Town or Elsewhere within the

Country, which is hereby left for the Majistrate to judge, It shall be lawful for any person or persons to apprehend any such person or Foreigner that shall be found amongst the Indians or elsewhere within the limits of the Country and him or them bring before the Governor or any one of the Council, who shall hereby have power to commit them to prison there to abide until they have paid Ten thousand pounds of Tobacco & Cask; otherwise to stand to the censure of the Governor.

III. And it is further declared that whatsoever Trade is found with the person apprehended one half thereof & one half of the Fine shall belong to the Apprehender & the other half to the Lords Proprietors.
—*State Records of North Carolina*, XXIII, 2.

25. THE ESTABLISHED CHURCH IN COLONIAL NORTH CAROLINA

According to the provisions of the proprietary charters the Church of England was the only one which could have official encouragement in Carolina. It was definitely established in North Carolina by an act of 1715. Nine parishes were created, for each of which vestrymen were selected, with the duty of procuring "an able & Godly Minister qualified according to the Ecclesiastical Laws of England," at an annual stipend of not less than £50. They were likewise to build a church and chapel in each parish. In spite of the law, there were no regular pastors in the colony for many years; only missionaries came, being sent out by the Society for the Propagation of the Gospel. As late as 1732 there was not a regular minister of the Church of England in the whole province. A law passed in 1741 required that vestrymen take an oath that they "would not oppose the liturgy of the Church of England." Another law prohibited justices of the peace from performing marriage ceremonies in any parish where a minister resided. The sheriffs were official tax collectors for the levies assessed by the vestry.

REV. JOHN BLAIR'S CLASSIFICATION OF THE RELIGIOUS GROUPS IN NORTH CAROLINA, 1704

FOR the country may be divided into four sorts of people: first, the Quakers, who are the most powerful enemies to Church government, but a people very ignorant of what they profess. The second sort are a great many who have no religion, but would be Quakers, if by that they were not obliged to lead a more moral life than they are willing to comply to. A third sort are something like Presbyterians, which sort is upheld by some idle fellows who have left their lawful employment, and preach and baptize through the country, without any manner of orders from any sect or pretended Church. A fourth sort, who are really zealous for the interest of the Church, are the fewest in number, but the better sort of people, and would do very much for the settlement of the Church government there, if not opposed by these three precedent sects; and although they be all three of different pretensions, yet they all concur together in one common cause to prevent any thing that will be chargeable to them, as they allege Church government will be, if once established by law.—*Colonial Records of North Carolina*, I, 601-2.

AN ACT FOR ESTABLISHING THE CHURCH & APPOINTING SELECT VESTRYS, 1715

I. This Province of North Carolina being a Member of the Kingdom of Great Britain; & the Church of England being appointed by the Charter from the Crown to be the only Established church to have Publick encouragement in it. . . .

II. . . . It is hereby Enacted that this province of North Carolina be divided into parishes, . . . Chowan precinct into two parishes. . . . Pasquotank precinct into two parishes, . . . Perquimins, Carrituck & Hyde to be parishes, . . . the remaining part of Pamlico River and the Branches thereof, commonly called Beaufort precinct to be one parish by the name of St. Thomas parish : And Neuse River & the Branches thereof by the name of Craven parish to which all the Southern settlements shall be accounted a part of the same parish until further divisions be made.

III. . . . that there shall be a Vestry in each & every of the aforesaid precincts & parishes consisting of the Minister of the parish, when any such shall be there resident, & Twelve men. . . .

VIII. . . . that the Vestrymen of every Precinct or Parish, or the the greatest part of them shall choose two persons who are Vestrymen to be Church Wardens, who shall continue in that Office one year & no longer unless he or they shall be willing. . . .

X. . . . that the Several Church-Wardens & Vesteries or the greatest part of them shall use their best & utmost endeavour to procure an able & Godly Minister qualified according to the Ecclesiastical Laws of England, and a person of a sober life & Conversation to be Clerk, & to raise for him or them such Stipends yearly as they shall think convenient, so as such sum or stipend for the Minister be not less than Fifty Pounds yearly. . . .

XI. . . . that the Church Wardens & Vestrymen shall have full power & Authority to purchase Land for a Glebe to build one Church & one or more Chappels in every respective precinct or parish. . . .

XII. . . . that for the defraying or paying whatsoever charges shall or may from time to time arise by force of this Act, or which shall properly be a parish charge. . . . It shall & may be lawfull for the several Church-Wardens & Vestrymen, . . . to raise & levy money by the Poll so as the same do not exceed five Shillings by the Poll per Annum. . . . —*State Records of North Carolina*, XXIII, 6-10.

AN ACT CONCERNING MARRIAGES, *1741*

I. For preventing clandestine and Unlawful Marriages, . . . it is hereby enacted. . . . That every Clergyman of the Church of England, or for want of such, any lawful Magistrate, within this Government, shall, and they are hereby directed, to join together in the Holy Estate of Matrimony, such Persons who may lawfully enter into such a Relation. . . .

II. . . . That no Justice of the Peace of any County in this Government, shall join together in Marriage, any Persons whosoever in any Parish where a Minister shall reside, . . . without Permission first had and obtained from such Minister, under the Penalty of Five Pounds Proclamation Money, to the Use of the Minister.— *State Records of North Carolina*, XXIII, 158.

VESTRY LAW, *1741*

III. . . . That no Person shall be admitted to be of any Vestry within this Government, that doth not take the Oaths by Law appointed to be taken, for the Qualification of Public Officers, and subscribe the following Declaration, viz. :

I, A. B., do declare, that I will not oppose the Liturgy of the Church of England, as it is by law established : And all and every Vestryman who shall neglect or refuse to do the same, shall (if he be not a known Dissenter from the Church of England), forfeit and pay the sum of Three Pounds. . . . —*State Records of North Carolina*, XXIII, 187.

VESTRY LAW, *1764*

XXI. . . . That the Vestry of each respective Parish shall have full Power and Authority, and are hereby directed and required, . . . yearly, to lay a Poll Tax on the Taxable Persons in their Parish, not exceeding Ten Shillings, for building Churches & Chappels, paying the Minister Salary, purchasing a Glebe, erecting a Mansion, and convenient Out-houses thereon, encourageing Schools, maintaining the Poor, paying Clerks and Readers, and defraying other incident Charges of their Parish. . . .

XXII. . . . That the Incumbent of each and every Parish within this province shall, at the Time of performing Divine Service, appear in the reading Desk and Pulpit, either in a Surplus or Gown, agreeable to the Rubrick of the Church of England.

XXIV. . . . That every Sheriff in this Government shall be, and is hereby appointed Collector of all such Taxes as shall be assessed, by the Vestry or Vestries within his County. . . . —*State Records of North Carolina*, XXIII, 605.

26. AN ATTEMPT TO REGULATE MORALS

The following law enacted in 1715 by the colonial legislature is one of the first attempts of the province to regulate the morals of the inhabitants. The lawmakers hoped "to prevent the grievous sins of cursing and swearing," to check drunkenness, to enforce Sunday observance, and in other ways improve public morality.

AN ACT FOR THE BETTER OBSERVING THE LORD'S DAY CALLED
SUNDAY, THE 30TH OF JANUARY—AND ALSO, FOR THE
SUPPRESSING PROPHANENESS, IMMORALITY, AND
DIVERS OTHER VICIOUS & ENORMOUS CRIMES.

I. Forasmuch as by the great neglect in keeping Holy the Lord's Day & the little regard had to all other days & times appointed to be kept religiously, Impiety is likely to grow to a very great height, if not timely prevented, to the great Dishonour of the Almighty and scandal of this Province, Wherefore for the Speedy & Effectual Redressing thereof,

II. Be it Enacted by his Excellency the Palatine and the rest of the True & Absolute Lords Proprietors, by & with the advice & consent of the General Assembly now met at Little River for the North-East of the Province of Carolina,

III. And It is hereby Enacted by the Authority aforesaid, that from & after the Ratification of this Act, all & every person and persons whatsoever shall on every Lord's Day apply themselves to the holy Observation thereof by exercising themselves publickly & privately in the required duties of Piety & true Religion & that no Tradesman, Artificer, Workman, Labourer, or any other person or

persons whatsoever shall do or exercise any Worldly Labour, Business or work of their Ordinary Callings, or shall employ themselves either by Hunting or Fishing on that Day or any part thereof (Works of Necessity & Charity only excepted,) and that every person being of the Age of fourteen years or upwards, Offending in the Premises, shall for every such offence forfeit & pay the sum of Ten Shillings.
. . .

VI. And be it Further Enacted that no Planter, Merchant, their Servants or Slaves, nor any other person or persons whatsoever shall Use, Employ, or Trade with any Boat, Cannoe,—on the Lord's Day—upon Pain that every person so offending shall forfeit & pay for every offence the sum of Ten Shillings.

And if any Ordinary or Punch-House Keeper shall sell any Wine, Beer, Punch or other Liquors on the Lord's Day—(except it be for necessary occasions, for Lodgers or Sojourners) every person so offending shall for every such offence forfeit & pay the sum of Ten Shillings.

VII. And Forasmuch as Prophane Swearing and Cursing is forbidden by the Word of God, Be it therefore Enacted by the Authority aforesaid that no person or persons shall prophanely Swear or Curse, upon pain of forfeiting & paying the sum of Two Shillings and six pence for every Oath or Curse if a private person; But if any person in Office, shall prophanely swear or curse, then such person shall forfeit and pay the sum of Five Shillings. And further, in case any person or persons shall prophanely swear or curse in any Court-House Sitting the Court, He or She shall upon Conviction, Immediately pay the sum of Five Shillings or be set in the Stocks for the space of three Hours by order of the Court before the Offence was committed.

VIII. And whereas the odious & loathsome Sin of Drunkenness is of late grown into common use within this Province & being the Root & Foundation of many Enormous Sins,

IX. Be it therefore Enacted that all & every Person & persons that shall after the Ratification hereof be drunk upon the Sabbath Day—shall forfeit & pay the sum of Ten Shillings, if on any other day the sum of Five shillings for every such offence.—*State Records of North Carolina*, XXIII, 3-4.

27. Staple Commodities Rated, 1715

Most of the early settlers of North Carolina were poor. They brought practically no money with them and no gold or silver was mined in the province. The colony had some trade, particularly with the West Indies, but this did not bring in sufficient quantities of specie. Consequently the colonial government issued paper money and also adopted a system of commodity money. England eventually prohibited the issuance of the former. The latter never proved very satisfactory, although it was retained throughout the colonial period. The following list is taken from the law of 1715. Several other commodities were added to the sixteen which were rated in the original act.

II. AND It Is Hereby Enacted that for establishing a Certainty in Trade & in the payment of Publick Levys all Debts due or which hereafter may become due on acct. of the Publick or to any Inhabitant or foreignor trading amongst us or in our private dealing amongst ourselves or otherwise howsoever the Debt being contracted or due in Money not expressing Sterling such person or persons to whom such money shall be due shall take & receive of the same any Specie hereafter expressed & all the Rates hereby appointed or Publick Bills of Credit any thing in this Act contained to the Contrary Notwithstanding.

	£	s.	d.
Tobacco per Cwt.	0	10	0
Indyan Corn per Bush.		1	8
Wheat " "		3	6
Tallow Tryed, per lb.			5
Leather Tanned & Uncured, per lb.			8
Beaver & other Skins per lb.		2	6
Wild Cat Skins per piece.		1	0
Butter per lb.			6
Cheese per lb.			4
Buck & Doe Skins (raw) per lb.			9
do do (drest) "		2	6
Feathers per lb.		1	4
Pitch (Full Gauged) per Barl.	1	0	0
Whale Oil " "	1	10	0
Porke " "	2	5	0
Beef " "	1	10	0

III. And Be It Further Enacted by the Authority afors'd none of the aforementioned Comodities shall be forced upon any Creditor or Publick Receiver or other at the Rates & Prices aforementioned unless they be good in their kind & Merchantable & approved by Two substantial Freeholders Indifferently chosen & sworn before

some Magistrate justly & impartially to give their opinion thereon.
—*State Records of North Carolina*, XXIII, 54-55.

28. PAPER MONEY IN COLONIAL NORTH CAROLINA

North Carolina was a poor colony from the beginning, and was slower
in developing its industry and commerce than many of the colonies.
There was very little specie in the province and as early as 1712 paper
currency was issued in order to "defray the charges of an Indian War
then kindled." These notes bore interest and were to be redeemed out
of tax receipts. The law made them "current in all payments." Another
issue of £8,000 was made in 1713, which "depreciated the value of the
whole about 40 per cent." An additional sum of £24,000 was printed in
1714. In 1729 an issue of £40,000 was made, which depreciated rapidly.
By 1731 one pound sterling was worth seven or eight pounds of paper
currency, and the Governor wrote home that the paper was "worse than
any of the Comoditys." Most of the royal governors complained about
the issuance of paper. English merchants memorialized Parliament against
it. Yet issues continued to be made, and the paper continued to depreciate in value. Finally, Parliament took steps to stop inflation in the
colonies. An act of 1764 prohibited any colony from issuing bills of credit
and making them a legal tender for debts. This did not keep North Carolina from issuing treasury notes. So in 1773, Parliament expressly prohibited their issue.

AN ACCOUNT OF THE STATE OF THE PAPER CUR-
RENCY OF NORTH CAROLINA FROM THE FIRST
EMISSION OF ANY BILLS OF CREDIT TO
THE YEAR 1740.

1712. The first emission of any paper currency in the Province of
North Carolina was in the year 1712 at which time the Trade of it
was carried on chiefly by barter (for want of a silver or gold medium)
and the commodities so changed generally reckoned of proclamation standard.

To defray the charges of an Indian War then kindled the Assembly passed an act for emitting the sum of £4000 in paper currency
supposed to be equal in value to so much proclamation money and
past as such for some small time.

1713. The charges of the Government increasing by the continuance of the war another emission was made of £8000 which made
the sum of £12000, and was this year partly sunk by a tax on the
Inhabitants.

This last emission depreciated the value of the whole about 40 per cent.

1714. This year an additional sum of £24000 was emitted by an act for paying the remaining part of the debts of the Government and for sinking the remaining part of the sum of £12000.

1715. The above act was continued and altho from that time to the year 1722 several Sums were sunk out of the currency then subsisting yet the bills were depreciated nigh 8 per cent from the value of their first emission.

1722. There not appearing to be more than £12000 paper bills current in this Province and those defac'd and torn. An Act was past for making the sum of £12000 for exchanging such of the paper bills as were then current &c:

From this year to 1729 the above sum subsisted and generally past current at the proportion of five to one sterling.

1729. An Act past the Assembly for making and emitting the sum of £40000 paper bills of credit £10000 was appropriated to exchange as much of the old currency (£2000 of which being then supposed to be lost) and the other £30000 let out on land security for fifteen years at the rate of 6s. 4d. per cent interest. . . .

At the same time another law past for making the sum of £1250 additional currency to be sunk by a Tax and Duty upon liquors in 5 years. so that There is now subsisting in this Province the sum of £52500 bills of credit. The difference between sterling and the said bills has been adjudged for these four years past to be as ten for one and is so paid and received at this time which is at the rate of 52 s. 4 d. paper currency for an ounce of silver.

THE PETITION OF MERCHANTS IN LONDON WHO TRADE TO NORTH
CAROLINA AND OF GENTLEMEN AND MERCHANTS IN AND
FROM THAT COLONY, 1759

Humbly Sheweth

That there is now in force in North Carolina, two different Acts of Assembly passed Anno. 1748 and 1754 for the Emission of Paper Currency, in which it is expressly mentioned, that the Paper Currency made by virtue of those Acts, shall be a lawful Tender, in all payments, whatsoever, at the rate of Proclamation money, that is at the rate of four shillings paper Currency, for three shillings sterling.

The plain meaning thereof is, that £133.6.8. paper Currency, shall be a good Tender in Law in payment of a real debt of £100 sterling: when in fact £133.6.8 paper Currency, will not purchase more than £70 sterling.

This is such a breach of Public Faith, so contrary to Justice and equity, that it totally destroys the credit of that Province, no person can trust any property, where such Laws are subsisting, and it is evidently contrary to the real interests of the people in that Colony, as well as highly prejudicial to the interests of those in Britain concerned with or for them.—*Colonial Records of North Carolina*, IV, 576-77.

REPORT OF PAPER MONEY IN NORTH CAROLINA, 1764

That in April 1748 the sum of Twenty one Thousand three Hundred and Fifty pounds, and in March 1754, the sum of Forty Thousand pounds, . . . and for Redeeming and sinking the said Bills, an Annual Poll Tax of one Shilling per poll, was laid on each Taxable person; as also a duty of four pence per Gallon on all Spirituous Liquors Imported. . . .

That in the Year 1760, there was Emitted in Bills the sum of Twelve Thousand pounds . . . to be Redeemed by an Additional poll Tax of one Shilling per poll. . . .

That in the year 1761, there was Emitted in Bills, Twenty Thousand Pounds, . . .

. . . For the encouragement of the late War there was issued in the year 1756, Treasury Notes bearing interest at 6 per cent . . . amounted to three Thousand six Hundred Pounds; . . .

That in the year 1757 a further sum in Notes . . . amounting to Five Thousand three Hundred and six pounds; . . .

That in the same year, a further sum in Notes on Interest, . . . amounting to . . . nine Thousand five hundred pounds. . . .

That in the year 1758, there was issued, Notes bearing Interest . . . the sum of seven Thousand Pounds; and for redeeming the same a poll Tax of four shillings and six pence was laid, . . . and two pence per Gallon on all Spirits to be imported, . . .

. . . There has been emitted from April 1748 to the present time in Bills of Credit at Proclamation standard the sum of Ninety three Thousand three hundred and Fifty Pounds; and of Notes on Interest Thirty Thousand seven hundred and seventy six pounds; making in the whole, One Hundred and Twenty four Thousand, one hundred and Twenty six pounds; . . . —*Colonial Records of North Carolina*, VI, 16-17, 1308-11.

GOVERNOR MARTIN'S DESCRIPTION OF THE FINANCIAL SITUATION IN NORTH CAROLINA, 1771

Governor Martin to Earl Hillsborough, Dec. 26, 1771

A great part of the time of this Session . . . was consumed in the most disorderly speculations such as I am informed are constantly the offspring of a necessity to raise money in this Country. A Majority from the Southern district in which the people are almost universally necessitous and in debt and whose policy it seems it has been to overflow the province with paper money would have availed themselves of this exigence and made it a pander to that pernicious design. The minority from the Northern districts as warmly opposed this system ; . . . I was . . . glad at last to close with the only expedient they would adopt that could serve the present emergency, and I have given my assent to an act for raising the sum of sixty thousand pounds proclamation money the vast amount of the expense of suppressing the late insurrection for which stamped debenture notes are to be issued forthwith. . . . —*Colonial Records of North Carolina*, IX, 76.

29. REQUEST OF A MISSIONARY FOR SLAVES, 1716

Slaves were to be found in North Carolina at an early date, though they were not numerous until the late eighteenth century. They were considered an economic necessity, and there was little religious opposition to them in the colonial period. No more impressive illustration could be given of the toleration with which slavery was regarded than this request of a missionary for slaves. John Urmstone labored for many years in the Carolina settlements as a missionary for the Society for the Propagation of the Gospel in Foreign Parts. A neighbor described him as a devout man, although there were some complaints about his drunkenness.

NORTH CAROLINA, DECR 15TH, 1716

SIR.

. . . I pray you therefore desire the Treasurer to the Society to pay to Joseph Jekyll Esqr His Majesty's Collector of Customs at Boston in New England, or his order 20 pounds sterling (bills of equal date being produced) and if his correspondent the Bearer hereof will undertake it pay likewise 40 pounds of like money to be invested in goods to buy me 3 or 4 Negroes in Guinea ; but if he refuse I beg some body may be employed to engage some Guinea

Captn or Merchant to be delivered to the aforesaid Jno. . . . Jekyll
or to me 3 Negroes men of middle stature about 20 years old and
a Girl of about 16 years. there is no living without servants there
are none to be hired of any colour and none of the black kind to be
sold good for anything under 50 or 60 pounds white servants are
seldom worth keeping and never stay out the time indented for. . . .
I shall be glad to hear my requests are complied with and till then
must struggle with a hard Winter, scarcity of Provisions, and rub
through many more difficulties with all the patience I am endued
with and ever be, Sir,

Your most humble Servt

Jon Urmstone

Missionary

—*Colonial Records of North Carolina*, II, 260-61.

30. Representation of the Board of Trade to the
King upon the State of His Maj: Plantations
in America. 8 September 1721

The following report by the Board of Trade is one of the best descriptions given of conditions in North Carolina in the last years of proprietary government. Special emphasis was placed upon products, population, Indian relations, and land grants.

The natural Produce of this Country is Rice, Pitch, Tar, Turpentine, Buck skins, Hides Corn Beef Pork Soap Mirtle Wax-Candles various sorts of Lumber as Masts Cedar Boards, staves shingles, and Hoop-poles But the soil is thought capable of producing Wine, Oyle, Silk, Indico, Pot-Ashes, Iron, Hemp and Flax.

The number of White Inhabitants in this Province have some time since been computed at 9000 and the Blacks at 12000. But the frequent massacres committed of late years by the neighboring Indians at the Instigation of the French and Spaniards has diminished the white men whilst the manufactures of Pitch and Tar has given occasion to increase the number of Black Slaves. . . .

The Indian Nations lying between Carolina and the French settlements on the Mississippi are about 9200 fighting men of which number 3400 whom we formerly Traded with are entirely debauched to the French Interest. . . . About 2000 more that lye between your majesty's subjects and those of the French King, Trade at present indifferently with both, . . .

The remaining 3800 Indians are the Cherokees, a Warlike nation

Inhabiting the Apalatche Mountains these being still at enmity with the French might with less difficulty be secured, . . .

This Province having hitherto but few Inhabitants the Quit Rents of the Lords Proprietors amount to only about 500 pounds per annum.—*Colonial Records of North Carolina*, II, 420-23.

31.   William Byrd's Description of North Carolina Settlers

William Byrd of Westover, Virginia, was one of the most prominent men of the colonial period. Planter, author, and colonial official, he played an active part in the early history of Virginia. In 1728 he was one of the commissioners appointed to run "the dividing line betwixt Virginia and Carolina." His *History of the Dividing Line* gives a good description of the region along the Virginia-Carolina line, but his portrayal of the early North Carolina people is very unfavorable and prejudiced. He makes numerous references to the indolence of North Carolinians, their lack of religion, their poverty, laziness, and disrespect for law and order. It is interesting to note that Byrd's *Secret History*, edited by W. K. Boyd, in 1929, contains but one unfavorable criticism of the North Carolina settlers—that they ate so much hog meat that it ruined their dispositions. The excerpts below are from the *History of the Dividing Line betwixt Virginia and Carolina*.

The only Business here is raising of Hogs, which is manag'd with the least Trouble, and affords the Diet they are most fond of. The Truth of it is the Inhabitants of N Carolina devour so much Swine's flesh that it fills them full of gross Humours. . . .

One thing may be said for the Inhabitants of that Province, that they are not troubled with any Religious Fumes, and have the least Superstition of any People living. They do not know Sunday from any other day, any more than Robinson Crusoe did, which would give them a great Advantage were they given to be industrious. But they keep so many Sabbaths every week, that their disregard of the Seventh Day has no manner of cruelty in it, either to Servants or Cattle.

Most of the Rum they get in this country comes from New England, and it is so bad and unwholesome, that it is not improperly call'd "Kill-Devil." It is distill'd from foreign molasses, which, if Skilfully manag'd yields near Gallon for Gallon. . . .

Surely there is no place in the World where the Inhabitants live with less Labour than in N Carolina. It approaches nearer to the Description of Lubberland than any other, by the great felicity of the Climate, the easiness of raising Provisions, and the Slothfulness of the People.

Indian Corn is of so great increase, that a little Pains will Subsist a very large Family with Bread, and then they may have meat without any pains at all, by the help of the Low Grounds, and the great Variety of Mast that grows on the High-land. The Men, for their Parts, just like the Indians, impose all the Work upon the poor Women. They make their Wives rise out of their Beds early in the Morning, at the same time they lye and Snore, till the Sun has run one third of his course, and disperst all the unwholesome Damps. Then, after Stretching and Yawning for half an Hour, they light their Pipes, and, under the Protection of a cloud of Smoak, venture out into the open Air; tho', if it happens to be never so little cold, they quickly return Shivering into the Chimney corner. When the weather is mild, they stand leaning with both their arms upon the corn-field fence, and gravely consider whether they had best go and take a Small Heat at the Hough: but generally find reasons to put it off till another time.

Thus they loiter away their Lives, like Solomon's Sluggard, with their Arms across, and at the Winding up of the Year Scarcely have Bread to Eat.

To speak the Truth, tis a thorough Aversion to Labor that makes People file off to N Carolina, where Plenty and a Warm Sun confirm them in their Disposition to Laziness for their whole Lives.

What little Devotion there may happen to be is much more private than their vices. The People seem easy without a Minister, as long as they are exempted from paying Him. Sometimes the Society for propagating the Gospel has had the Charity to send over Missionaries to this Country; but unfortunately the Priest has been too Lewd for the people, or, which oftener happens, they too lewd for the Priest. For these Reasons these Reverend Gentlemen have always left their Flocks as arrant Heathen as they found them. This much however may be said for the Inhabitants of Edenton, that not a Soul has the least taint of Hypocrisy, or Superstition, acting very Frankly and above-board in all their Excesses.

Provisions here are extremely cheap, and extremely good, so that People may live plentifully at triffleing expense. Nothing is dear but Law, Physick, and Strong Drink, which are all bad in their Kind, and the last they get with so much Difficulty, that they are never guilty of the Sin of Suffering it to Sour upon their Hands. Their Vanity generally lies not so much in having a handsome Dining-Room, as a Handsome House of Office; in this Kind of Structure they are really extravagant.—*William Byrd's Histories of the Dividing Line betwixt Virginia and North Carolina* (edited by William K. Boyd), pp. 54, 72, 90-92, 96.

32. LETTER FROM CAPT BURRINGTON, GOVR OF NORTH CAROLINA, DATED 20TH OF FEBRUARY 1731/2

Throughout the colonial period the British government was interested in the promotion of certain industries in the colonies which would not compete with English industries, especially oil, silk, potash, and naval stores. The following letter indicates Governor Burrington's interest in these "industrial experiments." It also shows that the aversion of people to taxation is not something new.

___

To THE RIGHT HONOURABLE THE LORDS OF TRADE & PLANTATIONS.

It has been a Policy of the Subtle People of North Carolina never to raise any money but what is appropriated, to pretend and insist that no Publick money can, or ought to be paid, but by a Claim given to, and allowed by the House of Burgesses; insomuch that upon the greatest emergency there is no coming at any money to fitt out Vessells against a Pirate, to buy Arms, Purchase Ammunition, or on any other urgent occasion. This I hope will be redressed. The whole amount of the Publick Levys, and Powder Money, paid by shiping, little Exceeds two Hundred Pounds sterling a Year. . . .

It cannot be expected that this Province should increase in People, if the Quit Rents are higher here, than in Virginia, and other Governments that are more commodious upon many Accounts and Healthier.

Great Improvements may be made in North Carolina Here is Iron Oar enough to serve all the world, and I believe other sorts will be found when the upper Parts of the Province are Inhabited.

Great quantitys of Potash might annually be made, if the true Method was known.

The soil in some Places produces Wild Hemp, . . .

Flax and Cotton are very good and easily Produced. Mulberry Trees that bear the thin leaf proper to feed silk worms grow naturally, this Country is certainly as proper and Convenient to produce silk as any in the world, the reason so little has been made is that the very time required to look after the silkworms, is the season of Planting and Cultivating Rice, Tobacco, Indian Corn and Pulse.

The soil and Climate is particularly adapted for producing seeds make Oyl. . . .

The Inhabitants of North Carolina, are not Industrious but subtle and crafty to admiration, allways behaved insolently to their Governours, some they have Imprisoned, drove others out of the Country, at other times sett up two or three supported by Men under Arms, all the Governours that ever were in this Province lived in fear of the People (except myself) and Dreaded their Assemblys.

The People are neither to be cajoled or outwitted, whenever a Governour attempts to affect anything by these means, he will loose his Labour and show his Ignorance.—*Colonial Records of North Carolina*, III, 331-39.

33. John Lawson's Description of Indians in Colonial North Carolina

The following account of Indian life in the colony is taken from Lawson's history, which was published in London in 1709. Lawson was killed by the Indians in 1711. See page 39 above.

THE *Indians* of North-*Carolina* are a well-fhap'd clean-made People, of different Statures, as the *Europeans* are, yet chiefly inclin'd to be tall. They are a very ftreight People, and never bend forwards, or ftoop in the Shoulders, unlefs much overpower'd by old Age. Their Limbs are exceeding well-fhap'd. As for their Legs and Feet, they are generally the handfomest in the World. . . . Their Eyes are black, or of a dark Hazle; The White is marbled with red Streaks, which is ever common to thefe People, unlefs when fprung from a white Father or Mother. Their Colour is of a tawny, which would not be fo dark, did they not dawb themfelves with Bears oil, and a Colour like burnt Cork. . . .

Their Eyes are commonly full and manly, and their Gate fedate and majeftick. . . . They are dexterous and fteady both as to their Hands and Feet. . . .

Their Teeth are yellow with Smoaking Tobacco, which both Men and Women are much addicted to. They tell us, that they had Tobacco amongft them before the *Europeans* made any Difcovery of that Continent. It differs in the Leaf from the fweet-fcented, and *Oroonoko*, which are the plants we raife and cultivate in *America*. . . . Although they are great Smokers, yet they never are feen to take it in Snuff, or chew it. . . .

They have no Hair on their Faces (except fome few) and thofe but little. . . . They are continually plucking it away from their Faces, by the Roots. . . .

No People have better Eyes, or fee better in the Night or Day, than the *Indians*. Some alledge, that the Smoke of the Pitch-Pine, which they chiefly burn, does both preferve and ftrengthen the Eyes. . . .

They let their Nails grow very long, which, they reckon, is the Ufe Nails are defigned for, and laugh at the *Europeans* for paring theirs. *. . .*

They are not of fo robuft and ftrong Bodies as to lift great Burdens, and endure Labour and flavish Work, as the *Europeans* are; yet fome that are Slaves, prove very good and laborious; But, of themselves, they never work as the *Englifh* do, taking care for no farther than what is abfolutely neceffary to fupport Life. In Traveling and Hunting, they are very indefatigable; becaufe that carries a Pleafure along with the Profit. . . .

These Savages live in *Wigwams*, or Cabins, built of Bark, which are made round like an Oven, to prevent any Damage by hard Gales of Wind. They make the Fire in the middle of the Houfe, and have a Hole at the top of the Roof right above the Fire, to let out the Smoke. Thefe Dwellings are as hot as Stoves, where the *Indians* fleep and fweat all Night. The Floors thereof are never paved nor swept. . . .

The Cabins they dwell in have Benches all round, except where the Door ftands; on thefe they lay Beafts-Skins and Mats made of Rufhes, whereon they fleep and loll. In one of thefe, feveral Families commonly live, though all related to one another. . . .

As to the *Indians* Food, it is of feveral forts, which are as follows Venifon, and Fawns . . . Bear and Bever; Panther; Pole-Cat; Wild-Cat; Poffum; Raccoon; Hares; and Squirrels. . . .

Some of the *Indians* wear great Bobs in their Ears, and fometimes in the Holes thereof they put Eagles and other Birds, Feathers, for a Trophy. . . .

Their Money is of different forts, but all made of Shells, which are found on the Coaft of *Carolina*. . . .

All the *Indians* give a name to their Children which is not the fame as the Father or Mother, but what they fancy. This Name they keep, (if Boys) till they arrive at the Age of a Warriour, which is fixteen or feventeen Years; then they take a Name to themfelves, fometimes *Eagle, Panther, Allegator*, or fome fuch Wild Creature, efteeming nothing on Earth worthy to give them a Name, but thefe Wild-Fowl, and Beafts. . . .

The King is the Ruler of the Nation, and has others under him, to affift him, as his War-Captains and Counfellors, who are pick'd out and chofen from among the ancienteft Men of the Nation he is King of. These meet him in all general Councils and Debates, concerning War, Peace, Trade, Hunting, and all the Adventures and Accidents of Humane Affairs, which appear within their Verge. . . .

The Succeffion falls not to the King's Son, but to his Sifter's Son. . . . Sometimes they poifon the Heir to make way for another. . . .

They are fo well verfed in Poifon, that they are often found to poifon whole Families; nay, moft of a Town; and which is moft to be admired, they will poifon a running Spring, or Fountain of Water. . . .

Moft of the Savages are much addicted to Drunkenefs, a Vice they never were acquainted with, till the Chriftians came amongft them. . . . Their chief Liquor is Rum, without any mixture. This the *Englifh* bring amongft them, and buy Skins, Furs, Slaves and other of their Commodities therewith. They never are contented with a little, but when once begun, they muft make themfelves quite drunk. . . . In these drunken Frolicks . . . they sometimes murder one another.—John Lawson, *A New Voyage to Carolina*, pp. 171-211.

34. Religious Sects in the Colony

One of the most interesting accounts of the social and economic life of the colony is found in *The Natural History of North Carolina*, written by Dr. John Brickell of Edenton about 1731 and published in Dublin in 1743. Although he copied much from Lawson's *A New Voyage to Carolina*, he went far beyond that writer and gave detailed descriptions of many things not even mentioned by Lawson. The following document is a brief account of the religious sects in the colony and their places of settlement. No mention is made of Lutherans, Moravians, or Methodists because they were not numerous or important at this early date.

THE Religion by Law eftablished, is the *Proteftant*, as it is profeffed in *England;* and tho' they feldom have Orthodox Clergymen among them, yet there are not only Glebe Lands laid out for that Ufe, commodious to each Town, but likewife convenient for building Churches. The want of thefe Proteftant Clergy, is generally fupply'd by School-Masters, who read the Lithurgy, and then a Sermon out of Doctor Tillitfon, or fome good practical Divine, every Sunday. . . .

I shall treat of the other Religions as they are to be regarded according to their Numbers; and firft of the *Quakers:* Thefe People enjoy the same Privileges as with us in *Ireland,* and live for the moft part in *Albemarle* County, wherein they have a decent Meeting-House.

The *Prefbyterians* fucceed next, and have had a Minifter of their own Order for many Years paft; they are chiefly fettled in and about the River *Neus*.

Roman-Catholicks are the next confiderable, and are fettled in Many Parts of the Country, but moftly in and about *Bath-Town*, they have likewife a Clergyman of their own Order among them at Prefent.

Next succeed the *Anabaptifts*, who live moftly in *Albemarle* County.

There are likewife many Sectaries in *Carolina*, who have little or no appearance of Religion, except fome few Forms of Prayers . . . It is common to see here numbers of Men, Women, and Children, Baptized all together, when a Clergyman arrives in thofe Parts, and I have actually feen the Grandfather, his Son, and Grandfon, receive this Sacrament at one time. There are numbers who never require Baptifm, and confequently never covet to be made Christians, yet ufe some few Forms of Prayer.

By what I have already urged, my Readers will naturally obferve that there is Liberty of Confcience allowed in the whole Province; however, the Planters live in the greateft Harmony imaginable, no Difputes or Controverfies are ever obferved to arrife among them about their Religious Principles. They always treat each other with Friendfhip and Hofpitality, and never difpute over their Liquor, . . . By this Unity of Affection, the Profperity of the Province has increafed from its firft rise, to this Day. But though they are thus remarkable for their Friendfhip, Harmony and Hospitality, yet in regard to Morals, they have their fhare of the Corruptions of the Age, for as they live in the greateft Eafe and Plenty, Luxury of Confequence predominates, which is never without its attendant Vices.—John Brickell, *The Natural History of North Carolina*, pp. 35-37.

35. SOCIAL AND ECONOMIC CONDITIONS IN THE COLONY

The following description of the social and economic life of North Carolina in the early colonial period is taken from Dr. Brickell's *Natural History of North Carolina*, described on page 61 above.

THE Planters by the richnefs of the Soil, live after the moft eafie and pleafant Manner of any People I have ever met with; for you shall feldom hear them Repine at any Misfortunes in life, except the loss of Friends, there being plenty of all Neceffaries convenient for Life : Poverty being an entire Stranger here, and the Planters the most hofpitable People that are to be met with, not only to Strangers but likewife to thofe who by any Miffortune have loft the ufe of their Limbs or are incapable to Work, and have no vifible way to support themfelves ; to such Objects as thefe, the Country allows *Fifty Pounds per Annum* for their Support. So there are no Beggars or Vagabonds to be met with Strowling from place to place as is too common amongft us.

The Country in general is adorned with large and Beautiful Rivers and Creeks, and the Woods with lofty Timber which afford most delightful and pleafant Seats to the Planters, and the Lands very convenient and eafie to be fenced in, to fecure their Stocks of Cattle to more ftrict Bounderies, whereby with fmall trouble of Fencing, almoft every Man may enjoy to himfelf an intire Plantation. . . .

The Men are very ingenious in feveral Handycraft Busineffes, and in building their Canoes and Houfes ; though by the richness of the Soil, they live for the moft part after an indolent and luxurious Manner ; yet fome are laborious, and equalize with the *Negro's* in hard Labour, and others quite the Reverfe ; for I have frequently feen them come to the Towns, and there remain Drinking Rum, Punch, and other Liquors for Eight or Ten Days succeffively, and after they have committed this Excefs, will not drink any Spirituous Liquor, 'till fuch time as they take *the next Frolick*, as they call it, which is generally in two or three Months. These Exceffes are the occafions of many Difeafes amongft them. But the better Sort, or thofe of good OEconomy, it is quite otherwife, who feldom frequent the Taverns, having plenty of Wine, Rum, and other Liquors at their own Houfes, which they generally make ufe of amongft their Friends and Acquaintance, after a moft decent and difcreet Manner, and are not fo fubject to Diforders as thofe who Debauch themfelves in such a Beaftly Manner. . . .

Their Houfes are built after two different Ways ; *viz.* the moft fubftantial Planters generally ufe Brick, and Lime, which is made of Oyfter-fhells, for there are no Stones to be found proper for that purpofe, but near the Mountains ; the meaner fort erect with Timber, the outfide with Clap-Boards, the Roofs of both Sorts of Houfes are made with Shingles, and they generally have Safh Windows, and affect large and decent Rooms with good Clofets, . . .

Their Furniture, as with us, confifts of Pewter, Brafs, Tables, Chairs, which are imported here commonly from *England:* The better fort have tollerable Quantities of Plate, with other convenient, ornamental, and valuable Furniture.

The Cloathings used by the Men are *English* Cloaths, Druggets, Durois, Green Linnen &c. The Women have their Silks, Calicoes, Stamp-Linen, Calimanchoes and all kinds of Stuffs, some whereof are manufactured in the Province. They make few Hats tho' they have the best Furrs in plenty, but with this Article, they are commonly supplied from New-*England* and sometime from *Europe*.

The *Liquors* that are common in *Carolina* at present, and chiefly made use of, are, Rum, Brandy, Mault Drink; these they import. The following are made in Country, viz. Cyder, Perfimon-Beer, made of the Fruit of that Tree, Ceder-Beer, made of Ceder-Berries; they also make Beer of the green Stalks of *Indian-Corn*, . . . They likewise make Beer of Mollaffes . . . there is no Malt Drink made, notwithstanding all kind of Malt Liquors bear a good Price. . . .

The *Fireing* they use is Wood, and especially Hickery, though we discovered Pit-Coal in our Journies towards the Mountains, yet it is not worth their while to be at the expence of bringing it, Timber being so plenty.

The chiefest Diverfions here are Fishing, Fowling; and Hunting, Wild Beafts, such as Deer, Bears, Raccoons, Hares, Wild Turkies, with several other forts, . . .

Horse-Racing they are fond of, for which they have Race-Paths near each Town, and in many parts of the Country. . . .

They are much addicted to *Gaming*, especially at Cards and Dice, Hazard and All-fours, being the common Games they use. . . .

Cock-Fighting they greatly admire, which Birds they endeavor to procure from *England* and *Ireland*. . . .

Wreftling, Leaping, and fuch Activities are much ufed by them; yet I never obferved any Foot Races.

Dancing they are all fond of, efpecially when they can get a Fiddle or Bag-pipe; at this they will continue Hours together, . . .

But they have a particular Seafon, which is only at their *Wheat-Harveft*, not to be omitted; this they celebrate with great Solemnity, it is in the beginning of *June*, at which time the Planters notify to each other, that they defign to reap the aforefaid Grain, on a certain Day, fome send their *Negroes* to affift, others only go to partake of the great Feafts &c. Some will frequently come twenty nay thirty Miles on this Occafion, the Entertainments are great, and the whole Scene pleafant and diverting; . . .

This Colony boafts more Advantages than feveral others on this Continent, both for Pleafure, Eafe, and Profit: Were the Inhabitants as induftrious as the Soil is bountiful, they might fupply themfelves with all the Neceffaries of Life? With little Induftry they may

have Wines, Oil, Silk, Fruits, and many forts of Drugs, Dyes, &c.
. . . If the plenty and cheapnefs of Provifions, and the low rate of
Lands, may tempt People to this delightful Country, fure those who
have but fmall Beginnings, with moderate induftry, may here live
more comfortably, and provide for their Families better than in
any place I have yet feen in Europe. . . .

The produce of this Country for Exportation to *Europe* and the
Iflands, are Beef, Porke, Tallow, Hides, Deer-Skins, Furs, Wheat,
Indian-Corn, Peafe, Potatoes, Rice, Honey, Bees-wax, Myrtle-wax,
Tobacco, fnake-root, Turpentine, Tar, Pitch, Mafts for Ships,
Staves, Planks and Boards of most forts of Timber, Cotton, and
feveral forts of Gums, Tears, with some medicinal Drugs; Bricks
and Tile are made here, likewife feveral ufeful Earths, such as Bole,
Fullers-Earth, Tobacco Pipe Clay. . . . They export abundance
of Horses to the Islands of *Antegua, Barbadoes, &c.* . . .

The Chriftians or Planters of *North Carolina*, Barter the Commod-
ities that are produced in the Country for Rum, Sugar, Molloffes,
Negroes and the like.—John Brickell, *The Natural History of North
Carolina*, pp. 30-34, 37-44.

36. CAPT BURRINGTON'S REPRESENTATION OF THE PRESENT STATE AND CONDITION OF NORTH CAROLINA JANUARY 1ST 173⅔

Governor Burrington made a report to the Board of Trade and Plantations, in which he described religious and economic conditions, commercial difficulties, and the need of labor. He said, "Land is not wanting
for men in Carolina, but men for land." Land was held subject to a
"quit rent." This was a rent, the payment of which quit or exempted the
person paying it from further obligations, such as military service. Quit
rents were very unpopular in all of the American colonies, and collections were made in North Carolina with difficulty, if at all.

To THE RIGHT HONOURABLE THE LORDS OF TRADE AND PLANTA-
TIONS

There is not one clergyman of the Church of England, regularly
setled in this Government. The former Missionarys were so little
approved of, that the Inhabitants seem very indifferent, whither any
more come to them.

Some Presbyterian, or rather Independent Ministers from New
England have got congregations, more may follow; many of them
being unprovided with liveings in that Country; where a Preacher

5

is seldom pay'd more than the value of twenty Pounds sterling a year by his Parishioners.

The Quakers in this Government are considerable for their numbers, and substance; the regularity of their lives, hospitality to strangers, and kind offices to new settlers induceing many to be of their persuasion.

Plantations continue to sell very cheap. . . .

The Trade of this Country is on so bad a footing, that it is thought, the People who traffick with the New England and Virginia Merchants, loose half the value of their goods; the way to remedy this, will be to open a Port on Ocacock Island, . . .

It is by most Traders in London believed, that the Coast of this Country is very dangerous, but in reality not so. There are no more than three shoals in about four hundred miles on the sea-side. Cape Fear river, Beaufort & Ocacock are very good harbours, will admitt the largest Merchant ships, . . .

Great is the loss this Country has sustained in not being supply'd by vessells from Guinea with Negroes; in any part of the Province the People are able to pay for a ships load; but as none come directly from Affrica, we are under a necessity to buy, the refuse refractory and distemper'd Negroes, brought from other Governments; It is hoped some Merchants in England will speedily furnish this Colony with Negroes, to increase the Produce and its Trade to England. . . .

. . . There are millions of acres of Savanna Land in this Country, if they were taken up the King's rents would be much increased.

. . . Not an hundredth part of the grounds are Plantable; the barren Pine lands will never be cultivated; the several sorts of wet lands, called in these parts, Dismals, Pocosans, Swamps, Marishes and Savannas cannot be cleared and drained, without great charge, and labour, therefore not hitherto attempted. . . .

I am able to demonstrate, that the two Provinces of North and South Carolina contain above one hundred Millions of Acres.

It is computed at this time, not five millions are Patented in both Countrys.

Land is not wanting for men in Carolina, but men for land.

Several Saw mills have been lately erected in the South Parts of this Government and others are now building. . . .

The granting of five thousand acres or more, to each owner of a mill, cannot be a prejudice to any person, and may increase the quitt rents, . . .

. . . The Militia I am certain consists of five thousand men, and there are at least another thousand not enrolled. I compute the White men, women, and children, in North Carolina; to be full thirty thousand, and the Negroes about six thousand. The Indians, men, women, and children, less than eight hundred.—*Colonial Records of North Carolina*, III, 429-33.

37. Iron Collars for Certain Runaways, 1741

The following law illustrates the colonial attitude toward one of the social problems of that day. Though the wearing of an iron collar must have been very uncomfortable, it was far less brutal than branding and other punishments of the period. As late as 1842 a North Carolina man was branded with a large "B" on his cheek for bigamy.

XXXIII. And be it further Enacted by the Authority aforesaid, That when the Keeper of the said Public Gaol shall, by Direction of such Court as aforesaid, let out any Negro or Runaway to Hire to any Person or Persons whomsoever, the said Keeper shall, at the Time of his Delivery, cause an iron Collar to be put on the Neck of such Negro or Runaway, with the Letters P.G. stamped theron; and that thereafter the said Keeper shall not be answerable for any Escape of the said Negro or Runaway.—*Laws of North Carolina, 1741; State Records of North Carolina*, XXIII, 199.

38. The Spread of Population into Piedmont and Western North Carolina

About the middle of the eighteenth century settlers began to move into Piedmont North Carolina, and in a short time they "had reached the foot of the mountains." Most of these newcomers were Scotch-Irish and Germans who had left Pennsylvania because of increasing land rents and other economic difficulties. They came down the "Wagon road" and settled largely in the Catawba, Eno, and Yadkin valleys. The Scotch-Irish were Presbyterians. Three religious groups were found among the Germans: Lutheran, Moravian, and Reformed. Wachovia (Salem) was settled about 1753 by Moravians under the leadership of Bishop Augustus Gottlieb Spangenberg. Bethania and Betharaba were likewise settled by the Moravians at an early date. The most important towns to develop in this portion of the colony were Salisbury, Salem, and Charlotte, The expansion of population into the mountain region is shown by the fact that Asheville was incorporated in 1797.

EXTRACTS FROM BISHOP SPANGENBERG'S DIARY, 1752

TRADE and business are poor in North Carolina. With no navigable rivers there is little shipping; with no export trade of importance the towns are few and small. Edenton is said to be one of the oldest towns in America, but it is hardly one quarter so large as Germantown [Pennsylvania], though it is well situated on a rather large sound. There are other towns mentioned in the law books, but they have neither houses nor inhabitants, are towns only by Act of Assembly. . . .

Of handicrafts I have seen practically nothing in the 150 miles we have traveled across this Province. Almost nobody has a trade. . . . In 140 miles I saw not one wagon or plough, nor any sign of one.

. . . From here we go through Orange and Anson, which is the last County lying toward the west.

The land that we have seen is not particularly good, and yet we are told that it has all been taken up; I presume this is so, for otherwise people would not go 200 miles further west to settle. . . .

You see from the enclosed Act of Assembly that the western part of North Carolina has been made a separate County and Parish, the County being called Anson. All the land that we have taken up, and what we expect to take, lies in Anson County. . . .

From the camp in the upper fork of the Second or Middle Little River, flowing into the Catawba, not far from Quaker Meadows. We are here in a region that has perhaps been seldom visited since the creation of the world. We are some 70 or 80 miles from the last settlement in North Carolina, and have come over terrible mountains, and often through very dangerous ways. . . .

Jan. 8, 1753. *From the camp in the three forks of Muddy Creek,* . . . The land on which we are now encamped seems to me to have been reserved by the Lord for the Brethren [Moravians].

It lies in Anson County, about ten miles from the Atkin, on the upper road to Pennsylvania, some twenty miles from the Virginia line. . . .

This tract lies particularly well. It has countless springs, and numerous fine creeks; as many mills as may be desired can be built. . . .

The entire tract, with which we here complete our allotment, contains from 72,000 to 73,000 acres. We have surveyed it in fourteen pieces, not of exactly the same size, and yet not very different. . . .

Everybody who knows the country says that this is the only place where we could find so much good land together, and decidedly the best land yet vacant. Our impression is the same.—*Records of the Moravians in North Carolina* (edited by Adelaide L. Fries), I, 26-64.

MATTHEW ROWAN TO THE BOARD OF TRADE, JUNE 28, 1753

In the year 1746 I was up in the Country that is now Anson, Orange and Rowan Countys, there was not then above one hundred fighting men there is now at least three thousand for the most part Irish Protestants and Germans and dayley increasing.—*Colonial Records of North Carolina*, V, 24.

LETTER OF GOVERNOR TRYON TO BOARD OF TRADE, AUG. 2, 1766

I am of opinion this province is settling faster than any on the continent, last autumn and winter, upwards of one thousand wagons passed thro' Salisbury with families from the northward to settle in this province chiefly; some few went to Georgia or Florida, but liked it so indifferently, that some of them have since returned. . . . These inhabitants are a race of people differing in health and complexion from the natives in the maritime parts of the province.— *Colonial Records of North Carolina*, VII, 248.

RECORDS OF ST. LUKE'S PARISH, SALISBURY, 1771

Whereas in the counties of Rowan, Orange, Mecklenburg and Tryon, situated in the province of North Carolina in America, are already settled near three thousand German protestant families, and being very fruitful in that healthy climate, are beside, vastly increasing by numbers of German protestants almost weekly arriving from Pennsylvania, and other provinces of America ; . . . and having been hitherto without the means of grace, and being unable to maintain a learned and orthodox minister of their language and persuasion, . . . In order that such an evil, which must provoke the Almighty God to anger and vengeance, may be effectually removed, near sixty German Lutheran Protestant families have united themselves to implore his Excellency TRYON, . . . to countenance, . . . that two of their members . . . are deputed by them humbly to beg of the protestant brethren . . . their benevolence and charity to enable them in supporting a learned and orthodox protestant minister. . . .

His Excellency Governor Tryon has . . . referred the case to the Honorable Society for the propagation of the gospel in foreign parts.

established in London; which society has likewise piously countenanced . . . this undertaking.—*Colonial Records of North Carolina,*
VIII, 630.

AN ACT ESTABLISHING A TOWN AT THE COURT-HOUSE IN THE COUNTY OF BUNCOMBE, 1797

Whereas it is reprefented to this General Affembly, that the ef-
tablishing a town at the court-houfe in Buncomb county would be
of great utility, and accord with the defire of the inhabitants of faid
county; and there being a number of lots already laid off at the faid
court-houfe; and Zebulon Baird, Efquire, the proprietor of the
lands adjoining the fame, having fignified his confent to lay off
as much more land as will amount to fixty-three acres including
faid lots for the purpofe aforefaid: . . . Be it enacted . . . That
the aforefaid fixty-three acres of land be . . . eftablifhed a town
by the name of Afhville; . . . —*Laws of North Carolina, 1797,* Chap.
LIV, pp. 19-20.

39. INDIAN TREATIES

As England began to realize the international complications that would
follow her occupation of the North American continent, she gradually
shaped her Indian policy to conform with her imperial needs. Towards
France, the major contender for colonial prizes, the English directed
many thrusts, to be delivered later by Indian nations bound to England
by treaties. While referring to amity and friendship, the following treaty
relieves its tedium by offering gifts of "striped duffles" and "white cloth
to be dyed blue"; but when admonishing the Indians to keep their lands
clear of all white men except the English, appropriate gifts of "five hundred pounds weight of swan shot and five hundred pounds weight of
bullets" are extended, the implication being that they were to be used
upon foreign intruders.

The Dumplin Creek treaty of 1785, made by North Carolina officials,
has its chief significance in the fact that land-hungry whites received
much, while the Indians, except for vague promises, had to content
themselves with very little.

CHEROKEE NATION'S TREATY WITH ENGLAND, 1730

WHITEHALL MONDAY SEPT. 7. 1730

Present

MR PELHAM. MR BLADEN. MR BRUDENELL

The seven Indian Chiefs of the Cherokee Nation attending as
thay had been desir'd with their Interpreter, Col. Johnson, Govr

of South Carolina Sir William Keith and several other gentlemen
Their Lords explained to them by their Interpreter (who was sworn)
the Form of a Treaty with them agreed at the last meeting in the
words following

Whereas you Scay-agusta Oukah Chief of the Town Tassetsa You
Scalilasken Ket-agusta, You Tethtowe, You Clogoittah, You Col-
annah, You Unnaconoy, You Oucounacon have been deputed by
the whole nation of the Cherokee Indians to come to Great Britain
where you have seen the great King George and in token of your
obedience have laid the Crown of your Nation with the scalps of
your enemies and feathers of peace at his Maj. feet. . . .

Hear then the words of the Great King whom you have seen and
who has commanded us to tell you

That the English everywhere on all sides of the Great Mountains
and Lakes are his people and his children whom he loves That their
Friends are his Friends and their Enemies are his Enemies That he
takes it kindly that the Great Nation of Cherokees have sent you
hither a great way to brighten the chain of friendship between him
and them & between your people and his people. . . .

The Great King and the Cherokee Indians being thus fastened
together by the chain of friendship he has ordered his people and
children the English in Carolina to trade with the Indians and to
furnish them with all manner of goods that they want and to make
haste to build houses and to plant corn from Charles Town towards
the Town of the Cherokees behind the great Mountains for he desires that the English and the Indians may live together as the children of one Family whereof the Great King is a kind & loving
Father And as the King has given his land on both sides of the Great
Mountains to his own children the English so he now gives to the
Cherokee Indians the privilege of living where they please and he
has order'd his Governor to forbid the English from building houses
or planting corn near any Indian Town for fear that your young
people should kill the cattle and young lambs and so quarrel with
the English and hurt them And hereupon we give two other pieces
of white cloth to be dyed blue. . . .

The Nation of The Cherokees shall on their part take care to
keep the trading path clean and that there be no blood in the path
where the English white men tread even though they should be
accompanied by any other people with whom the Cherokees are
at war Whereupon we give four hundred pounds weight of gun-
powder.

That the Cherokees shall not suffer their people to trade with the white men of any other Nation but the English nor permit white men of any other Nation to build any Forts Cabins or plant corn amongst them or near to any of the Indian Towns or upon the land which belong to the Great King and if any such attempt should be made you must acquaint the English Governor therewith and do whatever he directs in order to maintain & defend the Great King's right to the Country of Carolina Whereupon we give five hundred pounds weight of bullets. . . .

That if by any accidental misfortune it should happen that an Englishman should kill an Indian The King or Great Man of the Cherokees shall first complain to the English Governor and the man who did it shall be punished by the English laws as if he had killed an Englishman and in like manner if any Indian kills an Englishman the Indian who did it shall be delivered up to the Governor & be punished by the same English law as if he was an Englishman Whereupon we give twelve dozen of spring knives four dozen of brass kettles and ten dozen of belts. . . .

Their Lordships then showed them the samples of the above-mentioned presents and the chief of the Indians said to the Board by his Interpreter that they were not come hither as enemies but as friends That altho' they did not expect to see the King yet they had seen him And that they would give their Answer to the said Treaty on Wednesday morning next.—*Colonial Records of North Carolina*, III, 129-32.

TREATY OF DUMPLIN CREEK, 1785

At a Treaty of Amity and Friendship begun and held with the Cherokees at the mouth of Dumplin Creek on French Broad River And Continued by Adjournment the 31st day of May, Anno Domini 1785, Present, John Sevier, Commissioner; The King of the Cherokees; Aucoo, Chief of Chota; Abraham, Chief of Chelhowa; The bord Head Warrior of the Valley towns; The Sturgion of Tallassee; The leach from Settico; The bigg man Killer from Tallassee, and near thirty more Wariors, &c., of the Cherokee Nation, together With Charles Murphy, half breed Indian and Linguister of the Treaty.

Aucoo, chief of Chota, Chosen for the Speaker On the part of the Cherokees, begun & Spoke as follows:

It is agreed by us, the Warriors, Chiefs & representatives of the Cherokee Nation, that all lands lying and being on the South side of Holeson and French Broad Rivers, as far South as the ridge that divide the Waters of Little River from the Waters of Tenesee, That the same may be peaceably inhabited & Cultivated, Resided upon, enjoyed and inhabited by our elder brother, the white people, from this time forward and allways. And do agree on our part and in behalf of our Nation, That the white people shall never be by us or any of our Nation, molested or interupted, Neither in there persons or property in no Wise, or in any Manner or form whatever, in Consequence of there Setling or Inhabiting the said territory, tract of land and Country Aforesaid, or any part of the same whatever.

John Sevier, for and in behalf of the white people, and for and in behalf of the State or Government, or the United States, as the case may hereafter be Settled & concluded on, with respect to the Jurisdiction and Sovereignty over the said Tract and territory of land. That there shall be a reasonable & liberal compensation made the Cherokees for the lands they have herein ceeded and granted to the white people, and to the State or States that may hereafter legally possess & enjoy the lands and Country aforesaid, in good faith that this bargain And engagement now made and entered into between Us, the white people, & the Cherokees, may never be Broken, disanuled or dissolved, in consequence of Any Claim, right or sovereignty over the soil herby Mention and described as aforesaid.

Done in open Treaty the 10th June, 1785.

Signed,
JOHN SEVIER
THE KING
AUCOO, Chief of Chota
And Chiefs of the different towns.
—*State Records of North Carolina*, XXII, 649-50.

40. CATAWBA INDIANS PROTEST AGAINST SALE OF STRONG DRINK AND OCCUPATION OF THEIR LANDS, 1754-1756

The following documents illustrate the attitude of certain Indian leaders toward the white people in regard to two important matters, the sale of strong drink and the occupation of Indian lands.

AT A TREATY HELD ON THURSDAY THE TWENTY NINTH DAY OF AUGUST ONE THOUSAND SEVEN HUNDRED AND FIFTY FOUR. "KING HAGLAR AND SUNDRY OF HIS HEADMEN AND HIS WARRIORS."

KING—Brothers here is One thing You Yourselves are to Blame very much in, That is You Rot Your grain in Tubs, out of which you take and make Strong Spirits You sell it to our young men and give it them, many times; they get very Drunk with it this is the Very Cause that they oftentimes Commit those Crimes that is offencive to You and us and all thro' the Effect of that Drink it is also very bad for our people, for it Rots their guts and Causes our men to get very sick and many of our people has Lately Died by the Effects of that strong Drink, and I heartily wish You would do something to prevent Your People from Dareing to Sell or give them any of that Strong Drink, upon any Consideration whatever for that will be a great means of our being free from being accused of those Crimes that is Committed by our young men and will prevent many of the abuses that is done by them thro' the Effects of that Strong Drink. . . .

KING—As to our Liveing on those Lands we Expect to live on those Lands we now possess During our Time here for when the Great man above made us he also made this Island he also made our forefathers and of this Colour and Hue (Showing his hands & Breast) he also fixed our forefathers and us here and to Inherit this Land and Ever since we Lived after our manner and fashion we in those Days, had no instruments To support our living but Bows which we Compleated with stones, knives we had none, and as it was our Custom in those days to Cut our hair, which we Did by Burning it of our heads and Bodies with Coals of Fire, our Axes we made of stone we bled our selves with fish Teeth our Cloathing were Skins and Furr, instead of which we Enjoy those Cloaths which we got from the white people Ever since they first Came among us we have Enjoyed all those things that we were then destitute of for which we thank the white people, and to this Day we have Lived in a Brotherly Love & peace with them and more Especially with these Three Governments and it is our Earnest Desire that Love and Friendship which has so long remain'd should Ever Continue. . . .

COPY OF A CONFERENCE HELD WITH THE KING AND WARRIORS OF THE CATAUBAS BY MR. CHIEF JUSTICE HENLEY AT SALISBURY, NORTH CAROLINA IN MAY, 1756.

To which the King replied. . . .

I go very much among the White people and have often my Belly filled by them and am very sorry that they should at any time be distracted.

I return the Governour thanks for his care in purchasing Corn for my people which has saved the lives of many of our old men women and children.

As my people and the White people are Brethren I desire that when they go to their houses they may give them victuals to eat, some of the White People are very bad and quarrelsome and whip my people about the head, beat and abuse them but others are very good.

I desire a stop may be put to the selling strong liquors by the White people especially near the Indian Nation. If the White people make strong drink let them sell it to one another or drink it in their own Families. This will avoid a great deal of mischief which otherwise will happen from my people getting drunk and quarrelling with the White people. Should any of my people do any mischief to the White people I have no strong prisons like you to confine them for it, Our only way is to put them under ground and all these men (pointing to his Warriors again) will be ready to do that for those who shall deserve it.—*Colonial Records of North Carolina*, V, 143, 144a, 581.

41. WILD GAME IN THE MORAVIAN SETTLEMENTS, 1760

The following extract from the Moravian Records shows that there was a great abundance of wild game in colonial North Carolina. It seems almost unbelievable. Yet the Moravians had a reputation for truthfulness.

Nov. 2nd it is recorded that there were many bears and wolves about. The Moravians killed several of the former, one weighing 300 pounds. . . . Also on the 20th neighbors from the South Fork came for their share of corn they had helped to plant. On their way home they found the roosting place of wild pigeons of which there are remarkably many, and they killed 1200, of which they sent us a number. Next week some of the Brethren went to the same place and brought in 1800. In the morning the pigeons go off in clouds, at sunset return to their camp, crowding so closely together that branches are broken off, and trees that have withstood many a heavy storm fall to the ground. Every night many pigeons come to the ground with the falling branches and trees. People who have often seen wild pigeons before say they have never seen anything like this.—*Records of the Moravians in North Carolina* (edited by Adelaide L. Fries), I, 233.

42. REPORT OF GOVERNOR ARTHUR DOBBS TO THE BOARD OF TRADE, DECEMBER, 1761

The Board of Trade and Plantations sent Governor Dobbs seventeen questions relative to the soil, relief, climate, boundaries, population, resources, industries, government, Indians, militia, and other matters. Some of his answers are given here.

THE COLONY, ITS CLIMATE, SOIL, POPULATION, GOVERNMENT, RESOURCES, &C

AN ANSWER TO THE SEVERAL QUERIES SENT BY THE LORDS COMMISSIONERS FOR TRADE AND PLANTATIONS.

THE natural produce and Staple Commodities of this Province, for of Manufactures there are none ; Consist of Naval Stores Mast yards Plank and Ship Timber, Tar pitch and Turpentine Lumber of all Kinds, furs and peltry Beef pork Hides, and some tanned Leather— Indian Corn pease Rice and of late flour Hemp flax and flax seed, Tobacco Bees and Myrtle wax and some Indigo : We export little or no bullion or Sterling the whole Trade being carried on by paper Currency, . . .

The only Regulation made to prevent Frauds in the Exports are some inspecting Laws made some of them lately to inspect Beef Pork Pitch Tar Tobacco, and Turpentine in several parts the Inspectors not nominated by nor under the power of the Crown, but are chosen by the Justices in their Inferior Courts of Session, given in Jobs to their Friends & therefore not properly taken care of. . . .

No Mines are discovered opened or worked but great quantities of Iron ore have been found upon the surface of the ground, but not followed so as to find a Vein.

No Forges or Bloomeries have been yet erected occasioned by the Sloth or poverty of the Inhabitants, . . . Lead Ore has been found near the Virginia Line . . . there are also Symptoms of Copper ore.

The Taxables when I came over in 1754 were computed at about 26000, and now are computed at 34000. . . .

The only Tribes or remains of Tribes of Indians residing in this Province are the Tuskerora Sapona Meherin and Maramuskito Indians. The Tuskerora have about 100 fighting men the Saponas and Meherin Indians about 20 each and the Maramuskitos about 7 or 8. the first 3 are situated in the Middle of the Colony upon and near Roanoak and have by Law 10,000 acres of Land allotted to them in Lord Granville's District they live chiefly by hunting and are in perfect friendship with the Inhabitants.

The Catauba Indians who are also in close friendship with the Inhabitants . . . consisted within these few years of about 300 fighting men but last year the small pox ravaged in their towns which made them desert them and leave their sick behind them to perish; by an account from their King Haglar to me they are reduced to 60 fighting and about as many old men and boys and a suitable number of Women, . . .

The Cherokee Indians are situated among and beyond the Mountians to the Westward of our present Settlements . . . they were lately esteemed to be a powerful Tribe, and to consist of about 3000 fighting men, they are now upon account of the War Sickness and famine supposed to be reduced to about 2000. . . .

The only standing Revenue in this Province belonging to the Crown are the Quit Rents and what may arise from fines and forfeitures for the publick Revenue raised by the Assembly is temporary and trifling except what has been raised upon Account of the present War.—*Colonial Records of North Carolina*, VI, 605-23.

43. TRADE BETWEEN ENGLAND AND CAROLINA, 1767

The following account of the trade and navigation of Great Britain was written by Joshua Gee, a London merchant, in 1767. Gee maintained that the surest way for a nation to increase its riches was to prevent the importation of such foreign commodities as might be raised at home.

CAROLINA lies in as happy a climate as any in the world, from 32 to 36 degrees of northern latitude; the foil is in general fertile; the rice it produces is faid to be the beft in the world; and no country affords better filk than has been brought from thence, tho' for want of fufficient encouragement, the quantity imported is very fmall; 'tis said both bohea and green tea have been raifed there extraordinary good of the kind; the olive tree grows wild, and thrives very well, and might foon be improved fo far as to fupply us with large quantities of oil; 'tis faid the fly, from whence the cochineal is made, is found very commonly; and if care was taken, very great quantities might be made; the indigo plant grows exceeding well; and 'tis thought, if rightly improved, we might be fupplied with both the aforefaid commodities, not only to anfwer our home confumption, but with large quantities for re-exportation; the country has plenty of iron in it; and would produce excellent hemp and flax, if encouragement was given for raifing it; it lies as convenient as any of our colonies in America for carrying on the fkin trade, and fupplying the Indian nations with Englifh commodities; the rice trade, fince it hath been made an enumerated commodity, is under great difcouragement; for it cannot be fent directly to Portugal and Spain, as formerly; and it will not bear the charge of bringing home and refhipping, unlefs it be at the time when the crops in the Milanefe and Egypt prove bad. . . .

N. B. The rich grounds that lie under the Apalachean hills, and through Virginia, &c. are inviting places for raifing filk, hemp and flax, the air being accounted healthy and pure; and the country is large enough to canton out into diftinct lots all the inhabitants we fhall be capable of fending, from whence they will have the convenience of fending all their goods down by navigable rivers.—Joshua Gee, *The Trade and Navigation of Great-Britain Considered—A New Edition, with many Interesting Notes and Additions. By a Merchant*, pp. 51-53.

44. Agriculture and Stock Raising in Colonial North Carolina

Agriculture in colonial North Carolina was not very progressive or scientific. There was too much land and too little labor. "The bounty of nature and the great abundance of land made careful and systematic methods of culture seem unnecessary to the colonist and he consequently adopted wasteful and extravagant practices." Extensive cultivation of the soil was the general practice, and before the close of the colonial period complaints were being made about "soil exhaustion" and "land butchery." Like other colonies, North Carolina experimented unsuccessfully with a number of European crops. She finally adopted many of the Indian crops and methods. In many respects, however, the Indian was a more scientific farmer than the average white farmer of that day.

The following observation is from one of the best accounts written about agriculture in the American colonies in the late eighteenth century.

THE products of North Carolina are rice, tobacco, indigo, cotton, wheat, peas, beans, Indian corn, and all sorts of roots, especially potatoes. Rice is not so much cultivated here as in South Carolina; but in the latter they raise no tobacco, whereas in North Carolina it is one of their chief articles. It grows in the northerly parts of the province, on the frontiers of Virginia, from which colony it is exported. Indigo grows very well in the province, particularly in the southern parts, and proves a most profitable branch of culture. Cotton does very well, and the sort is so excellent, that it is much to be wished they had made a greater progress in it. The greatest articles of their produce which is exported are tar, pitch, turpentine, and every species of lumber, in astonishing quantities. . . .

Notwithstanding these great advantages, there are very few people in North Carolina; this has been owing to several causes: there were obstructions in settling it, which occasioned some to leave the country, and a general idea was spread to its disadvantage; but the principal evil was the want of ports, of which there was not one good one in all North Carolina . . . . And this want of good ports, and a trading town, has checked the culture of rice a good deal; but it has had another effect, which may probably prove a great advantage; it has driven the new settlers back into the country, and thrown them very much into common husbandry. . . .

The two great circumstances which give the farmers of North Carolina such a superiority over those of most other colonies, are, first, the plenty of land; and, secondly, the vast herds of cattle kept by the planters. The want of ports, as I said, kept numbers from settling here and this made the land of less value, consequently every settler got large grants; and, falling to the business of breeding cattle, their herds became so great, that the profit from them alone is exceeding great. It is not an uncommon thing to see one man the master of from 300 to 1200, and even to 2000 cows, bulls, oxen, and young cattle; hogs also in prodigious numbers. Their management is to let them run loose in the woods all day, and to bring them up at night by the sound of a horn: sometimes, particularly in winter, they keep them during the night in inclosures, giving them a little food, and letting the cows and sows to the calves and pigs; this makes them come home the more regularly. Such herds of cattle and swine are to be found in no other colonies; and when this is better settled, they will not be so common here; for at present the woods are all in common, and people's property has no other boundary or distinction than marks cut in trees, so that the cattle have an unbounded range; but when the country becomes more cultivated, estates will be surrounded by enclosures, and consequently the numbers of cattle kept by the planters will be proportioned to their own lands only.

It may easily be supposed that these vast flocks of cattle might be of surprising consequence in the raising manure, were the planters as attentive as they ought to be to this essential object: they might by this means cultivate indigo and tobacco to greater advantage than their neighbours; some few make a good use of the advantage, but more of them are drawn from it by the plenty of rich land, which they run over, as in the northern colonies, till it is exhausted, and then take fresh, relying on such a change, instead of making the most of their manure, which would add indefinitely to their profit.

Their system is to depend (where they have no navigation, and are at a considerable distance from it, which however is not the case in many parts) on the hides of their cattle, and on barrelled meat, with some corn, roots, and pitch and tar, ec. for the profit of their plantation; but the most bulky of these commodities yield but little, unless near some river; accordingly there are not many plantations at any distance from water, since it is not an inland navigation that is wanted in North Carolina, but ports at the mouths of the rivers that will admit of large ships.

The mode of common husbandry here is to break up a piece of wood land, a work very easily done, from the trees standing at good distances from each other; this they sow with Indian corn for several years successively, till it will yield large crops no longer: they get at first fourscore or an hundred bushels an acre, but sixty or seventy, are common: when the land is pretty well exhausted they sow it with peas or beans one year, of which they will get thirty or forty bushels per acre; and afterwards sow it with wheat for two or three years: it will yield good crops of this grain when it would bear Indian corn no longer, which shews how excellent the land must be. But let me remark that this culture of wheat to such advantage is only in the back part of the province, where the climate is far more temperate than on the coast; upon the latter it does not succeed well, a circumstance much deserving attention; for we may lay it down as a universal rule, that where wheat thrives well, there the climate is healthy, and agreeable to the generality of constitutions: it does well neither in extreme cold, nor in great heat.

In this system of crops they change the land as fast as it wears out, clearing fresh pieces of wood land, exhausting them in succession; after which they leave them to the spontaneous growth. It is not here as in the northern colonies, that weeds come first and then grass; the climate is so hot, that, except on the rich moist lands, any sort of grass is scarce; but the fallow in a few years becomes a forest, for no climate seems more congenial to the production of quick growing trees. If the planter does not return to cultivate the land again, as may probably be the case, from the plenty of fresh, it presently becomes such a wood as the rest of the country is ; and woods are here the pasture of the cattle, which is excellent for hogs, because they get quantities of mast and fruit; but for cattle is much inferior to pastures and meadows.—*American Husbandry*, by an American (London, 1775), I, 331-49.

45. FUNERAL CEREMONIES, 1775

In the early days of North Carolina history, funerals were public affairs. They were among the most important social functions. Private burials were illegal, and every planter was required to "set apart a Burial Place & fence the same for the interring of all such Christian Persons whether Bond or Free that shall die on their [his] Plantations." but nobody could be buried until "at least Three or Four of the Neighbours [had been called] to view the Corpse." Considerable publicity was given to the burial of the dead. Invitations were sent to relatives and friends. There was much eating and drinking. Seven gallons of whiskey were drunk at a funeral in Mecklenburg County in 1767, at the expense of the estate.

In her charming *Journal of a Lady of Quality*, Miss Janet Schaw gives an interesting account of the funeral of Jean Corbin at "Point Pleasant," near Wilmington, in 1775. Mrs. Corbin was the widow of James Innes and of Francis Corbin, and she was buried between her two husbands, "in a manner suitable to her fortune."

EVERYBODY of fashion both from the town and round the country were invited, but the Solemnity was greatly hurt by a set of Volunteers, who, I thought, must have fallen from the moon ; above a hundred of whom (of both sexes) arrived in canoes, just as the clergyman was going to begin the service, and made such a noise, it was hardly to be heard. A hogshead of rum and broth and vast quantities of pork, beef and corn-bread were set forth for the entertainment of these gentry. But as they observed the tables already covered for the guests, after the funeral, they took care to be first back from it, and before any one got to the hall, were placed at the tables, and those that had not room to sit carried off the dishes to another room, so that an elegant entertainment that had been provided went for nothing. At last they got into their canoes, and I saw them row thro' the creeks, and suppose they have little spots of ground up the woods, which afford them corn and pork, and that on such occasions they flock down like crows to a carrion.

They were no sooner gone than the Negroes assembled to perform their part of the funeral rites, which they did by running, jumping, crying and various exercises. They are a noble troop, the best in all the country ; . . . —Janet Schaw, *Journal of a Lady of Quality* (edited by E. W. and C. M. Andrews), p. 171.

III

TRANSITION FROM COLONY TO STATEHOOD

46. Resistance to the Stamp Act, 1765-1766

The history of the Stamp Act controversy is well known. Although the primary purpose of the act was to raise money for colonial defense, it met with bitter opposition in America. North Carolina, like other colonies, resisted it from the first. According to tradition, Speaker Ashe notified Governor Tryon that North Carolina would "fight it to the death." For years North Carolina people had maintained that the right of taxation could be lawfully exercised only by their own representatives. The Assembly of 1760 had positively stated that it was the indubitable right of the Assembly to frame and model every bill whereby an aid was granted to the King, and that every attempt to deprive them of the enjoyment thereof was an infringement of the rights and privileges of the Assembly.

There were demonstrations against the Stamp Act in a number of the towns of eastern Carolina. Resistance was most conspicuous at Wilmington and Brunswick. Armed force was most in evidence at Brunswick, though the story of the Wilmington riots is better known. On October 19, 1765, about five hundred people assembled in Wilmington and burnt Earl Bute in effigy because he had "several times expressed himself much in favor of the Stamp duty." They drank toasts to LIBERTY, PROPERTY and NO STAMP DUTY. On November 16, 1765, they compelled the resignation of Dr. William Houston, the recently appointed stamp master. The *North Carolina Gazette* was published on unstamped paper and with a skull and bones at the place where the stamp was to have been placed.

On November 18, 1765, "near fifty merchants and gentlemen of New Hanover and Brunswick" were invited to dine with Governor Tryon, who "urged to them the expediency of permitting the circulation of stamps." The next day they replied in writing that they thought it was the "securer conduct" to prevent to the utmost of their power the operation of the Stamp Act in any of its features.

In January, 1766, two ships, the *Dobbs* and the *Patience*, came into the Cape Fear and were seized because their clearance papers were not stamped, and were held by the British men-of-war, the *Diligence* and the *Viper*. This action aroused the people of that region, and on February 18, an association was entered into "by the principal gentlemen, freeholders and inhabitants of several counties of the Province." On February 19, the collector's desk at Brunswick was broken into and the clearance papers that had been seized for want of stamps were forcibly taken from him. On the same day one hundred and fifty armed men went to the Governor's house in Brunswick to demand the person of Captain Lobb, of the royal sloop *Viper*, who had made the seizures. Captain Lobb was not there; so on the next day a committee of the "inhabitants in arms" went aboard the *Viper* and demanded possession of the vessels which had been seized. The vessels were released. On February 21, Colonel Pennington. the comptroller of the province, was taken from the Governor's own house and from his very presence by the militia of the district and compelled to take an oath that he would not perform any duty with regard to the stamps. The Stamp Act was thus annulled in North Carolina. Not a stamp was sold in the province. Parliament repealed the Stamp Act in 1766.

The first document given below is taken from a pamphlet issued by Maurice Moore, an outstanding North Carolina leader. It is unique in that it challenged the British theory of "virtual representation" in Parliament and maintained that North Carolina could be taxed only by its own representatives.

THE JUSTICE AND POLICY OF TAXING THE AMERICAN COLONIES IN GREAT BRITAIN, CONSIDERED, 1765

. . . THE inhabitants of the Colonies upon the Continent, . . . have always thought, and I believe ever will think, all the constitutional rights and liberties enjoyed in Great-Britain, at the time they departed from it, their Birth-Right, and that they brought them over with them to America; among which, that of being taxed only with their own consent, is one of the most essential.

It is certainly very natural, that those who transport themselves from one country to another, should as well carry with them the Laws and Policy, as the Customs and Manners of the country from whence they came. . . . The Colonists seem to stand on the same footing with those who leave their own country, and settle themselves in a new one which was not inhabited before: If they do, . . . the Colonists have brought over with them every constitutional right, liberty and privilege; and if being taxed only by their own consent is one of them, they cannot, with the least degree of justice, be taxed by the British parliament, in which they are not represented, no person in that assembly being authorized to signify their consent: Few persons there, are acquainted with their circumstance, and perhaps none know what mode of taxation would be least burdensome to them.

It hath indeed pleased some of the honourable members of that august assembly to say, that the Colonies are virtually represented in parliament; but this is a doctrine which only tends to allow the Colonists a shadow of that *substance* which they must ever be slaves without. It cannot surely be consistent with British liberty, that any set of men should represent another, detached from them in situation and interest, without the privity and consent of the represented. . . .

The notion of virtual representation, may, for all I know, be consistent enough, while it is confined to Great-Britain only; its inhabitants intimately reside together; the interest and circumstance of those who do not vote for representatives, are the same with those that do; and are equally well known to, and understood by such representatives. . . . But hath the Colonies any of these advantages? They certainly have not: They live above a thousand leagues from Great-Britain; their interest and circumstance are not similar to those of the British inhabitants; nor have they been well considered or understood by the British parliament. The Colonists have suffered many impositions, as may be seen by the several acts of trade which have been borne by them alone, . . .

The Stamp Duty is itself a burthen too great for the circumstances of the Colonists to bear, considering the many restrictions that have been put upon their trade, which are at present rigorously enforced throughout America: It will occasion a discontinuance of industry, and must in the end, reduce them to a state of beggary; they will no longer be able to purchase the manufactures of the Mother Country, or furnish her with materials for making new ones. Great Britain then loses a trade, from which she hath derived her greatest opulence and dignity, and this too by insisting on a measure destructive of the peace and happiness of many thousands of as loyal subjects as any the King has. . . . The act imposing a Stamp Duty, will surely be repealed, as soon as its consequences are well considered. I am persuaded, the more closely united the Mother Country and the Colonies are, the happier it will be for both; but such an union will never take effect, but upon a foundation of equality: They must be upon such a footing, as that each may advance the other's interest, while he labours for his own. . . . It would be no injustice that the Colonies should bear a proportionable part of the heavy expense that hath been incurred in the course of the late war; and I am persuaded, that no man of sense in the Colonies would oppose it: but they should be allowed to consent to it, according to their constitutional right, in their own provincial assemblies, where they are really represented. And in estimating such proportion of expence, their number, circumstance, and the restrictions on their trade, should be considered : But if the British parliament will insist on taxing the Colonists, as their virtual representatives, then are they stripped of that constitutional right on which their liberty and property depends, and reduced to the most abject state of slavery; a situation, in which, it is very unnatural to think, a Mother can take pleasure in viewing her Children.—*Some Eighteenth Century Tracts Concerning North Carolina* (edited by William K. Boyd), pp. 157-74.

THE WILMINGTON DEMONSTRATIONS AGAINST THE STAMP ACT, 1765.

WILMINGTON, November 20.

On Saturday the 19th of last Month, about Seven of the Clock in the Evening, near Five Hundred People assembled together in this Town, and exhibited the Effigy of a certain HONOURABLE GENTLEMAN; and after letting it hang by the Neck for some Time, near the Court-House, they made a large Bonfire with a Number of Tar-Barrels, &c. and committed it to the Flames.—The Reason assigned for the People's Dislike to that Gentleman, was, from being informed of his having several Times expressed himself much in Favour of the STAMP-DUTY.—After the Effigy was consumed, they went to every House in Town, and bro't all the Gentlemen to the Bonfire, and insisted upon their drinking, LIBERTY, PROPERTY, and no STAMP-DUTY, and Confusion to Lord B-te and all his Adherents. . . . They continued together until 12 of the Clock, and then dispersed, without doing any Mischief, And,

On Thursday, 31st of the same Month, in the Evening, a great Number of People again assembled, and produced an Effigy of Liberty, which they put into a Coffin, and marched in solemn Procession with it to the Church-Yard. . . . But before they committed the Body to the Ground, they thought it adviseable to feel its Pulse ; and when finding some Remains of Life, they returned back to a Bonfire ready prepared, placed the Effigy before it in a large Two-arm'd Chair, and concluded the Evening with great Rejoicings, on finding that LIBERTY had still an Existence in the COLONIES.—Not the least Injury was offered to any Person.

On Saturday the 16th of this Inst. WILLIAM HOUSTON, Esq; Distributor of STAMPS for this Province, came to this Town ; upon which three or four Hundred People immediately gathered together, with Drums beating and Colours flying, and repaired to the House the said STAMP-OFFICER put up at, and insisted upon knowing, "Whether he intended to execute his said Office, or not?" He told them, "He should be very sorry to execute any Office disagreeable to the People of the Province." But they, not content with such a Declaration, carried him into the Court-House, where he signed a Resignation satisfactory to the Whole. . . .

Immediately after . . . they call'd upon Mr. A STUART, the Printer,—(who had not printed the GAZETTE for some weeks before the ACT took Place, it having pleased GOD to afflict him with a dangerous Fever) when he appeared, they ask'd him, if "He would continue his Business, as heretofore?—And Publish a NEWSPAPER?" . . . Mr. STUART then answer'd, "That rather than run the Hazard of Life, being maimed, or have his Printing-Office destroy'd, that he would comply with their Request"; but took the WHOLE for Witness, that he was compell'd thereto. . . . —*Colonial Records of North Carolina*, VII, 123-25. Reprinted from the *North Carolina Gazette*, November 20, 1765.

ASSOCIATION AGAINST THE STAMP ACT, FEBRUARY 18, 1766.

We the subscribers, free and natural born subjects of George the Third, . . . whose sacred person, crown and dignity, we are ready and willing, at the expense of our lives and fortunes to defend, being fully convinced of the oppressive and arbitrary tendency of a late Act of Parliament, imposing Stamp duties on the inhabitants of this Province, and fundamentally subversive of the liberties and Charters of North America; truly sensible of the inestimable blessings of a free Constitution, gloriously handed down to us by our brave Forefathers, detesting Rebellion, yet preferring death to slavery, Do, with all loyalty to our most gracious Sovereign, with all deference to the just Laws of our Country, and with a proper and necessary regard to ourselves and Posterity, hereby mutually and solemnly plight our faith and honour, that we will at any risque whatever and whenever called upon, unite, and truly and faithfully assist each other, to the best of our Power, in preventing entirely the operation of the Stamp Act.—*Colonial Records of North Carolina*, VII, 168-c-e. Reprinted from the *North Carolina Gazette*, February 26, 1766.

ARMED RESISTANCE TO THE STAMP ACT AT BRUNSWICK

It was about 10 o'clock when I observed a body of men in arms from four to five hundred move towards the house, A detachment of sixty men came down the avenue, and the main body drew up in front in sight and within three hundred yards of the house. Mr. Harnett a representative in the Assembly for Wilmington, came at the head of the detachment and sent a message to speak with Mr. Pennington. . . . I answered, "Mr. Pennington came into my house for refuge, he was a Crown Officer, and as such I would give him all the protection, my roof, and the dignity of the character I held in this Province, could afford him." Mr. Harnett hoped I would let him go, as the people were determined to take him out of the house if he should be longer detained; an insult he said they wished to avoid offering to me: An insult I replied that would not tend to any great consequence, after they had already offered every insult they could offer, by investing my house, and making me in effect a prisoner before any grievance, or óppression had been first represented to me. Mr. Pennington grew very uneasy, said he would choose to go to the gentlemen; . . . I told him he had better resign before he left me: Mr. Harnett interposed, with saying that he hoped he would not do that: I enforced the recommendation for resignation. He consented, paper was brought and his resignation executed and received. . . . He was afterwards obliged to take an oath that he would never issue any stamped paper in this province. The above oath the Collector informed me he was obliged to take, as were all the clerks of the County Courts, and other public officers. . . .

By the best accounts I have received the number of this insurrection amounted to 580 men in arms, and upwards of 100 unarmed. The Mayor and Corporation of Wilmington and most all of the gentlemen and planters of the counties of Brunswick, Newhanover, Duplin, and Bladen with some masters of vessels composed this corps. I am informed and believe the majority of this association were either compelled into this service, or were ignorant what their grievances were. I except the principals.—*Colonial Records of North Carolina*, VII, 172-74. Reprinted from Tryon's Letter Book, February 21, 1766.

47. THE REGULATOR MOVEMENT, 1766-1771

The Regulator movement, which culminated in the Battle of Alamance, was largely a struggle between the small farmers of the West and the large planters of the East. It was a protest of the western counties against inefficient and dishonest local government. Orange, Granville, Halifax, and Anson counties were the centers of the agitation. The outstanding leaders were Herman Husband, Rednap Howell, and James Hunter. The Regulator Association was organized in 1768. Its members agreed: (1) To pay no more taxes until satisfied they were according to law and lawfully applied; (2) To pay no fees greater than provided by law; (3) To attend meetings of the Regulators as often as possible; (4) To contribute, each man according to his ability, to the expenses of the organization; (5) In all matters to abide by the will of the majority.

The Regulators were defeated by the eastern militia at the Battle of Alamance, May 16, 1771. Seven were put to death, and over six thousand accepted Governor Tryon's pardon proclamation. The failure of the movement hastened the settlement of the country beyond the mountains.

Herman Husband's *Impartial Relation* is the best contemporary account of the grievances of the Regulators. The account of the riot was written by Judge Richard Henderson to Governor Tryon. Judge Henderson was at the time holding superior court in Hillsboro, the political and social center of western North Carolina of that day.

AN IMPARTIAL RELATION OF THE FIRST RISE AND CAUSE OF THE PRESENT DIFFERENCES IN PUBLIC AFFAIRS IN THE PROVINCE OF NORTH CAROLINA

IN *Orange* County the first Disturbance is generally ascribed to have arisen; but *Granville* and *Halifax* Counties were deeply engaged in the same Quarrel many Years before *Orange:* So that it may be necessary to give a few Paragraphs out of some of their Papers, to shew, that it was the same Grievance and Oppression that incensed all the Counties, without corresponding with each other. . . .

The Paragraphs in the *Granville* Paper runs as follows. . . .

"Well, Gentlemen, it is not our Form or Mode of Government, nor yet the Body of our Laws that we are quarreling with, but with the Malpractices of the Officers of our County Court, and the Abuses that we suffer by those that are impowered to manage our public Affairs: This is the Grievance, Gentlemen, that demands our serious Attention.—And I shall,

. . . Shew the notorious and intolerable Abuses that has crept into the Practice of the Law, in this County, and I doubt not but into other Counties also; though that does not concern us. In the first Place, there is a Law that provides that a Lawyer shall take no more than Fifteen Shillings for their Fee in the County Court.— Well, Gentlemen, which of you has had your Business done for Fifteen Shillings? They exact Thirty for every Cause: And Three Four and Five Pounds for every Cause attended with the least Difficulty, and laugh at us for our Stupidity and same Submission to these D-m-d, &c."

Another Paragraph runs thus in Substance.

"A poor Man is supposed to have given his Judgment Bond for Five Pounds; and this Bond is by his Creditor thrown into Court. —The Clerk of the County has to enter it on the Docket, and issue Execution, the Work of one long Minute, for which the poor Man has to pay him the trifling sum of Forty-one Shillings and Five-pence.—The Clerk, in Consideration he is a poor Man, takes it out in Work, at Eighteen-pence a Day.—The poor Man works some more than Twenty-seven Days to pay for this one Minute's-writing.

"Well, the poor Man reflects thus,—At this Rate, when shall I get to Labour for my Family? I have a Wife and Parcel of small Children suffering at Home, and here I have lost a whole Month, and I don't know for what; for my Merchant is as far from being paid yet as ever.—However, I will go Home now, and try to do what I can.—Stay, Neighbour, you have not half done yet,—there is a D . . . d Lawyer's Mouth to stop yet; —for you impowered him to confess that you owed this Five Pounds, and you have Thirty Shillings to pay him for that, or go and work nineteen Days more; and then you must work as long to pay the Sheriff for his Trouble; and then you may go home and see your Horses and Cows sold, and all your personal Estate, for one Tenth Part of the Value, to pay off your Merchant. And Lastly, if the Debt is so great, that all your personal Estate will not do to raise the Money, which is not to be had,—then goes your Lands the same way to satisfy these cursed hungry Caterpillars, that will eat out the very Bowels of our Common-wealth, if they are not pulled down from their Nests in a very short time. . . . But as these Practices are contrary to Law, it is our Duty to put a Stop to them before they quite ruin our Country, or that we become willing Slaves to these lawless Wretches, and hug our Chains of Bondage, and remain contented under these accumulated Calamities.

"Oh, Gentlemen, I hope better Things of you. I believe there are few of you but has felt the Weight of those Iron Fists. And I hope there are none of you but will lend a Hand towards bringing about this necessary Work; and in order to bring it about effectually, we must proceed with Circumspection; not fearful, but careful.

"1st. Let us be careful to keep sober,—nor do nothing rashly,—but act with Deliberation.

"2dly. Let us do nothing against the known established Laws of our Land, that we appear not as a Faction, endeavoring to subvert the Laws, and overturn the System of our Government;—But let us take Care to appear what we really are, Free Subjects by Birth, endeavoring to Recover our lost native Rights, of reducing the Malpractices of the Officers of our Court down to the Standard of our Law."

This Paper was large, and deserved to have been printed at Length, but my Ability would not afford it.—It was dated, "*Nutbush, Granville* County, the 6th of *June*, Anno Dom. 1765. . . ."

"We the Subscribers do voluntarily agree to form ourselves into an Association, to assemble ourselves for Conference for Regulating publick Grievances and Abuses of Power, in the following Particulars, with others of the like Nature that may occur.

"1st. That we will pay no more Taxes until we are satisfied they are agreeable to Law, and applied to the Purposes therein mentioned; unless we cannot help it, or are forced.

"2nd, That we will pay no Officer any more Fees than the Law allows, unless we are obliged to it; and then to shew our Dislike, and bear an open Testimoney against it.

"3d. That we will attend our Meetings of Conference as often as we conveniently can, and is necessary, in order to consult our Representatives on the Amendment of such Laws as may be found grievous or unnecessary; and to choose more suitable Men than we have done heretofore for Burgesses and Vestry-men; and to petition the Houses of Assembly, Governor, Council, King and Parliament, &c. for Redress in such Grievances as in the Course of the Undertaking may occur; and to inform one another, learn, know, and enjoy all the Privileges and Liberties that are allowed and were settled on us by our worthy Ancestors, the Founders of our present Constitution, in Order to preserve it on its ancient Foundation, that it may stand firm and unshaken.

"4th. That we will Contribute to Collections for defraying necessary Expenses attending the Work, according to our Abilities.

"5th. That, in Case of Difference in Judgment, we will Submit to the Judgment of the Majority of our Body."—Herman Husband's *Impartial Relation*, in *Some Eighteenth Century Tracts Concerning North Carolina* (edited by William K. Boyd), pp. 247-333.

RIOT OF THE NORTH CAROLINA REGULATORS, 1770

SIR, GRANVILLE Septr 29th 1770

With the deepest concern for my Country I have lately been witness to a scene which not only threatened the peace and well being of this Province for the future, but was in itself the most horrid and audacious insult to the Government, perpetrated with such circumstances of cruelty and madness as (I believe) scarcely has been equalled at any time. However flattering your Excellency's prospects may have been with respect to the people called Regulators, their late conduct too sufficiently evince that a wise, mild and benevolent administration comes very far short of bringing them to a sense of their duty. They are abandoned to every principle of virtue and desperately engaged not only in the most shocking barbarities but a total subversion of the Constitution.

On Monday last being the second day of the Hillsborough Superior Court, early in the morning the Town was filled with a great number of these people shouting. hallooing & making a considerable tumult in the streets. About 11 o'clock the Court was opened, and immediately the House filled as close as one man could stand by another, some with clubs others with whips and switches, few or none without some weapon. When the House had become so crowded that no more could well get in, one of them (whose name I think is called Fields) came forward and told me he had something to say before I proceeded to business. . . . Upon my informing Fields that he might speak on he proceeded to let me know that he spoke for the whole Body of the People called Regulators. That they understood that I would not try their causes, and their determination was to have them tryed, for they had come down to see justice done and justice they w^d have, and if I would proceed to try those causes it might prevent much mischief. They also charged the Court with injustice at the preceding term and objected to the Jurors appointed by the Inferior Court and said they would have them altered and others appointed in their room, with many other things too tedious to mention here. Thus I found myself under a necessity of attempting to soften and turn away the fury of this mad people, in the best manner in my power, and as much as could well be, pacifie their rage and at the same time preserve the little remaining dignity of the Court. The consequence of which was that after spending upwards of half an hour in this disagreeable situation the mob cried out "Retire, retire, and let the Court go on." Upon which most of the regulators went out and seemed to be in consultation in a party by themselves.

The little hopes of peace derived from this piece of behaviour were very transient, for in a few minutes Mr Williams an attorney of that Court was coming in and had advanced near the door when they fell on him in a most furious manner with Clubs and sticks of enormous size and it was with great difficulty he saved his life by taking shelter in a neighbouring Store House. M[r] Fanning was next the object of their fury, him they seized and took with a degree of violence not to be described from off the bench where he had retired for protection and assistance and with hideous shouts of barbarian cruelty dragged him by the heels out of doors, while others engaged in dealing out blows with such violence that I made no doubt his life would instantly become a sacrifice to their rage and madness. However M[r] Fanning by a manly exertion miraculously broke holt and fortunately jumped into a door that saved him from immediate dissolution. During the uproar several of them told me with oaths of great bitterness that my turn should be next. . . .

It would be impertinent to trouble your Exc[y] with many circumstances that occcured in this barbarous riot, Messrs. Thomas Hart, Alexander Martin, Michael Holt, John Litterell (Clerk of the Crown) and many others were severely whipped. Col. Gray, Major Lloyd, M[r]. Francis Nash, John Cooke, Tyree Harris and sundry other persons timorously made their escape or would have shared the same fate. In about four or five hours their rage seemed to subside a little and they permitted me to adjourn Court and conducted me with great parade to my lodgings. Col[o] Fanning whom they had made a prisoner of war in the evening permitted to return to his own House on his word of honour to surrender himself next day. At about ten o'clock that evening, I took an opportunity of making my escape by a back way, and left poor Col. Fanning and the little Borough in a wretched situation. . . .

The number of Insurgents that appeared when the Riot first began was, I think, about one hundred and fifty, tho' they constantly increased for two days and kept a number with fire arms at about a mile distance from Town ready to fall on whenever they were called for. This amount is contradicted by some and believed by others; certain it is that a large number of men constantly lay near the Town, whether they had arms or not is not yet sufficiently determined.

As the burden of conducting Hillsborough Superior Court fell on my shoulders alone, the Task was extremely hard and critical. I made every effort in my power consistent with my Office and the Duty the Publick is entitled to claim to preserve peace and good order, but as all attempts of that kind were ineffectual, thought it more advisable to break up Court than sit and be made a mock Judge for the sport & entertainment of those abandoned wretches. . . .

p. s. My Express has this instant arrived from Hillsborough with the following accounts, Colonel Fanning is alive and well as could be expected. The Insurgents left the Town on Wednesday night having done very little mischief after spoiling Mr Fanning's House except breaking the windows of most of the Houses in Town. . . .
—Letter of Judge Richard Henderson to Governor Tryon, in *Colonial Records of North Carolina*, VIII, 241-44.

48. North Carolina and the Non-Importation Movement, 1774

Following the Boston Tea Party, the British Government ordered the Port of Boston closed in 1774. This stirred the colonies to action, and non-importation associations sprang up all over the country. The following resolutions, adopted by the freeholders of Rowan County a month before the Continental Congress agreed to such a policy, show the attitude of one of North Carolina's western counties toward British taxation. It is interesting to note the condemnation of the African slave trade.

AUGUST 8TH 1774.

At a meeting August 8th 1774, The following resolves were unanimously agreed to. . . .

Resolved, That the Right to impose Taxes or Duties to be paid by the Inhabitants within this Province for any purpose whatsoever is peculiar and essential to the General Assembly in whom the legislative Authority of the Colony is vested. . . .

Resolved, That a general Association between all the American Colonies, not to import from Great Britain any Commodity whatsoever (except such things as shall be hereafter excepted by the general Congress of this Province) ought to be entered into and not dissolved till the just Rights of the said Colonies are restored to them, and the cruel Acts of the British Parliament against the Massachusetts Bay and Town of Boston are repealed.

Resolved, That no friend to the Rights and Liberties of America ought to purchase any Commodity whatsoever, except such as hereafter shall be excepted, which shall be imported from Great Britain after the general Association shall be agreed upon.

Resolved, That every kind of Luxury, Dissipation and Extravagance, ought to be banished from among us.

Resolved, That manufactures ought to be encouraged by opening Subscriptions for that purpose, or by any other proper means.

Resolved, That the African Trade is injurious to this Colony, obstructs the Population of it by freemen, prevents manufacturers, and other Useful Emigrants from Europe from settling among us, and occasions an annual increase of the Balance of Trade against the Colonies.

Resolved, That the raising of Sheep, Hemp and flax ought to be encouraged.

Resolved, That to be cloathed in manufactures fabricated in the Colonies ought to be considered as a Badge and Distinction of Respect and true Patriotism.—*Colonial Records of North Carolina*, IX, 1024-26.

49. PROTESTS AGAINST TEA AT WILMINGTON, 1774-1775

On November 23, 1774, the Wilmington Committee of Safety began to exert its authority. Captain Foster notified this body that tea was being imported in the brig *Sally* by himself, Messrs. Ancrum, Brice, Hill, and others, and asked the advice of the committee as to the proper disposition of the tea. A letter was directed to Mr. Hill, inquiring whether the tea might not be re-exported in the same ship. Mr. Hill replied that, in the absence of both collector and comptroller, he could not answer for them; but, said he, "The safety of the people is, or ought to be, the supreme law; the gentlemen of the committee will judge whether this law or an act of Parliament should, at this particular time operate in North Carolina. I believe every tea importer will cheerfully submit to their determination." The following is an extract from the Letter Book of William Hill.

"BRUNSWICK, JULY 26, 1774

"MESSRS. KELLY & CO., LONDON, ENGLAND:

"The tea, though repeatedly written for, is not come at all, but I need not find fault or make any objections now; for the flame into which this whole continent is thrown by the operation of the Boston port bill will presently show itself in a universal stop to all intercourse between Great Britain and the colonies. . . . Though the want of the tea has for some time past been a serious hurt to me, yet 'tis now a lucky omission, as I am very doubtful our committee would have ordered it back. But I hate politics, and your papers are by this time filled with the resolutions of the different provinces, towns, etc., in America. It may not be amiss to say that they are sending large contributions from every port on the continent to Boston for the relief of the suffering poor," etc., etc.

"Brunswick, August 17, 1774.

"The tea I am as much surprised to see now as I have been disappointed in the want of it these eleven months past. Had it come agreeably to my request, in July, 1773, it would have afforded a profitable sale; but it is now too late to be received in America. If I were ever so willing to take it, the people would not suffer it to be landed. Poison would be as acceptable. I hope you will not be surprised, therefore, to receive it again by the same ship. By this you will easily perceive how vastly mistaken your correspondents have been, in their opinion of disunion among the American provinces; and I can venture to assure you that North Carolina will not be behind any of her sister colonies in virtue and a steady adherence to such resolves as the Continental Congress now sitting at Philadelphia shall adopt."

Mr. Hill added that he would "decline, until the present difficulties are happily over, further intercourse with Great Britain."

"Brunswick, December 1, 1774

"Gentlemen: "The *Mary* luckily arrived two days before the importation limit expired; for, from and after this day, all goods imported from Great Britain are to be vendued—the first cost and charges to be paid to the importer; the profit, if any, to go to the relief of the sufferers by the Boston port bill.

"The tea of Ancrum & Company and Hewes & Smith was inadvertently landed; but they delivered it to the collector for the duties, and it is now lodged in the custom house."

"Brunswick, June 3, 1775.

"The whole continent seems determined, to a man, to die rather than give up taxation to those over whom they can have no constitutional check."—Extract from the Letter Book of William Hill, in S. A. Ashe, *History of North Carolina*, I, 425-26.

50. Resolutions of the First Provincial Congress, August 27, 1774

Four provincial congresses were held in North Carolina in the years 1774-1776. The first of these, which met at New Bern, August 25, 1774, was called as a result of a Wilmington mass meeting, which had declared it "highly expedient" that a provincial congress independent of the governor be held. Governor Martin had refused to call the Assembly in time to elect delegates to the Continental Congress. Hence it was deemed expedient to call a provincial congress for that purpose. Thirty counties and six towns were represented in the first Provincial Congress by seventy-one delegates. John Harvey was chosen "moderator." The Congress remained in session only three days, but during that time "it fully launched North Carolina into the revolutionary movement." It drew up a set of resolutions, which severely criticized the acts and policies of the British government, at the same time professing loyalty to the mother country.

WE HIS Majesty's most dutiful and Loyal Subjects, . . . impressed with the most sacred respect for the British Constitution, and resolved to maintain the succession of the House of Hanover, . . . and avowing our inviolable and unshaken Fidelity to our sovereign, . . . but at the same time conceiving it a duty which we owe to ourselves and to posterity, in the present alarming state of British America, when our most essential rights are invaded by powers unwarrantably assumed by the Parliament of Great Britain to declare our sentiments in the most public manner, lest silence should be construed as acquiescence, . . .

Resolved, That His Majesty George the third is lawful and rightful King of Great Britain, and the dominions thereunto belonging, and of this province as part thereof, and that we do bear faithful and true allegiance unto him as our lawful sovereign, that we will to the utmost of our power, maintain and defend the succession of the House of Hanover as by law established against the open or private attempts of any person or persons whatsoever.

That we claim no more than the rights of Englishmen, without diminution or abridgement, . . .

That it is the very essence of the British Constitution that no subject should be taxed but by his own consent, freely given by himself in person or by his legal representatives, . . .

That as the British subjects resident in North America, have nor can have any representation in the Parliament of Great Britain, Therefore any act of Parliament imposing a tax is illegal and unconstitutional, That our Provincial Assemblies, . . . solely and exclusively possess that right.

That the duties imposed by several acts of the British Parliament, upon Tea and other articles consumed in America for the purpose of raising a revenue, are highly illegal and oppressive, . . .

That the inhabitants of the Massachusetts province have distinguished themselves in a manly support of the rights of America in general and that the cause in which they suffer is the Cause of every honest American. . . .

That trial by Juries of the vicinity is the only lawful inquest that can pass upon the life of a British subject. . . .

That we will not directly or indirectly after the first day of January 1775 import from Great Britain any East India Goods, or any merchandize whatever, medicines excepted, nor will we after that day import from the West Indies or elsewhere any East India or British Goods or Manufactures, nor will we purchase any such articles so imported of any person or persons whatsoever, . . .

That unless American Grievances are redressed before the first day of October 1775, We will not after that day directly or indirectly export Tobacco, Pitch, Tar, Turpentine, or any other articles whatsoever, to Great Britain, nor will we sell any such articles as we think can be exported to Great Britain, . . .

That we will not import any slave or slaves, nor purchase any slave or slaves imported . . . after the first day of November next.

That we will not use nor suffer East India Tea to be used in our Families after the tenth day of September next, . . .

That we approve the proposal of a General Congress to be held in the City of Philadelphia, on the 20th of September next, then and there to deliberate upon the present state of British America and to take such measures as they may deem prudent to effect the purpose of describing with certainty the Rights of Americans, . . .

That William Hooper, Joseph Hewes and Richard Caswell . . . be Deputies to attend such Congress.—*Colonial Records of North Carolina*, IX, 1041-49.

51. THE EDENTON TEA PARTY, OCTOBER 25, 1774

On October 25, 1774, fifty-one Edenton ladies held a meeting and declared that they could not be indifferent to whatever affected the peace and happiness of the country. The provincial deputies of North Carolina had already resolved not to drink any more tea, or wear any more British cloth. The Edenton ladies, anxious to give proof of their patriotism, entered into the following association and discontinued use of East India tea. Miss Janet Schaw, who was traveling in North Carolina at the time. wrote, "The Ladies have burnt their tea in a solemn procession, but they had delayed, however, till the sacrifice was not very considerable, as I do not think any one offered above a quarter of a pound." (*Journal of a Scotch Lady of Quality*. p. 155.)

EDENTON, NORTH CAROLINA, OCTOBER 25 (1774)

As WE cannot be indifferent on any occasion that appears nearly to affect the peace and happiness of our country, and as it has been thought necessary, for the public good, to enter into several particular resolves by a meeting of members deputed from the whole province, it is a duty which we owe, not only to our near and dear connections, who have concurred in them, but to ourselves, who are essentially interested in their welfare, to do everything, as far as lies in our power, to testify our sincere adherence to the same; and we do therefore accordingly subscribe this paper as a witness of our fixed intention and solemn determination to do so:—S. A. Ashe, *History of North Carolina*, I, 427-29.

52. A "Scotch Lady of Quality" Observes North Carolina on the Eve of the Revolution, 1775

Miss Janet Schaw, a "Scotch lady of quality," visited North Carolina shortly before the outbreak of the Revolution. The following letters were written from Wilmington and Schawfield, which was near Wilmington. They were written to a private correspondent and not for the press.

The ports are soon to be shut up, but this severity is voluntarily imposed by themselves, for they were indulged by Parliment and allowed the exclusive privilege of still carrying on their trade with Europe, by which means they would not only have made great fortunes themselves by being the mart for the whole continent, but they would have had the power to serve the other colonies by providing them in those commodities, the want of which they will ill brook, and which is a distress they themselves must soon suffer, as European goods begin to be very scarce and will daily be more so, as the merchants are shipping off their propertys, either to Britain or the West Indies. I know not what my brother proposes to do with himself or me; for if he stays much longer, he will find himself in a very disagreeable situation. He is just now up the country at a town called Newbern, where Govr Martin resides, whose situation is most terrible. He is a worthy man by all accounts, but gentle methods will not do with these rusticks, and he has not the power to use more spirited means. I wish to God those mistaken notions of moderation to which you adhere at home may not in the end prove the greatest cruelty to the mother country as well as to these infatuated people.—*Journal of a Lady of Quality* (edited by E. W. and C. M. Andrews), pp. 156-57.

53. THE MECKLENBURG DECLARATION OF INDEPENDENCE, MAY 20, 1775

The genuineness of the "Mecklenburg Declaration of Independence" of May 20, 1775, has long been a controversial subject in North Carolina history. Books and articles have been written about it. The best books on the question, pro and con, are Moore's *Defence of the Mecklenburg Declaration of Independence* and Hoyt's *The Mecklenburg Declaration of Independence*.

In May, 1775, North Carolinians were alarmed. The port of Boston had been closed by the British government. and "the cause of Boston was felt to be the cause of all." "The situation having been discussed by some of the leading citizens of Mecklenburg County, and several local meetings having been held at different points in the county, Colonel Thomas Polk called for the election of two delegates from each of the militia districts of the county to take into consideration the state of the country, and to adopt such measures as to them seemed best to secure their lives, liberties, and property from the storm which was gathering and had burst on their fellow-citizens to the eastward by a British army." The delegates, having been chosen, met at Charlotte. The news of the Battle of Lexington had arrived and the people were excited. "Resolutions were adopted that were with great formality read by Colonel Polk to a large concourse of citizens, composed of nearly one-half of the men of the county, drawn together by their interest in the occasion."

"The manuscript records of these proceedings appear to have been in the possession of John McKnitt Alexander until the year 1800. In 1794 he sent a copy of them to Dr. Hugh Williamson. In April, 1800, his residence was destroyed by fire and these original records were then burnt." (Ashe, *History of North Carolina*, I, 437, quoting a statement of G. Graham and others.)

The attempt to reproduce these records from memory resulted in the famous document known as the "Mecklenburg Declaration of Independence" of May 20, 1775.

---

1 RESOLVED That whosoever directly or indirectly abetted or in any way form or manner countenanced the unchartered and dangerous invasion of our rights as claimed by Great Britain is an enemy to this country to America and to the inherent and inalienable rights of man.

2 Resolved That we the citizens of Mecklenburg County do hereby dissolve the political bands which have connected us to the mother country and hereby absolve ourselves from all allegiance to the British Crown and abjure all political connection contract or association with that nation who have wantonly trampled on our

rights and liberties and inhumanly shed the blood of American patriots at Lexington.

3 Resolved That we do hereby declare ourselves a free and independent people, are and of right ought to be a sovereign and self-governing association under the control of no power other than that of our God and the General Government of the Congress to the maintenance of which independence we solemnly pledge to each other our mutual co-operation our lives our fortunes and our most sacred honor.

4 Resolved That as we now acknowledge the existence and control of no law or legal officer civil or military within this County we do hereby ordain and adopt as a rule of life all each and every of our former laws—wherein nevertheless the Crown of Great Britain never can be considered as holding rights privileges immunities or authority therein.

5th, Resolved, That it is further decreed that all, each and every Military Officer in this County is hereby reinstated in his former command and authority he acting conformably to these regulations. And that every member present of this delegation shall henceforth be a civil officer viz, a justice of the peace in the character of a "committee man" to issue process, hear and determine all matters of controversy according to said adopted laws and to preserve peace, union and harmony in said county, and to use every exertion to spread the love of Country and fire of freedom throughout America, until a more general and organized government be established in this Province.—*Colonial Records of North Carolina*, IX, 1263-65.

54. THE MECKLENBURG RESOLVES, MAY 31, 1775

On May 31, 1775, a committee of Mecklenburg County citizens drew up a set of resolves, declaring that all commissions theretofore issued by the Crown were to be considered null and void. They proceeded to reorganize their local government, saying that they should "hold and exercise their several powers by virtue of this choice and independent of the Crown of Great Britain and former constitution of this province." These resolves were printed in the *North Carolina Gazette*, New Bern, June 16, 1775.

CHARLOTTE TOWN,
MECKLENBURG COUNTY, MAY 31. 1775

THIS day the Committee of this county met and passed the following resolves:

Whereas by an address presented to his majesty by both Houses of Parliament in February last, the American colonies are declared to be in a state of actual rebellion, we conceive that all laws and commissions confirmed by or derived from the authority of the King and Parliament are annulled and vacated and the former civil constitution of these colonies for the present wholly suspended. To provide in some degree for the exigencies of this county, in the present alarming period, we deem it proper and necessary to pass the following resolves, viz:

1. That all commissions civil and military heretofore granted by the Crown to be exercised in these colonies are null and void and the constitution of each particular colony wholly suspended.

2. That the Provincial Congress of each Province under the direction of the great Continental Congress is invested with all legislative and executive powers within their respective Provinces and that no other legislative or executive power does or can exist at this time in any of these colonies.

3. As all former laws are now suspended in this Province and the Congress has not yet provided others we judge it necessary for the better preservation of good order, to form certain rules and regulations for the internal government of this county until laws shall be provided for us by the Congress.

4. That the inhabitants of this county do meet on a certain day appointed by the committee and having formed themselves into nine companies . . . eight in the county and one in the town of Charlotte do choose a Colonel and other military officers who shall hold and exercise their several powers by virtue of this choice and independent of the Crown of Great Britain and former constitution of this Province.

5.. That for the better preservation of the peace and administration of justice each of those companies do choose from their own body two discreet freeholders who shall be empowered . . . to decide and determine all matters of controversy arising within said company under the sum of twenty shillings and jointly and together all controversies under the sum of forty shillings that so as their decisions may admit of appeal to the convention of the selectmen of the county and also that any one of these shall have power to examine and commit to confinement persons accused of petit larceny.

6. That those two select men thus chosen do jointly and together choose from the body of their particular body two persons properly qualified to act as constables who may assist them in the execution of their office.

7. That upon the complaint of any persons to either of these selectmen he do issue his warrant directed to the constable commanding him to bring the aggressor before him or them to answer said complaint.

8. That these eighteen selectmen thus appointed do meet every third Thursday in January, April, July and October, at the Court House in Charlotte, to hear and determine all matters of controversy for sums exceeding forty shillings, also appeals, and in cases of felony to commit the person or persons convicted thereof to close confinement until the Provincial Congress shall provide and establish laws and modes of proceeding in all such cases.

9. That these eighteen selectmen thus convened do choose a clerk to record the transactions of said convention and that said clerk upon the application of any person or persons aggrieved do issue his warrant to one of the constables . . . directing said constable to summon and warn said offender to appear before the convention at their next sitting to answer the aforesaid complaint. . . .

12. That all receivers and collectors of quit-rents, public and county taxes, do pay the same into the hands of the chairman of this committee to be by them disbursed as the public exigencies may require, and that such receivers and collectors proceed no further in their office until they be approved of by and have given to this committee good and sufficient security for a faithful return of such monies when collected.

13. That the committee be accountable to the county for the application of all monies received from such public officers.

14. That all the officers hold their commissions during the pleasure of their several constituents.

15. That this committee will sustain all damages that ever hereafter may accrue to all or any of these officers thus appointed and thus acting on account of their obedience and conformity of these resolves.

16. That whatever person hereafter shall receive a commission from the Crown or attempt to exercise any such commission heretofore received shall be deemed an enemy to his country and upon information being made to the captain of the company in which he resides, the said company shall cause him to be apprehended and conveyed before the two selectmen of the said company, who upon proof of the fact, shall commit him the said offender to safe custody until the next sitting of the committee, who shall deal with him as prudence may direct.

17. That any person refusing to yield obedience to the above

resolves shall be considered equally criminal and liable to the same punishment as the offenders above last mentioned.

18. That these resolves be in full force and virtue until instructions from the Provincial Congress . . . shall provide otherwise or the legislative body of Great Britain resign its unjust and arbitrary pretensions with respect to America.

19. That the eight Militia companies in this county do provide themselves with proper arms and accoutrements and hold themselves in readiness to execute the commands and directions of the General Congress of this Province and of this Committee.

20. That the committee appoint Colonel Thomas Polk and Dr. Joseph Kennedy to purchase three hundred pounds of powder, six hundred pounds of lead and one thousand flints for the use of the militia of this county and deposit the same in such place as the committee hereafter may direct.

Signed by order of the Committee,

EPH. BREVARD,

Clerk of the Committee.

—*Colonial Records of North Carolina*, IX, 1282-85.

55. THE HALIFAX RESOLVES, APRIL 12, 1776

There was some feeling for independence in North Carolina prior to 1776. On April 8, 1774, Governor Martin dissolved the last Assembly to meet in North Carolina under British rule, and wrote Lord Dartmouth that "Government is here as absolutely prostrate as impotent, and nothing but the shadow is left." About the same time William Hooper declared that the colonies were "striding fast to independence," and Samuel Johnston predicted a complete separation from England unless the mother country yielded. This was not the general feeling in North Carolina, however. There was talk of reconciliation with England throughout 1774 and 1775, but the course of events in the winter of 1775-1776, particularly the Battle of Moore's Creek Bridge, in February, 1776, converted North Carolina to the cause of independence. Hewes wrote, "I see no prospect of a reconciliation; nothing is left now but to fight it out." Samuel Johnston said. "All our people here are up for independence." William Hooper declared. "It would be more than unpopular, it would be Toryism to hint the possibility of future reconciliation."

The fourth Provincial Congress met at Halifax, April 4, 1776, with 148 delegates present from 34 counties and 8 towns. The North Carolina delegates from Philadelphia arrived, April 7, and the next day a special committee was appointed, consisting of Cornelius Harnett, Abner Nash, Thomas Burke, Thomas Person, John Kinchen, and Allen Jones, "to take into consideration the usurpations and violences attempted and committed by the King and Parliament of Britain against America. and the further measures to be taken for frustrating the same, and for the better defence of this Province." On April 12, they submitted a report which was adopted unanimously by the Congress. "This was the first authoritative, explicit declaration, by more than a month, by any colony in favor of full, final separation from Britain." The state flag commemorates this date.

IT APPEARS to your committee, that pursuant to the plan concerted by the British Ministry for subjugating America, the King and Parliament of Great Britain have usurped a power over the persons and properties of the people unlimited and uncontrouled ; and disregarding their humble petitions for peace, liberty and safety, have made divers legislative acts, denouncing war, famine, and every species of calamity, against the Continent in general. The British fleets and armies have been, and still are daily employed in destroying the people, and committing the most horrid devastations on the country. That Governors in different Colonies have declared protection to slaves, who should imbrue their hands in the blood of their masters. That ships belonging to America are declared prizes of war, and many of them have been violently seized and confiscated. In consequence of all which multitudes of people have been destroyed, or from easy circumstances reduced to the most lamentable distress.

And whereas the moderation hitherto manifested by the United Colonies and their sincere desire to be reconciled to the mother country on constitutional principles, have procured no mitigation of the aforesaid wrongs and usurpations, and no hopes remain of obtaining redress by those means alone which have been hitherto tried, your committee are of opinion that the House should enter into the following resolve, to wit :

Resolved, That the delegates for this Colony in the Continental Congress be impowered to concur with the delegates of the other Colonies in declaring Independency, and forming foreign alliances, reserving to this Colony the sole and exclusive right of forming a Constitution and laws for this Colony, and of appointing delegates from time to time (under the direction of a general representation thereof), to meet the delegates of the other Colonies for such purposes as shall be hereafter pointed out.—*Colonial Records of North Carolina*, X, 512.

56. THE CONSTITUTION OF NORTH CAROLINA, 1776

On August 9, 1776, the State Council of Safety issued a call for a constitutional convention. Delegates were elected October 15, and the Convention assembled at Halifax on November 12. Most of the prominent men of the new state were in attendance and Richard Caswell was chosen president of the meeting. The East controlled the Convention, which completed its labors December 18, 1776. The dominant ideas in the Bill of Rights and the Constitution were quite similar to those found in the Virginia Constitution. Some of the salient features were: legislative supremacy, weakness of the executive and the judicial branches of government, property and religious qualifications, borough representation in the legislature, free Negro suffrage, separation of Church and State, and a belief in public education. The Constitution was not submitted to popular vote for ratification.

A DECLARATION OF RIGHTS MADE BY THE REPRESENT-ATIVES OF THE FREEMEN OF THE STATE OF NORTH CAROLINA

I. That all political Power is vested in and derived from the People only.

II. That the people of this State ought to have the sole and exclusive Right of regulating the internal Government and Police thereof.

III. That no Man or set of Men are entitled to exclusive or separate Emoluments or Privileges from the Community, but in Consideration of Public Services.

IV. That the Legislative, Executive and Supreme Judicial Powers of Government ought to be forever separate and distinct from each other.

V. That all Power of Suspending Laws, or the Execution of Laws, by any Authority without Consent of the Representatives of People, is injurious to their rights and ought not to be exercised.

VI. That Elections of Members to serve as Representatives in General Assembly, ought to be free.

VII. That in all criminal Prosecutions every Man has a Right to be informed of the Accusation against him, and to confront the Accusers and Witnesses with other Testimony, and shall not be compelled to give Evidence against himself.

VIII. That no Freeman shall be put to answer any criminal Charge, but by Indictment, Presentment, Impeachment.

IX. That no Freeman shall be convicted of any Crime, but by the unanimous verdict of a Jury of good and lawful Men, in open Court as heretofore used.

X. That excessive Bail should not be required, nor excessive Fines imposed, nor cruel or unusual punishment inflicted.

XI. That General Warrants . . . are dangerous to Liberty, and ought not to be granted.

XII. That no Freeman ought to be taken, imprisoned or disseissed of his Freehold, Liberties or Privileges, or outlawed or exiled, or in any Manner destroyed or deprived of his Life, Liberty, or Property, but by the Law of the Land.

XIII. That every Freeman restrained of his Liberty is entitled to a Remedy to enquire into the Lawfulness thereof, and to remove the same if unlawful, and that such Remedy ought not to be denied or delayed.

XIV. That in all Controversies at Law respecting Property, the ancient Mode of Trial by Jury is one of the best Securities of the Rights of the People, and ought to remain sacred and inviolable.

XV. That the Freedom of the Press is one of the great Bulwarks of Liberty, and therefore ought never to be restrained.

XVI. That the People of this State ought not to be taxed or made subject to the Payment of any Impost or Duty, without the Consent of themselves or their Representatives in General Assembly freely given.

XVII. That the People have a right to bear Arms for the Defence of the State; and as standing Armies in Time of Peace are dangerous to liberty, they ought not to be kept up; and that the military should be kept under strict subordination to, and governed by, the civil Power.

XVIII. That the People have a right to Assemble together to consult for their common good, to instruct their Representatives, and to apply to the Legislature for Redress of Grievances.

XIX. That all Men have a natural and unalienable Right to worship Almighty God according to the Dictates of their own Conscience.

XX. That for redress of Grievances and for amending and strengthening the Laws, Elections ought to be often held.

XXI. That a frequent Recurrence to fundamental Principles is absolutely necessary to preserve the Blessings of Liberty.

XXII. That no Hereditary Emoluments, Privileges or Honours ought to be granted or conferred in this State.

XXIII. That Perpetuities and Monopolies are contrary to the Genius of a free State, and ought not to be allowed.

XXIV. That retrospective Laws, punishing Facts committed before the Existence of such Laws, and by them only declared criminal, are oppressive, unjust, and incompatible with Liberty, wherefore no Ex post Facto Law ought to be made.

XXV. The Property of the Soil in a free Government, being one of the essential Rights of the collective Body of the People, it is necessary in order to avoid future Disputes, that the limits of the State should be ascertained with Precision. . . . —*State Records of North Carolina*, XXIII, 977-78.

THE CONSTITUTION, OR FORM OF GOVERNMENT, &C.

Whereas Allegiance and Protection are in their Nature reciprocal, and the one should of Right be refused when the other is withdrawn. And whereas George the Third . . . by an Act of the British Legislature declared the inhabitants of these States out of the Protection of the British Crown. . . . And the said George the Third has also sent Fleets and Armies to prosecute a cruel War against them, for the Purpose of reducing the Inhabitants of the said Colonies to a State of abject Slavery. . . . And whereas the Continental Congress . . . have therefore declared, that the Thirteen United Colonies are of Right, wholly absolved from all Allegiance to the British Crown. . . . Wherefore, in our present State, in order to prevent Anarchy and Confusion, it becomes necessary that a Government should be established in this state : Therefore, We, the Representatives of the Freemen of North Carolina, chosen and assembled in Congress for the express Purpose of framing a Constitution under Authority of the People, most conducive to their Happiness and Prosperity, do declare that a Government for this State, shall be established in Manner and Form following, to-wit,

I. That the Legislative Authority shall be vested in two distinct Branches, both dependant on the People, to-wit, a Senate and House of Commons.

II. That the Senate shall be composed of Representatives annually chosen by Ballot, one from each County in this State.

III. That the House of Commons shall be composed of Representatives annually chosen by Ballot, two for each County, and one for each of the Towns of Edenton, New Bern, Wilmington, Salisbury, Hillsborough and Halifax.

IV. That the Senate and House of Commons, assembled for the Purpose of Legislation, shall be denominated the General Assembly.

V. That each Member of the Senate shall have usually resided in the County in which he is chosen, for one Year immediately preceding his Election; and for the same Time shall have possessed, and continue to possess, in the County . . . not less than three hundred Acres of Land in Fee.

VI. That each Member of the House of Commons shall have usually resided in the County in which he is chosen, for one Year immediately preceding his Election, and for Six Months shall have possessed, and continue to possess . . . not less than one hundred Acres of Land in Fee. . . .

VII. That all Freemen of the Age of twenty-one Years, who have been Inhabitants of any one County within the State twelve Months immediately preceding the Day of any Election, and possessed of a Freehold within the same County of fifty Acres of Land for six Months next before and at the Day of Election, shall be entitled to vote for a Member of the Senate.

VIII. That all Freemen of the Age of twenty-one Years, who have been inhabitants of any County within this State twelve Months immediately preceding the Day of any Election, and shall have paid public Taxes, shall be entitled to vote for Members of the House of Commons for the County in which he resides. . . .

X. That the Senate and House of Commons when met, shall each have power to choose a Speaker and other their Officers, be Judges of the Qualifications and elections of their Members. . . .

XI. That all Bills shall be read three times in each House before they pass into Laws, and be signed by the Speaker of both Houses. . . .

XIII. That the General Assembly shall, by joint Ballot of both Houses, appoint Judges of the Supreme Courts of Law and Equity, Judges of Admiralty, and an Attorney-General, who shall be commissioned by the Governor, and hold their Offices during good Behavior.

XIV. That the Senate and House of Commons shall have Power

to appoint the Generals and Field-Officers of the Militia, and all Officers of the regular Army of this State.

XV. That the Senate and House of Commons, jointly at their first Meeting after each annual Election, shall by Ballot elect a Governor for one Year; who shall not be eligible to that Office longer than three Years in six successive Years: That no Person under thirty Years of Age, and who has not been a Resident in this State above five Years, and having in the State, a Freehold in Lands and Tenements above the Value of one Thousand Pounds, shall be eligible as Governor.

XVI. That the Senate and House of Commons . . . shall by Ballot elect seven Persons to be a Council of State for one Year; who shall advise the Governor in the Execution of his Office. . . .

XVII. That there shall be a Seal of this State, which shall be kept by the Governor, and used by him as occasion may require; and shall be called The Great Seal of the State of North Carolina, and be affixed to all Grants and Commissions.

XVIII. That the Governor for the Time being, shall be Captain-General and Commander in Chief of the Militia; and in the Recess of the General Assembly, shall have Power, by and with the Advice of the Council of State, to embody the Militia for the public Safety.

XIX. That the Governor for the Time being, shall have Power to draw for and apply such Sums of Money as shall be voted by the General Assembly for the Contingencies of Government, and be accountable to them for the same; He also . . . shall have the Power of granting Pardons and Reprieve, except where the Prosecution shall be carried on by the General Assembly, or the Law shall otherwise direct. . . . And on his Death, Inability, or Absence from the State, the Speaker of the Senate . . . shall exercise the Powers of the Governor. . . .

XX. That in every Case where any Officer, the Right of whose Appointment is by this Constitution vested in the General Assembly, shall during their Recess die, or his Office by other Means become vacant, the Governor shall have Power, with the advice of the Council of State, to fill up such Vacancy by granting a temporary Commission, which shall expire at the End of the next Session of the General Assembly.

XXI. That the Governor, Judges . . . and Attorney-General, shall have adequate Salaries during their Continuance in Office.

XXII. That the General Assembly shall, by joint Ballot of both Houses, annually appoint a Treasurer or Treasurers for this State. . . .

XXIV. That the General Assembly shall, by joint Ballot of both Houses, triennially appoint a Secretary. . . .

XXVIII. That no Member of the Council of State shall have a Seat either in the Senate or House of Commons. . . .

XXXI. That no Clergyman, or Preacher of the Gospel, of any Denomination, shall be capable of being a Member of either the Senate, House of Commons, or Council of State, while he continues in the exercise of the pastoral Function.

XXXII. That no Person who shall deny the being of God, or the Truth of the Protestant Religion, or the Divine Authority of the Old or New Testament, or who shall hold Religious Principles incompatible with the Freedom and Safety of the State, shall be capable of holding any Office or Place of Trust or Profit in the Civil Department, within this State.

XXXIII. That the Justices of the Peace . . . shall in Future be recommended to the Governor for the Time being, by the Representatives in General Assembly, and the Governor shall commission them accordingly. . . .

XXXIV. That there shall be no Establishment of any one Religious Church in this State in Preference to any other; neither shall any Person, on any Pretence whatsoever, be compelled to attend any Place of Worship, contrary to his own Faith or Judgment; nor be obliged to pay for the Purchase of any Glebe, or the building of any House of Worship, or for the Maintenance of any Minister or Ministry, contrary to what he believes right. . . .

XXXV. That no Person in the State shall hold more than one lucrative office at any one Time, . . .

XXXVIII. That there shall be a Sheriff, Coroner or Coroners, and Constables in each County within this State.

XXXIX. That the Person of a Debtor, where there is not a strong Presumption of Fraud, shall not be confined in Prison after delivering up, bona fide, all his Estate, real and personal, for the Use of his Creditors, in such Manner as shall be hereafter regulated by Law. . . .

XL. That every Foreigner who comes to Settle in this State, hav-

having first taken an Oath of Allegiance to the same, may purchase, or by other just Means acquire, hold, and transfer Land or other real Estate; and after one Year's Residence, shall be deemed a Free Citizen.

XLI. That a School or Schools shall be established by the Legislature for the convenient Instruction of Youth, with such Salaries to the Masters paid by the Public, as may enable them to instruct at low Prices; and all useful Learning shall be duly encouraged and promoted in one or more Universities.

XLII. That no Purchase of Lands shall be made of the Indian Natives, but on Behalf of the Public, and by Authority of the General Assembly. . . . —*State Records of North Carolina*, XXIII, 980-84.

57. NORTH CAROLINA LOYALISTS

From the beginning of the Revolution there was considerable criticism of the patriot cause in North Carolina, but the number of active loyalists in the state was smaller than is generally believed. Throughout the war there were British sympathizers in North Carolina, but at no time after 1776 was there any general movement to support Great Britain. There were many conflicting reports about the number and activity of the loyalists, or Tories as they were usually called. Samuel Johnston declared that "not one man of any influence" had any share in their uprisings. The British Government, on the other hand, believed that the state was literally swarming with loyalists. Governor Martin, the last royal governor, was of the opinion that "loyal subjects yet abound and infinitely outnumber the seditious throughout all the very populous Western Counties of the Province." Early in 1776 he estimated that he could raise an army of 6,000 men in North Carolina for the British cause. As late as 1780 he declared that no less than 1,400 North Carolinians had joined the British army. To the very close of the war the British Government considered North Carolina more loyal than the other colonies. In the fall of 1780 Cornwallis entered the state "only to raise men." He was disappointed when only a few rallied to his support.

The chief source of loyalism in North Carolina was to be found in the merchant class and among the Scotch Highlanders. The imperial commercial policy had protected their trade, safeguarded their markets, and thus compelled the loyalty of the merchants. The Scotch Highlanders had taken an oath of allegiance to the Crown before coming to America. They held their lands direct from the Crown and disliked the group in control of the legislature of North Carolina. In the Battle of Moore's Creek Bridge, near Wilmington, some 1,600 loyalists were overwhelmingly defeated by North Carolina troops under the leadership of Colonel Moore.

After the Revolution 2,560 loyalist claims were filed with the British Government. Of these only 139 designated themselves as from North Carolina, and only ten of that number classified themselves as natives. The majority of the North Carolina claimants had recently migrated from the British Isles.

Soon after the war began, the state took steps to punish loyalism. In May, 1776, the Provincial Assembly ordered the imprisonment of the loyalists who had fought at Moore's Creek Bridge. In November of the same year British partisans were denied all civil rights and their property was made liable to seizure. In April, 1777, a law was passed defining treason and attempting to check loyalism in the state. Persons guilty of giving aid and confort to the enemy were to be imprisoned for the remainder of the war and half their estates were to be confiscated. Loyalist merchants were allowed three months in which to dispose of their property and leave the state.

The result of this punitive legislation was a great exodus of British sympathizers, especially of Scotch Highlanders. It was estimated that one-half of the population of Cumberland County left. Many loyalists returned to their native country. Others went to Canada, Nova Scotia, and Florida.

A number of confiscation laws were enacted by the legislature, and commissioners were appointed to take possession of the confiscable property. An act of 1779 specified the estates of 68 persons whose property was confiscable absolutely by the state. A report of November, 1783, indicates that loyalist property to the amount of £583,643-8-0 had been sold. Much real property remained unsold at the close of the war. All this was divided into lots of 640 acres and, between 1784 and 1790, sold at auction. It brought £284,452-4-0. British subjects made a number of efforts to regain their property after the Revolution, but these failed.

CIRCULAR FROM LORD DARTMOUTH TO GOVERNOR MARTIN, MAY 3, 1775

THE Addresses from the four counties of Guilford, Dobbs, Rowan and Surry breathe a spirit of loyalty to the King and Attachment to the Authority of Great Britain which cannot be too much encouraged and it will be necessary that you lose no time in acquainting the Inhabitants of those counties that these testimonies of their duty and affection have been most graciously received by his Majesty, . . . In the meantime it is his Majesty's Pleasure that you do pursue every step that may improve so favorable a symptom in the present state of general frenzy . . . I hope we may yet avoid the necessity of drawing the Sword, but it is prudent to provide as far as we are able against every possible mischief. . . . —*Colonial Records of North Carolina*, IX, 1241.

LETTER FROM GOVERNOR MARTIN TO THE EARL OF DARTMOUTH, NOVEMBER 12, 1775

I have the satisfaction, I think on good information, to assure your Lordship that the Scotch Highlanders here are generally and almost without exception staunch to Government, and on the same authority I am persuaded to believe that loyal subjects yet abound and infinitely outnumber the seditious throughout all the very populous Western Counties of this Province. I am also told for a certainty that their indignation against the late Congress held at Hillsboro ran so high that they would have broke it up if they had been provided but with a small quantity of ammunition. . . . —*Colonial Records of North Carolina*, X, 325.

DECLARATION OF THE PROVINCIAL CONGRESS AT HALIFAX, 1776

DECLARATION

To other Provinces, at a distance from their own places of residence, without that circle where their personal and family influence may be exerted to the prejudice of the Continent, and of this Province in particular, we have deemed it absolutely necessary for the public safety to remove a body of men, whose residence fortune had cast in the very bowels of our country, . . . this misguided people, disregarding the duty which they owe to that country, under the just and equal laws of which they have enjoyed protection, . . . were equally bound, by every tie divine and human, to defend and maintain the cause of liberty, which in common with ourselves, all virtuous men on this Continent, at the hazard of everything dear to them, are laboring at this day to defend. Those men, confederating with our unnatural enemies, and taking advantage of their residence amongst us, . . . have raised their hands against us, and endeavored to imbrue them in the best blood of our fellow citizens. God in his Providence hath hitherto defeated their wicked machinations, . . .

These have been our motives for exercising a severity, which regard to the common safety, and that first principle of nature, self-preservation, prompted. . . . We shall hail their reformation with increasing pleasure, and receive them to us with open arms.—*Colonial Records of North Carolina*, X, 547-49.

8

LAWS RELATING TO LOYALISTS, 1777

I. Be it Enacted . . . That all and every Person and Persons (Prisoners of War excepted) now inhabiting or residing within the limits of the State of North-Carolina, or who shall voluntarily come into the same hereafter to inhabit or reside, do owe, and shall pay Allegiance to the State of North Carolina.

II. . . . That if any Person or Persons belonging to, or residing within this State, and under the Protection of its Laws, shall take a Commission or Commissions from the King of Great Britain, or any under his Authority, . . . or shall levy War against this State, or the Government thereof; or knowingly and willingly shall aid or assist any Enemies at open War against this State, or the United States of America, by joining their Armies, or by inlisting, or procuring or persuading others to inlist for that Purpose, or by furnishing such Enemies with Arms, Ammunition, Provision, or any other Article for their Aid or Comfort; or shall form, or be in any way concerned in forming any Combination, Plot, or Conspiracy, for betraying this State, or the United States of America, into the Hands or Power of any foreign Enemy; or shall give or send any Intelligence to the Enemies of this State for that Purpose; every Person so offending, and being thereof legally convicted by the Evidence of two sufficient Witnesses, . . . in any Court of Oyer and Terminer, or other Court that shall and may be established for the Trial of such Offences, shall be adjudged guilty of High-Treason, and shall suffer Death without the Benefit of Clergy, and his or her Estate shall be forfeited to the State. . . .

V. . . . That all the late Officers of the King of Great Britain, and all Persons (Quakers excepted) being Subjects of this State, and now living therein, who have traded immediately to Great Britain or Ireland within ten Years last past, in their own Right, or acted as Factors, Storekeepers or Agents, here or in any of the United States of America, . . . or Ireland, shall take the following Oath of Abjuration or Allegiance, or depart out of the State, viz. I will bear faithful and true Allegiance to the State of North Carolina, and will to the utmost of my power support and maintain, and defend the independent Government thereof, against George the Third, King of Great Britain, and his Successors, . . . —*State Records of North Carolina*, XXIV, 9-12, 86.

EXODUS OF LOYALISTS

On Saturday last, sailed from this Port (New Bern), on an intended Voyage to Jamaica, a second Scotch Transport, having on Board a Number of Gentlemen of that Nation, particularly Mess. Archibald and John Hamilton, Gentlemen that have long resided in America, and with great Reputation, acquired very considerable Fortunes, but are unhappily under the fatal ministerial Delusion, which has driven such Numbers of their Countrymen away, the sure and certain Subjugation of America by the British Troops, when they may return in Safety, and not only re-possess their own Estates, but, for their Loyalty, share among those of their Neighbors, the rebellious Americans.—*North-Carolina Gazette*, October 31, 1777.

58. SIGNIFICANT REVOLUTIONARY BATTLES IN NORTH CAROLINA

It is unnecessary to recount the military history of North Carolina during the Revolution, but the significance of two important engagements should be noted: Moore's Creek Bridge, February 27, 1776, and King's Mountain, October 7, 1780.

Aptly called the "Lexington and Concord of the South," the battle of Moore's Creek Bridge (eighteen miles above Wilmington) served the double purpose of crushing the loyalists and awakening the Whigs of North Carolina. The late royal Governor Martin, in the safety of his ship's cabin, had conceived plans whereby the embryo revolt in North Carolina could be quickly ended. Coöperating with a force of British regulars to be raised and placed under the commands of Lord Cornwallis and Sir Henry Clinton, the refugee governor was to collect a band of Tories, and the combined force was to be employed in stamping out the rebellion. The plans went awry, however, for the leisurely dispatch with which Cornwallis moved his men to the American continent caused the over-eager Tories of the state to begin the fight alone. Falling into the neatly-sprung trap of Colonel Lillington and Richard Caswell, the Scotch Highlanders were met by a whining storm of swan-shot and bullets. For three minutes they faced the devastating fire and attempted to cross the bridge; then, leaving their commander and many comrades dead, the survivors hastily left the scene of carnage. This short engagement preceded an exodus of loyalists from North Carolina and served to strengthen the colony in the coming struggle for independence.

Having met defeat in the North, the British determined to make another stand in the South in an effort to redeem their sinking fortunes. Major Ferguson, therefore, was detailed to march his band of 1,100 Loyalists into western North Carolina, there to collect supplies and enlist more of the colonists in the royal cause. This efficient officer, however, tactlessly broadcast threats of rapine and death to the Whig mountaineers, promising to reduce the countryside with fire and sword if the inhabitants persisted in their disloyalty. These threats served to embolden the colonists, for as Ferguson lay encamped on King's Mountain (a ridge about sixteen miles long, running from Cleveland County, North Carolina, southwest into York County, South Carolina), these mountaineers laid aside farm work and, coöperating with more seasoned troops, stormed the mountain, killed Ferguson and a great part of his command, and took the remainder prisoners. Lord Cornwallis, who had been nervously waiting in Charlotte, found the "hornet's nest" too uncomfortable and speedily made his way into South Carolina, only to find that region in a "state of confusion and rebellion." Denied the reinforcements he had hoped Ferguson's expedition would bring, Cornwallis's surrender at Yorktown the following year can, in part, be traced to the disastrous battle of King's Mountain.

THE BATTLE OF MOORE'S CREEK BRIDGE, FEBRUARY 27, 1776

On the earliest intelligence that the tories were collecting and embodying at Cross Creek, which I received on the 9th of February, I proceeded to take possession of Rockfish-bridge, within seven miles of Cross Creek, which I considered as an important post. This I effected on the 15th, with my own regiment, five pieces of artillery and a part of the Bladen militia; but as our numbers were by no means equal to that of the tories, I thought it most advisable to entrench and fortify that pass, and wait for reinforcement. By the 9th I was joined by Col. Lillington with one hundred and fifty of the Wilmington minute-men, Colonel Kenon with 200 of the Duplin militia, and Col. Ash with about 100 of the volunteer independent yagers, making our number then in the whole about 1100; and from the best information I was able to procure, the tory army, under command of General McDonald, amounted to about 14 or 1500.—Extract of a letter from Brigadier General James Moore to Cornelius Harnett, President of the Provincial Council, Wilmington, March 2, in *Colonial Records of North Carolina*, XI, 283.

REPORT OF THE BATTLE OF MOORE'S CREEK BRIDGE

This morning [February 27, 1776], the North Carolina minute men and militia, under the command of Brigadier General James Moore, had an engagement with the Tories, at Widow Moore's Creek bridge. At the break of day an alarm gun was fired, immedi-

ately after which, scarcely leaving the Americans a moment to prepare, the Tory army, with Captain McCloud at their head, made
their attack on Cols. Caswell and Lillington, posted near the bridge,
and finding a small intrenchment vacant, concluded that the Americans had abandoned their post. With this supposition, they advanced in a most furious manner over the bridge. Col. Caswell had
very wisely ordered the planks to be taken up, so that in passing
they met with many difficulties. On reaching a point within thirty
paces of the breastworks, they were received with a heavy fire,
which did great execution. Captains McCloud and Campbell were
instantly killed, the former having nine bullets and twenty-four
swan shot through and into his body. The insurgents retreated with
the greatest precipitation, leaving behind them some of their wagons
&c. They cut their horses out of the wagons, and mounted three
upon a horse. Many of them fell into the creek and were drowned.
Tom Rutherford ran like a lusty fellow :—both he and Felix Keenan
were in arms against the Carolinians, and they by this time are
prisoners, as is Lieutenant-Colonel Cotton, who ran at the first fire.
The battle lasted three minutes. Twenty-eight of the Tories, besides
the two Captains are killed or mortally wounded, and between
twenty or thirty taken prisoners, among them is his Excellency
General Donald McDonald. This, we think, will effectually put a
stop to Toryism in North Carolina.—"Diary of the Revolution," I,
209-10, in *Colonial Records of North Carolina*, XI, 289-90.

OFFICIAL REPORT, BATTLE OF KING'S MOUNTAIN, 1780

A state of the proceedings of the Western Army, from the 25th of
September, 1780, to the reduction of Major Ferguson and the army
under his command.

On receiving intelligence that Maj. Ferguson had advanced as
high up as Gilbert Town, in Rutherford County, and threatened to
cross the mountains to the western waters, Col. William Campbell,
with four hundred men from Washington County, Virginia, Col.
Isaac Shelby, with two hundred and forty from Sullivan County
of North Carolina, and Lieut. Col. John Sevier, with two hundred
and forty men of Washington County, assembled at Watauga, on
the 25th of September, where they were joined by Col. Charles
McDowell, with one hundred and sixty men from the Counties of
Burke and Rutherford, who had fled before the enemy to the western waters.

We began our march on the 26th, and on the 30th we were
joined by Col. Cleveland, on the Catawba River, with three hun-

dred and fifty men from the Counties of Wilkes and Surry. No one officer having properly a right to command in chief, on the 1st of October we dispatched an express to Maj. Gen. Gates, informing him of our situation, and requesting him to send a general officer to take command of the whole. In the meantime Col. Campbell was chosen to act as commandant till such general officer should arrive. We marched to the Cowpens, on Broad River in South Carolina, where we were joined by Col. James Williams, with four hundred men, on the evening of the 6th of October, who informed us that the enemy lay encamped somewhere near the Cherokee Ford of Broad River, about thirty miles distant from us.

By a council of the principal officers, it was then thought advisable to pursue the enemy that night with nine hundred of the best horsemen, and leave the weak horsemen and foot-men to follow as fast as possible. We began our march with nine hundred of the best men, about eight O'clock the same evening, and marching all night, came up with the enemy about three O'clock P. M. of the 7th, who lay encamped on the top of King's Mountain, twelve miles North of the Cherokee Ford, in the confidence that they could not be forced from so advantageous a post. Previous to the attack, on the march, the following disposition was made : Col. Shelby's regiment formed a column in the centre, on the left Col. Campbell's regiment, another on the right, with part of Col. Cleveland's regiment, headed in front by Maj. Winston and Col. Sevier's regiment, formed a large column on the right wing. The other part of Cleveland's regiment, headed by Col. Cleveland himself, and Col. Williams' regiment, composed the left wing. In this order we advanced, and got within a quarter of a mile of the enemy before we were discovered. Col. Shelby's and Col. Campbell's regiments began the attack, and kept up a fire on the enemy, while the right and left wings were advancing to surround them, which was done in about five minutes, and the fire became general all around. The engagement lasted an hour and five minutes, the greater part of which time a heavy and incessant fire was kept up on both sides. Our men in some parts, where the regulars fought, were obliged to give way a small distance, two or three times, but rallied and returned with additional ardor to the attack. The troops upon the right having gained the summit of the eminence, obliged the enemy to retreat along the top of the ridge to where Col. Cleveland commanded, and were there stoped by his brave men. A flag was immediately hoisted by Capt. DePeyster, the commanding officer, (Maj. Ferguson having been killed a little before,) for a surrender. Our fire immediately ceased, and the enemy laid down their arms, the greatest part of them charged, and surrendered themselves to us prisoners at discretion.

It appears from their own provision returns for that day, found in their camp, that their whole force consisted of eleven hundred and twenty-five men, out of which they sustained the following loss: Of the regulars, one Major, one Captain, two Sergeants and fifteen privates killed, thirty-five privates wounded, left on the ground, not able to march, two Captains, four Lieutenants, three Ensigns, one Surgeon, five Sergeants, three Corporals and one Drummer, and forty-nine privates taken prisoners. Loss of the Tories, two Colonels, three Captains, and two hundred and one privates killed ; one Major and one hundred and twenty seven privates wounded and left on the ground, not able to march, one Colonel, twelve Captains, eleven Lieutenants, two Ensigns, one Quarter-master, one Adjutant, two Commissaries, eighteen Sergeants, and six hundred privates taken prisoners. Total loss of the enemy, eleven hundred and five men at King's Mountain.

Given under our hand at camp,

> WILLIAM CAMPBELL.
> ISAAC SHELBY.
> BENJ. CLEVELAND.

The losses on our side were, one Colonel, one Major, one Captain, two Lieutenants, Four Ensigns, nineteen privates killed ; total, twenty-eight killed ; one Major, three Captains, three Lieutenants and fifty-five privates wounded ; total, sixty-two wounded.

Published by order of Congress.

> CHARLES THOMSON, Secretary.

—From the *Virginia Gazette*, November 18th, and *Massachusetts Spy*, November 30th, 1780, in *Colonial Records of North Carolina*, XV, 163-65.

IV

THE INDEPENDENT STATE

59. The Cession of the Western Lands, 1784

One of North Carolina's most perplexing post-Revolutionary problems was the disposition of its transmontane lands. The colonization of the Tennessee country began with the Watauga Settlement just prior to the Revolution, and there was a steady stream of settlers into that region throughout the war. By 1783 there were about twenty-five thousand people beyond the mountains, and four counties had been created: Washington, Sullivan, Greene, and Davidson.

As early as 1780, Congress recommended the cession of all western lands to the central government in the interest of the national debt. New York ceded her lands in 1780, followed by Virginia in 1781. Sentiment for cession was growing in North Carolina. There was talk of a continental land tax and the apportionment of requisitions according to population. If Congress adopted this policy, it would be to North Carolina's advantage to cede her western lands. The less territory owned, the less would be its part in meeting future expenditures.

By act of cession, April, 1784, North Carolina ceded its western lands to Congress, subject to the following restrictions: "That neither the land nor the inhabitants should in the future be counted in estimating North Carolina's share of the expenses in the Revolution, that the bounties provided for officers and soldiers should be protected, that the territory granted should be considered a common fund for the benefit of the states, that one or more states should be created out of it, and that if Congress should not accept the cession, the lands should revert to the state." North Carolina was to retain its sovereignty over this country until the United States accepted the cession.

I. Whereas, the United States in Congress assembled, . . . have earnestly recommended to the respective States in the Union claiming or owning vacant Western territory to make cessions of part of the same; and whereas by their resolution of the eighteenth of April, 1783, as a further means as well as hastening the extinguishment of the debts as of establishing the harmony of the United States, it was recommended to the States which have passed no acts towards complying with the said resolutions, to make the liberal cessions therein recommended; and this State ever desirous of doing ample justice to the public creditors as well as establishing the harmony of the United States, . . .

II. Be it Enacted, . . . That this State do hereby cede to the Congress of the United States for the said States, all right, title and claim which this State has to the lands west of the Apalachian or Alleghany mountains, . . . and delegates from this State in the Congress of the United States are hereby authorized and impowered to execute a deed or deeds on the part of this State conveying to the Congress of the United States all the right, title and claim to the government and territory thereof, . . . upon the following express conditions and reservations, . . . That neither the lands nor the inhabitants of the territory westward of this said line shall be estimated after this cession shall be accepted in the ascertaining of the proportion of this State with the United States in the common expence occasioned by the late war . . . and that all and every right of occupancy and pre-emption, . . . and all reservations of hunting grounds for the use of the Indians, shall continue to be in full force in the same manner as if this cession had not been made, and as conditions upon which the said lands are ceded to the United States : . . . That all the lands hereby ceded to the United States and not reserved or appropriated as before shall be considered as a common fund for the use and benefit of such of the United American States as now or shall become members of the confederation or federal alliance of the said States, North Carolina inclusive, according to their respective and usual proportion in the general charge and expenditure ; . . . That the territory so ceded shall be laid out and formed into a State or States, . . . Provided always, That no regulations made or to be made by Congress shall tend to emancipate slaves, otherwise than shall be directed by the Assembly or Legislature of such State or States. . . . That if Congress do not proceed to accept the lands hereby ceded in due form and give official notice thereof to the delegates of this State, if in Congress, or to the executive or legislative authority within twelve months from the passing of this Act, then this Act shall and will be of no force, and the lands hereby ceded revert to the State.—*State Records of North Carolina*, XXIV, 561-63.

60. Governor Alexander Martin's Manifesto against the State of Franklin, 1785

On October 7, 1763, soon after the close of the French and Indian War, the British Crown issued a Royal Proclamation concerning America, which reserved the lands between the Appalachian mountains and the Mississippi River to the Indians. This action was resented by many Americans who were eager to settle the transmontane country, and it did not prevent westward expansion.

Under the leadership of James Robertson, Richard Henderson, Daniel Boone, and others, settlement of the Tennessee country began soon after this date and continued at a rapid rate until the Revolution. After the defeat of the Regulators at Alamance in 1771, hundreds of North Carolinians moved into the Watauga River valley of eastern Tennessee. The Watauga Association was organized in 1776, and in 1777 North Carolina was petitioned to "annex" the new settlement. In 1777 the North Carolina legislature transformed Watauga into Washington County.

In 1779 James Robertson and Richard Henderson founded Nashborough (Nashville). On May 13, 1780, the Nashborough settlers signed the Cumberland Agreement, by the provisions of which the colony was governed until the creation of Davidson County by North Carolina in 1783.

Because of social and economic differences the Tennessee settlers had no feeling of loyalty to North Carolina. So, when the latter ceded its western lands to the central government in 1784, the inhabitants of the Tennessee country organized the State of Franklin, adopted a constitution, and established a government, with John Sevier as governor. Congress refused to recognize the new state, because North Carolina, in the meantime, had withdrawn her act of cession. The result was the collapse of the State of Franklin. In 1788 North Carolina succeeded in establishing her authority over this disaffected region. She definitely surrendered her western lands to the United States in 1790, and Tennessee was admitted to the Union as a state in 1796.

The following manifesto by the Governor of North Carolina is an excellent illustration of the attitude of the East toward the rising West.

STATE OF NORTH CAROLINA

BY HIS EXCELLENCY ALEXANDER MARTIN, ESQUIRE, GOVERNOR, CAPTAIN-GENERAL, AND COMMANDER-IN-CHIEF OF THE STATE AFORESAID—

TO THE INHABITANTS OF THE COUNTIES OF WASHINGTON, SULLIVAN AND GREENE:

A MANIFESTO

Whereas, I have received letters from Brigadier General Sevier, under the style and character of Governor, and from Messrs. Landon Carter and William Gage, as Speakers of the Senate and Commons of the State of Franklin, informing me that they, with you, the Inhabitants of part of the territory late ceded to Congress, had declared themselves independent of the State of North-Carolina, and no longer considered themselves under the Sovereignty and jurisdiction of the same; stating their reasons for their separation and revolt, among which it is alledged that the western Country was ceded to Congress without their consent by an Act of the Legislature, and the same was repealed in the like manner. . . .

. . . The Last Assembly having learned what uneasiness and discontent the Cession act had occasioned throughout the State, whose inhabitants had not been previously consulted on that measure, in whom, by the Constitution the soil and territorial rights of the State are particularly vested, judging the said Act impolitick at this time, more especially as it would, for a small consideration, dismember the State of one-half of her territory, and in the end tear from her a respectable Body of her Citizens, when no one State in the Union had parted with any of her citizens or given anything like an equivalent to Congress but vacant lands of an equivocal and disputed title and distant Situation; and also considering that the said Act, by its tenor and purport was revocable at any time before the Cession should be completed by the Delegates, repealed it by a great majority. At the same time, the Assembly, to convince the people of the Western Country of their affection and attention to their interest, attempted to render Government as easy as possible to them by removing the only general inconvenience and grievance they might labour under, for want of a regular administration of criminal Justice and a proper and immediate command of the Militia; a new District was erected, an assistant Judge and a Brigadier-General were appointed. . . .

In Order therefore to reclaim such Citizens, who by specious pretences, and the Acts of designing Men, have been seduced from their Allegiance; to restrain others from following their example who are wavering, and to confirm the attachment and affection of those who adhere to the old Government, and whose fidelity hath not yet been shaken, I have thought proper to issue this manifesto hereby warning all persons concerned in the said revolt that they return to their duty and allegiance, and forbear paying any obedience to any self-created power and authority unknown to the Constitution of the State, and not sanctified by the Legislature . . . that the honor of this State has been particularly wounded by seizing that by violence, which in time no doubt, would have been obtained by consent, when the terms of separation could have been explained and stipulated to the mutual satisfaction of the Mother and the new

State. That Congress, by the Confederation, cannot countenance such a separation wherein the State of North-Carolina hath not given her full consent; and if an implied or conditional one hath been given, the same hath been rescinded by a full Legislature, . . .

That you be not insulted or led away with the pageantry of a mock Government without the essentials, the shadow without the substance, which always dazzles weak minds, and which will in its present form and manner of existence not only subject you to the ridicule and contempt of the World, but in general, rouze the indignation of the other States in the Union at your obtruding yourselves as a power among them without their consent. Consider what a number of men of different abilities will be wanting to fill the civil list of the State of Franklin and the expense necessary to support them suitable to their various degrees of dignity; when the District of Washington with its present officers, might answer all the purposes of a happy Government, until the period arrive when a separation might take place to mutual advantage and satisfaction, on an honourable footing. The Legislature will shortly meet, before whom the transactions of your leaders will be laid. Let your representatives come forward and present every grievance in a Constitutional manner that they may be redressed, and let your terms of separation be proposed with decency; your proportion of the public debts ascertained, the vacant territory appropriated, to the mutual benefit of both parties in such manner and proportion, as may be just and reasonable. . . .

But, on the contrary, should you be hurried on by blind ambition to pursue your present unjustifiable measures, which may open afresh the wounds of this late bleeding Country, and plunge it again into all the miseries of a Civil Warr, which God avert, let the fatal consequences be charged on the authors. It is only time which can reveal the event. I know with reluctance the State will be driven to arms; . . . but if no other ways and means are found to save her honour, and reclaim her head-strong, refractory Citizens, but this last sad expedient, her resources are not Yet so exhausted, or her spirits damped but she may take satisfaction for this great injury received, regain her Government over the revolted territory, or render it not worth possessing. But all these effects may be prevented at this time by removing the causes; by those who have revolted to return to their duty, and those who have stood firm still to continue to support the Government of this State, until the consent of the Legislature be fully and constitutionally had for a Separate sovereigny and jurisdiction. . . . —*State Records of North Carolina*, XXII, 642-47.

61. THE NORTH CAROLINA PRECEDENT FOR THE DOCTRINE OF JUDICIAL REVIEW: THE CASE OF BAYARD *vs.* SINGLETON, 1787

The case of *Bayard* vs. *Singleton* is the first reported case under a written constitution in which a law was held to be unconstitutional. It antedates John Marshall's well known decision in *Marbury* vs. *Madison* by many years.

The cause was an action of ejectment for the recovery of a house, lot, wharf, and other property in the town of New Bern. The defendant held under a title derived from the State of North Carolina, by a deed from a superintendent of confiscated estates. The plaintiffs claimed title under a deed from Cornell, who was the father of Mrs. Bayard, and whose estates had been conficated during the Revolution. The Bayards were not citizens of North Carolina, but of another state; Cornell had refused to become a citizen of North Carolina, remaining loyal to Great Britain.

Nash, for the defendant, moved that the suit be dismissed according to an Act of the Assembly for securing and quieting the possession of the purchases of property sold by commissioners of forfeited estates. This act required the courts, in all cases in which the defendant made affidavit that he held the disputed property under a sale from a commissioner of forfeited estates, to dismiss the suit on motion. Singleton had filed such an affidavit.

The courts declared this Act of the Assembly unconstitutional, stating that every citizen had a constitutional right to a decision in regard to his property by a trial by jury. The court also held that aliens could not hold land in the state and that alien enemies had no political rights at all.

As a result of this decision, there was a trial by jury in the November term, 1787, in which the jury found a verdict for the defendant. Twenty-seven other cases of a similar nature were dropped from the docket at this time.

EJECTMENT. This action was brought for the recovery of a valuable house and lot, with a wharf and other appurtenances, situate in the town of New Bern.

The defendant pleaded *not guilty*, under the common rule.

He held under a title derived from the State, by a deed, from a Superintendent Commissioner of confiscated estates.

At May Term, 1786, *Nash* for the defendant, moved that the suit be dismissed, according to an act of the last session, entitled an act to secure and quiet in their possession all such persons, their heirs and assigns, who have purchased or may hereafter purchase lands and tenements, goods and chattels, which have been sold or may hereafter be sold by commissioners of forfeited estates, legally appointed for that purpose, 1785, 7, 553.

The act requires the Courts, in all cases where the defendant makes affidavit that he holds the disputed property under a sale from a commissioner of forfeited estates, to dismiss the suit on motion.

The defendant had filed an affidavit, setting forth that the property in dispute had been confiscated and sold by the Commissioner of the district.

This brought on long arguments from the counsel on each side, on constitutional points. . . .

At May term, 1787, Nash's motion was resumed, and produced a very lengthy debate from the bar.

Another mode was proposed for putting the matter in controversy on a more constitutional footing for a decision, than that of the motion under the aforesaid act. The Court then, after every reasonable endeavor had been used in vain for avoiding a disagreeable difference between the Legislature and the Judicial powers of the State, at length with much apparent reluctance, but with great deliberation and firmness, gave their opinion separately, but unanimously for overruling the aforementioned motion for the dismission of the said suits. . . .

That by the constitution every citizen had undoubtedly a right to a decision of his property by a trial by jury. For that if the Legislature could take away this right, and require him to stand condemned in his property without a trial, it might with as much authority require his life to be taken away without a trial by jury, and that he should stand condemned to die, without the formality of any trial at all : that if the members of the General Assembly could do this, they might with equal authority, not only render themselves the Legislators of the State for life, without any further election of the people, from thence transmit the dignity and authority of legislation down to their male heirs forever.

But that it was clear, that no act they could pass, could by any means repeal or alter the constitution, because if they could do this, they would at the same instant of time, destroy their own existence as a Legislature, and dissolve the government thereby established. Consequently the constitution (which the judicial power was bound to take notice of as much as of any other law of the land whatever,) standing in full force as the fundamental law of the land, notwithstanding the act on which the present motion was grounded, the same act must of course, in that instance, stand as abrogated and without any effect. . . .

Both the plaintiffs and the defendant admitted the title cf the premises to have been in Samuel Cornell, Esq., at and before the time when independence of this State commenced.

The case appeared to be this : Mr. Cornell, once an inhabitant of New Bern, leaving his family, together with the premises in question, and a variety of property in this town, took shipping on the 19th of August, 1775, and went to Great Britain, where he continued till some time in the latter part of 1777, when he came to New York, then occupied by a British garrison ; and as a British subject came from thence and arrived in New Bern, on the 11th of December, 1777, and under the protection of a British flag.

His principal design, in coming to this State at that time, was to take his wife and family with him, to reside under the British Government, if he did not find our new government agreeable to his wishes. Not being pleased with the appearance of things here, and thereupon preparing to leave the State, and to carry with him his wife and family, he executed on board the vessel he came in, a deed to his daughter, one of the plaintiffs (under which they claim) for the premises in question, on the 19th of December, 1777.

This deed for the purpose of execution had been handed to him without a date, and being asked what date he chose it should bear, he hesitated and said he would look at the copy of a bill which was then in his possession, which bill he understood to be on its passage in the legislature, for confiscating the property of all persons of his description, who should not within a limited time come into this State, and be made citizens thereof, which bill afterwards in the same session passed into a law. After looking at the aforesaid copy of that bill, he chose that the deed should bear date on the 11th of the same month, being the day he arrived in the harbour of New Bern ; which deed was accordingly dated that day. After which Mr. Cornell returned with his family from this State, and from thenceforth lived and died a British subject, under the British Government.

The Court, ASHE J., SPENCER J., and WILLIAMS J., gave their opinion *seriatim*, but unanimously.

They observed that the cause turned chiefly on the point of *alienage* in Mr. Cornell. For this gentleman, having from his birth to the time of his death, been always a British subject, and having always lived under the British government, he owed allegiance to the King of Great Britain, and consequently was never a citizen of this, or any other of the United States, nor owed allegiance thereto. For when here, at the time of the transaction aforementioned, he was under the protection of a British flag. That he was therefore, in contemplation of law, as much an *alien*, and at the time of executing the deed, and, from the time of our independence as much an *alien enemy*, as if we had been a separate and independent nation, for any number of years or ages before the commencement of the war which was then carried on.

That it is the policy of all Nations and States, that the lands within their government should not be held by foreigners. And therefore it is a general maxim, that the allegiance of a person who holds land ought to be as permanent to the government who holds it, as the tenure of the soil itself.—That therefore by the civil, as well as by the common law of England, *aliens* are incapacitated to hold lands. For that purpose the civil law has made the contracts with *aliens* void. The law of England, which we have adopted, allows them to purchase, but subjects them to forfeiture immediately; and does not allow an *alien enemy* any political rights at all.

That the premises in question, upon these invariable principles of law, could not from the time our government commenced, have been held by Mr. Cornell; because that in consequence of his owing no allegiance to the State, he had no capacity to hold them, and according to the letter of the law of the land, they must have consequently been forfeited to the sovereignty of the State. That the act of confiscation, in which Mr. Cornell was expressly named, and more particularly the act which especially directed the sale of the very premises in question, must have been at least as effectual in vesting them in the State, as any *office found*, according to the practice in England can be, for vesting any forfeited property in the King.

That the circumstances and limited privileges of persons who were sent out of this State under a particular act of our General Assembly, are not applicable to this case. . . .

The jury found a verdict for the defendant.

Iredell, Johnston, and *Davie*, for the plaintiffs.

Moore and *Nash*, for the defendant.—*North Carolina Reports*, Vol. I. Cases Adjudged in the Superior Courts of Law and Equity and in the Court of Conference of North Carolina from November term, 1778, to December term, 1804, pp. 5-10.

62. LETTERS OF SYLVIUS, 1787

Dr. Hugh Williamson, the author of the "Letters of Sylvius," came to the state from Pennsylvania in 1777 and made his home at Edenton. He was surgeon to the North Carolina troops during the Revolution, member of the state legislature, in 1782 and 1785, delegate to the Continental Congress, 1782, 1783, and 1784, commissioner to the Annapolis Convention, 1786, member of the Constitutional Convention, 1787, and of both the Hillsboro and Fayetteville conventions. He also represented the state in the first and the second United States Congress.

The "Letters of Sylvius" appeared in the *American Museum*, in August, 1787. They were also printed and circulated in pamphlet form. They discussed the inherent evils of paper money, advocated excise rather than taxes on land and poll, and urged the promotion of domestic manufactures. They sound distinctly modern in that they advocated a "live at home program," favored the reduction of taxes on land, and suggested a "luxury tax."

ESSAY ON THE CONSEQUENCES OF EMITTING PAPER MONEY: ON THE NECESSITY AND ADVANTAGES OF ENCOURAGING AMERICAN MANUFACTURERS: OF THE BENEFICIAL EFFECTS OF AN ALTERATION IN THE PRESENT MODE OF TAXATION. . . .

Friends and Fellow Citizens:

In every part of these states, the great scarcity of money is become a common subject of complaint. This does not seem to be an imaginary grievance, . . . The misfortune is general, and in many cases it is severely felt. The scarcity of money is so great, or the difficulty of paying debts has been so common, that riots and combinations have been formed in many places, and the operations of civil government have been suspended. This is the more remarkable, because three years have not passed since money was very plenty. A calamity of such magnitude has deservedly drawn the attention of every legislature in the Union. In some of the states, paper-money has been emitted, as the best or most convenient remedy by which the sufferings of the people can be relieved. The General Assembly of this state has already had recourse to two emissions of paper. . . .

The more I consider the progress of credit, and the increase of wealth in foreign nations, the more fully I am convinced that paper money must prove hurtful to this country; that we cannot be relieved from our debts except by promoting domestic manufactures; and that, during the prevailing scarcity of money, the burdens of the poor may be relieved by altering the mode of taxation. . . .

In public measures, as in the conduct of private life, it will constantly be found that "honesty is the best policy." . . . A paper cur-

9

rency which is a legal tender, even when it may be depreciated 20 or 30 per cent is not generally considered as an honest tender : . . . I never have heard any man say, that it would be perfect justice to pass a law, by which every creditor should be compelled to receive three-fourths or two-thirds of his debt, instead of the whole debt, and yet such a law would be perfectly similar to the tender of depreciated paper, . . .

If we are willing to take a lesson from other governments, we shall find that money is not to be made out of paper, for there is not an empire, kingdom, or state under the sun, where debts may be legally discharged by paper money, except in some of the United States of America. . . .

I have said, that paper-money, which is a legal tender, must prove hurtful to this country; when made, it must depreciate, and the effects of depreciation are unfriendly to industry, injurious to the poor and destructive of good morals. . . .

Thus it is, that our citizens are universally involved : many of the debts are due to merchants; but a much greater amount is due to people who are not merchants : and we seem not to have discovered, that we are nearly ruined by foreign luxuries. Let any man cast his eye on this account : let him think of a state whose citizens are given up to indolence and vanity—who, in the space of three years, have plunged themselves in debt at least three hundred thousand pounds : let him observe how the property of our citizens is daily mortgaged to strangers and foreigners, and the inheritance of our children bartered away for fineries and fopperies : let him observe the desperate situation to which we are reduced, merely to obtain a transient release. The dignity of government is wounded—base money is declared to be a legal tender—the diligent man is plundered for the benefit of the indolent and extravagant—industry languishes—the orphan is defrauded—and the most atrocious frauds are practiced under the sanction of the law. . . .

We shall be told, in excuse for imported luxuries, that we buy goods cheaper than we can make them; and that a man earns more in his tobacco or corn-field, than he could earn at a loom, or by other manufactures. These positions are fallacious and ill-founded. Both experiment and calculation prove them to be false. . . . Every domestic manufacture is cheaper than a foreign one, for this plain reason : by the first nothing is lost to the country, by the other the whole value is lost; it is carried away never to return. . . . Let the manufacturer demand what he pleases for the produce of his labor, the farmer can easily settle his account by selling his provisions accordingly. The annual consumption of goods in this state has been estimated at a million, or rather a million two hundred thousand dollars in specie, or produce to that value, have been sent out of the state and we are so much the poorer. Suppose the whole of those goods had been manufactured within the state, or a sufficient quantity for our consumption, and that they had cost the consumers, or been valued at two millions of dollars; would the citizens of this state have lost eight hundred thousand dollars by this difference in price? The very reverse would have happened. . . .

Perhaps the most easy and effectual method of preventing the poor man from being distressed in the payment of taxes, is by altering the general form of taxation, or by substituting an excise in the place of a tax on property, which is common in North Carolina. . . .

The capitation-tax, and land-tax, such as are usual among us, are inevitable and positive taxes; they are not to be averted. The industrious man cannot elude them; the unfortunate cannot escape them. . . . But the excise is a negative or indirect tax. . . .

When I say that an excise is more favorable to the poor, than a poll-tax, or a land-tax, or any other tax on property, and that it tends to promote industry and wealth, I must constantly be supposed to mean an excise on luxuries, or imported goods: and I would also be understood to mean an excise that is impartially laid and fairly collected. . . .

The general advantage of a sumptuary law, or an excise upon imported goods, is so obvious, that I question whether any objections can be made to it, except the possibility of frauds being committed in secreting the goods.—*Historical Papers Published by the Trinity College* [Duke University] *Historical Society*, Series XI (1915), pp. 1-46.

63. JOURNAL OF A TOUR TO NORTH CAROLINA, 1787

William Attmore, a Philadelphia merchant, came to North Carolina in the winter of 1787 to collect debts owing to his firm and to obtain new business. While on his tour he kept a diary, of which some parts have been lost. Enough remains, however, to form an interesting narrative.

HORSE RACING

Saturday Nov. 24

Races again today . . . The Riders were young Negroes of 13 or 14 years old who generally rode bareback.—

. . . The objections and inconveniences attending this kind of Amusement, obvious to me, are,

1st. Large numbers of people are drawn from their business, occupations and labour, which is a real loss to their families and the State.

2nd. By wagering and betting; much quarreling wrangling, Anger, Swearing & drinking is created and takes place, I saw it on the present occasion prevalent from the highest to the lowest—I saw white Boys, and Negroes eagerly betting 1 / 2 / a quart of Rum, a drink of Grog, &c, as well as Gentlemen betting high.—

3rd. Many accidents happen on these occasions. . . .

FUNERAL CUSTOMS

Sunday, Nov. 25.

It is the custom here With some, if they can afford it, when a burial happens in their families, to give the Minister and bearers white scarffs and Bands the Scarff is composed of about 3 yards & a half of white linen and hangs from the right shoulder & is gathered in a knot below the left Arm, with a Rose and Ribbands, also white; from the knot the two ends hang down; the Band for the Hat is of white linen also, about 1½ yards or sometimes that quantity will make two Bands if split down the middle—This is tied round the Crown of the Hat and the two ends streaming down. . . .

FORCING THE SCHOOLMASTER TO GRANT A HOLIDAY

Thursday, Dec. 20

We were alarmed in our Quarters before day, by the firing of Muskets at some little distance from the house in which we lay— We found that the firing was at a school House in the neighborhood, of our Quarters, with powder only; tis the custom here for School Boys upon the approach of Christmas, Easter and Whitsuntide, to rebel against their Schoolmaster, in order to force him to grant them a holiday; the boys rise early in the Morning and go to the School House, which is considered as their Fort, they barricade the Door and Windows, carry into the house with them victuals and blankets, with water and wood, sufficient to sustain the Siege that they expect from the Master; Upon his approach at the usual School hours, he finds himself shut out, he demands the cause, the Garrison acquaints him that they are determined to have a holiday, this is frequently denied, and now commences the Siege, the Master tries to force his way into the house, they resist him by every means in their power, and sometimes give him some very hard knocks; throw Stones, &c. It is generally looked upon as a piece of fun; the

Master pretends to be solicitous to subdue them, and if he catches any Stragler from the Fort, he will flog him heartily & it is understood on these occasions that the boys are to be peaceable, except during the actual storm of the enemy, when they are at liberty to maul him to their hearts content. . . . This Scene is sometimes continued many days, at last the Master proposes terms, that he grants them so many days holiday; which if satisfactory being accepted by the Garrison, peace is again established in the little community.

EGG NOG DRINKING

Sunday Dec. 23.

It is very much the custom in North Carolina to drink Drams of some kind or other before Breakfast; sometimes Gin, Cherry-bounce, Egg Nog &c. several of the Assembly Men, this Morning indulged themselves in this respect. . . .

Tuesday, Dec. 25.

This Morning according to North Carolina custom we had before Breakfast, a drink of EGG NOG, this compound is made in the following manner: In two clean Quart Bowls, were divided the Yolks and whites of five Eggs, the yolks & whites separated, the Yolks beat up with a Spoon, and mixt up with brown Sugar, the whites were whisk'd into Froth by a Straw Whisk till the Straw wou'd stand upright in it; when duly beat, the Yolks were put to the Froth; again beat a long time; then half a pint of Rum pour'd slowly into the mixture, the whole kept stirring the whole time till well incorporated.—*Journal of a Tour to North Carolina by William Attmore* (edited by Lida Tunstall Rodman, in "The James Sprunt Historical Publications," Vol. XVII, No. 2. Chapel Hill, 1922), pp. 1-43.

64. NORTH CAROLINA'S ATTITUDE TOWARD THE FEDERAL CONSTITUTION, 1788-1789

In the period during and following the American Revolution, North Carolina displayed a strong feeling of individualism. The people were jealous of their rights and sensitive to any encroachments by the central government. Going into effect in 1781, the Articles of Confederation proved to be generally unpopular throughout the United States, and in North Carolina much criticism and many amendments were offered. When delegates were sent to the Philadelphia Convention (the Constitutional Convention) in the summer of 1787, there was a feeling in the state that the Articles would be revised. Instead of this, however, an entirely new Constitution was drawn up, and North Carolina was asked to give its approval to the new frame of government.

From the very first there was bitter opposition to the Constitution, based upon the allegations that it endowed the central government with too much power. This opposition found most of its strength in the "back country," while eastern counties, for the greater part, fought for the ratification of the Constitution. In the election of delegates to the state convention feeling ran so high that it culminated in a small riot in Edenton, in the course of which the courthouse was thrown into darkness and many Federalist heads were clubbed. Judge James Iredell and Colonel William R. Davie threw the weight of their prestige and popularity behind the fight for ratification, but the shrewd Willie Jones led the opposition and in the Hillsboro Convention defeated the Constitution by a vote of 184 to 83. In spite of this action, however, the instrument became effective in 1789 with the launching of the new government. Fearing that she would be subjected to economic pressure, North Carolina, in the autumn of 1789, voted at the Fayetteville Convention to come "under the federal roof."

JAMES IREDELL'S DEFENSE OF THE CONSTITUTION

EDENTON, NOVEMBER 12, 1787.

WE, the Grand Jury for the district of Edenton, considering the present as a very important crisis in the affairs of America, and being deeply sensible of the necessity of a firm and lasting union among the American States, to ensure the common safety and liberty of all, hope it will not be deemed presuming in us, that we take this occasion to express our sentiments on the subject of the new Constitution, proposed by the late respectable Convention. We believe that none can be so ignorant as not to know, and we hope few are so unfeeling as not to regret, the disordered and distracted state in which the affairs of the Union have been for a long time past. No sooner was the danger of a common enemy removed, than the States immediately detached themselves from the general concerns of the whole, as if our future fate was out of the power of fortune. The consequence has been, our public debts unpaid, the treaty of peace unfulfilled on both sides, our commerce at the very verge of ruin, and all private industry at a stand, for want of a united, vigorous government. Quotas demanded which we can never pay, and Congress preserving merely the shadow of authority, without possessing one substantial property of power. These evils dictated the necessity of a change, and the same happy expedient of an union of counsels which formed the confederation, was adopted to remedy its defects. Experience had pointed these out, and we believe it would be difficult to draw together in any country, a body of abler men than the persons appointed on this important occasion. They were not only able men, but entitled to the highest confidence which can be bestowed by any people upon illustrious and successful leaders; and the same patriotism of character which formerly distinguished so many of them in the most trying scenes, was visible in the anxious and deep attention they employed on this momentous subject. A work coming from such men, after such long deliberation, is entitled to the utmost respect, especially as all the States assembled were unanimous, a circumstance that strongly shows the purity of their intentions, their sense of the absolute necessity that a new constitution should be immediately formed, and that little subordinate attentions to local interests ought to give way to the great object of the general good. There is nothing we hold in greater disdain, nor is there any thing more inconsistent with common prudence, as well as the most ordinary share of public spirit, than that we should cavil about trifles when our all is at stake; that we should slight the present favorable opportunity, which may be the only one we may ever enjoy, to establish a free and energetic government, when we now lie at the mercy of the most inconsiderable enemy, and have a union in nothing but in name. We admire in the new Constitution a proper jealousy of liberty mixed with a due regard to the necessity of a strong authoritative government. Such a one is as requisite for a confederated, as for a single government, since it would not be more ridiculous or futile for our own Assembly to depend for a sanction to its laws on a unanimous concurrence of all the counties in the State, than for Congress to depend for any necessary exertion of power on the unanimous concurrence of all the States in the Union. One weak, corrupted, or unprincipled State might in such a case destroy the whole. This evil, the effect of which we have already felt, is, in our opinion, happily remedied by the constitution proposed, with an advantageous addition of a popular representative of the people at large, accompanied with useful checks to guard against possible abuses. It is also a part of the constitution, that we observe with particular pleasure, that nine States may at any time make alterations, so that any changes which experience may point out can be made without the danger of such calamities as are incident upon changes of government in all other countries, where they can be only brought about by a civil war. Nor can we avoid dwelling with delight upon those many provisions, calculated to make us as much one people as possible, and to impress upon the minds of all that useful and important truth, that our strength consists in union, and nothing can hurt us but division. May this great truth, so important for us, so formidable to our enemies, rest upon the minds of all well-wishers to their country, as the watch-word of American liberty and safety! The various attempts that were made to divide us during the war, and the danger of similar efforts being used on the present occasion to make us distrust our best and ablest characters, ought to put us upon our guard, that we may not suffer ourselves to be the dupes of an insidious policy, working for our destruction. But we trust in God, that the same all-powerful Providence, which has hitherto so wonderfully preserved us, will still continue to protect us from the machinations of all our enemies, internal and external, and that by a wise use of the vast advantages in our possession, this country may become, as it seems destined to be, an asylum for all the oppressed upon the globe.

Entertaining these sentiments, which the warmth of our feelings hath carried to a greater length than we intended, we most earnestly wish that the General Assembly may appoint the meeting of a Convention on as early a day as possible, that no reproach of unnecessary delay may lie on us, when, in all human probability, upon our speedy adoption or rejection of this constitution it may depend, whether we shall be truly a nation, happy in ourselves, and respected by the rest of mankind; or an inconsiderable scattered people, perpetually driving to and fro, in search of a perfection which never can be found, amusing ourselves with visionary ideas, when we might be enjoying real blessings, and at length doomed to feel the curse of all human discontent, the consciousness that, by rejecting the means Providence had put into our power, we had become both wretched and contemptible.—*Life and Correspondence of James Iredell* (edited by Griffith J. McRee), II, 181-83.

THE CONVENTION ELECTION RIOT AT KINSTON, 1788

The whole number of voters was three hundred and seventy-two; at sunset on Saturday the Poll was closed and the sheriff proceeded to call out the tickets; two hundred and eighty-two tickets were called out, the hindmost in number on the Poll of the Antifederalists had one hundred and fifty-five votes, the foremost in number of the Federalists had only one hundred and twenty-one, and the tickets coming out fast in favor of the Antifederalists, the other party seemed fully convinced they should lose their election and appeared to be much exasperated at the same, especially Colonel

B. *Sheppard*, who with sundry others cast out many aspersions and very degrading and abusive language to the other candidates, which was not returned by any of the candidates, or any person on their part with so much as one provoking word. At length Colonel A. Sheppard went upon the bench where the sheriffs, inspectors, and clerks were attending their business, and swore he would beat one of the inspectors who had been peaceably and diligently attending to his business, and having a number of clubs ready prepared, the persons holding the candles were suddenly knocked or pulled down and all the candles in the Court House were instantly put out; many blows with clubs were heard to pass (but it being dark they did the most damage to the Federalists). The Antifederal candidates being unapprized of such a violent assault, and expecting better treatment, from men who would wish to wear the character of gentlemen, were in no posture of defense, and finding their lives in danger, thought it most advisable to retire privately in the dark, but one of them (to wit) Isaac Groom was overtaken in the street, by a party of their men consisting of twelve or fifteen—with clubs, who fell on him and much abused him, in so much that he was driven to the necessity of mounting his horse and riding for his life; the sheriff also related that in the time of the riot on the Court House he received a blow by a club and that the ticket box was violently taken away.—*Norfolk and Portsmouth Journal*, April 30, 1788. (This and the following appear in the *Historical Papers* cited below.)

LETTER OF TIMOTHY BLOODWORTH TO GENERAL JOHN LAMB, *1788*

The importance of the subject on which you address us needs no apology but confers an obligation on those patrons of liberty whose attention to the public welfare merits our most candid acknowledgments. . . .

Although additional powers to the federated system meet our fullest approbation, yet we cannot consent to the adoption of a Constitution, whose revenues lead to aristocratic tyranny, or monarchical despotism, and opens a door wide as fancy can paint, for the introduction of dissipation, bribery and corruption to the exclusion of public virtue, whose luxuriant growth is only discoverable in the fertile soil of Republicanism, the only Asylum for the Genius of Liberty, and where alone she can dwell in safety. . . .

We acknowledge the obligation to our country, posterity, and the rights of mankind and will join in our feeble efforts to effect the ends you propose but we are apprehensive that Virginia will accede to the measure: by a late report we hear that a majority of thirty are in favor of its adoption: should this be the case, it will probably have a prevailing influence on our State, a decided majority of which, have hitherto appeared averse to the proposed Constitution.

LETTER OF THOMAS PERSON TO GENERAL JOHN LAMB, AUGUST 6, 1788

It is my decided opinion (& no man is better acquainted with the publick mind) that nine tenths of the people of this State are opposed to the adoption of the New System, without very considerable Amendments & I might without incurring any great hazard to err, assure you, that very Considerable numbers conceive an idea of a General Government on this extension impracticable & dangerous.
. . .

Our Convention met at Hillsborough on the day appointed & on the 22nd resolved itself into a committee of the whole house & continued thro discussion from day to day (Sundays excepted) until the 1st Inst on which we called the decisive question when there appeared, for non-concurrence 184 & 83 for adopting—but recommending numbered amendments which were repugnant to their Eloquence & reasoning in debate; a circumstance somewhat surprising; but proves nevertheless that even its advocates think the plan radically bad, by these exertions to render it virtually better.

A "CITIZEN OF NORTH CAROLINA" ON THE FEDERAL CONSTITUTION, AUGUST, 1788

But regret, with whatever poignancy it may be felt, is now useless. The danger is incurred. Eleven other states have a common united government: We have no share in it. If we can derive pride from the consideration our independence is increased. We are now not only independent of all other nations of the world, but entirely independent of the other states, except for our share in the debt hitherto incurred, which we are now utterly unable to pay. . . .

There are some men possibly, inflated with ridiculous ideas of their own importance, to whom this prospect may be pleasing. There are many weak men perhaps, who think danger never exists but when evils are actually and immediately felt. There may be a few . . . to whom confusion and disorder may be the most acceptable objects. But among the great majority, including both parties, those who are averse to the new constitution as well as those who are friends to it, I believe the idea of an entire disunion is reprobated with horror. I have had the pleasure to hear that was the case with by far the greatest part of the majority in our late convention, who unfortunately did not scruple to rush into a temporary one. . . .

In our present situation what are we reduced to? Have we any national character? Is the state of North Carolina known to any nation in Europe? No? *The United States of America are known.* But alas! We are to be no longer one of them. We have no alliance with any power on earth. We have no right, if attacked, to call on the other states for assistance. Can we much longer bear so humiliating, so dangerous a condition? What must our feelings be, when we see the prosperity of the other states derived from the energy of their new government, while we are deriving additional weakness from the dissolution of the old, without partaking of any of the benefits of the new? We have had our option allowed us. We have unfortunately chosen for the present a path leading to misery and ruin, if we continue to pursue it.—"News, Letters and Documents Concerning North Carolina and the Federal Constitution" (edited by William K. Boyd, in *Historical Papers Published by the Trinity College* [Duke University] *Historical Society*, Series XIV, 1922), pp. 75-95.

65. PRESIDENT WASHINGTON'S TOUR OF NORTH CAROLINA, 1791

In 1791, President Washington made a tour of the southern states. The purpose of this trip, he said, was "to acquire knowledge of the face of the country, the growth and agriculture thereof, and the temper and disposition of the inhabitants towards the new government." As we have observed, the "disposition of the inhabitants" of North Carolina toward the Constitution had been very unfavorable in 1788, when they rejected that document. Apparently there was a marked change of sentiment in 1789 in favor of the federal government. Washington visited most of the towns in Eastern Carolina—and there were not many—in April, 1791. A month or so later, on his return trip from the South, he passed through Charlotte, Salisbury, Salem, Guilford Courthouse, and other places in western Carolina.

NORTH CAROLINA : HALIFAX, TARBOROUGH, GREENVILLE

[April 15, 1791, reached Halifax.]

Hallifax is the first town I came to after passing the line between the two States, and is about 20 miles from it.—To this place vessels by the aid of Oars & Setting poles are brought for the produce which comes to this place, and others along the River ; and may be carried 8 or 10 miles higher to the falls which are neither great nor of much extent ; . . . This town stands upon high ground ; and it is the reason given for not placing it at the head of the navigation there being none but low ground between it and the falls—It seems to be in a decline & does not it is said contain a thousand Souls.

[April 18, 1791]

Set out by six o'clock . . . lodged at Tarborough 14 Miles further. This place is less than Hallifax, but more lively and thriving ; —it is situated on the Tar River which goes into Pamplico Sound and is crossed at the Town by means of a bridge a great height from the water, and notwithstanding the freshes rise sometimes nearly to the arch.—Corn, Porke, and some Tar are the exports from it.—We were recd. at this place by as good a salute as could be given by one piece of artillery.

[April 19, 1791]

At 6 o'clock I left Tarborough accompanied by some of the most respectable people of the place for a few miles—dined at a trifling place called Greenesville 25 miles distant—and lodged at one Allan's 14 miles further a very indifferent house without stabling which for the first time since I commenced my Journey were obliged to stand without a cover.

Greenesville is on Tar River and the exports the same as from Tarborough with a greater proportion of Tar—for the lower down the greater number of Tar makers are there—This article is contrary to all ideas one would entertain on the subject, rolled as Tobacco by an axis which goes through both heads—one horse draws two barrels in this manner.—Archibald Henderson, *Washington's Southern Tour, 1791,* pp. 77-101.

66. JEFFERSONIAN DEMOCRACY IN NORTH CAROLINA

Despite the fact that Thomas Jefferson evinced a gloomy concern over the state of political affairs in North Carolina, the electors of the commonwealth, when they met and voted in Raleigh in 1796, gave the Sage of Monticello eleven of their twelve votes, awarding Adams only one. As the election of 1800 approached Jefferson again had unfounded fears and pronounced North Carolina to be in "the most dangerous state." This was caused, he explained, by the political ascendency of lawyers, who were "all tories, the people substantially republican, but uninformed and deceived by the lawyers who are elected of necessity because [there are] few other candidates." Jefferson knew the remedy, however. "The medicine for that state must be very mild and secretly administered."

This medicine was quite effective, for in 1800 Jefferson received all but four of the electoral votes. In 1804 the electors again met and cast their votes "uniformly" for Jefferson and Clinton, and North Carolina was then deemed "as firmly attached to Republicanism as any in the Union."

In producing this political condition two men, Willie Jones and Nathaniel Macon, played a most important part. Of the two, Macon probably had more influence; it is certain that his voice in national affairs gave him more prestige, and he was more active politically in later years than Jones. Elected to the House of Representatives in 1791, Macon began a quarter-century of congressional membership and soon became North Carolina's foremost enunciator of Jeffersonian principles. In the following speech, which was provoked by the Alien and Sedition Acts, Macon gives a typically Republican view of relations between the states and the central government, concluding with an early acceptance of the doctrine of judicial review, which was to be of so much importance later.

MR. MACON said, the same section of the Constitution which forbids any interference with the freedom of speech and of the press, extends also to religious establishments, and says, "Congress shall make no law respecting an establishment of religion, or prohibiting the free exercise thereof." This bill [the Sedition Act] ought to be considered, therefore, as the commencement of a system which might as well be extended to the establishment of a national religion, as to a "restraint of speech and of the press." He acknowledged the bill was less exceptionable than when it came from the Senate; but it yet contained the principle which he considered as violating the Constitution. . . .

Gentlemen, Mr. M. said, might call this a harmless bill; but however harmless it may be, it is a beginning to act upon forbidden ground, and no one may say to what extent it may hereafter be carried. He thought this subject of the liberty of the press was sacred, and ought to be left where the Constitution had left it. The States have complete power on the subject, and when Congress legislates, it ought to have confidence in the States, as the States ought also to have confidence in Congress, or our Government is gone. This Government depends upon the State Legislatures for existence. They have only to refuse to elect Senators to Congress, and all is gone. He believed there was nowhere any complaint of a want of proper laws under the State Governments; and though there may not be remedies found for every grievance in the General Government, what it wants of power will be found in the State Governments, and there can be no doubt but that power will be duly exercised when necessity calls for it.

Mr. M. concluded with observing, that from the best examination he had been able to give to the subject, he was convinced that Congress does not possess the power to pass a law like the present; but if there be a majority determined to pass it, he could only hope that the Judges would exercise the power placed in them of determining the law an unconstitutional law, if, upon scrutiny, they find it to be so.—*Annals of Congress, 5th Cong., 2nd Sess.*, 2151, 2152.

67. Banking Problems in the Early Nineteenth Century

The first banks organized in North Carolina were the Bank of the Cape Fear and the Bank of New Bern, which received their charters in 1804. The former had a capital of $250,000 and the latter of $200,000. The amount of notes and debts of the Bank of the Cape Fear was not to exceed $750,000 over the moneys on deposit; of the Bank of New Bern, $600,000. The state had the right to subscribe 250 shares in each.

The State Bank of North Carolina was incorporated in 1810. It was thought that this would absorb the two existing banks and "equalize the relation between currency and specie." There was to be a central bank in Raleigh with branches at Edenton, New Bern, Wilmington, Fayetteville, Tarboro, and Salisbury. The capital of the bank was not to exceed $1,600,000, of which $250,000 was reserved for the state. In subscriptions preference was to be given to the banks of New Bern and of Cape Fear.

At first the banks had a wholesome effect on finance and commerce in the state. Rapid expansion of the currency and widespread speculation, however, led to confusion, commercial depression, and finally to the "panic of 1819." The total authorized capital of the banks had increased from $450,000 in 1804 to $3,200,000 in 1814. From 1815 to 1819 there was a tremendous increase of bank-note issues. In the latter year there was a very rapid return of the notes for redemption. Eventually the banks were forced to suspend specie payment. This action, together with "innumerable bankruptcies and insolvencies of individuals," led to an anti-bank movement. Governor John Branch was one of the leaders in criticising practices of the banks.

The anti-bank and pro-debtor elements in the state demanded drastic reforms in banking, but the legislature was controlled by a pro-bank majority. Accordingly all efforts at reform failed. It was not even possible to get an investigation of the banking situation. The majority in the legislature was so favorable to the State Bank that the legislature came to its aid by authorizing the public treasurer to purchase stock with the surplus money in the State Treasury.

While this criticism was being made of the state banks, a bitter attack was launched against the branch of the United States Bank, which was located at Fayetteville. In 1816 the legislature had requested the establishment of the branch of the United States Bank. Then in 1818 a tax of $5,000 was levied on this institution, probably for the purpose of "taxing it out of existence," though there is no proof of this intention. This tax was not collected and the president of the branch bank expressed surprise that North Carolina even attempted to collect it, in view of the fact that the Supreme Court of the United States, in the case of *McCulloch* vs. *Maryland*, had ruled that a state could not tax an agency of the federal government. The branch bank was denounced as a "Colossus," a "menace to State Rights," and a "Monster feeding upon our Vitals."

REPORT OF THE COMMITTEE ON INCREASING THE CAPITAL STOCK OF THE STATE BANK, *1817*

About twenty Years ago we had no Bank in this State: But we had a Paper Currency issued by the State, supposed to amount to about three hundred thousand Dollars . . . at least one half of our then Circulating Medium, was composed of Paper Currency; And this fact seems to prove that our Circulating Medium at that day did not exceed six hundred thousand Dollars.

Until within the last six Years, the Banks of Newbern and Cape-Fear were the only Institutions of that Description in this State. The Capital of both amounted to about four hundred thousand Dollars, And the Notes issued by them, not only composed almost entirely *our* Circulating Medium, but they overflowed into other States, and became considerably depreciated. . . .

When the State Bank was established six Years Ago, with a Capital of one Million, six hundred thousand Dollars, it was thought by many that the Capital was larger than could be profitably employed in supplying the Circulating Medium required by the State: And the Legislature itself seems to have thought that more Banking Capital could not be advantageously employed: for they invited the Newbern and Cape-Fear Banks to subscribe their Capital Stock into the State Bank, and did not require that the Stock of the State Bank should be all subscribed Until the Year 1820, When the Charters of the Newbern and Cape Fear Banks would expire: And they pledged the Faith of the State that no Other Bank should be established, during the Continuance of the Charter then granted. The Newbern and Cape Fear Banks did not accept the invitation, and the Legislature has since not only extended their Charters, but increased their Capital to the Sum of one Million, six hundred thousand Dollars. And at the last Session, the Legislature invited the establishment in this State of a Branch of the Bank of the United States. That Branch is now about to go into Operation with a Capital entirely at the Arbitrary Will of the President and Directors at Philadelphia.

These facts shew that the present Banking Capital of North Carolina is nine or ten times greater than it was seven Years Ago, and yet at that time it was quite sufficient for the State. These Facts also shew that an Increase of Banking Capital to any large Amount, would endanger in an eminent Degree, the Honour and Interests of the State and the People, And the very existence of the Banks of this State.

. . . When the Banks to the West and South of New-England suspended Specie Payment, the Notes issued by the State Bank of North Carolina became, in a great Degree, a Continental Currency. In Georgia they were at Par received and issued by the Banks of that State. In South Carolina, they were always at Par, except occasionally in the City of Charlestown, . . . Every where else they bore a Premium, often a very considerable one. This occasioned a very great Proportion of them to be carried out of this and circulated in Other States, . . . and left in a great degree, the Circulating Medium of North Carolina to be supplied by the Notes issued by the Banks of Newbern and Cape Fear. The Case hereafter will be very different: The State Banks have resumed specie Payments, and the Bank of the United States has been established. This Bank having the Collection of the Revenue of the United States, and having Branches in almost every State, its Notes will undoubtedly not only form the Circulating Medium between the different States, but they will very much circumscribe the Notes of all the Banks established by State Authority, even within their own State. Without attributing to this Bank premeditated Hostility, its Operations will be found to be very oppressive and injurious to all State Banks, and to none more so, than to those of North Carolina. They must hereafter be content with supplying a Part of their own Circulating Medium, instead of supplying as they have done for some Years past, the whole of that, and Part of the Circulating Medium of other States.—*Senate Journal, 1817-18*, pp. 89-91.

"LEONIDAS" ON THE EVILS OF THE STATE BANKS, 1819

The Banks in our State, (for reasons best known to themselves, have refused to pay specie for their notes. The consequence of such a measure, must add to the present embarrassment of the times, and greatly dishonor the State. . . .

I cannot but consider the banks, as the primary source of the present evils, and if they are not crushed in time, or properly regulated and corrected by the people, they will, ere long, destroy the peaceful equality of our government, and overthrow the present establishment of public liberty. Already we have experienced the unjust influence which the banks have in this State . . . several counties in this State have changed their politics, have degenerated from true Republican principles to those understood and practised by Federalists. The time will shortly arrive, unless the people keep a proper look out, when the banks will wield the democracy of the State, . . . and, it is to be feared, our Legislature, too, will feel its mighty influence.

This mighty colossus will, one day, put one foot upon the shores of Currituck, and the other on the mountains of Buncombe, straddle the State, and look down with contempt and derision on the State House; for money will, in every age and in every clime, have its force and influence.—*The Raleigh Minerva*, July 7, 1819.

GOVERNOR JOHN BRANCH'S CRITICISMS OF STATE BANKS AND BANKING PRACTICES, 1819-1820

The Banks, . . . in their . . . inordinate solicitude for the dividend, have led the citizens of our once happy country into the wilds and mazes of speculative life, . . . and so long as it is in the power of the Banks to increase or diminish the Currency of the country at their pleasure, . . . so long shall we be liable to a recurrence of similar embarrassments. . . . They have embosomed in their vaults or driven from the country all the specie, and the notes which have been substituted instead thereof, not being convertible into gold and silver, the country presents the melancholy spectacle of a people deeply involved in debt without a legitimate circulating medium. Never indeed have our citizens experienced such a pressure and unless something is done for their relief they must inevitably fall a prey to the iron grasp of their unrelenting creditors. . . .

That . . . very much of those embarrassments may be fairly attributed to the unreasonable multiplication of banks, and the excessive issue of their paper far beyond their capacity to redeem, will not be denied. . . . It is your duty to legislate efficiently on the subject, . . . and to place those monied institutions on such basis as will promise stability and the greatest uniformity in their issues, and thereby prevent those rapid appreciations and depreciations.

. . . For, by the establishment of Banks, money is not only made; but, by their failure to pay specie, the value thereof is indirectly regulated, and thus the salutary provisions of our constitution are virtually defeated.—*Journals of the House of Commons*, November 17, 1819, and November 22, 1820.

"CAROLINIUS" ON THE EVILS OF THE BRANCH BANK, *1819*

We . . . are shamefully prostrated at the feet of this Colossus. . . . With its immense capital, its ubiquity of presence, and its command of the whole revenue of the United States, we may truly say it is a thing fearfully and wonderfully made. Every thing beneath it must be ground to dust under its pressure.

I advise then . . . that we pertinaciously adhere to *state rights*. It is enough to suffer from our credulity & the schemes of others, without going the length of laying down our dignity as freemen.— *The Raleigh Minerva*, November 12, 1819.

MURPHEY'S OPPOSITION TO THE BRANCH BANK, *1821*

. . . I am convinced, that the Branch of the United States Bank at Fayetteville, which is literally a Broker's Shop and kept for this purpose by the Mother Bank, is the greatest Curse that has befallen us since the Year 1791 ; and that the local Banks as well as Individuals will continue to be pressed, if not ruined, Unless we get Rid of it. We can't bank in this State, with this Monster feeding upon our Vitals.—*The Papers of Archibald D. Murphey* (edited by W. H. Hoyt), II, 216-17.

68. NORTH CAROLINA'S OPPOSITION TO THE TARIFF, 1828

North Carolina was the only state in the Old South which consistently opposed all protective tariff legislation. Her representatives in Congress were particularly hostile to the so-called "Tariff of Abominations." South Carolina took the lead in resisting this unpopular tariff measure and called on her sister states for "aid and comfort." Governor Burton, in his message of November 21, 1827, referring to the exertion of South Carolina against the proposed increase in tariff duties, declared that "the dignity and interest of the State requires that North Carolina should not be silent." The General Assembly, acting upon his suggestion, adopted the following report.

THE committee are aware that there is no portion of the American People more attached to the Union, and more deeply sensible of the great benefits which might be expected to flow from it, conducted upon the principles upon which it was first formed, than the People of North Carolina: they have never, at any period of our history, even under the strongest political excitement, endeavored to embarrass the Government, or the administration of those to whom it was entrusted, otherwise than by the right of suffrage. . . .

The people of North Carolina . . . have seldom expressed a legislative opinion upon the measures of the General Government; being at all times, willing to give a full and fair opportunity to those charged with the management of public affairs, of being "judged by their measures." But a crisis has arisen in the political affairs of our country, which demands a prompt and decisive expression of public opinion. Under such circumstances, silence would be injustice to ourselves, and a want of candor to the other States of the Union.

The committee are of opinion, that interest, either pecuniary or political, is the great point of union, from the smallest association up to the Confederacy of the United States; and that, whenever a system or policy is pursued by the General Government which strikes at the very foundation of the Union, it is the right of every member of the Confederacy to call their attention to the fundamental principles upon which the Government was formed; and if they persist in measures ruinous in themselves, the question may fairly be discussed whether the checks and balances of the Government have not been overthrown; whether they have been instrumental in producing so onerous an effect; and whether the benefits of the Union are not more than counterbalanced by the evils.

The committee will not assert that Congress has no power, under the Constitution, to lay duties on imports, which are intended to operate as a *protection* to manufactures; they maintain, however, that the *exercise* of such a power, as contemplated by the Woollens Bill, is a direct violation of the spirit of that instrument, and repugnant to the objects for which it was formed. . . . It is conceded, that Congress has the express power to lay imposts; but it is maintained, that *that* power was given for the purpose of revenue, and revenue alone and that any other use of the power is usurpation on the part of Congress. . . .

Manufactures, in the United States, are not an object of *general* but of *local* interest; and yet they have received from the Government, not only a moderate and just encouragement, under the operation of a tariff of duties on imports, for purposes of revenue, but a protection by an enormous duty upon importations; which palsies every effort of the agriculturist, withers the product of his industry and greatly impairs foreign commerce.

The committee are of opinion, that the Woollens Bill, which received in the Congress of the United States, at its last session, so full and fair an investigation, is a measure, above all others which has occupied the attention of that enlightened body calculated to produce an enormous tax on the agriculture of the South, and to be destructive of revenue. They believe it to be a bill artfully designed for the advancement of the incorporated companies of New England, and admirably adapted to its end. They believe it fatal to the happiness, the morals, and the rights of a large portion of our common country; for it has its foundation in avarice, and consumes every patriotic feeling. . . .

Resolved, as the opinion of the Legislature of North Carolina, that it is inexpedient for the Congress of the United States to increase the duties on imports.—*Document No. 62, House of Representatives, 20th Cong., 1st Sess.*

69. NORTH CAROLINA'S ATTITUDE TOWARD NULLIFICATION, 1832-1833

When the South Carolina Convention issued the Ordinance of Nullification, November 24, 1832, it issued a call to the other states urging them to resist the federal tariff law. The reaction to this call surprised and displeased South Carolina. All of the state legislatures adopted resolutions condemning the action of the Palmetto State, and most of them expressed approval of President Jackson's method of handling the situation. The General Assembly of North Carolina declared that the tariff law was "impolitic, unjust and oppressive." At the same time it expressed a "warm attachment to the Constitution of the United States," declaring that the policy of nullification would lead to a dissolution of the Union. In January, 1833, the following resolves were adopted, by a vote of 47 to 7 in the Senate, and 98 to 22 in the House. "Union meetings" were likewise held throughout the state, all of which adopted resolutions condemning the action of South Carolina.

THE General Assembly of this State think, that the doctrine of Nullification avowed by South-Carolina, and declared in an Ordinance made by a Convention which recently assembled in Columbia, is revolutionary in its character, will, in its operation, be subversive of the Constitution of the United States, and leads to a dissolution of the Union. . . . We cherish sentiments of the highest respect for the virtue, talents and chivalry of the citizens of that State.

They no doubt believe, that a crisis of fearful and oppressive extremity has arrived, when no other alternative is left to patriotism, but boldly to stand forth in defence of reserved rights, and valorously to resist the oppressor. . . .

This is an awful crisis. The attitude which our Southern Sister has assumed, and the relation in which she now stands to the Federal Government, fill us with the deepest solicitude, and the most heart-thrilling anxiety. North-Carolina is not only deeply implicated in the existing controversy, as a member of the Union, but from her proximity to one of the contending parties, and their community of interests, may be vitally involved in the issue of the conflict. She is the border State, and her fields may become the battle ground of the combatants. These considerations justify us in approaching, with feelings of kindness our sister State, and in soliciting her to pause ere she takes a leap, the consequences of which are not within the reach of human eye. . . .

Resolved, That the General Assembly of the State of North-Carolina doth entertain, and doth unequivocally express a warm attachment to the Constitution of the United States.

Resolved, That the General Assembly doth solemnly declare a devoted attachment to the Federal Union, believing that on its continuance depend the liberty, the peace and prosperity of these United States.

Resolved, That whereas diversity of opinion may prevail in this State as to the Constitutionality of the Acts of Congress imposing duties on imposts; yet it is believed, a large majority of the people think those acts unconstitutional; and they are all united in the sentiment that the existing Tariff is impolitic, unjust and oppressive; and they have urged, and will continue to urge its repeal.

Resolved, That the doctrine of Nullification avowed by the State of South-Carolina, and lately promulgated in an Ordinance, is revolutionary in its character, subversive of the Constitution of the United States, and leads to a dissolution of the Union.

Resolved, That our Senators in Congress be instructed and our Representatives be requested to use all constitutional means in their power, to procure an adjustment of the existing controversy between the State of South Carolina and the General Government.
—*Journal of the House of Commons, 1833*, p. 224.

RESOLUTIONS ADOPTED AT WILMINGTON MEETING

Resolved, That in the opinion of this meeting, the assertion of South-Carolina, of a right in herself, to judge, in the last resort, of

the extent of the powers of the General Government, and to withhold obedience to its laws, when she may deem them to transgress
the limits of its authority, is unwarranted by the Constitution, is
the assumption of a power not incident to her as a State, and not
resulting from the nature of our political institutions, and in its exercise utterly incompatible with the allegiance which her citizens
owe to the General Government, with the peace of the Country,
and the existence of the Union. . . .

Resolved, That we cherish an ardent attachment to the Union
of these States, and of the people thereof; that we venerate it as the
work of our ancestors, and value it as the source of our public prosperity and our private security; as the certain pledge of domestic
concord, and the sure guarantee of public liberty; that as a bond
of brotherhood among those who have a common ancestry, a common glory, and a common country, we are prompted by every
motive of interest and affection, to preserve it unbroken.

Resolved, That in the opinion of this meeting, a further material
reduction of the duties collected on imports, is required by the condition of the agricultural states and by the exigencies of the country.—*Raleigh Register and North Carolina Gazette*, January 4, 1833.

70. SECTIONALISM IN NORTH CAROLINA

Sectionalism was apparent in North Carolina at an early date. When
the state adopted the Constitution of 1776, most of its population lived
in the East, and that section, dominated by the slaveholding aristocracy
controlled the government. In the nineteenth century there was a rapid
expansion of population west of Raleigh. Accordingly western leaders
began to clamor for constitutional changes which would give their section equitable power in the legislature. Charles Fisher and John Motley
Morehead, who has been called the "Architect and Builder of Public
Works in North Carolina," were among the early leaders in the move
ment for constitutional revision. On December 11, 1821, Fisher intro
duced a series of resolutions into the House of Commons, stating that rep
resentation of the people of the state under the 1776 Constitution wa
"greatly unequal, unjust, and anti-republican," and calling for an
election on the question of a constitutional convention. Fisher and More
head failed to win their point at that time, and it was not until 1835
that the much desired constitutional changes were made.

DEBATE ON THE CONVENTION QUESTION IN THE HOUSE OF COMMONS
DECEMBER 18, 1821

WHAT, Mr. M. asked, was the situation of things at the time when
our present Constitution was formed? The Eastern part of the State

was almost the only part which was inhabited. The West had but few settlers. But our lands are now rising in value, and our population is every day increasing, while the Eastern part of the State remains much the same. Take us, said he, poor as we are, and where is the boasted superiority of the East? . . .

Mr. M. said, he had made a few calculations on this subject, which he would offer to the committee. . . .

The total amount of population (including slaves and free persons of colour) is 638,829. The whole Federal population of the State is 556,839. The Federal population of the 27 Western Counties is 305,015, which . . . entitles them to 102 members instead of 81, which they now send. The Federal population of the 34 Eastern Counties is 234,100, which entitles her to 78 members only, instead of 102, which she now sends. . . .

Go to the next principle of representation; that of free white population and taxation. The taxation of the whole State (exclusive of clerks and auctioneers) is $65,735.60. Taxes of the Western counties are $31,184.09; of the Eastern, $32,203.41; of Wake County, $2,348.07. Estimating $353 for each member the Western counties will send 88; the Eastern 91; and Wake, 6.

Go to the next branch of the principle, that of free white population, to which the opposers of these resolutions have the greatest objection, and the Western part of the State, will be entitled to 31 more members than she has at present, and the Eastern part to 34 less.

For the total white population of the State is 419,200. The Western counties have 253,235, which . . . will give her 112 members. The Eastern counties have 154,014, which will give to them 68 members. The white population of Wake, being 11,951, gives to her 5 members.

Then compound the representation of the Federal population, free white population and taxation, and the Western counties are entitled to 101 members, 20 more than at present, and the Eastern counties will be entitled to 79 members, 23 less than at present. So that . . . the West evidently labor under important grievances.

Wealth fattens upon the necessity of poverty; it can bribe; it can corrupt: and whenever it shall have a predominant weight in our government, we may bid farewell to the boasted freedom of our Republic, and ignominiously submit to the yoke of Aristocratic Slavery. . . .

It will be to the East, if we are ever invaded. It may be expected your protection will not be found in your negroes; it will be found in yourselves, or in the strength of the West.—*Raleigh Register*, February 1, 1822.

71. CONSTITUTIONAL REFORM, 1835

The North Carolina Constitution of 1776 was never wholly satisfactory. From the time of its adoption to 1835, western North Carolina complained of the undemocratic form of government that it created, and demanded constitutional reform. In 1776 the East was the more populous section, but by 1830 more than one half of the state's population lived west of Raleigh. With this shifting of population, sectionalism became intense and more and more complaints were made about the unjust system of representation which gave the East control of the government.

Revision of the Constitution was linked with a number of other public questions, particularly those of internal improvements and the construction of a new capitol to replace the one which had been burned in 1831. From 1831 to 1835 North Carolina appeared to be on the verge of revolution. Finally western North Carolina succeeded in having a convention called, which met in Raleigh in June, 1835, and which made many significant changes in the organic law of the state. The most important reforms were: abolition of property and religious qualifications for voting and office holding, popular election of the governor, abolition of borough representation, disfranchisement of the free Negro, and reapportionment of representation in the legislature. The amendments were adopted by a very close popular vote, the western counties voting solidly for them and the eastern counties solidly against them.

ARTICLE I

Section 1.

1. THE Senate of this State shall consist of fifty Representatives, biennially chosen by ballot, and to be elected by districts, . . . *Provided*, that no county shall be divided in the formation of a Senatorial district. . . .

2. The House of Commons shall be composed of one hundred and twenty Representatives, biennially chosen by ballot, to be elected by counties according to their federal population, that is, according to their respective numbers, which shall be determined by adding to the whole number of free persons, including those bound to service for a term of years, and excluding Indians not taxed, three-fifths of all other persons; and each county shall have at least one menber in the House of Commons, although it may not contain the requisite ratio of population. . . .

Section 3.

2. All free men of the age of twenty-one years . . . who have been inhabitants of any one district within the State, twelve months immediately preceding the day of any election, and possessed of a freehold within the same district of fifty acres of land . . . shall be entitled to vote for a member of the Senate.

3. No free negro, free mulatto, or free person of mixed blood, descended from negro ancestors, to the fourth generation inclusive, (though one ancestor of each generation may have been a white person,) shall vote for members of the Senate or House of Commons.

ARTICLE II

1. The Governor shall be chosen by the qualified voters for the members of the House of Commons, at such time and places as members of the General Assembly are elected.

2. He shall hold his office for the term of two years from the time of his installation, and until another shall be elected and qualified; but he shall not be eligible more than four years in any term of six years. . . .

ARTICLE III

Section 1.

1. The Governor, Judges of the Supreme Court, and Judges of the Superior Courts, and all other officers of this State, (except Justices of the Peace and Militia officers,) may be impeached for wilfully violating any Article of the Constitution, mal-administration, or corruption. . . .

3. The House of Commons shall have the sole power of impeachment. The Senate shall have the sole power to try all impeachments. . . .

ARTICLE IV

Section 1.

1. No Convention of the People shall be called by the General Assembly, unless by the concurrence of two-thirds of all the members of each House of the General Assembly. . . .

2. No part of the Constitution of this State shall be altered, unless a Bill to alter the same shall have been read three times in each House of the General Assembly, and agreed to by three-fifths of the whole number of members of each House respectively; nor

shall any alteration take place until the Bill so agreed to shall have been published six months previous to a new election of members to the General Assembly. . . .

Section 2.

2. The thirty-second section of the Constitution shall be amended to read as follows : No person who shall deny the being of God, or the truth of the Christian Religion, or the divine authority of the Old or New Testament, or who shall hold religious principles incompatible with the freedom or safety of the State, shall be capable of holding any office or place of trust or profit in the civil department within this State.

Section 3.

1. Capitation tax shall be equal throughout the State upon all individuals subject to the same.

2. All free males over the age of twenty-one years, and under the age of forty-five years, and all slaves over the age of twelve years, and under the age of fifty years, shall be subject to Capitation tax, and no other person shall be subject to such tax. . . . —*The Proceedings and Debates of the Convention of North Carolina, Raleigh, 1835, pp. 409-24.*

EDUCATION IN NORTH CAROLINA TO 1860

72. Free School in Beaufort: James Winwright's Will, 1744

There was nothing like a public school in colonial North Carolina. Nevertheless, many prominent citizens were vitally interested in the promotion of education. Some of them left property by will for the establishment of "free schools for the benefit of the youth of North Carolina." One of the earliest wills of this nature was that of James Winwright of Beaufort, in 1744.

I WILL and appoint that the yearly Rents and profits of all The Town land and Houses in Beaufort Town Belonging unto me with the other Land adjoining thereto (which I purchased of John Pindar) after the Decease of my wife Ann to be Applyed to the Uses hereinafter Mentioned for Ever (to Wit) for The encouragement of a Sober discreet Quallifyed Man to teach a School at Least Reading Writing Vulgar and Decimal Arithmetick in the aforsd. Town of Beaufort, wch said Man Shall be Chosen and appointed by the Chair Man (or the Next in Commission) of Carteret County Court House and one of Church Wardens of St. John parish in the aforesd. County and Their Successors for Ever, also I Give and Bequeath the Sum of Fifty pounds Sterling (provided that my estate Shall be Worth so much after my Just Debts and other Legacys are paid and Discharged) to be applyed for the Building and finishing of a Creditable House for a School and Dwelling house for the said Master to be erected and Built on Some part of my Land, . . . and my True Intent and Meaning is that all the yearly profits and advantages arising by the aforesd. Town Lotts and Lands thereunto . . . be entirely for the use and Benefit of ye sd. Master and his Successors During his and their Good Behavior,—Also that the sd. Master Shall not be obliged to teach or take under his Care any Scholars Imposed on him by the Trustees herein Mentioned or their Successors or by any other person, But shall have free Liberty to teach and take under his care Such and so many Scholars as he shall think Convenient and to Receive his Reward for the Teaching of them as he and the persons tendering them shall agree.

Aug. 13, 1744.—C. L. Coon, *The Beginnings of Public Education in North Carolina: A Documentary History, 1790-1840*, I, 2-3.

73. NORTH CAROLINA'S FIRST COLLEGE

There were no public schools in colonial North Carolina. Elementary education was carried on largely by private tutors, most of whom were clergymen. For higher education, students were sent to colleges in Virginia and the North, or to English and Scotch universities. Near the close of the colonial period, considerable public interest was manifested in a movement to establish schools and colleges in the province.

Queen's College at Charlotte was the first college chartered in North Carolina. It was incorporated by the North Carolina Assembly, January 15, 1771, and was authorized to confer degrees. This law was vetoed by King George III, April 22, 1772. It was a year, however, before Governor Martin was officially notified of this action, and in the meantime the college had been well started. For several years it operated without a charter. Finally, in 1777, the legislature of the independent state granted it a new charter under the name of Liberty Hall. The school operated for three years and permanently closed its doors in 1780.

The money to be raised for founding, establishing, and endowing this college was to be raised "by placing a duty of six pence per gallon on all rum brought into and disposed of in Mecklenburg county for ten years following the passing of the act." The president of the College was required to be of the Established Church and also to be "a learned, pious, exemplary, and discreet person."

AN ACT FOR FOUNDING ESTABLISHING AND ENDOWING OF QUEEN'S
COLLEGE IN THE TOWN OF CHARLOTTE IN MECKLENBURG
COUNTY, JANUARY 15, 1771

WHEREAS the proper education of Youth has always been considered as the most certain source of tranquility, happiness and improvement both of private families and of States and Empires and there being no Institution or Seminary of Learning established in this Province, whither the rising generation may repair, after having acquired at a Grammar School a competent knowledge of the Greek, Hebrew and Latin Languages to imbibe the principles of Science and virtue and to obtain under learned, pious and exemplary teachers in a collegiate or academic mode of instruction a regular and finished education in order to qualify them for the service of their friends and Country, and whereas several Grammar schools have been long taught in the western parts of this Government, in which many students have made very considerable progress in the languages and other literary attainments, and it being thought by many pious, learned and public-spirited persons that great and singular benefits & advantages would be derived to the Publick, could some one of them receive the encouragement and sanction of a Law, for the Establishment thereof on a lasting & permanent basis, wherefore Be it enacted by the Governor, Council and Assembly and by the authority of the same that Messrs. Edmund Fanning, Thomas Polk, Robert Harris, Junior, Abraham Alexander, Hezekiah Alexander, John McNitt Alexander, Ezekiel Polk, Thomas Neal, Wm. Richardson, Hezekiah T. Balch, Joseph Alexander, Waitstell Avery, Henry Patillo and Abner Nash, be and they are hereby formed and incorporated into a Body Politic or Corporate, by the name of the Fellows and Trustees of the incorporated Society, for founding establishing and endowing Queens College in Charlotte Town and by that name to have perpetual succession and a Common Seal, and that they and their Successors by the Name aforesaid shall be able and capable in Law to purchase, have receive enjoy possess and retain to them and their Successors for ever, in special trust and confidence to and for the uses and purposes of founding establishing & endowing the said College, and supporting a President of the same and the number of three or less tutors, and Lands, Rents, Tenements and Heriditaments of what kind nature or quality whatsoever and also to sell, grant, demise, alien or dispose of the same, and also receive and take any charity, gift or donation, whatsoever to the said College and by the same name to sue implead be sued and impleaded, answer and be answered in all Courts of Record whatsoever.—*Colonial Records of North Carolina*, VIII, 486-90.

74. FOUNDING THE UNIVERSITY OF NORTH CAROLINA

The University of North Carolina was the second state university to be chartered in the South and the first to open its doors to students. Its origin may be traced to section 41 of the State Constitution of 1776, which declared that "all useful learning shall be duly encouraged, and promoted in one or more universities." Thirteen years elapsed before the legislature carried out this mandate. During the Revolution no serious effort was made to establish a university, and after the war political considerations caused delay. Most of the Federalists were in favor of a university; most of the Anti-Federalists were opposed. In fact, the Anti-Federalist legislature of 1784 definitely refused to establish a university. The Federalists, led by William R. Davie, kept up the fight, and in 1789 the General Assembly enacted a measure chartering the University of

North Carolina. This act, which was ratified December 11, "was carried through by the same men who had just procured the ratification of the Federal Constitution." Anti-Federalists continued their opposition, attacking the new institution because of its efforts "to give direction to the minds of students on political subjects, favorable to a high-toned aristocratic government."

The first serious problem to confront the University was that of finance. The legislature had chartered the institution, but had failed to make any appropriations for its support. Accordingly, the trustees had to depend on gifts, fees, arrears due the state, and escheated property. A number of donations were made by individuals, the largest being 20,000 acres by Benjamin Smith, 13,000 acres by Charles Gerrard, and $1,025 in cash by Thomas Person. Many smaller donations were made. Every person who subscribed ten pounds towards the University, to be paid within five years, was to be entitled to have one student educated at the University free from any expense of tuition.

Another problem was the location of the University. The charter provided for the "fixing on and purchasing a healthy and convenient situation, which shall not be situate within five miles of the permanent seat of government, or any of the places of holding the courts of law or equity." After consideration of many places, a committee headed by William R. Davie, selected New Hope Chapel, now Chapel Hill, as the site for the University. This place was twelve miles from Hillsboro. It was about the geographical center of the state, where the most important roads running north and south and east and west intersected. The name Chapel Hill is found in the report of the trustees, November, 1792, and a contemporary account gives the following description: "The seat of the University is on the summit of a very high ridge. . . . The ridge appears to commence about half a mile directly east of the building, where it rises abruptly several hundred feet. This peak is called Point Prospect. The flat country spreads out below like the ocean, giving an immense hemisphere in which the eye seem lost in the extent of space."

The cornerstone of the Old East Building was laid in 1793, and the University was formally opened, January 15, 1795. The first student was Hinton James, of Wilmington, who appeared "on the Hill" February 12.

The trustees were given authority to appoint a president of the University, and professors and tutors, whom "they may remove for misbehaviour, inability, or neglect of duty." They could "make all such laws and regulations for the government of the University and preservation of order and good morals therein as are usually made by such seminaries, and as to them may appear necessary: Provided, the same are not contrary to the inalienable liberty of a citizen or to the laws of the State." The power of conferring degrees was given to the Faculty, but the trustees must concur.

No president was chosen for the University. Instead there was a pre-

siding professor, who occupied the president's house and who was responsible for all the teaching. He was called "Professor of Humanity" and
received a salary of $300 a year and two-thirds of the tuition money.
Dr. David Kerr was the first presiding professor. The number of students
reached forty-one by the close of the first term, and during the second
term they rose to nearly one hundred. So it became necessary to employ
a tutor in Mathematics. Charles Wilson Harris was chosen.

Dr. Joseph Caldwell, for some years a presiding professor, was the first
president of the University of North Carolina, being chosen for that
position in 1804.

In December, 1795, the institution was divided into two branches,
called "The Preparatory School" and "The Professorships of the University." This was largely the idea of William R. Davie, whose "Plan of
Study" is given below.

AN ACT TO ESTABLISH A UNIVERSITY IN THIS STATE

WHEREAS, in all well regulated governments it is the indispensable
duty of every Legislature to consult the happiness of a rising generation, and endeavor to fit them for an honorable discharge of the
social duties of life, by paying the strictest attention to their education: And whereas, an university supported by permanent funds
and well endowed, would have the most direct tendency to answer
the above purpose.

I. Be it therefore enacted by the General Assembly of the State
of North Carolina. . . . That Samuel Johnston, James Iredell,
Charles Johnson, Hugh Williamson . . . (forty men in all) . . .
shall be and they are hereby declared to be a body politic and corporate, to be known and distinguished by the name of The Trustees
of the University of North Carolina; and by that name shall have
perpetual succession and a common seal; and that they the Trustees and their successors . . . or a majority of them, shall be able
and capable in law to take, demand, receive and possess all monies,
goods, and chattels that shall be given them for the use of the said
university, and the same shall apply according to the will of the
donor, and by gift, purchase or devise to take, have, receive, possess, enjoy and retain to them and their successors forever, any
lands, rents, tenements and hereditaments, . . . in special trust
and confidence that the same or the profits thereof shall be applied
to and for the use and purposes of establishing and endowing the
said university. . . .

That the said Trustees shall choose a President and Secretary. . . .
And . . . That when the Trustees shall deem the funds of the

said University adequate to the purchase of a necessary quantity of land and erecting the proper buildings, they shall direct a meeting of the said Trustees for the purpose of fixing on and purchasing a healthy and convenient situation, which shall not be situate within five miles of the permanent seat of government, or any of the places of holding the courts of law or equity; which meeting shall be advertised at least six months in some gazette in this state, and at such superior courts as may happen within that time.

That the Trustees shall have the power of appointing a President of the University, and such professors and tutors as to them shall appear necessary and proper, whom they may remove for misbehaviour, inability or neglect of duty; and they shall have the power to make all such laws and regulations for the government of the University and preservation of good order and morals therein, as are usually made in such seminaries, and as to them may appear necessary. . . . And the Faculty . . . the President and professors, by and with the consent of the Trustees, shall have the power of conferring all such degrees or marks of literary distinction, as are usually conferred in colleges or universities.

That every person who within the term of five years shall subscribe ten pounds towards this University, to be paid within five years . . . shall be entitled to have one student educated at the University free from any expence of tuition.

That the public hall of the library and four of the colleges shall be called severally by the names of one or another of the six persons who shall within four years contribute the largest sums towards the funds of this University, the highest subscriber or donor having choice in the order of their respective donations. . . . *Laws of North Carolina, 1789*, Chap. XX, pp. 21-25.

DAVIE'S PLAN FOR STUDY

A. THE PREPARATORY SCHOOL.

1st. (a) The English language, to be taught grammatically on the basis of Webster's and South's Grammar.

(b) Writing in a neat and correct manner.

(c) Arithmetic with the four first rules. . . .

(d) Reading and pronouncing select passages from the purest English authors.

(e) Copying in a fair and correct manner select English Essays.

2nd. After this preliminary course the student must learn the

Latin Language, beginning with Ruddiman's Rudiments and then studying Cordery, then Erasmus, then Eutropius, then Cornelius Nepos, with translations. After these came Caesar's Commentaries, and Sallust, without translations, but at the request of parents translations might be used with them. . . .

When the students can render Eutropius into correct English and explain the government and connection of the words, then they must begin the study of the French Language. . . .

The study of Greek is optional. . . .

The rudiments of Geography must be studied on the plan of Guthrie. . . .

It is allowable to study all three of the above mentioned languages, in which case the student must finish the Gospels in Greek when he is through the Preparatory School.

The English language shall be regularly continued, it being considered the primary object, and the other languages but auxiliaries.

Any language, except English, may be omitted at the request of the parents.

II. Plan of Education under the PROFESSORSHIPS OF THE UNIVERSITY

 1st. The President.
     Rhetoric on the plan of Sheridan.
     Belles-Lettres on the plan of Blair and Rollin.

B. PROFESSORSHIPS OF THE UNIVERSITY.

a. PROFESSOR OF MORAL AND POLITICAL PHILOSOPHY AND HISTORY ; the study of the following authors :

     Paley's Moral and Political Philosophy.
     Montesquieu's Spirit of Laws.
     Civil Government and Political Constitutions.
     Adam's Defence of DeLolme.
     The Constitution of the United States.
     The Modern Constitutions of Europe.
     The Law of Nations.
     Vattel's Law of Nations.
     Burlamaqui's Principles of Natural and Political Law.

On History,
     Priestly's Lectures on History.
     Millot's Ancient and Modern History.
     Hume's History of England, with Smollett's Continuation.
     Chronology on the most approved plan.

11

b. PROFESSOR OF NATURAL PHILOSOPHY, ASTRONOMY AND GEOG-
RAPHY

1. General properties of Matter, Laws of Motion, Mechanical
   Powers, Hydrostatics, Hydraulics, Pneumatics, Optics,
   Electricity, Magnetism.
2. Geography. The use of Globes, the Geometrical, political
   and commercial relations of the different nations of the
   earth. Astronomy on the plan of Ferguson.

c. PROFESSOR OF MATHEMATICS.

1. Arithmetic in a scientific manner.
2. Algebra and the application of Algebra to Geometry.
3. Euclid's Elements.
4. Trigonometry and its application to the Mensuration of
   Heights and Distances of Surfaces and Solids, Surveying
   and Navigation.

ELECTIVES. Thus far the mathematical studies are obligatory. The
following might be pursued if desired. Conic Sections, The Doctrine
of the Sphere and the Cylinder, The Projection of the Sphere,
Spherical Trigonometry, The Doctrine of Fluxions, The Doctrine
of Chances and Annuities.

d. THE PROFESSOR OF CHEMISTRY AND THE PHILOSOPHY OF MEDI-
CINE, AGRICULTURE AND THE MECHANIC ARTS.

Chemistry upon the most approved plan.

e. PROFESSOR OF LANGUAGES.

1. The English Language—Elegant Extracts in Prose and Verse.
   Scott's Collections.
2. The Latin Language—Virgil, Cicero's Orations, Horace's
   Epistles, including the Art of Poetry.
3. The Greek Language—Lucian, Xenophon.—Kemp P. Battle,
   History of the University of North Carolina, I, 6-96.

75. HENRY PATILLO'S GEOGRAPHICAL CATECHISM, 1796

Henry Patillo was a Presbyterian preacher and teacher in Orange and
Granville counties. Born in Scotland in 1726, he came to Virginia about
1740. He moved into North Carolina in 1765 where he conducted schools
at Hawfields, Williamsboro, and Granville Hall until his death in 1801.
He was one of the men appointed by Governor Tryon to pacify the disaffected Regulators. He was likewise a delegate to the Hillsboro Provincial Congress in 1775.

Patillo's *Geographical Catechism*, the first textbook written in North Carolina, was published at Halifax in 1796. According to the author the purpose of this text was : (1) "to smooth the way to the study of Geography" ; (2) to enable the farmers and their families to read with more intelligence ; (3) to bring all to know something of the works of God, and "to attempt to lead common readers to some more just conception of the divine works" ; and (4) to make a few dollars, "which will be welcome guests when they arrive."

In his Catechism he leads the students around the world, giving questions and answers about the earth, stars, and various phenomena of nature.

WE COME in the last place to the freest, happiest, most plentiful part of the globe; and the fartherest removed from tyranny, wars, and those commotions that curse and agitate the nations. . . . A country in which religion is unrestrained ; morality in repute ; education promoted ; marriage honourable, and age reverenced.

Q. 104. Pray sir, where lies this terrestrial paradise?

A. Within the limits of the UNITED STATES ; and the spot you stand on, makes a part of it. . . .

North-Carolina has Virginia on the north, by a dividing line in 36° 30', South-Carolina on the south, and the Atlantic ocean on the east. It extended to the Mississippi, but the Assembly gave up its western territory to the United States. The southern line is in 35° till it turns to the southeast, and extends on the sea coast about 200 miles. Its chief rivers are Pasquotank, Chowan, Roanoak, Tar-river, Neuse and Cape-Fear. Its rivers and extensive coast, render it as convenient for trade as any of its sister states, if the entrance from the ocean were not shallow and sandy ; which confines the trade to small vessels ; but Cape-Fear admits ships of any burden. The productions of this state are numerous and valuable. It sends by land to Virginia annually, 6 or 7000 hogsheads of tobacco ; and exports a number from its own inspections. Its other exports are wheat, flour, pease, beef, pork, butter, cheese, lumber, pitch, tar, turpentine, and I wish I could add to the exports of my country pot and pearl ashes, which it is well calculated to produce. The numerous landings in this state, are also unfriendly to large towns. It has however, some small towns on navigation, as Halifax, Edenton, Washington, Tarborough, Newbern, Fayetteville, and Wilmington, besides some inland towns that are represented in the Assembly. The seat of Government is fixed at the city of Raleigh. . . . A University is established by act of Assembly, in Orange county, with liberal appointments by the state, and numerous benefactions. It is yet in its infancy, has about sixty students, and is under the government of good and learned men, ... What can more loudly call for the prayers of all good people, than that GOD'S blessing may reside on our principal seat of learning, from which fountains are to flow those streams, that must poison, or purify and nourish our country. Its short progress has been rapid ; may its success be glorious! The population of this state in 1790, was 394,000, and the proportion of whites to slaves nearly as three to one. North Carolina sends ten representatives to Congress, besides two Senators, which is common to all the states. Religion is here also happily free.—*Patillo's Geographical Catechism* (edited by N. W. Walker and M. C. S. Noble, in "University Reprints" No. 1, Chapel Hill, 1909).

76. ARCHIBALD DeBOW MURPHEY'S REPORT ON EDUCATION, NOVEMBER 29, 1817

Archibald D. Murphey might well be called the "Father of Public Education in North Carolina." For years he carried on agitation for public schools, academies, and colleges. In 1816, as a member of the education committee of the legislature, he proposed to refer the Governor's remarks on education to a special committee. He was appointed to the chairmanship of that committee and wrote a report declaring that "the State's strength lay in the great mass of the people, that the State should offer to all the means to become enlightened without distinction of class, and that primary and secondary schools should be established leading directly to the University. At the close of this report he proposed the appointment of a committee "to digest a system of public instruction" and submit it to the next General Assembly.

When the General Assembly met in 1817, Murphey submitted his plan for the establishment of public schools. His report provided for a school fund to be managed by six commissioners with the governor at their head, with power to locate schools, to fix salaries of teachers, and to appoint the trustees of secondary schools. Counties were to be divided into townships with primary schools in each, and incorporated towns were also to establish such schools, all of which were to be aided by a combination of state and local funds. Secondary schools were to be aided by the state's paying one-third the salaries of teachers. His plan included the details of organization, courses of study, methods of instruction and discipline, education of the poor children at public expense, and the establishment of an asylum for the deaf and dumb.

Charles L. Coon said that "this measure and the report on it embraced the profoundest and most comprehensive educational wisdom ever presented for the consideration of a North Carolina legislature." Nevertheless, a bill to carry his recommendations into effect did not get past the first reading in either House of the General Assembly. Some extracts from the report are given in the following reading.

. . . ENLIGHTENED statesmen will avail themselves of this auspicious period to place the fortunes of the State upon a basis not to be shaken; to found and cherish institutions which will guarantee to the people the permanence of their government, and enable them to appreciate its excellence. The legislature of North Carolina, giving to their ambition an honorable direction, have resolved to improve this period for the best interests of the State; to adopt and carry into effect liberal plans of internal improvements; to give encouragement to literature, and to diffuse the lights of knowledge among all classes of the community. . . .

To give effect to any plan of general education, it is essentially necessary that ample funds be provided, and that these funds and also the execution of the general plan, be committed to the care and direction of a board composed of intelligent and efficient men. . . . Your committee do therefore recommend—

1st. That there shall be elected by joint ballot of the two Houses of the General Assembly, six directors who shall be styled, "The board of public instruction"; . . . The board may at any time enact, alter or amend such rules as to them may seem proper for the purpose of regulating the order of their proceedings; . . . They shall have power to establish and locate the several academies directed by law to be established; to determine the number and title of professorships therein; to examine, appoint and regulate the compensation of the several professors and teachers; . . . to provide some just and particular mode of advancing from the primary schools to the academies, and from the academies to the university, as many of the most meritorious children educated at the public expense, as the proceeds of the fund for public instruction may suffice to educate and maintain, . . . to manage the fund for public instruction, and apply its proceeds in carrying into execution and supporting the plan of education committed to their care; . . .

In arranging the system of schools, your committee have endeavored to make the progress of education natural and regular; beginning with primary schools, in which the first rudiments of learning are taught, and proceeding to academies, in which youth are to be instructed in languages, ancient and modern history, mathematics and other branches of science, preparatory to entering into the university, in which instruction is to be given in all the

higher branches of the sciences and the principles of the useful arts.
. . . The primary schools are of the first importance in any general plan of public education; every citizen has an interest in them, as the learning is indispensable to all, of reading, writing and arithmetic, is here to be taught. By judicious management and a proper selection of books for children while they are learning to read, much instruction in their religious and moral duties may be given them in these schools. . . . Your committee do therefore recommend that as to

THE PRIMARY SCHOOLS

1. Each county in this State be divided into two or more townships; and that one or more primary schools be established in each township, provided a lot of ground not less than four acres and a sufficient house erected thereon, be provided and vested in the board of public instruction. And that every incorporated town in the State containing more than one hundred families, shall be divided into wards. . . . Each ward upon conveying to the board of public instruction a lot of ground of the value of two hundred and fifty dollars, shall be entitled to the benefits and privileges of a primary school. . . .

4. The teacher of each primary school shall receive a salary of one hundred dollars, to be paid out of the fund for public instruction.

. . . Were these schools in full operation in every section of the State, even in the present state of our population, more than fifteen thousand children would annually be taught in them. These schools would be to the rich a convenience, and to the poor, a blessing.

ACADEMIES

. . . The Academies shall be located in different districts of the State for the convenience of the people, and the expenses of purchasing suitable sites and erecting thereon the necessary buildings, shall be divided between the public at large and several districts. Private liberality has of late erected many small Academies in the State, which deserve the consideration and patronage of the Legislature. . . .

The trustees of any academy may fix the salaries of their respective teachers, subject to the control of the board of public instruction; one third part of the salaries shall be paid by the board at such times and in such way as they shall prescribe.

The professors and teachers in any academy shall be bound to instruct free of charge for tuition, the pupils whom the board of public instruction may designate to be taught in said academy at the public expense. . . .

THE UNIVERSITY

This institution has been in operation for twenty years, and has been eminently useful to the State. It has contributed perhaps more than any other cause, to diffuse a taste for reading among the poor, and excite a spirit of liberal improvement; it has contributed to change our manners and elevate our character; it has given to society many useful members, not only in the liberal professions, but in the walks of private life; . . . When this institution was first founded, it was fondly hoped that it would be cherished with pride by the legislature. But unfortunately the nature of the funds with which it was endowed, in a short time rendered it odious to some, and cooled the ardor of others. The torrent of prejudice could not be stemmed; the fostering protection of the legislature was withheld and the institution left dependent upon private munificence. . . .

It is due to North Carolina, . . . to foster it with parental fondness and give to it an importance commensurate with the high destinies of the State. . . .

This institution has uniformly labored under the double disadvantages of a want of funds, and the want of subsidiary institutions, in which youth could be instructed preparatory to their entering upon a course of the higher branches of science in the University. . . .

THE EDUCATION OF POOR CHILDREN AT THE PUBLIC EXPENSE

One of the strongest reasons which we can have for establishing a general plan of public instruction, is the condition of the poor children of our country. Such has always been and probably always will be the allotment of human life, that the poor will form a large portion of every community; and it is the duty of those who manage the affairs of a state, to extend relief to this unfortunate part of our species in every way in their power. . . .

AN ASYLUM FOR THE DEAF AND DUMB

If there be any of our species who are entitled to the public consideration of the government, it is surely the deaf and dumb. Since the method of instructing them in science and language has been discovered, numerous asylums in different countries have been established for their instruction. While we are engaged in making provisions for others, humanity demands that we make a suitable provision for them. Your committee do therefore recommend that as soon as the state of the fund for public instruction will admit, the board who have charge of that fund, be directed to establish at some suitable place in the State, an asylum for the instruction for the deaf and dumb.—*Senate Journal, 1817-18*, pp. 30-49.

77. ACADEMIES IN NORTH CAROLINA

The State Constitution of 1776 provided "that schools for the convenient instruction of youth should be established." Friends of education interpreted this to mean the establishment of public schools. The legislature, however, failed to carry out this provision of the Constitution. Instead of a public school system, education centered around subsidized academies. The first academy in North Carolina was established at Wilmington by the Reverend James Tate, in 1760. Crowfield Academy, the forerunner of Davidson College, was founded the same year. Between 1790 and 1840 there were over three hundred academies chartered in the state.

The academies were usually private, although they were chartered by the state. Most of them were sectarian in character. They were allowed to grant certificates but not diplomas or degrees. The trustees ordinarily selected the teachers, fixed the curriculum, gave the examinations, and, in some cases, administered discipline. The academy was primarily a boys' school. Of one hundred and seventy-seven chartered before 1825, only thirteen were for girls. There were a few academies which gave instruction to free Negroes. The best known of the colored school teachers was John Chaves, who taught white children in the day-school and Negroes at night. Lotteries were frequently used as a means of financing the academies. A variety of subjects were taught, ranging from reading, writing, and arithmetic to the "ornamental subjects" of needlework, bookkeeping, and astronomy. There were many rules governing conduct and much emphasis was placed upon the moral training of students. The following documents illustrate various phases of academy education in North Carolina.

HILLSBOROUGH ACADEMY RULES, 1818

THE exercises of this Institution closed the 20th ult. and will be resumed on the first Monday in January next. A few pupils in addition to the number engaged may be accommodated with Board in the subscriber's family. Every attention will be paid to the discipline, Classical, and Religious instruction of Youth, sent to this Institution. In order that Parents and Guardians at a distance may learn the Principles upon which this Institution is conducted, the following Rules are subjoined.

1. Each Scholar must be present at morning and evening Worship, at the opening and close of the exercises of the day.

2. No profane, abusive or indecent language shall be permitted among the pupils—but each conduct himself with propriety and decorum on all occasions.

3. The use of ardent Spirits is strictly forbidden, unless as a medicine, and the severest discipline will be used when such cases occur.

4. No Scholar shall be permitted to lounge about any Store or Tavern, or the public streets, nor play therein.

5. Every Student is required to pay strict regard to the Lord's Day, attending regularly public Worship, refraining from ordinary studies, and every kind of amusement, as riding, walking, visiting and the like.

6. Every Student shall attend such recitations from the Scriptures on the Sabbath as shall be prescribed.

7. Should any Member of the School continue to use profane, indecent or licentious language, or be guilty of any immoral course of conduct, so as to render him an improper and dangerous companion for his fellow students, he shall (after due discipline being exercised) be dismissed from the institution.—*Raleigh Register*, December 11, 1818.

JOHN WITHERSPOON, PRINC'L.

COURSES OF STUDY AND TUITION CHARGES RALEIGH ACADEMY

Terms of TUITION in the Department of the Academy under the care of Doct. Freeman, will be per session—

1. For Spelling and Reading.........................$5.00
2. For Spelling, Reading, Writing and Tables.......... 7.00
3. Spelling, Reading, Writing, Arithmetic, English Grammar, Geography, History and Composition........12.00
4. Spelling, Reading, Writing, Arithmetic, English Grammar, Geography, History, Logic, Natural and Moral Philosophy, Chemistry, Astronomy, and Composition 15.00
5. Languages and Mathematics, with the above Studies and Composition...............................15.00

Raleigh, 12th June.

Raleigh Register, June 13, 1828.

WILL TAKE PAY IN BRANDY

AN ENGLISH SCHOOL,

On Low Terms,

Is opened by the Subscriber, for the term of twelve months from the 9th instant, in a secluded room in the house of Mr. C. Christopher, opposite Mr. C. Parish's Tavern. The terms of Tuition is Ten Dollars per annum, payable quarterly. I should be glad to take two or three Boarders, at Sixty Dollars for Board and Tuition the year. One great advantage to the scholars in boarding in my house will be that they will have the benefit of a night School, which I shall keep six months in the year, gratis. For board payment may be made in Corn, Bacon, or Brandy, and a generous price allowed—one half paid in advance the other at the end of the Year.

Those who please to encourage this school may depend on the strictest attention being paid to the instruction and morals of the pupils by their Preceptor.

The Public's humble servant,

ARCHIBALD WILLS

Raleigh Star, January 26, 1809.

JOHN CHAVES' SCHOOL, 1808

John Chaves takes this method of informing his Employers, and the Citizens of Raleigh in general, that the present Quarter of his School will end the 15th of September, and the next will commence on the 19th. He will, at the same time, open an Evening School for the purpose of instructing Children of Colour, as he intends, for the accomodation of some of his employers, to exclude all Children of Colour from his Day School.

The Evening School will commence at an hour by Sun. When the white children leave the House, those of colour will take their places, and continue until ten o'clock.

The terms of teaching the white children will be as usual, two and a half dollars per quarter; those of colour, one dollar and three quarters. . . .

Those who think proper to put their Children under his care, may rely upon the strictest attention being paid, not only to their Education but to their Morals, which he deems an *important* part of Education.—*Raleigh Register*, August 26, 1808.

A TEACHER WANTED

A Man well acquainted with teaching the English Language grammatically, writing, and Arithmetick, will meet with liberal encouragement by applying to the subscriber; provided he comes well recommended as to his moral character and abilities: Without which none need apply.

Should any person undertake a school at this place calculated to please, he may expect on a birth for several years.

Mount-Prospect, Edgecomb County, N. C.

EXUM LEWIS
Raleigh Star, December 11, 1812

WANTED IMMEDIATELY,

A TEACHER, to take charge of Pomona Academy, 14 miles North east of Raleigh.—The situation is very healthy, the water good, the neighborhood agreeable. It is necessary the Teacher should possess the following qualifications, viz: understand the English & Latin Languages, and have some knowledge of Mathematics, and be of undoubted moral character.—To such an one, a salary will be given equal in amount to $800. . . . —*Raleigh Register*, May 3, 1830.

ENGLISH GRAMMAR TAUGHT IN SEVEN WEEKS
SCHOOL NOTICE

I take this method of informing the public, that I shall, on Monday the 11th of July next, open my school again at Wake Forest Pleasant Grove Academy. . . . For the information of those who are unacquainted with my school, it may not be improper for me to remark, that it is an institution in which the English Grammar is taught upon a completely new and successful plan in seven weeks, at seven dollars per scholar. Any evidences of the superiority and efficacy of the system can be had by application to the subscriber. Board can be procured in respectable houses at $4 per month.

EDWARD T. FOWLKES
—*Raleigh Star*, June 30, 1831.

RULES OF STOKES COUNTY ACADEMY, 1848

Lashes

1. Boys and Girls Playing Together........................ 4
2. Quareling... 4
3. Fighting.. 5
4. Fighting at School.................................... 5
5. Quareling at School.................................. 3
6. Gambleing or Beting at School........................ 4
7. Playing at Cards at School...........................10
8. Climbing for Every foot Over three feet up a tree.......... 1
9. Telling Lyes.. 7
10. Telling Tales Out of School........................... 8
11. Nicknaming Each Other................................ 4
12. Giving Each Other Ill names.......................... 3
13. Fighting Each Other in time of Books.................. 2
14. Swaring at School.................................... 8
15. Blackgarding Each Other.............................. 6
16. For Misbehaving to Girls.............................10
17. For Leaving School Without Leave of the Teacher.......... 4
18. Going Home with each other without Leave of the Teacher.. 4
19. For Drinking Spirituous Liquors at School............. 8
20. Making Swings & Swinging on Them.................... 7
21. For Misbehaving when a Stranger is in the House.......... 6
22. For waring Long Finger Nails......................... 2
23. For Not Making a bow when a Stranger Comes in or goes out. 3
24. Misbehaving to Persons on the Road................... 4
25. For Not Making a bow when you Meet a Person.......... 4
26. For Going to Girl's Play Places...................... 3
27. Girles Going to Boys Play Places..................... 2
28. Coming to School with Dirty face and Hands.............. 2
29. For Caling Each Other Liars.......................... 4
30. For Playing Bandy....................................10
31. For Bloting Your Copy Book........................... 2
32. For not making a bow when you go home or when you come
     away 4
33. For Wrestling at School............................... 4
34. Scuffling at School................................... 4
35. For Not Making a bow when going out to go home........ 2
36. For Weting Each other Washing at Play time............ 2
37. For Hollowing & Hooping Going Home.................. 3
38. For Delaying Time Going home or Coming to School...... 4

Lashes

39. For Not Making a bow when you Come in or go Out...... 2
40. For Throwing Any Thing Harder than your trab ball...... 4
41. For Every word you mis In your Hart Leson without Good
Excuse.. 1
42. For Not Saying yes Sir & no Sir or yes marm or no marm.. 2
43. For Troubleing Each others Writing affares............... 2
44. For Not washing at playtime when going to Books.......... 4
45. For Going & Playing about the Mill or Creek............. 6
46. For Going about the Barn or doing any Mischief about the
Place 7

November 10, 1848   Wm. A. Chaffin

—C. L. Coon, *North Carolina Schools and Academies, 1790-1840: A Documentary History*, pp. 282-83, 494, 512-15, 763-64, 815.

78. LOTTERIES IN NORTH CAROLINA

A lottery is an arrangement for the distribution of prizes by chance among persons purchasing tickets. Slips or lots numbered in correspondence with the tickets and representing prizes are drawn from a wheel. Lotteries are illegal now, but they were used extensively in the late eighteenth and early nineteenth centuries. At a time when taxation was extremely unpopular, people were "willing to take a chance." Thus the lottery became a favorite method of financing academies, churches, bridges, canals, and other public works. From 1797 to 1825, it is estimated that North Carolina raised more than $150,000 by lotteries for educational purposes alone.

Sometimes the first prize in a lottery scheme would be $10,000 or more. Many times the total prizes would amount to more than $100,000. Some of the lottery notices sound like modern advertising, for instance; "Look Here. $8,000 For $4 only!!" (Salisbury Lottery, 1837). The following documents illustrate popular types of lotteries, and give some idea of the amount of money involved. In the Salisbury Academy Lottery, 1837, drawings were held in Salisbury, Fayetteville, Wilmington, New Bern, Asheboro, Raleigh, Hillsboro, and other towns.

CAPE FEAR CHURCH LOTTERY, 1759

AN ACT for raising Money for finishing the Churches in the Parishes of St. James and St. Philip, in New Hanover County, by a Lottery.

I. Whereas, the Churches in the Parishes of St. James and St. Philip, in New-Hanover County, remain unfinished for Want of a sufficient Fund for defraying the Expense thereof, besides the Money arising by the late Tax on the Inhabitants of the said Parishes, and the Method of raising Money by Lottery, in the Manner hereinafter mentioned, being a more easy Way than by an additional Tax for that Purpose.

II. Be it therefore Enacted . . . that Mr. Jehu Davis, Mr. Marmaduke Jones, Mr. Alexander Duncan, Mr. John Paine, or any Three of them, shall be, and are hereby appointed Managers, for undertaking, carrying on, and drawing a Lottery in Wilmington for the Purposes aforesaid; with Power and Authority to issue Two Thousand Tickets, to be signed by themselves, at the Price of Thirty Shillings, Proclamation Money. . . .

IV. And be it Further Enacted, by the Authority aforesaid, That it shall and may be lawful for the said Managers to deduct, out of the Amount of every Prize, Fifteen per Cent, to be applied as hereinafter mentioned: But before the said Managers shall issue any Tickets for the said Lottery, they shall give Bond, payable to his Excellency the Governor, and his Successors, in the penalty of £3,000, Proclamation Money, with Condition, for their faithful Discharge in the Trust reposed in them by this Act: Which Bond shall be recorded in the County Court of New Hanover. . . .

VI. And for the more speedy Disposal of the said Tickets; be it Enacted, that the Managers shall have Power, and they are hereby authorized to take out Tickets, for and in behalf of the said Churches, to the amount of the Sum of £400, Proclamation Money, or any lesser Sum, if they shall think it will be for the Advantage of the Churches aforesaid, and the Tickets so by them taken, shall be paid for out of the Fifteen per Cent to be deducted out of the several Prizes, and the Money that may arise by the same, and also, the Money arising by the Sale of the other Tickets, after deducting £50 for their Trouble and Expense of drawing the Lottery, Keeping the Accounts, paying the Prizes, and all other Charges attending the same, shall, by the said Managers, so soon as the drawing of the said Lottery shall be over, be paid one half to the Commissioners of the Church of St. James, and the other half to the Commissioners of the Church of St. Philip, to be by them severally applied for finishing the respective Churches. . . . —*State Records of North Carolina*, XXV, 391-92.

SALISBURY ACADEMY LOTTERY, 1834

NORTH CAROLINA STATE
LOTTERY,

For the Benefit of

THE SALISBURY ACADEMY

1st Class—High and Low System

To be drawn at Salisbury, on the 10th day of July.

Capital 3,000 Dollars!

SCHEME:

					$
1	Prize	of	$3,000	is	$ 3,000
5	"	of	1,000	is	5,000
4	"	of	500	is	2,000
5	"	of	300	is	1,500
10	"	of	200	is	2,000
50	"	of	100	is	5,000
60	"	of	50	is	3,000
100	"	of	20	is	2,000
250	"	of	10	is	2,500
20,000	"	of	470	is	94,000

20,485 Prizes, amount'g to $120,000

MORE PRIZES THAN BLANKS

Whole Tickets..............$4
Halves 2
Quarters 1

MODE OF DRAWING

This scheme, founded on the High and Low System, has 40,000 tickets, numbered from 1 to 40,000 inclusive. On the day of the drawing the 40,000 numbers will be put into one wheel; and all the prizes above the denomination of $4 70 in another; they will be drawn out alternately, first a number and then a prize, until all the prizes are drawn. From 1 to 20,000, inclusive, are low; and from 20,001 to 40,000, inclusive, are high. The prizes of $4 70 are to be awarded to the high or low division, will be determined by that which may draw the capital prize of 3,000 dollars. The prizes of $4 70 will be payable in tickets in the next scheme—all other prizes payable in cash forty days after the drawing. All prizes subject to a deduction of 15 per centum.—*Raleigh Star*, June 5, 1834, in C. L. Coon, *North Carolina Schools and Academies, 1790-1840: A Documentary History*, pp. 371-80.

79. DISCUSSION OF THE MORALITY OF LOTTERIES, 1826-1831

The legislature of 1826-27, after passing several lottery bills, refused to grant lottery privileges to Richmond Academy and indulged in a heated debate over their morality. Opponents of lotteries, led by Charles A. Hill of Franklin, contended that they were merely gambling devices. Defenders of the system maintained that they were not immoral, that they aided good causes, kept money at home, and should be considered in the same class as insurance risks. In 1831 a lottery to promote the publication of a North Carolina History was refused on moral grounds. By that date the sale of North Carolina lottery tickets outside the state had become very small. So it seemed expedient to discontinue their use. They were prohibited by North Carolina law in 1834.

THE bill authorizing the Trustees of the Richmond Academy to raise by Lottery, ten thousand dollars, was read the second time, and the question having been put on its passage—

Mr. Leake rose and said, . . . that when at the last session, he had the honor of introducing a similar bill, . . . his bill had failed —Gentlemen voted against it, either because they could not reconcile lotteries to their principles, or because they did not believe the School was in danger. . . . Without wishing to discuss the question whether lotteries were immoral, Mr. L. said, he would merely remark, that his principles were more pliable than theirs, inasmuch as he could vote for a lottery intended for some useful public purpose (to prop a declining school for instance) with as much cheerfulness, and as little reproach of conscience, as he could enter into a cotton or other speculation where there was a chance (as is always the case) of involving his family in ruin. . . .

Mr. Hill, of Franklin, was opposed to the bill. . . . However anxious he might be for the cultivation of the human mind, and the general diffusion of the benefits of education, he could not agree to promote these desirable objects in this way. He was willing to do anything not contrary to the principles of sound morality, to disseminate useful learning, but he had yet to be convinced, that the utility of the end, sanctified the impurity of the means put in requisition for its attainment. He never would aid by his vote, any measure which savored of the damning influence of gambling. He thought Lotteries were a species of gambling, and he thanked God he had never voted for their encouragement. That Lotteries participated of the nature of this pernicious evil, he thought could be proved, . . . Look around at the increase of the evil. Formerly it was but nominal—now, we cannot take up a country paper, but flaming lottery notices attract the attention. It was high time indeed to frown down this monstrous evil; . . .

Mr. Pickett entertained very different views on this subject. He seemed to deprecate the passage of the bill, on account of the immoral tendency of the principles which it involved—but as for himself he could not believe that Lotteries were inherently vicious. . . . It was known that our laws licensed the lottery system, and that in every part of the State, individuals were engaged in vending tickets in lotteries created for the benefit of other States. He could see no reason for withholding from the friends of literature the privilege of raising funds for purposes connected with the best interests of our citizens. It is certainly good policy to keep our money at home, . . . From the first establishment of our government, acts have been passed, authorizing Lotteries. The practice was not confined to our own State, but had been sanctioned, he believed, by every member of the Union. . . .

Mr. Seawell said. . . . If he understood the matter, the rejection of the bill was contended for, on the ground of immorality and impolicy of the measure. He thought a fair statement of the case was this—is the evil which would result from the passage of this bill of sufficient magnitude to counterbalance the good which would flow from the successful operation of the Academy in question. . . . Like all other speculations it holds out a prospect to adventurers, to gain a large sum by risking a small one. Gentlemen talking about restraining the people from indulging a gambling propensity. It cannot be done; . . . Everybody acts on the principle of gain; we are then, strictly speaking, all adventurers.—C. L. Coon, *The Beginnings of Public Education in North Carolina; A Documentary History, 1790-1840*, I, 330-36.

LOTTERY FOR PUBLICATION OF A NORTH CAROLINA HISTORY REFUSED, 1831

TO THE HONOURABLE THE GENERAL ASSEMBLY OF THE STATE OF NORTH CAROLINA:

THE MEMORIAL OF ARCHIBALD D. MURPHEY OF ORANGE COUNTY RESPECTFULLY SHEWETH,

That he has heretofore represented to the General Assembly that he has been for several years engaged in collecting materials for a correct history of North Carolina and that he was unable to complete the work, without liberal pecuniary aid. The General Assembly upon this representation passed an act authorizing him to raise by way of lottery the sum of fifteen thousand dollars, but restricted him to three drawings. This restriction and the smallness of the sum authorized to be raised put it out of his power to dispose of the Lottery. A subsequent act was passed authorizing the president and directors of the Literary Fund to raise by way of lottery the sum of fifty thousand dollars, and to pay over to your Memorialist one half thereof but no steps have been taken to carry this act into effect . . . The materials for our Colonial history are deposited in the public offices in England, and among the early records of the State of Virginia, South Carolina, and Georgia: . . . If sufficient aid be given to your Memorialist, he himself will proceed to London, or send an agent of Intelligence to procure copies of the papers and documents aforesaid, and after writing our Colonial history, he will present them to the General Assembly to be deposited in the Public Library. . . . He asks for no appropriation from the Treasury. I will, he hopes, answer his purposes, to be authorized to raise a sufficient sum by way of Lottery. . . .

The Committee to whom was referred the Memorial of Archibald D. Murphey, praying for the enactment of a law, and authorizing him to raise by way of Lottery the sum of fifty thousand dollars have considered the same and

REPORT,

That however anxious they are to see a correct History of North Carolina, yet a failure of a similar attempt made by the petitioner, not many years since, connected with the system of hazard, contemplated in the Memorial, upon the morality of the community induces your Committee to return the Bill and Memorial to the House and recommend its rejection.—Unpublished Legislative Doc uments, 1831, in C. L. Coon, *The Beginnings of Public Education in North Carolina: A Documentary History, 1790-1840*, I, 529-31.

80. The Rise of the Denominational Colleges

The first efforts for higher education in North Carolina centered around the University. By 1830 a second movement was under way, which led to the establishment of a number of denominational colleges. The causes of this movement were largely economic and religious. Inadequate transportation facilities and sectionalism kept the University from serving all regions of the state. Consequently, the citizens of western North Carolina began to urge the creation of a Western College "somewhere southwest of the Yadkin River." A charter for such an institution was granted by the legislature in 1820. $60,000 was subscribed, but when the trustees selected Lincolnton as the site of the college, they found themselves unable to collect more than 20 per cent of this amount. An effort was made to locate the college in Mecklenburg County in 1824, but it was unsuccessful. The Western College was never organized.

There was a rather general feeling that the University was too expensive, that it did not reach the masses, and that it was teaching skepticism and free thought. The great revival which swept North Carolina in 1810 and 1811 deepened the religious feelings of the people. It led them to demand the creation of institutions of higher learning that were sound in doctrine, safe for their children, and a proper place for the training of ministers. The church was the strongest social organization in the state, and it was natural that the demand for more educational institutions should come from church organizations. The Baptists took the lead, followed closely by the Presbyterians and the Methodists.

Wake Forest College had its beginning in "The Wake Forest Institute," a manual labor and classical school, chartered in 1833 and located in the "forest" of Wake County, seventeen miles north of Raleigh. Samuel Wait, a native of New York State, was principal of the school, which opened February 3, 1834, with sixteen pupils. In 1838 the Institute was rechartered as "Wake Forest College." Dr. Samuel Wait was president of the College from that date to 1845. The manual labor plan was dropped in 1838.

At the spring meeting of Concord Presbytery in 1835, the Reverend Robert Hall Morrison secured the adoption of a resolution appointing a committee to take charge of the raising of funds and the selection of a site for an institution of learning. At the fall meeting in 1835, this committee reported and the Presbytery passed a resolution saying that the institution should be called "Davidson College," as a tribute to the memory of "that distinguished and excellent man, General William Davidson, who, in the ardor of patriotism, fearlessly contending for the liberty of his country, fell (universally lamented) in the battle of Cowan's Ford." A few months later, the Presbyteries of Bethel and Morganton came to the support of Concord. The churches raised over thirty thousand dollars for the new college, which began on March 1, 1837, with Dr. Morrison as president, and with sixty-six students in attendance.

Trinity was the last of the large denominational colleges established. In the year 1838 some citizens of Randolph County established a school with the Reverend Brantley York as principal. In 1839 this school was enlarged and named Union Institute. In 1841 it was incorporated as the Trustees of the Union Institute Academy. In 1842 Braxton Craven became principal of the school, under whose leadership the institution in 1851 was rechartered as Normal College. The college was permitted to license teachers. In 1852 it was given the authority to grant degrees. As a training school for teachers the institution did not prosper, and in 1856 the curriculum was changed so as to make it a school of liberal arts. On February 16, 1859, the charter was amended and the name of the institution changed to Trinity College.

WAKE FOREST INSTITUTE

THE following is the general outline of the Plan of this Institution, adopted at the late sitting of the Board of Managers:

1. The name of the Institution is "The Wake Forest Institute."

2. The object of the Institute is to enable young Ministers to obtain an education on moderate terms, and to train up youth in general to a knowledge of Science and practical Agriculture.

3. Every pupil shall labor three hours a day, under the direction of an experienced and scientific farmer, subject to the control of the principal teacher, who is to be a Minister of the Gospel.

4. The total expenses of the Academic year shall not exceed $60, of which $25 are to be paid in advance, and an allowance shall be made to each student according to the value of his labor.

5. No pupil shall be admitted under 12 years of age.

6. Every pupil shall furnish himself with an axe and a hoe, a pair of sheets and a pair of towels.

7. There shall be one vacation in the year, from the middle of December to the first of February.

8. This Institute shall be open to the reception of all youth of good moral character, who will comply with the above regulations.

Arrangements are now making to carry into effect the objects of the Institute by the first of February.

The Board of Managers have limited the number of students to fifty for the first year.

All Editors of the State friendly to the Institute are requested to give the above an insertion in their papers.—*Raleigh Register*, Nov. 23, 1832.

MINISTERIAL EDUCATION

THE WAKE FOREST INSTITUTE, . . . has recently commenced operations. The forming of the Baptist State Convention of North Carolina, connected with the ministerial labors of its former President; the exertions of the Rev. Mr. Wait, while traveling as Agent of the Convention, before he became Principal of the Institution to conduct the instruction of its pupils; and the influence of the pen of the Rev. Thomas Meredith, Editor of that valuable publication, the Baptist Interpreter, are manifestly reckoned among the means that have, in the gracious Providence of God, been honored in developing a state of things in North Carolina, truly interesting and promising—out of which very much good may be expected to grow—out of which has sprung up the Wake Forest Institute. This is based upon the Manual Labor System. . . . —*Baptist Interpreter*, July 5, 1834.

THE MANUAL LABOR SYSTEM

Brother Meredith.—Taking it for granted that you would be pleased to learn some of the particulars of our operations here, I have taken it upon myself to give you a brief detail of our internal movements, and I might say, external movements; for never was a set of fellows kept so constantly on the go. I will begin at the dawn of day, when the loud peals of the bell arouse us from our sweet repose. We are allowed about fifteen minutes to dress ourselves and wash, when the bell summons us to prayers. At this second sound of the bell, the whole plantation seems alive with moving bodies; a stream of students is seen pouring in from every direction . . . Prayers being over, just as the sun raises his head from behind the distant forest, the Virgil class to which I belong, commences recitation. Other classes are reciting at the same time. At half past seven, the bell rings for breakfast; a few minutes after which, study hours commence. Every one is now kept at the top of his speed; some in recitation, and others preparing for recitation, until 12 o'clock, when the bell announces the dinner hour; and almost immediately after this we start on the same mental race. This is kept up through all the classes until three o'clock, when the bell rings long and loud for the toils of the field: While the bell is ringing the students assemble—some with axes, some with grubbing hoes, some with weeding hoes and some empty-handed, all in a thick crowd. . . . Those with axes make for the woods, where they fell the sturdy

oaks and divide them into rails; the grubbers take the field, . . .
Those with weeding hoes find much variety in their employment;
. . . We students engage in everything here, that an honest farmer
is not ashamed to do. If we should draw back from anything here
that is called work, we should feel that we had disgraced ourselves.

Those who are empty-handed make up the fences, . . . That you
may form some idea of our execution, I will state that two of our
corps yesterday mauled one hundred and twenty seven rails in two
hours and a half, and that the fence . . . corps made a fence and
staked it near a half mile in length, . . . A little bell calls from the
field— we enter the chapel for prayers, and immediately after take
supper. We now have about half an hour for amusement, when the
bell again calls to study. There is no place like Wake Forest at night.
. . . O what a place for meditation!

G. W.

—*Raleigh Register*, May 5, 1835.

DAVIDSON COLLEGE

The friends of education and religion in the Western part of
North Carolina and the adjoining districts of South Carolina have
long felt and acknowledged the necessity of an Institution of learning under the control of Christian principles, and accessible in its
privileges to that large and deserving part of Society who are not
able to reap the advantages of expensive Colleges. In the Spring
of 1835, the Presbytery of Concord, resolved with confident reliance
upon the blessing of God to undertake the establishment of a Manual Labor Seminary. In this noble attempt the Presbyterians of
Morganton and Bethel have since manifested the most cordial co-
operation.

After due investigation, a farm was selected in the upper part of
Mecklenburg County, distinguished for its healthy and central location. 469 acres of Land were procured . . . Agents were immediately appointed to lay before the public the claims of this benevolent enterprise. . . . In a few months over thirty thousand dollars
were subscribed.

It was determined to call it Davidson College, in commemoration
of Gen. W. L. Davidson, a brave, generous and intelligent officer,
who was killed in 1780, at Cowan's Ford, 7 miles from its site, opposing Lord Cornwallis, in crossing the Catawba river.

Three buildings for students, two Houses for professors and a
steward's House, with the necessary outbuildings will soon be completed. . . .

It has been determined to commence the exercises of the College on the 1st day of March, 1837. The year will be divided into two Sessions of five months each. August and February will be the vacation months.

All the Students will be required to perform labor, Agricultural or Mechanical, three hours each working day. . . .

The price has been fixed at six dollars per month, or thirty dollars a Session. The students will be divided into three classes of labor. . . .

The 1st class of laborers will be allowed a reduction on their board $15 by the session, or $30 by the year.

The 2nd class will be allowed a reduction of $12 by the session, or $24 by the year.

The 3d class a reduction of $9 by the session or $18 by the year.

Prices of tuition to the Students in the Languages and Sciences will be $15 by the Session.

Prices of tuition to those who may enter to study English Grammar, Geography and other branches of an English Education, will be $10 by the Session. . . .

Nothing will be required for room rent or fuel. . . .

Many promising and enterprising youths may receive the benefits of a Liberal Education in this way, whose circumstances prevent them from encountering heavy expenses. Every effort has been made to redeem the pledge given, that the expenses should be as small as they could be made. . . . But the diminution of expense will not be the only advantage of the Manual Labor Department. The regular and cheerful exercise afforded by it, will preserve and promote the health of the Students. . . . The great object of a good Education is, to train and cultivate a sound mind in a sound body. . . .

Another salutary result . . . will be the cultivation of independence and good habits among the Students. . . . The undivided and practical influence of all educated men should be given to render labor honorable, and the most efficient way to do this, is not to shrink from it themselves.—*Southern Citizen*, February 18, 1837.

THE BEGINNINGS OF TRINITY COLLEGE, 1838-1840

In the latter part of 1837, I was invited by several gentlemen in the neighborhood of Trinity College, to teach a school in that community; after some deliberation, I consented.

Early in the spring of 1838, I opened a school in a house known as Brown's Schoolhouse. . . . It was a very inferior building, built of round logs, and covered with common boards. The floor was laid with puncheons and slabs. . . . This house was entirely too small to accomodate the students, . . .

As soon as the farmers had laid by their crops, the citizens met in order to select a place to build a better house. A committee was appointed, . . . to select a suitable site; and after examining several places, the place where Trinity College now stands was finally chosen as the most convenient situation, and in a few weeks a log building 30 x 20 ft. was erected.

Early in the month of August, we moved from Brown's Schoolhouse to the one just completed. We commenced teaching in this new building with sixty-nine students. It was soon ascertained that this building, . . . was inadequate to accomodate our present number of students.

The first examination held in this new building was in the spring of 1839. Previous to this examination, I had resolved to attempt to establish a permanent institution of learning at this place, based upon an Education Association, and with a view of reaching the common walks of life with a more thorough education than had been previously afforded them. . . .

UNION INSTITUTE EDUCATIONAL SOCIETY

At the time appointed, the people of the neighborhood met at the place designated in order to organize an Educational Society, and to do such other things as might be deemed important in advancing the interest of the Institution. Up to this time the Institution had a "local habitation," but no name. The principal of the School was requested to give it a name; the name which he gave it was Union Institute, which name it held till it became Normal College. . . .

This organization was the beginning or origin of what is now Trinity College. . . .

In the Spring of 1841, the Educational Society held its third annual meeting. . . . During this year the Rev. Braxton Craven, a young man of some nineteen or twenty entered the school, and soon after was employed as assistant teacher, and continued to officiate in that capacity till the resignation of the Principal. The school continued to flourish; the number of students falling under fifty but it generally far exceeded that number.

Early in the year 1842, I (the Principal) was elected the Principal of Clemmonsville High School, . . .

According to the arrangement made between Mr. Craven and

myself he was to go with me to Clemmonsville, and still officiate as Assistant teacher; but as the time drew near for the election of another Principal, and no candidate offered his services, some of the leading members of the Society, inquired of me as to the fitness of Mr. Craven for the Principal. Though I was anxious for him to go with me, yet such was his studious habit, and his ability to learn, that I willingly recommended him as a suitable person for that position; consequently he was chosen principal at the ensuing election, and has continued there from that time to the present (June 20, 1876), except two years during the war, during which time he was stationed in Raleigh, Edenton Street Church.—*Autobiography of Brantley York* ("The John Lawson Monographs of the Trinity College Historical Society," Vol. I).

81. LETTERS ON POPULAR EDUCATION, 1832

One of the greatest exponents of education in North Carolina history was Joseph Caldwell. He was born in Iredell County in 1808, studied law, was a member of the state legislature for a short period, and represented North Carolina in Congress from 1849 to 1853. For a number of years he was the "presiding professor" of the University of North Carolina, and in 1804 was selected as the first president of that institution. In 1812 he resigned the presidency in order to "complete his work on geometry and perfect himself in the knowledge of astronomy." In 1824 he was sent to Europe to purchase supplies for the laboratories.

Caldwell wrote a series of letters on popular education addressed to the people of North Carolina. The substance of these letters first appeared in the *Raleigh Register* about 1830, under the signature of "Cleveland." The collected letters were published in 1832 by Dennis Heartt, Hillsboro.

ANOTHER obstruction meets us in our aversion to taxation beyond the bare necessities of government and the public tranquillity. Any scheme of popular education must be capable of deriving existence originally, and of maintaining it perpetually, without taxing us for the purpose, or we are well aware that we shall not as a people consent to its establishment.

A still further difficulty is felt in the indifference unhappily prevalent in many of our people on the subject of education. Vast numbers have grown up into life, have passed into its later years and raised families without it: and probably there are multitudes of whose fore-fathers this is no less to be said. Human nature is ever apt to contract prejudices against that which has never entered into its customs. . . . So strangely may the truth be inverted in the minds of men in such circumstances, that they become the avowed partizans of mental darkness against light, and are sometimes seen glorying in ignorance as their privilege and boast. . . .

I might mention further, as one of the greatest obstructions, the scattered condition of our population, over a vast extent of territory, making it difficult to embody numbers within such a compass as will make it convenient or practicable for children to attend upon instruction.

A most serious impediment is felt in our want of commercial opportunities, by which, though we may possess ample means of subsistence to our families, money is difficult of attainment to build school houses and support teachers. Could the avenues of trade be opened to this agricultural people, funds would flow in from abroad, and resources would be created at home, which would make the support of schools and many other expenses to be felt as of no consequence. Excluded as we now are from the market of the world, the necessity of rigid economy is urged against every expenditure however small, and the first plea which meets us, when the education of children is impressed upon parents is their inability to bear the expense. . . .

It appears then how numerous are the discouragements we have to encounter in framing any plan for popular education. Our habits of legislation have been long established, and their uniformity has in few instances been broken, from our first existence as a state. To provide for the education of the people, has unhappily never entered as a constituent part of these habits. . . . Our aversion to taxation, even to provide for the education of the poor children, is invincible, and extinguishes at once the hope of any plan to the execution of which such means are necessary. . . . Through the influence of inveterate habit, large portions of our population have learned to look with indifference on education. . . .

. . . We are a people whose habits and wishes revolt at everything that infringes upon an entire freedom of choice upon almost every subject. It would be easy to elucidate how this has come to be a trait so deeply marked in our character, but its reality is unquestionable. Provision for general instruction can scarcely be effected, without some compulsory measures regulating the action of individuals into particular channels directed upon the object. . . .

The evil which is the greatest of all, is the want of qualified masters. It may be difficult to obtain a teacher at all, but it is pretty certain in the present state of the country, not one is perfectly fitted for the occupation. Do we think that of all the professions in the world, that of a schoolmaster requires the least preparatory formation? If we do, there cannot be a more egregious mistake. . . . Yet in our present mode of popular education, we act upon the principle that school-keeping is a business to which scarcely any one but an idiot is incompetent, if he only knows reading, writing and arithmetic. . . .

In the present condition of society and of public opinion, the occupation of a school master in comparison with others, is regarded with contempt. It would be wonderful were it otherwise, when we look at the manner in which it is very often, if not most usually filled. . . . To teach a school is, in the opinion of many, little else than sitting still and doing nothing. . . . In short, it is no matter what the man is, or what his manners or principles, if he has escaped with life from the penal code, we have the satisfaction to think that he can still have credit as a school-master. . . .

It is apparent then that popular education cannot be efficient, when left to the insignificancy into which it sinks, with no other security for its prosecution than the accidental and voluntary action to which it is now left. . . . This plan of popular schools, hitherto, the only one we know, is so meagre and deformed in its features, and rickety in its constitution, that its repulsiveness prevents many from the use of it, who have not a doubt that education is of the utmost importance to the young, to families and to the population of a free state. . . .

Our country presents to ourselves and to the world the spectacle of a strange abstraction from light and knowledge, impenetrable to their beams, while they are falling upon her externally with the meridian splendor of science, religion and the arts. Can anyone who feels toward her any affectionate desire, who wishes for her respectability, who would see her raised out of intellectual darkness and desolation that hovers over her and settles with pervasion through the minds of her offspring, fail to be impressed with a conviction that we can no longer postpone the day of action upon the subject?

Shall we still plead that our physical ability is inadequate; that we possess not the means? To what distant period then are we to look, in what more auspicious condition must we be placed, to be conscious of strength enough to set forth in the attempt? What future prosperity of growth is in our prospect, which shall take from us all excuse of delay, and dispossess the spirit of supineness that reigns in our bosoms, of the sceptre which by its torporific touch benumbs all our faculties? . . . We have a country inferior to none of the original states in soil; in climate it is far superior to most, in the mildness of its winters, in the diversity of its productions, and in the renovation of its crops. In the midst of these sources of wealth and opportunity, our children are left to grow up unpruned and uncultivated as the forest of the brake which the hand of our industry has never touched—*Caldwell Letters on Popular Education*, printed by Dennis Heartt, Hillsborough, 1832.

82.   NORTH CAROLINA'S FIRST PUBLIC SCHOOL LAW, 1839

North Carolina's first public school law was ratified January 8, 1839. In 1817 Murphey had submitted a plan for the establishment of public schools, but little had been accomplished along that line for twenty years. A real educational revival began in the state about 1836. The immediate cause of this was the fact that North Carolina had received $1,433,757.39 as its portion of the national surplus. All of this amount, except $100,000, "ultimately went to the cause of education." Some members of the legislature wished to enact a school law immediately. Others advised delay. Finally, the legislature instructed the Literary Board to submit a plan for public schools at the 1838-39 session. The Board, guided largely by Murphey's report of 1817, recommended: the division of the state into 1,250 districts, estimating an average school population for each district of 108 children between the ages of eight and fifteen; the establishment of normal schools; the holding of an election in each county to vote on the issue of "schools" or "no schools." The law, as finally enacted, was a compromise measure, which carried out most of these recommendations, except those relating to normal schools and the election of a state superintendent.

AN ACT TO DIVIDE THE COUNTIES INTO SCHOOL DISTRICTS, AND FOR OTHER PURPOSES.

. . . That it shall be the duty of the Sheriffs of the several Counties in this State . . . to give notice . . . by public advertisement in every election precinct that an election will be held to ascertain the voice of the people upon the subject of Common Schools; And all who are in favor of raising by taxation, one dollar for every two dollars proposed to be furnished out of the Literary Fund, for the establishment of Common Schools in each School district, will deposit their vote with the word "School" written on it. Those opposed to it will vote "No School" upon their ticket; and all who vote for members of the House of Commons, shall be entitled to vote; . . . and if a majority shall be found in favor of Schools, it shall be the duty of the Sheriff to furnish a certificate of the same to the next County court of his County. . . .

That the several Courts of Pleas and Quarter Sessions in each County of the State . . . shall, in such County as shall determine to accept these terms . . . proceed to elect not less than five nor more than ten persons, as Superintendents of Common Schools, for such County. . . .

That said Superintendents . . . shall have power to choose one of their number as Chairman, and shall proceed to divide their respective Counties into School Districts, for the purpose of establishing Common Schools, containing not more than six miles square. . . .

That the aforesaid Boards or Superintendents, in each County . . . shall appoint not less than three, nor more than six School Committee Men, in each district, whose duty it shall be to assist said Superintendents in all matters pertaining to the establishment of Schools for their respective districts. . . .

That in every County in the State, where the vote shall be in favor of Common Schools, it shall be the duty of the said County Courts . . . to levy a tax to the amount of twenty dollars for each district in said County, in the same manner that other county taxes are now levied for other county purposes. . . .

That forty dollars out of the nett income of the Literary Fund, for the year one thousand eight hundred and thirty nine, is hereby appropriated to each district in said counties where the vote shall be in favor of the establishment of Common Schools, which shall be paid by the Public Treasurer, upon the warrant of the Governor, upon the certificate of the Chairman of the Board of Superintendents of said Counties, that taxes have been levied to the amount of twenty dollars for each School District in their respective counties and that School houses have been erected in each district sufficient to accomodate at least fifty scholars.—*Laws of North Carolina, 1838-39*, Chap. VIII.

83. GOVERNOR EDWARD B. DUDLEY'S REPORT TO THE LEGISLATURE IN REGARD TO THE UNIVERSITY OF NORTH CAROLINA, DECEMBER 17, 1840

The legislature had requested the Governor to report to the General Assembly "the whole amount of property received by the University of North Carolina, from its establishment in 1789, to this time, designating what kind of property received . . . from what source derived, expenses incurred; number and condition of buildings erected; and the number of professors."

THE act of incorporation declares "that in all well regulated governments, it is the indefensible duty of every Legislature to consult the happiness of a rising generation, and endeavor to fit them for an honorable discharge of the social duties of life, by paying the strictest attention to their education; and that a University supported by permanent funds, and well endowed, will have the most direct tendency to answer this purpose."

A supplemental act, passed at the same session, endowed the Institution, with all the arrearages due the State, from receiving officers of the present and late governments, up to the 1st day of January, 1783; and with all the property that had theretofore, or should thereafter, escheat to the State.

By other statutes, grants of certain confiscated estates were made; and by an act passed in 1809, all monies remaining in the hands of executors and administrators, unclaimed by legatees or next of kin, and debts due to the State, up to December, 1799, were vested in the Trustees. In 1803, two Lotteries were drawn in aid of the University, under the authority of the General Assembly, from which the sum of $5,080.80 appears to have been realized.

The first meeting of the Trustees was held in Fayetteville, on the 15th November, 1790. . . .

The Board of Trustees adopted energetic measures to obtain donations from the friends of education throughout the State, and to realize the greatest amount of benefit from the endowment, by the collection of the public land claims transferred to the Institution, and by securing and disposing of escheated estates. The anticipated degree of success was not realized from either of these sources. . . .

On the 3d August, 1792, more than two and a half years after the charter was granted, the entire amount of the property held by this Institution, consisted of the sum of $2,706.41, invested in the funded debt of the United States; $423.84 cash: subscriptions payable, . . . $200; lands in Orange county, yielding an annual rent of $33; and the lands before mentioned. . . .

The loan of $10,000, granted by the State in 1791, was subsequently converted into a gift; and since that donation, no direct advancement has at any time been made from the Public Treasury. . . .

The largest donations received from individuals were the conveyance of 20,000 acres of land, by Governor Smith; the devise of 13,000 acres of valuable land, by the late Major Charles Gerard; and the gift, by General Thomas Person, of Granville, of $1,025 in cash. . . .

Shortly after the selection of Chapel Hill as the seat of the University, twelve individuals residing in the vicinity, conveyed to the Trustees, for no other consideration than that of enlightened patriotism, 1392 acres, including all the real estate at present held by the corporation. . . .

In 1802, the ladies of Raleigh presented a pair of globes, with a compass; and in 1804, the ladies of Newbern a quadrant, "the best they could procure," as an evidence that the "sex could never be indifferent to the promotion of science, connected as it is with the virtues that impart civility to manners and refinement to life." . . .

The aggregate amount of Receipts into the Treasury of the University, from the 15th November, 1790, to 20th November, 1840, is composed of the following items:

From the sale of lands in Tennessee acquired under the laws regulating escheats, and of 33,000 acres acquired by donation or devise	\$ 195,294.82½
From the sale of lots in Chapel Hill and other lands in North Carolina	13,520.00
Profits on two lotteries	5,080.80
From Donations from the State	10,000.00
From Subscriptions obtained in 1796	7,684.40
From Dividends on Bank Stock	33,028.50
From Tuition fees since July, 1804	111,581.91
From Subscriptions obtained by Dr. Caldwell, in 1809 and 1810	10,535.00
From all other sources	134,066.99
	\$ 520,782.42½

. . . The College buildings are five in number, constructed of brick, and in good repair. . . .

The Faculty is composed of

1. The President, who is Professor of National and Constitutional Law.
2. A Professor of Chemistry, Mineralogy & Geology
3. A Professor of Mathematics & Natural Philosophy
4. A Professor of the Latin Languages and Literature
5. A Professor of the Greek Language and Literature
6. A Professor of Rhetoric and Logic

7. A Professor of the French Languages and Literature
8. A Tutor of Ancient Languages
9. A Tutor of Mathematics

—*Raleigh Register*, January 8, 1841.

84. RULES AND INSTRUCTION FOR READING, 1851

In 1851 Calvin H. Wiley published the *North Carolina Reader*, from which the following extract is taken. According to Weldon N. Edwards, the object of this reader was "to sow in the young minds of North Carolina the seeds of a true, healthy, and vigorous North Carolina spirit; and that it may effect its end, it is designed for universal use in the state, to go, with the Bible and the Almanac, into every home."

Wiley believed that most of the school books then in use were overloaded with rules and instructions; that the scholars were bewildered and fatigued with them; that a few simple rules, with good teachers, would be sufficient.

GENERAL RULES (Mostly from Worcester)

1. When reading, you should look forward a little, as you do in walking, to see what is before you, what things will make you pause, and where you must stop.

2. Read so slowly that you can speak all the words distinctly; but do not drawl or sing your words.

3. Do not read as though you were reading or talking to yourself, but as though you were telling something to others.

4. Read to any person as loudly as you would speak if talking to him.

5. Avoid reading rapidly and carelessly as you approach the end of a sentence.

6. Sit or stand erect, when you read. Leaning the head and shoulders forward causes the voice to sound badly.

7. Be careful to learn and remember the stops and marks so well that you will know their meaning whenever you meet them.

8. Do not read easy lessons too fast; but always think of what you are reading, and carefully watch the meaning as you read.

9. Do not repeat your words; and do not omit the sound of *f* in *of*, where it always sounds like *v*.

10. Read questions as you would ask them; and let your voice fall at the end of answers to questions.

11. Both poetry and prose that relate to religious subjects should

be read more slowly, distinctly, and seriously, than what relates to other subjects.

12. In reading humorous pieces, the reader must not laugh; but in reading melancholy tidings or pathetic pieces, he may properly manifest emotions.

13. Above all things, when reading or speaking, endeavour to think only of the *subject* of discourse.

14. Avoid the habit of coughing and making other unpleasant noises, just as you are beginning to read.

15. Do not read as if you were hurrying through a task.

16. Never run your words together: always pronounce every word in the sentence.

17. Keep a dictionary always by you, a standard pronouncing dictionary; and look in it for every word which you do not know how to pronounce, or whose meaning you do not understand.

18. Endeavor to look often at the persons to whom you read; and look at them as if you were talking to them.

19. When you are alone, think of your faults; when with others correct those faults. Apply this rule in all things.

20. Listen to corrections and heed them, being willing to be corrected.

21. In reading blank verse, pause only where the sense requires it, and not at the end of every line.

22. In reading poetry, you should be careful not to try to make rhymes where the author has made none; and while avoiding a drawling or monotonous tone, should read with more attention to cadences and inflections than in reading prose. . . .

23. The Italic words in the Bible are not emphatic words: they are words supplied by the translator for words not expressed, but understood, in the original text. We should read the Scriptures, not as though they were our own words, but as if we were seriously and meekly telling what they say to *us* and *to others*. What we read there is given to *teach us*, as well as the persons who hear us read.

24. All the words used to designate the Almighty should be pronounced *reverently, seriously*, and with a low, but distinct tone of voice.

Enunciate distinctly; and give every word, every syllable, and every letter its proper sound.

Draw your breath before you begin, and read so as not to get out of breath.

Do not hiss your words through your teeth; and be careful not to cough and make unpleasant noises in your throat while reading.

Observe all the stops and learn to be guided by them, without making awkward pauses.

Study the author's meaning; and imagine yourself to be talking in his place. . . .

Read to be instructed: study, therefore, the meaning and ideas of the author, observe his style, and reflect on what he says.—Calvin H. Wiley, *The North Carolina Reader, Number III*, pp. 19-20.

VI

SOCIAL AND ECONOMIC PROBLEMS OF ANTE-BELLUM DAYS

85. FRONTIER INNS OF CAROLINA

Inns and taverns were very important in the social life of the ante-bellum period. Most of the outstanding foreign travelers in the United States commented on them—usually adversely. The following descrip-tion is given by John Bernard, one of the most prominent travelers and one of the brightest English comedians of his day. It was published in *Retrospections of America, 1797-1811*.

IN ORDER that the nature of a Carolina ordinary (or, as it ought properly to have been termed, extraordinary) may be accurately apprehended, I will venture to depict one, as a sample of some dozen I was doomed to encounter during the journey in question. They were mostly log-huts, or a frame weatherboarded; the better sort consisting of one story and two rooms; the more numerous having no internal divisions, with a truly sociable character placing all upon a level, and forbidding the existence of parties. One corner of the room would be occupied by a "bunk," containing the family bed; another by a pine-wood chest, the family clothes-press and larder; a third would be railed off for a bar, containing a rum-keg and a tumbler. The rest of the furniture consisted of two chairs and a table, all in the last stage of palsy. Their external distinctions were few, but peculiar. You might always know an ordinary, on emerging from the woods, by an earthen jug suspended by the handle from a pole; the pipe of the chimney never rising above the roof; or a score of black hogs luxuriating in the sunshine and mud before the door. On pulling up at one you usually found the land-lord gone to market, the landlady cutting wood in the swamp, "Joe" hoeing corn in a field, and only a squalling child upon the floor and a ferocious house-dog to receive you. On some of the family arriving, you were stared at as a God-send, destined to be made the most of. If hunger and fatigue compelled you to remain, a little Indian corn for your horse, and a blanket on the hearth, with your saddle for a pillow, to represent a bed, were the most you would obtain. In summer a man would sometimes vary his enjoyment by stretching himself outside near the pigs, under the said blanket stretched over four stakes, to keep off the dew and mosquitoes. As to edibles, whether you called for breakfast, dinner, or supper, the reply was one—eggs and bacon; but the meal brought not a gratification, but a task. Here the motto was—ultra independence; every man his own servant. Ten to one you had to cook the meal yourself, while the landlady was searching for a trencher; and, when it was before you, you were sure of only one thing—to pay for it. No sooner were you seated than the house-dog (of the large wolf breed) would arrange himself beside you, and lift his lank, hungry jaws expressively to your face. The young children, never less than a dozen (the women seeming to bear them in a litter in those regions), at the smell and sight of the victuals would set up a yell enough to frighten the wolves. . . . —John Bernard, *Retrospections of America, 1797-1811* (New York, 1887) pp. 203-4.

86. GANDER PULLING—AN EARLY AMUSEMENT

The following highly-colored, satirical account of a gander pulling well illustrates the amusements with which early North Carolinians beguiled away the hours. The employment of horses in the sport, the liberal use of whiskey to sustain flagging spirits, and the almost universal betting on the outcome lent to this amusement something of the tone of King Arthur's tournaments, mixed with the crudeness and sensual pleasure of rural sport.

ANOTHER of our games which is more especially worthy of attention than the rest is that of gander pulling. This consists in hanging an old tough gander by the heels, rubbing his neck well with grease and soap, then riding under him with speed, seizing him by the neck as you pass, and endeavouring to pull his head off. The amusement consists in the frequent failures of the rider to lay hold on the long necked animal, and the danger he is in of being pulled from his horse, while he endeavours to pull off the poor animal's head. I cannot help recommending this as a most delightful amusement to all lovers of fun. It is one of the games which are assigned to Easter. The arrival of this period is for some weeks anticipated with rapture, by all bruisers either at fist or grog, all heavy bottomed well balanced riders, all women who want a holiday, and who have a curiosity to see the world, and particularly by all buxome young lasses, who wish to see the weight and prowess of their sweethearts tried in open field. In short all sporters, blackguards, mongrels and negroes take warning to collect their shillings and pence, that they may have wherewithal to buy whiskey, be generous to their companions, grow conspicuous by rattling their chink, or at least by showing that sort which is much of the colour and consistency of ground leaf tobacco. Then shall all overseers and enterprisers, have an opportunity to recount their exploits in beating up negro-quarters on a patrol night, in gouging a champion who was stout-hearted enough to attack them, or in shouting, quizzing, or chuckling at a gentleman traveller on a tobacco rolling. They shall then be able to prove their alertness in beating the earth with the body of a wrestler, by lifting & tossing him with a crotch lock or a cross buttock.

When the day has arrived and the company assembled, the whiskey is diligently plied in half broken tumblers, gourds and teacups. The ardour of joy springs up, and soon is lighted in every face. The target is fixed and many a bullet winged with invisible and unerring speed evinces the skill of the marksman, and sends his name on a shout of triumph to the skies. At length the rumour is abroad that the business of the day is prepared, and the hour of trial arrived, when champions, ponies and wagerers are to hold themselves in readiness, while all spectators, gentlemen, simpletons and raggamuffins are warned to enjoy the dodging, the gobbling and pulling of the great gander of the day. They flock in crowds to the appointed scene. On high you behold suspended by the heels from the flexile bough of some neighboring tree, or from some elastick pole, the grand object on which all eyes are fixed—A gander venerable for age, the sinews of whose neck hardened by years, are to contend in force with the sinews of many an arm that is the boast of its owner in the doughty field. In such a contest the chief hope of this prime emblem of all the geese and ganders on the plain above which he hangs, must be found in the armour of soap with which his limber neck is overlaid. On another side is raised to view the richly glittering hat which is to crown the head of him, who shall carry away the head of the father of goslings. The signal is given and the candidates appear in the lists with their proud and prancing ponies. Away they fly in successive career to the destined prize, the high object of their aspiring hopes, while the hearts of the multitude whose due bills are at stake, but especially the hearts of those fond damsels whose muscular and sinewy lovers are to vindicate their prowess, beat high with expectation. A centinel is stationed to urge the lingering nag from the reeking victim. The rider rises forward in his might, to seize the squalling prize; the noble gander waves his easy neck, and laughs in triumph at the disappointed grasp.

Another follows and is still succeeded till at length a resolute spirit determined on success lays hold with vigorous gripe, and lies sprawling on the ground. His successor sees his fate, but still more firm to his purpose hangs dangling in the air. The air is rent with peals of applause, but it remains for one of greater power of muscles and weight of flesh and bone, to accomplish the glorious victory; he is found at last, and clinging to his beast with a force that almost stops him in mid career, he bears off in triumph and with the inmost exultation of his mistresses' heart the [gander's head]."— Thomas Henderson's Letter-Book, 1810-1811. Manuscript in possession of the North Carolina Historical Commission.

87. TRAVEL IN NORTH CAROLINA, 1816-1817

Francis Hall, a British officer, arrived in the United States in March, 1816, and traveled through the northern and southern states. Except for his denunciation of "the spirit of speculation in all professions of life" and his strong condemnation of slavery, his views of the American people were favorable. He gives an interesting description of Raleigh and its vicinity. The following extract is taken from his *Travels in Canada and the United States in 1816 and 1817* (Boston, 1818).

RALEIGH is the capital of North Carolina, and seems a clean, little country town. At one end of the principal, or rather, only street, stands the Governor's brick-house, and at the other the senate, or court-house, surrounded by a grass plot neatly laid out. The houses are small, and built of scantling. Some of them have their foundations of the talcous granite of the ledge, which is the only stone in the country. The total want of limestone, and scarcity of brick earth, render it extremely difficult and expensive, to give buildings any degree of stability. The stage stops half a day at Raleigh, which enabled me to have a morning's quail shooting with two gentlemen, one of whom had fallen in love with my pointer, on my alighting at the tavern; and if any conclusion can be drawn from two chance specimens, society at Raleigh is by no means in a pitiable condition. . . .

At Fayetteville the road again crosses the granite ledge, and traverses a desolate tract of swamp and sandy pine-woods in Georgetown. In all this distance, Lumberton is the only clump of houses to which courtesy can apply the name of a village: the tavern here is kept by a general of militia, who seemed, indeed, to have more of the spirit of the soldier than of the landlord, for he declined

taking payment for the refreshment he very civilly prepared for
me. A tract of country like the above can have little variety of
scenery; the heavy dreariness of the pine-barrens was, however,
sometimes relieved by the verdure of the swamps, which were
covered with bright evergreens, through which the road frequently
ran for some distance, as through a park shrubbery.—Allan Nevins,
American Social History as Recorded by British Travelers, p. 103.

88. MEMOIR ON THE INTERNAL IMPROVEMENTS CONTEM-PLATED BY THE LEGISLATURE OF NORTH CAROLINA AND ON THE RESOURCES AND FINANCES OF THAT STATE, 1819

North Carolina was very backward economically in the first half of
the nineteenth century. It was called "Old Rip," the "Ireland of America," and was considered a "good State to be from." There were many
reasons for its undeveloped condition—poor farming, lack of manufacturing, inadequate transportation facilities, dependence upon Virginia and
South Carolina ports, and general indifference to education and progress.
There were a few dissatisfied spirits, however, a few voices "crying in
the wilderness" of economic despair. The most prominent of these was
Archibald D. Murphey. For a generation he carried on a veritable crusade for education and internal improvements. His "Memoir on Internal
Improvements" in 1819 gave an excellent statement of trade conditions
and the general conduct of business in the state. It likewise pointed out
the great possibilities of North Carolina.

FOR thirty years past, the climate and soil of North-Carolina have
been much underrated, and at no time have her physical resources
been understood. She has sent half a million of her inhabitants to
people the Wilderness of the West; and it was not until the rage for
emigration abated, that the public attention was directed to the
improvement of those advantages, and to the appreciation of those
blessings, which Providence has planted in abundance within her
own bosom. The delusion in favor of new Countries, which has
drained our population, is passing away; good sense is returning,
and we are beginning seriously to reflect how we may make our
fortunes *here*, instead of going to hunt for them in a Wilderness six
hundred or a thousand miles distant. . . . It is mortifying to look
around and witness the general ignorance which prevails of the resources and character of the State: to see, both in the Legislature
and out of it, men of respectable understanding, almost totally ignorant of our Geographical Situation, of the state of our Population,

our Finances, our Agriculture, our Commerce, our Soil and our Climate —We thank Heaven that a change is taking place, and that we begin to be as anxious to acquire a knowledge of our resources and of our capacities for improvement, as we have heretofore been indifferent. . . . The Legislature of 1815, availed themselves of this enthusiasm to commence a system of policy, which had for its object the prosperity and greatness of the State. They spread abroad a zeal, which distinguished in a peculiar manner the Legislature of 1816. They directed the public attention to the improvement of our internal condition : To the opening of new channels of intercourse : To the construction of good roads, to the opening of our rivers, to the improvement of our inlets, to the concentration of our commerce, and the growth of markets at home for the productions of our soil. . . .

. . . The events of the year 1819, have taught us lessons of the most impressive character. If we do not profit by them, we deserve to be lashed still more severely. It is true the distress in pecuniary matters which now prevails in this State is not attributable to one cause only ; but it is obvious to a common observer that the greatest and most operative cause of this distress is the scattered condition of our commerce and the want of a home market. Having no commercial city in which the staples of our soil can be exchanged for foreign merchandize, our Merchants purchase their Goods and contract their debts in Charleston, Petersburg, Baltimore, Philadelphia and New-York. Part of those debts are discharged by shipments of produce ; the balance in cash. Once in every year the State is literally drained of its money to pay debts abroad. . . . If North-Carolina had her commerce concentrated at one or two points, one or more large commercial cities would grow up ; markets would be found at home for the productions of the State ; foreign merchandize would be imported into the State for the demands of the market ; our debts would be contracted at home ; and our Banks would be enabled to change their course of business. They could give activity to the commerce of the State, and yet issue but a small amount of paper, . . .

In North Carolina, the cultivation of the soil will form the basis of public prosperity. To develop the resources of our soil, it is necessary to give facilities to our commerce. Industry will be inactive whilst there is no demand for its productions. An active commerce is the aliment of labour ; and at this day, when Political Economy has attained to the rank of a science, Statesmen will not seek to promote the Agriculture of a country by bounties and premiums, but will turn their attention to those ways and means by which, in the first place, the products of Agriculture can easily find a good market, and by which, in the second place, the profits of that commerce which sustains the market, shall be contributory to the wealth of their own, rather than of other States. . . .

The Internal Improvements contemplated by the Legislature of North-Carolina, relate

1. To the Inlets on our Coast.
2. To the Sounds along the Coast.
3. To the Primary Rivers.
4. To the junction of two or more of those Rivers by navigable Canals.
5. To the Public Highways.
6. To the Draining of the Marshes and Swamps of the Eastern and Southern Counties. . . .

The Legislature has granted charters to Companies for improving the navigation of each of the primary Rivers, and has subscribed a portion of the capital stock in all the Companies, except that for the Broad River. These Rivers generally intersect the State from North to South, and afford greater facilities of Inland Navigation than are found in any of the Atlantic States. . . .

Heretofore the productions of the Northern parts of the State, lying on the Roanoke and its branches, and also on the upper parts of the Tar and Neuse, have been sent to the markets of Virginia; and the trade of the Broad River, the Catawba and Pedee, has gone to South-Carolina. Thus it has happened, that we have shipped from our own Ports not more than one-third of our Agricultural products; and even a considerable portion of our Staves, Lumber and Naval Stores, have been sent to other ports by the Dismal Swamp Canal, on one side; or by the Wackamaw, Little Pedee and Lumber River, on the other. This unfortunate division of our trade produces many bad effects.

1. It makes us appear a poor state in the union.
2. It leaves us without markets at home: and thus we lose the profits upon our Commerce. The annual loss of Commercial Profit sustained by North-Carolina by not having markets of her own, is estimated at more than half a million of dollars.
3. Our trade being scattered and most of it sent to the neighboring states, we have no large Commercial City: and our whole population is devoid of that animating pride, which a large City and an extensive concentrated Commerce contribute to inspire.

COMMERCE OF NORTH CAROLINA

STATEMENT

Of the value of Exports of Domestic Produce from each of the Ports of North-Carolina, during the year ending the 30th September, 1816.

	Dlls.	Cts.
Wilmington	1,061,112	00
Newbern	84,281	
Washington	33,933	
Edenton	71,484	
Camden	12,982	
Plymouth	36,314	
Ocracocke	28,165	
Total	1,328,271	

COMMERCE OF THE CAPE-FEAR.

STATEMENT

Of the value of Exports of Domestic Produce from the Port of Wilmington, for six months, commencing 1st October, 1815, and ending the 31st March, 1816.

PRODUCE OF THE FOREST.

Lumber, (Boards, hewn Timber, Staves, Shingles, &c.)	$ 157,200
Naval Stores, (Tar, Turpentine, Rosin, Pitch, &c.)	131,000

PRODUCE OF AGRICULTURE.

Live Cattle—Horses, Hogs, Bacon Hams, &c.	4,800
Wheat, Flour, Indian Corn Meal	29,500
Rice	48,000
Tobacco	92,000
Cotton	216,000
Flax Seed	54,000
Produce Shipped Coastwise	380,000
	1,112,500

SPECIES OF MERCHANDIZE

23,650 Barrels of Tar
 1,000 do. of Turpentine
22,500 do. Rosin
  400 do. Pitch
  100 do. Varnish
  250 Casks Spirits of Turpentine
 2,900 Bales of Cotton
 1,309 Hhds. of Tobacco
  220 Casks of Flaxseed
 1,320 Tierces of Rice
 5,560 Bushels, rough do.
 3,250 Bbls. Flour
 9,660 Bushels Wheat
  62 Casks Bees Wax
  11 Hhds. Tallow
150,000 Ft. Flooring Plank
13,000 W. O. Hhds. Staves

STATEMENT

Of Domestic Produce boated from Fayetteville during the year
ending 30th September, 1816

Species of Produce	Value
2,337 hhds. Tobacco ....$	400,000
8,292 bales of Cotton.........................	621,900
11,813 bushels of Wheat.......................	17,719
10,341 bushels of Corn........................	10,341
5,164 casks Flaxseed	77,460
29,761 gallons Spirits	23,808
12,962 bbls. Flour............................	129,629
Tallow, Wax, Bacon, Furs, Lard, Feathers, &c...	50,000
	$ 1,331,398

STATEMENT

Of the value of Lands and Slaves in North-Carolina, as assessed
for the Direct Tax of 1815.

Total Value of Land	Total Value of Slaves
$53,521,513	$40,667,314

REVENUES OF NORTH-CAROLINA.

The revenues of North-Carolina are derived from

1. Taxes.
2. Dividends on Bank Stock.
3. Dividends on Navigation Stock.
4. Sales of vacant Lands. . . .

The amount of Taxes paid into the Treasury, exclusive of the Tax on Bank Stock, was in

1801	$ 37,076.85
1802	42,624.04
1803	42,759.97
1804	47,094.75
1805	47,951.08
1811	52,207.10
1812	61,481.60
1814	68,803.92
1815	84,923.78
1816	87,568.84
1817	84,701.88

Of the ability of the State to provide ample Funds for Internal Improvements. . . . There can be little doubt, that the revenue derived by the General Government from North-Carolina, since the adoption of the Federal Constitution, has exceeded twenty millions of dollars. This fact reminds us more sensibly than any other, of the humiliating condition of the State. Whilst we have thus liberally contributed to the support and the aggrandizement of the Union, how have we been viewed by the General Government, or by our Sister States? Have we not been uniformly treated with cold neglect by the one, and open contempt by the others? . . . We have been considered the outcasts of the Union, . . .

Why do we remain in this humiliating condition? No other cause has ever yet been assigned for it in the General Assembly, than that we are too poor to get out of this condition. A view of the resources of the State, will shew to any man of common sense, that this is only an apology to men for not doing their duty; an *off-hand* excuse to weak and timid minds, that can be offered on all occasions, whilst the true cause is to be found in the want of public spirit, of State pride, and of State feeling. . . .

Few men have the courage to impose taxes; and any plan for Internal Improvements which is bottomed upon an increase of the taxes, light as they are, will not be likely to meet with success. This renders it necessary to enquire what resources are at the disposal of the General Assembly, for public works, without resorting to further taxation—These resources are

1. The surplus monies remaining in the Treasury.
2. The lands in the Cherokee Nation of Indians, within our Boundary.
3. The sum of $160,000 which the Banks of Newbern and Cape-Fear are bound to loan to the State during the continuance of their Charters. . . . The Banks will find ample reasons for making extensive loans to the State for Public Works.

1. The money loaned will be expended within the State.
2. The wealth of their dealers, and of the State at large, will be increased.
3. The great object, desirable to all, but particularly to the Banks, will be gained : We shall ship our own productions and have markets at home.—*The Papers of Archibald D. Murphey* (edited by W. H. Hoyt), II, 103-96.

89. INTERNAL IMPROVEMENTS THE REMEDY FOR EMIGRATION, 1828-1829

During the second quarter of the nineteenth century there was such a steady stream of emigration from North Carolina to other states that this state was frequently called the "Ireland of America." Soil exhaustion, the lure of the West, lack of educational facilities, and improper internal improvements were some of the reasons why North Carolinians were "leaving home." The following extract from Governor Iredell's message to the legislature shows that he believed internal improvements would be the best remedy for the situation.

GOVERNOR JAMES IREDELL'S MESSAGE TO THE LEGISLATURE

THE subject of opening and improving our outlets to the ocean, of removing obstructions in our rivers, and of providing, by canals or roads, for the more convenient transportation of our produce to market, has so often engaged the attention of the Legislature, that I feel, when I touch upon these topics, all the awkwardness of addressing you upon trite matters. Yet when I look at the situation of our State, I can not forbear urging upon you what has so often elicited the earnest recommendation of my predecessors. We now occupy, from our population and territory, an elevated position among the States of the Union. Our relative rank can not be stationary, nor can it be maintained without exertions on our part. Almost every State is calling forth its powers to improve its internal condition. Shall we alone, who have such resources, and who could bring them into action by so small a comparative expenditure, shrink from the adoption of the means which are promoting the prosperity of others and leading to their superiority? Let us, too, press forward in the career of Internal Improvement. Let us, too, leave for the benefit and gratitude of posterity, memorials of that wise policy which consists not in hoarding our money, but in applying it to useful and profitable objects.

It were superfluous to dwell upon the happy effects on our prosperity, which would follow in the train of a judicious system of improvements, faithfully executed. A new life would be infused into every branch of industry; our agriculture would be relieved from a heavy burthen, which now oppresses it; our commerce would increase ten fold; the tide of emigration would be checked; and our population and wealth would advance with a rapidity equal to our most sanguine desires. Are we not prepared to commence such a system? Why should we delay? It will require much time for its completion, and the necessary expenditures will be divided among several years. You will discover, from the Treasurer's report that we have a large available fund, not required for the ordinary expenses of Government, and not otherwise appropriated. What this sum cannot supply, may be furnished by our credit. Every other State has resorted to loans for a similar purpose. The usual objection to loans, that it burthens posterity with a debt which we have contracted for our advantage, does not here apply. The benefit will descend to our posterity with the burden, and will be more than a compensation. We are but tenants for life; the estate will be theirs forever; and it is but just that they should pay the greater part of what we may expend in its permanent improvement.—*House Journal, 1828-1829*, pp. 136-37.

90. STAGE COACH TRAVEL

Prior to the advent of the railroad in North Carolina, stage coaches constituted the chief means of transportation. There were regular lines connecting the leading towns of the state, over which the coaches usually ran tri-weekly. Some of the lines continued to operate after the coming of the railroad. The following accounts throw some light on the speed and expense of this form of transportation.

STAGE LINE FROM RALEIGH TO ROXBOROUGH

THE Subscriber having contracted to run a Horse Stage from Raleigh to Roxboro', in Person county, informs the public that the line is now in full operation. The Stage is comfortable, and with good Horses and careful Drivers, he hopes to give entire satisfaction. . . .

The Stage leaves Raleigh every Friday morning, at 10 o'clock, and arrives at Roxboro' on Saturday at 3 o'clock in the afternoon. Leaves Roxboro' within an hour after its arrival, and reaches Raleigh on Sunday evening, at 8 o'clock. The distance between the two places is nearly sixty miles, & the price of passage is only $3.50 which is lower in proportion than on any Stage Route in the State. . . . Seats to be taken at the House of the Subscriber.
Raleigh, Feb. 7, 1828

GREEN BOBBITT
—*Raleigh Register*, February 22, 1828.

THE EXPENSES OF STAGE COACH TRAVEL

MY DEAR SIR:

I left here in the stage on the evening of the 10th ult., on a South-western tour, taking the Salisbury Convention in my way. I returned after an absence of 29 days on the 8th instant, having travelled about 1,550 miles—210 of which were along the stage route from Goldsborough to Charlotte. . . .

Along the line of our proposed Rail Road from Goldsborough to Charlotte, the stages run tri-weekly. If you reach Goldsborough precisely at the hour of departure, which is only possible, three times in the week, and meet with no delay from any cause, you may arrive in Charlotte in three days and a half, or 84 hours. Your expenses will be, stage-fare from Goldsborough to Raleigh $4.50— thence to Salisbury $10.50—to Charlotte $3—$18.

In tavern bills—dinner at Smithfield, 50 cents—a day's board in Raleigh $1.50—supper at Moring's 50—breakfast at Holt's 50— dinner at Greensborough 50, supper 50, (if you get any)—breakfast in Salisbury 50—dinner in Concord 50—$5.

Making the aggregate expense $23 for 210 miles stage travel, per-formed at the rate of less than 2½ miles an hour, at the average expense of about 11 cents per mile. . . .

You travel along the route of the proposed Rail Road at a fifth of the speed and at four times the expense, in approaching the cap-ital of your own State, that is required to take a Georgian or South

Carolinian to his capital, or to any of the great commercial markets of these States. This journey from Goldsborough to Charlotte cost me $23—the same distance in South Carolina and Georgia a fraction over $5. I paid a tax therefore on this single jaunt of about $18 for the omission of the government to provide a great highway for her citizens. . . . There are many citizens of North Carolina who pay a larger amount.—Letter from Governor Swain to Governor Morehead, Chapel Hill, July 13, 1849, *Raleigh Register*, August 3, 1849.

91. CUTTING OFF EARS ABOLISHED, 1831-1832

Many cruel and unusual punishments were inflicted on criminals a century or so ago. Some of the most prevalent were whipping, ducking, stocks and pillories, branding, and cutting off ears. The idea of vengeance seems to have dominated the whole system of criminal procedure. About the second quarter of the nineteenth century many humanitarian reforms were made in North Carolina and elsewhere in this country. The criminal code was ameliorated, though it was still far from humane. The following act illustrates the nature of punishments in use and the kind of reforms which were made.

AN ACT TO ABOLISH THE PUNISHMENT OF CUTTING OFF EARS

THAT it shall not be lawful hereafter to inflict the punishment of cutting off the ears, but the same is hereby abolished ; any law or usage to the contrary notwithstanding : *Provided*, that in all cases where by the existing laws the cutting off an ear or ears is prescribed, or part of the prescribed punishment, the offender on conviction shall in lieu thereof be sentenced to receive one or more public whippings, not less than thirty-nine lashes on his bare back : And *provided also*, that this act shall not extend to the punishment of any perjury or subornation of perjury, committed upon the trial of any capital offence.—*Laws, 1831-32*, Chap. XII, p. 10.

92. SOCIAL AND ECONOMIC CONDITIONS IN THE STATE, 1833

The following report of a legislative committee on internal improvements throws considerable light on economic and social conditions in the state a century ago. Agriculture was depressed and North Carolinians were emigrating in large numbers. The population generally seemed to be discouraged. A scheme of internal improvements, particularly the building of railroads, was proposed as the remedy for these evil conditions.

REPORT OF LEGISLATIVE COMMITTEE ON INTERNAL IMPROVEMENTS

Upon comparing the present languishing condition of the agricultural resources of North Carolina with the improved and prosperous condition of even the most inconsiderable member of the Union, the picture portrays the contrast, characteristic of a community worn down by the hand of adversity, in colours too strong to be concealed. That in North Carolina, it is apparent the reward of labor has ceased to be a stimulus to industry and enterprise; that agriculture has ceased to yield to the land owner a compensation equivalent to the expense attending the transportation of his surplus produce to market. The consequent result of this state of things is, that real estate throughout the country has so depreciated in the hands of farmers, as to be considered not to possess a fixed value estimated upon its products. Hence our citizens are daily abandoning the places of their birth for situations in other States less healthy, and often not superior in fertility of soil; but which, by the improvement of those States, rendered so by the fostering aid of Legislative patronage, the profits of labor hold out stronger inducements to agricultural pursuits than is to be found in North Carolina. Nor does the evil stop here. The tide of emigration, which never ebbs, not only carries with it a great portion of the enterprise and prime of our youth, but much of the productive and most valuable description of the State's wealth. . . . Can it be to our interest so to shape our policy as to render our State the mere nursery for the Western and Southwestern States? Surely not. We not only thereby lessen the political influence of the State in the councils of the General Government, but we evidently weaken the ties of patriotism of our citizens to the land of their nativity.

. . . Go into any neighborhood, and inquire of the seniors or heads of families, "how many children they have raised, and in what State do they reside?" and in nine cases out of ten, the answer will be, "I have raised some six or eight children; but the major portion of them have migrated to some other State"; and adds the parent, "I am anxious to sell my lands, to enable me to follow them." Thus, it will appear that the lands of nine-tenths of the farmers of the State are actually in market; and what does it arise from? Evidently from the fact, that the distance to, and expense of sending the staple products of the soil to market, so far lessen the profits upon agricultural labor, that the farmer has no inducements to effort. Therefore, it is that all our farmers are land sellers, and no land buyers.

14

The cause of these evils is apparent; but no less so, than is the remedy. Throw open the agricultural interest of our State to the action of trade or commerce; open its wide spread avenues, by constructing railroads from the interior of our fertile back country to markets within the State, at least, so far as nature in the distribution of her favors has rendered them feasible; connect by railroads the rivers of the State at given points, whereby the produce of their fruitful valleys may be sent to an export market. This done, and it will reflect to the State all the substantial benefits to be derived from an export depot—such at least as will locate a capital within its influence, equal to the amount of exports. . . .

. . . The utility and practical use of rail roads will be admitted by all. Their direct effect upon the landed interest of the country is also admitted. The action they necessarily produce to enterprise and the mechanic arts and the commerce of the country, all tend to stimulate industry in a degree only to be realised by such like improvements. These considerations constitute some of the advantages to be derived from commercial intercommunications of the country. They show that it is labour which developes the resources of any country. Should it not then be an object with the Legislature to promote, by such means as shall be found within its control, the industry and enterprise of the State with a liberal hand? . . .

It is a mistaken idea, as many suppose, that banks or the monied institutions of the country will of themselves render what is called "money plenty." Money must circulate by means of the products of labor or else it will ever be scarce, and the community poor. . . .

The policy of North Carolina should be to increase the products of her soil, by increasing the reward and wages of labor.

Our course of reasoning upon this subject for the last 30 years has been to evade rather than to investigate its merits; whilst the doctrines promulgated against a general system of improvement have unhappily had a serious and deleterious effect upon the public mind. . . .

The people now perceive that they have endured a state of privation, which sad experience shows to be a downward course, and when long forbearance would be but an aggravation of the evil. But the people, knowing their interest, with a voice not to be resisted hath proclaimed aloud that the period has arrived when SOMETHING OUGHT, SOMETHING CAN, and when SOMETHING MUST BE DONE to arrest the progress of our down hill march.—*Legislative Documents, 1833.*

93. PLIGHT OF A TRAVELER IN THE SOUTH, 1835

One of the most conspicuous foreign visitors in the thirties was Harriet Martineau, the French "deaf lady." She traveled in America for more than two years and wrote extensively about her observations. In the following she depicts the hardships of travel by stage coach in the Carolinas and Virginia.

I FOUND, in travelling through the Carolinas and Georgia, that the drivers consider themselves entitled to get on by any means they can devise; that nobody helps and nobody hinders them. It was constantly happening that the stage came to a stop on the brink of a wide and deep puddle, extending all across the road. The driver helped himself, without scruple, to as many rails of the nearest fence as might serve to fill up the bottom of the hole, or break our descent into it. On inquiry, I found it was not probable that either road or fence would be mended till both had gone to absolute destruction.

The traffic on these roads is so small, that the stranger feels himself almost lost in the wilderness. In the course of several days' journey, we saw, (with the exception of the wagons of a few encampments) only one vehicle besides our own. . . .

An account of an actual day's journey will give the best idea of what travelling is in such places. We had travelled from Richmond, Virginia, the day before, (March 2nd, 1835), and had not had any rest, when, at midnight, we came to a river which had no bridge. The "scow" had gone over with another stage, and we stood under the stars for a long time hardly less than an hour. The scow was only just large enough to hold the coach and ourselves; so that it was thought safest for the passengers to alight, and go on board on foot. In this process I found myself over the ankles in mud. A few minutes after we had driven on again, on the opposite side of the river, we had to get out to change coaches; after which we proceeded, without accident, though very slowly, till daylight. Then the stage sank down into a deep rut, and the horses struggled in vain. We were informed that we were "mired," and must all get out. I stood for sometime to witness what is very pretty for one; but wearisome when it occurs ten times a day. The driver carries an axe, as a part of the stage apparatus. He cuts down a young tree, for a lever, which is introduced under the nave of the sunken wheel; a log serving for a block. The gentlemen passengers all help; shouting to the horses, which tug and scramble as vigorously as the gentlemen. We ladies sometimes gave our humble assistance by blowing the driver's horn. Sometimes a cluster of negroes would assemble from a neighbouring plantation; and in extreme cases, they would bring a horse, to add to our team. The rescue from the rut was effected in any time from a quarter of an hour to two hours. . . .

Half a mile before reaching the place where we were to have tea, the thorough-brace broke, and we had to walk through a snow shower to the inn. We had not proceeded above a quarter of a mile from this place when the traces broke. After this, we were allowed to sit still in the carriage till near seven in the morning, when we were approaching Raleigh, North Carolina. We then saw a carriage "mired" and deserted by driver and horses, but tenanted by some travellers who had been waiting there since eight the evening before. While we were pitying their fate, our vehicle once more sank into a rut. It was, however, extricated in a short time, and we reached Raleigh in safety.—Harriet Martineau, *Society in America* (London, 1837), II, 172-76.

94. ESTABLISHMENT OF STATE HOSPITAL FOR THE INSANE

As early as 1817 Archibald D. Murphey had advocated "An Asylum for the Deaf and Dumb" as a part of his comprehensive plan of public education for North Carolina. It was many years, however, before the state legislature seriously considered this problem. In his message of 1842, Governor Morehead advocated "the establishment of asylums for the Deaf, Dumb, and Blind, and for the protection of the unfortunate Lunatic." Again in 1844, in a special message, he directed the attention of the General Assembly to the problem of the dependent, defective, and delinquent classes in the state. He estimated the number of deaf and dumb in the state to be 283, the blind, 223, and the insane, 582. He advocated a legislative appropriation of $75,000 to cover buildings and equipment for the education and care of these unfortunates. The legislature took action on part of his recommendation and enacted a law in 1845 establishing a school for the education of the deaf, dumb, and blind. $5,000 was appropriated from the Literary Fund, to be supplemented by local county taxes of $75 for each student. Mr. W. D. Cooke was the head of the school thus established, holding this position until 1860. A department for the education of the blind was postponed until 1851 owing to the lack of applicants as well as to the scarcity of trained teachers.

The Act of 1845 made no provision for the care of the insane. Consequently an intensive "campaign of education" now began, which finally led to the establishment of the institution commonly known as "Dix Hill." The most outstanding leader in this movement was Dorothea Lynde Dix, of Massachusetts, one of America's most prominent humani tarian reformers. Miss Dix spent ten weeks in the state collecting data about North Carolina's insane population. She went from county to county investigating the county homes and jails, and even going into private homes to study the care of the insane there. She found more than one thousand cases of insanity in the state, cared for by four different methods. In a forty-eight page memorial to the General Assembly of North Carolina, she reviewed the conditions existing throughout the state and made an eloquent appeal for the establishment of a state hospital for the care of the insane. Governor Graham endorsed her memorial, but the legislature was afraid that the establishment of such an institution would lead to increased taxes. Several legislative efforts to establish an insane asylum failed and the cause seemed lost, when, on December 22, 1848, Mr. James C. Dobbin procured a reconsideration of the measure. He introduced an amendment to the original bill calling for a tax of 1¾ cents on the $100 valuation of land and 5¼ on the poll for four years. "Supporting his proposal with an impassioned appeal, traditions of which still linger about the Capitol, he won a great triumph and secured the passage of his amendment by a vote of 91 to 10." The bill passed the Senate a few days later.

A beautiful hill near Raleigh was chosen as the site for the hospital. The first building was begun in 1850 and the first patients were admitted in 1856. In 1852 the tax of 1848 was continued for three years. Since 1856 direct appropriations have been made, supplemented by local county taxes for the care of the indigent insane. The first head of the institution was Dr. E. C. Fisher.

GOVERNOR MOREHEAD'S MESSAGE TO THE GENERAL ASSEMBLY, 1844

ASYLUMS

FOR more than a century and a quarter the Legislature of this State has been engaged in making laws for the benefit of that class of its citizens which least needed aid, while the helpless and afflicted children of misfortune, are almost wholly disregarded. Although we possess a large fund applied to the purposes of general education, no provision whatever is made whereby the deaf and dumb and blind, those most needing its aid, are benefitted. The facility with which they can be taught is truly surprising. . . .

Again : no provision is made for their maintenance and support, except what is to be found in the poor laws. Many of them, if educated and instructed in useful employments, would be able to maintain themselves and enjoy life as rational creatures. Without these advantages, we often find them huddled together within the confines of a loathsome Poor House, doomed to while away a miserable existence in wretchedness to themselves, and at an increased expense to those whose duty it is to make for them more ample provision.

The condition of the insane merits your earnest attention. Many of them might be restored to themselves and to their usefulness if an asylum were provided, where skilful and experienced managers could have the supervision and control of the patient. . . . I therefore most earnestly recommend that ample provision be made for the education of the deaf, dumb and blind; for the restoration of the insane, if practicable, and for the comfortable sustenance of all. —*Legislative Documents, 1844-45,* pp. 12-13.

MEMORIAL OF DOROTHEA DIX SOLICITING A STATE HOSPITAL FOR THE INSANE, NOVEMBER, 1848

I come not to urge personal claims, nor to seek individual benefits. I appear as the advocate of those who cannot plead their own cause; I come as the friend of those who are deserted, oppressed, and desolate. In the Providence of God, I am the voice of the maniac whose piercing cries from the dreary dungeons of your jails penetrate not your Halls of Legislation. I am the Hope of the poor crazed beings who pine in the cells, and stalls, and cages, and waste rooms of your poorhouses. I am the Revelation of hundreds of wailing, suffering creatures, hidden in your private dwellings, and in pens and cabins—shut out, cut off from all healing influences, from all mind-restoring cures. . . .

Could the sighs, and moans, and shrieks of the insane throughout your wide-extending land reach you here and now, how would your sensibilities to the miseries of these unfortunates be quickened; how eager would you be to devise schemes for their relief. . . . Could their melancholy histories be spread before you . . . how earnestly would you search out the most approved means of relief; how trifling, how insignificant, by comparison, would appear the sacrifices you are asked to make; . . .

At present there are practiced in the State of North Carolina, four methods of disposing of *more than one thousand* insane, epileptic, and idiotic citizens, viz: In the cells and dungeons of the County jails, in comfortless rooms and cages in the county poor-houses, in the dwellings of private families, and by sending the patients to distant hospitals, more seasonably established in sister States. . . .

It may be here stated that by far the larger portion of the insane, epileptic, and idiots, are detained in or near private families. . . .

If the plea of suffering humanity is insufficient to quicken Legislative interposition, an argument based on indisputable evidence, may be advanced, whose force cannot be slighted; I mean the *economy* directly to individuals, towns, and counties, and remotely, but not less actually to the State, of establishing without delay, a Hospital for the treatment and protection of the insane. . . .

In nearly every jail in North Carolina, have the insane at different times, and in periods varying in duration, been grievous sufferers. . . .

Bereft of reason, man loses everything that renders life valuable. . . . Have pity upon him. . . . Talk not of expense—of the cost of supporting and ministering remedies for these afflicted ones. Who shall dare compute in dollars and cents the worth of one mind! Who will weigh gold against the priceless possession of a sound understanding? You turn not away from the beggar at the door, ready to perish, you open your hand, and he is warmed, and fed, and clothed: will you refuse to the maniac the solace of a decent shelter, the protection of a fit asylum, the care that shall raise him from the condition of the brute, and the healing remedies that shall reillume the temple of reason? Who amongst you is so strong that he may not become weak? Whose reason so sound that madness may not overwhelm in an hour the noblest intellect?—*Memorial Soliciting a State Hospital for the . . . Insane, . . .* House of Commons, Doc. No. 2.

ACT ESTABLISHING A STATE HOSPITAL FOR THE INSANE

That John M. Morehead, of Guilford; Calvin Graves, of Caswell; T. N. Cameron, of Cumberland; G. W. Mordecai, of Wake; C. L. Hinton, of Wake; J. O. Watson, of Johnston, be, and are hereby appointed Commissioners, to select and purchase a tract of land, at fair price, embracing not less than one hundred acres, capable of cultivation . . . for the purpose of prescribing its location. . . .

That a tax of three-fourths of a cent shall be levied on every hundred dollars worth of land; and five and one-quarter of a cent shall be levied on every taxable poll, for the space of four years; and that the proceeds arising from said taxation shall be annually during that period, appropriated for the erection of a Hospital for the Insane. . . .

The admission of insane patients from the several counties of the State shall be in the ratio of their insane population. . . .

Patients in indigent circumstances, while resident in the Hospital, shall, in their own right, or by the State bearing their expenses, be chargeable no more than the actual cost of clothing, nursing, board and medical attendance: paying patients, whose friends pay their expenses, and who are not chargeable upon the counties of the State, shall pay in measure with the care received, the terms being subject to the decision by the Trustees.

The Courts of the State shall have power to commit to said Hospital any individual who has been charged with an offence punishable by imprisonment or death, and who shall have been found to have been insane at the time the offence was committed, and who still continues insane; and the expenses of said individual, if in indigent circumstances, shall be paid by the State.—*Laws of North Carolina, 1848-49*, Chap. I.

95. LIFE AMONG THE CHEROKEES, 1848

Most of the Indians were removed from western North Carolina as a result of a series of treaties negotiated between 1777 and 1835. At the latter date there were 3,644 Cherokees in the region between Asheville and the Tennessee line. These Indians protested vigorously against the removal treaty of 1835. Thereupon an army of seven thousand men, headed by General Scott, was sent to enforce the treaty provisions. This was no easy matter as most of the Indians hid in the fastnesses of the rugged mountains. Eventually Scott decided to allow many of them to remain, probably one thousand or more. A treaty was negotiated with them in 1846, which recognized their rights and which granted them an annual allowance of $3.20 per capita. William H. Thomas, a sincere friend of the Indians, was appointed Indian Agent.

Charles Lanman visited the Cherokee country in 1848 and wrote a series of letters describing their civilization. These were first published in the *National Intelligencer*. They later appeared in book form under the title *Letters from the Alleghany Mountains*.

LETTER XII. QUALLA TOWN, N. C., MAY, 1848.

QUALLA TOWN is a name applied to a tract of seventy-two thousand acres of land, in Haywood county, which is occupied by about eight hundred Cherokee Indians and one hundred Catawbas. . . . This portion of a much larger number of aborigines, in consideration of their rank and age, and of valuable services rendered to the United States, were permitted by the General Government to remain upon their native soil, while the great body of the Cherokee nation were driven into exile. They (the exiles) amounted in all to more than sixteen thousand souls, *eighteen hundred and fifty* having died on their way to the *"promised land"* beyond the Mississippi. . . . In addition to the Indians above mentioned, it ought to be stated that there is a remnant of two hundred still remaining in the county of Chero-kee. . . .

The Indians of this district, having formed themselves into a regular company, with appropriate regulations, they elected an old friend of theirs, named *William H. Thomas* . . . to become their business chief . . . the Qualla town people are divided into seven clans, and to each clan is assigned what is called a town, over each of which presides a regular chief. . . . The names of the clans are: In-e-chees-quah, or Bird Clan; In-egil-lohee, or Pretty-faced Clan; In-e-wo-tah, or Paint Clan; In-e-wah-he-yah, or Wolf Clan; In-e-se-ho-nih, or Blue Clan; In-e-co-wih, or Deer Clan; and In-e-eo-te-ca-wih, the meaning of which is not known. And among the customs which prevail among these clans is one which prevents their marrying among themselves, so that they have to select their wives from a neighboring fraternity. . . .

About three-fourths of the entire population can read in their own language, and, though the majority of them understand English, a very few can speak the language. They practice, to a considerable extent, the science of agriculture, and have acquired such a knowledge of the mechanic arts as answers them for all ordinary purposes, for they manufacture their own clothing, their own ploughs, and other farming utensils, their own axes, and even their own guns. Their women are no longer treated as slaves, but as equals; the men labor in the fields and their wives are devoted entirely to household employments. They keep the same domestic animals that are kept by their white neighbors, and cultivate all the common grains of the country. They are probably as temperate as any other class of people on the face of the earth, honest in their business intercourse, moral in their thoughts, words, deeds, and distinguished for their faithfulness in performing the duties of religion. They are chiefly Methodists and Baptists, and have regularly ordained ministers who preach to them on every Sabbath, and they have also abandoned many of their mere senseless superstitions. They have their own courts and try their criminals by a regular jury. Their judges and lawyers are chosen from among themselves. They keep in order the public roads leading through their settlement. By a law of the State they have the right to vote, but seldom exercise that right, as they do not like the idea of being identified with any of the political parties. Excepting on festive days, they dress after the manner of the white man, but far more picturesquely. They live in small log houses of their own construction, and have everything they need or desire in the way of food. They are, in fact, the happiest community I have yet met with in this Southern country, and no candid man can visit them without being convinced of the wickedness and foolishness of that policy of the Government which has always acted upon the opinion that the red man could not be educated into a reasonable being.—Charles Lanman, *Letters from the Alleghany Mountains*, pp. 93-94.

96. SOCIAL AND ECONOMIC CONDITIONS IN NORTH CAROLINA, 1850-1860

Frederick Law Olmsted, a landscape architect by profession and an abolitionist by avocation, was one of America's most outstanding travelers and observers in the ante-bellum period. In the years 1852-1856, he traveled extensively in the South and Southwest, and later published three volumes based upon his observations. His books throw much light upon the economic and social history of the "cotton kingdom."

NEGROES ON PUBLIC CONVEYANCES

Among our inside passengers, in the stage-coach, was a free colored woman; she was treated in no way differently from the white ladies. My roommate said this was entirely customary at the South, and no Southerner would ever think of objecting to it. Notwithstanding which, I have known young Southerners to get very angry because negroes were not excluded from the public conveyances in which they had taken passage themselves, at the North; and I have always supposed that where they were so excluded, it was from fear of offending Southern travellers, more than anything else. . . .

GASTON TO RALEIGH—NIGHT TRAINS

The train by which we were finally able to leave Gaston arrived the next day an hour and a half after its advertised time. The road was excellent and speed good, a heavy U rail having lately been substituted for a flat one. A new equipment of the road, throughout, is nearly complete. The cars of this train were very old, dirty, and with dilapidated and moth-eaten furniture. . . . The country passed through, so far as I observed, was almost entirely covered with wood; and such of it as was cultivated, very unproductive. . . .

RALEIGH

The city of Raleigh, the capital of North Carolina, is a pleasing town—the streets wide and lined with trees, and many white wooden mansions, all having little courtyards of flowers and shrubbery around them. The State-House is, in every way, a noble building, constructed of brownish-gray granite, in Grecian style. It stands on an elevated position near the centre of the city, in a square field—which remains in a rude state of undressed nature, and is used as a hog-pasture. . . .

There are several other public buildings and institutions of charity and education, honorable to the State. A church, near the Capitol, not yet completed, is very beautiful; cruciform in ground plan, the walls of stone, and the interior wood-work of oiled native pine, and with, thus far, none of the irreligious falsities in stucco and paint that so generally disenchant all expression of worship in our city meeting-houses. . . .

The country, for miles about Raleigh, is nearly all pine forest, unfertile, and so little cultivated, that it is a mystery how a town of 2,500 inhabitants can obtain sufficient supplies from it to exist. . . .

FARMING CONDITIONS BETWEEN RALEIGH AND FAYETTEVILLE

Stopping frequently, when I came to cultivated land, to examine the soil and the appearance of the stubble of the maize—the only crop in three different fields I made measurements at random of fifty feet each, and found the stalks had stood, on an average, five feet by two feet one inch apart, and that, generally, they were not over an inch in diameter at the butt. . . . A farmer told me that he considered twenty-five bushels of corn a large crop, and that he generally got as much as fifteen. . . . Cotton was the only crop they got any money for. I, nevertheless, did not see a cotton-field during the day. . . .

I do not think I passed in ten miles, more than half a dozen homesteads, and of these but one was above the character of a hut or cabin. . . .

TURPENTINE AND NAVAL STORES

There are very large forests of the long-leafed pine in North and South Carolina, Georgia, and Alabama; and the turpentine business is carried on, to some extent, in all these States. In North Carolina, however, much more largely than in the others; because, in it, cotton is rather less productive than in the others, in an average of years. Negroes are, therefore, in rather less demand; and their owners oftener see their profit in employing them in turpentine orchards than in the cotton-fields. . . .

The farmer, in the forest, makes nothing for sale but turpentine, and, when he cultivates his land, his only crop is maize; and of this not more than five bushels from an acre is usually obtained. Few turpentine farmers raise as much maize as they need for their own family; and those who carry on the business most largely and systematically, frequently purchase all the food for their hands. Maize and bacon are, therefore, very largely imported into North Carolina, chiefly from Ohio. . . .

If we enter, in the winter, a part of the forest that is about to be converted into a "turpentine orchard," we come upon negroes engaged in making boxes, in which the sap is to be collected the following spring. They continue at this work from November to March, or until, as the warm weather approaches, the sap flows freely, and they are needed to remove it from the boxes into barrels. These "boxes" are cavities dug in the trunk of the tree itself. A long, narrow ax, made in Connecticut, especially for this purpose, is used for this wood-pecking operation; and some skill is required to use it properly.

The boxes are made at from six inches to a foot above the roots, and are shaped like a distended waist-coat pocket. The lower lip is horizontal—the upper, arched. On a tree of medium size, a box should be made to hold a quart. An expert hand will make a box in less than ten minutes. . . .

The sap begins to flow about the fifteenth of March, and gradually fills the boxes, from which it is taken by a spoon or ladle, of a peculiar form, and collected into barrels. The turpentine barrels are made by negro coopers; the staves split from pine-logs, shaved and trimmed. They are hooped with split oak-saplings. Coopers wages, when hired out, are from $1.50 to $2.00 a day. A good cooper is expected to make six or seven barrels a day. They are of the rudest construction possible—thirty inches long and eighteen inches diameter, headed up at both ends, with a square hole in one end, where the turpentine is poured in.

The stills used for making spirits or oil of turpentine from the crude gum, are of copper, not materially different in form from common ardent-spirit stills, and have a capacity of from five to twenty barrels.

The turpentine lands were valued at from $5 to $20 an acre. . . .

A North Carolina turpentine orchard, with the ordinary treatment, lasts fifty years. The turpentine business is considered to be extremely favorable to health and long life.

The negroes employed in this branch of industry seemed to me to be unusually intelligent and cheerful. Decidedly they are superior to the great mass of white people—inhabiting the turpentine forest. Among the latter there is a large number, I should think a majority, of entirely uneducated poverty-stricken vagabonds. . . . They are poor, having almost no property but their own bodies; and the use of these, that is, their labor, they are not accustomed to hire out statedly and regularly so as to obtain capital by wages, but only occasionally by the day or job, when driven to it by necessity. A family of these people will commonly hire, or "squat" and build, a little log cabin, so made that it is only a shelter from rain—They will cultivate a little corn, and possibly a few roods of potatoes, cow-peas, and colewarts. They will own a few swine, that find their living in the forest . . . and the men, ostensibly occupy most of their time in hunting.

A gentleman of Fayetteville told me that he had, several times, appraised, under oath, the whole household property of families of this class at less than $20. . . .

NORTH CAROLINA FISHERIES—SLAVE FISHERMEN

The shad and herring fisheries upon the sounds and inlets of the North Carolina coast are an important branch of industry, and a source of considerable wealth. The men employed in them are mainly negroes, slave and free; and the manner in which they are conducted is interesting, and in some respects novel.

The largest sweep seines in the world are used. One sweep seine was over two miles in length. It was manned by a force of forty negroes, most of whom were hired at a dollar a day, for the fishing season, which usually commences between the tenth and fifteenth of March, and lasts fifty days. In favorable years the profits are very large. . . .

NORTH CAROLINA CHARACTER

North Carolina has a proverbial reputation for the ignorance and torpidity of her people; being in this respect, at the head of the Slave States. I do not find the reason of this in any innate quality of the popular mind; but, rather, in the circumstances under which it finds its development. Owing to the general poverty of the soil in the Eastern part of the State, and to the almost exclusive employment of slave labor on the soils productive of cotton; owing, also, to the difficulty and expense of reaching market with bulky produce from the interior and western districts, population and wealth is more divided than in the other Atlantic States; industry is almost entirely rural, and there is but little communication or concert of action among the small and scattered proprietors of capital. For the same reason, the advantages of education are more difficult to be enjoyed, the distance at which families reside apart preventing children from coming together in such numbers as to give remunerative employment to a teacher. . . . More than one fourth of the native white adults cannot read and write. . . . —Frederick Law Olmsted, *A Journey in the Seaboard Slave States* (New York, 1856), pp. 353-407.

97. COURT PROCEDURE AND SOCIAL LIFE IN THE MOUNTAIN COUNTIES, 1853-1854

The following extracts are taken from A. S. Merrimon's "Journal on the Circuit, beginning with the Fall Term of the Superior Court for Buncombe County, October 8th, 1853." At that time Merrimon was practising law in Asheville. He was a Whig and a Unionist. In 1862 he was one of the leaders in the campaign which led to Vance's election as governor. He was judge of the Superior Court, 1865-67. He was defeated for the governorship in 1872, but in November of that year he defeated Vance for the United States Senate, where he served one term. He was associate justice of the North Carolina Supreme Court from 1883 to 1889 and chief justice of that body from 1889 to 1892, the date of his death.

The circuit covered by the Merrimon Journal included Buncombe, Madison, Cherokee, Jackson, Haywood, Henderson, and Yancey counties. Jewell Hill, which the Journal referred to frequently, was the county seat of Madison, and was a few miles north of Marshall. This document, which consists of 115 pages of manuscript, throws much light on social conditions in the mountain counties and contains splendid characterizations of the lawyers in that part of the state.

THURSDAY OCT. 13TH. 1853.

. . . THE Court opened this morning at 10 O'Clock, the usual hour. A case of Slander has occupied the greater portion of the time of the Court to day. . . . I noticed a good deal of drinking going on to day, and whiskey drinkers have to day, I suppose, been carrying out this very consistent principle of that class: That to drink in damp and cold weather will warm them and to drink in hot weather it will cool them. . . .

MONDAY OCT. 17TH. 1853.

This morning I reached Jewell Hill about ten O'Clock. Had a rough ride over mountains and hills.—I found quite a crowd of people awaiting the arrival of the Court Judge Caldwell arrived about the same time with myself and opened Court in a verry bad house.—Open, without seats fit to sit on and without any place to do business. . . . The Crowd in attendance were "getting in a weaving way" about night. Some twenty or thirty women were present and most of them were drunk, or partially so, and the majority of the men were drunk.—I do not know any rival for this place in regard to drunkeness, ignorance, superstition and the most brutal debauchery. I regret that it is so, yet it is true. Scores of women attend this court for the sole purpose of drinking and pandering to the lustful passions of dirty men, and I regret so exceedingly to say, that some men, I will not say gentlemen, are guilty of intercours with these dirty, filthy strumpets, that ought to be, and one would think that are far above doing such things. . . .

TUESDAY OCT. 18TH. A. D. 1853.

. . . Yesterday the Judge ordered the whiskey wagons to be removed, and thus we have not been so much disturbed with drunkeness as yesterday. As soon, however, as court adjourned this evening the whole crowd hurried to the Court House Door—and such a drunken crowd, I have seldom seen. . . . I saw persons so drunk they could not walk, and their friends were dragging them along to their homes. . . .

CHEROKEE COUNTY COURT
THURSDAY DEC. 1ST. 1853.

. . . We travailed thirty five miles today, over bad road. This is a good day's ride for this season of the year. We stopped at a house, that did not look the most inviting in the world and stayed all night. We expected rough accomodations and we received them. . . . The house was small, a common log cabin, not put up in the best style by any means and not the most comfortable Our host was kind and accomodating however, and we made the best of our evening. . . . Our hostess was a plain and unfashionably dressed old lady that did not (have) much to say. Several lasses, enlivened the scene. These were the daughters of our host. They relished the various topics of conversation, which were principally "unmarked hogs," "wild hogs," "boars," "mountain boomers," and the like. . . .

The beds were all in the same room. Our covering was stiff as pasteboards and our pillows about as large as my fist. We made the best of the night, learned something of the ways of many in this world. . . . Our host only charged fifty cents. . . .

MONDAY DEC. 5TH. 1853.

. . . The new State road traversing the country from Asheville to the extreme Western limit of the State, has greatly improved the county and its travail will be felt more sensibly every year. Several Rail Road projects are comeing forward that are expected to benefit this part of N. C. greatly if carried out. The county is beautiful, the soil very productive, the mountain rich and the range in summer unsurpassed. The County deserves to be improved and it will be. Murphy is a small place and poorly improved. . . . The situation of the village is beautiful. and a most beautiful town might be built here. . . .

NEAR WEBSTER, JACKSON COUNTY
JACKSON COUNTY COURT.

. . . Almost every man at court had some business with me, and in a majority of cases the business amounted to nothing. . . . I think I can say with safety, that I have never been at a place, or in a County, where there seemed to be as much Mallice and diabolical revenge.—Revenge seems to rankle in the bosom of every one. . . .

HAYWOOD COUNTY COURT.

. . . Haywood is probably the highest county, above the level of the sea, east of the Rocky Mountains. I have never received much encouragement from this county. . . . Waynesville is a dirty small village and there is no place of entertainment in it fit to stay at.—One would suppose it to be a large negro quarter to see it from a distance. The buildings are poor and decayed. The Court house is a verry bad one. The best building in the place is the Jail, a new building. . . .

MADISON COUNTY COURT.

MONDAY JANUARY 16TH. 1854.

. . . I am glad to see that there is not quite so much drunkeness here as usual, though as it is, one could scarcely credit a recital of the scenes that occur here. A crowd of filthy whisky drinkers collect around a wagon and drink and curse and blackguard beyond description, women and men, and women sell themselves to prostitution of the basest character not unfrequently for whisky. O, wretched state of morals.

YANCY COUNTY COURT

TUESDAY JANUARY 24TH. 1854.

. . . I feel confident in saying that I have never seen a court behave so badly and *keep* such confusion. . . . It is disgraceful that in a country like our own, distinguished for its freedom and equality, justice is permitted to be trampled upon. Men are placed in office, and that by the Legislature of our State, who are ignorant as heathen, and corrupt as demons, to adjudicate the rights of men and to administer the laws of our country. . . . Our public men are too selfish and think too little of the public interest. . . .

WEDNESDAY JANUARY 25TH. 1854.

. . . Only two or three cases have been disposed of and they have been *handled* in the rudest manner. The more I see of the County Courts, the more I wish to see them abolished. Drunkeness has reigned today. A portion of the Court has been drunk all day. . . . One can learn little by conversation here, save how depraved men are.—A. S. Merrimon's "Journal on the Circuit, beginning with the Fall term of the Superior Court for Buncombe County, October 8th, 1853," *North Carolina Historical Review*, VIII (July, 1931), 300-30.

VII

ANTE-BELLUM ECONOMIC DEVELOPMENT

98. THE IRON INDUSTRY IN NORTH CAROLINA PRIOR TO 1860

Iron-making has been called "a forgotten industry of North Carolina." A small amount of pig iron was shipped to England during the colonial period, but the industry amounted to little in North Carolina until the Revolution. There were only two furnaces in active operation in the colony as late as 1770. During the Revolution the iron industry was stimulated by bounties offered by the Provincial Congress for the production of pig iron, nails, steel, and other products. There was talk of making the Deep River country the "Sheffield of North Carolina." After the Revolution the iron industry declined.

The North Carolina General Assembly enacted a law in 1788 "to encourage the building of iron works in the State," offering three thousand acres of vacant land to every set of works erected in the state, and if the works went into operation within three years of the grant and produced five thousand weight of iron the land was to be tax exempt for ten years. This was a boon to the iron industry and many small furnaces and forges were erected between 1790 and 1800.

Some iron was produced in Nash, Johnston, and other eastern counties, but most of the iron works were in the Piedmont. Lincoln County was the leader. In 1823 there were ten forges and four furnaces in active operation in that county, with a total output of over nine hundred tons of bar iron. Most of the large iron works were owned by a few men, the most important of whom were Peter Forney, Alexander Brevard, Joseph Graham, and John Fulenwider.

Iron-making in North Carolina could hardly be called an independent industry. It was subsidiary to the agricultural operations of the plantation, and the risks of iron production were greater than those of cotton culture. Some individuals made money in iron-making, but most of them did not. The peak of production was reached about 1830 with an output of one thousand eight hundred tons of pig iron. By 1840 the problem of wood for charcoal was causing difficulty, and by 1850 production had dropped to four hundred tons. Efforts were made to revive the iron industry in the fifties, following the discovery of bituminous coal in the Deep River Valley. One of the arguments used for railroad construction at that time was that it would stimulate iron production.

The following extracts are taken from the geological reports of Olmsted, Mitchell, and Emmons.

OLMSTED'S REPORT, 1824

I HAVE been informed that the iron of Nash County was wrought for some years—that the works rented for fifteen hundred dollars per annum, and the manufacture was a profitable concern, but the works were consumed by fire and have not since been rebuilt. A bloomery was also established some years since in Johnston, five miles west of Smithfield, where a quantity of bar-iron was manufactured, which is said to have been of excellent quality, and to have met with a ready sale on the spot at ten dollars per hundred.
. . .

The Iron beds of Stokes and Surry are numerous, consisting of parallel ridges that lie chiefly between the Yadkin on the south, and the Virginia line on the north, and are opened in various places over a space not less than thirty miles broad. . . . The Iron beds of Lincoln occupy a ridge of mica slate . . . which runs nearly parallel with the Blue Ridge, at the distance of fifty miles, extending from the base of Little mountain on the north, to the foot of King's mountain on the south . . . this ridge traverses nearly the whole of the county of Lincoln. . . .

The manufacturing of these ores, constitutes one of the most enterprising objects of the western district. In Lincoln, there are ten forges and four furnaces, where, in the year 1823 (as I learned from Gen. Graham) were made about 900 tons of bar-iron, and 200 tons of castings. . . . In the northern counties bar-iron alone is manufactured, and this is made altogether in bloomeries without the aid of a furnace . . . most of the Iron Works of the west, are kept in operation only in the fall and winter months, the remaining seasons of the year being devoted to agriculture. . . .

The ores which occur in the northern counties are almost wholly of the magnetic kind; more of those of Lincoln are unmagnetic, though the former are very abundant. . . .

The ponderous character of the cinders, that are found in the vicinity of all the bloomeries that I have visited in this State, suggests that, by the aid of a blast furnace and limestone, this slag itself might be profitably wrought.—Denison Olmsted, *Report on the Geology of North Carolina, November, 1824*, pp. 102-3, 118-22.

MITCHELL'S REPORT, 1827

It is probable therefore, that the mineral riches of the western counties will be limited to their beds of limestone and iron ore, and as the county of Lincoln was the first to embark in the iron manufacture, so it is probable that she will maintain the standing she has acquired. The superior excellence of the ores from which the metal is extracted contributing along with the skill and judgment with which the business is conducted, to produce an excellent kind of iron, warrants this conclusion. Nor is the demand just at present, greater than this single county might supply.—Elisha Mitchell, *Report of North Carolina, Part III, November, 1827*, p. 26.

EMMONS' REPORT, 1856

Chatham county . . . can furnish within the radius of seven or eight miles, five kinds of ore in abundance. . . . Pennsylvania. . . . can make iron cheaply by her anthracite, but no cheaper than it can be made on Deep river by bituminous coal or coke . . . What I wish to say is, that in the coal of Deep river, the manufacturer has all the material he can want for this purpose; and if a better article of iron can be made from coke than by anthracite, then in a district of equal extent, North-Carolina has advantages over Pennsylvania, for the manufacture of iron. In proof of this, I repeat that she has, 1st. The peculiar ore of the coal fields; 2nd. The magnetic, specular and haematitic ores of the primary and palaeozoic rocks in immediate proximity; 3d. The use of coke by which to make the iron; 4th. A fine agricultural region for the cereals, and 5th. A milder climate and rivers both for moving machinery and transportation, which is unobstructed in the winter. The cost of living, and the means for conducting the business, will be much cheaper. . . . — Ebenezer Emmons, *Geological Report of the Midland Counties of North Carolina, 1856*, pp. 123-24.

99. PLANK ROADS—THE "FARMERS' RAILROADS"

One of the first phases of the "good roads" movement in North Carolina is to be found in the plank road experiments of the fifties. Toll roads, operated by private companies, had been in operation in the state for many years. The plank road was the last stand of the toll road as a major factor in our transportation system.

Plank roads were first used in Russia. The earliest experiment in America was in Canada in 1834. This proved successful, and in a few years a veritable plank road fever seized the United States. Between 1849 and 1860, North Carolina incorporated no less than eighty-one companies, whose authorized capital stock aggregated $5,807,500. Much of this stock was never paid, and consequently many of these roads were not constructed.

The "farmers' railroads," as the plank roads were called, were built by private companies and were operated as toll roads. In organization, privileges, and liabilities they were quite similar to the old turnpike companies. They were considered as "feeders" of the railroad, not as rivals to it. Advocates of plank roads declared that they were the best roads imaginable. "All classes profited, but the farmer gained most directly. Their peculiar merit was the diminution of friction, by which a horse was enabled to draw from two to three times as great a load as he could do on the ordinary road." The speed on the plank road was greater. It would make the farmer more independent. Instead of being forced to market his crops in dry weather, when his labor was needed on the farm, he could deliver his goods to market when bad weather prevented farm work. De Bow declared, "The plank road is the road of the people, open to all, affording relief to the beast of burden and affording a delightful means of travel. . . . Even in country where stone is abundant and wood comparatively scarce, they are one-half cheaper than macadamized roads, and one-fourth the cost of railroads. In the whole history of internal improvement there is scarcely anything to surpass the rapidity with which this system has developed itself." *Hunt's Merchant's Magazine* said, "The railroad is the thoroughfare of the citizen away from home—for travel; but the plank road is for home use."

On the whole, the North Carolina plank roads were very small enterprises, ranging in capital from $200,000 to $2,500. Few of them exceeded $50,000 in authorized capital. In the main, they were financed by the people living along the road and the business interests of the towns in which they centered. The State of North Carolina invested a total of $180,000 in three of the plank road companies: $120,000 in the Fayetteville and Western, $50,000 in the Fayetteville and Centre, and $10,000 in the Fayetteville and Warsaw.

The principal plank roads radiated from Fayetteville, which was the center of the wagon trade of the state. The name of Fayetteville appeared in seven companies. Most of the roads were located in the naval stores section, though some were to be found in all parts of the state.

The first plank road in North Carolina was the Fayetteville and Western, incorporated in. 1849 and completed about 1854. The "Appian Way" of North Carolina, as this road has been called, ran from Fayetteville via Salem to Bethania a distance of 129 miles. It was the longest plank road ever built in the world. "For fifteen years it served as a commercial artery from the inland section to the wharves at the head of navigation in Fayetteville."

Another prominent and profitable road was the Greenville and Raleigh Plank Road, which did much to promote the naval stores industry in that section of the state.

There was considerable criticism of the Fayetteville and Western road when it began. One newspaper called it a "monument of folly." Other critics maintained that the work was progressing too slowly, that the contracts had been improperly let, that the grading had been poorly done, that the lumber and sills were of poor quality, that the planks would wear out and decay in a short time, and that the road was not properly located. As the road progressed and as trade along its route increased, criticism practically disappeared.

The roads were surveyed, graded, and allowed to settle; heavy sills or sleepers made out of pine were then placed end to end, lengthwise. These hewed stringers cost about $3 per 1,000 feet. The planks were of heart pine, 9 to 16 inches wide, and 3 to 4 inches thick, laid directly across the sills at right angles to the line of the road. Most of the roads were 8 feet wide or more. Necessary culverts and ditches were made in order to insure a dry road bed. "Turnouts" were provided at intervals along the road. The cost of construction averaged about $1,500 per mile. It was estimated that a plank road would last five to seven years before serious repairs were needed and that within ten years the entire flooring would have to be replaced.

According to the laws of incorporation, "reasonable tolls" were to be charged after five miles of the road were completed. Plank road companies were not to be allowed to make more than 20 to 25 per cent on their capital in any one year. The toll levied on the Fayetteville and Western Plank Road was ½c per mile for a man on horseback; 1c for a one-horse team; 2c for a two-horse team; 3c for a three-horse team; 4c for a six-horse team. There was a fine of $5 for riding or driving between the toll gates for the purpose of avoiding tolls. Toll gates were constructed at intervals along the roads. There were fifteen such toll houses between Bethania and Fayetteville.

The plank roads were prosperous for a few years. It was a short-lived prosperity, however. The first cost was not so great, but depreciation was tremendous. The planks wore out rapidly and decayed more rapidly. The "excessive cost of maintaining a usable surface doomed the plank roads to failure." Bad crops, the panic of 1857, and the competition of the railroad also contributed to the decline and failure of the "farmers' railroads." They had practically disappeared by 1860.

THE FARMERS' RAILROADS

To AN inland town like ours, roads are substitutes for navigable rivers. The more widely they radiate in every direction, and the better their condition, the greater will be our prosperity. . . . Of all modes of improving their surface, Plank Roads are the most effectual, at the smallest cost. . . .

Plank roads, therefore, enable a horse to do more than any other arrangement, except railroads. But invaluable as the latter are to the hurrying traveller—the ordinary roads, on which every farmer can drive his own team, when not needed for the farm labors, are incomparably more useful to the community at large—and of all

such, plank roads are the perfection. They are the *Farmers' Railroads.—Raleigh Register,* February 28, 1849.

THE FAYETTEVILLE AND WESTERN PLANK ROAD COM-
PANY INCORPORATED, *1849*

Sec. 1. That it shall be lawful to open books in the town of Fayetteville . . . and in the town of Salisbury . . . and at such other
places . . . for the purpose of receiving subscriptions to the amount
not exceeding two hundred thousand dollars, in shares of fifty dollars each, for the purpose of communicating by means of a plank
road from the town of Fayetteville to the town of Salisbury, by the
most practicable route, to be determined by the said company, after
the same shall have been formed. . . .

Sec. 3. When $25,000 shall be subscribed, the subscribers are to
be incorporated into a company by the name and style of "The
Fayetteville and Western Plank Road Company," and by that name
shall be capable in law of purchasing, holding, selling, leasing and
conveying estates, real and personal and mixed. . . .

Sec. 15. The President and directors may demand and receive,
at some convenient toll gates to be by them erected, a reasonable
toll from all persons using said plank road, or any of its branches,
which toll so to be collected, shall be so regulated, that the profits
shall not exceed 20 per cent of the capital of said company in any one
year.

Sec. 16. The road shall be not less than ten feet nor more than
thirty feet wide. . . .

Sec. 20. Whenever one-fifth of the capital stock of said company
shall be subscribed by individuals or corporations . . . the Treasurer of the State . . . shall be directed to subscribe one-fifth of
said capital stock of said company for and on behalf of the State ;
and whenever another fifth of such capital stock shall be subscribed
. . . the treasurer of the State . . . shall subscribe two-fifths more
of the capital stock for and on behalf of the State, so that the State
shall hold an interest of three-fifths of the proposed capital stock of
said company. . . .

Sec. 22. The State shall issue bonds to pay for stock. . . . —
Laws of North Carolina, 1848-49, pp. 183-92.

ADVANTAGES TO BE DERIVED FROM PLANK ROADS

This system of improved transportation is exactly adapted to the
wants of our State and particularly middle and western North
Carolina. These roads can be built cheap. These roads work no

violent change in their habits. They double the value of the means which every farmer has for going to market. He does the work with two horses that he would do with four; his wagons and gear are doubled in value, for they will last double the time they would on roads he has been accustomed to travel to market.

Our people will find it to their interest to extend the construction of these roads. Simple and cheap as they will be found to be they will radiate it is to be hoped, from every market town and spread over the whole state. . . .

The tolls should be so low as to induce travel, yet they should be so laid as to produce a revenue to the stockholders and thus induce capital to be applied to the extension of this system of roads. The use of teams with more than two horses should be discouraged, until the road is extended. . . .

The line of road is well located for branches. . . . The present capital must be used to complete the line designated by the charter, but the capital can be increased to $300,000. On the north, a branch may be very profitably thrown out for 9½ miles, striking Deep River at Watson's Bridge. Another through a populous and wealthy region of country, to Salem and Greensborough, both important and thriving points, particularly the latter.—*First Annual Report of the President of the Fayetteville and Western Plank Road Company, April, 1850.*

COST OF CONSTRUCTION

The cost of the Road to Little River, 12⅝ miles, was $19,468.62. Of the six miles beyond Little River, $7,727.95. Of the 23 miles to Carthage, $30,628.58. To this should be added, cost of bridges, right of way, toll houses, land &c., which with the above amounts to $57,825.18, or an average of $1468.27. . . . The President estimates the cost of the road from Fayetteville to Johnsonville, 88 miles at $125,384.15. . . . Beyond Johnsonville, the cost is estimated at $1750 per mile. . . . Lines have been surveyed to Lexington, the Yadkin River, Mocksville and Salisbury; about 14 miles on the route to Salem.

The Report states . . . that the increase in the value of land between this place and Carthage, has been more than the whole cost of the Road between those points. The increase in the value of property in Carthage has been more than the amount of stock subscribed in the whole county of Moore and the appearance of that place has generally improved. More than 20 buildings, including the Saw Mills, have been erected along the line of the

Road, and a Turpentine Distillery is going up about 8 miles from this place.

A Dividend of one per cent was declared, equal to more than 7 per cent on the cost of the Road from which tolls were collected. —*Fayetteville Observer*, April 15, 1851.

EXTENSION OF ROAD URGED

We have received for Tolls collected the past year the gross amount of $2,718.44. Tolls have been collected for three months on 12 miles, and for nine months on 18 miles.

The number of vehicles passing the Toll-gate at Fayetteville is 9546.

The amount received for Tolls would have been very largely increased if the crops the past year had been good. . . .

The surveys have extended on through Lexington to Mocksville, about 14 miles on towards Salem, to Salisbury, to Deep River. . . .

We have paid for the right of way, to this date, $714.23. . . .

In selecting lines of location, if, without any sacrifice of the interests of the Company, an individual, a neighborhood or a village could be accommodated, it should be done. . . .

We have paid for Steam Mills to this date $15,380.07. There are charges yet to go to this account, which will make the average cost of the five Mills now owned by the Company $3,200. . . . The Mills are doing good work, and make from 40 to 50,000 feet of Plank Road Lumber every 24 hours. . . .

We have paid for land for Toll-houses, and fencing, to this date, $900.85, which includes the Toll-house, &c. at Fayetteville, and the one at Little River. . . .

From Johnsonville, in Randolph county, it is thought that the line could be located to a point from which a branch could be thrown off to Salem, and thence go on to the Virginia line. . . .

The citizens of that prosperous, enterprising and interesting Town have always looked to the Cape Fear as the channel of their trade, Fayetteville has experienced its benefits, and it would be strange if she did not appreciate the wishes of Salem to unite more closely their interests and welfare. . . .

My wish has always been that a line of Plank Road should pass on to Lexington, thence to Mocksville, Statesville, and on to join the Turnpike to the Georgia line, and also the Ashe and Watauga Turnpike,—thus establishing the connection between Western Carolina and the Cape Fear.

If this connection had been made twenty-five years ago, how

vastly improved would be the condition of the middle region of the State. . . .

These roads are extending North, South, East, and West. The Raleigh and Greenville Road has been commenced, and steps taken for the organization of the Taylorsville Plank Road Company.— *Second Annual Report of the President of the Fayetteville and Western Plank Road Company, April 10, 1851, pp. 3-10.*

PLANK ROAD TRAVEL

One of our most successful farmers, a few days ago, brought to town, on the plank road, at one load, with 4 mules, 117 bushels of meal, 200 lbs. of lard, weighing in all about 6,200 pounds. The distance travelled to and fro was 26 miles which was done with ease in one day.

This gentleman is the largest individual stockholder in the road. He is now realizing the benefit of his liberal investment, in the ability to do in one day what would formerly have required three days. —*Fayetteville Observer*, July 15, 1851.

EXTENSION OF WESTERN PLANK ROAD URGED

The extension of the Fayetteville and Western Plank Road, by a branch from a point West of Johnsonville, to Lexington, and thence to Mocksville, is a subject which we hope our friends in that section will not abandon. The trade of this place and we think the income of the Road, would be greatly benefitted by such a branch. There is a scope of country lying South of Salem, in the direction of Salisbury, that would give a fine trade to Fayetteville. . . .

Should the road be extended still further west from Mocksville, either to Statesville or Taylorsville, intersecting the Caldwell and Wautauga Turnpike, which runs from Taylorsville to the Tennessee line, and also the projected Western Turnpike, (a State work), extending to the Georgia line, our western friends will have the benefit of a *Home Market*, and not be compelled to seek a foreign one.— *Fayetteville Observer*, March 25, 1852.

PLANK ROAD DIVIDENDS

It will be seen that the Fayetteville and Western Plank Road. . . the pioneer work of that kind in the South, and we suppose the longest Plank Road in the world, pays the stockholders a semi-annual dividend of *four* per cent. Besides this . . . all the current repairs have been paid for, and 10 per cent of all receipts been invested as part of the permanent fund for reconstruction. . . . We learn that the main road will probably be finished to Salem within two months.—*Fayetteville Observer*, April 14, 1853.

ROAD DOING WELL—STATE MAKING MONEY ON INVESTMENT

The earnings of the Road for the last 6 months amounted to about $6,000; for the last month $1368. . . . A resolution was adopted authorizing the Board to open books of subscription . . . for three branches, to the Coal Mines in Moore and Chatham, to Lexington, and to Greensborough. . . .

The State's Dividend was $7,800. Interest paid by State on-Bonds issued in payment for Stock, is $6,288.75. From which, deduct premium received for the bonds, $1,136.12. Leaving a net profit of $2,647.37. This is the first time the State has made money directly by a subscription to Internal Improvements.—*Fayetteville Observer*, April 13, 1852.

DIVIDENDS OF THE ROAD

We understand that the receipts of tolls exceed those of last year by about $10,000. A semi-annual dividend of 4 per cent has been declared. . . . A meeting has been held in Lexington for the purpose of constructing a branch from this road to Lexington and thence to Mocksville, Davie county. Sufficient stock to build a road from Lexington to Mocksville has already been taken.—*Fayetteville Observer*, April 13, 1854.

FAYETTEVILLE AND WESTERN PLANK ROAD NEARLY COMPLETE

The road is nearly complete, and in successful operation, and the annual meetings now are held, merely for the purpose of electing officers and receiving the encouraging reports of the road's prosperity. . . . The capital stock of the Company now amounts to $253,200; of which $241,294 have been paid in. . . . There are now under toll 140 miles of road—120 on the main road; 20 on branches. The gross tolls for the year ending March 31, 1854 amount to $27,419.77 against $17,398.60 for the year ending March 31, 1853—an increase of rather more than $10,000.—*Fayetteville Observer*, April 17, 1854.

PLANK ROAD GIVES WAY TO MACADAMIZED ROAD

The plank road leading out west, by Fries' factory and the Wachovia steam mills, has been improved by removing the plank and macadamizing it. The need of a renovation of this road was becoming more and more apparent, as the greater portion of the plank was either partly or wholly decayed, and the pieces which yet remained were scattered about in such a manner as to prove dangerous to the traveller, especially after dark.—*Salem Press*, October 1, 1858.

100. THE ADVENT OF THE RAILROAD

The second quarter of the nineteenth century marked the beginning of railroad construction in North Carolina. Two years after the building of the first American railway, Dr. Joseph Caldwell, of the University, published a series of anonymous newspaper articles, which later appeared in book form, *The Numbers of Carlton*. In these articles, he advocated the development of transportation facilities throughout the state and showed the advantages of railroads over canals and turnpikes. Low prices of cotton, soil exhaustion, migration to the West, and other causes had placed the state in dire condition. He proposed to cure these economic ills by the construction of railways. He wanted to develop Beaufort and New Bern. He advocated a railroad from the coast to the mountains, to be built of wooden rails. He thought "iron railways for any considerable distance would be out of the question in this country, as the expense would be far too great." He estimated the cost of a wooden railroad at $2,649 per mile. A poll tax of 37 cents levied by the state would yield sufficient revenue to begin the road. Later work would be financed by tolls from the road. Horsepower was to be used.

Caldwell's proposals evoked considerable newspaper discussion. During the next five years many railroad meetings were held throughout North Carolina. The first meeting of this nature ever held in the state met in the home of William Albright, in Chatham County, August 1, 1828. More than two hundred delegates were present from Chatham, Orange, Guilford, and Randolph. The construction of a central railroad through the state, from east to west, was advocated, and an address on that subject was directed to the citizens of North Carolina.

The first railroad chartered by the legislature was the Fayetteville-Campbellton, 1830-31, although this was not the first road built. The legislature of 1831-32 incorporated three others: the Cape Fear and Yadkin, the North Carolina Central, and the Tarboro and Hamilton. No less than ten railroad companies were chartered by the 1833-34 legislature.

The Raleigh Experimental Railroad was the first railroad actually constructed in North Carolina. This was a little road 1½ miles long, built in 1834 for the purpose of transporting stone from the quarry for the rebuilding of the capitol, which had burned in June, 1831. This road proved to be a great success and stimulated general interest in railroad building.

The first real railroads constructed in North Carolina were the Wilmington and Raleigh and the Raleigh and Gaston. Both of these were begun in 1836 and completed in 1840. The Wilmington and Raleigh, completed March 7, 1840, was 161½ miles long, and was reported to be the longest railroad in the world 'at the time. It had one straight stretch of 48 miles. The gauge of the road was 4 feet 8½ inches. The rails were of heart pine covered with iron strips. The road was built by private enterprise and cost $1,909,755.54. The Raleigh and Gaston, completed in April, 1840, was 85 miles long and ran from Raleigh to Weldon. It was also built by private capital. The total cost was $1,343,380.44.

THE ADVANTAGES OF RAILROADS OVER CANALS

IN THE remarks now to be made, the object is to show in what respects rail-roads are preferable to canals.

1. It is obvious that in determining the course of a canal we must be continually hampered by the necessity of carrying it where there will be at all times a sure and sufficient supply of water. This occasions the meandering of canals along the banks of rivers, and leading them to intersect at proper places, so that their length is extended far more than would be necessary, could this circumstance so essential to *them* be wholly set aside. . . . It would not be extravagant to say, with regard to canals of much extent, that at least one fourth, if not one third, is likely to be added by this single object. . . . Let us remember too, that such a difference has its effects, not only in the first construction and expense, but in all travelling and transportation upon it, and in the maintenance of it in repair through all future time. . . .

2. It is proved by experience that upon an average of one mile with another, a railroad is less costly in its construction than a canal. . . . The excavation, or removal of earth or rocks for the former is much greater than for the latter. The iron necessary is far less costly than we are apt to suppose . . . And let it be considered that a lock cannot be properly completed . . . for less than eight or ten thousand dollars. . . .

3. At least as large a burden, or as many tons, can be transported in the same time and by the same force upon a rail-road as upon a canal. . . . It has been common to remark, and it has been until lately received as a maxim, that conveyance by water must always be less expensive than conveyance by land. This did continue true till the perfection now attained in the construction of roads and carriages, and it is no longer correct in a comparison of rail-roads and canals. . . .

4. The expense of making canals, and for ever attending them, in repairing and keeping them in good condition, and in the erection and maintenance of bridges over them, is greater than any such expense necessary to railroads. When a canal is made through a country, means must be provided at convenient distances for crossing it, to prevent the communication between one part of a farm or neighborhood from being cut off from another. This brings on a multitude of contracts between the public and the owners of lands along the line of a canal, for making and keeping up bridges through all future time. . . .

5. It is much to be apprehended that canals may render unhealthy the parts of the country along their route. The motion of water in a canal, if there be any, is exceedingly slow, so as to approach stagnation. . . .

6. Our principal rivers originate towards the western extremity of the state. Were a canal attempted from the same distance in the interior, the long summers of our southern latitude, drying up all our smaller streams, . . . would make it necessary for such a canal, that it might be fed with certainty, to confine its course to the margin of some main river. . . .

7. It is now ascertained that rail-ways may be constructed with all the necessary strength and firmness, out of wood, at a cost of little more than half of that which must be incurred in making them of iron. . . . The lasting and substantial pine abounding in our low country, and the no less solid oak of the western part, would leave us nothing to desire in compactness, durability, and cheapness of materials. The work, too, would be of a sort that could be executed by our own people, under the direction of an engineer,
. . .

8. Another disadvantage incidental to canals in a comparison with rail-roads, is the interruption of business upon the former for a considerable time in the winter, from their becoming frozen, . . . On such causes as these the rail-road is wholly independent.

9. It is continually evinced by present practice that steam can be employed in transportation by a rail-road. A locomotive engine of ten horse power goes four miles an hour with ninety tons in its train, and twelve miles an hour with twenty-five tons. As to canals for ships or steamboats, they are wholly out of consideration, in speaking of such as are ordinarily constructed through a country.
. . .

Were a rail-way constructed from the mountains to Beaufort on the sea-coast, produce could be transported from one end of it to

the other, through a distance of three hundred miles, in three days.
. . .

. . . The number of taxable polls in the state of North Carolina, is a hundred and thirty-five thousand. . . . An annual payment of thirty-seven cents by each individual, raises at once the sum of fifty thousand dollars a year. It cannot be that the payment of 37 cents a year upon the poll for five years, is so great that we ought not to consent to it, provided we are sure of the result. It is upon this condition then that it is proposed, and upon this alone, that it shall be adequate to procure to the citizens of our state, so easy and cheap a conveyance for their goods and productions, their manufactures and their mines that where it now costs them thirty dollars, it shall not cost them one. . . .

A central rail-road is the common benefactor of all, but it is especially the poor man's friend. . . . The want of it bears with particular hardship upon him. The rich man with his waggon and horses, who can send or go to the best market, distant or near, can do without it, and rarely feels the extremities of distress. To be without the rail-road, is to the poor to be shut out from every opportunity, except selling for such prices as he is forced to take in the little circle of his immediate neighbourhood. . . . —Joseph Caldwell, *The Numbers of Carlton, addressed to the People of North Carolina, on A Central Railroad through the State* (New York, 1828), pp. 9-15, 23, 30, 39, 158, 206-9.

CHATHAM COUNTY RAILROAD MEETING, 1828

A number of inhabitants of Chatham, Randolph, and Orange, and some from Guilford, having assembled for the special purpose of comparing our views respecting the expediency of a central railroad, first from some seaport to the capital of the state, and then by a middle course to its western extremity, solicit your attention. . . .

. . . While other states of this union have for many years actively and successfully exerted themselves in opening the opportunities of commerce to their people, North Carolina has unhappily languished under a spirit of despondency in regard to the possibility of ever attaining to similar privileges. Time was when a vast portion of the interior settlers of other states were in a situation similar to our own. They were intercepted from the market of the world by immense distances, and almost insuperable obstacles. So long as this continued to be the case, they and we went into that market upon some terms of equality. . . . But this no longer continues to be the case. The different states of the union have for many years augmented their population, and while they extended their settlements far into their interior territories, two consequences have resulted which it is important to distinguish. One is the vast abundance of agricultural productions of every description which have been thrown into the market, and the other, a prevention of increased expense and labour in transportation, by making the improvement of their roads and rivers, and the opening of canals keep pace with the extension of their settlements. In our state these improvements have never been realized. . . . Our resources and exertions have been limited in supply, inefficient by dispersion, and we are left to contend with all the primitive obstructions of a natural state. . . . Of most of our people it must certainly be said, that to them no rivers have been made navigable, no canals have been dug, no turnpike roads levelled and paved, no rail-ways constructed. . . . We still remain destitute of all this instrumentality of action, with all its animating and inspiring motives. Hence, though we could once rival, upon something like equal terms, the people of other states in the general market, we can now do it no longer. . . . To enter now the general market from our interior country, and cope with the prices, we must have rail-roads, or canals, or navigable rivers. . . .

. . . Cotton is now almost the only article which bears transportation. But it is much to be apprehended that even cotton will not long remain a source of profit in our present manner of conveyance. . . .

And is this a time, fellow-citizens, for us to continue in supineness and inaction, when even the last remaining prop of our interest in the market of the world is ready to be undermined, and to leave us prostrate in the dust? . . . —Joseph Caldwell, *The Numbers of Carlton*, . . . Appendix, pp. 221-24.

THE EXPERIMENTAL RAILROAD

The State-House of North Carolina, which (together with a large portion of the town) was destroyed by fire, is now in the course of being rebuilt, with the beautiful and excellent granite furnished by the neighboring quarries. . . . A Railway of 1¼ miles, was made from the quarry to the State-House square, solely to bring the stone, and has yielded profitable dividends to the proprietors, and at the same time enabled the transportation of the stone to be effected at one third of the expense that it would otherwise have cost. . . .

This little railroad has doubtless had much effect in promoting the present zeal for similar and more extensive works.—We are

much more ready to be impressed by what we see, than what we hear, . . . and very many, who have come to the seat of government, from every quarter of the state, have been first convinced of the advantages of railways by seeing the enormous masses of stone conveyed as fast and as easily as the empty car could be drawn on good common roads. Of the 2200 yards of the whole road, 1304 required excavation or embankment, the greatest depth being apparently 4 feet and the greatest height eight feet. . . . The total cost of the railway amounted to only $2700 or $2100 the mile.—
Raleigh Register, January 28, 1834.

STATE AID TO RAILROADS

The state of North Carolina, so long taunted as the Rip Van Winkle of the confederacy, has at last been awakened—and has adopted highly important measures, and offered liberal aid, for improving the physical state of the country, and the moral and pecuniary condition of its population. It may be said, . . . that it required the great and unlooked-for treasure furnished in her share of the surplus revenue of the United States, to make North Carolina commence the noble work of aiding her great improvements and developing her great but dormant resources. This, it must be confessed, is true. . . .

Subscription to Railways

By recent enactments, the state of North Carolina has adopted, for certain works only, the plan . . . of paying two-fifths of the expense of all such useful public improvements, by roads, railways, and canals, as shall have the remaining three-fifths paid by individual subscribers. And the great works to which this state bounty has been extended, are the *Central Rail Road*, proposed to run from Beaufort to Fayetteville—the *Fayetteville and Western Rail Road*, (from Fayetteville to the Narrows of the Yadkin, and thence by one branch to Wilkes county, and another to join the Charleston and Cincinnati route)—and the *Wilmington and Halifax Rail Road*, which is already in progress. While heartily applauding the liberal aids offered to these works, we must also condemn the refusal to extend the like measure to the Raleigh and Gaston Rail Road and its continuation towards Columbia, both constituting a most important, and, no doubt, a most profitable part of the great northern-southern line of mail carriage and travel, which will, before long, be complete from Boston to New Orleans. . . . It is true that North Carolina owes this first great railway that is entirely in her

16

territory—and which has led to the success of all the other schemes
now proposed—to the citizens of other states having more confidence
in the value of such a work, than the government of North Carolina,
or many of her citizens. To the enterprise and capital of these "foreigners" (most of whom we are proud to say, are Virginians) North
Carolina will owe, not only this great source of value and profit to
her agriculture, but, *indirectly*, also the establishment of her whole
system of such improvements.—*Farmers' Register*, IV, No. 12 (1837),
pp. 766-68.

OPENING OF THE RALEIGH AND GASTON RAILROAD, 1840

Phizzz-zzz-zzz. This is near, as we can come in type, towards expressing the strange sound which greeted the ears of the assembled
population of our city, on Saturday evening last. About 6 o'clock
of that day, the first Steam Locomotive, that ever snorted amongst
the hills of Crab-tree, reached the limits of our City, and was en-
thusiastically welcomed with every demonstration of joy. The bells
rang, the artillery roared and the people cheered. Huzza! Huzza!!
Huzza!!! The Raleigh and Gaston railroad is completed, and no
mistake. . . .

Magnificent enterprise! We have now ocular demonstration of
that, which no man would have believed thirty years ago, to be
within the compass of human power. . . .

The Raleigh and Gaston railroad is 86 miles in length, and has
been constructed altogether by individual stockholders, the State
having uniformly declined embarking in the enterprize. More than
usual difficulties have presented themselves in the progress of the
work over and above the *natural* obstacles, but they have all vanished
before a determined purpose and nevertiring energy—The whole
line is now finished, is said to be admirably built. . . . We hail the
rumbling of the first locomotive, as the glad omen of future prosperity to our city and county, and feel that we shall not be disappointed.—*Raleigh Register*, March 24, 1840.

BEGINNINGS OF THE NORTH CAROLINA RAILROAD

The late session of the Legislature will mark a new era in the history of the State. . . . A great system of Internal Improvements
has been adopted, which will redeem and disenthrall the State and
the people. A movement has been made which will shake off the
incubus of lethargy and sloth for which we as a people have become
proverbial. . . .

The Central Rail Road, from the day of its commencement, must infuse a spirit of industry and enterprise among the people which has not been felt in many years; and we anticipate a sensible increase in the value of real estate. The expenditure of some three millions of dollars in the employment of the surplus labor of the people, and in the purchase of the products of the soil, will of itself be productive of great good; but this is only an incidental and transient advantage. The permanent benefits it will confer will consist in the facilities of sending agricultural products, as well as those of the mines to market, and of receiving their value in the goods and merchandise of other regions. . . . —*Raleigh Register*, January 31, 1849.

101. GOLD MINING IN NORTH CAROLINA—A FORGOTTEN INDUSTRY

Prior to the discovery of gold in California in 1848, North Carolina was the leading gold producing state. The total amount of the precious metal mined in North Carolina has been estimated at about $24,000,000. There are at least three hundred and fifty localities in the state which have been worked for gold at one time or another. Warren County on the northeast, Moore County on the southeast, and the Tennessee line on the west, mark the approximate limits of the North Carolina gold field. It extends into Virginia on the north, and into South Carolina and Georgia on the south.

According to tradition several gold mines were worked by the Indians before the advent of the white man, but evidence to support this theory is lacking. Indeed, it is very doubtful if any gold was mined during the colonial period.

The first authentic discovery of gold in North Carolina occurred at the Reed mine in Cabarrus County, in 1799, at which date a nugget weighing 3½ pounds was picked up in a creek on the plantation of Joel Reed. Reed carried it to Concord and showed it to a silversmith, who did not know what kind of metal it was. Reed kept it for several years on his house floor, as a door stop. In 1802 he took it to Fayetteville, where he sold it for the "big price" of $3.50. The Reed mine is said to have been the first gold mine in the United States.

Further investigations led to the discovery of many large nuggets, the largest of which weighed 28 pounds and was worth about $8,000. The *Mining Magazine*, October, 1853, estimated that the Reed mine had yielded $10,000,000. This estimate was probably too high, however.

The "gold fever" spread rapidly. As early as 1829, the state was producing more than $100,000 a year. In 1830 there were no less than 56 mines in operation. The *North Carolina Spectator* declared that Mecklenburg County had as many mines as it had square miles, which was probably true. More than 60 mining companies were incorporated in the state between 1817 and 1861. There was "a large demand for native gold by jewelers on account of its beauty."

The principal veins, those in the Gold Hill section of Rowan and adjoining counties, were not discovered until 1842. In a short time, active prospecting was taking place throughout the whole Piedmont section, and the slate formation of that area was commonly called the "Gold Country." Prospectors were referred to as "Gold Hunters."

A branch mint was established at Charlotte in 1838, which coined $5,059,188 worth of gold between that date and 1861. $3,625,840 was coined and fluxed by the private Bechtler mint near Rutherfordton, between 1831 and 1849.

The peak of gold production was reached about 1847, the Charlotte mint coining $478,820 in that year. The "gold rush" to California did not stop gold mining in the state, although production fell off slightly. Yet North Carolina seems to have produced almost as much gold in the fifties as it had mined in the forties. Very little was mined during the Civil War, and at the close of that conflict only one gold mine was in active operation.

The mines were not opened up until some years after the Civil War. When work was resumed, better and more extensive machinery was installed and attempts were made to mine both gold and copper but with indifferent success. An unofficial report in 1891 listed 35 mines in operation. The North Carolina Geological Survey for 1896 named 18 gold mines.

The first official report on the gold mines of North Carolina was made by Denison Olmsted in 1824. This report was made before the discoveries in the Gold Hill section. The earliest geological study of that region was made by Ebenezer Emmons in 1856. Extracts from both of these reports are given in the documents below. John H. Wheeler was superintendent of the Charlotte mint for some time.

DESCRIPTION OF NORTH CAROLINA GOLD MINES, 1824

THE Gold Mines of North-Carolina, which have recently become an object of great inquiry, both at home and abroad, are situated between the 35th and 36th degrees of North Latitude, and near the 81st degree of West Longitude. They are in the southern part of the State, not far from the borders of South-Carolina, and somewhat westward of the centre. Through the Gold Country flows the River Peedee, receiving within the same district two considerable streams, namely, Rocky River from the south, and Uwharee River from the north. Above the junction with the Uwharee, the Peedee bears the name of Yadkin. The Gold Country is spread over a space of not less than 1000 square miles. On a map of the State, one may easily trace the general boundaries, so far at least as they have been hitherto observed. From a point taken 8 miles west by south of the mouth of the Uwharee, with a radius of 18 miles, describe a circle—it will include most of the County of Montgomery, the northern part of Anson, the north-eastern corner of Mecklenburg, Cabarrus as far as a little west of Concord, and corners of Rowan, Davidson, and Randolph. In almost any part of this region, Gold, in greater or less abundance, may be found at or near the surface of the ground. . . .

The Gold Country occupies the southern part of the Slate Formation, . . .

The principal Mines are three—the Anson Mine, Reed's Mine, and Parker's Mine.

The *Anson Mine* is situated in the County of the same name, on the waters of Richardson's Creek, a branch of Rocky River. This locality was discovered only two years since by a "Gold Hunter," one of an order of people that begin already to be accounted a distinct race. . . .

Reed's Mine in Cabarrus, is the one which was first wrought, and at this place indeed were obtained the first specimens of Gold that were found in the Country. A large piece was found in the bed of a small creek which attracted attention by its colour and lustre; but it was retained sometime in the hands of the proprietor, through ignorance whether it was Gold or not. . . .

The first glance is sufficient to convince the spectator, that the business of searching for Gold is conducted under numerous disadvantages, without the least regard to system, and with very little aid from mechanical contrivances. . . .

Large pieces of Gold are found in this region, although their occurrence is somewhat rare. Pieces of 400, 500, or 600 pennyweights are met with; and one mass was found weighing 28 pounds. This was dug up by a negro at Reed's Mine, within a few inches of the surface. Its value was towards 8000 dollars. Various marvellous stories are told respecting this rich mass; as that it had been seen by Gold Hunters at night reflecting so brilliant a light when they drew near to it with torches, as to terrify them and deter them from further examination. . . . No unusual circumstance attended the discovery of this mass. . . . It was melted down and cast into bars soon after its discovery. Another mass weighing 600 pennyweights, was found on the surface of a ploughed field in the vicinity of the Yadkin; and, . . . a piece has been found at Parker's Mine that weighed four pounds and eleven ounces. . . .

Parker's Mine is situated four miles South of the Yadkin, in Montgomery. . . .

The Gold Mines are rented at various rates, the proprietor receiving from one-fourth to one-third, according to the reputation of the Mine. Parker's Mine rents as high as one-half. The Gold obtained at these Mines is of almost unequalled purity, being 23 carats fine; that is 23 parts out of 24 are pure Gold. The remainder is Silver and Copper. It is usually, when found, kept in goose quills and exchanged by weight, constituting a part of the currency of the Country. Almost every man in the immediate vicinity of the Mines, has a quill of it in his pocket, and a pair of money scales and the commodities of trade are paid for by *weighing out the price* as in the day of the Patriarchs. I saw a bottle of whiskey paid for by weighing out 3½ grains of gold.—Denison Olmsted, *Report on the Geology* of *North Carolina, November, 1824*, pp. 33-39.

A PRIVATE MINT IN NORTH CAROLINA, 1837

September 20. . . . After breakfast I walked a few miles to visit a German of the name of Bechler, who issued a gold coinage of which I had seen several pieces. . . . He had resided seven years in this country, and had established for himself a character for integrity, as well as skill in his profession.

The greater part of the small streams in this part of the gold region have more or less gold in them, so that all the settlers upon the streams were engaged, more or less, in washing for gold. Each of them possessing but a small quantity, and there being no general purchaser, it was an article not easily disposed of without taking the trouble to go great distances. Bechler had also obtained some in the usual manner, and having made a die, coined his gold into five dollar pieces, of the same intrinsic value as the half eagles of the United States, which are worth five dollars each. He also coined pieces of the value of two dollars and a half, and stamped the value, as well as his own name, upon every piece that he coined. These after a while found their way to the mint of the United States, were assayed and found to be correct. This becoming known, all the gold finders in his vicinity, and indeed from greater distances, began to bring their gold to his mint to be coined. At the period of my visit, his gold coinage circulated more freely than that of the United States, which was very scarce. He told me that his books showed that he had coined about two millions of dollars from the gold found by the settlers, putting his name, with its weight and quality to every piece. On receiving the gold from the country people, which in this part of the gold region is alloyed with silver, he first reduced it to a common standard, then made the five dollar pieces equal to those of the United States in value, and when coined delivered it to the respective proprietors, deducting two per cent. for the seignorage. . . .

The North Carolina Spectator, Rutherfordton, Aug. 27, 1831 "To Gold Miners and Others"

The undersigned having coined a great quantity of North Carolina gold into pieces of $2.50 and $5.00 value, of 20 carats fine, and being well prepared to increase the business to any extent, is established 3½ miles on the road leading from Rutherfordton to Jeanstown, invites the attention of Miners in South Carolina and Georgia as well as North Carolina to the advantage which would result from having the product of their mines coined or made into ingots bearing their just value rather than disposing of it in its fluxed state, without an assay and therefore liable to produce an improper value; gold in a fluxed state of 22 or 23 carats is generally sold for 84 cents per dwt. in the bank, whereas its intrinsic value, if coined, is 90 or 94 cents, consequently an actual saving of 6 cents per dwt. will be made by having it coined after paying all the expenses of coining. . . .

The following are his prices; for fluxing 400 dwts. or less $1.00; for assaying (by a fire ordeal) 1000 dwts. or less, $1.00; for coining 2½ per cent. When the gold is to be coined no charge is made for the assay.

"C. BECHTLER"

—Thomas Featherstonhaugh, "A Private Mint in North Carolina," *Publications of the Southern History Association*, X (1906), 67-77.

WEIGHT OF DIFFERENT PIECES OF GOLD FOUND AT REED'S MINE

1803	28 lbs.		1824	16 lbs.	
1804	9 "		"	9½ "	
"	7 "		"	8 "	
"	3 "		1835	13¼ "	
"	2 "		"	4½ "	
"	1¼ "		"	1 "	
			"	8 "	

115¼ lbs.
(steelyard weight)

—Report by John H. Wheeler, Supt. of Branch Mint, to the Secretary of the Treasury, in 1838.

DESCRIPTION OF THE GOLD COUNTRY, 1856

It is only fourteen years since mining began at Gold Hill. In the progress of the operations required in the business, and in consequence of the direction of the attention of the operators to the character of the country, many new discoveries have been made since the first surface-mine was worked on the land of Andrew Troutman, in 1842. The first veins discovered were upon the lands of John Troutman. By this discovery, $400,000 were obtained, the deepest shafts reaching only to the depth of 100 feet.

The Honeycut vein was discovered in the same year. This mine yielded $101,665.

The next year, (1854), the mine known as the Barnhardt was discovered on the land of George Heilick. . . .

The veins of Gold Hill have not all proved remunerative, but the aggregate production of gold from all the veins up to the present time, 1856, has been $2,000,000.

Gold Hill is on the southern border of Rowan county, adjoining Cabarrus county. It is fourteen miles south from Salisbury. . . . It is only one mile east of the granite belt upon which Salisbury is situated.

The machinery employed at Gold Hill for separating gold, consists, first of the Chilian mill for crushing and grinding after being broken by hammers, the Tyrolese bowls, the Burke rockers, and the Drag mill. Amalgamation is always resorted to, though it has been frequently suggested that the ore is sufficiently rich to be reduced in the furnace.

The work for a Chilian mill of this ore is seventy bushels per day; and our mills run for twenty-four hours, with one or two short interruptions. They are all moved by steam power, and all the water used in the mills is pumped from the mine. . . .

The force employed at Gold Hill, for working the Earnhart vein, consists of sixty-six miners paid by the month, and thirty-nine negroes hired by the year. The day of twenty-four hours is divided into three shifts of eight hours each, for underground work. The expenses per month for the whole year amount to four thousand and thirty-eight dollars and forty-five cents, ($4,038.45). . . .

Rudersill gold mine is near Charlotte, Mecklenburg county, and was at one time regarded as the most productive mine in the State. . . . This mine was reopened about two years ago.—Ebenezer Emmons, *Geological Report of the Midland Counties of North Carolina, 1856,* pp. 155-60, 166, 176.

THE GOLD HILL MINES, 1853

Some very interesting notices have recently appeared of the mineral wealth of North Carolina and South Carolina. Dr. Daniel Asbury of Charlotte, North Carolina, has recently published a report on the gold and copper mines of Gold Hill, Rowan county, North Carolina. From the statistics given by Dr. Asbury, it appears that the Gold Hill mines have afforded $1,500,000 since their discovery in 1843 and that their exploration has led to the growth of a village of above eight hundred inhabitants, situated directly over the mines. The gold region covers about one square mile. The veins are numerous, well defined, of large size, and are judged to be of unending depth, as they are entirely vertical in their positions. They are already down in some places as deep as 350 feet. The average yield of the ores, by the first process, is $1.50 per 100 lbs. The sands are then re-washed 5 times by different parties. . . . Equally remarkable is the abundance of copper found in North Carolina.—*DeBow's Review,* XV (September, 1853), 320.

102. EARLY EFFORTS TO PROMOTE TEXTILE MANUFACTURING

In the first part of the nineteenth century North Carolina was inclined to become a textile manufacturing state. Cotton spinning machines were to be found at Fayetteville as early as 1802, and a cotton mill was established at Lincolnton by Michael Schenck in 1813. This was probably the first cotton mill south of the Potomac. The original contract for its machinery is now preserved in the Archives of the North Carolina Historical Commission.

During the next two decades other mills were erected at Rocky Mount by Joel Battle and Henry A. Donaldson, at Greensboro by Henry Humphries, at Alamance Creek by E. M. Holt, at Great Falls by John W. Leak, at Salem by Francis Fries and Dr. Schumann, and at Leaksville by John W. Morehead.

The 1840 census listed twenty-five cotton mills in the state : in Chatham, Caswell, Davie, Davidson, Edgecombe, Guilford, Lincoln, Montgomery, Rockingham, Richmond, Surry, and Stokes.

In spite of the momentum of an early start, however, the textile industry grew slowly in the state. By 1860 North Carolina had only 761 looms and 41,834 spindles. Many reasons have been given for this slow development—the damper climate of New England, improper transportation facilities, plantation slavery, inertia and indifference of the people, lack of capital, lack of skilled labor, and the belief so prevalent in the whole South that cotton production was more profitable and more desirable than cotton manufacture.

Between 1820 and 1840 there were many complaints about soil exhaustion, the low price of cotton, and the constant drain of North Carolina population to the West. The newspapers were filled with discussions of these matters, and legislative committees were appointed to study the situation and to suggest remedies. A report made by Mr. Charles Fisher of Rowan to the House of Commons, January 1, 1828, gave the most lucid account of the economic ills of the state and proposed the promotion of manufacturing and wool growing as the solution of its agricultural and industrial problems.

CONTRACT FOR MACHINERY IN NORTH CAROLINA'S FIRST COTTON MILL, 1816.

Articles of agreement made & entered into this 27ʰ day of April 1816 between Micheal Shenk & Absolam Warlick of the County of Lincoln & state of North Carolina of the one part, and Micheal Beam of the County & state aforesaid of the other part, Witnesseth that the said Micheal Beam obliges himself to build for the said Shenk & Warlick within twelve months from this date, a spining machine, with one hundred & forty four fliers, with three sets of flooted rolers, the back set to be of wood, the other two sets to be of Iron, the machine to be made in two frames with two sets of wheels, one carding machine with two sets of cards to run two ropings, each to be one foot wide, with a picking machine to be attached to it with as many saws as may be necessary to feed the carding machine, one roling machine with four heads. all the machinery to be completed in a workmanlike manner—and the said Beam is to board himself & find all the materials for the machine, & set the machine going on a branch on Ab. Warlicks land, below where the old machine stood, the said Shenk & Warlick are to have the house for the machine, & the running gears made at their expense but the said Beam is to fix the whole machinery above described thereto ; the wooden cans for the roping & spining & the real to be furnished by the said Shenk & Warlick, all the straps & bands necessary for the machinery to be furnished by said Shenk & Warlick—In consideration of which the said Shenk & Warlick are to pay the said Beam, the sum of thirteen hundred dollars as follows to wit three hundred dollars this day two hundred dollars three months from this date, one hundred dollars six months from this date, and the ballance of the thirteen hundred dollars, to be paid to the said M. Beam, within twelve months after said machine is started to spining—In testimony whereof we have hereunto set our hands & seals the day & year above written.

ABSOLOM WARLICK
MICHAEL SHENK
MICHAEL BEAM

—Manuscript in archives of the North Carolina Historical Commission.

MANUFACTURES AND WOOL GROWING IN NORTH CAROLINA

REPORT ON THE ESTABLISHMENT OF COTTON AND WOOLEN MANUTURES TO THE HOUSE OF COMMONS, JAN. 1, 1828

The Select Committee, to whom was referred the Resolution, on the subject of *Cotton* and *Woolen* Manufactures, and on the growing of Wool in North Carolina, have had the same under consideration, and REPORT,

That the subject of the Resolution is one, which deeply concerns the citizens of this state, and is vitally connected with their best interest and prosperity. A crisis is at hand, when our citizens must turn a portion of their labor and enterprize into other channels of industry; otherwise, poverty and ruin will fall on every class of our community. It is a lamentable fact, that the people of North-Carolina are indebted to one another, and to the Banks, to an amount appaling to the mind. . . . The debts due to the local institutions alone, amount to $5,221,877. . . .

Owing to the want of navigable streams in our state, leading to good marts, hithertò but few of our Agricultural products would admit the expense of carrying to market. Cotton and Tobacco from the interior, are almost the only articles that will bear transportation, while rice and naval stores, on the sea-board, are the principal exports. When the prices of these articles were up, the farming interest of North-Carolina presented something like the appearance of prosperity, but a great depression has taken place in their value, and at this time they are scarcely worth producing. The loss of the West Indian Trade has lessened the demand for lumber. Tobacco is now taxed in the British markets, more than 600 per cent, while the demand for cotton, our other great staple, does not keep pace with its increased production. . . . If the planter in North-Carolina can barely afford to raise cotton at 8 cents per lb. he must soon be driven from its culture altogether, by the farmers of the West, whose new rich lands enable them to produce it with less labour and expense. . . . The balance of trade against us, for several years past, has greatly increased.

The balance of trade against us, produces another state of things on the monied concerns of North-Carolina, which threatens not only the ruin of our local institutions, but as an inevitable consequence, bankruptcy and distress throughout the community.

In setting about to ameliorate our condition, the first step is to adopt some system that will enable us to buy less and sell more,—that will enable us to supply within ourselves, our own wants and necessities. . . . But how is this important revolution to be accomplished? We unhesitatingly answer—by introducing the Manufacturing System into our own State, and fabricating, at least to the extent of our own wants. We go further. Instead of sending off at great expense of transportation, our raw material, convert it into fabrics at home, and in that state, bring it into market. In this way, our want of navigation will not be so severely felt. . . .

North-Carolina, during good crop years, is estimated to have shipped for the North and Europe, through her own ports and those of her sister states, at least 80,000 bales of cotton. Eighty thousand bales at $30 per bale, amounts to $2,400,000. But 80,000 bales, thus worth $2,400,000 in the raw state, when converted into fabrics, are increased in value four fold, which will make the sum of $9,600,000 or $7,200,000 more than we obtained for it. . . .

The hand of nature itself seems to point out North-Carolina as a region of country well adapted to manufactories. Cut off from the ocean by a sound-bound coast, her rivers filled with shoals and obstructions along their whole extent, and their mouths inaccessible to large vessels, she can never be greatly commercial. On the other hand, her climate and soil are equal to those of any of her sister states, and she abounds with all the facilities necessary to the manufacturing arts. . . .

COTTON—The soil and climate of North-Carolina, excepting the mountainous regions, are well adapted to the growth of this great staple. . . . The fibres are not so long, but in texture they are finer and more silky than further south or west. . . . The advantages of having the raw material on the spot, are much more important than at first may appear. First, the expense of transportation is saved. This is equal, on an average, to 25 per cent. . . . 2d. Another advantage in our favor is, that the Cotton here would be delivered in the seed. Cotton taken from the gin is in the best state for spinning. Besides, we should save the bagging, roping and wastage—all of which, Mr. Donaldson of Fayetteville, estimates equal to ten per cent in our favour.

WOOL. . . . The Committee entertain the opinion, that the climate and soil of North-Carolina, are well adapted to the raising of Sheep and the growing of Wool. . . .

In the business of raising Sheep, North-Carolina has two very important advantages over the Northern States. First, the price of lands. Second, the climate. . . .

One thousand dollars in North-Carolina will purchase a more extensive Sheep-walk than ten thousand will command in New England, New York, or Pennsylvania. In the Northern States, sheep require to be fed nearly six months in the year; while here, six weeks is as long as is necessary. . . . In addition to this, the severity of climate at the north, requires more care and attention to be paid to the young than is necessary here. All these things considered, it is evident that we can raise sheep at least 35 or 40 per cent. cheaper than they can be raised at the north. . . .

Now, the cultivation of cotton requires the best of soil; it exhausts the land and requires much labour, while the raising of sheep gives value to lands not suited to ordinary cultivation, and makes worn-out fields productive of profit to the farmer. Further, it requires but little labour, and that of the lightest kind.

IRON.—In addition to cotton and wool, we may add iron ore, as a raw material abounding in our State. . . .

WATER-POWER.—Few States in the Union abound more in sites of Water-Power than North-Carolina. . . . Much of this power is found in that range of country where the cotton grows well, and is extensively cultivated; and higher up, near, and in the mountains, there is no limit to this power. It being thus abundant, it must forever remain cheap, while at the North it is dear. . . . When those extensive Lakes, Mattamuskeet and others, are drained, the Canals drawing off the water, will furnish admirable sites for Mills and Manufacturing Establishments.

LABOUR.—It has hitherto been urged against the establishment of manufactures in North-Carolina, and in the Southern Country generally, that the price of labour is too high to yield profits, or to enable us to compete with the Northern States and England, where population is more dense. This is a great mistake. . . .

We have two species of labour—*white* labour and *black* labour. As to *white labour*, we hazard nothing in saying, that it is cheaper in North-Carolina than it is either in England or at the North. . . .

We are aware, that the opinion is entertained at the north, and even by some persons among ourselves, that our slaves cannot be advantageously employed in Manufactories. 1st. Because, as is alleged, that they are deficient in intellectual qualifications; and 2d, because they have no moral principle.—Now, that the Northern Manufacturers should hold out these ideas is not to be wondered at, when we consider it is their interest to do so; but that these notions should be entertained by any well informed persons acquainted with our black population, is strange indeed. What branch of Mechanics have we in our country, in which we do not find negroes often distinguished for their skill and integrity? In every place, we see them equalling the best white mechanics. . . . With the blacks there is no turning out for wages, and no time lost in visiting musters and other public exhibitions.

But one of the great advantages of black labour is, that you can attach it permanently to the establishment by purchase. . .

PROVISIONS.—The soil and climate of North-Carolina are well suited to the production of all the necessaries of life depending on agriculture.

CLIMATE, HEALTHY AND MILD.—The rigor of the New England climate is a drawback on the profits of manufacturing. 1st. It requires more fuel there to keep the establishments comfortable. 2d. The operatives have to be more thickly and expensively clothed. And 3d. The streams often freeze up and stop operations altogether. . . .

SKILL AND CAPITAL

In these two requisites, North-Carolina acknowledges her deficiency; but they are wants that can be supplied; they are elements that may be created. For skill, we must in the beginning, be indebted to the North and to Europe; but let the system once take root among us, and experience will create skill at home. . . .

As to capital, owing to the pursuits of our people, it is hard to be commanded here. The wealth of our citizens consists in property that is not easily converted into money; in lands and negroes. . . .

We have nearly reached the lowest point of depression, and it is time for the reaction to begin. Our habits and prejudices are against manufacturing, but we must yield to the force of things, and profit by the indications of nature. . . .

Let the Manufacturing System but take root among us, and it will soon flourish like a vigorous plant in its native soil; it will become our greatest means of wealth and prosperity; it will change the course of trade, and, in a great measure, make us independent of Europe and the North.

Nature has made us far more independent of them than they are of us. They can manufacture our raw material, but they cannot produce it. We can raise it and manufacture it too. Such are our superior advantages, that we may anticipate the time, when the manufactured articles of the South will be shipped to the North, and sold in their markets cheaper than their own fabrics, and when the course of trade and difference of exchange will turn in our favor.
—*Legislative Reports on the Establishment of Cotton and Woolen Manufactures,* 1828.

MANUFACTURES IN NORTH CAROLINA, 1840

The South is rapidly becoming independent in almost every branch of manufactures. There are in North Carolina alone, at this day, a greater number of factories of different kinds than ten years ago there were in the whole of the southern states.

The enterprise of the citizens of this state is rapidly enabling it to become independent of the north in almost every branch of manufactures . . .

A convention of those interested in the manufacturing business in North Carolina, is to meet in Raleigh, on the 13th instant. The object of the Convention is stated to be for the purpose of arranging the domestic market of cotton yarns, and to take such steps as may be deemed of importance in circulating information calculated to show the usefulness and propriety of a more extensive operation.—
Niles' National Register, May 2, May 16, June 13, 1840.

REVOLUTION IN NORTH CAROLINA MANUFACTURING, 1836-1843

A complete revolution in the trade in cotton yarns has been effected in North Carolina within a few years by the establishment of a number of factories in that state. Prior to the year 1836, immense quantities of the article were imported into the state from the north. In that year a factory was established in Fayetteville; others were soon after established throughout the state; and now, instead of drawing their supplies from abroad, large quantities are annually exported. In Fayetteville, there are six factories which cost about $347,000. Three of these manufacture brown sheetings; the fourth has just commenced to weave heavy Oznaburgs, weighing half a pound to the yard; the other two make yarns only. Sheetings, shirtings, and bagging manufactured there have acquired a reputation second to none in this country.—*Niles' National Register*, June 24, 1843.

NORTH CAROLINA WAKING UP TO IMPORTANCE OF MANUFACTURING, 1849

Nearly all the Southern States are waking up to the importance of the establishment of manufactories in their limits, which will not only render them *independent* within themselves, but also be to them an immense source of wealth and importance. We should be proud to see an emulative spirit in this respect prevail in North Carolina; for in no State in the Union, perhaps, are there greater inducements for embarkation in works of this kind than in our own.

By means of the Rail Road project . . . it is hoped that at no distant day, the two extremes of the State will be connected together, offering great facilities for the transportation of its varied productions from one part to the other. Our agricultural operations must be regarded as the basis, the solid foundation, upon which our national prosperity rests. Yet to render them effective, there must be a co-operating agent—and that is the Manufactory—an agent working along by the side of the farm, ready to take up the farm material and convert it into a suitable form for use. We use the term Manufactory, in its broadest signification—embracing all the Mechanical Trades. . . . Merchant Flour Mills, Tobacco and Cotton Manufactories, &c. . . .

The establishment of Manufactures and Mills of every description, would have the tendency to arouse the energies of the people, to quicken their inventive genius, to concentrate their capital, and to enhance it, to cause an influx of capitalists and operatives, to create a market for the productions of the farm, and by a reflex influence, the refuse of all such consumption being returned to the soil, to increase its value.—*Raleigh Register*, June 16, 1849.

103. NORTH CAROLINA AGRICULTURE, 1850-1860

In spite of the fact that North Carolina was a backward rural state, which was frequently called "Old Rip," there were many evidences of agricultural progress in the decade preceding the Civil War. Many agricultural journals were established, the most important of which were the *Farmers' Advocate*, the *Farmers' Journal*, the *Arator*, the *Carolina Cultivator*, and the *North Carolina Planter*. Most of these were published in Raleigh. A State Agricultural Society was created in 1852 and soon there were local societies in many counties. Several investigations of the state's agri-

cultural resources were made, the most significant being those of Ebenezer Emmons, state geologist from 1852 to 1863. Some interest was manifested in soil chemistry and a chair of Applied Chemistry was set up at
the University in 1854.

Judge Thomas Ruffin's address to the State Agricultural Society in
1855 gives a very clear description of North Carolina agriculture at that
time. Ruffin was one of the greatest jurists, if not the greatest, in all
North Carolina history. He was likewise a great farmer, owning several
plantations. For more than thirty-five years, in the recess of his courts,
he tried to improve agriculture in the state. He was president of the
State Agricultural Society from 1854 to 1860.

. . . TRUE, the soil is not what it once was, and our task is not
merely to preserve fertility but in a great degree to restore that
which has been more or less exhausted. We must not blame our
ancestors too hastily or too severely, for the system under which the
rich vegetable loam they found here was used up. . . . Land was
in plenty—timber an incumbrance and labor scarce and costly; so
that in reality, it was cheaper, and the sounder economy in them to
bring new fields . . . into culture, rather than manure those which
they had reduced by imperfect tillage and scourging cropping. . . .

If not to the lowest, certainly to a very low condition, much of
the land in the State, had been brought; and the time came, when,
if improvement was ever to be made, it would be commenced. . . .

. . . Of the counties ranging along our northern border, from
Warren to Stokes, inclusive, I have had for about fifty years, considerable knowledge. That was the principal region of the tobacco
culture. According to the course of that culture, wherever it
prevailed in our early annals, the country was cut down rapidly,
cropped mercilessly with a view to quantity rather than quality, then
put into corn, and exhausted quickly and almost entirely. When I
first knew it, and for a long time afterwards, there were abounding
evidences of former fertility, and existing and sorrowful sterility.
Corn and tobacco and oats were almost the only crops. But little
wheat and no grasses were to be seen in the country. Warren and
Granville bought the little flour they used from Orange wagons.
Large tracts were disfigured by galls and frightful gulleys, turned
out as "old fields," with broomstraw and old field pines for their
only vesture, instead of their stately, primitive forests, or rich crops
for the use of man. This is a sad picture. But it is a true one; and
there was more fact than figure in the saying by many, whose work
of destruction rendered that region so desolate, that it was "old and

17

worn out." Happily, some thought its condition not so hopeless, and cherishing this attachment for the spots of their nativity, within these few years—since the time of railroads and river navigation began—set about repairing the ravages of former days. Do you suppose they were content with less crops, and therefore that they cultivated less land than before, leaving a larger portion for recovery by rest? That was not their course. They did not give up the cultivation of tobacco, but gradually increased it, and corn also; and they added to their rotation wheat, when so much more easily and cheaply carried to market. But they gradually increased the collection and application of manures from the stables and cattle yards, with considerable additions of the concentrated manures obtained from abroad, and protected the land from washing by judicious hill-side trenching and more thorough plowing. The result has been that many old fields have been reclaimed and brought into cultivation, that lands generally much increased in fertility, and, of course, in actual and market value in a like proportion. . . .

. . . I cannot close, however, without asking you once more to cleave to North Carolina. Stay in her, fertilize her, till her, cherish her rising manufactures, extend her railways, encourage and endow her schools and colleges, sustain her institutions, develop her resources, promote knowledge, virtue and religion throughout her borders, stimulate State pride and exalt her to renown. . . . —*The Papers of Thomas Ruffin* (edited by J. G. de R. Hamilton), IV, 323-37.

104. AGRICULTURAL, GEOLOGICAL, AND DESCRIPTIVE SKETCHES OF LOWER NORTH CAROLINA, 1861

Edmund Ruffin was one of the most prominent farmers and agricultural publicists in American history. He lived near Petersburg, Virginia, on a large estate called "Marlbourne." For a decade he edited the *Farmer's Register*, one of the earliest and most important farm papers in the antebellum South. Through the columns of this publication he advocated the rotation of crops, better drainage, proper seed selection, and the use of manures and fertilizers, particularly marl. His book *Calcareous Manures* was one of the most widely read books on agriculture in the nineteenth century. In politics Ruffin belonged to the radical group of southerners known as "fire eaters." Soon after South Carolina seceded from the Union, Ruffin "seceded" from Virginia and joined the Palmetto Guard in South Carolina, firing the first shot on Fort Sumter.

Ruffin's description of eastern North Carolina is one of the best written about that section of the state just prior to the Civil War.

. . . THE whole country, and especially from Perquimans county to Currituck Sound, is pervaded by broad and deep estuaries near to the Sound; and their head waters, extending near or into the Dismal Swamp, make, with their many branches, a net-work of natural still-water canals, narrow and crooked, indeed, but as deep, as smooth, and as sluggish as artificial canals, and free from the changes of levels and the obstruction of lock-gates, which accompany the benefits of canal navigation. . . .

In travelling along the public road from Elizabeth city, North Carolina, to Currituck Court House, within the distance of seven miles, we passed four navigable water courses, including the Pasquotank and two of its branches. Three of these had draw-bridges for the passage of masted-sea-vessels. The fourth stream had no draw-bridge, because it was not needed in such close vicinity to others; . . . Such great and numerous natural facilities for navigation, as in the many rivers of this region, are unequalled; and they are exceeded by the aid of art, only in the canal navigation of the Dutch Netherlands. . . .

The great crop, of the North Carolina counties is corn. Next to this, and especially in Perquimans, is wheat. These two are the only great crops for market. The lands generally, if not suffering from wetness, produce corn well. On the new clearings of firm swamp lands, ditched well on the ordinary plan, fifty bushels to the acre may be made. . . .

It was with much surprise, some years ago, that I heard that the best and largest crops of wheat in Perquimans, and in some other parts of this region, were still reaped by the sickle, or reap-hook. . . . Neither is this practice confined to small crops. The best farmers and largest wheat growers, who sometimes make crops of more than five thousand bushels, reap them with the sickle. I knew that, by this mode, there might be avoided much of the great waste of wheat that is usually made by cradling; but had supposed that the slower operation of the sickle, and the high prices of harvest labor, and the scarcity of laborers at any price, had caused this implement to be abandoned everywhere in the United States, except for sports of rank and tangled wheat, or on steep hill sides. . . .

Except corn and wheat there is scarcely a crop of large culture raised for market in the North Carolina counties. Cotton, which is so universally and extensively cultivated in the nearest higher counties in North Carolina, and even to some extent in those of Virginia, is not attempted here, as a crop for market. The general prevalence of wet soil is a sufficient cause for the absence of this crop. Oats, and

especially hay, would be good crops for this humid climate and soil.
But neither is raised for market, and hay scarcely at all, the fodder
and shucks of corn serving in the place of hay, as everywhere in our
corn-growing country. Yet vessels load of coarse and mean hay,
from the northern States, are continually brought here for the use
of the towns, and for the teams of the lumberers working in the
swamp forests. There is no better country for grass east of the mountains. . . .

Taking the whole space within the outlines of Pamlico, Albemarle
and Currituck sounds, and their connecting waters, and of all the
deep, still and unobstructed waters of the many rivers discharging
therein, there is not one of the Atlantic States, which has such great
extent of good and smooth navigable water—and safe from storms
also, by its topographical features, and entirely secured from any
invasion, or effective blockade, by a hostile naval force. . . . But
these remarkable and otherwise valuable characteristics are rendered
almost nugatory by another remarkable feature of this region. There
is now no access to the ocean, through the sand-reef, so good and
deep as the narrow Ocracoke inlet, which now only permits vessels
of six feet draft to pass over the bar across the inlet, after tedious
delays and much danger, and which passage opens upon an un-
sheltered and most dangerous sea coast. The whole ocean shore of
North Carolina is a terror to navigators, and is noted for the number of shipwrecks, and especially near Cape Hatteras. . . .

Beaufort Harbor is the only deep inlet through the whole reef.—
This will safely pass ships drawing seventeen feet, and into a secure
and excellent harbor. But this noble harbor is connected with the
Pamlico and more northern sounds, only by the long and shallow
strait called Core sound. This water affords barely four feet depth
for navigation, over a bottom (as I was told) of loose and shifting
sand, and that extending for so long a distance, that the deepening
the channel, and keeping it open by dredging, would be of enormous cost, and probably impossible to effect. Thus, the noble harbor of Beaufort has continued almost unused, and heretofore useless to the great back country, because it was thus cut off from the
deep navigable waters of the interior. There is now in progress of
construction a railroad of about ninety miles in length, to connect
Beaufort harbor with the back country, by joining the existing
Wilmington railroad at Goldsborough. As this new branch of railway will pass through a very unproductive country (east of Goldsborough) and lead to where (at present) there is neither a town, a
market, nor purchasers, nor capital to buy with, it may well be

questioned whether the existing trade can be thus diverted from Wilmington. This is already a busy, growing and thriving town, and a mart of much trade and enterprise, having good navigation of twelve feet draft to the ocean, and to which, the approach by railroad (long in use) from the intersection of the two roads, (according to the map), not longer than, if so long as the other new branch, which will indeed go to a port of deeper passage to the ocean, but which as a market, as yet, is nothing. . . .

There are ducks of various kinds, of which the canvas-back is the most esteemed. There are also wild geese, and swans. Altogether they congregate in numbers exceeding all conception of any person who had not been informed. The shooting season continues through the winter. From description, I cannot imagine any other sport, . . . that can be more likely to gratify a hardy sportsman. . . The returns, in game killed and secured through any certain time, to a skilful and patient and enduring gunner, are as sure as the profits of any ordinary labor of agriculture or trade, and far larger for the capital and labor employed.—Edmund Ruffin, *Agricultural, Geological, and Descriptive Sketches of Lower North Carolina* (Raleigh, 1861), pp. 56, 57, 83-87, 113-18, 151, 152, 163.

VIII

THE NEGRO IN NORTH CAROLINA PRIOR TO 1860

105. White, Slave, and Free Negro Population of North Carolina, 1790-1860

The number and distribution of Negroes, slave and free, their relative increase, and the number of slave-holding families may be seen in the following statistical table based on the United States Census of 1860. From these tables, it is to be observed that Negroes were increasing more rapidly than whites from 1790 to 1860, and also that there was a marked tendency toward concentration in ownership.

Year	White	Per cent of Increase	Per cent of Population	Free Colored	Per cent of Increase	Per cent of Population
1790	289,143	....	73.2	5,135	....	1.3
1800	337,764	17.19	70.6	7,043	41.56	1.04
1810	376,410	11.44	67.6	10,266	45.76	1.83
1820	419,200	11.36	65.6	14,612	42.33	2.3
1830	472,823	12.79	64.1	19,534	33.74	2.6
1840	484,870	2.54	64.3	22,732	16.31	3.01
1850	553,028	14.05	63.6	27,463	20.81	3.2
1860	629,942	14.42	63.4	30,463	10.92	3.1

Year	Slaves	Per cent of Increase	Per cent of Population	Total Population	Slave Owning Families	Per cent of Families
1790	102,726	....	25.5	395,005	16,310	31.0
1800	133,296	32.53	27.8	478,103	....	....
1810	168,824	26.65	30.3	555,500	....	....
1820	205,017	21.43	32.1	638,829	....	....
1830	245,601	19.79	33.1	737,987	....	....
1840	245,817	.08	32.6	753,419	....	....
1850	288,548	17.38	33.2	869,039	28,303	26.8
1860	331,059	14.73	33.3	992,622	....	....

—*Eighth Census of the United States, 1860.*

106. SLAVE CODE AND PRACTICES

There were many cases of harsh and cruel punishment of slaves in North Carolina during the latter part of the eighteenth century. According to the Fundamental Constitutions the master was to have "absolute power and authority" over the slave. Many barbarous punishments were inflicted upon the slaves, who enjoyed no legal protection. Runaway slaves were outlawed upon refusal to surrender. There are a few cases of Negroes' being burned at the stake for murder, by order of the court. Such an instance took place in Duplin County in 1787.

PUNISHMENT FOR PERJURY, 1741

To BE ordered by Court "to have one Ear nailed to the Pillory, and there stand for the space of One Hour, and the said Ear to be cut off, and thereafter the other Ear nailed in like manner, and cut off at the Expiration of one other Hour; and moreover, to order every such Offender Thirty Nine Lashes well laid, on his or her bare Back, at the Common Whipping Post.—*Laws of 1741*, Chap. XXIV.

RUNAWAY SLAVES OUTLAWED, 1741

It shall be lawful for any Person or Persons whatsoever to kill and destroy such Slave or Slaves by such Ways and Means as he or she shall think fit, without Accusation or Impeachment of any Crime for the same.

Provided always, . . . That for every Slave killed in Pursuance of this Act, or put to death by Law, the Master or Owner of such Slave shall be paid by the Public.—*State Records of North Carolina*, XXIII, 202-3.

ADVERTISEMENT FOR RUNAWAY SLAVE, 1774

Ran away last November from the subscriber, a negro fellow, named Zeb; aged 36. As he is outlawed, I will pay twenty pounds currency to any person who shall produce his head severed from his body, and five pounds if brought home alive—John Moseley.— *North Carolina Gazette*, 1774.

NEGRO BURNED AT STAKE BY ORDER OF COURT, 1787

Whereupon the Court doth pass this Sentence in the word following to wit that the said Negro Man Darby be immediately committed to Gaol under a good Guard and that on Tomorrow between the Hourse of one and Four o'clock in the afternoon he be taken out thence and tied to a Steak on the Court House Lott and there burned to Death and to Ashes and his ashes strewed upon the Ground.—Manuscript Records of Duplin County Court, March 15, 1787.

107. RUNAWAY SLAVES

The accompanying advertisements for fugitives and stolen slaves are taken from North Carolina newspapers during the year 1818. They reveal one of the most serious problems of the slave-owner—the retention of his slave property. They also show the dangers and punishments to which fugitives were subject. Rewards frequently ran as high as a hundred dollars. As the value of slaves increased, rewards for their return likewise increased.

SHOOTING AT RUNAWAYS

FIFTY DOLLARS REWARD. Ran Away from the subscriber, living in Franklin county, North-Carolina on the 12th. of January, 1817, a Negro Man named Randol about 26 or 27 years of age, between 5 and 6 feet high, rather yellow complected; appears humble when spoken to. It is expected he has some marks of shot about his hips, thighs, neck and face, as he has been shot at several times. His wife belongs to a Mr. Henry Bridges, formerly of this county, who started with her about the 14th. instant, to South-Carolina, Georgia or Tennessee. It is supposed he will attempt to follow her. This is to caution all persons harbouring or trading for said Negro. And all masters of vessels are forbid having anything to do with him at the penalty of the law. The above reward and all reasonable charges will be paid to any person who will secure the said negro, so that I get him.

WOOD TUCKER

December 23, 1817.

—*Raleigh Register*, February 20, 1818.

BOUNTY FOR HEAD OF OUTLAWED SLAVE

ONE HUNDRED DOLLARS REWARD. The subscriber having legally outlawed his negro man Harry, offers the above reward for his head, or the same if delivered alive to me. Harry is a stout well made fellow about five feet six inches high, small eyes, and an impudent look; he took with him when he absconded two coats, one grey and the other blue, and a home made suit of winter clothes, together with some other articles of clothing not recollected.—The above mentioned negro is legally outlawed.

JOHN Y. BONNER

Fairfield, near Washington, N. C.—*Carolina Sentinel* (Newbern), August 8, 1818.

"FOR SALE AS HE RUNS"

TWENTY-FIVE DOLLARS REWARD. Ranaway from the Subscriber two months since, a Negro man named John ; he is about 27 years of age, 5 feet 5 or 6 inches high, of a dark complexion, has a lean face, round body, and is well made—speaks plain, can read tolerably well, and has a scar on one of his heels. He has been lurking about Vine Swamp, in this county, and about my own neighborhood—and has frequently been seen with a gun, and other weapons for defense. It is thought that he will endeavor to get to Portsmouth, in Virginia, where he was sold by Mr. H. Harboard, to Mr. Andrew Hurst of Duplin County N. Carolina.

The above reward will be given to any person who will apprehend said negro & secure him in any Jail so that I get him.

Should any person be disposed to purchase him as he runs, I will take six hundred dollars, and give a good title. He is an excellent ditcher, can Hew, farm, or turn his hand to almost anything.

All masters of vessels and others are forewarned from harbouring, employing, or carrying him away under the penalty of the law.

FRANCIS GOODING

Lenoir County, 25th. April, 1818.

—U. B. Phillips, *Plantation and Frontier Documents*, II, 87-93.*

108. A SLAVE PLOT IN EASTERN NORTH CAROLINA, 1831

Prior to 1830 there was considerable anti-slavery feeling in North Carolina, and apologies were made for the "peculiar institution." After that date, however, North Carolinians, like other southerners, defended slavery as an economic and moral good. There were three significant reasons for their change of heart: the growing profitableness of cotton culture, the agitation of abolitionists, and Negro uprisings, particularly Nat Turner's insurrection in Southampton County, Virginia, August 21, 1831.

In 1821 there was a small revolt among the Negroes of Bladen, Carteret, Jones, and Onslow counties. Several slave plots were discovered in North Carolina in 1831, and there was widespread alarm in the state

---

*Reprinted by permission of the publishers, The Arthur H. Clark Company.

following Turner's insurrection. In the fall of that year six Negroes were placed in jail at Wilmington for attempting to incite an insurrection. They were convicted and executed. There were no other important outbursts, although there was general fear of trouble for some time.

The following news item from Fayetteville appeared in the *Federal Union*, Milledgeville, Georgia, October 6, 1831.

Two of the gentlemen who went from this place to Clinton on Monday night, have this moment returned, there being no danger, though the existence of the plot is clearly established. We have procured from one of them the following statement, drawn up by himself yesterday at Clinton. It is worthy of entire reliance.

On Sunday, the 4th inst., the first information of the contemplated rising of the blacks was sent from South Washington. The disclosure was made by a free mulatto man to Mr. Usher, of Washington, who sent the information to Mr. Kelly of Duplin. It appears from the mulatto's testimony, that Dave, a slave belonging to Mr. Morissey, of Sampson, applied to him to join the conspirators; stated that the negroes in Sampson, Duplin, and New Hanover, were regularly organized and prepared to rise on the 4th of October. Dave was taken up, and on this testimony convicted. After his conviction, he made a confession of the above to his master, and, in addition, gave the names of the four principal ringleaders in Sampson and Duplin, and several in Wilmington, named several families that they intended to murder. Their object was to march by two routes to Wilmington, spreading destruction and murder on their way. At Wilmington they expected to be reinforced by 2,000, to supply themselves with arms and ammunition, and then return. Three of the ringleaders in Duplin have been taken, and Dave and Jim executed. There are 23 negroes in jail in Duplin county, all of them no doubt concerned in the conspiracy. Several have been whipped, and some released. In Sampson 25 are in Jail, all concerned directly or indirectly in the plot. The excitement among the people in Sampson is very great, and increasing; they are taking effectual measures to arrest all suspected persons. A very intelligent negro preacher, named David, was put on his trial to-day, and clearly convicted by the testimony of another negro. The people were so much enraged, that they scarcely could be prevented from shooting him on his passage from the Court house to the jail. All the confessions made induce the belief that the conspirators were well organized, and their plans well understood in Duplin, Sampson, Wayne, New Hanover, and Lenoir. Nothing had transpired to raise even a suspicion that they extended into Cumberland or Bladen, except that Jim confessed that Nat, Col. Wright's negro, (who has been missing since the discovery of the plot,) had gone to Bryant Wright's, in the neighborhood of Fayetteville, to raise a company to join the conspirators. The rumors respecting a large force having been seen collected together, are unfounded, though there seems no doubt but that small armed bands have been seen. I cannot believe that any danger is to be apprehended, where the citizens are so constantly on the watch, and pursue such rigorous measures towards the offenders. The militia are assembled in ample force.

The Raleigh *Star* of Thursday last says—"We understand that about 21 negroes have been committed to jail in Edenton, on a charge of having been concerned in concerting a project of rebellion."—U. B. Phillips, *Plantation and Frontier Documents*, II, 101-3.*

109. A Large Cotton and Rice Plantation on the Lower Cape Fear

The following advertisement of Orton, a large estate on the lower Cape Fear, appeared in the Charleston *City Gazette*, January 17, 1825.

WILL be sold at Public Auction, at the Court House, in the town of Wilmington, N. C. on the first day of December next—

All that Plantation, lying in the county of Brunswick, State of North-Carolina, known by the name of Orton, late the residence of Gov. Benjamin Smith, containing 4975 acres, more or less. Of this tract between 400 and 500 acres is swamp land, of a strong and fertile soil, which, it is believed, will produce at least 1000 lbs. of Cotton, or 4 tierces of Rice, to the acre, and is more capable of being well drained than any on the river, the fall of the tide being at least 4½ feet. Orton is a valuable and beautiful Plantation, situate on the Cape-Fear river, about 16 miles below Wilmington, which affords a good market for all kinds of produce, and about 14 miles above Smithville, a place in high repute for its salubrity and pleasantness as a summer retreat. Included in the premises is a very superior and never failing Mill Stream, with an excellent Dam, wanting only flood gates—the Rice Machine, Mill and Gin having been recently destroyed by fire. The Pond may be used at all times as a reservoir of water to flow the low lands, thus rendering Orton one of the most valuable Rice Plantations in the country.

A liberal credit will be given, the particulars of which will be

*Reprinted by permission of the publishers, The Arthur H. Clark Company.

made known on the day of the sale, or sooner, if application be made to the subscriber. The premises can be viewed at any time, and possession will be delivered immediately after the sale.

W. ANDERSON, Cashier of the Bank of Cape Fear.
Wilmington, August 28, 1824.

—U. B. Phillips, *Plantation and Frontier Documents*, I, 251.*

110. MANUMISSION SOCIETIES IN NORTH CAROLINA, 1826

In the early part of the nineteenth century there was considerable opposition to slavery in North Carolina and there was much talk of emancipation in some of the newspapers. Much propaganda was spread by the North Carolina Manumission Society. This anti-slavery organization was founded in 1816 and in a short time had some forty branches. It proposed to emancipate slaves gradually, to ameliorate the slave laws, and to educate the people to the evils of slavery. The Greensboro *Patriot* seems to have been the unofficial organ of the society. The following extract gives some evidence of the activities of the organization in the state.

AT THE annual meeting of the Society of Friends in this State, held last Fall, that respectable body came to the resolution of manumitting and removing all the coloured people held by them, that were willing to leave the country; and since that time thay have been concerting measures for carrying their intentions into effect, and in consulting the wishes of the coloured people themselves in relation to their future destination, which has resulted in the following arrangement: 120 of the number are desirous of going to Hayti; 316 to Liberia; and about 100 wish to be sent to the non-slaveholding States of Ohio and Indiana—which we believe embrace the whole of the population of this description held by this Society, except a few who have formed family connections which they are unwilling by removal to dissolve, and where the husband or wife is held by persons from whom they cannot be purchased. . . .

The 316 of this population who have chosen to go to Liberia, and the 100 who wish to be removed to Ohio or Indiana, will also be sent there at the expense of the Society of Friends; the former, by one of the first vessels to the African Settlement; and the latter, by means of wagons, which will be engaged to convey them and the little property of which they may be possessed.

Besides the above mentioned coloured people, we learn, that this Society have already sent off 64 persons to the State of Ohio, 47 by

*Reprinted by permission of the publishers, The Arthur H. Clark Company.

the Indian Chief, which lately sailed from Norfolk to Liberia, and
11 by another vessel which sailed about the same time to Africa.

It ought also to be mentioned to the credit of this Society that it
contributed 800 dollars to the funds of the African Colonization
Society soon after its establishment.—*Raleigh Register*, May 30, 1826.

III. SLAVES MUST NOT BE TAUGHT TO READ, 1830-1831

The period around 1830 is a turning point in the history of Negro
slavery in the United States. Prior to that date the South had more or
less apologized for its "peculiar institution." After that date it defended
slavery as a "positive good," and as northern abolitionists became more
active, the South became more defensive. Laws pertaining to slaves became more severe. The movements of slaves were watched more carefully than ever, and practically all of the southern states passed laws to
"prevent all persons from teaching slaves to read or write, the use of
figures excepted." Members of the North Carolina legislature maintained
that teaching the slaves to read and write afforded them "facilities of
intelligence and communication, inconsistent with their condition, destructive of their contentment and happiness, and dangerous to the community." "To prevent these evils," the law reprinted below was enacted.

AN ACT to prevent all persons from teaching slaves to read or write,
the use of figures excepted.

Whereas the teaching of slaves to read and write has a tendency
to excite dissatisfaction in their minds and to produce insurrection
and rebellion, to the manifest injury of the citizens of the State:

THEREFORE,

Be it enacted by the General Assembly of the State of North
Carolina, and is hereby enacted by the authority of the same, That
any free person, who shall hereafter teach or attempt to teach, any
slave within this State to read or write, the use of figures excepted,
or shall give or sell to such slave or slaves any books or pamphlets,
shall be liable to indictment in any court of record in this State
having jurisdiction thereof; and, upon conviction, shall, at the discretion of the court, if a white man or woman, be fined not less
than one hundred dollars, nor more than two hundred dollars, or
imprisoned; and if a free person of color, shall be fined, imprisoned
or whipped, at the discretion of the court, not exceeding thirty-nine
lashes, nor less than twenty lashes.

II. Be it further enacted, That if any slave shall hereafter teach,
or attempt to teach, any other slave to read or write, the use of

figures excepted, he or she may be carried before any justice of the peace, and on conviction thereof, shall be sentenced to receive thirty-nine lashes on his or her bare back.

III. Be it further enacted, That the judges of the Superior Courts and the justices of the County Courts shall give this act in charge to the grand jurors of their respective counties.—*Laws of North Carolina, 1830-31*, Chap. VI.

112. THE UNDERGROUND RAILROAD

The Underground Railroad was the name given to an organized system of aiding fugitive slaves to escape from the South. The "railway" had "stations" at regular intervals at the homes of anti-slavery people who were known as "agents." It was the duty of an "agent" secretly to transport the fugitive to the next "station." "Conductors" went into the border states and encouraged discontented slaves to flee from their masters. Probably 2,000 slaves escaped from their masters every year from 1830 to 1860 by traveling over the Underground Railroad.

Underground methods were first used in North Carolina about 1819. In that year, Vestal Coffin organized the Underground Railroad near the present Guilford College. Levi Coffin, his cousin, was the "reputed President" of the national organization. The Coffins were Quakers and were unflinching in their opposition to slavery. Levi's early years were spent in North Carolina. In 1826, he moved to southeastern Indiana, where his house at Newport (now Fountain City) became a center at which three distinct lines of the Underground Railroad converged. It is estimated that Coffin personally assisted in the escape of about one hundred slaves annually for many years. He always had a carriage in readiness to convey the fugitives to a place of safety and he organized sewing circles to provide clothing for the destitute. The 1850 Census showed that North Carolina had sixty-four fugitive slaves; in 1860 there were only sixty-one. The following extracts are from Levi Coffin's *Reminiscences.*

FUGITIVES IN CONCEALMENT

RUNAWAY slaves used frequently to conceal themselves in the woods and thickets in the vicinity of New Garden, waiting opportunities to make their escape to the North, and I generally learned their places of concealment and rendered them all the service in my power. My father, in common with other farmers in that part of the country, allowed his hogs to run in the woods, and I often went out to feed them. My sack of corn generally contained supplies of bacon and corn bread for the slaves, and many a time I sat in the thickets with them as they hungrily devoured my bounty, and listened to the stories they told of hard masters and cruel treatment, or spoke in language, simple and rude, yet glowing with native eloquence, of the glorious hope of freedom which animated their spirits in the darkest hours, and sustained them under the sting of the lash. . . .

We often met at night in a thicket where a fugitive was concealed, to counsel in regard to his prospects and lay plans for getting him safely started to the North. We employed General Hamilton's Sol, a gray-haired, trusty old negro, to examine every coffle of slaves to which he could gain access, and ascertain if there were any kidnapped negroes among them. When such a case was discovered, Sol would manage to bring the person, by night, to some rendezvous appointed, in the pine thicket or the depth of the woods, and there Vestal and I would meet them and have an interview. There was always a risk in holding such meetings, for the law in the South inflicted heavy penalties on any one who should aid or abet a fugitive slave in escaping, and the patrollers, or mounted officers, frequently passed along the road near our place of concealment. . . .

In the spring of 1822, I opened my first school, having previously served as assistant teacher.

I continued this business for more than three years, in different neighborhoods, and assisted in organizing Sabbath-schools in various places.

ANTI-SLAVERY MATTERS

During the time I was engaged in teaching, I was not idle in anti-slavery matters. The subject of gradual emancipation, or manumission of slaves, was agitated in various parts of the State. A paper, called the Greensboro *Patriot*, was started at Greensboro, edited by William Swaim, a young man of rare talent. He advocated the manumission of slaves, and though he met with a storm of opposition and was assailed by other papers, he continued his course boldly and independently. He received letters from various parts of the State full of threats and warnings. These he published in his paper, and replied to them in editorials. . . .

Some plan of gradual manumission was the theme of general discussion at that day, but none of the advocates spoke or seemed to think of immediate and unconditional emancipation. Manumission societies were organized in different counties. The first, I believe, was organized at New Garden, Guilford County. . . . We also had several State Conventions, which were largely attended, and at which addresses were delivered and speeches made, by prominent

men. The various branches were represented by delegates. . . .
Several lenient slave-holders united with us in those meetings, and
advocated plans for gradual manumission.

Quite a number of slave-holders were present who favored gradual manumission and colonization. They argued that if the slaves
were manumitted, they must be sent to Africa; it would not do for
them to remain in this country; they must return to Africa, and
this must be made a condition of their liberty. A motion was made
to amend our constitution, so that the name of our organization
would be "Manumission and Colonization Society". . . . Many of
us were opposed to making colonization a condition of freedom, believing it to be an odious plan of expatriation concocted by slave-
holders, to open a drain by which they might get rid of free negroes,
and thus remain in more secure possession of their slave property.
They considered free negroes a dangerous element among slaves.
We had no objection to free negroes going to Africa of their own
will, but to compel them to go as a condition of freedom was a movement to which we were conscientiously opposed and against which
we strongly contended. When the vote was taken, the motion was
carried by a small majority. We felt that the slave power had got
the ascendency in our society, and that we could no longer work in
it. The convention broke up in confusion, and our New Garden
branch withdrew to itself, no longer co-operating with the others.
. . .

The laws relating to slavery were constantly made more oppressive. A law was finally passed prohibiting slaves who had been set
free by their masters from remaining in the State, except in exceptional cases, where they had been manumitted for meritorious conduct.

Slavery and Quakerism could not prosper together, and many of
the Friends from New Garden and other settlements moved to the
West. . . .

In the winter of 1826-27, fugitives began to come to our house,
and as it became widely known on different routes that the slaves
fleeing from bondage would find a welcome and shelter at our house,
and be forwarded safely on their journey, the number increased.
. . .

The Underground Railroad business increased as time advanced,
and it was attended with heavy expenses . . . I found it necessary
to keep a team and a wagon always at command, to convey fugitive
slaves on their journey. . . . Every precaution to evade pursuit had
to be used, as the hunters were often on the track, and sometimes

ahead of the slaves. We had different routes for sending the fugitives to depots, ten, fifteen, or twenty miles distant, and when we heard of slave-hunters having passed on one road, we forwarded our passengers by another.—*Reminiscences of Levi Coffin, the Reputed President of the Underground Railroad*, pp. 20-22, 71-76, 108-12.

113. STEALING OF NEGRO SLAVES, 1849

One of the most serious problems of the slave-owner was the retention of his slave property. Some Negroes ran away of their own accord. Quite a number were stolen. The following newspaper notice reveals the attitude of the governor toward this grave problem.

$300 REWARD

A PROCLAMATION

By His Excellency Charles Manly, Governor of North Carolina.

Whereas, Nathaniel H. Simpson and Andrew F. Gibson stand charged by the Grand Jury of the County of Guilford with stealing a Negro Slave, named Bob, the property of one Ludwick Summers, of the said County of Guilford : and whereas it has been made to appear to me, that the said Nathaniel H. Simpson and Andrew F. Gibson have fled from justice and escaped probably beyond the limits of the State.

Now to the end that the said Nathaniel H. Simpson and Andrew F. Gibson may be arrested and brought to trial for said offence. I do hereby issue this my Proclamation, offering a reward of *three hundred* dollars for the apprehension and delivery of them to the Sheriff of the said County of Guilford or for their confinement in any Jail in this State; or a reward of one hundred and fifty dollars for the arrest and confinement of either of them as aforesaid. . . . — *Raleigh Register*, April 18, 1849.

114. REWARD FOR A RUNAWAY SLAVE, 1853

Probably fewer slaves fled from their masters in North Carolina than in many other southern states. Yet the problem of runaways was serious. For more than a generation prior to the Civil War the newspapers of the state carried notices similar to the accompanying one.

18

FIFTY DOLLARS REWARD!

RANAWAY from the Subscriber, on the 19th inst., a Negro man named LUKE, about five feet six or eight inches high, dark complected, has a scar on the side of one of his eyes, (which one not recollected, but believed to be the right eye,) stout built, weighs about 175 or 180 pounds.

He was purchased in 1846 from Mr. Josiah E. Bryan of this town. He has relatives in the County of Sampson, among them a half-brother named Sam Boon,—a free man of color,—and may possibly be lurking in that neighborhood, as I am informed he was seen about there a short time since. Possibly he may have obtained free papers, and is endeavoring to escape to a free State, as I understand some free persons of color removed from Sampson County last week to Indiana.

A reward of Ten Dollars will be given for his apprehension and delivery to me, if taken in this county, Fifteen Dollars if taken in any other county in this State and lodged in a safe Jail; or Fifty Dollars if taken out of the State,—so that I get him again.

M. H. LEARY

Fayetteville, March 29, 1853

—*Fayetteville Observer*, April 25, 1853.

115. LAW FOR THE EMANCIPATION OF A SLAVE, 1855

Laws pertaining to slaves were rather lenient before 1830; after that year they became more severe. Much public feeling was displayed against the free Negro. In 1835 he was deprived of suffrage. Many laws were passed restricting his freedom. Marriages between slaves and free Negroes were forbidden. They were not allowed to preach or teach. Free Negroes who left the state and remained absent as long as ninety days were forbidden to return under penalty of fine and imprisonment, and manumitted slaves who did not leave the state within ninety days after their manumission, or who, having left, returned, could be sold into slavery. Owners who freed slaves were required to give bond for the good behavior of the emancipated Negroes. The following law is illustrative.

AN ACT TO EMANCIPATE JERRY, A SLAVE

Sec. 1. Be it enacted by the General Assembly of the State of North Carolina, and it is hereby enacted by the authority of the same, That Jerry, a slave, the property of H. B. Williams and S. A. Davis, of Mecklenburg county, be, and he is hereby, with the consent, and

at the request of the said owners, emancipated and set free, and by
the name of Jerry Bethel, shall hereafter possess and exercise all the
rights and privileges which are enjoyed by other free persons of
color in this State: Provided, nevertheless, That before the said
slave is emancipated, the said Williams and Davis, or either of them,
shall give bond and approved security, payable to the Governor and
his successors in office, in the county court of Mecklenburg county,
in the sum of one thousand dollars, that the said Jerry shall honestly and correctly demean himself as long as he shall remain in the
State, and shall not become a county charge, which bond may be
sued upon in the name of the governor for the time being, to the
use of the said county, and of any person injured by the misconduct
of the said slave hereby emancipated. (Ratified 8th day, January
1855).—*Laws of North Carolina, 1854-1855,* Chap. CIX, pp. 90-91.

116. A NORTH CAROLINIAN'S DEFENSE OF SLAVERY, 1855

Thomas Ruffin was one of North Carolina's most distinguished men.
As associate justice and chief justice of the State Supreme Court from
1829 to 1853, he acquired the reputation of being one of the greatest
"legal minds" in the United States. He owned a large plantation on the
Haw river in Alamance County and another in Rockingham County.
He took much interest in farming and defended slavery vigorously.

In his address before the State Agricultural Society in 1855, he stated
his case for slavery and answered the criticisms which had been made by
the abolitionists. He contended that slave labor was more productive
than free labor, especially in the South. He did not believe that the presence of slavery tended to degrade white labor, insisting that labor among
the whites was respectable and respected. He thought the northern belief
that slaveholders led a life of ease and luxury was fallacious.

THE nature of the labor employed in our agriculture is the next
subject for our consideration. It is a most important element in the
cost, amount, and value of production. I very frankly avow the
opinion, that our mixed labor of free white men of European origin
and of slaves of the African race, is as well adapted to the public
and private ends of our agriculture as any other could be . . . that
it has a beneficial influence on the prosperity of the country, and
the physical and moral state of both races, rendering both better
and happier than either would be here, without the other. . . .
. . . My purpose, . . . is merely to maintain that slavery here is
favorable to the interests of agriculture in point of economy and
profit, and not unwholesome to the moral and social condition of

each race. In support of the first part of the proposition, a decisive argument is furnished by the fact that the amount and value of the productions of slave labor in this country exceeds those of similar productions, nay, of all other agricultural productions, of an equal number of men in any other country. . . . The blacks . . . can labor, without detriment, under degrees of heat, moisture, and exposure, which are found to be fatal to the whites. Men who are thoroughly versed in the practical operation of any institution, certainly will not, to their own prejudice, uphold it from generation to generation, and cling the closer to it as by its natural extension it becomes more and more destructive. . . . It was much easier for those who now condemn so strenuously our toleration of slavery, to capture and enslave the helpless Africans and bring them here, than for us, without crime yet more heinous, to renounce our dominion over them and turn them loose to their own discretion and self-destruction. Their fate would soon be that of our native savages or the enfranchised blacks of the West Indies, the miserable victims of idleness, want, drunkenness, and other debaucheries. . . . When did any man, . . . leave North Carolina in order to get clear of his slaves or of slavery? We have, indeed, a respectable and peaceful religious society—who are forbidden by an article in their creed from holding men in slavery. Even they never warred or contended against this institution here, . . . With that slight exception, the public sentiment is so generally satisfied with the existence of slavery and its propriety here, that it may properly be called universal. Some men have emancipated some or all of their slaves by sending them to other States. But I know not of an instance in which the former owner went with them, or left North Carolina because other owners would not follow their example. . . .

. . . It cannot but excite a smile in us, who know the contrary so well, when we are told that white men do not work here, and that they do not because it is considered disgraceful. Why, there is not a country on earth in which honest labor and diligence in business in all classes and conditions, is considered more respectable, or respected. We, like every other people, have the idle and vicious amongst us. But they are chiefly those who have the least connexion with slaves, and particularly those employed in agriculture, . . .

It is a mistake, too, equally notable, that slaveholders are above or exempt from the cares and business of life ; and it is a gross calumny to represent them as ruthless and relentless tyrants, . . . Slavery, indeed, is not a pure and unmixed good. Nor is anything that is human. There are instances of cruel and devilish masters,

and of turbulent and refractory slaves, . . . But these are exceptions. Great severity in masters is as much opposed to the usages of
our people as to the sentiment of the age, and, indeed, to the interest
of the master. . . .

But the interest of the owner is not the only security to the slave
for humane treatment; there is a stronger tie between them. Often
born on the same plantation, and bred together, they have a perfect knowledge of each other, and a mutual attachment. . . .

. . . Slaves are no part of this State, with no political power, and
seek no violent or sudden change in the law or policy of the country;
and where slavery exists labor and capital never come in conflict,
because they are in the same hands, and operate in harmony. It is
not, then, a blot upon our laws, nor a stain on our morals, nor a
blight upon our land. . . . —*The Papers of Thomas Ruffin* (edited by
J. G. deR. Hamilton), IV, 329-37.

117. THE IMPENDING CRISIS OF THE SOUTH: HOW TO MEET IT, 1857

Hinton Rowan Helper was born near Mocksville, North Carolina, December 27, 1829. Coming from a "poor white" family he early learned
to despise the institution of slavery. In 1857, he published *The Impending
Crisis of the South: How to Meet It*. This was a scathing arraignment of
slavery from the point of view of the small southern farmer. Helper took
the census figures from 1790 to 1860 and showed how the North had made
much greater economic and social progress than the South. He made
comparisons between certain northern states and certain southern states.
He was very uncritical in method. Without considering all the complex
factors involved in economic progress, he attributed southern backwardness to slavery alone. His book became immensely popular in the North
and was used as a campaign document by the Republican party. The
book was just as unpopular in the South, and caused as much excitment
in some sections as Harriet Beecher Stowe's *Uncle Tom's Cabin*. The following selections give comparisons between North Carolina and several
northern states.

MASSACHUSETTS AND NORTH CAROLINA

IN 1790, Massachusetts contained 378,717 inhabitants; in the same
year North Carolina contained 393,751; in 1850, the population of
Massachusetts was 994,514, all freemen; while that of North Carolina was only 869,039, of whom 288,548 were slaves. Massachusetts
has an area of only 7,800 square miles; the area of North Carolina
is 50,704 square miles. . . . Massachusetts and North Carolina

each have a harbor, Boston and Beaufort, which harbors, with the States that back them, are, by nature, possessed of about equal capacities and advantages for commercial and manufacturing enterprise. Boston has grown to be the second commercial city in the Union ; her ships, freighted with the useful and unique inventions and manufactures of her ingenious artisans and mechanics, . . . glide triumphantly through the winds and over the waves of every ocean. . .

How is it with Beaufort, in North Carolina, whose harbor is said to be the safest and most commodious anywhere to be found on the Atlantic coast south of the harbor of New-York, and but little inferior to that? Has anybody ever heard of her? Do the masts of her ships ever cast a shadow on foreign waters? Upon what distant or benighted shore have her merchants and mariners ever hoisted our national ensign, or spread the arts of civilization and peaceful industry? . . .

In 1853, the exports of Massachusetts amounted to $16,895,304, and her imports to $41,367,956 ; during the same time, and indeed during all the time, from the period of the formation of the government up to the year 1853, inclusive, the exports and imports of North Carolina were so utterly insignificant that we are ashamed to record them. In 1850, the products of manufactures, mining and the mechanic arts in Massachusetts, amounted to $151,137,145 ; those of North Carolina, to only, $9,111,245. In 1856, the products of these industrial pursuits in Massachusetts had increased to something over $288,000,000, a sum more than twice the value of the entire cotton crop of all the Southern States! In 1850, the cash value of all the farms, farming implements and machinery in Massachusetts, was $112,285,931 ; the value of the same in North Carolina, in the same year, was only $71,823,298. In 1850, the value of all the real and personal estate in Massachusetts, without recognizing property in man, or setting a monetary price on the head of a single citizen, white or black, amounted to $573,342,286 ; the value of the same in North Carolina, including negroes, amounted to only $226,-800,472. In 1856, the real and personal estate assessed in the City of Boston amounted in valuation to within a fraction of $250,000,000, showing conclusively that so far as dollars and cents are concerned, that single city could buy the whole State of North Carolina. . . .
In 1850, there were in Massachusetts, 1,861 native white and free colored persons over twenty years of age who could not read and write ; in the same year, the same class of persons in North Carolina numbered 80,083 ; while her 288,548 slaves were, by legislative en-

actments, kept in a state of absolute ignorance and unconditional subordination.

Hoping, however, and believing, that a large majority of the most respectable and patriotic citizens of North Carolina have resolved, or will soon resolve, with unyielding purpose, to cast aside the great obstacle that impedes their progress, and bring into action a new policy which will lead them from poverty and ignorance to wealth and intellectual greatness, and which will shield them not only from the rebukes of their own consciences, but also from the just reproaches of the civilized world, . . . we will . . . forbear . . .

In 1856, there were assessed for taxation in the State of

NEW YORK

Acres of land...............................	30,080,000
Valued at ....$	1,112,113,136
Average value per acre	36.97

NORTH CAROLINA

Acres of land...............................	32,450,560
Valued at ....$	98,800,636
Average value per acre......................	3.06

It is difficult for us to make any remarks on the official facts above. Our imagination is struck almost dumb at this outstanding and revolting display of the awful wreck that slavery is leaving behind it in the South. We will, however, go into a calculation for the purpose of ascertaining as nearly as possible, in this one particular, how much North Carolina has lost by the retention of slavery. As we have already seen, the average value per acre of land in the State of New York is $36.97; in North Carolina it is only $3.06; why is it so much less, or even any less, in the latter than in the former? The answer is *slavery*. In soil, in climate, in minerals, in water-power for manufactural purposes, and in area of territory, North Carolina has the advantage of New York, and, with the exception of slavery, no plausible reason can possibly be assigned why land should not be at least as valuable in the valley of the Yadkin as it is along the banks of the Genesee.

The difference between $36.97 and $3.06 is $33.91, which, multiplied by the whole number of acres of land in North Carolina, will show, in this one particular, the enormous loss that Freedom has sustained on account of Slavery in the Old North State. Thus :—

32,450,560 acres at $33.91........$1,100,398,489.

Let it be indelibly impressed on the mind, however, that this amount, large as it is, is only a moity of the sum that it has cost to maintain slavery in North Carolina. From time to time, hundreds upon hundreds of millions of dollars have left the State, either in search of profitable, permanent investment abroad, or in the shape of profits to Northern merchants and manufactures, who have become the moneyed aristocracy of the country by supplying to the South such articles of necessity, utility, and adornment, as would have been produced at home but for the pernicious presence of the peculiar institution.

A reward of Eleven Hundred Millions of Dollars is offered for the conversion of the lands of North Carolina into free soil. The lands themselves, desolate and impoverished under the fatal foot of slavery, offer the reward. How, then, can it be made to appear that the abolition of slavery in North Carolina, and, indeed, throughout all the Southern States—for slavery is exceedingly inimical to them all—is not demanded by every consideration of justice, prudence, and good sense?—Hinton Rowan Helper, *The Impending Crisis of the South: How to Meet It* (New York, 1857), pp. 14-17, 325-30.

118. SLAVE TRADING IN NORTH CAROLINA, 1859-1860

In the markets of the Southwest, dealers specialized in slaves from Virginia and South Carolina, or "Carolina," but very seldom did they advertise slaves from North Carolina. Few persons boasted of birth in North Carolina unless "up near the Virginia line" or "down near the border of South Carolina." Traders profited by this fact of social snobbishness. North Carolina slaves bought in either Richmond or Charleston were readily resold as natives of Virginia or South Carolina, and the ease with which they could be sent from Raleigh to Richmond and from Wilmington to Charleston was favorable to these markets. North Carolina, therefore, possessed no first-class slave markets. Slaves were sold in the state, however. Hector Davis, the Richmond trader, regularly advertised in Raleigh.

In February, 1856, a traveler saw thirty or forty slaves on a ferryboat crossing the Cape Fear River at Wilmington, "chained together in gangs and accompanied by their owner or overseer. They were being taken to the slave-mart in this city [Charleston], to be sold at auction to the highest bidder . . . the men had a stolid look, as if devoid of sensibility and were, to all appearance, as unconcerned and indifferent to their fate as a flock of sheep on their way to the butcher's shambles."

The Wilmington *Journal* advertised for slaves a great deal. The following advertisement is taken from that paper, January 3, 1860.

CO-PARTNERSHIP NOTICE THE UNDERSIGNED have entered into co-partnership in the town of Wilmington, North Carolina, under the firm of SOUTHERLAND & COLEMAN, for the purpose of buying and selling NEGRO SLAVES, where the highest cash prices will be paid.

They also have a house in Mobile, Alabama, where they will receive and sell slaves on commission. Liberal advances made upon slaves left with them for sale.—Wilmington *Journal*, January 3, 1860.

119. FREE NEGROES BY COUNTIES IN NORTH CAROLINA, 1860

North Carolina had more free Negroes than any other southern state with the exception of Virginia and Maryland. Their origin can be traced to many sources: (1) manumission, (2) immigration, (3) military service in the Revolution, (4) intermarriage, (5) cohabitation of white women and Negro men. Their number by counties is given below. It is to be observed that all the counties having more than a thousand free Negroes were in the East. All having less than one hundred free Negroes were in the West.

Alamance	422	Columbus	355
Alexander	24	Craven	1,332
Alleghany	33	Cumberland	109
Anson	152	Currituck	223
Ashe	142	Davidson	149
Beaufort	728	Davie	161
Bertie	319	Duplin	371
Bladen	435	Edgecombe	389
Brunswick	260	Forsyth	218
Buncombe	111	Franklin	566
Burke	221	Gaston	111
Cabarrus	115	Gates	361
Caldwell	114	Granville	1,123
Camden	274	Greene	154
Carteret	153	Guilford	693
Caswell	282	Halifax	2,452
Catawba	32	Harnett	103
Chatham	306	Haywood	14
Cherokee	38	Henderson	85
Chowan	150	Hertford	1,112
Cleveland	109	Hyde	257

Iredell	26	Polk	106
Jackson	6	Randolph	432
Johnston	195	Richmond	345
Jones	113	Robeson	1,462
Lenoir	178	Rockingham	409
Lincoln	81	Rowan	136
McDowell	273	Rutherford	123
Macon	115	Sampson	488
Madison	17	Stanly	45
Martin	451	Stokes	86
Mecklenburg	293	Surry	184
Montgomery	46	Tyrrell	143
Moore	184	Union	53
Nash	687	Wake	1,446
New Hanover	640	Warren	402
Northampton	659	Washington	299
Orange	528	Watauga	81
Onslow	162	Wayne	737
Pasquotank	1,507	Wilkes	261
Perquimans	395	Wilson	281
Person	318	Yadkin	172
Pitt	127	Yancey	67

—*Eighth Census of the United States*, 1860, pp. 358-59.

IX

FOUR YEARS OF STRIFE: THE CIVIL WAR

120. A Constitutional Union, 1860

There was strong Union sentiment in North Carolina in 1860. The *North Carolina Standard*, edited by W. W. Holden, expressed the opinion of many people when it advocated a "Constitutional Union." It believed that there was no reason why North Carolina should contemplate a dissolution of the Union at that time. It further declared, "while we would surrender no right of our State, and while we would preserve her honor untarnished among her sisters, yet disunion is one of the last things to be thought of." Holden believed that Lincoln's election would cause the secession of the "cotton States," but he thought that, even then, North Carolina might remain within the Union. Causes might arise for the dissolution of the Union, but he was not willing to hasten this event. It is interesting to note that Holden, in the following editorial, referred to North Carolina as a "bread-stuff State" rather than a "cotton State."

NORTH Carolina has been for the space of seventy years a member of the federal Union. She entered this great sisterhood of States after mature deliberation. She did so believing she would thereby best promote her own interests, and more effectually than in any other situation protect herself from encroachments by foreign States. Strong in her own arm and in her own determined purpose to maintain the right under all circumstances, she was nevertheless not unmindful of the fact that in union there would be strength beyond that which any individual could possess. During this long period she had been faithful to all her Constitutional obligations; and on the other hand, while her rights as a slaveholding State have not always been as fully respected and maintained as they should have been, yet no deliberate wrong has been put upon her, and none of her vital interests have been assailed or threatened by the common government. When her co-states of the South have complained of unjust tariff laws, or protested against the encroachments of non-slaveholding States upon their rights in the common territories, she has sympathized with them in these complaints and protests; but when they have nullified the laws, or taken steps to dissolve their relations with the other States, she has mildly but firmly interposed to prevent the calamitous consequences which would flow from nullification and disunion. She has never been either a nullifying or a disunion State, and she is not so now. Some great cause must move her—some great wrong must either be inflicted or must overshadow her, before she will seriously contemplate by her own act a severance of the Union. She feels that while Virginia, and Tennessee, and Maryland, and Kentucky are safe in the Union she will be safe also; and that her honor, as sensitive and as untarnished as theirs, has been confided to her own keeping, and not to that of South Carolina, Alabama, and Mississippi. She is a bread-stuff rather than a "cotton-State." Her interests are central among the southern States, relying as she does for protection not more on the slave-holding States south of her than on those of the north and west. She is not so much of a "cotton State" as to be ready just now to pitch into the vortex of disunion and revolution. She will not rush into this vortex herself, and she will hold others back, if she can.

. . .

In a word, no reason exists why North Carolina should contemplate at this time a dissolution of the Union.

While we would surrender no right of our State, and while we would preserve her honor untarnished among her sisters, yet disunion is one of the last things to be thought of. Disunion would be fraternal strife, civil and servile war, murder, arson, pillage, robbery, and fire and blood through long and cruel years. It would unsettle all business, diminish the value of all property, put the lives of both sexes and all ages in peril, and launch the States on a sea of scenes which no eye has scanned and no navigator sounded. It would bring debt, and misrule, and oppressive taxes, to be followed, perhaps, by the military rule of titled tyrants. It would wrench apart the tenderly entwined affections of millions of hearts, making it a crime in the North to have been born in the South, and a crime in the South to have been born in the North. It would convert the great body of the conservative men of the North, who are now our friends, into either deadly enemies or indifferent spectators of our intestine struggles, which would increase in intensity until law, order, justice, and civil rule would be forgotten or unknown. We repeat, there is no good cause *now* for dissolving the Union. The cause may arise, but let us not hasten to make or meet it. . . . —*Southern Editorials on Secession* (edited by D. L. Dumond), pp. 142-44, citing the *North Carolina Standard* (Raleigh), July 11, 1860.

121. NORTH CAROLINA LEAVES THE UNION, 1861

North Carolina had little desire to secede, but the events of April, 1861, left her no alternative. When President Lincoln asked Governor Ellis for two regiments, North Carolina's course in the war was decided. In a short telegram the Governor replied that he regarded "the levy of troops made by the administration for the purpose of subjugating the States of the South as in violation of the Constitution and a gross usurpation of power." To aid "this wicked violation" of the country's laws and "this war upon the liberties of a free people," Lincoln could "get no troops from North Carolina." And forthwith the secessionist governor dispatched men and arms to Virginia soil, acting upon the urgent requests of Confederate Secretary of War L. P. Walker. Even the staunch Unionists now admitted the necessity of war, and all elements in the state began to prepare for the coming conflict. Federal forts and arsenals were seized, together with the United States mint at Charlotte, the use of which Ellis promptly offered to the Confederacy. Thirty thousand volunteers were called, and a training camp was established at Raleigh. The legislature, meeting in a special session on May 1, immediately and with an almost unanimous vote called a convention without submitting the question to a popular vote.

The convention met in Raleigh on May 20, 1861, with one hundred and twenty delegates present. It was "an able body, but their political antipathies were deep and strong." The aged Weldon N. Edwards, an outspoken secessionist, was chosen president, defeating ex-Governor William A. Graham, a "revolutionist," by a vote of 65 to 48. Two ordinances of separation were proposed at the first day's session. One, introduced by George E. Badger, Whig leader in the state, was based on the right of revolution, and denied by implication the right of secession. The other, which was adopted, was the handiwork of Judah P. Benjamin and was based squarely upon the right of secession. On the same day the Convention ratified the Provisional Constitution of the Confederate States.

ON THE VERGE OF SECESSION

RALEIGH, N. C., APRIL 15, 1861.

HON. SIMON CAMERON, SECRETARY OF WAR

Your dispatch is received, and if genuine, which its extraordinary character leads me to doubt, I have to say in reply that I regard the levy of troops made by the administration for the purpose of subjugating the States of the South as in violation of the Constitution and a gross usurpation of power. I can be no party to this wicked violation of the laws of the country, and to this war upon the liberties of a free people. You can get no troops from North Carolina. I will reply more in detail when your call is received by mail.

JOHN W. ELLIS,

Governor of North Carolina

MONTGOMERY, APRIL 22, 1861.

GOV. J. W. ELLIS, RALEIGH, N. C. :

Sir : Your patriotic response to the requisition of the President of the United States for troops to coerce the Confederate States justifies the belief that your people are prepared to unite with us in repelling the common enemy of the South.

Virginia needs our aid. I therefore request you to furnish one regiment of infantry without delay to rendezvous at Richmond, Va. It must consist of ten companies, of not less than sixty-four men each. . . .

L. P. WALKER,

Secretary of War.

RALEIGH, APRIL 24, 1861.

HON. L. P. WALKER :

You shall have from one to ten thousand volunteers in a few days, with arms, and I wish them to go as State troops. Many of our men will enlist in the Confederate Army. Will have a regiment ready in four days. Funds will be required for transportation, as I cannot lawfully draw on the State treasury for this purpose. I am anxious to send at least three regiments. Our legislature will meet in a few days. I will not await, however.

JOHN W. ELLIS.

MONTGOMERY, APRIL 25, 1861.

GOV. J. W. ELLIS, RALEIGH, N. C. :

I shall have to supply with arms three regiments from Tennessee and one from Arkansas that rendezvous at Lynchburg, Va. Can you send this Government two thousand percussion muskets to be sent to Lynchburg?

L. P. WALKER.

RALEIGH, APRIL 25, 1861.

L. P. WALKER:

Arms at Fayetteville off the railroad. Two thousand percussion muskets are at your service soon as can be procured. Where will you have them sent?

JOHN W. ELLIS.

RALEIGH, MAY 1, 1861.

JEFFERSON DAVIS:

Convention bill passed; also a resolution authorizing me to send troops to Virginia at once without limit. Our mint at Charlotte will coin for the Confederate Government if desired. Ships of war are hovering on our coast near the Cape Fear. Designs unknown. I am preparing to manufacture percussion caps. Will succeed. More troops are offering than can provide for.

JOHN W. ELLIS

RALEIGH, MAY 17, 1861.

L. P. WALKER:

I have already sent nine thousand five hundred muskets to Richmond. Cannot possibly spare more. Virginia has already more guns than men. North Carolina has not. I must beg of you to accept four regiments of twelve-months' men. They are now in camp. Two regiments are on their way to Richmond. Please answer.

JNO. W. ELLIS.

—*Official Records*, Ser. I, Vol. I, pp. 486-88.

THE BADGER ORDINANCE

An Ordinance Declaring the Separation of North Carolina from the United States of America.

Whereas, Abraham Lincoln . . . and Hannibal Hamlin . . . were chosen President and Vice President of the United States by a party in fact and avowedly entirely sectional in its organization, and hostile in its declared principles to the institutions of the Southern States of the Union . . . and, whereas, the people of North Carolina, though justly aggrieved by the evident tendency of this election . . . did, nevertheless, abstain from adopting any such measure of separation, and . . . did remain in the said Union. . . .

And, whereas, the said Abraham Lincoln . . . did, on the 16th day of April, by his proclamation, call upon the States of the Union to furnish large bodies of troops to enable him, under the false pretencè of executing the laws, to march an army into the seceded States with a view to their subjugation under an arbitrary and military authority . . . and, whereas in aid of these detestable plans and wicked measures, the said Lincoln, without any shadow of rightful authority, and in plain violation of the Constitution of the United States . . . [put the Southern ports] under blockade. . . .

And, whereas, since his accession to power, the whole conduct of the said Lincoln has been marked by a succession of false, disingenuous, and treacherous acts and declarations. . . .

And, whereas, he is now governing by military rule alone. . . .

Therefore, this Convention, now here assembled, in the name and with the sovereign power of the people of North Carolina, doth, for reasons aforesaid, and others, and in order to preserve the undoubted rights and liberties of the said people, hereby declare all connection of government between this state and the United States of America dissolved and abrogated, and this State to be free, sovereign and independent state, owing no subordination, obedience, support or other duty to the said United States, their Constitution or authorities, anything in her ratification of said Constitution or of any amendment or amendments thereto to the contrary notwithstanding; and having full power to levy war, conclude peace, contract alliances, and to do all other acts and things which independent states may of right do; and appealing to the Supreme Governor of the world for the justice of our cause, and beseeching Him for his gracious help and blessing, we will, to the uttermost of our power, and to the last extremity, maintain, defend and uphold this declaration.

THE CRAIGE ORDINANCE

An ordinance Dissolving the Union Between the State of North Carolina and the Other States United with her under the Compact Government Entitled "The Constitution of the United States."

We, the people of the State of North Carolina, in convention do declare and ordain, and it is hereby declared and ordained, That the ordinance adopted by the State of North Carolina in the convention of 1789, whereby the Constitution of the United States was ratified and adopted, and also all acts and parts of acts of the General Assembly, ratifying and adopting amendments to the said Constitution, are hereby repealed, rescinded, and abrogated.

We do further declare and ordain, that the union now subsisting between the state of North Carolina and the other states, under the title of "The United States of America," is hereby dissolved, and that the state of North Carolina is in full possession and exercise of all those rights of sovereignty which belong and appertain to a free and independent state.—*Journal of the Convention of the People of North Carolina, May 20, 1861*, pp. 10-13.

122. NORTH CAROLINA AND THE CONFEDERACY

North Carolina contributed heavily in men and supplies to the southern cause. She had 125,000 men in state and Confederate service, although the military population of the state in 1860 was only 115,369. It is no idle boast to say that North Carolina was "First at Bethel, Farthest at Gettysburg and Chickamauga, and Last at Appomattox." At the same time no state was more jealous of its rights than North Carolina. Governor Zebulon Baird Vance consistently and persistently protested against many acts and policies of the Confederate government, which he thought impaired the rights of his state. He objected strenuously to the Confederate conscription law, the suspension of the writ of habeas corpus, the impressment of property, and the use of Virginia officers in North Carolina. On one occasion he threatened to "take North Carolina out of the Confederacy," if President Davis did not change his policy in regard to the state. The correspondence between Vance and Davis became so heated that the latter asked Vance that it be discontinued.

The following extracts from Vance's letters throw considerable light on North Carolina's attitude toward the Confederacy.

RALEIGH, N. C., OCTOBER 25th, 1862

HIS EXCELLENCY JEFFERSON DAVIS:

DEAR SIR: When in Richmond, I had the honor to call your attention, in the presence of Mr. Randolph, to the subject of allowing the conscripts the privilege of selecting the regiments to which they should go. I understood you and the Secretary both to assent to it willingly.

A few days after my return home, therefore, I was much surprised and grieved to find an order coming from the Secretary to Major Mallet to disregard an order to this effect from Brigadier-General Martin and to place all of them in certain brigades under General French. I immediately addressed a letter to Mr. Randolph protesting against it, and giving my reasons for so doing. To this letter, after the lapse of two weeks, I have received no reply. Last week about one hundred men were brought into camp from one county above, from a region somewhat lukewarm, who had been got to come cheerfully, under the solemn promise made them by my enrolling officer that they should be allowed to join any regiment they desired, according to the published order. Under the circumstances, General Martin said they might have their choice, started them accordingly, and wrote to General French, begging his consent to the arrangement. He refused, and according to a note received from him, the men were stopped at Petersburg and distributed equally to certain regiments, as quarter-master's stores or any other chattel property, alleging that, by not coming in sooner, they had forfeited all claims to consideration.

On the shortsightedness and inhumanity of this harsh course towards our people I shall offer no comment. I wish not only to ask that a more liberal policy may be adopted, but to make it the occasion of informing you also of a few things of a political nature, which you ought to have.

The people of this State have ever been eminently conservative, and jealous of their political rights. The transition from their former opinions anterior to our troubles, to a state of revolution and war, was a sudden and very extraordinary one. Prior to Lincoln's proclamation the election of delegates to our proposed Convention, exhibited a popular majority of upwards of 30,000 against secession for existing causes. The late election after sixteen months of war and membership with the Confederacy, shows conclusively that the original advocates of secession no longer hold the ear of our people. Without the warm and ardent support of the old Union men North Carolina could not so promptly and generously have been brought to the support of the seceding States, and without that same influence constantly and unremittingly given, the present status could not be maintained for forty-eight hours. *These are facts.* I allude to them, not to remind you of my heretofore political differences, (which I earnestly hope are buried in the graves of our gallant countrymen), but simply to give you information.

The corrollary to be deduced is briefly this : that the opinions and advice of the old Union leaders must be heeded with regard to the government of affairs in North Carolina, or the worst consequences may ensue. I am candid with you for the cause's sake. I believe, sir, most sincerely, that the conscript law could not have been executed by a man of different antecedents from myself, without outbreaks among our people. And now, with all the popularity with which I came into office, it will be exceedingly difficult for me to execute it under your recent call, with all the assistance you can afford me. If, on the contrary, West Point generals, who know much less of human nature than I do of military service, are to ride rough-shod over the people, drag them from their homes, and assign them, or rather *consign* them to strange regiments and strange commanders, without regard to their wishes or feelings, I must be compelled to decline undertaking a task which will certainly fail. These conscripts *are* entitled to consideration. They comprise a number of the best men in their communities, whom indispensable business, large and helpless families, poverty and distress, in a thousand shapes, have combined to keep at home until the last moment. In spite of all the softening I could give to the law, and all the appeals that could be made to their patriotism, much discontent has grown up, and now the waters of insubordination begin to surge more angrily than ever, as the extended law goes into effect. Many openly declare that they want not another conscript to leave the State until provision is made for her own defense. Others say it will not leave labor sufficient to support the women and children, and therefore it must not be executed. Thousands are flying from our eastern counties, with their slaves, to the centre and west, to devour the very short crops, and increase the prospects of starvation. Governor Letcher is threatening to deprive the State of a contract we have for procuring salt in Virginia, and when the enemy secures Wilmington (which he no doubt will do when the pestilence abates) we shall have no assurance of obtaining it from any other source, hence I am importuned by many to defend our own coast myself. You see the difficulties that beset me. But through them all I have endeavored and shall endeavor to hold my course straight forward for the common good. It is disheartening, however, to find that I am thwarted in so small a matter as this, which is yet a great one to the conscript. I have thus spoken candidly and explicitly. I beg that you will not in any matter misunderstand me, or fail to appreciate my motives. I trust that, whether on the field or in the council, I have established my claim to respect and confidence. I can do much towards increasing our armies, if properly aided by the War Department. When the sowing of the wheat crop is completed, fifteen or twenty thousand men can be got out in a short time, especially if an assurance can be given that an adequate proportion will be sent to the defense of our own coast and suffering people. . . . A course of justice and fair treatment will do more than all besides in bringing our entire able bodied population in the field.

Earnestly requesting that my representation of things in North

Carolina may enable you to do that which is for the best, and will most advance the great cause for which the nation is suffering and bleeding, I remain, with kindest respect,

Your obedient servant,

Z. B. VANCE.

STATE OF NORTH CAROLINA, EXECUTIVE DEPARTMENT,

RALEIGH, NOVEMBER 11TH, 1862.

HIS EXCELLENCY PRESIDENT DAVIS:

MY DEAR SIR: By the recent expedition of our troops by the order of General French into eastern North Carolina some forty persons were arrested on suspicion of disloyalty and sent up to Salisbury for safe keeping. As Governor of the State of which they are citizens, it becomes my duty to see that they are protected in whatever rights pertain to them. First among them is the undeniable right of a trial of their alleged offenses. A number of others, it is proper to state, have been there in confinement for some time past under similar circumstances. I should be glad to know what disposition is to be made of them, or if there exists any grave public reason why these cases should not be investigated.

Very respectfully, your obedient servant,

Z. B. VANCE.

STATE OF NORTH CAROLINA, EXECUTIVE DEPARTMENT

RALEIGH, JANUARY 26TH, 1863.

HON. JAMES A. SEDDON, SECRETARY OF WAR, RICHMOND, VA.

SIR: I had the honor to complain to His Excellency, the President and your immediate predecessor, Mr. Randolph, in regard to the manner of enforcing the Conscript Act in this State, and of disposing of the men in regiments, during the month of October last. I am compelled again, greatly to my regret, to complain of the appointment of Colonel August as commandant of conscripts for North Carolina, who has recently assumed command here.

Merely alluding to the obvious impropriety and bad policy of wounding the sensibilities of our people by the appointment of a citizen of another State to execute a law, both harsh and odious, I wish to say, sir, in all candor that it smacks of discourtesy to our people to say the least of it. Having furnished as many (if not more) troops for the service of the Confederacy, as any other State, and being, as I was assured by the President, far ahead of all others in the number raised under the conscript law, the people of this State have justly felt mortified in seeing those troops commanded by citizens of other States, to the exclusion of the claims of their own. . . .

Without the slightest prejudice against Colonel August or the State from which he comes, I protest against his appointment as both unjust and impolitic. Having submitted in silence to the many, very many acts of the Administration, heretofore, so calculated to wound that pride which North Carolina is so pardonable for entertaining, it is my duty to inform you that if persisted in, the appointment of strangers to all the positions in this State and over her troops, will cause a feeling throughout her whole borders, which it is my great desire to avoid. . . .

Most respectfully, your obedient servant,

Z. B. VANCE.

STATE OF NORTH CAROLINA, EXECUTIVE DEPARTMENT

RALEIGH, FEBRUARY 25TH, 1863.

HON. J. A. SEDDON, SECRETARY OF WAR:

SIR: I had the honor some three weeks ago, to address you, respectfully asking the removal of a lot of broken down cavalry horses from the northwestern counties of this State, of General Jenkins' command, which were devouring the substance of a people threatened with famine. I have not had the pleasure of receiving a reply to that letter.

I beg leave to inform you that their depredations are still continued, and that they have become not only a nuisance but a terror to the community, . . . With every possible disposition to aid in the support of the army, I have the strongest reasons conceivable, the existence of my own people, for declining to permit these horses to remain in that section of the State. When the question of starvation is narrowed down to women and children on the one side and some worthless cavalry horses on the other, I can have no difficulty in making a choice.

Unless they are removed soon, I shall be under the painful necessity of calling out the militia of the adjoining counties and driving them from the State. I hope, however, to be spared such a proceeding.

Very respectfully, your obedient servant,

Z. B. VANCE.

STATE OF NORTH CAROLINA, EXECUTIVE DEPARTMENT

RALEIGH, DECEMBER 21ST, 1863

HON. JAS. A. SEDDON, SECRETARY OF WAR :

DEAR SIR : I desire to call your attention to an evil which is inflicting great distress upon the people of this State, and contributing largely to the public discontent. I allude to illegal seizures of property and other depredations of an outrageous character by detached bands of troops—chiefly cavalry. The department, I am sure, can have no idea of the extent and character of this evil. It is enough in many cases to breed a rebellion in a loyal county against the Confederacy, and has actually been the cause of much alienation of feeling in many parts of North Carolina. It is not my purpose now to give instances and call for punishment of the offenders—that I do to their commanding officers, but to ask if some order or regulation cannot be made for the government of troops on detached service, the severe and unflinching execution of which might not check this stealing, pilfering, burning, and sometimes murderous conduct.

I give you my word that in North Carolina it has become a grievance, intolerable, damnable, and not to be borne! If God Almighty had yet in store another plague—worse than all others which he intended to have let loose on the Egyptians in case Pharaoh still hardened his heart, I am sure it must have been a regiment or so of half armed, half disciplined Confederate cavalry! Had they been turned loose on Pharaoh's subjects with or without an impressment law, he would have become so sensible of the anger of God, that he never would have followed the children of Israel to the Red Sea. No, sir, not an inch!! Cannot officers be reduced to the ranks for permitting this? Cannot a few men be shot for perpetrating these outrages, as an example? Unless something can be done, I shall be compelled in some sections to call out my militia and levy actual war against them. I beg your early and earnest attention to this matter.

Very respectfully yours,

Z. B. VANCE.

—Letter from Vance's official letter book, in Clement Dowd, *Life of Zebulon B. Vance*, pp. 73-88.

123. W. W. HOLDEN'S INDICTMENT OF THE CONFEDERATE GOVERNMENT

William Woods Holden was one of North Carolina's leading political journalists before and during the Civil War. Born in Orange County in 1818, he moved to Raleigh in 1837, where he worked on the *Star*, the state's leading Whig paper. In 1843 he became editor and owner of the *North Carolina Standard*, a Democratic journal. According to Professor Hamilton, he made this "more powerful than any other newspaper has ever been in North Carolina." He was considered a radical secessionist, and when the state left the Union he pledged "the last man and the last dollar" to the southern cause.

Defeated for governor in 1858 and for the Senate in 1860, Holden became very critical of Democratic leadership in the state. At the same time he was making editorial attacks on the acts and policies of the Confederacy. He supported Vance for governor in 1862, hoping that the latter's election would cause a rupture within the South. When Vance refused to make the definite break which Holden desired, Holden assumed the leadership of the Peace party in the state and ran against Vance for governor in 1864. He was defeated by an overwhelming vote, Vance receiving an army vote of 13,209 to 1,824 for Holden, and a state vote of 58,065 to 14,471 for Holden.

From 1863 to 1865 Holden wrote many caustic editorials relative to the conduct of the war. He criticized the Confederate government for its mistreatment of North Carolina, for its failure to give the state a proper amount of patronage, for raking North Carolina for conscripts "as with a fine-tooth comb," for impressment of property, and for setting up a "military despotism." The following are excerpts from Holden's editorials.

. . . WE were told, when the government was broken up by the States south of us, that the contest was to be for liberty; that the civil power was to prevail over the military; that the common government was to be the agent of the States, and not their master; and that free institutions, not an imperial despotism, were to constitute the great object of our toils and sufferings. But the official paper (the *Richmond Enquirer*) has declared otherwise. That paper is opposed to a nobility to be established by law, but it favors a military despotism like that of France. . . .

We know that a military despotism is making rapid strides in these (Confederate) States. We know that no people ever lost their liberties at once, but step by step, as some deadly disease steals upon the system and gradually but surely saps the fountain of life. . . . The argument now is, we hate Lincoln so bitterly that in order to resist him successfully we must make slaves of ourselves. The answer of our people is, *we will be slaves neither to Lincoln, nor Davis, nor France, nor England.* North Carolina *is a State,* not a province, and she has eighty regiments of as brave troops as ever trod the earth. When she calls them they will come. If the worst should happen that can happen, she will be able to take care of herself as an independent power. She will not submit, in any event, to a law of Congress passed in deliberate violation of the Constitution, investing Mr. Davis with dictatorial powers; but she will resist such a law by withdrawing, if necessary, from the Confederation, and she will fight her way out against all comers. . . . For one, we are determined not to exchange one despotism for another. . . . —*North Carolina Standard,* May 6, 1863.

North Carolina is badly treated. She is ignored. She has no voice in the Cabinet. She is raked for conscripts as with a fine-tooth comb. Her troops are always placed in the forefront of the hottest battles. Her sick and wounded are scattered through every hospital in Richmond, and are treated by physicians appointed from other states. A large portion of her people are suspected of being disloyal. The people of North Carolina are long suffering; but Mr. Davis would do well to bear in mind that it is the last straw that breaks the camel's back. . . . North Carolina must be the equal of the other states of the Confederacy, or she will leave it, and endeavor to take care of herself.—*North Carolina Standard,* June 3, 1863.

124. CONDITIONS IN NORTH CAROLINA, 1864

One of the clearest accounts of political, social, and economic conditions in the state during the latter part of the sectional conflict is given in Governor Vance's message to the General Assembly at the opening of the 1864-65 session. In a document of eighteen pages he summarized the outstanding problems of North Carolina at that critical time. It is quoted, in part, below.

He called the attention of the legislature to the disorderly conditions prevailing in some sections of the state. He said that deserters, representing almost every state in the Confederacy, infested many counties, stealing, plundering, and murdering. He saw no remedy except to outlaw them and drive them from the state by force. He regretted to announce that some of the Home Guard had deserted and joined the enemy, and urged the legislature to adopt a rigorous policy in regard to desertion.

He hated to say that blockade-running operations of the state were pretty well stopped, and he blamed the policy of the Confederate government as much as he did the activities of the Federal fleet for this unhappy situation. Fortunately the state had an adequate supply of clothing and blankets. But he did not know where the winter supply of shoes was going to be obtained. There was an abundant supply at the Islands off the coast, but he now had no means of bringing them in.

It was going to be necessary to increase taxes considerably. Money was needed not only for the soldiers in the field, but also for their families at home. A supply of salt was likewise required. He asked legislative permission to spend money in the North for the benefit of North Carolina prisoners.

Some slaves had been employed by governmental authority and the report had been circulated that the state was going to arm the Negroes. Vance denied this emphatically. Under no circumstances would he consent to see them armed, and he considered the proposition to emancipate them by the Confederate government as entirely out of the question. He thought such a policy would defeat the purpose of the war and stultify the South in the eyes of the world.

He asked the legislators not to forget the public schools, declaring that "the Common Schools should be kept going at every cost."

SINCE the adjournment of your predecessors, the enemy have not encroached upon our territory, except the recapture of the town of Plymouth, and the consequent evacuation of Washington, events greatly to be deplored. The western border is however, subject to the constant raids and the situation of the inhabitants is distressing in the extreme. Bands of lawless men, many of them our own citizens, acting or pretending to act under commissions from the enemy, swarm in the mountain frontier, murdering, burning, and destroying. Totally regardless of the laws of civilized warfare, they have inaugurated a system of cruelty, at which humanity shudders. I have written to General Breckenridge and urged him to take such steps as may be in his power to stop such proceedings, but I do not yet know what may be the result. Nor is the interior of the State entirely free from the disorders naturally to be expected from a state of continued war. Deserters representing almost every state in the Confederacy infest the swamps and mountains of many counties, stealing, plundering and in many instances murdering the inhabitants. In some places they muster in such force as to almost amount to a suspension of civil authority, aided and protected as they are by their relatives and friends. All of my efforts to abate the nuisance by offers of pardon having proved fruitless, I see no remedy for the evil, but to outlaw them and drive them from the State by the strong hand. If my control over the Militia for this purpose were unrestrained, I am confident I could easily rid the community of this pest. I also recommend that the law against harboring, aiding and abetting desertion, be amended so as to facilitate the making of the proof required to convict, and that it be made the duty of all civil, as well as military officers to assist in their arrest under such penalties as will enforce obedience. . . .

I feel quite ashamed also to add that a number of the Home Guard in certain interior counties, holding both civil and military offices, actuated either by treason or cowardice or perhaps both, have recently deserted and fled to the enemy. I earnestly recommend that you take such steps for the punishment of such a crime by confiscation or otherwise as may deter others from such cowardly and degrading treason. There should be no more trifling in this matter. . . .

I regret to say that the blockade running operations of the State are pretty well stopped. The regulations imposed by the Confederate Government, in defiance as I think of the act of Congress to which I have heretofore adverted, have operated so injuriously as to compel me in a measure to withdraw our vessels from the trade, after losses by detention, the surrender of cargo space, &c., of not less than $200,000 in gold. I regret also to have to announce the loss of the State Steamer *Ad-Vance*, during the month of September. This noble vessel, the pride of the State, and the benefactor of our soldiers and people, was captured by the enemy after she had successfully made her way through the blockading squadron, in consequence of the seizure of her foreign coal for the use of the cruiser *Tallehassee*, compelling her to put to sea with North Carolina coal. This being unsuited to her furnaces and machinery, rendered her incapable of making more than half her usual speed, and left behind her a dense volume of black smoke, by which she was easily followed and captured. So obviously is her loss attributable to this unwarranted seizure of her coal, that I trust you will memorialize Congress for compensation. The unwise policy of making our only remaining seaport a resort for our cruisers cannot be too strongly condemned. It has trippled the stringency of the blockade, has already caused the loss of many valuable steamers, and will ultimately provoke the utmost efforts of the enemy for the capture of Wilmington. It is no exaggeration to say that the *Ad-Vance* alone in solid benefits has been worth more to our government than all the cruisers we have ever put afloat. . . .

Where our supply of shoes is to come from this winter I do not know. I have an abundant supply at the Islands, but have now no means of getting them in. I trust you will again instruct our representatives in Congress to ask for a repeal of these regulations. This done, our remaining steamers could soon bring in the many valuable supplies we have bought abroad. The act of Congress authorizing the President to impose regulations upon commerce expressly provides "that nothing in this act shall be construed to prohibit the Confederate States or any of them from exporting any of the articles herein enumerated on their own account." What policy so urgently requiring the States to be forced by executive construction out of the benefit of this proviso, influences our government, I have not been able to learn. . . .

Fortunately of clothing and blankets we still have an abundance . . . not only have the army and the people been supplied with indispensable articles without loss, but with actual profit to the State, notwithstanding the fears of some to the contrary. It has not been our aim to make money, but to supply the necessities of our people and army for simply cost and charges, which has been done. In regard to insinuations which have been indulged in against this enterprise, I can only say that I have heretofore and do now challenge the strictest investigation. . . .

There is also in the hands of and due to Major Dowd of the Clothing Department, the sum of $2,672,990, which if so ordered can be made available to the Treasury for the current fiscal year. My intention was to buy cotton, tobacco, &c., for exportation, so as to make the ship's cargo inward buy the cargo outward without any connexion with the Treasury, but perhaps it would be better to divert it to this purpose to aid in avoiding an increase of the public debt, and depend upon the proceeds of the supplies on hand to furnish the means for exportation. . . .

I can see great propriety in the retention by the State of a small military force in time of war, and very little in transferring absolutely all her physical power to other hands. The time has already come when, to say the least of it, the assertion of a right as pertaining to a sovereign State is worth much more if backed by some show of physical power to enforce it. Neither can I regard it as in any wise anomalous that the State should employ her militia in trying to arrest the numerous bands of deserters who infest the country robbing and murdering the citizens, and in some instances compelling a strong force to be under arms to protect the sittings of the courts. . . .

I . . . concur in the Treasurer's recommendation, that the taxes will have to be considerably increased for the next fiscal year. . . . I therefore recommend an appropriation of two millions in currency, and the imposition of a tax in kind, say one-twentieth bushel of corn, wheat and peas, gallon of syrup &c., so arranged and systematized as you may deem best. . . .

Contrary to the impression sought to be made by some, the resolution relating to the impressment or conscription of slaves, was by no means intended to include the arming of them, much less their final emancipation, which I take it would follow as a natural consequence. I supposed that as property their temporary services were within reach of the government like all other property, to be employed as pioneers, erecting fortifications, cooks, teamsters, hospital servants, laborers in the several Departments and wherever in short the negro could take the place of any ablebodied white man who could carry a musket. Under no circumstances would I consent to see them *armed*, which I would regard as not only dangerous in the extreme, but as less degrading only than their employment in this capacity by our enemies. . . . The proposition to emancipate them by the Confederate Government. . . . I regard as entirely out of the question. This course would, it seems to me, surrender the entire question which has ever separated the North from the South, would stultify ourselves in the eyes of the world, and render our whole revolution nugatory. . . . The slave, however, should certainly be made to do his part as a non-combatant. . . .

By a recent agreement entered into between our government and that of the enemy, it is provided that each may have the privilege of supplying its soldiers held as prisoners of war by the other with certain necessary articles. . . . I therefore ask your consent to expend, should it be necessary, a portion of our funds abroad, not exceeding £5,000 sterling, for the benefit of North Carolina soldiers held in Northern prisons—officers and men. . . .

The subject of our Common Schools is one which I beg you will not forget amid the great concerns of the war. The efforts making by the friends of education with our zealous and indefatigable Superintendent at their head, to prevent the public from losing sight of this great interest, is worthy of our admiration. . . . I also suggest that regular teachers be exempted from State military duty whilst engaged in teaching. The Common Schools should be kept going at every cost. . . .

The execution of the laws becomes more and more difficult, owing not so much to the increase of crime, in my opinion, as to the want of boldness in the civil magistrates. Many complaints continue to reach me from all parts of the State of depredations and outrages of straggling soldiers, illegal impressments of property by Confederate Agents and many high handed violations of civil rights by military commanders. Most of the sufferers appeal to me for redress which I am often unable to afford them. . . .

Nobody has yet starved, and with sufficient care nobody will, during the coming season. But the end of this war and the return of peace seems still hid from human vision. . . .

It is a matter of sincere consolation, however, that the good sense and conservatism of our people have rescued our State from the ruin of attempting to seek for it by separate action. Their unparalleled unanimity at the polls has put to rest all our apprehensions on that score, and satisfied our enemies and our friends that North Carolina will share the fate for weal or woe of her confederates. . . . If I have ever maintained a constant and abiding faith in our ultimate triumph, I owe that faith . . . to that pure and unselfish patriotism which glows in the bosom of our people.—*Legislative Documents, 1864-65,* Document No. 1.

125. BLOCKADE-RUNNING

On April 19, 1861, President Lincoln issued a proclamation declaring a blockade of southern ports. By a further proclamation of April 27, the blockade was extended to the ports of Virginia and North Carolina. The South had some three thousand miles of coast line and it was almost impossible for the Federal fleet to police it. This was particularly true of the North Carolina coast, with its numerous capes, sand banks, shoals, inlets, and sounds. Wilmington, situated twenty-eight miles from the sea, was an ideal port for blockade running. It was the last Confederate port to be closed. About $65,000,000 worth of goods, at gold prices, were brought into Wilmington during the war.

As the war progressed blockade runners multiplied. Profits were tremendous. A single trip frequently netted more than $100,000. "A steamer carrying one thousand bales of cotton sometimes realized a profit of a quarter of a million dollars on the inward and outward trip of two weeks. . . . Cotton could be purchased in the Confederacy for three cents in gold and sold in England from forty-five cents to a dollar a pound." There were probably one hundred blockade-runners operating from Wilmington in 1863. Many of these were captured later. At least sixty-five were captured or sunk by Federal ships during the war.

Governor Vance was determined to break the blockade. Ships were purchased from England for that purpose. The *Ad-Vance,* carrying 800 bales of cotton at a trip, made eleven successful voyages through the blockade before it was captured by the enemy. By 1864 no less than 50 Federal steamers were stationed at the entrances along the North Carolina coast. In spite of this, however, North Carolina ships made 365 successful trips to Nassau, and sixty-five to other ports. $12,000,000 worth of goods was brought in by ships belonging to the state. About half of this amount was resold to the Confederacy.

The first document below is a communication by Colonel J. G. Burr of Wilmington to James Sprunt. The second extract is Vance's statement of North Carolina's success in running the blockade. Both these accounts were written many years after the war by persons closely connected with the events they recorded.

EXPERIENCES OF A BLOCKADE-RUNNER

THE *Advance* was a first-class ship in every respect and had engines of great power and very highly finished, and her speed was good. With a pressure of twenty pounds to the square inch she easily averaged seventeen knots to the hour, and when it was increased to thirty pounds she reeled off twenty knots without difficulty. . . . The only objection to her was her size and heavy draught of water, the latter rendering it difficult for her to cross the shoals, which at that time were a great bar to the navigation of the river, and in consequence of which she could never go out or return with a full cargo of cotton or supplies.

She ran the blockade successfully seven or eight trips, bringing in all kinds of supplies that were much needed by our troops and people, thanks to the energy and wise foresight of our patriotic war governor. The regularity of her trips was remarkable and could be forecast almost to the very day; indeed, it was common to hear upon the streets the almost stereotyped remark, 'Tomorrow the *Advance* will be in,' and when the morrow came she could generally be seen gliding up to her dock with the rich freight of goods and wares so greatly needed by our people. In the meantime, however, she had several narrow escapes from capture. . . . But the most exciting trip was one made in the month of July, 1864, from Bermuda. . . . By some error in calculation, instead of making Cape Fear Light at 3 a. m., as was intended, they made the light on Cape Lookout, a long distance out of their course. What was best to be done was the question to be solved, and to be solved at once, for daylight comes very soon in July. The ship had scarcely enough coal in her bunkers to take her back to the port she had left and almost certain capture stared them in the face should they attempt to run in. It was determined, however, to make the attempt to get in. The ship was headed for New Inlet and, hugging the shore as closely as possible, with all steam on, she dashed down the coast with the speed of a thoroughbred on a hotly contested race-course. Fortunately, at that time many persons were engaged in making salt on the coast, and the smoke rising from the works created a cloud, or mist, which concealed the ship from the (Federal) blockaders, although it was broad day; but as she neared the inlet she was compelled to change her course further out to sea on account of a shoal, or spit, that makes out into the ocean at that point, and she was immediately discovered by the blockading fleet, that opened fire upon her and gave chase like a pack of hounds in eager pursuit of a much coveted quarry. It was a most trying situation, for the ship was compelled to keep her course, although it carried her nearer and nearer to the enemy, until she could round the shoal and run in towards the land, when she would be in comparative safety. Round shot and shell were flying around her in every direction, but she held steadily on, though rushing, as it seemed, to certain destruction, when suddenly a roar was heard from the fort—the heavy guns upon the mound had opened upon the pursuers and with such effect as to check their speed and force them to retire; and the gallant ship, which had been so hard pressed, soon rounded the shoal and was safe beneath the sheltering guns of the fort.

But the pitcher that goes often to the fountain is broken at last, and the time came when the career of the *Advance*, as a blockade runner was to cease forever. She was captured on her outward trip a few miles from our coast, owing to an inferior quality of coal she was compelled to use, which was very bituminous and emitted a black smoke that betrayed her to the watchful eyes of the fleet, and, being surrounded by them, she was obliged to surrender with her cargo of cotton, her officers and crew becoming prisoners. She was a noble ship, greatly endeared to the people of our State, and her capture was felt by all as a personal calamity.—James Sprunt, *Chronicles of the Cape Fear River, 1660-1916*, pp. 455-56.

VANCE'S SUMMARY OF NORTH CAROLINA'S SUCCESS IN BLOCKADE-RUNNING

By the general industry and thrift of our people, and by the use of a number of blockade-running steamers, carrying out cotton and bringing in supplies from Europe, I had collected and distributed from time to time, as near as can be gathered from the records of the Quartermaster's Department, the following stores: Large quantities of machinery supplies; 60,000 pairs of hand cards; 10,000 grain scythes; 200 bbls. bluestone for the wheat-growers; leather and shoes to 250,000 pairs; 50,000 blankets; gray woolen cloth for at least 250,000 suits of uniforms; 12,000 overcoats, ready-made ; 2,000 best Enfield rifles, with 100 rounds of fixed ammunition ; 100,000 pounds of bacon ; 500 sacks of coffee for hospital use ; $50,000 worth of medicines at gold prices ; large quantities of lubricating oils, besides minor supplies of various kinds for the charitable institutions of the State. Not only was the supply of shoes, blankets and clothing more than sufficient for the supply of the North Carolina troops, but large quantities were turned over to the Confederate government for the troops of other States. In the winter succeeding the battle of Chickamauga, I sent to General Longstreet's corps, 14,000 suits of clothing complete. At the surrender of General Johnston the State had on hand ready-made and in cloth 92,000 suits of uniforms, with great stores of blankets, leather, etc. To make good the warrants on which these purchases had been made abroad, the State purchased and had on hand in trust for the holders 11,000 bales of cotton and 100,000 barrels of rosin. The cotton was partly destroyed before the war closed and the remainder, amounting to several thousand bales, was *captured*, after peace was declared, by certain officers of the Federal army.—Clement Dowd, *Life of Zebulon B. Vance*, pp. 70-71, 489-90.

126. PUBLIC EDUCATION IN NORTH CAROLINA DURING THE CIVIL WAR

The public school system, which had been established under the leadership of Calvin H. Wiley before 1860, continued to operate throughout the Civil War. Efforts were made to transfer the school funds to military purposes, but Superintendent Wiley successfully resisted all such attempts. "No people," he said, "could or would be free who were unable or unwilling to educate their children." He appealed to all of the local school officials, showing them the advantages of preserving the schools of the state. Similarly, and with great success, he pleaded with Governor Ellis to keep the schools going at any cost. Clark and Vance, successors to Governor Ellis, adopted the same favorable attitude toward the public school system. The majority of the papers endorsed Wiley's position. The *North Carolina Standard* said, "In the name of the good people of the State, let none of the schools be abandoned." The Charlotte *Democrat* maintained that "the children of the State must be taught to read and write, war or no war." The office of superintendent of common schools was abolished in 1865, after the war.

Wiley's report for 1863 gave a splendid picture of public education at that date, and advocated the establishment of graded schools.

THE present generation does not need to be told that it was hard to keep up a general educational system in any part of the Confederate

States of America during the year 1863, . . . Considering the great trials through which the country is passing, we are prepared to hear, without surprise, of the temporary suspension of enterprises with which our best hopes are bound up; and it is, therefore, a subject of devout gratitude to me to be able to announce that our Common Schools still live and are still full of glorious promise! Through all this dark night of storm their cheerful radiance has been seen on every hill and in every valley of our dear old State, . . .

The number of schools taught, reported in fifty counties, is 1,076; and the number of teachers licensed in forty-four counties is males 524, females 348, total 872. The number of children reported to have attended school in fifty counties is, males 18,977, females 16,518, total 35,495; the average length of the schools was very near three months, and the average salary about $25 *per* month.

The receipts of money reported in fifty-four counties amount to $240,655 and 38 cents. The disbursements to 81,588.56½ cents. . . .

The depreciation in the value of the currency has made it impossible in many instances to employ teachers. . . .

In other instances there have been fears that the county courts would divert the moneys distributed for school purposes, to other crises; and in a number of cases schools are taught but the drafts are held back with the hope of obtaining funds of a higher market value. It should be added, that in some instances it is found impossible to get active district committees, as nearly every man of that useful class which is willing to assume, without remuneration, responsibilities in behalf of popular education and improvement, is gone to the army.

Still, everything considered, the statistical tables of this report are highly encouraging; they clearly show that the war has not exhausted the financial or the moral resources of North Carolina. . . .

The number of soldiers which she has contributed . . . will be an enduring monument of her patriotic devotion to the cause she has espoused. . . .

But the future historian of this stirring age will find authentic records which will enhance the honor of her character; and he will add, as her crowning glory, that in the darkest hour of the Confederacy, when every nerve and muscle of the country were wrought to the highest tension, in a terrible and unexampled struggle for existence and independence, North-Carolina still supported a vigorous and beneficent system of free and public schools, and that·

20

they were attended by fifty thousand of the children of her patriotic citizens. . . .

The great defect of our Common School system is the fact that it is a horizontal one, furnishing one kind of education for children of all ages, and of every degree of advancement. . . . —*Report of the Superintendent of Common Schools for the Year 1863*, Document No. 9, Sess. 1863.

127. ATTITUDE OF THE NORTH CAROLINA LEGISLATURE TOWARD THE CIVIL WAR, 1864-1865

Probably no southern state contributed more to the cause of the Confederacy than North Carolina. At the same time no state was more critical of Confederate policies and more insistent on its own rights. On several occasions the General Assembly, acting largely on the recommendation of Governor Vance, challenged the arbitrary powers being exercised by the Confederate government, even while both the Governor and the legislature were professing loyalty to the southern cause. As late as the Hampton Roads Conference, February 3, 1865, the legislators were still urging a "vigorous prosecution of the war to an honorable peace."

The following resolutions of the General Assembly relating to jury trial, conscription, the arming of slaves, and the peace movement, throw considerable light on the struggle within the Confederacy.

RESOLUTIONS CONCERNING CERTAIN ACTS OF THE LATE CONGRESS OF THE CONFEDERATE STATES, MAY 28, 1864

Resolved, That while the people of North-Carolina have ever been and still are anxious to strengthen the administration of the Confederate government in every legitimate way, and to promote the success of the common cause in order that we may have a speedy and honorable peace, they view with deep concern and alarm every infraction of the Constitution by the Congress of the Confederate States, and this General Assembly, in their name, protest against such infractions as of pernicious example and fatal tendency.

Resolved, That the act of the late Congress, entitled "An act to suspend the privilege of the writ of *habeas corpus* in certain cases," violates the fundamental maxim of republican government which requires a separation of the departments of power, clothes the Executive with judicial functions which Congress cannot constitutionally confer even on the judiciary itself, and sets at naught the most emphatic and solemn guarantee of the Constitution.

Resolved, That this General Assembly, representing the people of

North-Carolina, doth not consent to the sacrifice of the vital principles of free government in a war carried on solely to secure and perpetuate them, and doth declare that "no conditions of public danger,"—present or prospective, probable or possible, can render the liberties of the people incompatible with the public safety.

Resolved, That the act of the same Congress, entitled "An act to organize forces to serve during the war," declaring all white men, residents of the Confederate States, between the ages of seventeen and fifty, to be in the military service, embracing in its provisions every State officer in all the departments, executive, legislative and judicial, and subjecting all the industrial pursuits of the country to military supervision and control, reduces the State governments to mere provincial administrations, dependent on the grace and favor of Congress and the Executive, is destructive of state sovereignty, and imports an assertion of the power on the part of Congress to convert the Confederate government into a consolidated military despotism.

Resolved, That this General Assembly doth therefore request our Senators and Representatives in Congress to use their best endeavors to procure a repeal of the first mentioned act, and such modification of the second as shall secure the rights and preserve the integrity of the States of the Confederacy. . . .

RESOLUTION IN RELATION TO GOVERNOR VANCE, MAY 28, 1864

Resolved, That his Excellency, Z. B. Vance, is justly entitled to the confidence and thanks of this General Assembly for the able, faithful and successful manner in which he has heretofore discharged and is now discharging the complicated and arduous duties of the executive office, embarrassed as it has been by the difficulties growing out of the present unjust and fiendish war.—*Resolutions of a Public Nature passed by the General Assembly at its Adjourned Session, 1864*, pp. 23-25.

Resolutions against the Policy of arming the Slaves, Feb. 3, 1865.

Resolved, That the State of North-Carolina protests against the arming of slaves by the Confederate government, in any emergency that can possibly arise, but gives its consent to their being taken and used as laborers in the public service, upon just compensation being made.

Resolved, That North-Carolina denies the constitutional power of the Confederate government to impress slaves for the purpose of arming them, or preparing them to be armed in any contingency, without the consent of the States being first freely given—and then, only according to state laws. . . .

Resolution on Subject of Peace and Preparation for War, Feb. 6, 1865.

Whereas, We have heard with the greatest pleasure and heartfelt satisfaction that negotiations for peace have been inaugurated by the governments at Richmond and Washington, yet mindful of the maxim that in time of war, while "we hold the olive branch in one hand we should hold the sword in the other"; Therefore,

Resolved, That until the issue of these negotiations is known, North-Carolina will not abate one jot or tittle of her determination and zeal, for a vigorous prosecution of the war to an honorable peace.—*Resolutions of a Public Nature passed by the General Assembly, 1865*, pp. 33-35.

128. THE LAST NINETY DAYS OF THE WAR IN NORTH CAROLINA

One of the most vivid pictures of North Carolina during the closing days of the Civil War was given by Mrs. Cornelia Phillips Spencer in *The Last Ninety Days of the War in North Carolina*. Mrs. Spencer lived in Chapel Hill and knew most of the prominent people of the state. She was a very good friend of Governor Vance, who said of her on one occasion when he heard her called "the brightest woman in North Carolina," "Don't forget that she's the smartest *man* too!" Mrs. Hope Chamberlain says that she was "the equal in intellect and worth of any other woman in America."

In the fall of 1865, Governor D. L. Swain, writing in behalf of Governor Vance, then a prisoner in Washington, as well as for himself, asked Mrs. Spencer to write a series of articles giving her own personal knowledge of the last days of the Civil War. These articles were first published in *The Watchman*, a New York City paper. They later appeared in book form.

Mrs. Spencer's purpose, as stated in the Preface of the book, was "to do justice to North-Carolina, and to place beyond cavil or reproach the attitude of her leaders at the close of the great Southern States Rights struggle—to present a faithful picture of the times, and a just judgment, whether writing of friend or foe." In order to do this she wrote many of her friends who lived along the line of march of northern armies through the state. She took the information received and, combining it with her personal knowledge of conditions, wrote an interesting narrative. Mrs. Chamberlain says of it: "Alone among the Civil War narratives it gives the immediate feeling of things, the hysteria, the fear, the uncertainty, the indignation, the sorrow, the despair, which succeed each other in the minds of the watchers by the hearthstone when an enemy army is approaching."

By January, 1865, there was very little room left for "belief" of any sort in the ultimate success of the Confederacy. All the necessaries of life were scarce, and were held at fabulous and still increasing prices. The great freshet of January 10th which . . . carried off fences, bridges, mills, and tore up railroads all through the central part of the State, at once doubled the price of corn and flour. Two destructive fires in the same month, which consumed great quantities of government stores at Charlotte and Salisbury, added materially to the general gloom and depression. The very elements seemed to have enlisted against us. And soon, with no great surplus of food from the wants of her home population, North-Carolina found herself called upon to furnish supplies for two armies.

Early in January, an urgent and most pressing appeal was made for Lee's army ; and the people, most of whom knew not where they could get bread for their children in three months' time, responded nobly. . . . From the humble cabin . . . up through all grades of life, there were none who did not feel a deep and tender, almost heart-breaking solicitude for our noble soldiers. For them the last barrel of flour was divided, the last luxury in homes that had once abounded was cheerfully surrendered. Every available resource was taxed, every expedient of domestic economy was put in practice. . . . I speak now of Central North-Carolina, where many families of the highest respectability and refinement lived for months on corn-bread, sorghum, and peas ; where meat was seldom on the table, tea and coffee never ; where dried apples and peaches were a luxury ; where children went barefoot through the winter, and ladies made their own shoes, and wove their own homespuns ; where the carpets were cut up into blankets, and window-curtains and sheets were torn up for hospital uses ; where soldiers' socks were knit day and night, while for home service clothes were twice turned, and patches were patched again ; and all this continually, and with an energy and a cheerfulness that may be well called *heroic*.

There were a few localities in the State where a few rich planters boasted of having "never felt the war" ; there were ladies whose wardrobes encouraged the blockade-runners, and whose tables were still heaped with all the luxuries thay had ever known. . . . I speak not . . . of these, but of the great body of our citizens—the *middle* class as to fortune, generally the *highest* as to cultivation and intelligence. . . .

The fall of Fort Fisher and the occupation of Wilmington, the failure of the peace commission, and the unchecked advance of Sherman's army northward from Savannah, were the all-absorbing topics of discussion with our people during the first months of the year 1865. The tide of war was rolling in upon us. . . .

The smoke of burning Columbia, and of the fair villages and countless plantations that lay in the route, where, for hundreds of miles, many a house was left blazing, and not a panel of fence was to be seen, rolled slowly up our sky; and panic-stricken refugees, homeless and penniless, brought every day fresh tales of havoc and ruin. By the eleventh of March, General Sherman was in possession of Fayetteville. . . . The ladies, as usual, were especially active and indefatigable. . . . Who shall question the course of the women of the South in this war, or dare to undervalue their lofty heroism and fortitude, unsurpassed in story or in song? When I forget you, O ye daughters of my country! your labors of love, your charity, faith, and patience, all through the dark and bloody day, lighting up the gloom of war with the tender graces of woman's devotion and self-denial, and now, in even darker hours, your energy and cheerful submission in toil and poverty and humiliation—when I cease to do homage to your virtues, and to your excellences, may my right hand forget its cunning and my voice be silent in the dust! . . .

During the month of March our central counties were traversed by straggling bodies of Confederate soldiers, fragments of the once powerful army of Tennessee, hurrying down toward Raleigh to concentrate under General Johnston once more, in the vain hope of being able yet to effect something. . . .

Thousands of delicate women, bred up in affluence, are now bravely working with their hands for their daily bread; many in old age, and alone in the world, are bereft of all their earthly possessions. Thousands of families are absolutely penniless, who have never before known a want ungratified. . . . Nobody is ashamed of himself, or ashamed of his position, or of his necessities. What the South wants is not charity—but generosity. . . .

How shall the South begin her new life? How, disfranchised and denied her civil rights, shall she start the wheels of enterprise and business that shall bring work and bread to her plundered, penniless people? How shall her widows and orphans be fed, her schools and colleges be supported, her churches be maintained, unless her rights and liberties be regained—unless every effort be made to give her wounds repose, and restore health and energy to her paralyzed and shattered frame? . . .

The town of Goldsboro was occupied by General Schofield's army on the twenty-first of March. . . . On the twenty-third of March General Sherman's grand army made its appearance, heralded by the columns of smoke which rose from burning farm-houses on the south side of the Neuse. . . . The town itself was in a measure defended, so to speak, by General Schofield's preoccupation; but in the vicinity and for twenty miles round, the country was most thoroughly plundered and stripped of food, forage, and private property of every description. . . . Not a farmhouse in the country but was visited and wantonly robbed. Many were burned, and very many, together with out-houses, were pulled down and hauled into camp for use. Generally not a live animal, not a morsel of food of any description was left, and in many instances not a bed or sheet or change of clothing for man, woman, or child. . . .

While the Federal armies lay at Goldsboro, trains were running day and night from Beaufort and from Wilmington, conveying stores for . . . Sherman's army. The Confederate army, lying between Goldsboro and Raleigh, having no supplies or reinforcements to receive, waited grimly and despairingly the order to fall back upon Raleigh. . . . The scenes in Raleigh during the first week of April were significant enough. The removal of government stores, and of the effects of banks; the systematic concealment of private property of every description; the hurried movements of troops to and fro; the doubt, dismay, and gloom painted on every man's face, told too well the story of anticipated defeat and humiliation. . . .

On the same day that General Sherman entered Raleigh, General Stoneman occupied Salisbury, April 12-13th, thus completing the chain of events which was closing in upon the Confederacy. Among the prisoners kept at Salisbury were some of the better class, who were at large on *parole*. This they broke in the winter of 1864-'5, and, making their escape over the mountains into Tennessee, carried such accounts of the accumulation of stores, etc., at Salisbury, as made its capture an object of importance.

General Stoneman entered the State during the last week of March, by the turnpike leading from Taylorsville, Tennessee, through Watauga county to Deep Gap, on the Blue Ridge. His force was probably six or seven thousand strong, though rumor increased it to fifteen, twenty, thirty, and in one instance to sixty thousand.

They entered Boone, the county-seat of Watauga, on the twenty-sixth of March. . . . The jail was burned by order of General Gillam. . . . Private houses were of course plundered, and the cit-

izens were consoled by the assurance that "Kirk was to follow and
clean them out." Several citizens were shot under circumstances of
peculiar aggravation. . . . Kirk's raiders . . . came down after
Stoneman had passed on, and stripped the place of all that had
been left. . . .

Leaving Wilkesboro on the thirty-first of March, General Stoneman moved over into Surry county . . . he sent out various detachments to cut the North-Carolina Central Road and the Dan-
ville and Greensboro Road, destroy bridges, supplies, etc. One of
these parties . . . narrowly missed capturing the train conveying
the whole Confederate government, in its flight to Greensboro.
They burned the bridge at Jamestown. . . . At High Point they
burned the depot and large quantities of government stores, also
seventeen hundred bales of cotton. . . . The public buildings and
stores at Lexington and Thomasville were saved by the arrival of a
body of Ferguson's cavalry, who chased the raiders back to Salem.
. . .

At Salem and Winston private property was protected, no pillage
being permitted. . . .

But General Stoneman's policy toward the inhabitants of Salisbury is a very striking illustration of the principles which . . . were
the only true and generous and really politic guide for the commanders of an invading army. Private property was protected,
guards were stationed, and General Stoneman repeatedly gave
strict orders for the enforcement of quiet and protection of the citizens. He himself in person inspected the public stores, which were
of course by the laws of war doomed to destruction, and refused to
allow the Confederate Quartermaster's depot to be burned lest it
should endanger the town. . . . Whatever plundering and insolence
the people were subjected to—and there were a number of such
cases—was very evidently the work of unauthorized bummers. . . .

North-Carolina had nothing to retract, nothing to unsay, no pardon to beg. She had acted deliberately in joining the Southern
cause. She had given her whole strength to it, with no lukewarm
adherence; and now, in the hour of acknowledged defeat and failure, she did not attempt to desert, or abjectly bespeak any favors
for herself on the ground of her anti-secession record or proclivities.
. . . We had desired peace—an end to the bloodshed and to the
impending starvation of women and children. Peace we had longed
and prayed for; but not *this* peace.—Cornelia Phillips Spencer, *The
Last Ninety Days of the War in North Carolina*, pp. 29-31, 46-53, 71-75,
94-100, 192-235.

129. THE SALISBURY MILITARY PRISON

Sidney Andrews was special correspondent for the Chicago *Tribune* and the Boston *Advertiser*, writing under the name of "Dixon." September-November, 1865, he visited the Carolinas and Georgia, and his letters to the Boston and Chicago papers were brought together in 1866 and published in a 400-page volume, *The South Since the War*. His observations in the South furnished valuable information on the social, political, and economic conditions in the states he visited. His conclusions, however, were flavored with strong anti-southern sentiment.

SALISBURY, SEPT. 29, 1865

THE Salisbury military prison was established in the summer of 1863. At first and for more than a year, it was occupied as a penitentiary for the confinement of what were called State prisoners, —Southern Union men, captured naval officers, deserters from the Union armies, and Northern men held on suspicion or as hostages. It was first used as a place of confinement for soldiers captured in battle in the fall of 1864. Previous to that time persons confined here were treated much better than at the majority of the Rebel prisons; but some time in the summer of that year Major John H. Gee, of Selma, Alabama, a coarse and brutal wretch, was made commandant; and his cruelties not only soon balanced the account, but made the prison the terror of our army, and only less dreadful than Andersonville.

The prison proper was a brick building, forty by one hundred feet in size, and four stories in height, formerly a cotton factory. Connected with it were six small brick buildings,—formerly offices and tenement houses,—and a small frame hospital, large enough for no more than fifty or sixty beds.

At a later day these buildings were enclosed in a yard of about six acres, and, after the fall of 1864, were entirely used for hospital purposes. The stockade wall was a stout board fence some twelve feet in height, on which sentinels were stationed fifty feet apart. Inside the wall was a ditch, varying in width from six to ten feet, and in depth from three to six feet.

In the spring and summer of 1864 respectable citizens were allowed to visit Northern men confined here, and the condition of the prisoners at that time was comparatively good. I am satisfied that there were some genuine Union people resident in the town, and many more in the counties to the westward. These never wearied in good offices to the prisoners, and for a while they did much to mitigate the rigors of confinement. All this was changed, however, when Gee became commandant, and particularly after the Rebels began to confine soldiers here.

In the fall and winter of 1864 not less than fourteen thousand men were herded within this small enclosure like sheep, tortured with infernal malignity, cheated of food when the storehouses half a mile away were bursting with rations, cheated of shelter when fifty or sixty thousand feet of lumber originally intended for this use was lying useless at the upper end of the town, cheated of fuel when magnificent forests were almost within rifle-shot! The poor wretches fought for bones like dogs. . . . The number of deaths ran as high as seventy-five per day; in one period of eight days, 526 were tumbled out for the dead-wagon; for three months the daily average was not less than forty. . . .

The prisoners, thanks to the tender mercies of their captors, came to the place generally without shoes or blankets, rarely with overcoats, and often without blouses. The buildings in the stockade were soon overflowing with the sick. For those not admitted to the hospital there was very little shelter. . . . The winter of 1864-65 was unusually severe in this latitude. . . . —Sidney Andrews, *The South Since the War: as Shown by Fourteen Weeks of Travel and Observation in Georgia and the Carolinas*, pp. 102-7.

130. A Northern Newspaper Correspondent's Observations of North Carolina, 1865

The following account is a "Summary of Three Weeks' Observations in North Carolina" by Sidney Andrews, whose book, *The South Since the War*, is described on page 313 above. His observations were decidedly anti-southern in sentiment and created a false impression of the North Carolina people.

Spindling of legs, round of shoulders, sunken of chest, lank of body, stooping of posture, narrow of face, retreating of forehead, thin of nose, small of chin, large of mouth,—this is the native North-Carolinian as one sees him outside the cities and large towns. There is insipidity in his face, indecision in his step, and inefficiency in his whole bearing. His house has two rooms and a loft, and is meanly furnished,—one, and possibly two, beds, three or four chairs, half a dozen stools, a cheap pine table, an old spinning-wheel, a water-bucket and drinking gourd, two tin basins, half a dozen tin platters, a few cooking utensils, and a dozen odd pieces of crockery. Paint and whitewash and wall-paper and window-curtains are to him needless luxuries. His wife is leaner, more round-shouldered, and more pinched of face than her husband. He "chaws" and she "dips." The children of these two are large-eyed, tow-headed urchins, alike ignorant of the decencies and the possibilities of life. In this house there is often neither book nor newspaper; and what is infinitely worse, no longing for either. The day begins at sunrise and ends at dark; its duties are alike devoid of dignity and mental and moral compensation. The man has a small farm, and once owned six or eight negroes. How the family now lives, the propping hands of the negroes being taken away, is a mystery, even if one remembers the simple cheapness of mere animal life.

I am not speaking either of the white resident of the cities or of the "poor white" technically so named, but of the common inhabitant of the country,—the man who pays taxes and votes, but never runs for office. . . . His larder is lean, and his cookery is in the last degree wretched. He tenders "apple-jack," as an evidence of good-will, and wonders in a feeble way how a man can live who don't drink it at least half a dozen times a day. He likes to talk, and rarely has any work that prevents him from hanging on the fence to chat with the chance traveller who asks the road. . . . He receives two or three letters per year, perhaps, and wonders why a man should take a daily newspaper. He troubles himself very little about schools or education, but likes to go to meeting, and thinks himself well informed as to matters of theology. He believes the "abolishioners" brought on the war; but he doesn't love Jeff Davis or Governor Vance. He "allers dun hansumly by his niggers," and thinks them the "most ongratefullest creeturs on the face of the yerth." . . .

The complexion of these country residents is noticeable, and suggests many inquiries. . . . Their whiteness of skin is simply the whiteness of ordinary tallow. It is sallowness, with a suggestion of clayeyness. . . . The skin seems utterly without vitality, and beyond the action of any restorative stimulants; it has a pitiful death-in-life appearance. I am told the climate is in fault, but my judgement says the root of the matter is the diet of the people. . . .

The amount of tobacco consumed by the people is beyond all calculation. I hardly exaggerate in saying that at least seven-tenths of all persons above the age of twelve years use it in some form. . . .

The labor system of the State is not so badly disorganized as that of South Carolina, but it is thoroughly demoralized.—*The South Since the War: as Shown by Fourteen Weeks of Travel and Observation in Georgia and the Carolinas*, pp. 180-90.

X

THE TRAGIC YEARS OF RECONSTRUCTION

131. Proclamation Appointing a Governor for North Carolina, May 29, 1865

Soon after entering office, President Johnson issued a proclamation of amnesty, offering pardon to those southerners who would subscribe to an oath to "faithfully support, protect, and defend the Constitution of the United States, and the union of the States thereunder," and to "abide by and faithfully support all laws and proclamations" which had been made relative to the emancipation of slaves. Fourteen classes—which included nearly all of the reputable citizens of the South—were ineligible to take this oath.

On the same day, Johnson proceeded to put the "Presidential Plan" of reconstruction into effect by appointing William W. Holden governor of North Carolina. It was not long until Congress, jealous of executive power, rejected Johnson's plans of reconstruction and adopted their own scheme of restoring the South to the Union, that is to say, military government.

Whereas the fourth section of the fourth article of the Constitution of the United States declares that the United States shall guarantee to every State in the Union a republican form of government and shall protect each of them against invasion and domestic violence; and

Whereas the President of the United States is by the Constitution made Commander in Chief of the Army and Navy, as well as chief civil executive officer of the United States, and is bound by solemn oath faithfully to execute the office of President of the United States and to take care that the laws be faithfully executed; and

Whereas the rebellion which has been waged by a portion of the people of the United States against the properly constituted authorities of the Government thereof in the most violent and revolting form, but whose organized and armed forces have now been almost entirely overcome, has in its revolutionary progress deprived the people of the State of North Carolina of all civil government; and

Whereas it becomes necessary and proper to carry out and enforce the obligations of the United States to the people of North Carolina in securing them in the enjoyment of a republican form of government:

Now, therefore, in obedience to the high and solemn duties imposed upon me by the Constitution of the United States and for the purpose of enabling the loyal people of said State to organize a State government whereby justice may be established, domestic tranquillity insured, and loyal citizens protected in all their rights of life, liberty, and property, I, Andrew Johnson, President of the United States, and Commander in Chief of the Army and Navy of the United States, do hereby appoint William W. Holden provisional governor of the State of North Carolina, whose duty it shall be, at the earliest practicable period, to prescribe such rules and regulations as may be necessary and proper for convening a convention composed of delegates to be chosen by that portion of the people of said State who are loyal to the United States, and no others, for the purpose of altering or amending the constitution thereof, and with authority to exercise within the limits of said State all the powers necessary and proper to enable such loyal people of the State of North Carolina to restore said State to its constitutional relations to the Federal Government and to present such a republican form of State government as will entitle the State to the guaranty of the United States therefor and its people to protection by the United States against invasion, insurrection, and domestic violence : Provided, That in any election that may be hereafter held for choosing delegates to any State convention as aforesaid no person shall be qualified as an elector or shall be eligible as a member of such convention unless he shall have previously taken and subscribed the oath of amnesty as set forth in the President's proclamation of May 29, A. D. 1865, and is a voter qualified as prescribed by the constitution and laws of the State of North Carolina in force immediately before the 20th day of May, A.D. 1861, the date of the so-called ordinance of secession ; and the said convention, when convened, or the legislature that may be thereafter assembled, will prescribe the qualification of electors and the eligibility of persons to hold office under the constitution and laws of the State—a power the people of the several States composing the Federal Union have rightfully exercised from the origin of the Government to the present time.

And I do hereby direct—

First. That the military commander of the department and all officers and persons in the military and naval service aid and assist the said provisional governor in carrying into effect this proclamation ; and they are enjoined to abstain from in any way hindering, impeding, or discouraging the loyal people from the organization of a State government as herein authorized.

Second. That the Secretary of State proceed to put in force all laws of the United States the administration whereof belongs to the State Department applicable to the geographical limits aforesaid.

Third. That the Secretary of the Treasury proceed to nominate for appointment assessors of taxes and collectors of customs and internal revenue and such other officers of the Treasury Department as are authorized by law and put in execution the revenue laws of the United States within the geographical limits aforesaid. In making appointments the preference shall be given to qualified loyal persons residing within the districts where their respective duties are to be performed ; but if suitable residents of the districts shall not be found, then persons residing in other States or districts shall be appointed.

Fourth. That the Postmaster-General proceed to establish post-offices and post-routes and put into execution the postal laws of the United States within the said State, giving to loyal residents the preference of appointment ; but if suitable residents are not found, then to appoint agents, etc., from other States.

Fifth. That the district judge for the'judicial district in which North Carolina is included proceed to hold courts within said State in accordance with the provisions of the act of Congress. The Attorney-General will instruct the proper officers to libel and bring to judgment, confiscation, and sale, property subject to confiscation and enforce the administration of justice within said State in all matters within the cognizance and jurisdiction of the Federal courts.

Sixth. That the Secretary of the Navy take possession of all public property belonging to the Navy Department within said geographical limits and put in operation all acts of Congress in relation to naval affairs having application to the said State.

Seventh. That the Secretary of the Interior put in force the laws relating to the Interior Department applicable to the geographical limits aforesaid.—*Messages and Papers of the Presidents*, VI, 312-14.

132. THE RED STRINGS AND THE UNION LEAGUE IN NORTH CAROLINA

Soon after the Civil War many northern political organizations became active in the South. The chief purpose of these seems to have been to "educate the Negro to the Republican party." Many lawless acts were committed by the Union League, the Red Strings, and other secret societies. In some places the Negro was led to believe that the whites were attempting to re-enslave him. One of the main causes for the organization of the Ku Klux Klan in North Carolina was to combat the influence of the Union League. Governor Holden was the first president of the

League in North Carolina and James H. Harris, a Negro, was vice-president.

The following account reveals the sentiments of a North Carolina Unionist toward these societies.

THERE was an organization at the close of the war, which has existed since, called the Heroes of America, or the Red Strings. I became acquainted with it just at the close of the war, when some of the members were apprehended as being inimical to the confederacy and as having entered into a secret conspiracy to overthrow it. . . . They applied to me as a Union man for the purpose of getting them discharged from arrest. In that way I became acquainted with their organization and their oaths. The only objection I saw to any portion of their oath was, they swore to come to each other's aid in distress. . . . That organization continued some time after the war, as I understood. . . .

The next organization of which I have any knowledge was that of the Union League, which arose immediately after the colored people got power. . . . The avowed object of that was that they should all act in unison, and they have carried it out very faithfully. I have never seen a more compact league than that has been. . . .

Governor Holden was at the head of it. . . .

This danger to property arises from these Loyal Leagues. There have been a great many lawless acts committed by the Loyal Leagues, . . . the burning of barns, the destruction of cattle, horses, and mules. . . .

[The Leagues] are chiefly composed of negroes and low white people. In the county adjoining the one in which I live, . . . within the last eighteen months, there have been a great many outrages committed—burning of barns and dwelling-houses. . . . Those persons who had been arrested said that their directions to burn had come from the city of Raleigh, from the chief leader in Raleigh. . . . [The League] is governed in the most remarkable manner, controlled from one end of the State to the other. At our last congressional election a candidate was run on that side whose name had not been mentioned previous to the day of the election, that I had heard, or that had been heard by a great many others, yet there was an almost unanimous vote throughout the whole district for that person . . . on the part of the Radical party, or the League. . . .

Several gentlemen told me that they were in danger of their lives; that they were informed by some of the League-men that they were to be killed; that they were to be hanged; and the manner in which it was to be done was detailed; . . . that there were several men who were to be punished, just about the election or before the election. . . .

If there had been no Loyal League in North Carolina, there would have been no Ku-Klux, or clubbing together of the white people there. . . . Still the negroes operate upon each other, so that one dare not depart from the ranks; they are arrayed yet in a solid phalanx. . . .

The colored people of North Carolina have, since the passage of the reconstruction measures of Congress, been taught to believe by the leading members of the Leagues that the white men of the country are their enemies; that their only friends are the northern men, and those who have gone with the northern men in giving them suffrage, etc.; that it is the desire and deliberate purpose of the white people . . . to restore slavery at the earliest possible moment. The negroes themselves say that they have been taught to believe (they have told me so), that such is the purpose of the white people of the Southern country. As a matter of course the negroes are ignorant and superstitious. They are taught to believe that the armies of the United States emancipated them, that the Government of the United States was their only protector, that the Southern people were their enemies. . . . They have been alienated in that way from the white people, and remain so to a great extent, though a large number of them are willing to believe that the representations that have been made to them in regard to the restoration of slavery in the Southern States are false.

About the time the Leagues were being organized, or rather reorganized, in that country, the influence of these men was very bad indeed. As I stated awhile ago, the negroes were made to believe that the white people were their enemies; that they were seeking the first opportunity to put them back into slavery. That is being told to the negroes even to this day (1871) by a number of men. In fact it is the chief stock in trade of a number of men in that section of the country. A great many honest men, even on the Republican side, say there is no danger; but others . . . tell the negroes that there is. The negroes at one time expected the confiscation of the property of the Southern people. . . . They were told so. I have myself heard several negroes say that they were told that the lands of the Southern people would be confiscated, and that they were promised lands, horses, etc. forty acres in real estate for each negro, . . . and a horse or a mule. Some of the negroes of my county say that the chief man of the Leagues in 1867 and 1868—Mr. Elliott, who has since died—boldly stated in the League meetings that such would be the policy adopted.

I know instances in which their advice has led to riots and bloodshed on the same day they have held their public meetings. It was so in one case in my own village. Mr. Justice came to my town in 1868 and addressed some five hundred negro hearers, in a very excited manner, telling them that the white people were their enemies ; that they should believe nothing said to them by the southern people generally ; that they were only seeking to put the negroes back into slavery and would do it as soon as they got control of the State Government. . . . Mr. Justice said afterward that he did not advise riot at all ; but the manner in which such men have addressed these ignorant, superstitious people has caused them to commit many acts of violence that they would not otherwise have done. . . .

The negroes in my county had three places where they were meeting at night and drilling. One place was their League-house. They were stationing their sentinels on the highways . . . and were halting white people on the roads, and . . . not allowing them to go by. In the extreme northern part of my county where the Republican vote is strongest . . . the negroes had another place of meeting ; in the town of Shelby, in which I live, they had a place where they were meeting and drilling at night. The people were alarmed. . . . They did not know with what object the negroes were meeting and carrying on these operations. They thought that the lessons which the negroes were being taught in the League were leading them on.—*Documentary History of Reconstruction* (edited by W. L. Fleming) II, 21-23, quoting *Outrages in the Southern States*, 1871. Statement of B. F. Moore, a North Carolina Unionist.*

133. THE NORTH CAROLINA "BLACK CODE," 1866

During the "Tragic Era" of Reconstruction the southern state legislatures enacted many laws governing the conduct of Negroes. A large number of provisions in these "Black Codes" dealt with vagrancy and apprenticeship. This alarmed the North, which insisted that the South was attempting to "re-enslave the negro." Southerners maintained that these laws were necessary in order to put the Negro "in his place." North Carolina's "Black Code" was one of the most tolerant. "It is true that it did not admit the negro to entire equality before the law with the whites ; nevertheless it validated the marriages of former slaves ; changed the law of apprenticeship so as to apply, with one minor exception, to

*Reprinted by permission of the publishers, The Arthur H. Clark Company.

21

both races alike; declared negroes entitled to the same rights and privileges as whites in suits at law and equity; made the criminal law applicable to the two races alike except in the punishment for an assault with intent to rape; provided for the admission of the testimony of negroes in the courts; and made provision for the protection of negroes from fraud and ignorance in making contracts with white persons."—R. D. W. Connor, *North Carolina: Rebuilding an Ancient Commonwealth*, II, 278-79.

SECTION 1. *Be it enacted by the General Assembly of the State of North Carolina,* . . . That negroes, and their issue, even where one ancestor in each succeeding generation to the fourth inclusive is white, shall be deemed persons of color.

Section 2. All persons of color who are now inhabitants of this State shall be entitled to the same privileges, and are subject to the same burthens and disabilities, as by the laws of the State were conferred on, or were attached to, free persons of color, prior to the ordinance of emancipation, except as the same may be changed by law.

Section 3. Persons of color shall be entitled to all the privileges of white persons in the mode of prosecuting, defending, continuing, removing and transferring their suits at law and in equity; and likewise to the same mode of trial by jury, and all the privileges appertaining thereto. And in all proceedings in equity by or against them, their answer shall have the same force and effect in all respects as the answer of white persons.

Section 4. In all cases of apprenticeship of persons of color . . . the master shall be bound to discharge the same duties to them as to white apprentices . . . (and the word white is stricken from the code); Provided always, That in the binding out of apprentices of color, the former masters of such apprentices, when they shall be regarded as suitable persons by the court, shall be entitled to have such apprentices bound to them, in preference to other persons.

Chapter 5, section 3, of the revised code, as amended by this act, reads thus;

The master or mistress shall provide for the apprentice diet, clothes, lodging, and accommodations fit and necessary; and such apprentice shall teach or cause to be taught to read and write, and the elementary rules of arithmetic; and at the expiration of every apprenticeship shall pay to each apprentice six dollars and furnish him with a new suit of clothes, and a new Bible; and if upon complaint made to the court of pleas and quarter sessions it shall appear that any apprentice is ill-used, or not taught the trade, profession and employment to which he was bound or that any apprentice is not taught reading, writing, and arithmetic as aforesaid, the court may remove and bind him to some other suitable person).

(Section 6, chapter 5, of the revised code of North Carolina, as amended by this act, reads thus:

If any apprentice, whether colored or otherwise, who shall be well used by his master, and who shall have received from his said master not less than twelve months' schooling, shall absent himself, after arriving at the age of eighteen years, from his master's service before the term of his apprenticeship shall have expired, every such apprentice shall be compelled to make satisfaction to the master for the loss of his service; and in case any apprentice shall refuse to make such satisfaction, his master may recover by warrant before any justice of the peace such satisfaction, not exceeding sixty dollars, as the justice may determine ought to be made by such apprentice; or the master may have his action on the case against the apprentice, for his default; Provided, That no apprentice shall be compelled to make any satisfaction, but within seven years next after the end of the term for which he shall be bound to serve).

Section 5. . . . In all cases where men and women, both or one of them were lately slaves and are now emancipated, now cohabit together in the relation of husband and wife, the parties shall be deemed to have been lawfully married as man and wife at the time of the commencement of such cohabitation, although they may not have been married in due form of law. And all persons whose cohabitation is hereby ratified into a state of marriage shall go before the clerk of the court of pleas and quarter sessions of the county in which they reside, at his office, or before some justice of the peace, and acknowledge the fact of such cohabitation, and the time of its commencement, and the clerk shall enter the same in a book kept for that purpose; and if the acknowledgment be made before a justice of the peace, such justice shall report the same in writing to the clerk of the court of pleas and quarter sessions, and the clerk shall enter the same as though the acknowledgment had been made before him; and such entry shall be deemed prima facie evidence of the allegations therein contained. . . .

Section 7. . . . All contracts between any persons whatever, whereof one or more of them shall be a person of color, for the sale or purchase of any horse, mule, ass, jennet, neat cattle, hog, sheep or goat, whatever may be the value of such articles, and all contracts between such persons for any other article or articles of property whatever of the value of ten dollars or more; and all contracts executed or executory between such persons for the payment of money of the value of ten dollars or more, shall be void as to all persons whatever, unless the same be put in writing and signed by the vendors or debtors, and witnessed by a white person who can read and write. . . .

Section 9. . . . Persons of color not otherwise incompetent shall be capable of bearing evidence in all controversies at law and in equity, where the rights of persons or property of persons of color shall be put in issue, and would be concluded by the judgment or decree of court; and also in pleas of the State, where the violence, fraud, or injury alleged shall be charged to have been done by or to persons of color. In all other civil and criminal cases such evidence shall be deemed inadmissable, unless by consent of the parties of record: Provided, That this section shall not go into effect until jurisdiction in matters relating to freedmen shall be fully committed to the courts of this State: Provided, further, That no person shall be deemed incompetent to bear testimony in such cases because of being a party to the record or in interest. . . .

Section 11. . . . Any person of color convicted by due course of law of an assault with an attempt to commit rape upon the body of a white female, shall suffer death.

Section 12. . . . The criminal laws of the State embracing and affecting a white person are hereby extended to persons of color, except where it is otherwise provided in this act, and whenever the shall be convicted of any act made criminal, if committed by a white person, they shall be punished in like manner, except in such cases where other and different punishment may be prescribed or allowed by this act.—*Public Laws of North Carolina, 1866*, I, 99; *Senate Executive Document, No. 26, 39th Cong., 1st Sess.*, p. 197.

134. FEAR OF NEGRO INSURRECTION IN NORTH CAROLINA

During the decade following the Civil War, southern whites lived in constant fear of Negro insurrection. Negroes were supplied with arms in many parts of the South, and this naturally gave the whites a feeling of insecurity. In order to avert attack, the North Carolina Convention enacted an ordinance "directing the sheriffs and boards of magistrates to enroll and organize as many military companies as might be necessary to preserve law and order therein, and to act as an armed police until the regular organization of the State militia." The following extract is taken from the debate on this ordinance and explains conditions at that time.

MR. FEREBEE . . . said that in his county the white citizens had all been deprived of arms, while the negroes were almost all of them armed by some means or another. It was a fact that nearly every negro was supplied with arms, and there was a general feeling of insecurity on the part of the whites. There had been rumors of anticipated trouble in some of the counties at the commencement of next year. He did not know how well grounded the fears might be, but there certainly was much apprehension among the white citizens, especially among the female portion, of coming danger.

Gen. Dockery . . . stated that in his county the white residents had been disarmed, and were at present almost destitute of means to protect themselves against robbery and outrage. He had consulted with the General in command of this department, and found that he had no objection to the raising of such a police force as was contemplated by the bill.—*American Annual Cyclopedia*, V (1865), 627.

135. NEGRO EVIDENCE IN NORTH CAROLINA COURTS

Following the Civil War the Negro was enfranchised and the leading whites of the South were disfranchised. One of the first questions to come up was that of Negro testimony in the courts. Should it be allowed? Should the Negro be permitted to serve on juries? The extract below is a report of a committee of the North Carolina legislature on these momentous questions. The legislature was in the control of carpet-baggers and Negroes during this tragic period.

WE recommend that the courts should be fully opened to the negro race, for protection and property, and all the rights of freedmen, by being heard as witnesses whenever these rights are in controversy. The enactment recommended allows their evidence in civil cases only where the rights of person or property of persons of color would be precluded by the judgment or decrees made in those cases. And in criminal cases, only where violence, fraud, or injury charged to have been done by or on them is put directly in issue. . . .

The committee will proceed to give some of the reasons which have induced them to recommend the reception of the evidence of negroes. . . .

First. The present helpless and unprotected condition of the race demands it.

Their condition of personal security is greatly changed. Prior to emancipation they were grouped on farms which they seldom left, and were overlooked by their masters or overseers, surrounded by families of white children.

They were not only watched by the whites to preserve the discipline necessary for servitude, and to prevent spoliations, but were cared for and protected as property. It was the slave-holder's interest to prevent, and when committed to punish, any injuries done to the persons of their slaves. The interest of one slave-holder was the interest of all; so that their security was guaranteed by the common interest of the wealthiest and most powerful men in the country, and, of course, of all their kindred and adherents, among whom, generally, were their poorer white neighbors. Thus the person of the slave (without reckoning the feelings of humanity which have generally characterized the slaveholders of this State) became the subject of general protection by every class of white men, and any outrages on his person a general cause for common vindication. With this shield of security, the white aggressor was checked in his violence; and if not, his detection was almost sure. These sources of personal security are all removed by emancipation, and, without capacity to bear evidence, he stands in numerous cases utterly defenceless, except by opposing force against every species of outrage offered to himself or to his family. . . . If he should submit to the violence, and suffer the most grievous wrongs, there is no one who can be heard in his behalf; and he could expect, from his submission, nothing less than a repetition of his unredressed wrongs. If he should oppose force to force in the justest cause, whatever might be the result, his mouth and the mouths of all colored witnesses would be closed.

Secondly. The admission of such evidence is necessary to secure the colored people in their rights of property.

While in slavery they had no property. What was set apart for their use belonged to their master, and was under his protection. In their new state they enter on the broad ground of citizenship, and become actors in all the departments of social life. They are allowed to trade with the white man in every article of property; to possess and cultivate lands, and, by all wise means, should be encouraged to habits of industry and a desire for honest acquisition.

If the property which a negro shall own, his cattle, his money, may all be carried off, yea, his very house robbed of its furniture, and his person of his valuables, by abandoned white men, and he shall be unable to bring the robbers to justice because the witnesses are colored, can the race feel any ardent disposition to labor for themselves? On the contrary, will they not feel doubly tempted by such want of security for their own property to become depredators themselves, especially when they reflect that it is the white man's policy which thus exposes them to licentious white men? . . . Al-

eady the wicked white man and corrupt dependent negro have
)anded together in lawless thefts and frauds on industrious and
)eaceful citizens, both white and black; and the white associate,
f negro evidence shall be excluded, will stand secure in his villainy
)ehind his colored friend. . . .

Slaves were not allowed to bear testimony against free persons of
:olor until 1821.

The policy of excluding such testimony was founded on two con-
iderations. First, the entire and absolute dependence of a slave on
is master . . . which rendered him unfit to bear witness for or
.gainst his master . . . or for or against any person to whom his
naster extended his favor or dislike. Besides this, the settled policy
vas to humble the slave and extinguish in him the pride of inde-
)endence. This latter policy was extended in 1821 to the free negro,
vho, it was alleged, was greatly corrupting the slave by claiming
uperior privileges over him.

Emancipation having destroyed the distinction all legislation con-
:erning the colored race must be the same.

The rules regulating the admissibility of the evidence of white
)ersons, with a few exceptions, remain with us as they were a cen-
ury since. But all at once the slave has disappeared, and upward of
300,000 free persons of color are added to the population; these con-
titute one-third of our entire people. If it ever was, it is certainly
ot now our policy to degrade them. On the contrary, our true
)olicy, is to elevate them in every way consistent with the safety
ind good government of the community. They must be educated
)ut of their ignorance, and reformed out of their vicious habits.
. .

By the laws of all civilized Europe, regulating the competency of
vitnesses, none are excluded by reason of character, race, color or
religion. We ourselves admit the semi-barbarian of every continent
ind island; of every nation and tongue; of every religion—Christian,
ieathen and pagan; and of every color and race, unless he may
all under the ethnological varieties of the human species denomi-
ated Negroes and Indians.

We are not prepared to admit, nor indeed do we believe, that the
:olored man in North Carolina is entitled to less credit on his Chris-
ian oath than the colored Musselman or heathen of Asia or Egypt
, . . is when sworn on his Koran or other symbols of religious reverence. And when we consider the many thousands in the State who
ire in full fellowship as Christians, though we are quite sensible of
:he general demoralization which pervades them as a class, we feel

little dread for the consequences which may attend the admissibility of their evidence as reported. . . .

We have conceded the general demoralization of the colored population; but we should do great injustice to many of them if we should close this report without excepting from the stigma hundred who, throughout their lives, have conducted themselves in a manner altogether becoming the best of citizens, and deserving the very highest praise. . . . —*Senate Executive Document, No. 26, 39th Cong. 1st Sess.*, 152nd Report of a committee of the North Carolina legislature, January 22, 1866.

136. SCHOOLS ESTABLISHED BY THE FREEDMEN'S BUREAU IN NORTH CAROLINA, 1865-1869

On March 3, 1865, Congress passed an act to establish a Bureau for the Relief of Freedmen and Refugees. The North Carolina bureau was organized July 15, 1865, and remained in operation until January 1, 1869. Though very unpopular in certain sections of the state, it did much meritorious work. In North Carolina alone the Freedmen's Bureau distributed about $1,500,000 worth of food; established hospitals which cared for more than 40,000 patients; and organized 431 schools which had 439 teachers and more than 20,000 pupils. The following document shows the Negro's interest in education.

A GENERAL desire for education is everywhere manifested. In some instances, as in Halifax County, very good schools were found taught and paid for by the colored people themselves. Said a gentleman to me, "I constantly see in the streets and on the door-steps opposite my dwelling groups of little negroes studying their spelling-books." . . .

Not only are individuals seen at study, and under the most untoward circumstances, but in very many places I have found what I will call "native schools," often rude and very imperfect, but there they are, a group, perhaps, of all ages, trying to learn. Some young man, some woman, or old preacher, in cellar, or shed, or corner of a negro meeting-house, with the alphabet in hand, or a torn spelling book, is their teacher. All are full of enthusiasm with the new knowledge the book is imparting to them.

It is no infrequent occurrence to witness in the same rooms, and pursuing the same studies, the child and parent—youth and gray hairs—all eagerly grasping for that by which, obtained, they are intellectually regenerated. . . .

As an evidence of the great interest manifested for acquiring knowledge, an instance, probably never before equalled in the history of education, is to be found in one of the schools of this State, where side by side sat representatives of four generations in a direct line, viz.: a child six years old, her mother, grand-mother, and great-grandmother, the latter over 75 years of age. All commenced their alphabet together, and each one can read the Bible fluently.

Night schools have met with gratifying success, and are eagerly sought for by those whose labors are of such a character as to prevent their attendance during the day.

Sunday schools have been established at many points where teachers reside. . . . It is evident much good has been accomplished by their establishment, and no estimate can be made of the beneficial results of their full development.—Report of J. W. Alvord, superintendent of Schools for the Freedmen's Bureau, *Senate Executive Document No. 27, 39th Cong., 1st Sess.*

137. SCHOOLS FOR FREEDMEN

During the dark years of Reconstruction many northern societies and religious groups aided in the establishment and maintenance of schools for freedmen. In 1869 there were 11,826 pupils enrolled in North Carolina schools which were financed by northern organizations. By far the most active educational agency, however, was the Freedmen's Bureau. In September, 1865, J. W. Alvord was appointed general superintendent of schools for the Bureau of Refugees, Freedmen, and Abandoned Lands. Reverend F. A. Fiske, a Massachusetts carpet-bagger, was made superintendent of education in North Carolina. He was succeeded by H. C. Vogell, who made the following report, July 1, 1869.

THE work in this state has made gratifying progress during the last term. In February the superintendent reports a large increase as the result of unremitting energy and zeal. At that time there was a gain of 58 schools, 76 teachers, and 3,209 pupils, making a total of 19,635 pupils. There was also an increase of 25 Sabbath schools, 154 teachers, and 3,328 pupils, so that the whole number under instruction in the State was 22,334. . . .

Nor is the thirst for knowledge confined to the young. The aged in the State, though unable to devote much time to study, eagerly avail themselves of every opportunity of learning to read. . . . An aged woman of seventy years was in regular attendance upon school for five weeks; at the end of that time she could read easy passages in the New Testament. . . .

Educational meetings have been held at various points in the

State, the people, and especially the freedmen, attending in large numbers. . . .

In reviewing the history of schools in North Carolina for the six months ending June 30, 1869, the progress of education among freedmen awakens the liveliest interest. The contrast between the past and present is a matter of wonder and gratitude. From servile degradation and debasing ignorance they have awakened to a life of earnest and successful improvement.

Schools sought for—. Our schools everywhere are sought for by old and young, as time and opportunity admit. I am in receipt of letters daily, requesting aid for schools in different parts of the State. Today two men came to my office, noble specimens of their race, to ascertain for themselves all that was necessary in getting up a school for the education of their children, performing a journey on foot, to and from their residence, of one hundred and forty miles.

It seems to me the aspirations for knowledge existing everywhere among freedmen must silence the most skeptical and arouse the most lukewarm to effort in their education and elevation. Never has there existed a greater field or opportunity for Christian philanthropy and benevolence than is now offered among freedmen.

Missionary field—. This is in all respects a missionary field, where "faith and works" may be united in elevating a hitherto crushed manhood. . . .

To meet the demand of the freedmen for education the organization of the Freedmen's Bureau has been used in this State to good purpose. Their educational necessities have been, as far as possible provided for. The cause, however, needs the addition of all the facilities which northern societies can furnish for the prosecution of the work.

Results—.

There are now in North Carolina 430 schools. Sustained by Bureau, (rental of $5 to $10 per month,) 250 schools. Sustained by Northern societies, 150 schools. Of these 30 are graded schools, averaging about 150 per school, making the number in such schools 4,500.

There are 150 northern teachers in the field, averaging an expenditure to societies of $25 per month, making a total of $5,250 monthly

. . .

The highest number reported in all our schools for a single month was 20,000 pupils. . . .

Books—. Books are greatly needed. I am constantly importuned for them. I had 7,000 volumes given me for distribution, and y

ιe demand is as pressing as before. I have known of a few instances
ヽhere a class of 10 or 12 were obliged to use one book, passing it from
ιe to another as their turn to read came.

As the Bureau has no appropriation for school books, we appeal
ɔ benevolent individuals and to publishing societies to supply the
ϸove demand. Packages can be forwarded through these head-
ιarters.—*Bureau of Refugees, Freedmen. and Abandoned Lands, 8th Semi-
inual Report, July 1, 1869, pp. 24-28.*

138. WHY THE KU KLUX KLAN WAS ORGANIZED IN NORTH CAROLINA

The Ku Klux Klan, which probably originated in Tennessee in 1865,
ιst appeared in North Carolina in 1867. It grew rapidly for a period
ˊ two years and then declined. Since its operations were veiled in secrecy,
з total membership is not known, but estimates place it as high as 40,000.
olonel William L. Saunders took the lead in promoting the Klan's polit-
al activities, though it seems that he was not a member of the organiza-
ɔn. By means of warnings, threats, whippings, mutilations, and even
urder, the Klan was a great factor in the "restoration of white suprem-
ɔy." The reports of congressional investigating committees show that
ιere were at least 260 Klan "visitations" in twenty North Carolina
ɔunties, 174 of which were directed against Negroes. The rapid growth
ˊ the Klan in North Carolina. was due to several factors : the effort to
ɔmbat northern secret organizations in the South, the desire to "put
e negro in his place," the attempt of the whites to regain control of
ɔvernment, and the protection of southern womanhood. The accom-
ιnying document is taken from a report made to a congressional com-
ittee appointed to investigate reasons for the organization of the Ku
lux Klan.

THINK there were five persons hung in the county (Orange) ; three
ere hung for burning barns ; another was hung for having threat-
ιed to ravish a girl ; I never heard why the other was hung. . . .

. . . the poorer classes in the community, women who carry
lack-berries, cherries, eggs, butter, and things of that sort to town
ϸ sell, were afraid to go to town by themselves ; they would only
ɔ when they could form large companies for mutual protection.
ɔrmerly, and even now, they could go singly just when they were
ady. But just about that time they were afraid to go to town alone
r fear of being insulted or ravished by negroes. . . .

I can very readily state, as a general answer, that in my opinion
ιe cause of the troubles in the whole southern country is bad gov-
nment. . . . I am fortified in that belief by the fact that up to the

time that these governments and State constitutions so obnoxious to the people of that country were imposed upon them, nothing of this sort was occurring. From the close of the war up to 1867, affairs were perfectly quiet in the South; there were no occurrences of this kind. I attribute the whole thing to bad government, corrupt and incompetent officials, and bad advice to the ignorant negro population.

I know of no disposition on the part of the white people of that country to coerce the black people. . . . But I know that the colored people of North Carolina . . . have been taught to believe by the leading people of the Leagues that the white men of that country are their enemies; that their only friends are the northern men . . . that it is the desire of the white people of our portion of the country to restore slavery at the earliest possible moment.

In the county of Gaston, adjoining my own county, there were, a year and a half ago, as I have been told by Governor Vance, of our State, eleven barns burned within sight of the village of Dallas, the county seat of that county.

There is no necessity on the part of the higher and more intelligent classes for that jealousy toward the negroes which exists between the poor white and the negro; but there is a feeling among the poorer classes of white people that they and the country would be a great deal better off if the negroes were entirely out of the country; and they would unanimously vote for colonizing them, or anything else to get them away, simply because they believe and declare that they and their families are the sufferers. As to the commission of rapes and things of that kind, the wealthy and more intelligent classes do not, of course, feel under the same danger as do the poorer classes of white people in the country.

I do not know of any jealousy or hatred on the part of intelligent, wealthy men toward the negroes; . . . but I do think that the common white people of the country are at times very much enraged against the negro population. They think that this universal political and civil equality will finally bring about social equality; there are already instances in the county of Cleveland in which poor white girls are having negro children. Such things as these are widening the breach between these two classes of our population. The white laboring people feel that it is not safe for them to be thus working in close contact with the negroes. . . .

It was at a time when the republican party had three secret organizations in operation in the State, the Union League, the Heroes of America, and the Red Strings. They had a paper called he Red String, printed at Greensborough, edited by Mr. Tourgee. Our friends thought it was proper to organize a secret society for he purpose of counteracting that influence.—*Ku Klux Reports, North Carolina Testimony*, pp. 8, 309-10, 318, 363.

139. JUDGE THOMAS RUFFIN'S CRITICISM OF THE KU KLUX KLAN, 1869

Apparently most southerners considered the Ku Klux Klan a necessity and approved its methods of putting the Negro "in his place." Judge Ruffin was an exception. In a letter to his son, John K. Ruffin, July 8, 869, he stated his objections to the Klan.

BUT I am satisfied that such associations as that you mention are perilous to the parties, dangerous to the community, and highly immoral and wrong. . . .

Besides and mainly, the great objection is, that the whole proceeding is against Law and the Civil power of Government and assumes to supersede by taking the power of trying, condemning, and punishing in their own hands. That is a power not to be entrusted to any man or set of men. No man can trust himself with it, much less all those indiscriminately with whom he is associated. Supposing them to have the best intentions in such case; there is danger of mistake from want of a fair, open, and deliberate trial, by a responsible tribunal. But, at all events, it is in every case an attempt to do good by wrong means. . . . To do evil that good may come of it, is a horrible heresy in Religion, morals and public polity, even if the good hoped for really resulted. But, in truth, it hardly ever does, but evil almost certainly always follows evil and what was begun in good faith for useful ends, almost ever terminates in gross personal and private injuries. Perhaps at first only bad men are the subjects of the assumed jurisdiction ; but it may happen, and after a while, almost certainly does happen, that good and innocent men become the victims of their arrogant and self constituted tribunals, and gross outrages are perpetrated. It is wrong—all wrong . . and I beg you to have nothing to do with it. It is much better that offenders should escape punishment than to attempt to repress crime by such unlawful, presumptuous, and dangerous methods of repression. At best it is committing one crime, to prevent or punish another.—*The Papers of Thomas Ruffin* (edited by J. G. deR. Hamilton), IV, 226-27.

140. THE 1868 CONSTITUTION

The Reconstruction Act of March 2, 1867, divided the South into five military districts. The Carolinas constituted the second district. The Act also provided, "That when the people of any one of said rebel States shall have formed a constitution of government in conformity with the Constitution of the United States in all respects, framed by a convention of delegates elected by male citizens of said State, twenty-one years old and upward, of whatever race, color, or previous condition, who have been resident in said State for one year previous to the day of such election, except such as may be disfranchised for participation in the rebellion or for felony at common law, and when such constitution shall provide that the elective franchise shall be enjoyed by all such persons as have the qualifications herein stated for electors of delegates, and when such constitution shall be ratified by a majority of the persons voting on the question of ratification who are qualified for electors as delegates, and when such constitution shall have been submitted to Congress for examination and approval, and Congress shall have approved the same, and when said State, by a vote of its legislature elected under said constitution, shall have adopted the amendment to the Constitution of the United States . . . known as article fourteen, and when said article shall have become a part of the Constitution of the United States said State shall be declared entitled to representation in Congress."

Accordingly to General Canby's orders, the Constitutional Convention met in Raleigh, January 14, 1868, and drew up a document which has been called the "Canby Constitution." There were 107 Republicans present, of whom 18 were carpet-baggers and 15 negroes. Only 13 Conservatives were in attendance. Deweese referred to the Convention as "that assemblage of corrupt and doubtful representatives," while Conservative papers dubbed it "the Convention (so-called)." Calvin J. Cowles was the presiding officer. Albion W. Tourgée of Ohio was probably the most influential man in the proceedings of the Convention.

Some of the provisions were copied from the Ohio Constitution while others were in line with progressive legislation in northern states. Many of the changes were quite democratic. Some of the most significant were: the abolition of slavery, removal of religious tests for office-holding, popular election of all state and county officials, abolition of county court system and the adoption of the township-county commission form of government, and provision for "a general and uniform system of public schools." Four new executive offices were created: lieutenant-governor, auditor, superintendent of public works, and superintendent of public instruction. The elective Council of State was dropped.

Preamble

WE, the people of the State of North-Carolina, grateful to Almighty God, the Sovereign Ruler of Nations, for the preservation of the American Union and the existence of our civil, political, and religious liberties, and acknowledging our dependence upon Him for the continuance of those blessings to us and our posterity, do, for the better government of this State, ordain and establish this Constitution.

ARTICLE I

DECLARATION OF RIGHTS

Section 1. That we hold it to be self-evident that all men are created equal; that they are endowed by their Creator with certain unalienable rights : that among these are life, liberty, the enjoyments of the fruits of their own labor, and the pursuit of happiness. . . .

Sec. 4. That this State shall ever remain a member of the American Union; that the people thereof are part of the American nation; that there is no right on the part of this State to secede, and that all attempts—from whatever source or upon whatever pretext, to dissolve said Union, or to sever said nation, ought to be resisted with the whole power of the State.

Sec. 5. That every citizen of this State owes paramount allegiance to the Constitution and Government of the United States, and that no law or ordinance of the State in contravention or subversion thereof can have any binding force.

Sec. 6. To maintain the honor and good faith of the State untarnished, the public debt, regularly contracted before and since the rebellion, shall be regarded as inviolable and never be questioned; but the State shall never assume or pay, or authorize the collection of, any debt or obligation, express or implied, incurred in aid of insurrection or rebellion against the United States, or any claim for the loss or emancipation of any slave. . . .

Sec. 27. The people have a right to the privilege of education, and it is the duty of the State to guard and maintain that right. . . .

Sec. 33. Slavery and involuntary servitude, otherwise than for crime whereof the parties shall have been duly convicted, shall be, and are hereby, forever prohibited within this State.

Sec. 34. The limits and boundaries of the State shall be and remain as they now are.

ARTICLE II

LEGISLATIVE DEPARTMENT

Section 1. The Legislative authority shall be vested in two distinct branches, both dependent on the people, to wit: A Senate and House of Representatives.

Sec. 2. The Senate and House of Representatives shall meet annually on the third Monday in November, and when assembled, shall be denominated the General Assembly. . . .

Sec. 3. The Senate shall be composed of fifty Senators biennially chosen by ballot. . . .

Sec. 6. The House of Representatives shall be composed of one hundred and twenty representatives, biennially chosen by ballot, to be elected by the counties respectively, according to their population, and each county shall have at least one representative in the house of representatives. . . .

Sec. 12. The General Assembly shall have power to pass general laws regulating divorce and alimony, but shall not have power to grant a divorce or secure alimony in any individual case. . . .

Sec. 21. The Lieutenant-Governor shall preside in the Senate, but shall have no vote, unless it may be equally divided. . . .

Sec. 26. Each member of the General Assembly, before taking his seat, shall take an oath or affirmation that he will support the Constitution and laws of the United States, and the constitution of the State of North Carolina, and will faithfully discharge his duty as a member of the senate or house of representatives. . . .

ARTICLE III

EXECUTIVE DEPARTMENT

Section 1. The Executive Department shall consist of a Governor, (in whom shall be vested the Supreme executive power of the State,) a Lieutenant-Governor, a Secretary of State, an Auditor, a Treasurer, a Superintendent of Public Works, a Superintendent of Public Instruction, and an Attorney-General, who shall be elected for a term of four years, by the qualified electors of the State, at the same time and places, and in the same manner as members of the general assembly are elected. Their term of office shall commence on the first day of January next, after their election, and continue until their successors are elected and qualified. . . .

Sec. 14. The Secretary of State, Auditor, Treasurer, Superintendent of Public Works, and Superintendent of Public Instruction shall constitute, *ex officio*, the Council of the State, who shall advise the Governor in the execution of his office, and three of whom shall constitute a quorum. . . . The attorney-general shall be, *ex officio*, the legal advisor of the Executive Department.

Sec. 17. There shall be established in the office of Secretary of State a Bureau of Statistics, Agriculture, and Immigration, under such regulation as the general assembly may provide.

ARTICLE IV

JUDICIAL DEPARTMENT

Section 1. The distinction between actions at law and suits in equity, and the forms of all such actions and suits, shall be abolished, and there shall be in this State but one form of action for the enforcement or protection of private rights, or the redress of private wrongs, which shall be denominated a civil action; and every action prosecuted by the people of the State as a party, against a person charged with a public offence, for the punishment of the same, shall be termed a criminal action. Feigned issues shall also be abolished, and the fact at issue tried by order of court before a jury. . . .

Sec. 4. The Judicial power of the State shall be vested in a court for the trial of Impeachments, a Supreme Court, Superior Courts, Courts of Justices of the Peace, and Special Courts. . . .

Sec. 8. The Supreme Court shall consist of a Chief Justice and four Associate Justices.

Sec. 9. There shall be two terms of the Supreme Court held at the seat of Government of the State in each year, commencing on the first Monday in January and the first Monday in June, and continuing as long as the public interests may require.

Sec. 10. The Supreme Court shall have jurisdiction to review, upon appeal, any decision of the courts below upon any matter of law or legal inference; but no issue of fact shall be tried before this court. . . .

ARTICLE V

REVENUE AND TAXATION

Section 1. The General Assembly shall levy a capitation tax on every male inhabitant of the State over twenty-one and under fifty years of age, which shall be equal, on each, to the tax on property valued at three hundred dollars in cash. The Commissioners of the several counties may exempt from capitation tax in special cases, on account of poverty and infirmity, and the State and county capitation tax shall never exceed two dollars on the head.

Sec. 2. The proceeds of the State and County capitation tax shall be applied to the purposes of education and the support of the poor, but in no one year shall more than twenty-five per cent. thereof be appropriated to the latter purpose. . . .

Sec. 6. Property belonging to the State, or to municipal corporations, shall be exempt from taxation. The General Assembly may exempt cemetaries, and property held for educational, scientific, literary, charitable, or religious purposes; also, wearing-apparel, arms for muster, household and kitchen furniture, the mechanical and agricultural implements of mechanics and farmers, libraries, and scientific instruments, to a value not exceeding three hundred dollars.

ARTICLE VI

SUFFRAGE AND ELIGIBILITY TO OFFICE

Section 1. Every male person born in the United States, and every male person who has been naturalized, twenty-one years old or upward, who shall have resided in this State twelve months next preceding the election, and thirty days in the county in which he offers to vote, shall be deemed an elector. . . .

Sec. 4. Every voter, except as hereinafter provided, shall be eligible to office; but before entering upon the discharge of the duties of his office, he shall take and subscribe the following oath: "I, —— ——, do solemnly swear (or affirm) that I will support and maintain the Constitution and laws of the United States, and the constitution and laws of North Carolina not inconsistent therewith, and that I will faithfully discharge the duties of my office: so help me God."

Sec. 5. The following classes of persons shall be disqualified for office: First, All persons who shall deny the being of Almighty God. Second, All persons who shall have been convicted of treason, perjury, or of any other infamous crime . . . unless such persons shall have been legally restored to the rights of citizenship.

ARTICLE VII

MUNICIPAL CORPORATIONS

Section 1. In each county, there shall be elected, biennially, by the qualified voters thereof, as provided for the election of members of the General Assembly : A Treasurer, Register of Deeds, Surveyor, and Five Commissioners.

Sec. 2. It shall be the duty of the Commissioners to exercise a general supervision and control of the penal and charitable institutions, schools, roads, bridges, levying of taxes, and finances of the county, as may be prescribed by law.

Sec. 3. It shall be the duty of the Commissioners first elected in each county to divide the same into convenient districts, to determine the boundaries, and prescribe the names of the said districts . . . the said districts shall have corporate powers for the necessary purposes of local government, and shall be known as townships.. . . .

Sec. 9. All taxes levied by any county, city, town, or township shall be uniform and *ad valorem* upon all property in the same, except property exempted by this Constitution. . . .

ARTICLE IX

EDUCATION

Section 1. Religion, morality, and knowledge being necessary to good government and happiness of mankind, schools and the means of education shall forever be encouraged.

Sec. 2. The General Assembly at its first session under this Constitution, shall provide by taxation and otherwise for a general and uniform system of Public Schools, wherein tuition shall be free of charge to all the children of the State between the ages of six and twenty-one years.

Sec. 3. Each County of the State shall be divided into a convenient number of Districts, in which one or more Public Schools shall be maintained, at least four months in every year. . . .

Sec. 5. The University of North-Carolina, with its lands, emoluments and franchises, is under the control of the State, and shall be held to an inseparable connection with the Free Public School system of the State. . . .

Sec. 16. As soon as practicable after the adoption of this Constitution, the General Assembly shall establish and maintain in connection with the University, a Department of Agriculture, of Mechanics, of Mining, and of Normal Instruction.

Sec. 17. The General Assembly is hereby empowered to enact that every child of sufficient mental and physical ability, shall attend the Public Schools, during the period between the ages of six and eighteen years, for a term of not less than sixteen months, unless educated by other means. . . .

ARTICLE XI

PUNISHMENTS, PENAL INSTITUTIONS, AND PUBLIC CHARITIES

Section 1. The following punishments only shall be known to the laws of this State, viz: death, imprisonment with or without hard labor, fines, removal from office and disqualification to hold and enjoy any office of honor, trust, or profit under this State.

Sec. 2. The objects of punishments being not only to satisfy justice, but also to reform the offender, and thus prevent crime, murder, arson, burglary, and rape, and these only, may be punishable with death, if the General Assembly shall so enact. . . .

Sec. 7. Beneficent provision for the poor, the unfortunate, and orphan being one of the first duties of a civilized and Christian State, the General Assembly shall, at its first session, appoint and define the duties of a Board of Public Charities, to whom shall be intrusted the supervision of all charitable and penal State institutions, and who shall annually report to the Governor upon their condition, with suggestions for their improvement. . . .

ARTICLE XII

MILITIA

Section 1. All able bodied male citizens of the State of North-Carolina between the ages of twenty-one and forty years, who are citizens of the United States, shall be liable to duty in the Militia: *Provided*, That all persons who may be averse to bearing arms, from religious scruples, shall be exempt therefrom. . . .

ARTICLE XIV

MISCELLANEOUS

Sec. 2. No person who shall hereafter fight a duel, or assist in the same as a second, or send, accept, or knowingly carry a challenge therefor, or agree to go out of this State to fight a duel, shall hold any office in this State. . . .

Sec. 7. No person shall hold more than one lucrative office under the State, at the same time: *Provided*, That officers in the Militia, Justices of the Peace, Commissioners of Public Charities, and Commissioners appointed for special purposes, shall not be considered officers within the meaning of this section. . . . —*Constitution of the State of North Carolina together with the Ordinances, Resolutions of the Constitutional Convention, assembled in the City of Raleigh, January 14, 1868*, pp. 1-39.

141. THE IMPEACHMENT OF GOVERNOR W. W. HOLDEN,
1870-1871

The first impeachment of a governor in the United States took place
in North Carolina in 1870-71 when the state legislature impeached and
convicted Governor William Woods Holden. It is likewise the only instance of a North Carolina governor's removal by that process.

Holden's impeachment was the result of a long train of events and circumstances. He had made himself extremely unpopular with Democratic
leaders during the war by his criticisms of Vance, his denunciation of the
Confederacy, and his leadership of the Peace party. In fact, he had been
forced to suspend publication of the *Standard* in 1864.

After the war he became *persona non grata* to the Conservatives of the
state. His appointment to the governorship by President Johnson had
met with disapproval. He was later elected governor, and his administration was one of the most unfortunate in the history of the state. In
referring to it, Ashe says: "But they had wrecked the State. They had
dissipated the State's assets, opened no schools, closed the University,
and destroyed every hope of any early amelioration of the unfortunate
condition of transportation facilities; and worse than all else, the Assembly was odorous with fraud, bribery and corruption."

Things came to a head in 1870. Maintaining that there was disorder in
Alamance and Caswell counties because of the activities of the Ku Klux
Klan, Governor Holden proclaimed both of these counties in a state of
insurrection. Judge Tourgée, carpet-bag judge, refused to hold court in
Alamance; whereupon the Governor proceeded to organize two regiments, only one of which actually saw service. This regiment was under
the command of Colonel George W. Kirk of Tennessee, and the disastrous events of the following months are known in North Carolina history
as the "Kirk-Holden War."

Kirk had the reputation of being a "desperate and brutal character."
He had 670 men, more than 200 of whom were illegally recruited outside of North Carolina. Three hundred and ninety-nine of his regiment
were under and 64 over legal military age. A large number of Negroes
were included. Kirk's men proceeded to take charge of Alamance and
Caswell counties, occupying the courthouses at Graham and Yanceyville.
They roamed about the country, pillaging and insulting the people, and
instituting a regular reign of terror. Eighty-two military arrests were
made in Alamance and nineteen in Caswell.

Josiah Turner, editor of the *Sentinel*, was "making things hot" for the
Governor. Holden threatened to arrest him. Turner dared him to do it.
Holden made good his threat, had Turner arrested, carried to Yancey-
ville, and jailed.

The Conservatives, who were now in control of the legislature, could
stand no more. B. F. Moore declared that Holden's impeachment was

"demanded by a sense of public virtue and due regard to the honor of the State." Finally, on December 14, 1870, the House of Representatives resolved that the Governor "be impeached of high crimes and misdemeanors." There were eight charges of impeachment.

The trial began February 2 and the final vote was taken March 22, 1871. One hundred and seventy witnesses were called, 57 by the House managers and 113 by Holden. The Governor was found guilty on six of the eight charges. When the result was announced, the Senate adopted a resolution adjudging that William W. Holden "be removed from the office of governor and be disqualified to hold any office of honor, trust, or profit under the State of North Carolina." Lieutenant-Governor Tod R. Caldwell became governor, serving out the remainder of Holden's term. In referring to the impeachment trial, Vance remarked: "It was the longest hunt after the poorest hide I ever saw."

ARTICLES Exhibited by the House of Representatives of the State of North Carolina against W. W. Holden. . . .

I. . . . that William W. Holden, Governor of said State, unmindful of the high duties of his office, the obligation of his solemn oath of office, and the Constitution and laws of said State, and intending to stir up civil war, and subvert personal and public liberty, and the Constitution and laws of said State and of the United States and contriving and intending to humiliate and degrade the said State. . . . and especially the people of the county of Alamance, and to provoke the people to wrath and violence, did, under the color of his said office, on the seventh day of March eighteen seventy, in said State, of his own false, corrupt and wicked mind and purpose, proclaim and declare that the county of Alamance . . . was in insurrection, and did, . . . send bodies of armed, desperate and lawless men, organized and set on foot without authority of law, into said county, and occupy the same by military force, and suspend civil authority, and the Constitution and laws of the State; . . . and did detain, hold, imprison, hang, beat and otherwise maltreat and injure many of them, . . . [81 names are mentioned] . . . when in fact and truth there was no such or any insurrection in said county of Alamance. And he, . . . well knew that such and said proclamation was groundless and false, and that there was no insurrection in said County, and that all civil authorities, both State and County, in said county, were peacefully and regularly in the full, free and unrestrained exercise in all respects, . . . and the courts were all open, . . .

II. . . . That William W. Holden, . . . did . . . proclaim and declare the County of Caswell in said State in insurrection, . . .

and did detain, hold, imprison and otherwise maltreat and injure many of them, . . . [19 names are mentioned, and the same charges as those in Article I are restated].

III. That . . . Holden . . . in eighteen seventy, in the county of Orange, did then and there unlawfully, . . . order and command one John Hunnicutt and other evil disposed persons to assault, seize, detain and imprison and deprive of his liberty and privileges as a freeman and citizen of said State, Josiah Turner, . . .

IV. That . . . Holden, . . . in the year eighteen seventy, in the County of Caswell . . . did then and there unlawfully and without any lawful warrant and authority, . . . incite, procure, order and command one George W. Kirk, and one B. G. Burgen and other evil disposed persons, to assault, seize, detain and impress and deprive of their liberty . . . John Kerr, Samuel P. Hill, William B. Bow, and Nathaniel M. Roane, citizens and residents of the County of Caswell. . . .

V. That . . . Holden, . . . in the months of June, July and August in the year eighteen seventy, . . . unlawfully recruited, armed and equipped soldiers, a large number of men . . . 500 men and more and organized them as an army, and appointed officers to command, and . . . placed a large number of said armed men under the immediate command and control of one George W. Kirk as Colonel, . . . and sent such . . . men . . . into the County of Alamance, . . . the said armed men, . . . seized, held, detained and imprisoned, . . . one Adolphus G. Moore, a peaceable and law-abiding citizen, . . . That the said . . . Moore . . . made due application to the Honorable Richmond M. Pearson, Chief Justice of the Supreme Court of said State, . . . for the writ of *habeas corpus*, . . . directed to the said George W. Kirk, commanding him forthwith to produce the body of the said . . . Moore, before him the said Chief Justice, . . . in the City of Raleigh; that the said George W. Kirk . . . duly served with the said writ . . . made no return of or to the same and refused to produce the body of the said . . . Moore, . . . avowing and declaring that he had made such seizure and delivered and imprisoned the said . . . Moore, at the instance of and by the procurement, command and order of the said William W. Holden, . . . and would not produce the body, . . . unless compelled to do so by superior armed force, or by the express order and command of the said William W. Holden. . . .

VII. That the said William W. Holden, . . . did . . . in . . . June, July and August eighteen seventy, . . . without any authority of law, . . . and intending to provoke and stir up civil strife and war, recruit and call together from this State and the State of Tennessee, a large number of men, . . . Five hundred men and more, many of them the most reckless, desperate, ruffianly and lawless characters, and did then and there organize, arm and equip them as an army of soldiers, and place the same under the chief command of a notorious desperado from the State of Tennessee, by the name of George Kirk, having falsely proclaimed the counties of Alamance and Caswell . . . in a state of insurrection, and did send large numbers of such armed desperate men into said counties, . . . and did there and then without any warrant or authority, seize, hold, imprison and deprive of their liberty for a long time, . . . many of the peaceful law-abiding citizens of said counties, . . . and seize, hold, imprison and deprive of their liberty and hung by the neck William Patton, Lucien H. Murray and others, and did thrust into a loathsome dungeon Josiah Turner, Junior, and F. A. Wiley and to maintain, support and aid the lawless armed men so organized, . . . did, . . . without any lawful authority, make his warrant upon David A. Jenkins, Treasurer of the State for . . . the sum of 70,000 dollars and more and cause and procure the said . . . Treasurer . . . to recognize such unlawful warrant, and to pay out of the Treasury such said large sums of money. . . .

VIII. That . . . Holden, . . . with a view and for the purpose of supporting and maintaining an armed military force which he had then and there recruited, . . . without the sanction of the Constitution and laws of the said State, . . . did . . . make his warrants . . . upon the Treasury of the said State for the sum of eighty thousand ($80,000) dollars and more, to be used for the unlawful purposes aforesaid ; . . . —*Impeachment Trial of William W. Holden*, I, 1-17.

142. IGNORANT JUSTICES OF THE PEACE IN NORTH CAROLINA

In the decade following the Civil War there were many complaints of the ignorance, stupidity, and dishonesty of officials. The following statement of a Unionist Republican is indicative of the feeling toward the most numerous, and probably the most inefficient, group of local officers.

A LARGE portion of the gentlemen of North Carolina who had been in office in former times, who had taken just such a part in the rebellion, against their will and wishes, as to make them obnoxious to the provisions of reconstruction, were kept out of office. There is nothing that tends more to the security of life and property than the respectability of subordinate magistrates. . . . A great many of the new appointments were of men of known bad character, men convicted of theft, or accused and believed to have been guilty of theft, and men who could not read or write. Why, sir, precepts have been brought to me issued by justices who were not able to sign their names, but who made their mark. Justices who tried important cases, involving misdemeanors for which the parties might be sent to jail, could not write, and had to make their mark for their signature.—*Documentary History of Reconstruction* (edited by W. L. Fleming), II, 43, quoting *Outrages in the Southern States*, Part II, p. 17. Statement of B. F. Moore, a North Carolina Unionist, 1871.*

143. STATUS OF PUBLIC SCHOOL EDUCATION IN NORTH CAROLINA, 1872

The following report of Alexander McIver, State Superintendent of Public Instruction, October 1, 1872, gives a good picture of the North Carolina public school system at that time.

THE SCHOOL SYSTEM

The first general assembly which met under the present constitution provided for a general and uniform system of public schools. The failure of this system resulted from the fact that while the county commissioners were required to establish schools and authorized to order a tax for the purchase of sites, and for the building or renting of houses, they were given no authority to levy a county tax to pay the wages of teachers.

The State school fund consists of seventy-five per cent of the State and county capitation taxes, the income from taxes on auctioneers, and on licenses to retail spirituous liquors, and the income from the invested school funds. The whole amount which could be realized from these sources may be set down at fifty cents a year for each child in the State, It is true that the general assembly of 1868-69 appropriated $100,000 for the support of public schools, to be paid out of the State Treasury; but this amount was not paid except by the tax of one-twelfth of one per cent, which was levied the following year.

The present school law has, therefore, been on trial only since

* Reprinted by permission of the publishers, The Arthur H. Clark Company

March 14, 1872. It is not and was not intended to be a complete system. It is but the germ of a system to be developed by future legislation.

The extent to which the present beginning of a school system shall be made to meet the wants of the people will depend upon the action of the general assembly.

DEFECTS OF THE PRESENT LAW

The greatest defect in the practical operation of the law is, that incompetent teachers are allowed to get teacher's certificates. The county examiners yield to the idea that certificates must be given to a sufficient number of teachers to take charge of the public schools, and there the school money is wasted.

Another defect in the present law is, the want of uniformity in school books. However competent a teacher may be, if, when he goes into a school of forty or fifty pupils, or a less number he finds his pupils supplied with different kinds of school books, as is now the case, he will be unable to class them as he might otherwise do, and it will be impossible for him to instruct them to advantage.

Other defects noted are the failure to fix by law the time and manner of laying off districts, and the failure to make provision for the building and furnishing of school-houses. Concerning this the superintendent says : "It should be submitted to a vote of the townships, whether or not a tax should be levied to defray half the expenses of building and furnishing neat, substantial, and comfortable school-houses ; the other half being paid out of the general school fund."

COMPULSORY EDUCATION

The superintendent after quoting the most distinguished educators upon this subject, and giving copious extracts as indications of popular opinion on compulsory education says : "I am convinced of the necessity of adopting it in North Carolina."

His reasons for this conclusion he gives, as follows : "According to the census of 1870, there are in this State 38,647 white children and 40,955 colored children between the ages of 10 and 15 years, unable to read and write ; there are 31,911 white children and 44,-805 colored children in the State, between the ages of 15 and 21, unable to read and write. There are in the State, 191,961 whites and 205,032 colored, over the age of 10 years, unable to read and write. . . . The entire population of the State is 1,071,361. If from this number we deduct the whole number of children in the State under the age of 10 years, and divide the remainder by 2 we will find that about one-half the population of the State, over the age of 10 years, are unable to read and write."

INDUSTRIAL EDUCATION

The superintendent further remarks that "industrial education is a part of the system which cannot be omitted. All children should be instructed in some one of the industrial pursuits of the State. They should be instructed to make an honest living. Instruction in trades and industrial pursuits will be more valuable than instruction in books, but the latter is necessary to the former and bears to it the relation of means to an end. Every child in the State should be instructed in some trade, profession, or pursuit.—*House of Representatives, Executive Document 1, Part 5, 42nd Cong., 3rd Sess.*

144. FINANCIAL CONDITION OF NORTH CAROLINA, 1860-1872

Like other southern states, North Carolina was in critical financial condition during and following the Civil War. Property had been destroyed in large quantities, an investment of more than $250,000,000 had been lost as a result of emancipation, railroads had gone to ruin, banks had failed, land values had declined, but taxes had increased. In 1871, Plato Durham testified that taxation for state purposes had increased five fold under the 1868 Constitution.

The following report gives a brief summary of the state's financial affairs during a "critical period" of our history.

NORTH CAROLINA SUMMARY

1860

In 1860 the debt was $9,129,505 ; contingent liabilities, $150,000, and prospective liabilities $4,699,000; total $13,978,505. Assets $7,668,140. School, literary, and sinking funds, $3,428,950. Balance in the treasury, $615,691.

Property in the State was assessed at $292,297,602. Estimated value of slaves $115,870,650. The banks had capital of $6,626,470 ; and coin $1,617,687 ; circulation, $5,594,047. There were 889 miles of railway, which cost $16,709,793. The average expense of the government for 1858, 1859, and 1860, was $137,977.

Expended for common schools by State and County annually, $240,000. The number of white children of school age, in 1860, was 186,174.

1865

In 1865 the old debt and liabilities were $16,398,500; prospective liabilities, $3,571,000; debt contracted in rebellion, $18,117,836; total debt and liabilities, $38,087,336; increase, $24,108,831; assets $300,000; trust funds $153,250; loss $11,249,531. The bank capital was lost; the banks owed $8,555,000 and were able to pay one-tenth. There were 984 miles of railway in bad condition.

The first assessment of property was $120,900,000. Loss in property, exclusive of slaves, $55,526,902; loss of assets and trust funds, $11,249,531; increase of debt, $24,108,831; total loss since 1860, $90,885,264.

1868

The reconstructed government was inaugurated in 1868. The rebel debt had been repudiated, the recognized debt and liabilities were $20,638,445; prospective liabilities, $3,571,000; total, $24,-209,445; increase since 1865, $4,239,945; increase since 1860, $10,-230,000; loss of assets, $11,249,531; total $21,479,531.

1871

At the end of the fiscal year 1871 the debt and liabilities were $34,887,464; increase since 1865, $10,678,019. Part of this increase is interest unpaid; but it is mainly from aid to railroads granted by the convention of 1868 and the legislature of 1868 and 1869. The bonds were issued in October 1868—April 1869.

The acts were generally approved and passed by votes of members of both parties. The object was to extend and complete a general railroad system, and the popular belief was that immigration and consequent development would justify the improvement and secure the State against loss. These expectations have been disappointed.

Immigration was checked and prevented. Part of the bonds were sold at a sacrifice and the proceeds misapplied by officers of the companies. . . .

The probable loss to the State from railroad bonds issued since the war is estimated at from $6,000,000 to $10,000,000. . . .

The continued depression of values in North Carolina is attributed to several causes: the condition of the State credit, which prevents investment of capital from other States; the want of those internal improvements, which should have been made, and the disorders which have prevailed in the State, beginning in 1867 and culminating in 1868-69.—*Report of Joint Select Committee appointed "to enquire into the Condition of Affairs in the late Insurrectionary States," 42nd Cong., 2nd Sess., Report No. 41, p. 1.*

145. COST OF LIVING IN AN EASTERN NORTH CAROLINA TOWN, 1874

The following table, based on the report of a congressional investigating committee, shows the average weekly expenditures of a Tarboro family, with its weekly earnings, for the year 1874. This family consisted of two adults and five children.

Articles

Flour and bread	$ 1.20
meats	1.75
lard	.60
butter	.75
sugar and molasses	.60
milk	.10
coffee	.30
tea	.25
fish	.30
soap, salt, pepper, vinegar	.15
eggs	.10
potatoes and vegetables	.40
fruits	.20
fuel	1.00
oil and other light	.10
other articles	.15
spirits, beer and tobacco	.30
house rent	3.00
educational, religious and benevolent objects	.20
Total weekly expense	$ 11.80
Total expenses 52 weeks	613.60
Clothing per year	114.40
Taxes per year	4.00
Total yearly expenses	$ 732.00
Weekly earnings	14.00
Yearly earnings	728.00

—*Executive Document No. 21, 44th Cong., 1st Sess.*

146. CONSTITUTIONAL CHANGES, 1875-1876

Regardless of its merits, the 1868 Constitution was offensive to most native North Carolinians. It was considered the handiwork of carpet-baggers and Negroes, and there was a general feeling that the latter would be placed in control of local government, particularly in the East. The township form of local government had been unpopular from its inception. Therefore the Conservatives announced their intention of displacing the "Canby Constitution" at their first opportunity. In 1871 they made an unsuccessful attempt to call a convention to consider constitutional changes. In 1872-73 the legislature adopted a number of amendments which were ratified by the voters in August, 1873. But these changes were not sufficient. After the 1874 election, the Conservatives had more than a two-thirds majority in both Houses of the General Assembly. Early in 1875 a legislative resolution was adopted declaring "that the present Constitution is unsuited to the wants of the people of the State, is a check upon their energy, and impedes their welfare, and that the people demand that the burdens contained in the same shall be removed from their shoulders." Accordingly a call was issued for a Convention.

The Convention met in Raleigh, September 5, 1875. Membership stood Conservatives 58, Republicans 58, Independents 3. Edward Ransom, a Conservative, was chosen presiding officer. The Convention did not frame a new Constitution, but added thirty amendments, some of which were insignificant. Most of the changes were the result of the experiences of Reconstruction. Secret political societies were not to be tolerated; white and black schools were to be kept separate; marriages between whites and blacks were forbidden; residence requirements for voting were raised; the legislature was given control over justices of the peace; the legislature was given control over county government; the legislature was to meet in January instead of November; per diem for members of the legislature was fixed at $4 and mileage at ten cents; the number of supreme court judges was reduced from five to three; superior court judges were reduced from twelve to nine.

Only a few constitutional changes have been made since 1876. In 1928 an amendment was added increasing the compensation of members of the General Assembly to $600 per term.

ARTICLE II

Legislative Department

Sec. 2. The Senate and House of Representatives shall meet biennially on the first Wednesday after the first Monday in January next after their election. . . .

Sec. 28. The members of the General Assembly for the term for which they have been elected shall receive as a compensation for their services the sum of *four dollars* per day for each day of their session; for a period not exceeding sixty days; and should they remain longer in session, they shall serve without compensation. They shall also be entitled to receive ten cents per mile, both while coming to the seat of government and while returning home, the said distance to be computed by the nearest line or route of public travel. . . .

ARTICLE IV
Judicial Department

Sec. 10. The State shall be divided into nine judicial districts, for each of which a judge shall be chosen. . . . But the General Assembly may reduce or increase the number of districts. . . .

ARTICLE IX
Education

Sec. 2. The General Assembly . . . shall provide by taxation and otherwise for a general and uniform system of public schools. . . . And the children of the white race and the children of the colored race shall be taught in separate public schools; but there shall be no discrimination in favor of, or to the prejudice of, either race. . . .

ARTICLE XIV
Miscellaneous

Sec. 8. All marriages between a white person and a negro, or between a white person and white person of negro descent to the third generation inclusive, are hereby forever prohibited.—*Laws and Resolutions of the State of North Carolina passed by the General Assembly at its Session 1876-77*, pp. 8-12, 17, 30, 39.

147. RECONSTRUCTION AND ITS RESULTS IN NORTH CAROLINA

The following account of reconstruction in North Carolina was written by Zebulon B. Vance. It was published in 1890 in a series of essays entitled *Why the Solid South? or, Reconstruction and its Results*. Vance hoped that "this recital of these unhappy events" might tend "to soften the opinion and mitigate the judgment" of northerners toward the South.

CONGRESS, for purely partisan purposes, proceeded to treat these states as outside of the Union; and as alien communities who were to be dealt with anew under the laws of conquest and admitted to the Union on conditions of its own imposing. They happened to be Democratic in their politics; and it was not desirable to have the Union restored by the admission of eleven Democratic states; that would seriously endanger the Republican party. . . .

North Carolina, who had already, in obedience to the President's invitation, held a convention and remodeled her government . . . became a part of "Military District No. 2." Orders from "Headquarters" in Charleston, South Carolina, dissolved her state government . . . overturned her laws and displaced her officials. Anarchy reigned. . . . A new convention was called. . . .

The negroes were invited to vote, though their suffrage was not known to either State or Federal law; whilst many thousands, embracing nearly all of her leading citizens, were disfranchised. . . .

The excuse given for this legislation was that the states lately in insurrection were in a state of complete anarchy, entirely without civil law and a republican form of government. Each assertion was a lie. . . .

A saturnalia began. Our English-speaking race has not known its like since the plunder of Ireland in the sixteenth century. Detachments of the army were stationed at various points to overawe the people. Almost every citizen of experience of affairs in the state was disfranchised, and over the others hung the threat of confiscation. Under such circumstances the new convention was called by military orders: the qualification of its members, its electors, and the persons to hold the elections, the time and place, were all prescribed by the same authority. . . .

The returns . . . were examined in secret and the result announced.

That result was 110 Republicans and 10 Democrats!

The voting population of the state . . . was 214,222; the registration for that election in 1868 was 103,060 whites and 71,657 negroes—total 174,717. The result shows that about 40,000 were either disfranchised or in some other way deterred from voting.

Of the 110 Republicans . . . elected . . . were thirteen negroes and eight strangers, who came to be wittily called "carpet-baggers." They were not citizens of the state and were in no way entitled to the privilege of making laws for North Carolina; but they came to officer the negroes and to teach loyalty to the whites. The rest were disaffected white natives, mostly without property to be taxed or sympathy with their race, or regard for the misfortunes of their country. . . .

They met in January, 1868, and framed a Constitution after those of Ohio, Illinois and other Northern states. . . .

On the 4th of July, 1868, the new government was inaugurated. . . .

The Senate stood thirty-eight Republicans and twelve Democrats. The House stood eighty Republicans to forty Democrats. Of the Republicans there were twelve carpet-baggers and nineteen negroes —several of whom could not read or write. They made loud promises of a new generation of progress, and they were soon to bring about "a new heaven and a new earth." They told how the old order of things had been weighted down by slavery, and the poor had been oppressed by an aristocracy based upon it; and they declared that their divine mission was to regenerate a vast state and awaken the latent energies of a sleeping people and develop the hidden resources of buried wealth!

The better to do this, a number of outside carpet-baggers were called in to assist in the great work of progress by manipulating the negroes and the purchasable whites. Prominent among these strangers were one Milton S. Littlefield, Dewees and others—men whose reputations at home, if they ever had a home, entitled them to the contempt of their neighbors, and who, in their wanderings in search of plunder in the wake of devastating armies, left everywhere behind them a stench of foulness and corruption.

They immediately organized for a raid upon the depleted treasury of an impoverished people. It was soon stripped of every available dollar; then the school fund was robbed, its investments were sold to pay their *per diem*, which was spread out indefinitely by their protracted and unusual sittings. Four hundred and twenty thousand dollars of stock in the Wilmington & Weldon and the Wilmington & Manchester Railroads, which belonged to the educational fund, for the benefit of the poor children of the state, were sold by the Republican Treasurer for $158,000; which, with $100,000 more, borrowed from the Bank of George W. Swepson, was paid for their services, at the rate of eight dollars a day, to these negroes and carpet-baggers, who were professing to be the especial friends of education. . . .

A ring was formed, the chief of which were the said Littlefield and one George W. Swepson, a native, whose reputation for integrity was so bad as to make that of Littlefield tolerable. He was, perhaps, the most adroit agent of corruption who was ever known in North Carolina, as was evidenced by the way in which he manipulated lawyers, legislators and judges. This ring demanded, and in

23

most cases received, ten per cent on all appropriations passed by the Legislature. . . . Lavish entertainments were given and paid for in the same way; a regular bar was established in the Capitol, and it was said that . . . some of its rooms were devoted to the purposes of prostitution. Decency fled abashed; the spectacle of coarse, ignorant negroes sitting at table, drinking champagne and smoking Havana cigars, was not uncommon. . . .

Railroad companies were chartered right and left, and the friends and members of the thieving-guild were made president, directors and treasurers. . . .

Bonds were issued for the stock of the state in all these projects, and they were issued at once and in full. . . .

In this way, in less than four months the Legislature authorized the issuing of $25,350,000. In addition to this, bonds had been issued for various other schemes of minor importance. . . . The whole debt thus imposed upon our people exceeded $42,000,000; whilst the whole property of the state assessed for taxation in our then impoverished condition barely reached $120,000,000. . . .

The county authorities, emulating the example of the state, began a system of plunder in their municipal credit and plunged many of them so deeply in debt, that some of the wealthiest in the state had their script hawked on the streets at ten cents on the dollar. Many of the bonds of the state were paid out in fabulous sums to lawyers and in some cases even to judges. Hundreds of thousands were gambled away in New York. . . .

The administration of justice was conducted but little better. . . . It may without exaggeration be termed scandalous. A majority of the judges were either ignorant or corrupt. . . .

Several of them were known as $20 lawyers—that is, men who had never studied law, but had obtained a license to practice upon proof of good character and the payment of $20. . . .

It scarcely seems credible, and yet it is true, that with this $25,-000,000 of bonds authorized to be issued, $14,000,000 of which were actually issued, not one mile of railroad was built in the state. That, with all the school fund which the state had left from the war, supplemented as it was by a considerable taxation for school purposes, not one child in the state, white or black, was educated in any public school for two years. Not one public building or charitable institution of any kind was built. No single thing was done to sustain the credit of the state or to improve the condition of the people. They simply sank the state as low in the scale of progress as could possibly be done short of universal ruin.

To all of this, and more . . . the people of North Carolina submitted with long-suffering patience. They were spirit-broken by the results of the war—the desolation of their homes and the slaughter of their sons. They were worn down to the earth by the degradation imposed upon them by the negro-equality of the Civil Rights Bill and all the racking evils of the times. But a day was coming when their ancient spirit was once more to re-assert itself.—*Why the Solid South?* (by H. A. Herbert and Others), pp. 70-84.

XI

REBUILDING

148. The Rise of Farm Tenancy after the Civil War

One of the most significant effects of the Civil War was the break-up of plantations into smaller farms and the rise of farm tenancy. The slaves were freed and a new relationship existed between land owner and laborer. Some North Carolinians tried renting their land for cash; others paid their farm hands a money wage; the majority rented out their lands on the share system. Each method had its merits and demerits. Conditions favored the adoption of the share system, however. Money was very scarce. The landowner did not have money to pay wages; the Negroes and poor whites did not have money to pay rent. So the landowner agreed to furnish the land, the implements and seed, and in most cases the stock, and to receive from one-half to two-thirds of the crop when it was harvested. Some outstanding farmers and a few farm papers were hostile to the adoption of this method of farming. The logic of circumstances forced it upon the South, however. One of the chief complaints against it was that it accentuated the devotion of the South to the one-crop system.

THE great amount of land once tilled, but now unimproved, is chiefly due to the decrease in the number of plantation hands. Most estimate that the number of hands now at work in the fields is but half what it was in 1860. The causes of this diminution of farm laborers may be accounted for about as follows: The women, as a rule, no longer work out of doors. Sickness, particularly contagious diseases, contracted during and since the war, have carried off large numbers of both sexes. . . . Of those who are well, many flock to the large towns. . . . As a rule they seem inclined to change their location even when the new place offers no superior advantages over the old one. . . . Some work for wages, but the greater part . . . work the land and receive part of the crop. The land owner, in most cases furnishes the team, farming utensils and seed, and receives from one-half to two-thirds of the corn and cotton after it is harvested. He also furnishes the provisions for the family, receiving a like amount in the fall, or its equivalent in money or cotton. . . .

The freedmen (so-called) are generally working well, some for a share of the crop, some on wages. . . . They are in great demand for chopping out cotton, and some gentlemen in our township who have plenty of money and plenty of faith in the future of cotton, and probably backward and grassy crops, are giving as much as 75 cents and $1 per day for a hand. I believe in our township most of the contracts are made on what is called the "share system"—in my judgment a ruinous one to the interests of the country and its labor. . . .

We have some suggestions to make to our planting friends. First and foremost, hire by the year only, and for wages as a general rule. More labor, steady labor the year round, is what we want. The wages system is far better in the long run for both employer and employees. The farmer knows what he is to pay; the laborer knows what he is to receive. There is no room for a squabble over the division of the crop at the end of the year.

The share system has worked badly in Edgecombe, we think. In adopting it the laborer gives up a certainty for an uncertainty. . . . With such a season as '67, he not only does not make a living but falls into debt, and has to begin the next year with this debt hanging over him. . . .

What demoralizes the labor of our country more than anything else is *farming on shares*. . . . The manner in which share laborers are managed is a curse to the country, for in many instances they are put off on land (they having no better sense) that will not support them the first year, no matter how good the cultivation of the crop may be. . . .

Many of our farmers . . . buy meat, corn, seed and manures and every necessary article of family consumption from the North on time, paying as high as twenty-five per cent for the credit, hypothecating their prospective crop, and mortgaging their lands and other provisions as collateral security. . . .

We are in favor of that reconstruction which will cause one cow to yield as much milk and butter as from two to five now produce, and that which will make hogs weigh as much at one year old as they now do at two, and also for the use of reapers and mowers in place of the common cradle. . . . In short, we are in favor of everything that will make us a prosperous people.—*The Reconstructed Farmer* (Tarboro), I, 70-71, 82-83, 94, 147.

149. THE RISE OF TOBACCO MANUFACTURING

The Civil War stimulated smoking and drinking and thus greatly increased the demand for two of North Carolina's best known products, tobacco and corn whiskey. Small quantities of the weed were manufactured in the state during the war, but after the conflict "all over the country a new era opened for good tobacco." Durham took the lead in this manufacturing, more or less accidentally. During the war J. R. Green was producing a brand of tobacco known as the "Best Flavored Spanish Smoking Tobacco." Both Confederate and Federal soldiers, in passing through Durham, became acquainted with this brand, and northern soldiers ransacked Green's factory, liked his tobacco, and spread favorable reports about it. In a short time he reopened his factory and took W. T. Blackwell into partnership. In order to meet the somewhat unfair competition of other manufacturers, who were selling a product called "Spanish Flavored Smoking Tobacco," Green and Blackwell adopted the picture of a Durham bull for their trademark, and soon their "Bull Durham Smoking Tobacco" was making North Carolina famous.

In 1865 Washington Duke began the manufacture of tobacco on his farm in Orange County, but in a few years he moved his enterprise to Durham. Starting with practically nothing, he and his three sons built up one of the greatest tobacco interests in the world. In 1868 Durham had only one tobacco factory; in 1872 it had twelve.

Winston, like Durham, witnessed a very rapid development of the tobacco industry, the leaders of which were the Hanes brothers, Brown, and Richard J. Reynolds.

The 1870 census showed 111 tobacco factories in North Carolina, employing 1,465 hands, many of them Negroes, representing an investment of $375,882, and with an annual product valued at $718,765.

WINSTON

. . . Winston lived in humble obscurity as a courthouse village, until suddenly the spring was touched which gave her life and energy, . . . She has now a population of little less than four thousand, . . . and a business, based upon the sales and manufacture of tobacco, which makes it one of the most important centres of that stupendous interest.

In the town of Winston there are three sales warehouses, fourteen plug factories, one smoking factory, . . .

BROWN'S WAREHOUSE

In 1872, Mr. T. J. Brown was encouraged by the increasing cultivation of tobacco in this section, to venture upon the enterprise of opening a warehouse in Winston, . . .

The next ware house in date of erection is that of Phol & Stockton . . . built in 1874. . . .

One of the most extensive factories is that of Brown & Brother, who worked under the same firm name in Mocksville, North Carolina, as far back as 1858, but who subsequently removed to Winston. . . . Two hundred and twenty-five hands are employed, during eight months of the year, in making all styles and grades of plug and twist; the latter being a specialty for the Southern and Western trade. . . .

The prominent brands of this factory are "Honest 7," "Cottage Home," "Waverly," "Ruby," "Little Joker," "Archer," "Brick Factory," "Golden Link," "Gold Dust," "Oliver Twist," "H W's," "Slap Jack," "Dexter," "Brown's Mule," etc. "Oliver Twist" is a popular brand of twist. . . .

P. H. Haines & Co. began work in 1874. . . .

Bailey Brothers, consisting of W. D. Bailey & P. N. Bailey, removed from Statesville, where they had worked as manufactures since 1874, to Winston during the year 1880. . . .

R. J. REYNOLDS

began business at his present location in 1874, gradually enlarging his building as his business increased, until he now occupies a brick building, 38x128, three stories high, and employing one hundred and twenty-five hands, with a nett result of two hundred and seventy-five thousand pounds for the current working year. The steady increase of business will compel additions to the buildings next year. The trade is partly with the South, but more extensive with the North and West, exacting a great variety of styles and grades for so many different markets. The prominent brands are "Strawberry," twist; "Oronoko," pounds; "World's Choice," pounds; and Reynolds' "Bright 7 ounce twist." . . .

. . . Durham and Reidsville . . . have been called into being by the trade in tobacco, while Hillsboro, Henderson, and Oxford have enlarged greatly their original means of prosperity by adding this to their other branches of business.

The market in North Carolina which has made the most rapid development . . . is

DURHAM

in Orange County. Designated originally as a railroad station, and known at first only for its connection with the State University, for which it was the point of transfer, it lingered in undisturbed obscurity until the chance operations of the latter days of the war gave

it notoriety as the halting-place of the victorious army of Sherman.
. . .

This halt of Sherman's army was fruitful of unlooked-for consequences upon the destiny of Durham. The soldiery, idle in their camps . . . sought relief in such solace as accident might present. The little tobacco factory of J. R. Green had wafted its cheer through the war among the comfortless and half-starved ranks of the Confederate army. There was no more welcome visitor from home than a present of Green's tobacco. The Federal army struck at its fountain-head the source of the cheer which lightened the hours of the weary Confederates. Durham proved no Capua to it; but it made impressions and it begat tastes which became ineradicable. Durham Smoking Tobacco became a national necessity. The returned and disbanded soldiery turned wistful and longing eyes back to the scene which had relieved the monotony of peaceful camp-life by its grateful and luxurious resources, and impatient hands were stretched out from every part of the American Union for a modicum of the fragrant compound. The effect on the fortunes of Durham was immediate and surprising. Factories sprang rapidly into existence, warehouses were established, population flocked in, a town grew up around the once obscure station and now Durham is known throughout the wide world wherever the grateful incense of its tobacco ascends. Its six warehouses sell annually from ten to twelve million pounds of the planter's tobacco. . . . The population, the real growth of the last six years, has now reached 3,600, and continually increases. . . .

FACTORIES

W. T. BLACKWELL & COMPANY

This house has no merely local name. It is known the world over, . . . For the fortunes of Durham and Blackwell & Company are one and inseparable; . . .

It was in 1868 that W. T. Blackwell and I. R. Day, then tobacco jobbers, bought a half interest in the business of I. R. Green; and this partnership was continued until the death of Mr. Green, which took place the next year, when the other partners purchased his interest from the heirs. In 1870 Mr. Julian S. Carr, of Chapel Hill, N. C., bought a third interest in the business. In 1878 Mr. I. R. Day sold his share to the other partners, . . .

About five years ago the nucleus of the present large structure was erected . . . on which was emblazoned in colossal proportions the typical idea of the business—the great Durham bull, rampant and triumphant.

W. DUKE, SONS & CO.

have grown from the very modest beginnings to be among the largest and most successful manufacturers of Durham. The humble peddler of manufactured tobacco, ruined by the war, and compelled for sub-sistence to travel through the country selling from his wagon the small stock drawn by a pair of mules, all the ravages of war had left him, now presides over next to the largest business in the place.

Mr. W. Duke began the manufacture of smoking tobacco in the vicinity of Durham in the fall of 1865, removing to Durham during 1872 or 1873. He, or rather the firm of W. Duke, Sons & Co., for he has associated with him three enterprising and experienced members of his family, now occupy a building of wood, three stories high, seventy feet long, with a frontage of eighty feet, . . . The product is "granulated," the most widely known brand made being "The Duke of Durham," "Pro Bono Publico" is another fine brand, but "High Grab," unsurpassed in quality and selling readily at $1.00 per pound, is also largely made. . . . —J. D. Cameron, *A Sketch of the Tobacco Interests of North Carolina* (Oxford, N. C., 1881), pp. 13, 14, 16, 17, 19, 48, 49, 52, 53, 56.

150. The Resources of North Carolina: Its Natural Wealth, Condition, and Advantages, as Existing in 1869

Bannister, Cowan, and Company was established for the purpose of negotiating the sale of southern lands of all descriptions, and other property; also to induce immigration, organize joint stock companies, and negotiate loans. Its principal offices were at Wilmington and New York City. A list of references accompanying the following prospectus included many prominent men, North and South. Among others given were Zebulon Vance, Thomas Bragg, W. A. Graham, Asa Biggs, George Davis, R. H. Cowan, R. R. Bridgers, D. W. Bagley, and James Dawson of North Carolina, ex-Governor Seymour of New York, A. G. Cattrell, Samuel Bolton, and J. Drexel of Philadelphia, and D. P. Eells of Cleveland, Ohio.

The following prospectus was issued in the hope of promoting immigration to the South, and to encourage the investment of northern capital.

Presented to the Capitalists and People of the Central
and Northern States

by

Bannister, Cowan, and Company, Real Estate and Financial Agents.
New York and Wilmington

TO THE PUBLIC

We would respectfully state to capitalists and others desiring profitable investments in real estate, mining, or manufacturing interests, timber lands, water power, etc., that we are prepared to offer
them greater inducements than can elsewhere be found.

The principal fact which led to the establishment of this agency
was the existence in the South of so many very important, and, in
most cases, wholly undeveloped resources, which for their proper
development require capital, and which, by such development,
would undoubtedly result in great prosperity and wealth. The capital, in abundance, is in the North, seeking opportunities of profitable investment, while the opportunities, in like abundance, are in
the South, awaiting the capital. What is now needed is a means of
bringing them together. This our agency proposes to furnish.

We are prepared to negotiate loans upon the best of securities and
at liberal rates of interest. There are numerous industries in the
South which are crippled to a great extent for the want of a little
more capital. Loans can readily be negotiated upon abundant security, bearing interest at from 10 to 15 per cent. per annum. We invite attention to this branch of our business. . . .

North Carolina is conspicuous among the States of the Atlantic
seaboard for advantages of position calculated to develop every
feature of its natural wealth. Whatever it may produce through its
fertility of soil, its abundant growth of timber, or its extensive mineral deposits, is within easy reach of the best markets, and can be
forwarded by the cheapest modes of transportation. Facilities for
cheap production are also remarkably abundant. Machinery can
easily be sent to any point; the properties of every sort—land, water,
power, timber, and mines—are all purchasable at very reasonable
rates; labor is cheaper than in any other State of the Union, and
all these materials and appliances can be handled by any owner or
capitalist residing in any one of the States north of it without such
risk of loss or waste as is inevitable in attempting to own, hold, or
work productive property in the new Western States. . . .

GOLD MINING IN NORTH CAROLINA AND GOLD PROSPECTS

North Carolina has been celebrated for half a century as a gold-mining country, and the reports of the United States Mint show that more than ten million dollars worth of gold has come from this State to the Mint for coinage. Previous to 1869 there had been coined at the Branch Mint at Charlotte, North Carolina, $4,520,730 of North Carolina gold, and at the United States Mint at Philadelphia, $4,666,026 of the same production. While it is probable that at least $2,500,000 in value passed into use in the arts, was sent abroad, or was retained in some way from the Mint. Since the war about $400,000 in gold has been received at the Mint and Assay offices from North Carolina, the amount in 1868 being $100,000. In 1866 it was over $140,000.

The principal mines of the State are about half way from Raleigh to the foot of the Blue Ridge. Cabarrus County is distinguished as the place of original discovery, and one piece of pure gold, weighing twenty-eight pounds, was found there. All the counties of that section of the State, which is drained chiefly by the Yadkin and Catawba Rivers, abound in gold. . . .

It will be an inviting field to an Eastern or Northern man who would like to try gold mining without going to California, to buy a tract in this tempting region, and while he prosecutes farming or any other business as a general pursuit, try his hand at leisure times in obtaining gold from his own lands.—*Prospectus* of Bannister, Cowan, and Company (Wilmington, 1869), pp. 1-114.

151. SOCIAL AND ECONOMIC CONDITIONS IN THE STATE, 1875

The following description of North Carolina is taken from Edward King's book, *The Great South*. This study was undertaken at the instance of the publishers of *Scribner's Monthly*, who desired to present to the public, an account of the material resources and the social condition of the people in the southern states. The author and the artists associated with him traveled more than 25,000 miles, visited nearly every town and city in the South, and talked with men of all classes, parties, and color. They were "kindly and generously received by Southern people."

NEGRO SUFFRAGE

The evils of universal suffrage have been very great in this State. The great mass of densely ignorant and ambitious blacks suddenly hurled upon the field created the wildest confusion, and crushed the commonwealth under irredeemable debt. The villainy and robbery to which the white population of the State was compelled to submit, at the hands of the plunderers maintained in power by the negro, did much to destroy all possibility of a speedy reconciliation between the two races. Still, the citizens are loyal to the Union, and are anxious to be on friendly terms with the North; yet continue to regard Northerners as in some way the authors of the evils which have befallen them. . . .

At the close of the wild carnival of robbery and maladministration which marked the career of the first reconstruction government, North Carolina found that her debts were between $36,000,000 and $40,000,000. This was an appaling exhibit, for the mere payment of the interest was enough to stagger the impoverished and struggling agriculturists. . . . The plundered people only knew that out of $16,000,000 voted by the Legislature for "public works of improvement," but $500,000 had ever been devoted to that purpose.

EDUCATION

The State certainly needs to make progress in education, for the illiteracy at present within its borders is shocking. One of the United States Senators gave it [to] me [as] his belief that there were as many as 350,000 persons in North Carolina who could neither read nor write. The State Superintendent of Instruction said that, late in 1873, there were only 150,000 out of the 350,000 pupil-children actually at school. . . . The dollar tax demanded for the schools was odious to the masses. Still, from $250,000 to $400,000 is annually collected for school purposes. The same provision is made for whites and blacks; there is not much desire on the part of ex-Confederates to deprive the negro of the advantages of an education, as they now realize it helps him to become a better laborer. There are 40,000 colored children now in the free schools of the State; 530 black teachers passed the Board of Examiners in 1873, and these teachers were paid $46,000 per year. . . . There are several small colleges each having five or six score of students. Prominent among them are Trinity, Davidson, and the Wake Forest College, near Raleigh

The school law of the State requires that public free schools shall be maintained "four months every year in every school district in each county in the State in which the qualified voters shall vote to levy the additional school-tax for that purpose." This, of course, gives people an opportunity to reject the system entirely, but there are few counties so rude as to refuse all educational facilities, although the people in the back-country have a most unaccountable aversion to paying "school-taxes." . . . Raleigh, strange to say, is hindered from taxing itself to support a system of graded schools by the State law, . . .

WESTERN NORTH CAROLINA

Western North Carolina is not only exceedingly fertile, but abounds in the richer minerals, and needs but the magic wand of the capitalist waved over it to become one of the richest sections in the Union. Occupying one-third of the entire area of the State, and possessing more than a quarter of a million of inhabitants, its present prospects are by no means disagreeable; but its prominent citizens, of all walks of life, are anxious for immigration and development of the rich stores of gold, iron, copper, mica, and other minerals now buried in the hills.

Let no one fancy that this mountain region is undesirable as an agricultural country; there are fewer richer or better adapted to European immigration. . . . Give all that section immigration, and railroads cannot be kept out of it, even by the rascality of such gigantic swindles as have been forced upon North Carolina. The copper mines in Jackson were worked extensively before the war, and Northern capital and shrewd English mining experience are once more developing them. . . . Vast tracts of land in Western North Carolina can be sold to colonists or capitalists at from one to two dollars per acre. . . .

The town of Asheville now boasts of a population of 2,500 people. It will in future be the railroad centre of Western North Carolina, and must grow to be a large and flourishing city. The present poverty of the section as to railroad communication is largely due to the discouragement consequent on the manner in which the confidence of those subscribing to the principal enterprise has been betrayed. . . .

THE SMALL FARMER IN WESTERN NORTH CAROLINA

The tall, lean, sickly farmer, clad in a homespun pair of trowsers and a flax shirt, with the omnipresent gray slouched hat, minus rim, drawn down over his forehead, courteously greeted us. . . .

He cultivated a small farm, like most of the neighbors in moderate circumstances; only grew enough corn for his own support; "didn't reckon he should stay thar long; warn't no schools, and he reckoned his children needed larnin'; schools never was handy; too many miles away." There was very little money in all the region round about; farmers rarely saw fifty dollars in cash from year to year; the few things which they got from the outside world they got by barter. The children were, as a rule, mainly occupied in minding the numerous pigs about the cabin, and caring for the stock. The farmer thought sheep-raising would be "powerful peart," if folks had a little more capital to begin on. . . .

He welcomed the mineral movement gladly; reckoned may be we could send him some one to buy his farm, and let him go to a more thickly settled region; but seemed more cheerful when we suggested that emigrants might come in and settle up the country, bringing a demand for schools with them. "He reckoned there warn't no Ku Klux these days; never knew nothin' on 'em. Heerd nothin' furder from 'em sence the break-up," . . . The housewife was smoking her corn-cob pipe and sitting rather disconsolately before the fire place.

COMMERCE AT WILMINGTON

Commercially, Wilmington has every reason to hope for great development. The principal articles of export are spirits of turpentine in barrels, crude turpentine, rosin, tar, pitch, cotton, peanuts, and lumber in all shapes. . . . After the war, the exports of spirits of turpentine and rosin were encouraging until 1870; since their development has not been so great, but the constant growth of the cotton trade makes amends for their failure. . . . —*The Great South, a Record of Journeys in the Southern States* (Hartford, Conn., 1875), pp. 466-506.

152. ZEBULON B. VANCE'S INTEREST IN EDUCATION

Under the capable leadership of Calvin H. Wiley North Carolina had adopted a public school system a decade previous to the Civil War. In 1860 Wiley wrote: "The educational system of North Carolina is now attracting the favorable attention of the states south, west, and north of us. . . . All modern statistical publications give us a rank far in advance of the position which we occupied in such works a few years ago."

Though confronted with serious financial difficulties and other obstacles the schools kept open during the four years of civil strife. This was due in great measure to the efforts of Governor Vance. At the close of the war, the public school system collapsed—along with almost everything else. Very little progress was made during the carpet-bag régime of the reconstruction period. When Vance became governor of the state for the third time, in January, 1877, he made a determined effort to promote secondary and higher education. In particular he urged the establishment of a school for the training of teachers. The following extracts from his messages to the General Assembly of 1877 and of 1879 reveal his deep interest in the promotion of education.

PERHAPS the most effective action which your honorable body could take to promote the cause of public education would be the establishing of a school of normal instruction at the University for the exclusive education of teachers. This would be only a compliance with the plain provisions of the Constitution, and would be a long step in the direction of connecting the University with the common school system as the head and guide thereof, which is its natural position. It is impossible to have an effective public school system without providing for the training of teachers. The blind cannot lead the blind. . . . The schools in which this training is conducted, called normal colleges, or normal schools, have been found by experience to be the most efficient agents in raising up a body of teachers who infuse new life and vigor into the public schools. There is urgent need for one, at least, in North Carolina.

The Constitution of the State, in Section 4, Article IX, requires the General Assembly, as soon as practicable, to establish and maintain, in connection with the University, a department of Normal Instruction. I respectfully submit that it is now practicable to make a beginning in carrying out this provision of the Constitution. There cannot possibly be found in this State competent teachers for our public schools. The records of the county examiners show that most of the applicants for the post of imparting knowledge to others, are themselves deficient in the simplest elements of spelling, reading, writing and arithmetic. The University is now in successful operation. If the General Assembly should appropriate an amount sufficient to establish one professorship for the purpose of instructing in the theory and art of teaching, I am persuaded the best results would follow.

A school of similar character should be established for the education of colored teachers, the want of which is more deeply felt by the black race even than the white. In addition to the fact that it is our plain duty to make no discrimination in the matter of public education, I cannot too strongly urge upon you the importance of the consideration that whatever of education we may be able to give the children of the State, should be imparted under our own auspices, and with a thorough North Carolina spirit. Many philosophical reasons can be given in support of this proposition. I am conscious of few things more dangerous than for a State to suffer the education of an entire class of its citizens to drift into the hands of strangers, most of whom are not attached to our institutions, if not positively unfriendly to them.

There are in the State several very respectable institutions for the education of black people, and a small endowment to one of them would enable it to attach a normal school sufficient to answer the present needs of our black citizens. Their desire for education is an extremely creditable one, and should be gratified as far as our means will permit. In short, I regard it as an unmistakable policy to imbue these black people with a hearty North Carolina feeling, and make them cease to look abroad for the aids to their progress and civilization, and the protection of their rights as they have been taught to do, and teach them to look to their State instead; to convince them that their welfare is indissolubly linked with ours. . . .

I am happy to be able to state that an increased interest is manifested among all classes in popular education. This, I believe, is due to the action of the last Legislature in appropriating money for the establishment of normal schools. In accordance with the law, the Board of Education established the one for whites at the University, and decided to locate one for the blacks at Fayetteville, in a building tendered by the colored people of that place. They were established on somewhat different systems, regard being had to the circumstances of each race. It was considered that the white race already had many educated teachers who simply needed instruction on the art of teaching, whilst the blacks needed teachers instructed in both the elements of learning and the art of teaching. For the one, therefore, a six weeks' school was held at Chapel Hill during the summer vacations, and for the other, a permanent school was established in Fayetteville. Both have been remarkably successful. At the first session of the white school 225 teachers attended, and at the second one, the past summer, more than 400 teachers were present, representing about sixty counties. An excellent corps of instructors was employed. The University gave the use of its buildings, its libraries, laboratories and apparatus. The railroads very generously gave reduced rates. The agent of the Peabody Fund supplemented the appropriation with a handsome donation, and every dollar that could be spared was used to equalize the benefits of the State's bounty by paying the traveling expenses of the more indigent. Lectures by distinguished citizens of the State on popular themes were delivered almost daily with the best results. The undoubted effect of the whole was to arouse an enthusiastic interest in behalf of popular education among a large portion of our people, and to excite a spirit of honest pride in their noble calling among all the teachers present, which will, it is hoped, do much good.—Clement Dowd, *Life of Zebulon B. Vance*, pp. 206-9.

153. Position of the Negro in North Carolina Life Since 1865

One of the most perplexing problems confronting North Carolina after the War was the political, economic, and social status of the colored man. The Negro, in many instances, misused his newly acquired freedom. Within a few years, however, most of the Negroes adopted a sane attitude in regard to their position in society. From that time thay have shown marked signs of economic and social progress, particularly in Durham, Winston-Salem, Charlotte, Salisbury, Raleigh, and other communities.

There have been many contributory causes to this progress. The character of the Negroes, the tolerant attitude of the white people, and the ability of certain colored leaders have all been important.

In a letter to a Negro educational convention, in 1890, Washington Duke gave the Negroes friendly advice. The address of John Merrick, colored capitalist of North Carolina, delivered in 1898, is typical of the advice given by outstanding Negro leaders to their race.

LETTER OF WASHINGTON DUKE TO A NEGRO EDUCATIONAL CONVENTION, 1890

I HAVE always had a friendly feeling toward you, and now address you in the spirit of a friend, wishing if I can to help you to overcome the hard conditions of your lot.

I have no doubt that each of you would like to be a successful man. It is right that you should feel so, for a proper ambition is God's call to a higher life, but how shall that success be gained? . . . Be industrious, do not always be looking for an easy, soft place. I have made more furrows in God's earth than any man of forty years of age in North Carolina. And when you have made yourself industrious, you must be frugal. Establish it as a rule to always spend less than you make. I never closed a year's work in my life without being happy in the knowledge that I was better off than I was when it begun. Be sure to put away every week part of your earnings in a Savings Bank. And when people begin to find out that you are industrious and reliable they will offer you positions of profit. Do honest work for your honest dollar, put it in your pocket, and at night when you lie down with it under your pillow the eagle on its face will sing you to sleep, because it knows you have earned it and can spend it properly.

24

Be men of honest, upright lives; support your churches and your schools; regard your minister as your best friend and your school teacher as your next; work honestly for your money and give some of it to help support these institutions; cease to rely upon outside help, for you must work out your own salvation. Ever since I was twelve years old I have been trying to make the world better by having lived in it. Let this be the rule of your lives. I have never failed to give freely to the support of the gospel; I have regarded it as a part of my life. If I am anything, if my life has been successful, if from small beginnings I have brought myself to a successful point in life, then I say to you that it was by following these rules that I have gained it.—W. K. Boyd, *The Story of Durham, City of the New South*, pp. 281-83.

ADDRESS OF JOHN MERRICK TO DURHAM NEGROES, 1898

There has been lots and lots said about the Negro and his condition in North Carolina. So much so that I think that the least of us have a perfect right to give vent to our feelings if we wish; and on these grounds, I take the privilege to say a few words about me and my people the way I see it.

We are here and we are going to stay. And why not stay? We have the same privileges that other people have. Every avenue is open to us to do business there is to any other people. We are allowed to own homes and farms, run farms, do banking business, insurance, real estate business and all other minor businesses that are done in this Commonwealth. Therefore, I claim that the Negro's condition in North Carolina is as good or better than it's been since our Emancipation, if we go ahead and use them in the right direction.

We don't concur with Bishop Turner when he says the thing for Congress to do is to appropriate one hundred million dollars to colonize us to our mother country. And what would be the result? That land is controlled by the whites, and it's natural to suppose that the owner of everything ought to control it. And our condition would eventually be the same there as here, if we got over there and all of us want to be king. . . .

Now take the Negro all over the land. The most of our capital is invested in muscle. Now the thing for us to do is to do like other men. They do what is best to protect their land, railroad, mill, factory, and real estate interests. Now, we have no such interests; so let us do what will protect what we have. Our labor is what we have got to look after more carefully in the future than we have in the past if we would hold our own.

The Negroes have lots of offices in this State and they have benefitted themselves but very little comparatively; nothing comparing with what they could have done along business and industrial lines had they given it the same time and talent. And I claim they have done the masses harm in this way.

Now to show you why we have not been benefitted by politics and why we ought to let them alone. In the first place, our good men and lots of our best men have turned their attention to party and office. A man goes into politics a good man and he goes to pulling the wires and soon is classed a politician. This naturally makes him lose interest along business and industrial lines; then he has to stick to it for protection, as that settles him as a business man. This happens with very few exceptions.

Now I believe in paying debts and we owe the Republican party lots of gratitude. Now we have been paying it as a people, almost as a man, ever since the Emancipation. Now, don't you think we are about even, and the time has come when we can take that valuable ballot and vote it as we please, and not be considered by our own people as murderers?

What difference does it make to us who is elected? We got to serve in the same different capacities of life for a living. That reminds me of something I heard 14 years ago on Mangum Street. Cleveland's first term, John Bets, a Republican revenue officer, was passing and a countryman was sitting way up on a load of wood. In order to tease Bets, he yelled as Bets passed, "Hurrah for Cleveland." Bets stopt and said: "Never mind, damn you, you got to still haul that wood." That is what we ought to think when we are so grieved when the election don't go as we want it. We got to haul wood, and don't care who is elected.

Now let us think more of our employment and what it takes to keep peace and to build us a little house, and stop thinking we are the whole Republican Party and without us the whole thing would stop.

Now don't the writers of the race jump on the writer and try to solve my problem. Mine is solved. I solved mine by learning to be courteous to those that courtesy was due, working and trying to save and properly appropriate what I made.

I do think we have done well and I think we could have done better. Now let us make better use of the years we have left than the years that have past, as we have the past to look back over and see the many mistakes.—W. K. Boyd, *The Story of Durham, City of the New South*, pp. 281-83.

154. THE REVOLT OF THE FARMERS

Agriculture was North Carolina's basic industry during the nineteenth century. It had been stimulated during the Civil War, particularly in the production of foodstuffs. From 1865 to the close of the century, it fell on evil days.

During the dark years of reconstruction the North Carolina farmer faced many handicaps. Much of his property had been destroyed or had gone to ruin. His livestock had been killed or carried away. His money had become worthless, and banking facilities had almost disappeared. Transportation facilities had broken down. The slave had been freed, thereby wiping out a $250,000,000 investment in the state, and also introducing a new economic relationship between landowner and laborer. For three years after the war the federal cotton tax, amounting to from $10 to $15 a bale, extracted several millions of dollars from the state —money which was sorely needed for agricultural rehabilitation.

Few farmers were in more critical economic condition than those of North Carolina from 1865 to 1900. The situation was acute in the seventies. It became extremely serious in the eighties and early nineties. The farmer was "gradually but steadily becoming poorer and poorer every year." He lacked an adequate "reserve" to tide him over a "lean" year, of which there were many. Prices of things he sold were too low and getting lower. Prices of things he bought were too high and, in many instances, getting higher. Industry and commerce seemed to be prosperous; agriculture was languishing.

Prices, under the control of economic forces which the farmer did not understand, always seemed to be at the level of production, or lower. The price of cotton fell from a dollar a pound in 1865 to twenty-five cents a pound in 1868. It averaged about twelve cents during the seventies, nine during the eighties, and seven during the nineties, falling below five cents a pound in 1894.

Like other southern farmers, he did business on a credit basis. The country merchant agreed to "run" the farmer until harvest time, taking a lien on his unplanted crops. The merchant was assuming considerable risk. Therefore, he raised the price of supplies from 20 to 50 per cent above the prevailing cash prices. "Since the goods were purchased throughout the year and the payments were made in the fall, the average item ran for less than six months; so that the farmer paid in effect from 40 to 100 per cent annual interest." This crop-lien system helped to perpetuate the one-crop system because the merchant based his loans upon the amount of land to be planted in cotton and tobacco, the two "money crops."

The merchant was not wholly to blame for the one-crop evil. The farmer's ignorance of other crops was a noteworthy factor. *The Progressive Farmer* declared "We may join all the farmers' organizations that can be devised, but hard times will hover around our firesides so long as we buy our meat and bread, hay and fertilizers, and other farm supplies, and attempt to pay for them from the proceeds of one crop."

The farmers believed that there were many factors contributing to their distress. They blamed the credit system, with its excessive rates of interest. They complained of the evil practices of railways, particularly of high and discriminatory freight rates, and the lack of governmental regulation. They insisted that our tariff policy was building up industry at the expense of agriculture. They denounced "trusts," particularly the jute bagging "trust" which had doubled the price of cotton bagging within a few weeks. They believed that they were the victims of a vicious scheme of unequal and unjust taxation. They had bitter words of disapproval for the whole American financial system because it had failed utterly to provide a money supply adequate to meet the rapidly growing needs of the country. National banks were special objects of their attacks.

It was natural for the farmers to revolt against this situation. From the early seventies on, the "embattled farmers" showed a tendency to organize for redress of their grievances. There were three phases of this "agrarian crusade": (1) the Grange; (2) the Farmers' Alliance; (3) the Populist movement.

The Grange first appeared in the state in 1873, and reached its peak two years later when it had 477 chapters and about 10,000 members.

The Farmers' Alliance was first organized in North Carolina in 1887. Its leading spirit was Colonel Leonidas L. Polk; its leading organ, *The Progressive Farmer*. Polk began the publication of this agricultural weekly at Winston in 1886. He was soon called to Raleigh to become state commissioner of agriculture, and he moved the paper to Raleigh. Under Polk's leadership two large farmers' meetings were held in Raleigh in January, 1887. Many farmers' clubs suddenly sprang up, and many old "granges" were revived. The Farmers' Alliance first appeared in Robeson County in April of that year. Within one year there were 1,018 suballiances in the state, and by 1890 there were 2,147 representing every county, except one, and having over 90,000 members. It is doubtful if the Alliance ever had 100,000 members in North Carolina. After 1891 it declined in both membership and influence. Polk was secretary of the organization. S. B. Alexander was its first president. He was succeeded by Elias Carr in 1890. Marion Butler was president, 1891-1894.

At first the Alliance was not primarily political. In fact some of its leaders thought an educational program was more important than political activity. So the leaders tried to bring the people of the rural communities together for entertainment and education. Speakers were imported to discuss seed selection, stock-raising, fertilizers, crop rotation and other agricultural matters. Institutes, canning clubs, and agricultural fairs were encouraged and promoted. Active support was given to the movement to establish a State College of Agriculture and Mechanic Arts, a State Normal and Industrial College for Women, and to reorganize the State Department of Agriculture.

The business feature of the Alliance was likewise important. The act of incorporation conferred upon it "power to conduct mercantile and manufacturing businesses, operate warehouses, stock-yards, grain elevators, and packing establishments, and manufacture fertilizers." Not many of these powers were ever exercised, but a state agency was created to aid the farmers in buying agricultural implements, fertilizers, and even groceries direct from the manufacturers. Its capital eventually amounted to about $33,000 : Its total business in 1890 amounted to about $325,000, which represented a saving to those who made their purchases through it of from 10 to 60 per cent.

In general, the Alliance disapproved of the coöperative store movement. One of its prominent officials declared its purpose was "to protect the agricultural and laboring classes against monopolies—not to make merchants." Some coöperative ventures were tried nevertheless.

Fundamentally the Farmers' Alliance was interested in politics. Its leaders insisted that it was not a political organization, but they admitted that it was deeply concerned in the action of the major political parties. *The Progressive Farmer* said, "We don't advise bringing politics into the farmers' organizations, but we do advise taking agricultural questions *into politics*. Take these questions into your nominating conventions, have them put into your political platforms and see to it that your candidates shall stand strictly and squarely upon them."

The farmers eventually arrived at the conclusion that they could not hope for better times until something was done to remedy the financial ills of the country. They endorsed the idea of free and unlimited coinage of silver, which was attracting national attention at this time. But this would not go far enough. The panacea which they recommended was the sub-treasury scheme. Harry Skinner of North Carolina was accredited with the authorship of this plan, which provided for the creation by the federal government of a system of warehouses and a sub-treasury. To the former the farmer was to bring his non-perishable products for storage ; from the latter he was to receive legal tender notes up to 80 per cent of the local current value of the deposited crops and a certificate of deposit. These certificates were to be sold within a year to millers or other consumers for the difference between the current price and the sum the farmer received from the sub-treasury. A bill to establish this system was introduced into the United States Senate by Zebulon B. Vance, but it failed to pass.

The legislature chosen in 1888 had a larger proportion of farmers than any other since the Civil War, and an Alliance leader was selected speaker of the House.

The Alliance now threatened to become a political party.

The People's party, or the Populist party as it is usually called, was a direct outgrowth of the Farmers' Alliance. By 1892 this organization had abandoned all hope of reform through either of the old parties, and the radical wing of the Alliance was demanding separate political action. Colonel L. L. Polk definitely committed the North Carolina Alliance to the third party movement. The more conservative element, led by Elias Carr, remained within the Democratic party.

The Democratic press endeavored "to make Populism odious" in the state. Polk was their particular target. He died in 1892, and Marion Butler succeeded him as leader of the new political party.

The first Populist state convention was held in August, 1892. Seventy-two counties were represented by 495 delegates. W. P. Exum was nominated for governor, after Harry Skinner had declined the nomination. The platform adopted called for rigid economy in government; encouragement of education, agriculture, and manufacturing; a 6 per cent interest law, secret ballot, "purity" of elections, taxation of all railroads, and a ten-hour day in certain industries.

The Populist vote for president in the state was 44,723, the Democratic vote 132,951, and the Republican vote 100,746. The Populists captured three seats in each House of the legislature. For a new party it had made a good showing.

RESOLUTIONS OF THE FARMERS' MASS CONVENTION, 1887

RESOLUTIONS were introduced as follows: To regulate warehouse charges on tobacco; to work public roads by taxation, . . . to demand of the legislature a reduction of all public salaries, fees and appropriations to one half the present amounts, . . . that there be no further appropriations made for the State University, . . . that temperance, hard work and economy will benefit the farmer more than legislation; that the tax of $500 on each brand of commercial fertilizer be abolished and a ton tax be imposed, . . . that the tax to be imposed by this session of the General Assembly do not exceed twenty cents on the $100 worth of property, . . . to encourage immigration; to urge farmers to make less cotton and tobacco and more grain and grass; protect sheep; to reduce expense in the state departments and penitentiary and appropriate the savings to industrial and agricultural schools; to levy a tax of one dollar on every dog for the benefit of sheep growers and the free schools; to abandon commercial fertilizers; to establish agricultural clubs; to urge the General Assembly to repeal the present homestead and lien laws.—*News and Observer*, January 27, 1887.

WHERE IS THE WRONG AND WHAT IS THE REMEDY?

There is something radically wrong in our industrial system. There is a screw loose. The wheels have dropped out of balance.

The railroads nave never been so prosperous, and yet agriculture languishes. The banks have never done a better or a more profitable business, and yet agriculture languishes. Manufacturing enterprises never made more money or were in more flourishing condition, and yet agriculture languishes. Speculators and incorporations never accumulated fortunes more rapidly, and agriculture languishes. Towns and cities flourish and "boom" and grow and "boom," and yet agriculture languishes. Salaries and fees were never so temptingly high and desirable, and yet agriculture languishes. A city editor visits one of our flourishing towns. It is supported by "a splendid back country." . . . He sees magnificent commercial blocks and buildings going up on the streets and corners. The merchants are busy—the farmers are rushing to and fro trading and loading; beautiful cottages are going up in the suburbs. He is inspired by this splendid show of prosperity and writes to his home paper—"this is a magnificent country. It is on a rushing boom." . . .

The city editor looked at the pleasant but delusive surface. . . . He did not interview the register of deeds and find huge piles of mortgages and liens.

The *News and Observer* "rejoices in the progress of various towns throughout the State." . . . Our worthy contemporary sees the languishing condition of agriculture and ascribes it largely to the robbing of people by taxation under the form of law. This is true, but if the towns, railroads, manufactures, banks and all speculative enterprises flourish so prosperously and agriculture languishes under the same laws imposing these taxes, this is but another proof that something is radically wrong.—*The Progressive Farmer*, April 28, 1887.

THE MORTGAGE CROP-LIEN SYSTEM

The mortgage and lien bond system gets more attention perhaps than any other topic and very properly, because the facts gathered and presented show that more evils have come to the farmers of the State on account of the mortgage and lien bond system than from any other, and indeed from every other source. It has proved a worse curse to North Carolina than drouths, floods, cyclones, storms, rust, caterpillars, and every other evil that attends the farmer. Wherever they have depended upon this system to furnish them their supplies the farmers are in debt, and wherever it has been the custom of the farmers to raise their own supplies, then the people are free from debt and the community is thrifty. The cotton belt of North Carolina from the reports made is worse off financially than any other part of the State. This may be attributed to raising a money crop. It is an easy matter to sell cotton when it is gathered. Cotton is as easily handled almost as money, and therefore the merchant wants cotton for his supplies. He does not want hay, clover, grain, potatoes, &c., they are too much trouble to handle, and when a farmer proposes to raise these articles it is impossible to get supplies from a merchant. The merchant insists upon a cotton crop, because of the facility with which he can handle it. The same may to a large extent be said of a landlord—rent is usually demanded in lint cotton. All the tendencies in the cotton belt, therefore, is for the cultivation of a money crop, and the results are perfectly apparent— the farmers of the cotton belt are more heavily mortgaged than any other section of the State, and they are worse off generally. . . . Farm labor is also better paid in the western counties—the average price is represented at $9.50 per month and board, while in twenty of the best counties in the cotton belt the wages of farm laborers are $8.40 per month and board.

It is true in some of the western counties the mortgage system is beginning to be felt. It is said by some of the reports to be attributed to raising of tobacco in late years, but its blighting effect has not made itself apparent yet as it has in the eastern counties. The per cent paid in the west is not as great as it is in the eastern counties, the average per cent being about 25 per cent, while in the eastern counties the average is at least 40 per cent. The most profitable business in this country cannot pay such a per cent as that, much less farming. . . . It is useless to talk about diversified crops to a man who pays 40 per cent for supplies. There is no system of diversified crops that will enable him to pay such a price it makes no difference what kind of a crop may be raised. . . . The conclusion of the whole matter is therefore that there must be an increased production of farm supplies in the State if the farmers would better their condition and place themselves beyond the time-price system.

The reports received show that the average number of months which farm labor is employed is a fraction over seven. This means that there are five months for idleness or uncertain labor. . . . No such system will make a laborer reliable or keep him so. The system of farming which distributes labor over the whole year would doubtless be found to be the most satisfactory and the most profitable. . . .

In a great part of North Carolina they are badly in debt and it will take years of closest economy and good crops to free them from it. The bad crops for some years past, and the low prices for farm products, together with the evil effects occasioned by a failure to raise home supplies, have caused a reduction of wages in a great many counties. . . .

DENUNCIATION OF "TRUSTS"

One of the primal causes of the great upheaval among the farmers and industrial classes of this country is the steady and sure encroachments made by the moneyed power of the land, which threatens to impoverish and enslave them. . . . It struts into our halls of legislation and by bribery or intimidation controls and shapes legislation in its favor. Trusts and combines—names that should be synonymous with highway robbers—are being formed every day to extort through the power of money, exorbitant and ruinous prices from those who are compelled to buy. A few millionaires get together and agree that they will get control of the manufacture or product of a certain commodity—will stop its production if need be, and raise the price to whatever their greed may demand, and thus force the consumer to pay it.

It has just been discovered that a few firms, the manufacturers of bagging in St. Louis, Indiana, Boston, Louisville and New Orleans, have formed a "Bagging Trust," and that they control the product and the price for this whole country. At the time this robbery was concocted, bagging was selling for seven cents per yard, and the probabilities are that it would have gone no higher for the season, but for this scheme to plunder the struggling cotton planters of the South. But as soon as their plans were perfected and they got control of the mills, they advanced the price 4 and ¾ cents per yard. What does this mean to the cotton farmers of the South? It means simply that these half dozen firms have demanded and will force the cotton farmers of the South to pay into their pockets two millions of dollars.

Now is the opportunity and now the occasion for the farmers of North Carolina and of the South to show that they have the rights and they are determined they shall be protected. Let them covenant together that they will support no man for the State Legislature or for Congress who will not pledge himself to enact laws against the wholesale robbery that is grinding the industrial classes into a state of poverty and slavery, and put out of existence the "trusts," "combines" and speculators in futures.

The place and the only place to meet these combinations, is in our legislative halls. They must be throttled. Let it be done by the iron hand of law. To do this we must have men who are identified with us and who are in full sympathy with us, to represent us.—*The Progressive Farmer*, August 7, 1888.

RESOLUTIONS OF THE NORTH CAROLINA FARMERS' ALLIANCE, 1888

Resolved 1. That the North Carolina Farmers' State Alliance hereby enters its earnest protest against the policy of giving away the labor of our convicts, and demands of our Legislature the enactment of such laws as will hereafter prevent this outrage on the rights of the tax payers of your State.

Resolved 2. That we demand such changes in our laws as will reduce the costs in litigation in minor causes, and as shall enlarge the jurisdiction of our Justices of the Peace.

Resolved 3. That we demand that laws shall be enacted to prohibit our public officials from receiving or using free passes or free tickets on our railroads.

Resolved 4. That we demand that our Legislature establish a Commission for the regulation of freights and tariff on the railroads of our State.

MEMORIAL OF THE FARMERS' ALLIANCE OF CHATHAM COUNTY TO THE GENERAL ASSEMBLY OF NORTH CAROLINA, 1889

The failure of the crops in this county last year necessitates the buying of almost our entire supplies to make another crop, and there is very little money in the hands of the farmers. Almost every farmer is depressed; many are disheartened; labor is unremunerative; the value of land is depreciating, and there is a growing disposition to abandon the farm and seek other employment. Unless something is done to bring relief, many will be compelled to give up their farms. The boasted progress and increase of wealth in North Carolina is not shared by the farmers. They are gradually but steadily becoming poorer and poorer every year.—*Document No. 25, Session 1889.*

THE SUB-TREASURY BILL, 1890

Section 1. Be it enacted by the Senate and House of Representatives of the United States of America in Congress assembled, that there may be established in each of the counties of each of the States of these United States, a branch of the Treasury Department of the

United States to be known and designated as a Sub-Treasury, as hereinafter provided, where one hundred or more citizens of any county in any State shall petition the Secretary of the Treasury requesting the location of a Sub-Treasury in such county, and shall,

1. Present written evidence duly authenticated by oath or affirmation of county clerk and sheriff, showing that the average gross amount per annum of cotton, wheat, oats, corn and tobacco produced and sold in that county for the last preceding two years exceeds the sum of $500,000, at current prices in said county at that time, and

2. A certificate of election showing that the site for the location of such a Sub-Treasury has been chosen by a popular vote of the citizens of that county, and also naming the manager of the Sub-Treasury elected at said election for the purpose of taking charge of said Sub-Treasury under such regulations as may be prescribed.

. . .

Section 2. That any owner of cotton, wheat, corn, oats, or tobacco may deposit the same in the Sub-Treasury nearest the point of its production, and receive therefor treasury notes, hereinafter provided for, equal at the date of deposit to eighty per centum of the net value of such product at the market price, said price to be determined by the Secretary of the Treasury under rules and regulations prescribed based upon the price current in the leading cotton, tobacco, or grain markets of the United States; but no deposit consisting in whole or in part of cotton, tobacco or grain imported into this country shall be received under the provisions of this act.

Section 3. That the Secretary of the Treasury shall cause to be prepared, treasury notes in such amounts as may be required for the purpose of the above section . . . provided that no note shall be less than one dollar, or more than one thousand dollars.

Section 4. That the treasury notes issued under this act shall be receivable for customs, and shall be a full legal tender for all debts, both public and private, and such notes when held by national banking associations shall be counted as part of its lawful reserve.

Section 5. It shall be the duty of the manager of the Sub-Treasury when cotton, grain or tobacco is received by him on deposit . . . to give a warehouse receipt showing the amount and grade or quality of such cotton, tobacco or grain and its value at the date of deposit; the amount of treasury notes the Sub-Treasury has advanced on the product; that the interest on the money so advanced is at the rate of one per centum per annum; expressly stating the amount of insurance, weighing, classing, warehousing and other charges that will run against each deposit of cotton, grain or tobacco. All such warehouse receipts shall be negotiated by endorsement.

Section 6. That the cotton, grain or tobacco deposited in the Sub-Treasury under the provisions of this act may be redeemed by the holder of the warehouse receipt herein provided for, either at the Sub-Treasury, in which such product is deposited, or at any other Sub-Treasury by the surrender of such warehouse receipt and the payment in lawful money of the United States of the same amount originally advanced by the Sub-Treasury against the product, and such further amount as may be necessary to discharge all interests that may have accrued against the advance of money made on the deposit of produce, and all insurance, warehouse and other charges that attach to the product for warehousing and handling. . . . —*The Progressive Farmer*, December 2, 1890.

STATE PLATFORM OF THE PEOPLES' PARTY, 1892

That we favor the strictest economy in the administration of the State Government.

That we favor the fullest development of our educational system in all of its departments.

We favor the fullest encouragement to the great agricultural and mechanical and manufacturing industries of our State and all enterprises tending to build up our State and to develop its varied resources.

Whereas the last General Assembly of North Carolina failed to pass a bill reducing the legal rate of interest to 6 per cent, and whereas we endorse the position of those who used their efforts and votes to pass such a measure, Therefore

We demand of our General Assembly at its next session to pass a bill reducing the legal rate of interest to 6 per cent.

We demand of our General Assembly at its next session the passage of a secret ballot law, with a provision in said law that will secure to voters who cannot read an opportunity to vote.

We deplore the corrupting use of money in elections as tending to degrade manhood and to corrupt the ballot-box, and we do denounce all attempts to subvert the rights of the people at the ballot-box and an effort to deprive them of a fair and honest count when the votes have been cast.

Whereas, there are large railroad properties and interests in this State now escaping taxation in whole or in part; and whereas, further, it is in the province of the General Assembly of North

Carolina to make all property in this State bear its equal burden of taxation; now, therefore,

Resolved, That we demand of the General Assembly of North Carolina to force, as far as is in its power, all railroad property and interests that are now escaping taxation, in whole or in part, to pay its full and equal share of taxes for support of the Government of North Carolina as the property of farmers, laborers and other citizens are now taxed.

2. That we demand that no further franchises or privileges in the way of amended or extended charters or otherwise be granted any corporation claiming exemption of taxation, until such corporation or corporations make a complete and unqualified surrender of any claimed exemption from taxation.

Whereas, it is believed by many that there will be an effort to repeal the Railroad Commission bill or cripple it by amendment; therefore

We demand of the next General Assembly of North Carolina that it shall sustain the present Railroad Commission bill, that no amendment lessening or hampering the power of the Commission shall be passed, and that only amendments (if any at all) such as may or will increase the efficiency of the Commission and perfect the machinery and details of the same, shall be enacted into law.

Resolved, That this Convention endorses the platform adopted by the National Peoples' Party at Omaha, July 4, 1892.—*The Progressive Farmer*, August 23, 1892.

155. THE CAMPAIGN FOR A SEPARATE AGRICULTURAL AND MECHANICAL COLLEGE

The act granting public lands to the several states and territories, enabling them to establish colleges for the benefit of agriculture and mechanic arts, was approved by President Lincoln on July 2, 1862. It provided that there be granted to each state an amount of public land equal to 30,000 acres for each Senator and Representative to which the state was entitled under the 1860 census. All money derived from the sale of land or land scrip was to be invested in safe stocks constituting a perpetual fund, the interest from which was not to be less than 5 per cent of the par value of the stock, and which was to be used for "the endowment, support and maintenance of at least one college, where the leading subjects should be, not excluding other scientific and classical studies, and including military tactics, such branches of learning as are related to agriculture and mechanic arts, in such manner as the legislatures of the states may prescribe, in order to promote the liberal and practical education of the industrial classes in the permanent pursuits and professions of life."

Soon after the Civil War, North Carolina availed itself of the advantages of this act. It accepted the grant and transferred the land scrip to the University of North Carolina, on condition that an agricultural and mechanic arts college should be established and maintained. North Carolina was allotted 270,000 acres, the receipts from the sale of which amounted to $125,000. Although no agricultural college was established, the University received $7,500 annually for many years for the purpose of giving agricultural and mechanical education. In the early eighties many complaints were made about this situation. Finally, on February 10, 1886, Colonel Leonidas L. Polk founded *The Progressive Farmer*, which carried on a veritable crusade to take from the University the $7,500 annual grant and give it to a new institution designed to give more practical education in agriculture and the mechanic arts. The movement for a separate college was already gaining strength. In 1885 the Watauga Club, of Raleigh, had petitioned the state legislature to establish "an industrial school in North Carolina which shall be a training place for young men who wish to acquire skill in the wealth producing arts and sciences." About this time Mr. Stanhope Pullen, of Raleigh, donated eighty-three acres of land in the suburbs of Raleigh for the establishment of such an institution. The result was the creation of the State Agricultural and Mechanical College. It was chartered in 1887 and opened for students in 1889.

The following documents throw light on the campaign for the establishment of a separate agricultural and mechanical college.

REPORT ON NORTH CAROLINA'S DISPOSITION OF LAND GRANT, 1872

In compliance with a resolution of the House, January 16, 1872, instructing the Committee on Agriculture to "inquire and report the disposition made by the several States of land scrip issued to them," Mr. John T. Wilson made the accompanying report.

"Accepted the grant February 24, 1866, and received land scrip for 270,000 acres, which was transferred to University of North Carolina on condition that an Agricultural and Mechanics Arts College should be established and maintained in conformity with the requirements of the act of Congress of July 2, 1862. The scrip was sold for $125,000, which was invested in North Carolina State bonds, most of which were special tax bonds, and which are now largely below their par value. The college has not yet been opened and the State is at present deprived of the advantage which the institution was designed to confer."—*House of Representatives Report No. 83, 42nd Cong., 2nd Sess.*, p. 6.

AN AGRICULTURAL COLLEGE

The Catalogue of the State University for 1885-86, recently issued, informs us that there is an Agricultural College connected with and as a part of that institution. If this were literally true, or even approximately true, it would be agreeable information, but it is neither. The so-called "Agricultural" College which is paraded in the Catalogue is a sham, a mere pretence, a thing which has a mere technical existence, under cover of which the University continues to appropriate and to use the annual interest on $125,000 which belongs to the agricultural and mechanical classes of this State, and which should be used for their benefit only. We say this out of no hostility to the University, to which we are friendly, and which we wish to see well and liberally encouraged and supported, but because we believe in fair, honest dealing, and protest against taking the money which belongs to the Farmers and Mechanics of the State and turning it into the Treasury of the University, where it does not belong. . . .

In the first and second issues of *The Progressive Farmer* we gave a statement of the act of Congress of 1862 appropriating to the several States land scrip for the establishment of colleges for the benefit of the agricultural and mechanical classes where they might be trained and educated in their respective callings. The donation was specifically for this purpose and no other, and every state accepting the grant accepted it with that distinct understanding. We also gave a statement of the action of the legislature of 1866-67 in the resolution accepting the grant from the government amounting to 270,000 acres, and of the subsequent act of the Legislature February 11, 1868 transferring the grant to the trustees of the University for the purpose contemplated in the grant, with the proviso that the University comply with the act and make its "*leading* object to teach such branches of learning as are related to Agriculture and the Mechanic arts, without excluding other scientific studies, and including Military tactics." This scrip was turned into special tax (state bonds) bonds which were afterwards repudiated, but the Legislature in 1874-75, partially made good the loss by issuing to the trustees of the University certificates of indebtedness to the amount of $125,000, bearing six per cent interest payable semi-annually, which has since been paid regularly, $7,500 a year, amounting since, in the aggregate, to $82,500. And let it be remembered that the farmers who pay the bulk of the state taxes, are taxed to pay this $7,500 a year, of which they have been deprived for the benefit of the University; so that the farmers not only lose the original grant, but are also taxed to make it good for the benefit of some one else. And in the mean time, in these eleven years, where was the Agricultural and Mechanical College? Who ever heard of it until it put in its belated appearance in their 85-6 catalogue, where it appears as a new discovery, 20 years after the acceptance of the grant by the State and eleven years after the State had made good the stolen scrip? . . . It has had no existence except the technical existence that an occasional lecture on agricultural chemistry, botany, or something of that sort might give it, under cover of which this $7,500 a year is appropriated and used with utter disregard of both the spirit and letter of the Act of Congress and the subsequent act of the Legislature. . . .

The Progressive Farmer wants to see, and it demands it in the name of the people for whom it speaks, this money placed to the credit of the people to whom it belongs to the end that they may at some day if not now, have schools in which their children may be educated in accordance with the intent of the Government in making the grant and of the Legislature in accepting it, and in afterwards assuming responsibility for it. This is all that we, and all the people ask, and this is all we and all the people demand—simply justice and fair play. Nothing more is asked. Nothing less will satisfy.

We propose to continue this subject and follow it up until justice is done the people, or they know why it is not done.—*The Progressive Farmer*, May 19, 1886.

DEMAND FOR A REAL AGRICULTURAL COLLEGE

After a period of eleven years of laborious effort, and with an expenditure of $85,500 of money given our people by the Government, we have at last succeeded in getting a "College of Agriculture and Mechanic Arts"!

It is a model of architectural beauty and admirably equipped in all its departments. It is located on the forty-eighth page of the catalog of the University. The catalog says that "two courses are offered" in this elegant paper college. "Offered" is a good word! These "courses," we presume, have been offered to our farmer boys for these eleven years, but we search the catalog in vain to find one who has availed himself of the offer.

We make no war upon the University. We want to see it rise until it shall stand the equal of any similar institution in all the land, but an earnest conviction of duty to the farmers of our state shall enlist our utmost effort until we see that justice is done them in this matter.

25

We need an agricultural college for the practical training of the children of our farmers and other industrial classes, and there is but one way to get it—build it with the money given us by the government for that purpose. How are we to get it? By electing a legislature that will give it to us!—*The Progressive Farmer*, August 25, 1886.

A MISTAKE

It has been reported that the farmers of North Carolina are being organized to make war on the State University. This is a very great mistake. The farmers are not organizing to make war on anything. They are perfectly docile, and considering how they have to scuffle to get along, in remarkably good humor. They have no hostile designs on the University. They wish it well, but they want it to stand, so to speak, on its own feet. They don't see why the University should have and, through its managers continue to claim the Land Scrip fund which belongs to the farmers. That's all. They think the University (whose President pronounces it in a very healthy and prosperous condition) should, after eleven years use of this money, be able to get along without it—and they mean what they say. Thousands of people in North Carolina who are not farmers, believe that they are right and their demands reasonable. But this is not making war on the University.—*The Progressive Farmer*, January 26, 1887.

THE ESTABLISHMENT OF A SEPARATE AGRICULTURAL AND MECHANICAL COLLEGE

At the same time a formidable crusade was made, mainly by the eloquence of Colonel Leonidas L. Polk, former Commissioner of Agriculture, to take from the University the $7,500 Land Grant and give it to a new institution organized for the more practical education of the sons of farmers and mechanics than could be given at the University. Colonel Polk was possessed of a style of speaking very acceptable to his hearers and he had plausible ground for a new move. It was generally known that many States had concluded that cattle breeding, garden and orchard culture and the like could not well be gained in institutions like Harvard, Princeton, the Universities of North Carolina and Virginia, and had established separate colleges. Of course in his speeches he minimized unjustly the laboratory work of the University, but there was enough truth in his position to make the movement irresistible.

In order to bring pressure on the Legislature a public meeting of farmers was called, composed of all whose chief income was from the soil, the call being issued by the Board of Agriculture, of which President Battle was a member *ex officio*, that is, as president of the institution holding the Land Grant. The Board requested Governor Scales and him to explain to the Convention its policy, its work in the past and intentions in the future. They did so, and were accorded a respectful hearing, with one ill-mannered interruption by a delegate, although it was evident that the friends of Colonel Polk were present by concert, and were in the majority. Later in the meeting President Battle was allowed to answer some strictures on the scientific teaching at the University. It was evident, however, that the members had come together with a pre-judgment in favor of a separate institution, and that at Raleigh.

An adjourned meeting was held in the City Hall. President Battle was fully persuaded that the movement would be successful and that ultimately it would be best for the University to surrender the fund rather than have an endless wrangle on the subject. At his instance his friends induced the Convention to ask the General Assembly to appropriate $7,500 a year to replace what was taken away. This, however, did not obtain the approval of the law makers.

What made the new movement so readily successful was the fact that a citizen of Raleigh offered land for the establishment of the Agricultural and Mechanical College and the Board of Agriculture, by means of the tax on fertilizers, had ample funds to aid in the erection of buildings. Moreover the necessary bricks and labor were ordered to be furnished by the Penitentiary free of charge, the cost of which was not perceived by the taxpayer. Of course large sums have been appropriated since from the public treasury to the new institution, but in 1887 Members of the Legislature did not foresee this, nor was it revealed to them by those who were pushing the measure. . . .

The attitude of Colonel Polk was clearly shown by his exultation at the creation of the Agricultural and Mechanical College. He was overheard saying to a friend in the lobby, "Now we will let Battle alone!" He kept his promise. It was not long before death claimed him. It is not thought that he had special animosity against the University, although in the heat of oratory he may have criticised harshly its practical interpretation of the Land Grant Act. In the opinion of many, if not most, judicious persons he was right in the contention that the Land Grant college should be separate. President Battle was and is of this opinion, but to the best of his ability he carried out the will of his Trustees in endeavoring to retain the fund. His task was a delicate one, but he managed to keep his reputation as a man of truth, although in his heart convinced that the University could never satisfy the demand for hand work and keep up its reputation for theoretical training. . . . —Kemp P. Battle, *History of the University of North Carolina*, II, 374-77.

156. Founding of the State Normal and Industrial School, 1891

What is now the Woman's College of the University of North Carolina was established by an act of the North Carolina General Assembly in 1891 as "a normal and industrial school for white girls." It opened its doors to students October 5, 1892.

Charles Duncan McIver was the moving spirit in the establishment of this institution. He was a man of intense earnestness, energy, might, and common sense, who believed that the State of North Carolina should provide for its young women "an institution of higher learning, adequate for every need, and within the reach of all." He did not believe that the state could have an efficient public school system without well trained teachers. Accordingly he championed the cause of teacher training, and he was chiefly instrumental in securing the passage of the act establishing The State Normal and Industrial School. He was president of the institution for fifteen years and "he so laid its foundations and outlined its future growth that the college must ever remain a monument to his statesmanship."

The Act establishing the institution required that it be located at some suitable place, where the citizens would furnish the necessary buildings, or money sufficient to erect them. The Board of Directors accepted the offer made by the City of Greensboro, which was $30,000 in money and a beautiful ten-acre site located within the corporate limits, and donated by Messrs. R. S. Pullen, R. T. Gray, E. P. Wharton, and others. One hundred and sixteen acres of land were purchased later by the directors. The following report of Charles Duncan McIver to the State Superintendent of Public Instruction in 1890, throws much light on the question of teacher training in the state at that time.

To Hon. S. M. Finger, Superintendent of Public Instruction

During the school year just ending today, I have visited thirty counties and conducted educational Institutes at the county seats. . . .

My work has been conducted with a view to stimulating and encouraging the teachers, and to making friends to the cause of public education among the people. . . .

My Institutes last five days. The first four days are devoted mainly to the professional work of the teacher. Lectures are delivered on the different branches taught in the public schools; on school organization; discipline, methods of teaching, and methods of studying; on school law, and on the proper use of the books on the State list. Friday, the fifth day, is, in a special sense, "People's Day." The School Committeemen and people generally are urged to attend, and the exercises are arranged with a view to interesting and instructing them in the work of public education. Besides various other exercises a special address is made on that day, showing the necessity for education by taxation, and answering objections to it commonly heard among the people. Nearly 15,000 people have attended these Friday exercises in my Institutes since July 1, 1889. . . .

As bad a showing as our teachers make, I think they come nearer to doing their full duty than the people do. Parents often take no interest in the schools. Probably not one in fifty visits the school where his children are taught and the majority of the committeemen even do not visit the schools of which they have charge. The irregularity in attendance on the part of pupils is a universal trouble. Frequently fifty pupils are enrolled during the school-term and the average attendance is less than twenty. Under these circumstances good teaching is impossible. The law ought to give the teacher power to refuse to re-admit a pupil who has, without sickness or providential hindrance, been absent a certain number of times. Irregularity in attendance is doing more harm to the schools than any other one thing except lack of money. I found in some counties that the school-term was less than *four months* and still taxes were not levied up to the constitutional limit. . . .

As dark as the picture may appear in some respects, I think the future is bright. . . . The teachers are better, and are getting better still every day; the school-houses are greatly improved; the regular State-list books are more uniformly used than ever before. . . .

If the next Legislature will deal liberally with the public schools, and give the teachers a chance, our progress will be so rapid that we will surprise ourselves.

A STATE NORMAL AND TRAINING SCHOOL

Good teachers make good schools. . . . Three things are essential if one is to become an efficient teacher. They are *scholarship*, a *desire to teach*, and a knowledge of *how to teach*.

Professional training is as necessary to the teacher as it is to the doctor. A normal and training school is for teachers just what a medical school is for physicians.

The fact that the State Superintendent has, in his last two biennial reports, plead for the establishment of a training school, and the further fact that the Teacher's Assembly, has been asking for it for several years, and that the profession is a unit in its favor, ought to make additional argument unnecessary. But to those who are still skeptical as to the wisdom of the training-school movement, I would add one more reason why the school should be established and be liberally supported by the State. Under our present system of higher education, a white girl, unless her father is comparatively wealthy, cannot, as a rule, get the scholarship necessary to make her a first-rate teacher. Her brother can get it at the University and colleges of the State, because in those institutions about three-fourths of his tuition is paid by the State and the churches. Up to the present time the State and our leading churches have adopted the suicidal policy of refusing to help educate white girls, except in the public schools of the State. The average man cannot send his daughter to our female colleges long enough to make her a scholar. Those who are able to go at all do not intend to teach school. The girls of the ordinary well-to-do farmers, who would, if prepared, make the best teachers for the State's children cannot even get the scholarship necessary to become teachers. One of the results of this is, that two-thirds of our public school-teachers are men, whereas two-thirds, at least, ought to be women. . . . The State appropriates nothing for the training of white women, except the $4,000 for the Institutes. It appropriates $8,000 to the training of colored teachers, . . . By the help of the State, the churches and philanthropists, a fair opportunity of getting an education is given to every white boy, negro boy and negro girl in North Carolina. Neither of the three has to pay more than one-fifth of the expenses of his tuition. But the white girl must pay for every cent of hers. If the training school shall be established for white girls, it will make education possible to thousands of girls, who, under present conditions, must grow up in a state of ignorance and dependence worse than almost any other form of slavery. In addition North Carolina will get a set of teachers better than she has ever had, and a set, too, who will bless her because she blessed them.—*Biennial Report of the Superintendent of Public Instruction for the Scholastic Years 1889-1890*, pp. 15-22.

AN ACT TO ESTABLISH A NORMAL AND INDUSTRIAL SCHOOL FOR WHITE GIRLS, *1891*

1. That there shall be established an institution for the white race under the corporate name of "The Normal and Industrial School." . . .

2. That the institution shall be located by the board of directors as elected by the General Assembly of North Carolina, at some suitable place where the citizens thereof will furnish the necessary buildings or money sufficient to erect them. . . .

5. The objects of the institution shall be (1) to give to young women such education as shall fit them for teaching, (2) to give instruction to young women in drawing, telegraphy, type-writing, stenography, and such other industrial arts as may be suitable to their sex and conducive to their support and usefulness. Tuition shall be free to those who signify their intention to teach upon such conditions as may be prescribed by the board of directors.

6. The institution shall be in regular session for at least thirty weeks per annum, and the instructors, in addition to their duties at the institution, shall be required to hold institutes in the various counties of the state, under such regulations as may be made by their directors, and without other compensation than their regular salaries at the institution. The directors and faculty of the normal and industrial school, upon the completion of the prescribed course, shall grant certificates which shall entitle the holders to teach in any of the schools of the state, subject to the general school laws of the state as to character. . . .

10. When an institute is held in any county . . . it shall be the duty of the county superintendent to assist in the exercises and it shall be the duty of the teachers to attend. . . .

11. That it shall be the duty of the faculty of the normal and industrial school to extend its influence and usefulness as far as possible to persons who are unable to avail themselves of its advantages as resident students. . . . To this end they shall arrange a course of reading and study which may be pursued by others than those resident at the institution. . . .

12. The institution shall be located at a place where low rates of board can be secured in families; and for the benefit of those who may desire to avail themselves of it a matron's hall shall be established at which board shall be furnished at actual cost not to exceed eight dollars per month. . . . —*Public Laws, 1891*, Chap. 139.

157. RESOURCES AND ADVANTAGES OF NORTH CAROLINA, 1893

During the latter part of the nineteenth century North Carolina officials endeavored to attract northern capital and labor to the state. Pamphlets were issued advertising the climate, natural resources, water power, transportation facilities and possibilities, cheap lands, low taxes, and other "resources and advantages." The following extracts, taken from a pamphlet issued by Governor Elias Carr, are typical.

Immigrants and capitalists are at last turning their attention southward, and it behooves us, desiring their presence, to set forth some of the advantages we offer, and I confidently assert that North Carolina, . . . can and does offer more varied inducements to the homeseeker than any spot upon the habitable globe.

First, above all else desired by mankind, is health, and this, without cavil, must be conceded to North Carolina. . . .

Nearly the whole of Eastern North Carolina, containing an area of 25,000 square miles, is peculiarly adapted to truck growing, and its accessibility to the great urban population of this country; being within less than twenty four hours of New York by fast freight, destines North Carolina to be literally, as well as figuratively, the garden spot of the country. For lack of population and capital these lands can now be had at a very reasonable figure. Cotton is produced in a majority of the counties . . . and notwithstanding the low price at which it has ruled for the past few years (7 to 9 cents), it continues to be quite largely grown. . . . But it must be admitted that exclusive cotton growing, or any other crop does not pay in North Carolina. . . .

But it is in manufacturing enterprise that North Carolina has shown the greatest development during the past few years. The numerous streams furnish water power, which in the aggregate is estimated to be equal to 3,500,000 horse-power. The abundant supply of wood furnishes a cheap fuel to supplement coal. Labor is cheap and satisfactory, and the climate mild enough to allow uninterrupted work. . . . There are in the State at the present time 160 cotton mills, located in thirty-eight different counties. . . . The profits arising from many of these mills range from 10 to 25 per cent. on the capital invested. There are 13 woolen mills. . . . There are tobacco factories located at Winston, Durham, Reidsville, Henderson, Oxford, Raleigh, and elsewhere, 110 plug and smoking tobacco factories. There are 57 carriage factories. . . . 32 wagon factories, 25 furniture factories, 6 hub and spoke factories, 24 sash, blind and door factories, 3 paper mills, 8 knitting mills, 14 cotton seed oil mills, 16 fertilizer factories, and a considerable number of miscellaneous establishments. . . .

The demand for rapid transit for both travel and perishable freight has greatly stimulated the transportation lines. To meet this we have now more than 3000 miles of railroad and 1000 miles of waterways open to steamboat navigation. . . . Our facilities for foreign commerce at Wilmington have been greatly improved. . . .

Taxes in North Carolina are very light comparatively. A capitation tax is imposed which cannot exceed $2 upon the poll, and a constitutional restriction of 66 and ⅔ cents on each $100 worth of property. The total State debt amounts to $5,939,000, but this is offset by the State's interest in the North Carolina Railroad, amounting to $2,700,000, so that practically the State debt amounts to $3,219,000 at 4 per cent.—*Resources and Advantages of North Carolina* (Raleigh, 1893).

158. Populist-Republican Fusion

Colonel L. L. Polk, the leader of the Farmers' Alliance in North Carolina, distrusted both Democratic and Republican parties and advocated separate political action. So long as he lived he was able to steer the People's party of North Carolina along independent lines. After his death in 1892 the newly formed party began to make gestures to both major political organizations. Economic conditions became more critical in the state following the panic of 1893. This tended to strengthen the People's party. So eager were the Populists (People's party) to overthrow the Democracy in North Carolina that they fused with the Republican party, which was stronger in North Carolina than in almost any other southern state. The Fusionist ticket was very successful in 1894, electing the entire state ticket, six of seven superior court judges, four Populist and three Republican congressmen, and a majority in both houses of the legislature. Marion Butler, a picturesque Populist from Sampson County, was chosen United States senator.

Although Bryan carried North Carolina by 20,000 majority in 1896, the "Fusionist" state ticket received a plurality of about 8,000 and Daniel L. Russell was elected governor. Five Populist congressmen, three Republicans, and one Democrat were elected. The "Fusionists" had an overwhelming majority in both houses of the legislature. The Populist-Republican organization now controlled all three branches of the state government.

The Populist-Republican régime in North Carolina was unpopular and was severely criticized by the Democratic press. The Raleigh *News and Observer* insisted upon calling Cyrus Thompson a "Hyena" and Marion Butler a "Sampson Huckleberry."

By 1898 there were three factions in the Populist party. One, led by Marion Butler, wanted to fuse with the Democrats, Another group, led by Harry Skinner, wanted to continue the agreement with the Republicans. A third element was opposed to making gestures to either of the other parties. The platform of 1898 was severe in its criticism of the Republicans, and made a number of overtures to the Democrats. The *News and Observer* advocated fusion, but the Democratic organization, led by Charles B. Aycock, of Wayne, refused the offer of fusion. The Populists then decided to resume their alliance with the Republicans, although *The Progressive Farmer* opposed such action. In the election the Democrats swept the state, gaining control of both houses of the legislature. The Populists elected only six members to that body.

The sudden loss of Populist power may be attributed to three causes: (1) the Negro question had come to be associated with the Populist-Republican administration; (2) the Populists probably erred in "fusing" with the Republicans instead of maintaining an independent existence; (3) Populism had run its course. Many of the farmers' grievances had been settled, and the Democratic party was beginning to take cognizance of the agrarian troubles.

COLONEL L. L. POLK'S OPPOSITION TO FUSION, *1892*

LETTER from Polk to Mr. J. W. Denmark, March 12, 1892

Butler is here, and I trust we may arrive at some definite line of action. Of one thing, I am satisfied—there is a large element in our state who will go into no kind of fusion with the Democratic Party. The result will be People's Party Clubs formed all over the State. The more I think of it the more I am convinced, that the only true and manly course to take, is to strike out boldly on our own hook, and I shall so state to Mr. Butler. But I do not believe I can make him or Alexander see it. . . .

Letter from Polk to J. W. Denmark, March 15, 1892

Your two letters just received. Give yourself no concern about my being complicated with the fusion matter. I cannot give such a policy my indorsement, for I can see in it elements of great weakness and I think defeat. My honest opinion is, that any man who attempts to keep the people of North Carolina from an open and bold declaration for the People's Party will be run over. I verily believe, that if we would boldly unfurl the People's banner, throw down the gauntlet and make the issue squarely, we would carry the state by a tremendous majority. . . . It seems to me that trouble and embarrassment will hang heavily on the present plan. . . . You may look out for squalls in North Carolina. So far as I am concerned, I cannot in any manner, shape or form commit myself to any line of policy dictated by the Democratic Party. I am an out and out People's Party man, and shall conduct myself accordingly. . . .

Letter from Polk to Denmark, March 16, 1892

The *people* are ripe and ready and will not tolerate a dilly-dally policy. A straight manly fight will win. The outlook now is that we can carry 8 Southern States, and at least 14 Northern States. . . . —Letters from Colonel L. L. Polk to J. W. Denmark, in manuscript form.

STATE POPULIST PLATFORM, 1894

We condemn the election methods resorted to in certain counties and precincts in the election of 1892, concocted and executed by the Democratic machine of the State, by which thousands of citizens who had voted for years under the same registration were deprived of their suffrage, by which ballots to the People's party after being delivered to poll-holders to be properly deposited were destroyed in "bull pens" and other dark hole voting places, and ballots for the Democratic party were substituted ; by which county canvassing boards, with autocratic power, threw out many townships which gave majorities for the People's party, to such extent as to put in power a minority party. Such a party is unfit to govern. Such a party is an irresponsible despotism bottomed on fraud and all good citizens should strive to defeat and crush it. We favor such changes in our present election law and election machinery as will take from the party in power the absolute control of the suffrages of all of our people. We condemn the Democratic party for abusing this high and sacred trust. . . .

Resolved, That every man, white or black, must have free access to the ballot-box. His vote must be received, it must be counted, correct returns must be made and the man who has the majority, if it is only one vote, must be inducted into office and exercise its functions, or this government cannot endure.—*The Progressive Farmer*, October 16, 1894.

WHAT SHALL THE HARVEST BE?

In North Carolina the Coöperative ticket will be victorious. The majority will be not less than 20,000, probably 30,000 or 40,000. The Democratic party having all the election machinery and the courts, and a portion of the party being totally corrupt, may attempt to thwart the will of the majority by numerous well-known schemes for stealing elections. But will hardly succeed. Even if it does it will only hasten the total annihilation of the corrupt machine. The party is in bad repute locally and nationally. Ballot stealing is driving many of the best men out of the party, and if it adds another wholesale steal to the already long list every honest man left will quit it at once. Fraud and roguery will succeed for a time. . . . But the Democratic structure cannot stand longer if another black crime is committed.—*The Progressive Farmer*, November 6, 1894.

IT IS WICKED

The *News & Observer* made the point yesterday that a white man had been displaced in the organization of the Legislature by a negro. We hope our contemporary was betrayed into this intemperate and unwise utterance. . . . For whoever seeks to inflame the base passions of either race against the other is the enemy of both races. We speak plainly. But plain speech is necessary.

The negro is a citizen. He has to bear the burdens of citizenship. He is entitled to the dignities and honors of citizenship whenever his intelligence and character qualify him for them, and the white man is entitled to them upon no other ground.—*The Caucasian*, January 10, 1895.

"REDEEMING THE STATE"

Mr. Daniels takes up the editorship of the *News and Observer* determined to "redeem the State." This is a sort of high assumption, that might be the prerogative of angels, if they were not too modest, and which tempts persons of much humor to indulge in immoderate laughter, when they see it affected by mere mortality, and mere Democratic mortality, at that. . . .

Mr. Daniels intends to "redeem" the State. He means to take this old Commonwealth back into the hands of the aristocratic coterie that have held it, and selfishly used it, for the last twenty years. He means to subject all men and questions, in this State, to the machine methods, which have been employed for 20 years. He means to have our elections so conducted in the future that there shall be no possibility of ascertaining what the will of the people is —that is to say, he means to govern this State by the will of a minority.—*The Caucasian*, January 31, 1895.

COOPERATION A DISMAL FAILURE

In this State . . . it was found apparently both necessary and advantageous for the People's party to form a combination with the Republicans. . . . The advantage was the certainty of FIVE Populist Congressmen from North Carolina. . . . Enough men who were elected as Populists, however, failed to stand by either principle or party, and the most pronounced and rabid monopolistic administration ever known in this country was by the action of these men, given power to effect its designs and purposes. . . . The opportunity which the Populists of this State had for giving both the principles and party a tremendous impetus was thrown away—evidently swapped off for "pie"—and such an opportunity will never come to them again. Their failure to take advantage of such a grand chance as was open to them was disastrous—a crime. . . . This action will grow blacker as it grows older. So then, for all practical purposes and in all essentials, the cooperation of Populists and Republicans in this State has been a dismal and disastrous failure. Only the contemptible "pie hunters" see any good in it.—*The Caucasian*, February 4, 1897.

159. The Red Shirt Campaign and the Struggle for White Supremacy, 1898

The two years following 1896 were perilous ones in North Carolina. The new system of local self-government resulted in Negro control in most of the eastern counties and towns. Wilmington, the state's leading city, with a population of 8,000 whites and 17,000 blacks, was completely under Negro rule. New Bern, Greenville, and other cities were "negroized." Negroes ran the schools, controlled the courts, and dominated county and city politics. They likewise filled the post offices and held other federal positions in eastern North Carolina. The state was passing through a second "tragic era" somewhat similar to the horrible years of the reconstruction period.

The whites were determined to put an end to this Negro rule, and just as the Ku Klux Klan had come into existence in the state in 1868 to put the Negro "in his place," the Red Shirts now became prominent. The members of this secret organization wore red shirts and "represented the fixed determination of the whites to put an end to existing conditions." The Red Shirts probably originated in South Carolina when the white people of that state rose against Negro rule, and its success there probably led to its rapid spread in North Carolina. It was composed "in the main of respectable and well-to-do farmers, bankers, school teachers, and merchants—in many cases the best men in the community." The Red Shirts were most active in the southeastern part of the state. Ordinarily they did not resort to extreme measures. A few Negroes were killed, however.

Just before the election, F. M. Simmons, chairman of the Democratic Executive Committee, issued a very eloquent appeal to the voters of the state, asking them to "restore the state to the white people."

The election was much quieter than might have been expected. There was very little disorder. The Red Shirts were very active, but found it unnecessary to resort to force. Many Negroes simply remained away from the polls. The Democrats made a "clean sweep" of the state, capturing both houses of the legislature.

The only serious post-election troubles were the race riots at Wilmington, which resulted in the death of a number of Negroes, the overthrow of Negro rule, and the restoration of "white supremacy" with A. M. Waddell in charge of the new city government.

THE SITUATION AT WILMINGTON PRECEDING THE ELECTION, 1898

THE NEGROES will attempt to vote, and in the resistance which will be offered to them at the polls a conflict will surely come. . . .

The campaign in North Carolina, of which this Wilmington situation is but a part, recalls the stormy days when the State passed through the throes of reconstruction. Business is practically at a standstill, and merchants, lawyers and bankers gather in public meetings and in their offices to discuss the extreme measures necessary to keep the negroes from the polls. The color line is sharply drawn. It is the whites against the blacks—the former determined to rule at all hazards. . . .

Many of the leading citizens have sent their families out of the State. . . . Private houses are fortified against possible attack, and the local papers solemnly warn house-wives not to give up any rifles on orders purporting to be signed by their husbands, as this is said to be one of the schemes of the negroes to secure arms.—*News and Observer*, October 30, 1898.

RED SHIRT PARADE IN WILMINGTON

Wilmington, Nov. 3, 1898

The first red shirt parade on horseback ever witnessed in Wilmington electrified the people today. It created enthusiasm among the whites and consternation among the negroes. The whole town turned out to see it. It was an enthusiastic body of men. Otherwise it was quiet and orderly.—*News and Observer*, November 4, 1898.

CHAIRMAN F. M. SIMMONS' APPEAL TO THE VOTERS OF NORTH CAROLINA, 1898

To the Voters of North Carolina:

The most memorable campaign ever waged in North Carolina is approaching its end. It has been a campaign of startling and momentous developments. The issues which have overshadowed all others have been the questions of honest and economical State government, and WHITE SUPREMACY. These issues were not planned and inaugurated by parties or conventions, but they were evolved out of the extraordinary conditions of the situation. Strenuous efforts have been made by the Fusionist leaders to divert the attention of the people from these conditions, and to throw the campaign into other channels, but all their efforts in this direction have proven impotent. The people of North Carolina are sufficiently intelligent to discriminate between GOOD AND BAD government. They are sufficiently virtuous to want GOOD AND HONEST government. They have seen the government of the last two years, and they recognize it to be bad and corrupt. . . . The horrible condition of affairs in the eastern counties, and the progress there of negro domination over white communities raised the question of whether in any part of North Carolina white men of Anglo-Saxon blood should be subjected to the rule and mastery of the negro, and this issue burned itself into the hearts of the people and kindled a fire of indignation which cannot be smothered by "Executive Proclamation," or by the threat of Federal bayonets.

On these two issues, therefore, the Democrats have waged an aggressive and relentless campaign. Our enemies have been on the defensive from the very start. . . .

It was charged and proved that the Fusionists, coming into power under a promise to reduce expenses, had, in three years, increased the expenses of the State government more than THREE HUNDRED

THOUSAND DOLLARS.

It was charged and proved that the expenses of the Legislature, under Fusion government, had increased in two sessions, FOURTEEN THOUSAND DOLLARS. . . .

To the charge of extravagance was super-added the charge of corruption. . . .

It was charged and proved that public office was made a commercial commodity, and bartered and sold for a price, unblushingly, openly and systematically. . . .

Nor were the scandals and disgraces of the Fusion administration confined to venality, corruption and pilfering. As the superintendent of the penitentiary was removed for his misconduct in one line, so the physician for the insane at the penitentiary fled the State upon charges of vile conduct too repulsive to name, and the penitentiary farms were shown to be dens of iniquity, too foul to be described. . . .

In the midst of all this din and conflict, there came a voice from the East, like the wail of Egypt's midnight cry. It was not the voice of despair, but of rage. A proud race, which had never known a master, which had never bent the neck to the yoke of any other race, by the irresistible power of fusion laws and fusion legislation had been placed under the control and dominion of that race which ranks lowest, save one, in the human family.

The business of two of the largest and most prosperous cities in the State had been paralyzed by the blight of negro domination.

In another city a white majority had been discriminated against in favor of a black minority. . . .

WHITE WOMEN, of pure Anglo-Saxon blood, had been arrested upon groundless charges, by negro constables, and arraigned, tried and sentenced by negro magistrates. . . .

NEGRO CONGRESSMEN, NEGRO SOLICITORS, NEGRO REVENUE OFFI-CERS, NEGRO COLLECTORS OF CUSTOMS, NEGROES in charge of white institutions, NEGROES in charge of white schools, NEGROES holding inquests over the white dead. NEGROES controlling the finances of great cities, NEGROES in control of the sanitation and police of cities, NEGRO CONSTABLES arresting white women and white men, NEGRO MAGISTRATES trying white women and white men, white convicts chained to NEGRO CONVICTS, and forced to social equality with them. . . .

Before this overwhelming array of evidence, the weak and puny wall set up by the apologists of NEGRO rule, crumbled away, and then there came the collapse. They had seen the handwriting on the wall. Everywhere they read in the face of the brave and chival-rous white men of the State, a cool, calm, fixed resolution and de-termination that these things must stop; that hereafter white men should make and administer the laws; that negro supremacy should forever end in North Carolina. . . .

The battle has been fought, the victory is within our reach. North Carolina is a WHITE MAN's State, and WHITE MEN will rule it, and they will crush the party of negro domination beneath a majority so overwhelming that no other party will ever again dare to at-tempt to establish negro rule here. . . . —*News and Observer*, Novem-ber 3, 1898.

THE WILMINGTON RIOTS, 1898

Wilmington, Nov. 10, 1898.

Wilmington has been all excitement today, though comparative quiet reigns tonight. Yesterday, a large mass meeting of business men was held, and it was demanded of the negroes to have the plant and editor of the *Daily Record*, the negro paper which recently printed the vile slander on the white women of the State, removed from the town by 7 o'clock this morning. The demand was not acceded to by the negroes, and at 8:30 o'clock, 600 armed white citizens went to the office and proceeded to destroy the printing material. While this was in progress, in some unaccountable way, the building took fire and was burned to the ground. . . .

Incensed at this, a number of negroes assembled . . . and a clash between whites and blacks ensued. . . . Three negroes were killed. At various other times during the day seven negroes are reported to have been killed.

Business during the day has been suspended, and the town tonight is heavily guarded to prevent incendiary fires or further trouble. Ten or more negroes have been lodged in jail on the charge of being implicated in the instigation of a riot. . . .

Bumptious negro political leaders are being made to leave the town on almost every train.—*News and Observer*, November 11, 1898.

ORDER RESTORED IN WILMINGTON

Wilmington, Nov. 12, 1898.

The new city government has thoroughly established law and order. Under Mayor Waddell's direction order has been brought out of chaos, and the military patrol is to be dispensed with Monday. . . .

Negroes who fled to the woods in droves Thursday, and have since been in hiding, are coming back to town, many of them in a famished condition.

Many of them, however, are still leaving of their own accord. Ex-Mayor Wright left the city today. He bought a ticket to New York city, and it is not believed that he will ever return. Others will follow.

The coroner's inquest was held over the dead bodies this morning. . . .

They found in their verdict that the deceased came to their death by gun-shot wounds at the hands of unknown parties.

The new city government could not be a better one. It is headed by ex-Congressman Waddell. The board of aldermen is composed of the most prominent and wealthiest men in the city. . . .

Negro rule is at an end in North Carolina forever. The events of the past week in Wilmington and elsewhere place that fact beyond all question.—*News and Observer*, November 13, 1898.

A. M. WADDELL'S STORY OF THE WILMINGTON RACE RIOTS

The recent revolution, which resulted in the reformation of the city government, was occasioned by municipal misrule and the dictatorship usurped by Governor Russell. . . . Trouble was brewing for months. Before election, the city which was in the power of the Fusionists, was practically without a charter or effective government, and was dominated by negroes and negro sympathizers.
. . .

White women found it unsafe to walk through the streets in daytime without an escort. They were insulted and elbowed into the gutter by negro women and men. Children going to school were abused. . . .

On the day following the election, the prominent Democratic citizens banded together and determined to act. The Fusionist officials in power "resigned," and the revolutionary government assumed control. . . .

Immediately the revolutionists in power proceeded to make it warm for negro-rule leaders and sympathizers. Objectionable Fusionists were given to understand that they had become decidedly persona non grata in Wilmington. . . .

There was (but is no more) in the city of Wilmington an "Afro-American" newspaper called the "Record" published by a mulatto named A. L. Manley. . . . Proposals were made to lynch Manley.

When the revolutionary government took charge, Editor Manley was expelled from the city. . . . The feeling against Governor Russell is very bitter. The negroes are dubbed generally "Russell' savages."—*News and Observer*, November 27, 1898.

XII

THE DAWN OF A NEW ERA

160. THE ELECTION OF 1900 AND THE "GRANDFATHER CLAUSE"

The 1900 campaign and election is one of the most memorable in the annals of North Carolina politics. In that year Charles B. Aycock was elected governor. A new day dawned for education. Agriculture and industry seemed to take on new life. And white supremacy was held to be assured by the adoption of a suffrage amendment to the Constitution, commonly known as the "grandfather clause." This amendment was carried by a vote of 187,217 to 128,285. It is given below, as well as the platforms of the two major parties.

ARTICLE VI

SUFFRAGE AND ELIGIBILITY TO OFFICE

(Section 1.) Every male person born in the United States, and every male person who has been naturalized, twenty-one years of age, and possessing the qualifications set out in this Article, shall be entitled to vote at any election by the people in the State, except as herein otherwise provided.

(Sec. 2.) He shall have resided in the State of North Carolina for two years, in the County six months, and in the precinct, ward or other election district, in which he offers to vote, four months next preceding the election : Provided, that removal from one precinct, ward or election district, to another in the same County shall not operate to deprive any person of the right to vote in the precinct, ward or other election district from which he has removed until four months after such removal. . . .

(Sec. 3.) Every person offering to vote shall be at the time a legally registered voter, . . . and the General Assembly of North Carolina shall enact general registration laws to carry into effect the provisions of this article.

(Sec. 4.) Every person presenting himself for registration shall be able to read and write any section of the Constitution in the English language, and before he shall be entitled to vote, he shall have paid on or before the first day of May of the year in which he proposes to vote, his poll tax for the previous year. . . . But no male person who was, on January 1, 1867, or at any time prior thereto, entitled to vote under the laws of any State in the United States wherein he then resided, and no lineal descendant of any such person, shall be denied the right to register and vote at any election in this State by reason of his failure to possess the educational qualifications herein prescribed: Provided, he shall have registered in accordance with the terms of this section prior to December 1, 1908. The General Assembly shall provide for the registration of all persons entitled to vote without the educational qualifications herein prescribed, and shall, on or before November 1, 1908, provide for the making of a permanent record of such registration, and all persons so registered shall forever thereafter have the right to vote in all elections by the people in this State, unless disqualified under section two of this article. . . .

Sec. II. This amendment to the Constitution shall be submitted at the next general election to the qualified voters of the State . . . and . . . those persons desiring to vote for such amendment shall cast a written or printed ballot with the word "For Suffrage Amendment" thereon, and those with a contrary opinion "Against Suffrage Amendment."—*North Carolina Year Book, 1901*, pp. 58-65.

DEMOCRATIC STATE PLATFORM, 1900

We denounce the tariff legislation of the Republican party, which has increased the burdens of taxation upon our consumers and increased the powers of the trusts and monopolies to rob the people. Believing that under our present method of Federal taxation more than three-fourths of our national revenues are paid by people owning less than one-fourth of the property of the country, we protest against such inequality and injustice, and in order to remedy to some extent this great wrong we favor an income tax and favor all constitutional methods to sustain it.

We denounce the Republican party for its passage of the recent legislation by which the gold standard has been fixed upon our people.

We denounce the policy of the Republican party for its legislation by which the people in territory acquired by the United States are taxed without representation and deprived of the protection afforded by the principle that the Constitution follows the flag.

We are in favor of peaceful commercial expansion, but denounce imperialism and militarism. . . .

We denounce the administration of the Republican party in

North Carolina by which negroes were placed in high and responsible official positions which ought to have been filled with white people. . . .

We favor a government of the people, by the people, and for the people, economy in expenditure and the abolition of unnecessary offices.

We heartily commend the action of the General Assembly of 1899 for appropriating one hundred thousand dollars for the benefit of the public schools of the State, and pledge ourselves to increase the school fund so as to make at least a four months' term in each year in every school district in the State.

We point with pride to the record of the Democratic party in the building and management of the institutions for the care of the unfortunate insane, and pledge the party to so increase the appropriations for this purpose as that every needy insane person in the State may be cared for at public expense. . . .

We condemn free passes.

We denounce all trusts, monopolies, and trade combinations, and demand the passage of such legislation, State or national, as will suppress the same.

We favor the election of United States Senators by the people.

We favor the enactment of laws by the next General Assembly providing for the holding of primary elections for the nomination of State and County and Congressional officers. . . .

We heartily approve the action of the last Legislature in submitting the Constitutional amendment to the people, and we urge its adoption, because it will promote the peace, prosperity, the happiness of the people of North Carolina.—*North Carolina Year Book, 1901*, pp. 58-65.

REPUBLICAN STATE PLATFORM, 1900

We reaffirm our allegiance to the principles of the Republican party as set forth in the national platform of 1896. . . .

Every sound that greets the ear, and every sight that meets the eye, is an argument in favor of the continuance of Republican policies now in successful and beneficent operation throughout this broad land. . . .

In spite of the official records, which show that there has been no negro domination, and no possibility of negro domination in the State or in any of its counties, during the past quarter of a century, the Democratic leaders have determined to wage the coming campaign upon the race issue alone, and they go before the people with a scheme of disfranchisement which is the most impudent assault upon the Constitution of the United States, and the most shocking act of perfidy ever attempted by men who recognize the obligation of an oath or the sanctity of a public pledge. . . .

The highest court in our State has decided that provisions identical in purpose and effect with certain parts of this election law are unconstitutional, and that all proceedings held under such laws are null and void. We, therefore, warn the authors of this infamous, perfidious and invalid statute that they need not hope to enter the National Senate or House of Representatives with commissions based upon such a law. . . .

We denounce, with indignation and abhorrence, the Democratic proposition that the right to vote should be made dependent upon heredity and thus build up an aristocracy of birth upon the ruins of free government.

We denounce the frauds, robberies, violence and intimidation by means of which the Democratic party carried the last election. We point to the exposure of these unlawful methods in the contest election cases from the Sixth and Ninth Congressional districts. . . .

Notwithstanding the Democratic party has at all times in the past bitterly denounced force bills, we call attention to the fact that the present General Assembly passed an election law which authorizes the employment of over six election bailiffs at the polls, armed with deadly weapons, instead of legal warrants, for the sole purpose of intimidating the voters of the State. . . .

The administration of the affairs of the State and of the several counties during four years of Republican ascendancy, has been scrupulously clean, faithful and economical.

During this period the credit of the State, as shown by the market value of its bonds, has reached the highest point known in our history. . . .

The Republican party has always fostered public education, that party engrafted in the organic law of the State the mandatory requirements providing public schools for both whites and blacks, but that party will never brand ignorance as a crime, whose penalty is disfranchisement, so long as the cause of that ignorance is the neglect of the State. . . .

We can only judge the future by the past; this is especially true when we study the value of Democratic promises in the light of their performances. They tell us that they are the devoted friend of education; that their candidate for Governor is its especial champion. The impartial hand of history points to their record from 187 to 1895, during which period they had uninterrupted control of the Legislature, and during that quarter of a century the number of illiterate white voters instead of diminishing actually increased by more than twenty thousand. . . . The figures of the census show the number of illiterate white voters in North Carolina was, in

1870... 33,111
1880... 44,420
1890... 49,570

—North Carolina Year Book, 1901, pp. 58-65.

161. CHARLES BRANTLEY AYCOCK, "THE EDUCATIONAL GOVERNOR"

Probably no man has done so much for public school education in North Carolina as Governor Charles Brantley Aycock. He was born in Wayne County, November 1, 1859; graduated at the University in 1880; began the practice of law in Goldsboro in 1881; and became active in the Democratic party about the same time. In 1898 he was one of the most outstanding leaders in the "white supremacy" campaign and became known as the most effective Democratic speaker in the state. On April 11, 1900, he was unanimously nominated for governor. He became the leader in the campaign for the adoption of the constitutional amendment providing for the literacy test and "grandfather clause." He made 110 speeches and addressed upwards of 100,000 people. The result was his election by a majority of 60,354—one of the largest majorities in North Carolina history. The amendment carried by 53,932 majority.

Aycock promised the people if elected governor he would wage a persistent campaign for education. He carried out his pledge. As soon as he took office he began a crusade for public education for both races and both sexes. His interest in the cause did not falter with the expiration of his term of office as governor. He died April 4, 1912, at Birmingham, Alabama, while addressing the Alabama Educational Association on the subject of Universal Education.

The following excerpts from his speeches indicate his views and attitude on the subjects of education and the race question.

INAUGURAL ADDRESS, JANUARY 5, 1901

ON A hundred platforms, to half the voters of the State, in the late campaign, I pledged the State, its strength, its heart, its wealth, to universal education. . . . Men of wealth, representatives of great corporations applauded eagerly my declaration. I then realized that the strong desire which dominated me for the uplifting of the whole people moved not only my heart, but was likewise the hope and aspiration of those upon whom fortune has smiled. . . . Then I knew that the task before us . . . was not an impossible one. We are prospering as never before—our wealth increases, our industries multiply, our commerce extends, and among the owners of this wealth, this multiplying industry, this extending commerce, I have found no man who is unwilling to make the State stronger and better by liberal aid to the cause of education. Gentlemen of the Legislature, you will not have aught to fear when you make ample provision for the education of the whole people. . . . For my part I declare to you that it shall be my constant aim and effort during the four years that I shall endeavor to serve the people of this State to redeem this most solemn of all our pledges. . . .

SPEECH BEFORE NORTH CAROLINA SOCIETY IN BALTIMORE, DECEMBER 18, 1903

I am proud of my State, moreover, because there we have solved the negro problem. . . . We have taken him out of politics and have thereby secured good government under any party and laid foundations for the future development of both races. We have secured peace, and rendered prosperity a certainty.

I am inclined to give to you our solution of this problem. It is, first, as far as possible under the Fifteenth Amendment to disfranchise him; after that let him alone, quit writing about him; quit talking about him, quit making him "the white man's burden," let him "tote his own skillet"; quit coddling him, let him learn that no man, no race, ever got anything worth the having that he did not himself earn; that character is the outcome of sacrifice and worth is the result of toil; that whatever his future may be, the present has in it for him nothing that is not the product of industry, thrift, obedience to law, and uprightness; that he cannot, by resolution of council or league, accomplish anything; that he can do much by work; that violence may gratify his passions but it cannot accomplish his ambitions; that he may eat rarely of the cooking of equality, but he will always find when he does that 'there is death in the pot.' Let the negro learn once for all that there is unending separation of the races, . . . that they cannot intermingle; let the white man determine that no man shall by act or thought or speech cross this line, and the race problem will be at an end.

These things are not said in enmity to the negro but in regard for him. He constitutes one third of the population of my State: he has always been my personal friend; as a lawyer I have often defended him, and as Governor I have frequently protected him. But there flows in my veins the blood of the dominant race; that race that has conquered the earth and seeks out the mysteries of the heights and depths. If manifest destiny leads to the seizure of Panama, it is certain that it likewise leads to the dominance of the Caucasian. When the negro recognizes this fact we shall have peace and good will between the races.

But I would not have the white people forget their duty to the negro. We must seek the truth and pursue it. We owe an obligation to "the man in black"; we brought him here; he served us well; he is patient and teachable. We owe him gratitude; above all we owe him justice. . . . We cannot change his color, neither can we ignore his service. No individual ever "rose on stepping stones of dead" others "to higher things," and no people can. We must rise by ourselves. We must execute judgment in righteousness; we must educate not only ourselves but see to it that the negro has an opportunity for education.

As a white man I am afraid of but one thing for my race and that is that we shall become afraid to give the negro a fair chance. The first duty of every man is to develop himself to the uttermost and the only limitation upon his duty is that he shall take pains to see that in his own development he does no injustice to those beneath him. This is true of races as well as of individuals. Considered properly it is not a limitation but a condition of development. The white man in the South can never attain to his fullest growth until he does absolute justice to the negro race. If he is doing that now, it is well for him. If he is not doing it, he must seek to know the ways of truth and pursue them. My own opinion is, that so far we have done well, and that the future holds no menace for us if we do the duty which lies next to us, training, developing the coming generation, so that the problems which seem difficult to us shall be easy to them.

ADDRESS BEFORE DEMOCRATIC STATE CONVENTION AT GREENSBORO, JUNE 23, 1904

Coming into office at a new period, when our Constitution had been amended in such fashion that after 1908 no person then coming of age could vote unless he could read and write, my mind has naturally been much occupied with this all-important question. As one should do who is charged with the enforcement of the law, I turned for guidance to that document, the product of the great thoughts of your fathers and mine—the Constitution of North Carolina, and I read there—"Religion, morality, and knowledge being necessary to good government and the happiness of mankind, schools and the means of education shall forever be encouraged." I read again and found "That the people have a right to the privilege of education and it is the duty of the State to guard and maintain that right."

I have earnestly endeavored, with the cooperation of my associates, to carry out these high provisions of our Constitution. I believe with Thomas Jefferson that "intelligence should ever preach against ignorance as the enemy of liberty and of moral and material progress." . . .

. . . To-day we can boast for the first time in the history of the State that we have redeemed our pledge, kept faith with the people, and made provision for all the children. If the child is blind, we have teachers ready to open his eyes. If he is deaf, he can be taught to speak. If he is friendless and poor, the schoolhouse door stands wide open to shed its genial warmth upon him. . . .

To do these things has cost much money and to raise money in North Carolina by taxation has ever been a matter liable to cause offense. None of us pay taxes cheerfully or graciously. . . . This administration has spent much money and it is glad of it. There was need for expenditure of money. There was a demand for it, and we have met it. It undoubtedly appears cheaper to neglect the aged, the feeble, the infirm, the defective, to forget the children of this generation, but the man who does it is cursed of God, and the State that permits it is certain of destruction. . . .

When I was elected Governor it was after the revolution of 1898. It was in the same campaign in which we advocated and adopted the Amendment to the Constitution. These two campaigns were the occasion of much bitterness. They gave rise to intense passion. They set the two races in the State in fearful antagonism. The adoption of the Amendment was a cause of great anxiety to our colored citizens . . . and in a large measure cut them off from hope. I, in common with most of the thoughtful citizens of the State, realized this feeling of theirs. We had made the fight for the Amendment in no enmity to the negro, but for the sake of good government, peace and prosperity. When the fight had been won, I felt that the time had come when the negro should be taught to realize that while he would not be permitted to govern the State, his rights should be held the more sacred by reason of his weakness. I knew that our own passions had been aroused and that we were in danger of going too far. I realized to the fullest the peril of antagonizing the dominant and prevailing thought in the State, and yet I believed that the people who had chosen me Governor did so in the hope that I would be brave enough to sacrifice my own popularity—my future if need be—to the speaking of the rightful word and the doing of the generous act. I have proclaimed this doctrine in many places and in doing so I have frequently met the condemnation of friends whose good opinion I esteem and whose loyalty in the past I appreciate; but, holding my views, I could not have been worthy of the confidence of the great people of this State if I had contented myself to remain silent. My position has brought satisfaction and even happiness to many humble homes in North Carolina, and the negro, whose political control I have fought with so much earnestness, has turned to me with gratitude for my support of his right to a public school education.—R. D. W. Connor and Clarence Poe, *The Life and Speeches of Charles Brantley Aycock,* pp. 117-18, 161-63, 254-58.

162. The Temperance and Prohibition Movement

There were some temperance societies in North Carolina as early as 1831-32, but they accomplished very little. In 1865, the order of The Friends of Temperance was instituted at Petersburg, Virginia. It extended its influence into North Carolina, and the State Council of North Carolina was organized in 1867. By 1877 it had no fewer than 290 chapters, and had adopted as its official paper the *Friend of Temperance,* a "temperance and family newspaper, devoted to temperance, literature, agriculture and general news."

Through the columns of its official organ the Friends of Temperance carried on a vigorous agitation. Some of their favorite headlines were:—"What Drunkenness is Doing," "A Drunkard's Wife," "Poisoned," "Let It Alone and It Won't Hurt You," "Effects of Dram Drinking," "How He was Reformed," and "Total Abstinence a Good Thing."

The temperance advocates finally induced the 1881 legislature to order a popular referendum on the question. The results were disappointing. Prohibition was snowed under by a vote of 166,325 to 48,370. This defeat practically killed the Friends of Temperance and it put their official publication out of business.

The Democratic party took up the fight for prohibition about 1900. The North Carolina Anti-Saloon League was organized in 1902. The Watts Law providing for "local option" was passed in 1903. State-wide prohibition was adopted in 1908 by a vote of 113,612 to 69,416. The 18th Amendment to the Constitution, adopted in 1919, provided for nation-wide prohibition. This "noble experiment" did not work very well and in 1933 the 18th Amendment was repealed by the 21st Amendment. The General Assembly of 1937 enacted a state-wide county option liquor law and created a

State Board of Alcoholic Control. Since that date almost one-third of the state's counties have established Alcoholic Beverage Control (ABC) stores.

PENALTY AND RESULTS

Councils should always exercise the greatest amount of charity in the imposition of penalties upon an offending brother. Mild, but certain punishment is always the best, and a simple reprimand from the Chair, in open session, is often more effectual than the infliction of a fine or suspension.

THE PLEDGE

The pledge of total abstinence is, after all, the essence of the whole thing; and to restrain men from breaking it, when once made, should be our end and aim. . . . Once a temperance man always a temperance man, is the only safe principle for any of us.

SOMETHING FOR ALL TO DO

In the temperance reform there is something for everybody to do —a field for every variety of labor—and a sphere for every order of talent. . . .

The foe against which we do battle is a mighty one, and his emissaries are legion. . . .

In every land—in every clime—in every empire, kingdom, nation —in every state, city, municipality, township . . . the viceregents of the monarch Alcohol, are busy in the service of their master— sowing seeds of death, and dragging the victims of their wily arts down to misery and the grave.

To meet such a foe a vast army is needed—an army of pure men and women, with a moral courage that will not shrink from duty nor yield to the fierce assaults of the mighty foe—men and women who love their race, and who esteem virtue above everything else.

Intemperance is a foe to virtue—a foe to everything that is good —to everything ennobling. . . .

The temperance reform is a warfare. . . .

Join the Friends of Temperance and give your influence to that order.

Subscribe for the *Friend of Temperance,* and help to build up, in this our Southern land, a temperance paper that will wield a mighty influence for good and to the pulling down of the enemy's strong- holds—the grog-shops.

Make temperance speeches, and preach temperance sermons, and distribute temperance tracts, and wherever you go, let it be known that you belong to the cold water army.

Organize juvenile temperance societies and train the youth of the land to shun the path that leads by the still-house and through the grog-shop down to the drunkard's grave and drunkard's hell.

Discard the wine bottle from your tables and the brandy peaches from your closets and begin with the first dawnings of reason to instill into the minds of the little boys and girls a more than mortal hatred for that demon which has so long fatally cursed the world. . . .

The present annual outlay for intoxicating liquors in the United States is $680,000,000.

MESSAGE OF PRESIDENT OF STATE COUNCIL, JUNE 28, 1871

Never, perhaps, in the history of our State has there been such a widespread interest, such zeal and such encouraging hopefulness in the cause of Temperance as there is today. . . . One hundred and one Councils in full operation, with a combined membership of nearly six thousand, are zealously at work. . . .

From every quarter of the State the news reaches us that men of promise . . . are uniting themselves with our Order, and in many instances are becoming active workers in the cause. . . .

But do not imagine for one moment . . . that the necessity for vigorous, united effort is any the less urging. Every year fifteen hundred inebriates lie down in drunkard's graves and go to meet their last account with brains on fire from the accursed drink. More than one hundred thousand families are each year left among us homeless and penniless, by the agency of the arch-fiend—Intemperance.—*Friend of Temperance,* May 10, 17, 24, June 28; August 9, 1871.

AN ACT TO PROHIBIT THE MANUFACTURE AND SALE OF INTOXICATING LIQUORS IN NORTH CAROLINA, 1908

1. That it shall be unlawful for any person or persons, firm or corporation to manufacture or in any manner make, or sell, or otherwise dispose of, for gain, any spirituous, vinous, fermented or malt liquors or intoxicating bitters within the State of North Carolina: *Provided,* this act shall not be construed to forbid the sale of such . . . liquors by a legalized medical depository, or by any licensed and registered pharmacist, for sickness, upon the written

prescription of a regular licensed and actively practicing physician or surgeon: . . . *Provided,* . . . that wines and ciders may be manufactured or made from grapes, berries or fruits, and wine sold at the place of manufacture only. . . .

2. That all liquors or mixtures thereof, by whatever name called, that will produce intoxication shall be construed and held to be intoxicating liquors within the meaning of this act. . . .

5. Nothing in this act shall be construed as making it unlawful to sell to any minister of religion or other officer of a church wine to be used for religious or sacramental purposes. . . .

8. Any person violating any of the provisions of this act shall be guilty of a misdemeanor.

9. That the foregoing provisions of this act shall go into effect on the first day of January, in the year of our Lord one thousand nine hundred and nine, if a majority of the votes cast at the election hereinafter provided for shall be "Against the Manufacture and Sale of Intoxicating Liquors."—*Public Laws, 1908,* Chap. 71.

163. North Carolina a "Militant Mediocracy"

Judge Robert W. Winston has referred to North Carolina as a "militant mediocracy." The following is taken from his article in *The Nation,* (New York), February 21, 1923.

Her early settlers were for the most part plain people, neither rich nor aristocratic. "To be rather than to seem" her motto, North Carolina was willing to fight but not to brag about it. She cared nothing for state archives, historical associations, or written history. . . . North Carolina's development is the triumph of a vigorous middle class. The State never had the aristocratic tradition of either Virginia or South Carolina. To be sure, it had its planter class, the members of which cherish their escutcheons and family trees as the Virginia and South Carolina grandees cherished theirs; but this favored company never established itself so firmly in a holy of holies as its blood brethren to the north or south. It was closer to the ground, and when the big smash came the aura which had surrounded it was dissipated more quickly.

The more complete dominance of an upper class in Virginia had its advantages. It was favorable . . . to the growth of culture. No unbiased observer of the life of these two neighbors, no student of their history can fail to find that North Carolina has been behind

Virginia in polish, in the amenities of intercourse, in devotion to things literary and artistic.

The lesser gap between high and low in North Carolina in antebellum days has been reflected in a greater readiness to welcome new ideas, a lack of reverence for old allegiances and preconceptions. True, the dead hand of the past seemed to have as firm a grip here as elsewhere in the first quarter of a century after Appomattox, but more recent events have proved that this was not so.—*The Nation* (New York), February 21, 1923.

164. THE "GOOD ROADS STATE," 1920-1930

One of the most outstanding achievements of North Carolina in recent years has been its highway development. In 1921 the state began a program of road building which has been carried forward to such an extent that North Carolina is frequently called the "Good Roads State." The Highway Act of 1921 provided for a system of 5,500 miles. By 1929 the State Highway system embraced 7,515 miles, connecting all of the county seats and most of the towns of the state. The "Gardner Road Bill" of 1931 placed the county roads under state control.

The following report of the State Department of Conservation and Development gives a brief discussion of some aspects of highway development.

Increase in Automobiles.—

No more striking vindication of the bond issue, or "pay-as-you-ride" plan of highway construction adopted by North Carolina, can be found than in the 300 per cent increase in the number of automobiles operated in North Carolina during the past six years, or since the highway program actually started. In 1921, when the first bond issues of $50,000,000 was authorized, there were only 148,627 motor vehicles registered in the State; while in 1922 there were 182,550; in 1923 the number reached 246,812; in 1924 the registration was 302,232; in 1925 it was 340,287; in 1926, 385,047; in 1927, 430,499; and in 1928, 463,841. During 1927 North Carolina showed a greater percentage of increase in registration than any State in the Union, namely 11.8 per cent.

Revenues.—

The increase in motor vehicle registration has brought about a large increase in revenue from this source which is constantly increasing. In the last eight years since the highway act became effective, the State has received, approximately $70,000,000 in gasoline and motor vehicle fees. In 1926 these taxes amounted to approximately $13,000,000 and in 1927 to $15,000,000 and in 1928 to approximately $19,000,000.

Investment and Expenditures.—

Since the original bond issue of $50,000,000, was authorized by the General Assembly of 1921 additional bond issues to enlarge the system have been authorized by it at each successive biennial meeting. In 1923 a bond issue of $15,000,000 was voted; at the session of 1925 a $20,000,000 bond issue; and the session in 1927 added $31,850,000, making a total authorized of $116,850,000. In addition the State has received from the Federal Government, through the provisions of the Federal Aid Act of 1916, approximately $12,000,000, and this together with county loans and gifts and donations, has brought the total amount available for construction to approximately $155,000,000. . . .

Prior to the establishment of the State Highway System the upkeep of 7,500 miles of road operated by the State was a direct burden upon the taxpayers of the counties. In the majority of instances the work, because of inexperience and limited facilities, was done indifferently and expensively and at additional cost to the users through the poor condition of the roads and the wear and tear upon vehicles. The relief obtained by the counties from the construction and maintenance of these roads, carrying approximately 80 per cent of the traffic, is a dividend of no mean importance. The laboratory service and expert engineering advice of the State Highway has been made available to the local divisions of government, in maintaining the county roads and this promises to be one of the most important contributions that this enterprise will make to its citizens.

Benefits to Education.—

Our expenditure for the operation of public schools has grown from $9,000,000 in 1920 to $24,000,000 in 1927, and our investment in public school buildings from $1,000,000 in 1900 to $93,000,000 in 1927. The development of this public school system with its modern consolidated rural schools served by school busses would have been impossible but for the growth of the State Highway System. Today 1,050 of these schools are being served by 3,234 busses, transporting daily from the remote sections of the school districts 120,318 children. Exemplified in terms of educational advantages to the childhood of the State this dividend alone would justify the expenditure of the millions invested in highway construction.

Dividends to Agriculture.—

Notwithstanding its rapid development and leadership in industrial lines, North Carolina is equally important as an agricultural state, ranking second to Texas only, among the Southern States, in the annual value of its farm crops. In handling the two major crops, cotton, amounting to approximately $100,000,000 a year, and tobacco, bringing the farmers, in round figures, $111,000,000 annually, good roads have been of great value, by making possible transportation to market with greater ease and less expense. In the handling of perishable crops such as truck, fruit, and berries, good roads are practically indispensable. In season one may see in the central industrial section of the State trucks from the eastern portion of the State laden with fresh vegetables, fruits, berries, or fish and oysters from the coast. Trucks loaded with peaches from the famous "Sandhills" in the southern portion of North Carolina, are found in scores of towns all over the State where their loads find a ready market. In the fall trucks coming east from the mountain section loaded with apples, late potatoes and cabbage, find a good market in the industrial section. These markets are not confined to North Carolina as the interstate shipments by truck play an important part in this commerce. During 1928 truck shipments of strawberries equivalent to 132 carloads were moved from two small towns alone, in Eastern North Carolina, and many of these trucks placed the berries on the market in New York City twenty-four hours ahead of the refrigerator service of the railroads and it is reported that the berries were in better condition and commanded higher prices than those shipped by train.—*North Carolina Resources and Industries* (Raleigh, 1929), pp. 59-61.

165. WATER TRANSPORTATION AND THE MOVEMENT FOR PORT DEVELOPMENT IN 1920's

From the settlement of the colony to the present there have been complaints about the commercial dependence of eastern North Carolina upon Virginia ports. There has been much talk about port development, but little action. The completion of the inland waterway system focused public attention on this important question, and Governor Cameron Morrison, 1921-1925, endeavored to "educate" North Carolinians to the idea of port development. His "Port Bill," submitted to popular referendum, was narrowly defeated. The accompanying passage is taken from his message to the General Assembly, August 7, 1924.

THE railroad situation is not only not detrimental to a modern and up-to-date development of water carried commerce from North Carolina, but the facilities for getting commerce to and from our water towns into other parts of our State, except two or three remote counties in the East and West, are almost unprecedented for a southern or western state.

There is some thought in the State that we cannot build a great city upon our waterways because of lack of connection with great western trunk line railroads. The situation is not generally understood, for our connections are very far superior to what is commonly accepted as a fact. However, my primary and controlling reason for so earnestly desiring to see my beloved State develop water carried commerce is not in the hope of establishing some mighty commercial city upon our waterways, though if the recommendations found in the report of the State Ship and Water Transportation Commission are adopted by you, I confidently expect to see not one but several cities of large proportion established there; but my chief concern is not to build an important city there upon commerce from Tennessee or Kentucky carried through our State to such a city. This is desirable, but it is nothing like so desirable as to see an additional and far cheaper mode of transportation made available to the farm, factory, fishery, or other industrial establishments in North Carolina. I am far more interested in furnishing an additional and cheaper mode of transportation for the farmers, merchants, manufacturers and others engaged in industry in this State than I am in creating a more direct route for freight in the states west of ours, to pass through our State to the world.

We may never build a city at Wilmington, Southport or any other place in the Cape Fear basin, or at New Bern, Morehead City, or any other port near Cape Lookout, but this does not prevent our taking modern and up-to-date steps to carry to almost every nook and corner of North Carolina, in more or less degree, the blessings and opportunities which would go with the development of water commerce carrying facilities from and to our counties and towns situated upon navigable waters.

It may be true that we need other trunk line railroad systems penetrating the great West in order to successfully build a great commercial city upon our waterways, but there are literally hundreds of small towns and villages and wide areas of country around them, situated on or near navigable waters, who enjoy the blessings of competition between rail and water carried commerce. Our people are entitled to the same benefits and can have them if we will develop water carried commerce, although we may never have a city.

Primarily, the big thing to be accomplished through the undertaking under discussion is water carried commerce. This would be highly desirable for a great area of our State, and a large per cent of our population, absolutely independent of the freight rate question. It would be almost magically energizing and animating and practically helpful to twenty-five of our counties in North Carolina which are situated upon navigable waters, and to twenty-five more counties, over our good roads and with the truck, within fifty or sixty miles of navigable waters, although the benefit did not radiate beyond this area to the remainder of our people. . . .

The total cost annually of the progressive government which the State of North Carolina is now enjoying, and sometimes is criticized for its liberality and expenditures in the many activities which the State is engaged in, aggregate about twelve millions of dollars exclusive of expenditures for highways and permanent improvements. The total freight charges paid by the people of this State aggregate fifty-five millions of dollars annually. There are many lamentations from many sources in the State about the expenditures of twelve millions annually by the State government which carries so many blessings to the people of the State, but very little attention is given by the whole citizenship to the fifty-five millions expended in freight carrying charges upon our commerce. There are mighty outcries by certain watchers of State expenditures for good government against the small annual interest charges to be added to the expenditures by the State, if this water development project is carried through; but these same gentlemen are silent over the proposition which is being seriously made and pressed, in a readjustment and overhauling of freight rates going on before the Interstate Commerce Commission, wherein the rail carriers of this State seek to increase the freight charges upon only a part of the commerce of this State, a sum greater than ten millions of dollars annually.

In some way the art of publicity is so influenced or controlled in this State that no attention whatever, or scarcely any, is being given to the cold, cruel, and relentlessly pushed effort to add to the fifty-five millions of dollars paid the railroads in freight charges by this

State an additional ten millions annually—a sum amounting to nearly as much as the total cost of our State government. It would be interesting to know how such use of the mysteries and means of publicity in North Carolina are obtained.—*Public Papers and Letters of Cameron Morrison* (edited by D. L. Corbitt, compiled by W. H. Richardson), pp. 72-80.

166. THE LIVE-AT-HOME MOVEMENT IN 1920'S

For many years North Carolina has held high rank among the states in the production of tobacco, cotton, and other money crops, but the farmers of the state have neglected the production of adequate food to make agricultural life of the state independent. The result has been that bad crop years, slumps in prices of money crops, and other causes have led to considerable distress at times. The recent governors, particularly Morrison and Gardner have emphasized increased food production. The following appeal of Morrison to the people of North Carolina, in 1922, is typical.

TO THE PEOPLE OF NORTH CAROLINA:

North Carolina has been pushed to a high comparative position among the states of the Union in the production on our farms of money crops for the market; but our whole agricultural life is weakened by the fact that we have neglected the production of sufficient food on the farms of the State to make our agricultural life independent, and give it strength to stand the periodic vicissitudes of misfortune to the money crops, due to slump in prices, or other causes sure to occur. Much improvement has been made in the last few years in this well understood weakness of the State, but there is yet much to be done. It is hard to "get out of a rut."

A highly competent authority declared recently: "There is not a single county in the State in which there is raised enough food in value or quantity for the human and animal life of the county."

FIGHT WEEVIL WITH FOOD

Independently of the approach of the boll weevil, this phase of our agricultural life should be strengthened throughout the State; but the approach of the boll weevil threatens a serious blight to a large area of the State, particularly the great areas devoted largely to the growth of cotton. If the boll weevil should have the devastating effect upon the crops this year in the cotton sections of the State that it has had in some of the states to the south of us, and if the people in the cotton sections of the State do not raise more food supplies for themselves and their animals than they have heretofore raised, it will certainly result in widespread suffering and destitution. This threatened danger and distress can be largely averted, if it comes, as there is reasonable ground to fear it may, and at the same time a policy adopted in the agricultural life of the State which will greatly strengthen the whole life of our people, not only in the cotton sections, but in the entire State.

We must so order our agriculture as not to require the immense outlay of money rendered necessary largely to buy the food upon which the people live who grow money crops in the State for the market. The small farmers and tenants cannot stand the periodic slumps which occur from various causes, and the wealthier men and large landowners cannot withstand the boll weevil blight, if it comes, and feed their tenants and farm laborers through it. *Buying our food elsewhere and raising our money crops requires too much capital, and is too hazardous for our people to engage in on an extensive scale.*

WE MUST INCREASE OUR HOME SUPPLY OF MEAT

We cannot raise beef profitably in a large part of the State, but we can raise hogs and poultry of every description on account of our long summer seasons as easily and cheaply as it can be done anywhere in the Union. We must increase our meat supply through hogs and poultry. We can raise vegetables of almost every known variety; and keep and maintain milch cows probably more cheaply than it can be done elsewhere in the Union. If we would but realize the importance of this matter, we could make hog meat, chicken, turkey and other fowl meat, eggs, butter and milk so plentiful in the State, particularly on the farm, that our food bill would be trifling compared to the enormous outlay, with the business hazards accompanying it, which we now annually pay.

We urge the people of the State to a careful study of how to make this increase in food in the State economically, and that they adhere to it, not only during the threat of the boll weevil disaster, but until North Carolina becomes a great food raising State, independent of the threat of periodic disaster through failure to make profit on the crops.—Public Papers and Letters of Cameron Morrison, p. 144.

167. FARM TENANCY IN NORTH CAROLINA, 1900-1925

Farm tenancy has been one of the state's most serious social and economic problems. It has been closely related to "the supply-merchant—crop lien—time credit business," which Clarence Poe called "the greatest curse of the agricultural South." Tenancy has been partially responsible for North Carolina's high rank in adult illiteracy. With almost half of its farms operated by tenants, prior to 1940, North Carolina was one of the leading tenant states, and according to Dr. Hobbs, "is headed into farm tenancy more rapidly than any other state except Texas, taking the fifteen-year period from 1910 to 1925 as the basis of comparison." There have been many causes of tenancy in the South: (1) the collapse of the plantation system at the close of the Civil War; (2) lack of ready cash; (3) one-crop system of agriculture; (4) inertia of landholders and tenants; (5) land speculation and large inherited estates; (6) lack of interest in home and farm ownership.

The following extracts are from *The Progressive Farmer* and from S. H. Hobbs, *North Carolina Economic and Social,* published in 1929.

THE greatest curse of the agricultural South is our vicious time-prices credit system. It is a curse alike to landowners, tenants, merchants, bankers, professional men, and to county and state as units of government. It is holding our whole section back just as truly as it was forty years ago when that great Southern orator and statesman, Henry W. Grady, portrayed its blighting influence on our section. . . .

As *The Progressive Farmer* has shown by careful investigations made in 1915 and again in 1924, the average supply merchant charges from 15 to 22 per cent more for an article sold "on time" than when sold for cash. Around 20 per cent extra for "time-prices" credit seems to be the rule from North Carolina to Texas inclusive. And if a merchant charges 20 per cent extra for a credit item running six months, that is equal to the customer paying interest *at the rate of 40 per cent a year.* On the other hand, if (as many believe) the average time-price item runs only four months before the usual maturity of the store account on November 1, then paying 20 per cent extra to get credit for only four months *is equal to paying interest at the rate of 60 per cent per annum*—or ten times the standard rate of interest in most of the United States. No business on earth can succeed if it must pay at the rate of 40 per cent to 60 per cent a year for its operating capital, and for the tenant farmer to have to pay such rates foredooms him to poverty and failure.—*The Progressive Farmer,* January 19, 1929.

FARM TENANCY

Year	Number Farms	Number Farm Tenants
1900	224,637	93,008
1910	253,725	107,287
1920	269,763	117,459
1925	283,482	128,254

The Census of 1920 classifies farm tenants by types. The following table shows the distribution in North Carolina for that year:

Type	Number
Share Tenants	58,819
Croppers	39,939
Share-Cash	468
Cash Tenants	9,425
Standing Renters	6,491
Unspecified	2,317

It is thus seen that the bulk of our tenants are share tenants and croppers, the two often being hard to distinguish. Neither possesses very much as a rule; the cropper usually possesses next to nothing in the form of worldly goods. . . .

At this point it might be well only to outline the economic advantages and disadvantages of farm tenancy. . . . The economic advantages in part are as follows:

a. Affords a living to landless, moneyless labor.
b. Supports agriculture in regions lacking cash operating capital.
c. Is a school of experience and a stepping-stone into farm-ownership—to southern Negroes mainly. In the South one-fourth of the Negro farmers are owners, in Virginia nearly three-fourths, in North Carolina nearly one-third.
d. Produces large crop totals per year, large per acre totals, but small per man.

Some of the economic disadvantages are the following:

a. Steady decrease in the average size of farms. Southern farms are the smallest in the United States. North Carolina farms are the smallest of any state, counting only cultivated area.

Cultivated acres per farm in North Carolina were only 19.5 in 1925; 125 acres in 1860.

b. Depletion of soil fertility.

c. Handmade cash crops. Waste of human, horse, and machine power.

d. Crop farming mainly, hindering livestock development.

e. Lower standards of living.

f. Production of great farm wealth annually, but little of it retained where produced, mainly because of the crop-lien system and excessive labor cost in handmade crops.

g. An unstable, unsafe basis for agriculture.

h. Small farm dividends because cash crops are a gamble with market prices.

i. Home-raised supplies neglected, and farm operation on a credit basis.

j. An unsafe, unstable basis for agricultural labor, due mainly to the loose one-year contract. The social consequences are largely due to the constant migration of tenants.

SOCIAL EFFECTS OF TENANCY

From a social point of view tenancy is bad, chiefly because farm tenants are forever on the move. It is generally estimated that approximately 40 per cent of them in the South change farms every year. The rate is equally high in North Carolina. If this is true, then approximately 300,000 farm tenants and their families change farms in North Carolina each year. The highways in December, January, and February are literally dotted with tenants who are playing a game reminiscent of the childhood pastime called "fruit-basket." The reasons for their annual shift are almost as numerous as the farmers represented. Often they move for no apparent reason. They just have a habit of moving. It is common to find a tenant who has lived on a dozen different farms and perhaps in a dozen different communities. They often go from one state to another. Hundreds, even thousands, have recently come into North Carolina from boll-weevil-ridden Georgia and South Carolina. This wandering mass of humanity has no abiding interest in any community because the tenants have no stake in the land. They are strangers, sojourners, pilgrims, forever on the move, and always discontented. Nor can they be blamed for their discontent. They are forever trying to better their condition by trying new fields. This spells disaster to schools, school attendance, school consolidation, church membership, attendance, and support. It spells disaster to good roads development, public health sanitation, law and order, community organizations, and enterprises for progress and prosperity, welfare, and well-being. It spells disaster for coöperative marketing associations. A landless, homeless, wandering tenant population cannot become a coöperative machine.—S. H. Hobbs, *North Carolina Economic and Social*, pp. 119-27.

168. THE REHABILITATION OF A RURAL COMMONWEALTH

In an address delivered at the North Carolina meeting of the American Historical Association, in 1929, Professor R. D. W. Connor gave one of the best and most beautiful descriptions yet written about North Carolina's recent progress. In a brilliant manner he portrayed the "rehabilitation of a rural Commonwealth."

LENGTHENING transmission lines explain one important phase of the industrialization of North Carolina. They have industrialized this rural community without destroying its rural character. In North Carolina, eighty per cent of the people still live in rural areas, and the State cannot boast of a single city of a hundred thousand people. Nor have industries been localized. Variety rather than specialization characterizes their development. Cotton mills, tobacco factories, furniture plants, and other industrial enterprises exist side by side in the same communities. Winston-Salem and Durham are famed as tobacco centers, but both are also large manufacturers of cotton goods. In the Greensboro area are great cotton mills, but High Point, twenty miles away, is second only to Grand Rapids as a furniture mart. The Charlotte-Gastonia district is the textile heart of the South, but at Badin, in an adjoining county, is the world's largest aluminum plant. The 535 cotton mills of the State are found in sixty-two, the 109 furniture factories in twenty-four of the State's one hundred counties. . . .

. . . From 1900 to 1925, the number of wage-earners in industry in North Carolina increased from 72,000 to 173,000, their annual earnings from $14,000,000 to $127,000,000, the cost of the raw materials they used from $45,000,000 to $380,000,000, the value of their output from $85,000,000 to $952,000,000. Agriculture kept pace with industry. In the same period the value of North Carolina's farm products rose from $89,000,000 to $514,000,000, the value of farm lands from $233,000,000 to $1,050,000,000. The estimated true value

of all property in the State was $682,000,000 in 1900; it was $5,284,-
000,000 in 1925 . . . the per capita wealth of the State in 1890 at $361
was the same as it was in 1860; in 1925 it was $1,879.

At this point I must pause to brag a little; . . . For it would
never do to allow you to return to your homes without being told
that North Carolina leads the nation in the number of cotton mills;
that in the value of their output it challenges the primacy of Massachusetts; that in furniture it treads on the heels of Michigan; that
in tobacco it outstrips all competitors; that the value of its farm
products surpasses that of any Southern State except the empire of
Texas, which is five times its size, and that, excepting New York
alone, it pays the United States treasury a larger revenue than any
other State in the Union. . . .

It is only when this economic progress is translated into terms of
social development that its full significance appears. The old Commonwealth against which the farmers revolted in the 'nineties was
primarily a political institution; the new commonwealth of the
twentieth century is primarily a social institution. Public interest in
race relations, education, health, temperance, public welfare work,
the relations of labor and capital, and other similar questions, have
almost driven politics off the front pages of the newspapers. The
establishment by the State since 1900 of half a hundred charitable,
correctional, and educational agencies to meet the growing interest
in such problems is expressive of the popular conception of the State
as chief social agent of its people. To the solution of these problems
North Carolina, through both public and private sources, for twenty-
five years has been devoting her best thought and her treasure. . . .

North Carolina has made industry the handmaiden of social development. To the rejuvenating powers of universal education this
new Commonwealth pins its faith. In 1897 Walter Page summed
up the educational tragedy of "Bourbonism" in the single phrase,
"The Forgotten Man." At that time, twenty-six per cent of the
white population of North Carolina above ten years of age was illiterate! Public education had not then become an interest of the
average person; the traditions of education as a luxury and a privilege of the rich and the well-born still lingered in the mind of the
common man. In 1900, three years after Page coined his phrase,
North Carolina spent a trifle more than $1,000,000 on her public
schools, and for a like sum valued the entire public school property
of the State; twenty-five years later she spent $34,000,000 on public
education and valued her public school property at $70,000,000.

Higher education has had a similar development. The old university at Chapel Hill, with its fine classical traditions, has passed; a new university has arisen from its ashes—a university, which, in the words of a well-known journalist, is not merely "a picked battalion of youth shining their intellectual armor at the feet of learned men," but is also "a great service bureau for the State, eager to serve, and eagerly sought for its counsel"; while at Durham, within a stone's throw of the ruins of Washington Duke's first log tobacco factory, is rising a noble institution in which James Buchanan Duke, in a unique way and with rare vision, has linked together the industrial and intellectual resources of the New South.—R. D. W. Connor, "The Rehabilitation of a Rural Commonwealth," *The American Historical Review*, XXXVI (October, 1930), 44-62.

169. Views of North Carolina Liberals on Industry, 1930

The following document was written by Frank Graham, president of the University of North Carolina, and was signed by three hundred and ninety citizens of the state. It expresses the social attitude of these liberal leaders toward industrial changes. It emphasizes the rights of free speech and collective bargaining, calls for an economic and social survey of the textile industry, and advocates social adjustments to industrial changes.

In this time of economic transition and industrial struggle, social attitudes are in process of formation critical with human meaning as to the sort of Commonwealth we are to become. It is in keeping with our North Carolina traditions that interested citizens try to look through the confusion and antagonisms of the hour to a few simple working principles born of our democratic experiment and experience. In our present situation when the old struggle for self-government has advanced from the religious and political to include the industrial life, four principles, evolved out of historic movements, stand out for our guidance now. On the preservation and adaptation of these principles turns today the search in an industrial society for that freedom of personality and equality of opportunity which this Commonwealth was founded to win for all our people.

First, that the constitutional and legal rights of person and property and lawful freedom of speech and assembly be guaranteed equally to all persons in this Commonwealth without regard to birthplace, race, ownership or labor status, unionism or non-unionism, religion, politics or economic views. The essential Americanism of this constitutional bill of rights, without faithless violation, can stand against the fallacies, fanaticism and violence of communism, fascism and anarchism with the due processes of light, liberty and law. By this very preservation of the ideals of American freedom, the fair and open resources of American democracy will prevail over class hatreds and dictatorships, economic unreason and social injustice.

Second, that just as the American principle of liberty guarantees the right of individual capitalists and the individual laborers to organize or not to organize, so the American principle of equal rights makes it logical that if one group organizes and bargains collectively the corresponding group has the same right to do so, with all attendant legal rights and responsibilities. This equal right of the investors of capital ànd management and the investors of human life and labor to bargain collectively, has been and is declared for in the national platforms of both the Democratic and Republican parties: is a part of the general historic process, and, despite abuses on both sides, this equal right, when fairly recognized and co-operatively promoted, becomes economically productive, democratically stabilizing and humanly valuable.

Third, that it is one of the working principles of self-government to find facts as a basis for democratic action. Since the textile industry is one of the national economic resources, conditioned by sectional, national and world economics, and involves the way of life for millions of the American people; and since the sickness of this industry, due to many complex factors, entails financial costs to stockholders, mental costs to managers and social costs to workers, who are human resources of the industry and the nation, it is advisable for the industry and the nation that a nation-wide nonpartisan economic and social survey and analysis of the textile industry be made at once.

Fourth, that even without this survey we find already written in the record of every modern Commonwealth that social adjustment must be made to industrial change. Since, in our Commonwealth, some social adjustments lag behind the industrial advance, it is, therefore, the part of social and industrial wisdom to make such clearly needed adjustments as the reduction of the legal 60-hour week, the gradual abolition of night work for women and young people, the modification or the elimination of the fourth-grade clause in the child labor law, and the adequate provision for supervision and enforcement of this social code by the Commonwealth.

As friends of industry involved in its well-being, and as citizens of a Commonwealth whose people are concerned with building, in patient time, a more humanly creative and spiritually beautiful civilization, we make this declaration to which we now sign our names and pledge our support.—*News and Observer*, February 16, 1930.

170. GOVERNOR GARDNER'S SURVEY OF HIS ADMINISTRATION

For ten years after the World War North Carolina "drove ahead on a program of progress that for sheer advance matches the record of any state in the Union." The state seemed to experience a new awakening. It spent vast sums of money for public education as the consolidated school movement swept the state. Expenditures for higher education increased tremendously. Highway development went forward at a rapid rate. New governmental departments were created and governmental functions expanded all along the line.

Recently it became imperative to call a halt and to take stock of the financial condition of state and local government. More and more the state has been following a policy of consolidation and centralization. It has taken over the public school system, the supervision of county finance, county roads, and it has established a centralized purchasing agency.

In an article in *The Saturday Evening Post,* Governor Gardner showed how North Carolina had "cleaned house."

IN 1931, North Carolina passed four acts of legislation largely without precedent in this nation. Each was revolutionary, but each was designed to meet the situation prevailing under changed economic conditions. North Carolina is traditionally a conservative state—next to the last to join the Union when it was formed, and the last to leave it when it was broken up—but it is not afraid to stand by itself. . . . At any rate, it pioneered in road legislation, in public-school legislation, in legislation for the control of local public debt, and in university consolidation.

After the war, North Carolina—traditionally conservative and stubbornly individualistic—stretched herself like a strong man after sleep. For ten years she drove ahead on a program of progress that for sheer advance matches the record of any state in the Union. The 1921 General Assembly authorized the issuance of $50,000,000 in bonds for state highways, and $7,000,000 for permanent improvements at state institutions—roughly, one third of a program which contemplated the expenditure of $20,000,000 in six years. In eight years we spent $160,000,000 of state and local funds for the state highway system, $90,000,000 for school buildings, and $32,000,000 for enlargement of state institutions. The counties, cities and districts followed the example of the state in providing permanent improvements and increasing local operating expenses. The annual tax bill of the state and local governments grew from $23,500,000 to $100,000,000. And for every dollar levied in taxes we had on the average an additional fifty cents of borrowed money to spend.

In carrying out such a sizable governmental program, mistakes and waste were inevitable. On the whole, we stepped too fast. Under a delusion of grandeur attributable in part to the fact that the Federal Government was collecting on the average more than $200,000,000 annually in revenue from and through North Carolina—last year more than from any other state except New York—we doubtless extended our spending too rapidly and made mistakes accordingly. But our mistakes were honest mistakes of judgment.

The good times stopped. The panic did not wait until 1931 to strike North Carolina. The fog and darkness, forerunning our present economic upset, were gradually settling over this state even before the crash in 1929. One of the most serious aspects of the intricate maze of interlocking difficulties that the state was grappling with, and that we lumped together under the head of economic depression, was the fact that North Carolina agriculture had become unprofitable. The farmer gave expression to his financial distress by manifesting his dissatisfaction with his tax burden, but his real ailment was more deep-seated and profound than he was led to believe. Agriculturally, North Carolina is a cash-crop state. Cotton and tobacco represent 50 per cent of our total agricultural production, and the market value of these crops fell $45,000,000 in two years.

NORTH CAROLINA LIVES AT HOME

. . . A survey conducted for the governor in 1929 developed the fact that between $150,000,000 and $175,000,000 regularly went out of North Carolina each year for the most primary agricultural products—corn, hay, foodstuffs and feedstuff. It was apparent that one important way to increase the actual income of farmers was to check this annual outflow of cash. We adopted the slogan "Live at Home," which, being liberally interpreted, means produce for your families and animals all the foodstuffs and feedstuff they consume, and then produce the cotton and tobacco that you can profitably grow as a surplus. The program did not involve the growing of food and feed crops for export. It was designed to meet the home consumption of North Carolina farm families. . . .

The results for the first two years have been most gratifying. We reduced our cotton acreage 536,000 acres and increased our corn production 10,000,000 bushels. This year the farm women canned more than twice as much fruits and vegetables as two years ago. . . . We increased our production of molasses more than 1,000,000 gallons. . . .

Another aspect of the live-at-home movement . . . is the effect it has had upon public health. A disease to which certain farm families are peculiarly subject is pellagra. This disease is the simple and direct result, physicians state, of an unbalanced ration. . . . The milk cow, the chicken and the vegetable garden have saved the cotton and tobacco farmer from doctor's bills for his family and have given him new health and ambition. . . .

In spite of the live-at-home movement, however, the trend of profits from agriculture continued downward. This trend was just as pronounced in other fields. . . . The swelling chorus was, "Taxes on property must be reduced." Revenues suffered substantial shrinkage. The governor cut state appropriations $3,000,000.

STATE CONTROL FOR THE ROADS

The most advanced legislation enacted was embraced in the administration bill for the state to take over the county roads. The governor's message proposed that on a given day the maintenance of every mile of public road in North Carolina should be transferred from the counties and townships to the state, that their support should be lifted from the county property tax, and that county boards should be prohibited from levying any tax for road maintenance. It also recommended that county prisoners sentenced to jails and chain gangs be transferred to the state, to be used in the construction and maintenance of roads and highways. More than 3,800 prisoners not sentenced to the state penitentiary were serving sentences in county jails and chain gangs. . . .

The magnitude of this proposal when first made jarred the complacency of the public mind. This shock can be appreciated when I state that it involved the abolition of more than 175 county and township road boards and the elimination of some 600 local road officials. . . . The transfer involved the state's assumption of an expenditure that was costing $8,250,000 a year. . . . By way of parenthesis, it may be stated that from the first day of July, 1931, to November first, the purchasing agent has saved the state more than $400,000 in the purchase of state supplies, materials and equipment.

. . . During the past ten years the counties had invested $125,000,000 in roads, and $100,000,000 of this stood on the books in the form of bonded debt. . . .

The bill as passed provided for: First, the transfer of the maintenance and support of all county roads to the state, the abolition of all county and township boards, and no tax levy by the counties for road maintenance or construction. Second, the maintenance of county roads from the gasoline tax, which was increased from five cents a gallon to six cents, and an appropriation of $6,000,000 a year made for county roads. Third, the designation of the boards of county commissioners as liaison units between local communities and the State Highway Commission, and the appointment of a state director of local roads to deal with local communities. Fourth, the transfer of all county prisoners and chain-gang camps from the counties to the state, and the employment of county prisoners on roads and highways, thus ridding us of our spotted chain-gang systems, relieving the counties of a burdensome and annually mounting expenditure, and permitting better treatment of prisoners. Fifth, the reorganization of the State Highway Commission with a chairman and six members representing the state at large instead of a chairman and nine district commissioners, each with large independent powers in his own district.

THE LOCAL GOVERNMENT ACT

The act of the legislature that attracted widest attention, that stabilized the credit of North Carolina counties and towns, that increased the confidence of the holders of North Carolina securities, that gave a new meaning to the phrase "local self-government," was the Local Government Act.

. . . Until 1927 we did not know what the local governments owed. When it was figured up, the sum staggered us, but it did not check our bond issues. A beginning was made in local-government reform in 1927, through the creation of a County Government Advisory Commission. In 1929 a further step was taken by requiring counties and cities to get the approval of the State Sinking Fund Commission for all bonds they proposed to issue. . . .

. . . North Carolina made up her mind that, in so far as could be legally done, she would preserve and protect her character and credit. Instead of passing the local bills authorizing the funding of current deficiencies, the finance committees formulated a plan with teeth in it for protecting the taxpayers against the despotic power of five-men boards to pile up public mortgages on property without limitation. They then created a Local Government Commission to enforce the act.

The most important power of the commission was its power to limit the incurring of additional debt. . . .

The act provides that bonds and notes of local units shall be sold by the commission in Raleigh instead of by the local boards. On the whole, this means better sales and lower interest rates. . . .

The commission is given supervision of the investment of sinking funds of local units—a most important function—and specifies the kind of securities they can be invested in. . . .

The act of the General Assembly which will have the deepest and the most enduring effect on the future of this commonwealth was the consolidation and merger of the three major state educational institutions into a greater University of North Carolina. The General Assembly passed, with only three dissenting votes, the administration bill to consolidate the University of North Carolina, located at Chapel Hill, the North Carolina State College of Agriculture and Engineering at Raleigh, and the North Carolina College for Women at Greensboro. Their combined enrollment is more than 6,000 students. . . .

The legislation which brought about the largest decrease in the cost of government and the greatest reduction in taxes on property was the public-school legislation. Early in the session the General Assembly voted complete state responsibility for the state public-school system and, after a two months' deadlock, provided for direct state support. It went further: At the outset of its school legislation the Assembly passed an act pledging the state to support the constitutional term from sources other than ad-valorem taxes on property. In most states the public-school system is supported mainly by district property taxes supplemented by county property taxes and of late years further supplemented by state aid. . . .

In 1931 the General Assembly reversed this policy of thirty years and boldly stepped up and embraced the principle of state responsibility for the constitutional school term. It enacted the MacLean Law, which provided that the six months' constitutional term should be supported by the state from sources other than ad-valorem taxes on property. The total expenditure for the operation of the six months' term last year was $22,000,000. Roughly, $17,000,000 of this was raised by property taxes and $5,000,000 from indirect sources. . . .

. . . The most substantial contribution of the 1931 General Assembly was to tackle and stop in its tracks the advancing tax burden for the first time in the modern history of North Carolina. It went further—it turned the curve of taxation definitely downward. The total cost of government was reduced $7,000,000, but the tax burden on property was reduced by more than $12,000,000 by the school and road legislation alone. These two acts provided an average reduction in county rates of more than forty cents on the hundred dollars of assessed value.—*The Saturday Evening Post*, January 2, 1932.

171. A VIRGINIA EDITOR'S APPRAISAL OF NORTH CAROLINA NEWSPAPERS, 1932

North Carolina has a number of newspapers which have attracted national attention, although there is not a paper in the state with as large a circulation as those of some of the largest Southern cities. Virginius Dabney, author of several books about the South and editor of the Richmond *Times-Dispatch,* has made some very complimentary remarks about the North Carolina press and about five papers in particular.

No Southern state boasts a more liberal press than North Carolina. If the Charlotte *Observer* has abandoned the principles of Tompkins and Caldwell and become a mouthpiece of Bourbonism and reaction, and if the *Southern Textile Bulletin* of the same city is even worse, there are other journals in the Old North State which stand for decency and intelligence.

Foremost among them, perhaps, is the Greensboro *News,* edited by Earle Godbey. This paper is notable for the enlightenment of its views no less than for the urbanity of the language in which those views are expressed. When Gerald W. Johnson was on its editorial staff, the *News* held undisputed sway in the state, and was the mouthpiece of North Carolina liberalism. Mr. Johnson finally resigned to become professor of journalism at Chapel Hill and, incidentally, to contribute to leading magazines many brilliantly penetrating critiques dealing with various aspects of Southern civilization. Subsequently he joined the editorial staff of the Baltimore *Evening Sun,* where he is not only continuing his journalistic work, but at the same time is contributing frequently to periodicals and publishing characteristically provocative biographical studies of Southern figures. The loss of Mr. Johnson, whose contribution to liberal causes in the South during the past dozen years has been of the first importance, was naturally a heavy one for the Greensboro *News*. But Mr. Godbey is carrying on in the same liberal tradition, and his editorial page is read today by those who enjoy a combination of sound writing with equally sound ideas.

Josephus Daniels's Raleigh *News and Observer* has been metamorphosed since it led the pack against John Spencer Bassett nearly thirty years ago. It is still erratic in some respects, and its publisher's relationship with the Democratic party causes it to be astonishingly naive at times in its analyses of political issues. On the other hand the *News and Observer* is probably the most fearless paper in the South in its attitude toward economics and industrial questions. The textile and tobacco interests, the two most powerful commercial groups in North Carolina, are treated as cavalierly by Mr. Daniels as if they controlled no advertising. In his advocacy of the right of laboring men to organize in unions and his excoriation of the reactionary textile element, he has exhibited independence of the highest order. He has been fortunate, too, in having on his staff Miss Nell Battle Lewis, whose Sunday column has been a widely read feature of the paper for a good many years. In Miss Lewis's keenly discriminating mind are combined boldness and intelligence, unwavering resolution and openminded tolerance. Her liberal influence has extended beyond the confines of her native state.

Robert Lathan, who presides over the editorial page of the Asheville *Citizen*, was formerly with the Charleston, South Carolina, *News and Courier*, where his "The Isolation of the South" won a Pulitzer prize. This editorial set forth courageously and sanely the need for adequate political leadership below the Potomac.

Two smaller papers in North Carolina which are deserving of attention are the Elizabeth City *Independent*, edited by W. O. Saunders, and the Chapel Hill *Weekly*, edited by Louis Graves. Mr. Saunders has a penchant for clowning but he is in many ways a man of sense. Mr. Graves is a balanced liberal whose weekly paper has a distinctive flavor.—Virginius Dabney, *Liberalism in the South*, pp. 406-8.

XIII

NORTH CAROLINA IN RECENT YEARS

172. THE NEGRO IN MODERN NORTH CAROLINA

The Negro made marked progress in North Carolina during the two decades after 1920 and there was less evidence of race prejudice than in most Southern states. The most significant and the most hopeful aspect of this advancement was in the field of education.

One of the most distinguished Negro leaders in the state for many years was Dr. James E. Shepard, President of the North Carolina College in Durham. This able college executive commanded the respect of both races and his address on the race question on the Town Hall program received the praise of many national newspapers. One of Dr. Shepard's finest statements on this question was his speech delivered under the auspices of the Negro Grand Lodge of Masons and broadcast over various radio stations of the state.

Dr. Clyde Erwin, State Superintendent of Public Instruction, gave a good summary of Negro Education in the state in his Biennial Report for 1941-42.

THE PRESENT STATUS OF THE NEGRO: AN APPEAL TO THE PEOPLE OF NORTH CAROLINA, 1941

NORTH CAROLINA has always taken the lead in providing educational facilities for the Negroes of the State. There are five state-supported colleges for the education of the Negro. Each one of these institutions is accomplishing wonderful work. Each one is necessary, and each one is doing work which is reducing crime, promoting efficiency, teaching lessons of health and thrift, and thus reducing the load of the taxpayers, and at the same time promoting good will between the races. She has realized that it is far better to tax for the advancement of our educational institutions for both the white and colored race than to provide for the maintenance and establishment of penal institutions. It is far better to prevent the large waste of human material before it has drifted than to attempt to save it after it has drifted.

This is no time at present to speak about economy when it comes to the maintenance of our educational institutions, and the salaries of our public school teachers. These are the first line of defense.

We are proud of the fact that North Carolina was the first State to provide an insane asylum for the Negro race, the first deaf, dumb, and blind institution, the first department of public welfare, the first to start a public health program. This program has grown to such proficiency that it has been used as an example as to what a State can do along the line of public health for a minority group. North Carolina was the second State to establish a far-reaching set-up of the NYA for our group.

I believe that there is more good will between the races of North Carolina than can be found anywhere else. Therefore, I join in saying: "God Bless North Carolina!" Her sons both white and black are proud of her. While we live our best can be given to her. Our utmost strength shall be given to the development of her resources, and the spread of good will so that in the galaxy of states no state shall be more justly proud than our own glorious State.

There are certain things, however, which will greatly help in our program of peace, our general advancement, and prosperity. No one argues the question: "Does education pay?" Those who fail to recognize this indisputable fact are simply green and need to ripen. . . .

To the everlasting credit of North Carolina, the Gaines Decision did not frighten our State. Ten years before, Dr. N. C. Newbold and the North Carolina State Department of Education had envisaged a plan for the enriched education of the Negro. They had planned for teachers colleges which would grant degrees in education instead of two-year normal schools with a limited curriculum. They desired to see a university for Negroes. Their plans are almost consummated. Their ideals are almost realized. We have three four-year Teachers Colleges. We have an Agricultural and Technical College which is destined to be the greatest agricultural and technical college in the South, and we are on the way to having a great university for Negroes where they can be trained in liberal arts, science, home economics, law, library science, health, and to go even beyond the master's degree. In the first place because it is just, and in the second place because it is needed. There must be consecrated trained leadership for, where there is no vision the people perish.

North Carolina has advanced without any court decision to settle the matter of differential to pay between white and colored teachers holding the same certificate, and having the same experience and training. For two years the State School Commission has increased the salary of Negro teachers of North Carolina about

‹300,000 annually. This was done without pressure from any source, but simply as an act of justice because those who were in the lead desired to do so. As a result there is a spirit of hopefulness and satisfaction on the part of the Negro teachers, and they would not murmur nor complain. To the credit of white teachers, they have helped in this matter. They have stood aside willing to wait until salaries were equalized, and then let all go up the hill together, and work for a new day and a new order of things . . . when teachers would come fully into their own. . . .

I am moved to these optimistic remarks by the history of our State. There have been during these forty years of the present century eleven chief executives. I certify to the younger generation of my people that not one of them rose to his eminence by appeal to racial prejudices, and that most of them are esteemed today in proportion to their friendliness to the Negro. The glorious records of Aycock, Bickett, Morrison, McLean, Gardner, Ehringhaus, Hoey, and Broughton are testimonies in behalf of this statement. A few days ago our big-hearted Christian Governor joined in the celebration of the 75th anniversary of a great Negro church. I said to myself again, "God ʋless North Carolina!" What a contrast—governors in some states not as fortunate as ours seek to stir up strife and discord, instead of sowing the seeds of Christian love.

North Carolina, a great civilized and Christian community, recognizing substantially the rights and privileges of our group, has gone ahead of its neighbors as though they were of a different race of men. If North Carolina were not too Christian to indulge in race repression, it is too enlightened and too thoughtful of its intelligent self-interest to do so. That is a great gain for us all.

Because I believe so deeply in the innate righteousness of North Carolinians, I am standing against recourse to litigation to hasten the ending of those discriminations which were identified in the earlier moments of this address. Courts are very excellent institutions and both our state and federal jurisdictions have been quick to interpret the organic as well as the statutory laws favorable to our litigants. But I do not need to tell you that in most courts friendships end and feuds begin. What I regard as supremely important is the trend in current life. If the tendencies run in the direction of greater friendship and wider doors of opportunity, it is my conviction that rights are won more quickly and the gains from them are held more securely by the friendlier processes of our democracy. I hope that it will never be necessary to appeal to our courts.

After all, democracy is more than a form of government, and the democratic process means more than election by majorities, government by legislatures and congresses, laws executed by governors and presidents, interpreted by courts state and federal. Democracy is that audacious belief of our people that in the most ordinary men there are resident the most extraordinary possibilities, and that if we keep the doors of opportunity open to them they will amaze us with their achievements. For that reason I trust more to the generous and Christian attitude of our North Carolina people in making the needed social, political and economic re-adjustment than I do to congresses and all other legal parliaments. North Carolina has learned that it is not the public interest that any of its citizens should be reared in ignorance and live in poverty. And once we set ourselves with informed and illuminated consciences to these tasks all auxiliary and incidental questions will settle themselves. Whether we work through the social gospel into personal religion, or the other way around, we are coming to the gist of this whole matter when we agree that the saving of our democracy is personal religion, a belief in the divine parenthood of the human family. I, for one, do not believe it will ever be necessary again for any North Carolinian to stand up and ask his State to be democratic and Christian. In these two qualities will be found the soul of our State.—James E. Shepard, November 24, 1941.

STATE SUPERINTENDENT OF PUBLIC INSTRUCTION'S REPORT ON NEGRO EDUCATION, 1942-44

Beginning with the school year 1944-45 the salaries of white and Negro teachers paid from State funds were equalized. This final act of the State Board of Education was in accordance with the intention of the General Assembly of 1943, which made a final appropriation, under a plan begun several years ago, for the elimination of the differential existing between the two schedules used as a basis for the payment of teachers' salaries.

Believing that the schools for Negroes need further improvement, Governor Broughton recommended to the State Board of Education that a study be made of the Negro public schools and colleges of the State. That study has now been completed and a report including recommendations has been prepared and submitted to the State Board of Education. This report envisages a program covering a period of years for its final completion for im-

proving the public school facilities for Negroes. The report suggests a number of ways by which the Negro schools may be further
improved. I heartily endorse any plans that may be projected by
the General Assembly in line with the recommendations made by
the committee which made this study. If the State can render to the
local authorities any assistance in providing better educational facilities in order that the doors of educational opportunity of this race
may be opened wider, I hope this may be started at once. The
present provisions for education for many children of this race are
meagre, to say the least. Better education for Negroes will not only
raise the level of the race itself—it will improve the citizenship of the
State as a whole. I commend to your careful consideration, therefore,
this report in an attempt to help in the solution of some of the problems surrounding this question.—*Biennial Report of the Superintendent of Public Instruction of North Carolina*, Part I, p. 110.

173. NORTH CAROLINA'S CONTRIBUTION TO WORLD WAR II

The following documents give an excellent summary of North
Carolina's military, industrial, and financial contributions to World
War II. The first two statements are taken from addresses by Kenneth C. Royall of Goldsboro, Under Secretary of War, and the third
document is from a report by Allison James, Executive Manager of
the War Finance Committee for North Carolina.

NORTH CAROLINA'S MILITARY CONTRIBUTION
TO THE WAR

IT IS a North Carolina habit to furnish its full quota to America's
Armed Forces in every war—to do its full part in the military and
naval services. . . .

And in World War II we did our full share—and more. From
the State's total population of less than 3,600,000, 362,000 young
North Carolinians entered the Armed Services. About 258,000 of
these were in the Army, 90,000 in the Navy, 13,000 in the Marines,
and the remainder in the other Armed Services, including the Coast
Guard.

Most of these young men were inducted under the Selective
Service program, but many of them were volunteers. You will all
recall that, when the Selective Service Act first went into effect,
some counties in North Carolina did not have to furnish their first
quotas, because the volunteers already had furnished the required

number. At least 35,000 North Carolinians—perhaps more—volunteered for service. . . .

In the service of North Carolinians in our Armed Forces, "something new has been added" in this war—the large-scale service of women in uniform. There were many North Carolina women who served well and faithfully as members of the WAC, WAVES, as nurses, as medical technicians, and in other capacities.

About four thousand were in the Army, two thousand in the Navy. These women performed—in all echelons of command—valuable service for the nation—service that, in many instances, would have had to be performed by men in uniform—men who were thus available for combat or for heavier tasks. . . .

I know many will be interested to know that in this war the 30th division . . . took a leading part in the battles of France and Germany—and that the 81st, on the other side of the world, distinguished itself in the Pacific and helped in the liberation of the Philippines.

But in World War II North Carolina could not be associated primarily with any particular division or unit. North Carolinians served in every unit which fought in Africa and Europe under Eisenhower, or Patton, or Hodges, or Bradley—or, in the Pacific, under MacArthur, Kreuger, Nimitz or Vandergrift. . . .

Our State paid with the lives of between 7,000 and 8,000 of her young men. Many others were casualties—who will carry grievous wounds of war during the remainder of their lives. No North Carolina city, no town, no rural section escaped. These boys, the dead and living wounded, are real heroes of this war—these boys and those living who were awarded decorations for valor. These are the men to whom our State and every part thereof should never fail to pay tribute. . . .

After considering the record of our young men in the Armed Forces—particularly in the combat forces—any other subject must, in a sense, be an anti-climax. But there is one important fact that our State should never forget—its opportunity—during the entire war —to see and to help so many soldiers who came from other States.

North Carolina was a State of camps and military installations—many and large. Fort Bragg was—and is—one of the largest Army camps in the country—with its 122,000 acres and its 3,135 buildings and its maximum load at nearly 100,000 men. And it was the most comprehensive of Army installations, performing more different functions than any other camp.

Camp Lejeune on our mid-coast is the second largest Marine

camp in the country. There is Cherry Point, one of the largest Marine Air Bases in the nation—Camp Davis, one of the large Infantry camps. Camp Mackall, the second largest Airborne training center in the country, where the famous 82nd and 101st Airborne Divisions, and also the 11th and 13th trained.

There is Camp Butner, home of the 78th Infantry or Lightning Division and of the 35th Infantry Division and many service troops. There were large air installations at Greensboro and Goldsboro; and Marine and Navy air installations at Elizabeth City and Edenton, and the Navy receiving station and training center at Wilmington.

I cannot mention them all. The Army alone had installations in 37 communities. There were Army and Navy installations—large and small—air fields, specialized installations, others—throughout the State.

I cannot pass unnoticed the civilians, more than twelve thousand in number, who worked with and for the Army and Navy in the hundreds of camps, posts and stations in the State—and helped in the training and other functions.

In these installations were trained more than 2,000,000 of our fighting men. We take pride in the fact that many of these men and officers learned in our fields and woods, and on our hills and in our valleys, the fighting technique that won the battles of Europe and of the Pacific. . . .

Many of the men who later commanded divisions, corps, and armies—as well as thousands who commanded small units—and as well as many who served in the ranks—got their first real training in modern combat conditions here in North Carolina.—Kenneth C. Royall, May 23, 1946.

NORTH CAROLINA'S INDUSTRIAL CONTRIBUTION TO THE WAR

Almost $2,000,000,000 was spent in North Carolina directly by the Armed Forces in connection with the direct purchase of manufactured war supplies and material.

This figure does not include subcontracting, that is, the amounts sold by North Carolina industries to producers who, in turn, sold direct to the Government. Exact figures on this are not available. But it is certain that they would add a very large amount to the total—much larger than the figure for direct purchases on prime contracts. . . .

North Carolina's manufactured goods, which ultimately went to the Armed Forces, thus totalled several billion dollars. And there was another large business activity in our State—the construction industry—which produced nearly a half billion dollars in Army and Navy cantonments, airfields, and military installations—and also produced for defense homes, and housing projects, and public works connected therewith,—many more millions of dollars.

Rounding out the war supply picture were the products of our farms . . . and the products of our mines and our forests. Quantities of cotton, lumber, tobacco, mica, bauxite—even some uranium—went into the weapons and supplies of war. For example, mica, a scarce article, was essential for fractional motors. . . .

Eighty-three of North Carolina's major industrial plants manufactured and sold direct to these defense agencies $1,358,000,000 worth of war material.

But scattered throughout North Carolina were small plants, manufacturing goods for the Army and Navy. . . . These lesser shops manufactured many articles under subcontracts, the figures for which are not included in our totals. . . .

There is scarcely a town of any size in North Carolina which was not, during the war years, engaged in war production—usually in several plants, sometimes in many—turning out items that found their way to the Army and Navy for use on the battlefields or behind the lines. . . .

North Carolina delivered to the Quartermaster Corps more textile goods than did any other state—sheets, blanket, clothing, tents, bandages, parachutes—not to mention tire cords and fabrics, which were sold on subcontracts. We were the world center for fine-combed yarn.

At Kure Beach, the Ethyl-Dow plant manufactured all the tetraethyl lead used in the war—and almost all produced in the country. We supplied more than 50 per cent of all the sheet and punch and circle mica. We were the fourth state in the production of lumber for the Armed Forces.

Other outstanding contributions included the secret work at Durham by a sudsidiary of Sperry Corporation, also Corbitt trucks from Henderson, concrete floating dry docks at Wilmington, chemicals from Canton, more than 4,000 tons a month of aluminum from Badin, the cigarettes and tobaccos from several localities, two million pounds a month of high tenacity rayon from Enka.

There were also hosiery, surgical instruments, aeroplane components and parts, bedding, guns, explosives, electrical equipment, chemicals, foods, landing craft, and many other important products. . . .

And there was not only quantity and speed. There was also quality. Many North Carolina products became symbols for good workmanship. . . . Twenty-eight of the industrial plants in this State received a total of 72 Army-Navy "E" awards for outstanding war production records. . . .

Five plants won five awards each: Chatham Manufacturing Company, Cramerton Mills, Edwards Company at Sanford, National Munitions Corporation at Carrboro, and Wright's Automatic Machinery Company at Durham.

Three won four awards: Aluminum Company at Badin, Marshall Field and Company at Spray, and U. S. Rubber Company at Charlotte.

Four won three awards: Ethyl-Dow Chemical Company, Firestone Textiles at Gastonia, P. H. Hanes Knitting Company at Winston-Salem, and North Carolina Finishing Company at Salisbury. . . .

An "M", or Maritime award, was made to the North Carolina Ship Corporation at Wilmington, which turned out 126 Liberty ships and 232 other ships, up to the end of 1945, of the value of more than 475 million dollars.

These companies were of all sizes. . . . One of the plants employed more than 5,500 workers—one employed only 68. . . .

Such is the story of North Carolina industry in war. The results attained are a tribute not only to North Carolina patriotism, but also to North Carolina ingenuity in devising new and better ways to accomplish results. The credit for thus supporting our fighting forces goes to management for wise planning, sound industrial leadership, and improved production processes—and to North Carolina workers for long hours and intelligent work—and better results.— Kenneth C. Royall, May 24, 1946.

THE WAR FINANCE PROGRAM IN NORTH CAROLINA, MAY 1, 1941–JANUARY 3, 1946

The War Finance Program in North Carolina, as in other states, consisted of the promotion of the sale of Series E, F and G Savings Bonds continuously from May 1, 1941, through January 3, 1946, and the promotion of seven War Loan Drives and a Victory Loan Drive during this period in which Savings Notes and marketable securities also were offered.

The Series E Bond, the "people's" savings bond, was the security that was principally relied on for sale to small investors. From May 1, 1941, through January 3, 1946, a total of $527 million was invested in E Bonds by men, women and children of North Carolina.

Total sales of all securities including Series E Bonds in North Carolina from May 1, 1941 through January 3, 1943 amounted to $1,811,000,000. . . .

This greatest financing program of all times was carried out in North Carolina and in other states through the patriotic work of thousands of volunteers, men, women and children. Volunteer War Finance Committee chairmen in each county of the state were appointed by the State War Finance Committee, and had charge of organizing and directing the county volunteer workers who, during the eight War Loan Drives and the in-between-drive periods, made house-to-house, farm-to-farm, industry-to-industry canvasses to promote Bond sales. They distributed posters and pamphlets, and took part in special Bond rallies and Bond shows displaying military equipment made available by Army and Navy camps in North Carolina.

North Carolina schools, primary, grade schools, high schools and colleges were, and are continuing to be, a great factor in carrying the Savings Bond messages into the homes, as well as investing their savings in Bonds and Stamps through the Schools' Thrift Program. During the war teachers and pupils in North Carolina schools and colleges sponsored millions of dollars worth of planes, jeeps, ships, ambulances and hospital equipment, both by purchasing and selling more than $43,074,388.45 in Bonds and Stamps.—Allison James, Executive Manager of the War Finance Committee.

174. PLANNING FOR POSTWAR INDUSTRY IN NORTH CAROLINA

Much was said and written about postwar planning in North Carolina, and the state created a State Planning Board, whose work was of inestimable value. Two of the finest statements made on this important subject were by R. D. W. Connor, formerly National Archivist and later Craige Professor of Jurisprudence and History at the University of North Carolina, and by Harriet Herring of the Institute of Social Research of the University of North Carolina. The first document below is Professor Connor's statement, and the second that of Miss Herring.

POSTWAR PLANNING IN NORTH CAROLINA
AFTER WORLD WAR II

WE HAD by no means solved the problem inherited from the Civil War and Reconstruction when the irresistible forces of the past swept our country into the maelstrom of the First World War. Unlike our previous wars, the battles of the World War were fought in lands and on seas so remote from us that we failed to understand what they were doing to our American way of life; postwar prophets complacently assured us that when the boys came home all we had to do was to forget the war and take the road back to normalcy. And hardheaded, practical America fell for this soul-satisfying philosophy.

But the past is inexorable. History does repeat itself, and there is nothing new under the sun. In 1920 North Carolina, like the rest of the country, took up where she had left off in 1917 in the comfortable assurance that the future called for no new plans but merely for the continuance and expansion of the old. And so the State turned her energies to the construction of highways, the building of schools, the creation of modern social welfare agencies, and the conservation and development of her natural resources.

Nothing better illustrates her approach to her post-World War problems than the scientific manner in which the State and private enterprise have cooperated in the development of her waterpower. It was state surveys that revealed to the world the immense horsepower that lay dormant in streams which for centuries had been wasting their waters in the vastness of the Atlantic. Why not harness them in the service of man? The State propounded the query; private enterprise answered it. A North Carolina capitalist led the way, and hydroelectric power plants rose like magic along the banks of our streams; like magic, mills and factories sprang into being and following ever-lengthening transmission lines soon converted thousands of square miles of wilderness into hives of industry. Lengthening transmission lines explains one of the most striking phases of the industrialization of North Carolina. They have industrialized this rural commonwealth without destroying its rural character. The United States Census of 1940 classifies 73 per cent of the State's population as rural. Nor have industries become localized. Cotton mills, tobacco factories, furniture factories, aluminum plants, lumber mills, and a thousand other kinds of industrial enterprises exist side by side. This means, of course, that North Carolina has not concentrated her industries into one or two great centers by draining the rest of the State of its wealth and its population.

But it is only when this economic development is translated into terms of social development that its full significance appears. The old Commonwealth against which the farmers revolted in the nineties was primarily a political institution; the new Commonwealth of the twentieth century is primarily a social institution. Public interest in education, art, sports, health, public welfare, labor problems, race relations, and other social problems has almost driven politics off the front page of the newspaper. The half a hundred public charitable, correctional and cultural agencies and institutions, and as many private ones, created since 1900, bear witness to this fact. Since 1920 the public school budget has quadrupled, the value of public school property has increased five-fold. The old University at Chapel Hill, with its fine classical traditions, had been transformed into a university system of three constituent institutions devoted to research and teaching in all the branches of knowledge required by a modern state. Church colleges have kept pace and one of them, by linking together in a unique way the economic and intellectual resources of the State, has won its place among the great universities of the world.

North Carolina has not been unmindful of her promise of social justice for the Negro. Although much remains to be done, much has been done to make good that promise. Upward of 275,000 Negro children are enrolled in the public schools; the State supports three training schools for Negro teachers, and two colleges for Negro youths, and graduates of the North Carolina College for Negroes are accredited for admission into the graduate schools of the nation's leading universities—a distinction enjoyed by only three other colleges for Negroes. A state hospital for Negroes, a state orphanage for their fatherless children, and a state training school for their youthful delinquents, are guardians of the unfortunates of the race. The spirit of mutual confidence manifested by these things has tempered the prejudices of the whites and allayed the apprehensions of the blacks. You have heard *ad nauseam* that the Southern white understands the Negro; as a factor in the solution of the race problem it is even more important that the Negro understands the Southern white.

Since 1783 North Carolina has travelled far along the highway of progress. In January, 1837, when the American Union consisted of only twenty-five states, the first governor of North Carolina elected by the people summed up North Carolina's situation in his Inaugural Address in which he said: "As a state we stand fifth in population, first in climate, equal in soil, minerals and ores, with superior advantages for manufacturing and with a hardy, industrious and economical people. Yet, with such unequalled natural facilities, we are actually last in the scale of relative wealth and enterprise, and our condition daily becomes worse—lands depressed in price, fallow and deserted—manufacturing advantages unimproved—our stores of mineral wealth undisturbed, and our colleges and schools languishing from neglect."

In 1944, of course, we make a much better showing. Among the 48 states, we rank 27th in area, 14th in assessed valuation of property, and 11th in population. But by all the other tests of what constitutes a great American state, North Carolina still ranks among the lowest ten. It is evident that her destination is still over the hills and far away; but wise planning and intelligent, courageous leadership will enable her to surmount these obstacles.

North Carolina did not get to her present position by accident. Somebody charted her course, and what past generations can plan and do, the present and future generations can plan and do. If Governor Broughton and his successors, following the example of Governor Dudley, will furnish the leadership, they can count on the people of North Carolina to transform the field of jimson weed which Governor Martin saw in 1783 into the garden of roses which Governor Broughton visualized in 1943.—R. D. W. Connor, in *Popular Government*, August, 1944, pp. 14, 17.

PLANNING FOR POSTWAR INDUSTRY

. . . By the 1890's the great textile centers of the Northeast were uneasy over southern competition; soon after the turn of the century they conceded the manufacture of coarse yarns and cloth. By 1925 North Carolina had passed Massachusetts as a textile state.

FURNITURE AND TOBACCO

In this community effort and achievement North Carolina was part of a southern movement. The development of the furniture industry was more localized in this state. But many of the same features were present: local resources of suitable woods, plentiful labor already partially accustomed to the work through carpentry and saw-milling; young entrepeneurs like Snow, Wrenn, Tomlinson, the Tates, Harriss at High Point, Huntley at Winston-Salem, the Lambeths and Finch at Thomasville, Hedrick at Lexington, eager for fields of endeavor more promising than the old routine offered; their towns, as well as Statesville, Morganton, Asheboro, just as eager for pay rolls and more population, communities approving the manufactures, supporting them, proud of them.

The growth of the tobacco industry in North Carolina was similar to furniture in all these respects, though here the part of the enterpriser was more striking because it succeeded more strikingly. In 1880 North Carolina had 126 little tobacco manufactories. Several around Durham and Winston-Salem were already beginning to stand out in size compared with others in surrounding counties. Reynolds in Winston-Salem needed money for enlargements to keep abreast of the demand. He sought it from neighbors, employees, and fellow townsmen. They responded because they had confidence in him and his growing business. The foundations of many substantial fortunes in Winston-Salem go back to this community faith in the manufacture of a local product by a local enterpriser with drive and ability.

Duke, on the other hand, faced toward the bigger sources of bigger money. A promoter with financial as well as manufacturing and merchandizing genius, he gathered millions from investors all over the country to manufacture North Carolina tobacco in North Carolina and elsewhere. With capital built up from the profits, he entered the new field of hydroelectric power in 1904. The development of the Catawba River proceeded systematically and scientifically as markets for electric current increased; manufacturing increased in its power province because the current was available. This was a parallel process nudged along and stimulated by Southern Power, later Duke Power Company: a new dam when there were more customers; persuasion, sometimes it must be admitted, pinching deals to bring in established users to take the surplus current of the new dam. Duke Foundation with its ramifications followed after time had tempered some of the bitterness of the older battles. When Senator Cameron Morrison described the Duke Power Company as almost a benevolent institution, the cynical intelligentsia sneered a little; but many people in North Carolina, proud of the shining new university, grateful for hospital grants and minister's pensions, were inclined to agree.

These are the economic kingdoms that have been conquered by the enterprise of individual sons of North Carolina, carved out of its resources of material, labor, position, and climate, and aided by community support and approval. They all reached their maturity before the first world war. Since that time, though North Carolina has seen growth in these and other manufacturing lines, no new industry of similar magnitude has seized the imagination of individual enterprisers and of the community. During this period the

United States has seen great new industries rise or attain their major growth: automobiles, rubber, petroleum products, airplanes, mechanical appliances, chemicals, specialized food processing. Is North Carolina in a rut that it has had little or no share in the newer industries, in producing the goods which are commanding an increasing part of the consumer's dollar, which are demanding new skills and offering new opportunities?

TEXTILES, WOOD, TOBACCO

It is certainly undeniable that in its manufacturing industries North Carolina has concentrated on textiles, wood, and tobacco. In 1939 the state had 270,000 wage earners in manufacturing. Of these 180,000, or 66.7 per cent were in textile mill products. There were 37,600, or 14 per cent, in wood (about half in furniture) and 16,500, or 6.1 per cent, in tobacco. Thus these three groups account for 86.8 per cent of the state's wage earners in manufacturing.

In other great groups like rubber, products of petroleum and coal, non-ferrous metals and electrical machinery which together employ about three-fourths of a million workers, North Carolina had none. In iron and steel, machinery, transportation equipment, and leather, great groups which employ a total of nearly 2½ million workers, North Carolina had less than 5,000. Even in five great groups, food products, paper, printing, chemicals, stone, clay and glass—which include many industries carried on on a local service basis. North Carolina had less than 20,000 out of a total of over 2 millions.

The Census of Manufactures of 1939 divides manufacturing in the United States into 446 industries. North Carolina had establishments representing 191 of these classifications, though in 67 it had only one plant. . . .

FAVORABLE LOCATION

North Carolina is on the way between the raw sugar of the West Indies and the markets of the Northeast just as conveniently as Savannah is. It is on the way between the coffee, meat and hides of South America and the markets of the seaboard just as conveniently as New Orleans, Maryland, New Jersey, and Massachusetts. It is on the road by which the wool and grain of Australia come to the east coast via the Panama Canal, as well as the tin of Malaya when we regain access to it. . . .

In the case of wood products there are more possibilities for improvement. . . . With the experience and skill already existing it should not be difficult for North Carolina to make better furniture.

It might be necessary to secure fine woods from elsewhere but New York and Illinois do this and, for that matter, so does some of the North Carolina industry. There are a number of small wood industries which are growing and are desirable by all measures, among them screens, wood preserving, and to a lesser extent caskets and coffins.

But the forest resources of the state need not be used only as wood. . . . North Carolina has some pulp manufacturing and should have more, both because of its value as an industry per se, and because the long-term needs of such an industry work in well with planned forestry, another of the crying needs of North Carolina.

MORE FINISHED PRODUCTS

The manufacture of pulp brings us to another class of manufacturing which North Carolina needs, namely, the further processing of its semi-finished products. North Carolina has 4 per cent of the pulp industry in the United States. It has only 1 per cent of the paper and paper board industry, less than that of the converted paper products, about 0.2 per cent of the book and periodical printing. All these are growing industries. . . .

The wood-pulp-paper-printing series is an illustration of conditions in many branches of southern and North Carolina industry, the processing of natural resources through the primary stages and passing the semi-finished product on to other states and regions where more labor is employed, more skill applied, and more profits derived. Other examples are to be found in the processing of mica, peanuts, cottonseed, soybeans, fruits and berries. . . .

And the fact is that North Carolina's agriculture needs balancing quite as badly as its manufacturing. There is the same concentration in a single crop in some countries, cotton which North Carolina cannot produce profitably in competition with the deep South; in others, tobacco, a bonanza in some years and a tragedy in others; in one area peanuts, which are sold at the price of fodder and brought back at the price of confections; in smaller areas peaches or berries or watermelons which must go in their perishable freshness to the big centers of population whence they send back sometimes fat checks and sometimes bills for the freight. The state has an enormous deficit of animals and animal products which means a deficit in the diet of dairy products and protein meats, a deficit in animal manures for restoring the soil, a deficit in leguminous feed and cover crops which build up the soil and prevent erosion. . . .

North Carolina has 2.72 per cent of the population of the United States, but it has less than 1 per cent of the food manufacture. More of these industries would help the soil and the farmer, employ labor and capital and save hauling from half across a continent all sorts of food and feed from butter to laying mash.

There are other great branches of manufacturing which meet our tests of desirability and even the test of practicability for North Carolina if pushed with vigor and imagination. Chemicals is one. North Carolina has a reasonable proportion of only two, fertilizers and rayon. . . .

But the great recent expansion has been in industrial chemicals. The expansion in the immediate future is expected to be in an extension of industrial chemicals, namely, plastics. Is North Carolina to run along in its textile manufacturing rut as it did in its cotton growing rut until other states and regions have done the pioneering and skimmed the cream off the new industry? Will it, a decade or a century late, find its wood resources gone, need materials for its houses and tables and chairs and then by a super-human effort break into plastics after this exciting new industry has become an old settled member of the manufacturing hierarchy?

There is one other great group of industries which North Carolina lacks, the iron-steel machinery series. It seems unlikely, under present methods of utilization, that North Carolina has deposits of iron, coal and limestone rich enough for the first stages in this industry. . . . Nor does North Carolina have the skills to manufacture intricate machinery out of iron and steel purchased from Alabama and Pennsylvania. . . .

But it can begin in a small way to train some of its own people to make some of the less elaborate machinery and thus build up the skills as Connecticut, Ohio, and Illinois have built them up. North Carolina used much textile machinery and will need enormous replacements in the post-war period. It makes a little and so has a nucleus for beginning. The state would do well to offer more inducements and give more acclaim to a spinning frame works than to a shirt factory. North Carolina uses much woodworking machinery; it makes practically none. It uses some—not enough—farm machinery but when good oak wagons and plows were replaced by trucks and tractors some thriving North Carolina factories curled up and died. . . .

Can North Carolina build and operate these industries? Two generations ago North Carolina needed something to help its depressed agriculture, to employ its half idle, to enliven its dead little towns. Men motivated by the desire for profit and by the community need projected industries as unfamiliar as any of these. Citizens supported them by subscribing capital. Workers flocked willingly to the mills. Every community agency joined in acclaiming them and in defending them against every criticism.

Surely we have enterprisers now with as much vigor and daring, workers with as much will to learn. We have more citizens with more money. We have more newspapers and more people who know how to read them. We have more organizations with promotional machinery—chambers of commerce, state departments—to supply information. We even have a greater need. We must make it profitable —not just a duty—for our agriculture to preserve our soil. We must offer our workers employment that is worthy of their toil, not just a collection of what have become of the least desirable industries in the country. We must offer our gifted youth opportunities suited to their talents. What North Carolina has done once, surely in a changed and changing world it can do again.—Harriet Herring in The University of North Carolina *News Letter,* Vol. XXX, Nos. 7 and 8, April 5 and 19, 1944.

175. THE UNIVERSITY OF NORTH CAROLINA IN RECENT YEARS

The thirty year period 1935-65 witnessed a tremendous expansion in the physical plants and a great increase in the number of students at all three branches of the University of North Carolina. Student enrollment for the school year 1963-64 was: 10,887 at Chapel Hill, 8,200 at Raleigh, and 3,900 at Greensboro. By action of the General Assembly in 1963, the Woman's College was made co-educational and the name was changed to the University of North Carolina at Greensboro. The community (Junior) college at Charlotte became a four-year college and later was changed to the University of North Carolina at Charlotte. The General Assembly of 1965 changed the name of the Raleigh branch to North Carolina State University at Raleigh. Thus, in 1965, there were four "branches" of the University of North Carolina and there was a general feeling that more "branches" would be added in the future.

The first document below is taken from *A Ten Year Review: The University of North Carolina, 1934-1944* by President Frank Graham. The second document is from *The President's Report, 1963-1964* by President William Friday.

REPORT OF PRESIDENT FRANK P. GRAHAM, MAY 26, 1944

WITHIN the decade the University at Chapel Hill has been the subject of five surveys by agencies and experts outside North Carolina. In the survey conducted under the auspices of the American Council on Education which was taken through a secret ballot registering the appraisal of the graduate work of each department's work by all the other departments of the universities in the Association of American Universities, the University at Chapel Hill stood first of the universities south of Baltimore and east of the Mississippi River. In the survey of the natural sciences made by a national foundation, the University also stood first in the South. In a drastic appraisal of the deficiencies of higher education in the South, the only department accorded national preëminence in a Southern institution was found at the University of North Carolina. The University of North Carolina Press has been adjudged first in the Southern region and near the top in the University world. In two surveys conducted by the experts of the U. S. Navy as to the best place for the location of Pre-Flight Schools, North Carolina was adjudged first in the South and also first in the East. These verdicts and appraisals are no grounds for complacency, but rather, I wish to emphasize again and again, are challenges for us to recognize that in buildings, equipment, libraries, appropriations, and faculty salaries, the University at Chapel Hill, in fact all three of our institutions, are far behind. They urgently need for the great work they owe to the youth and people of North Carolina, more buildings, scientific equipment, larger provision for faculty salaries, teacher training, fellowships, scholarships, and student health and welfare. . . .

REPORT OF PRESIDENT WILLIAM FRIDAY, 1964

The vigor of the University is shown by the continued growth of its instructional and research programs. Enrollments are increasing rapidly, particularly at the graduate level, and the number seeking admission to the University is expected to continue to grow during the present decade.

As the numbers of students increase, the need for specialized training in new subject matter areas also increases; and to meet these demands for broader educational opportunities, the University has added new curricula leading to undergraduate and graduate degrees. . . .

The most conspicuous enrollment growth has been in the graduate schools of the University. At Chapel Hill and at Raleigh graduate students now make up approximately one-fifth of the total student population. At Greensboro, where the graduate program emphasizes the master's degree and where until recently only women were admitted, the number of graduate students now approaches one-seventh of the total enrollment. Graduate enrollment at Chapel Hill has increased by more than 15 per cent over last year; at Raleigh the increase has been something over 12 per cent. This rate of increase is imposing some strains upon the resources of the University. Because graduate students are the only source of future college and university teachers and the principal source of the research investigators upon which our technological society is so dependent, we have a responsibility to meet the needs that these increases in enrollment represent. . . .

We are virtually sure that our total college population will reach 125,000 in North Carolina by 1975. We have authorized the expansion of existing college facilities and the establishment of new institutions. Where will their faculties come from? Who will train the instructional staffs for the community colleges and the industrial education centers? What steps are we taking to share our resources with other institutions? The current widespread discussion among private foundations, educational agencies, and in the government about strengthening predominantly Negro colleges by various forms of assistance and other programs is a matter of particular interest.

It is predicted that within the next decade over 50 per cent of the population of North Carolina will be living in urban areas. Less than 14 per cent of the population will be employed on the farms. Much of the shift will, of course, be to industries based upon agriculture which will mean that agriculture and agricultural science will not be less important but different and more important. It is estimated that 1,300 new industries supplying 60,000 to 70,000 jobs will be established. Enormous educational opportunities are created by these population shifts and demands for new skills. Our leading industries will move toward greater automation and the change this will produce has significant consequences.

It has been said that there is no southern university, public or private, that ranks among the top twenty institutions in America. I regret that this is true. I also believe it to be true that no southern university will achieve this rank without a major administrative effort backed by the resources necessary to assemble a first-line faculty, excellent libraries, and modern laboratory and classroom equipment. In addition, the climate of university affairs must be at the optimum.

—*The President's Report: The University of North Carolina, 1963-1964,* Chapel Hill, 1964, pp. 4-5, 11.

176. WORK OF THE DUKE ENDOWMENT, 1924-1963

"To make provision in some measure for the needs of mankind along physical, mental and spiritual lines" was the "purpose of trust" as stated by James Buchanan Duke in the Indenture of December 11, 1924, which created the Duke Endowment. The first document below gives a summary of assistance to hospitals by the Duke Endowment; the second summarizes the total disbursements of this huge endowment since its creation.

HOSPITAL BEDS IN THE CAROLINAS

Hospitals assisted by The Endowment in the year (1963) had 92.0 per cent of the total number of general and special beds, excluding bassinets, in the Carolinas. The 22,540 beds (excluding 111 beds for long-term nursing care) in assisted hospitals were all except 1,954 of the 24,494 in use.

In the Carolinas there were 225 short-term general and special hospitals other than those operated by the federal government. These institutions demonstrated their concern for the need for hospital beds to serve the public by adding 881 during the year. Of the total number, which does not include bassinets, North Carolina had 16,450 and South Carolina 8,044. The last figure available on ratio of beds to each 1,000 of population showed 3.6 for the entire nation in 1962. The Carolinas remained in satisfactory position from this standpoint, as North Carolina's ratio was 3.4 and South Carolina 3.0. . . .

Financial assistance to hospitals was in three areas: to aid eligible nonprofit hospitals in operating expenses; to help in building, equipping, and purchasing hospitals; and to assist in educating health personnel and easing the personnel shortage. This was the thirty-ninth consecutive year in which The Endowment had provided funds for hospitals of the two states. . . .

With the 1963 appropriations, The Endowment has given $29,778,-050.95 to help hospitals care for charity patients, North Carolina receiving $17,547,407.35, and South Carolina $12,230,643.60. . . .

The 190 short-term general and special hospitals assisted had a total operating income of $176,744,258 as follows: $129,578,397 from inpatients; $11,401,784 from outpatients; $31,496,147 from contributions. . . .

Although definite figures on the amount paid to hospitals of the Carolinas by Blue Cross plans and insurance companies are not available, information from the Blue Cross plans . . . indicate that approximately $127,468,000 was paid from these sources in 1963 for hospital expenses in the Carolinas, $89,930,000 in North Carolina, and $37,538,000 in South Carolina.

From figures for hospitals assisted by The Duke Endowment, it is estimated that these payments amounted to 69.1 per cent of the total operating expenditures of the 217 nonfederal general hospitals in the Carolinas. . . .

For the 182 assisted general hospitals which were in operation the entire year, the average total cost per inpatient day, not including any expenses of replacement, depreciation, interest, rent, and taxes and counting three newborn days as one day of care, was $22.01. It was $22.48 for 127 North Carolina hospitals and $20.92 for 55 in South Carolina. . . . For the hospitals affiliated with medical schools, the average for the preceding fiscal year was $29.10, and the lowest average was $18.92 for 18 hospitals with 71 to 85 beds. . . .

Through the years, The Endowment has given a total of $14,655,-429.70 for these purposes (construction, equipment, or purchase of hospitals). The appropriations included $11,898,933.47 to 123 North Carolina hospitals and $2,756,496.23 to 50 in South Carolina.

For both operation of hospitals and the building, equipping, and purchasing of such institutions, the total amount is $44,433,480.65 for 272 hospitals, 189 in North Carolina receiving $29,446,340.82, and 83 in South Carolina, $14,987,139.83.—*Annual Report of the Duke Endowment, 1963* (Durham, 1963), pp. 24-28.

SUMMARY OF DUKE ENDOWMENT: INCOME AND ALLOCATIONS, 1924-1963

Income available for distribution and allocation in
   accordance with the terms of the Trust Indenture. . . . $206,921,089

Distribution and Allocation thereof:

Duke University	$106,573,274
Hospitals	44,976,391
Davidson College	7,106,867
Furman University	7,163,742
Johnson C. Smith University	4,653,707
Orphanages	7,447,848
Superannuated Preachers	1,461,427
Building Rural Churches	3,775,847

Operating Rural Churches 2,865,200
Funds set apart as principal and held for the benefit
   of specific beneficiaries 19,261,228
Funds held for appropriation 1,635,558
                                  $206,921,089

—*Annual Report of the Duke Endowment, 1963* (Durham, 1963),
pp. 49-50.

177. STATE OF NORTH CAROLINA REVENUES, 1933-1964

The following tables are taken from the reports of Edwin Gill,
State Treasurer. The largest items in the general fund revenue have
been: income taxes, sales taxes, franchise taxes, license taxes, beverage
taxes, insurance taxes, and inheritance and gift taxes, in that order.
Sales taxes yielded the largest amount of revenue to 1941, but since
that date income taxes have been the largest revenue producer. In
the highway fund, the gasoline tax has been by far the largest revenue
producer, with motor vehicle registrations coming second. More than
one-half of the agriculture fund revenue has come from the fertilizer
tax.

GENERAL FUND REVENUE

1933-34	$ 23,056,004
1934-35	26,006,816
1935-36	30,414,588
1936-37	38,613,475
1937-38	38,609,395
1938-39	36,181,205
1939-40	40,698,042
1940-41	47,280,139
1941-42	57,649,331
1942-43	70,445,137
1943-44	76,622,101
1944-45	80,697,290
1945-46	90,453-171
1946-47	119,996,404
1947-48	129,568,152
1948-49	140,843,645
1949-50	132,837,931
1950-51	162,072,863
1951-52	178,887,834

1952-53 180,978,102
1953-54 184,709,897
1954-55 189,111,046
1955-56 224,613,939
1956-57 237,768,203
1957-58 242,111,765
1958-59 253,670,563
1959-60 310,207,655
1960-61 325,986,671
1961-62 374,837,139
1962-63 415,327,825
1963-64 437,849,734

HIGHWAY FUND REVENUE

1933-34 . . . .$ 31,499,621
1934-45   29,810,866
1935-36   38,359,946
1936-37   32,684,400
1937-38   35,159,592
1938-39   36,710,898
1939-40   37,213,369
1940-41   42,954,940
1941-42   45,532,809
1942-43   35,920,039
1943-44   33,262,334
1944-45   33,855,933
1945-46   55,637,647
1946-47   64,742,166
1947-48   68,520,794
1948-49   63,343,984
1949-50   83,348,270
1950-51   98,267,452
1951-52 106,079,177
1952-53 111,575,730
1953-54 116,094,953
1954-54 122,674,672
1955-56 139,378,567
1956-57 171,938,131
1957-58 275,264,098
1958-59 164,344,012
1959-60 164,216,483

1960-61............................... 177,334,512
1961-62............................... 190,691,887
1962-63............................... 201,361,546
1963-64............................... 214,917,493

AGRICULTURE FUND REVENUE

1933-34................................$ 308,667
1934-35................................   367,693
1935-36................................   382,177
1936-37................................   414,649
1937-38................................   453,286
1938-39................................   477,365
1939-40................................   526,716
1940-41................................   558,251
1941-42................................   597,938
1942-43................................   751,914
1943-44................................   783,339
1944-45................................   820,382
1945-46................................   833,962
1946-47................................   910,909
1947-48................................   892,881
1948-49................................   969,956
1949-50................................ 1,186,409
1950-51................................ 1,629,987
1951-52................................ 1,734,761
1952-53................................ 2,047,058
1953-54................................ 1,767,906
1954-55................................ 2,145,168
1955-56................................ 2,065,831
1956-57................................ 2,021,367
1957-58................................ 2,167,272
1958-59................................ 2,452,109
1959-60................................ 2,521,536
1960-61................................ 2,738,036
1961-62................................ 2,942,594
1962-63................................ 2,972,409
1963-64................................ 3,322,345

REVENUES AND EXPENDITURES FOR THE FISCAL YEAR ENDING JUNE 30, 1964

REVENUES

GENERAL FUND:

Income:

Individual	$113,612,983	
Corporate	63,509,318	
Penalties and Interest	665,946	$177,788,247
Sales & Use		156,730,512
Franchise		35,674,041
Beverage		20,406,392
Insurance		17,470,342
Inheritance and Gift		10,886,352
License		5,704,768
Bank, Building and Loan		3,397,044
Other		9,792,036
Total General Fund		$437,849,734

HIGHWAY FUND:

Gasoline	$122,840,049	
Motor Vehicle Registration	40,788,358	
Property Owners, Cities and Towns Participation	3,427,668	
Other	1,983,712	
Total Highway Fund		$169,039,787

AGRICULTURE FUND:

Fees and Receipts		$ 1,517,709
TOTAL REVENUES		**$608,407,230**

EXPENDITURES

GENERAL FUND:

Education:

Public Schools	$271,129,277	
Higher Education	43,322,393	
Related Education Activities	5,204,531	$319,656,201
Health and Hospitals		40,292,885
Correction		14,984,565
Public Welfare		14,110,764

General Government	11,945,406	
Debt Service	10,440,791	
Agriculture	8,625,740	
Conservation and Development	4,932,752	
Miscellaneous Services	4,870,571	
Total General Fund		$429,859,675

HIGHWAY FUND:

Construction and Maintenance	$128,136,875	
Administration	21,599,787	
Debt Service	12,355,188	
State Aid to Municipalities	8,078,232	
Total Highway Fund		$170,170,082

AGRICULTURE FUND:

Total Agriculture Fund	$ 3,316,674
TOTAL EXPENDITURES	$603,346,431

178. THE BONDED INDEBTEDNESS OF THE STATE OF NORTH CAROLINA, 1965

The following document, taken from a report of Edwin Gill, State Treasurer, reviews the purposes for which the state has borrowed money through the issuance of long-term bonds. Mr. Gill, who has been State Treasurer since 1953, wrote: "A history of the public debt of North Carolina is a commentary on the efforts of our State to provide essential services for the people, such as schools, roads and hospitals. The statistics involved may appear cold and lacking in color, but the purposes for which the debt was incurred pulsate with life and tell us a great deal about the character of the people of North Carolina."

SINCE 1900 the amount of bonds issued by the State total $610,669,531. This amount plus supplementary appropriations of $13,708,090 was allocated as follows:

Fund		Amount
General Fund:		
Higher Education	$ 79,974,199	
Hospitals and Sanitoriums	46,679,387	
Training Schools and Institutions	19,187,547	
Public Education	96,000,000	
Miscellaneous	65,736,488	$307,577,621

Highway Fund:

Highway Construction	$115,000,000	
Secondary Roads	200,000,000	
Other	1,800	316,800,000
TOTAL		$624,377,621

When one considers that in addition to the proceeds of the bonds issued, North Carolina has annually invested in the purposes mentioned above millions upon millions of dollars in direct appropriations both for capital improvements and for current expenditures, we can begin to realize how public spirited the people of North Carolina are and how they have been willing to invest their economic resources, their hopes and their treasure in a program of progress for the State.

Our gross debt, as of July 1, 1964, was $211,868,000 which is modest when compared with the debts of other states similar in population and wealth and as compared with the total assessed valuation of all real and personal property in North Carolina of $10,695,139,747 (1963). The General Fund net debt is only $130,390,000.

Fund		*Amount*
General Fund:		
Payable from Revenues	$130,390,000	
Payable from Sinking Funds	11,228,000	$141,618,000
Highway Fund:		
Secondary Road Bonds	$ 70,250,000	70,250,000
		$211,868,000
Gross Debt:		
Less: Sinking Fund Bonds	$11,228,000	
Secondary Road Bonds	70,250,000	81,478,000
Net Debt July 1, 1964		$130,390,000

Probably the most significant act ever passed by the North Carolina General Assembly, from a fiscal viewpoint, was in 1945 when funds were set aside from the State's accumulated surplus to provide for the payment of the General Fund bonded indebtedness outstanding at that time in the amount of $51,585,079. This Act placed the State in the enviable position of providing for prior obligations, incurred for the purpose of increasing the facilities of the State's institutions when current revenues were not considered available, out of surplus funds created by abnormal revenues coming from abnormal war conditions.

The General Assembly of 1963, Chapter 1079, authorized the issuance of bonds in the amount of $100,000,000 subject to approval by the people. The proceeds of said bonds are to be used to aid the counties in the construction of public school facilities. The provision of the statute authorizing the issuance of said bonds directed that the proceeds be distributed among the counties of the State on the basis of student population during the school year 1961-62. The proposed bonds were approved by the voters in the General Election held on November 3, 1964; however, as of the date of this report the bonds have not been issued pending the ultimate approval of the proposed facilities of the counties by the State Board of Education. It is anticipated that the bonds will be issued during the fiscal year 1965-66.

The responsibility for the organization and administration of the public school system is both a State and local function of government. The State assumes the major responsibility for payment of salaries of teachers, clerical workers and janitors, transportation, fuel, water and lights. The counties provide funds for capital outlay, maintenance of plant, debt service and insurance. Supplements to the salaries and other current expenses paid by the State are made by the local governmental units. Federal grants are designated for specific purposes including vocational education.

In 1931, through action of the General Assembly, the State assumed full responsibility for the operation of the public schools of the State. Under this Act the State undertook to provide all funds required for the maintenance of school buildings and such fixed charges as debt service and insurance. The features of this Act have been carried forward and are still characteristic of the system of today. Of course the localities can by supplement provide extra compensation and services if they wish to exceed the minimum standards guaranteed by the State.

The expenditures for public schools in North Carolina during the years 1931 through 1963 are summarized as follows:

Expenditures—Current Operations

Source of Funds	Amount	Per Cent
State	$2,615,000,000	78.50
Local	542,000,000	16.27
Federal and other	174,000,000	5.23
TOTALS	$3,331,000,000	100.00

Expenditures—Capital Improvements

Source of Funds	Amount	Per Cent
State	$100,000,000	13.46
Local	621,000,000	83.58
Federal and other	22,000,000	2.96
TOTALS	$743,000,000	100.00

Total Expenditures

Source of Funds	Amount	Per Cent
State	$2,715,000,000	66.64
Local	1,163,000,000	28.55
Federal and other	196,000,000	4.81
TOTALS	$4,074,000,000	100.00

Included in the expenditures of the State for capital improvement purposes are the proceeds from the bond authorizations of 1949 and 1953. The bond authorization of 1949 of $25,000,000 was matched with a direct appropriation from the General Fund of $25,000,000. The 1953 bond issue amounted to $50,000,000.

In order to reflect the increase in total expenditures for public schools in North Carolina since 1931, the following figures are presented:

Year	Average Attendance	Total Expenditures	Per Pupil
1931	728,265	$ 25,700,000	$ 35.27
1941	779,850	40,800,000	52.30
1951	816,106	185,600,000	227.47
1961	1,035,933	337,200,000	325.46

During the year ended June 30, 1963, the State provided 80% of the operating funds of the public schools (68% of total including capital improvements) while the local units provided 16% and the Federal government 4%.

Operating funds to build and maintain North Carolina highways are derived from highway user taxes levied by the State and from Federal aid. Since 1921, $316,800,000 in borrowed funds have been used to build roads and bridges throughout the State. This amount represents about 10% of the total highway expenditures during such period. Thus, highway spending has been largely on a pay-as-you-go-basis.

Expenditures for highway activities since 1921, through the fiscal year 1963, total $2,978,341,609. The annual expenditures, using funds from all sources, range from a low of $21,657,427 in 1933 to a record high of $196,232,910 in 1961. To illustrate the expenditure trends, the following tabulation is shown:

Period Covering			Amount
1921-30			$ 218,613,666
1931-40			312,146,157
1941-50			512,319,118
	1951	$ 91,670,618	
	1952	104,125,560	
	1953	108,032,153	
	1954	112,472,434	
	1955	125,307,288	
	1956	133,213,269	
	1957	169,840,160	
	1958	177,695,348	
	1959	159,896,434	
	1960	180,204,832	
1951-60			1,362,458,096
	1961	$196,232,910	
	1962	191,445,825	
	1963	185,125,837	
1961-63			572,804,572
TOTAL			$2,978,341,609

Prior to 1931 most of the public roads were built and maintained by the counties of the State. In 1915, however, the General Assembly established the State Highway Commission to cooperate and advise with the counties in road building. After the Federal Highway Act was passed in 1916, the State began to receive Federal aid on a matching basis to improve the inter-state highways and under the State Highway Act of 1919 the State began its highway construction on a major scale. Then in 1931 the responsibility of constructing and maintaining the county roads was transferred to the State but not until the State had expended borrowed funds for road construction of more than $115,000,000. The State's policy during the 1920s was "build the roads with borrowed money and let the roads pay for themselves."—Edwin Gill, State Treasurer, *The Bonded Indebtedness of the State of North Carolina* (Raleigh, 1965), pp. 7-8, 9-10.

179. PUBLIC SCHOOLS IN NORTH CAROLINA, 1919-1964

North Carolina made much progress in public education after World War I, and educational facilities and opportunities in the state were greatly expanded. Though the state's school system ranked among the lowest third in the nation in 1964, it had climbed from the bottom past a number of states after 1900. Great advances were made in length of term, physical plants, salaries of teachers, library facilities, and other aspects of educational work, but the educational leaders of the state have not been satisfied with the progress which has been made and have worked unceasingly for the improvement of the public schools. The first document below summarizes public school progress made under the administrations of three successive Superintendents of Public Instruction. The next document is a statement by Charles F. Carroll, who has been Superintendent of Public Instruction since 1952. The following document gives a summary of public school expenditures since 1934. The last document indicates how the state's public school system ranks and shows that much more needs to be done to improve our national rank.

"PUBLIC EDUCATION, A STATE FUNCTION"

BROOKS' ADMINISTRATION, 1919-1923

DR. E. C. BROOKS, Professor of Education in Trinity College, now Duke University, was appointed State Superintendent of Public Instruction by Governor Bickett on January 1, 1919, and served until June 11, 1923.

During this period the public schools made noticeable progress. Perhaps the most outstanding facts during these 4½ years were the following:

1. The effective year of the six-months school term amendment (1919-1920).

2. The inauguration of salary schedules for teachers, principals and superintendents, and the strengthening of the certification regulations, including a plan for standardizing the teacher training facilities in the normal schools and colleges of the State (1920-21).

3. The first two $5,000,000 special building funds to be loaned to the counties for the erection of schoolhouses (1921 and 1923), thus stimulating the erection of many modern buildings for school purposes.

4. The increase in staff personnel of the Department of Public Instruction.

5. The decrease in number of districts and a corresponding in-

crease in larger school instructional areas by consolidation in accordance with a countywide plan of school organization, thus resulting in a decided decrease in the number of small schools.

6. The beginning of transportation at public expense.

7. A recodification of the public school laws.

8. The beginning of vocational education under the provisions of the Federal Smith-Hughes Act. The State Board for Vocational Education was created with the State Superintendent as executive officer.

ALLEN ADMINISTRATION, 1923-1934

A. T. Allen, Director of the Division of Teacher Training for the State Department of Public Instruction, was appointed by Governor Morrison as State Superintendent of Public Instruction and took office on June 11, 1923. He died while serving in this position on October 20, 1934.

During his more than 11 years service the public schools made remarkable progress. This period also witnessed the depths of the depression and consequently much retardation in school improvement. Perhaps the most outstanding facts during these years are the following:

1. The continuation of the building program under the stimulation of two additional special building funds, $5,000,000 and $2,500,000 (1925 and 1927).

2. The introduction by law of the countywide plan of school organization (1924).

3. The emphasis upon better elementary schools and their standardization.

4. The improvement in the training of teachers, including a scheme for rating the teachers employed in a unit.

5. The revision of the school curriculum.

6. The introduction of a monthly paper, *State School Facts,* for the dissemination of information about the schools.

7. An increased emphasis upon library facilities, with the addition of a person to the Department staff in charge of school libraries.

8. An increase in the Equalization Fund to $5,250,000 and a tax reduction of $1,250,000 (1930-31).

9. The assumption of the support of the six-months school term by the State, supported by a direct appropriation of $11,500,000, a 15-cent property tax levy estimated to yield $4,350,000, and $1,320,000 from fines, forfeitures and penalties. In addition an appropriation of

$1,500,000 was made toward the support of the extended term in schools operating eight months.

10. The provision for a State-supported uniform eight-months school term on State standards (1933).

ERWIN ADMINISTRATION, 1934-1947

Clyde A. Erwin, Superintendent of Schools of Rutherford County, was appointed State Superintendent of Public Instruction on October 24, 1934, by Governor Ehringhaus to succeed the late Dr. A. T. Allen. The State had just started on the second year of its eight-months term program at State expense. The appropriation for the operation of that first year's program was $16,000,000, and this sum, plus $2,296,364 from fines, forfeiture, penalties, and other local funds —a total of $18,296,364—was the amount of money expended for the current operation of the public schools.

Since that low point in our recent history, the public schools have fared better at each subsequent convening of the General Assembly. The trend both in funds made available and in expanded opportunities provided for the children of the State has been upward and outward. Public education is more fully realized now as a State function than ever before.

The annual State appropriation for the support of the regular school program has increased every year, as follows:

1935-36	$20,031,000
1936-37	20,900,000
1937-38	24,396,367
1938-39	24,986,160
1939-40	25,941,313
1940-41	27,000,000
1941-42	28,158,324
1942-43	29,454,233
1943-44	37,062,874
1944-45	38,140,941
1945-46	41,360,374
1946-47	41,997,738

In addition to this particular appropriation the appropriation for vocational education has increased from $146,000 in 1935-36 to $1,257,427 for 1946-47. Then, too, the appropriation for the purchase of school buses was separated from the regular support with a $650,000 appropriation for each of the years for the 1943-45 biennium and $1,338,764 and $960,000 respectively for 1945-46 and 1946-47.

Other significant advances made during this period have been the following:

1. The establishment of a rental system textbooks in 1935.

2. The provision for free basal textbooks for grades 1-7 in 1937.

3. The provision for voting taxes for supplementing school purposes in districts having a school population of 1,000 or more in 1939.

4. The establishment of a retirement system for all teachers and other State employees in 1941.

5. The provision for the introduction of a 12-year program of instruction in lieu of the 11-year plan in 1942-43.

6. The provision for a single State Board of Education to take the place of five existing State Agencies in 1943-44.

7. The extension of State support to a nine-months school term in 1943-44.

With free textbooks now furnished to all elementary school children; with transportation at State expense for approximately 350,000 pupils; with nearly 1,000 high schools in which more than 129,000 boys and girls are enrolled; with library facilities increased to more than 3,000,000 books; with many modern and adequately equipped buildings valued at nearly $130,000,000 located throughout the State; with vocational education greatly expanded; and with the curriculum extended to a 12-year program on the basis of a nine-months term—surely it can be said that educational opportunities in North Carolina have been greatly expanded.—*State School Facts*, Vol. XVIII, No. 12, September, 1946.

NORTH CAROLINA SCHOOLS HAVE MADE PROGRESS

North Carolina has made tremendous progress in public education since 1949, according to a recapitulation of some evidences of this progress by the State Department of Public Instruction:

1. School enrollment has increased by 200,000 children—from 893,745 to approximately 1,116,000 today. This has necessitated the employment of more instructional personnel—from 29,134 in 1948-49 to 38,155 last year (1958-59).

2. More pupils are transported at public expense—400,000 in 1948-49; more than 500,000 in 1958-59.

3. With transportation and consolidation, there are fewer and larger schools: there were 2,852 elementary schools in 1949; in 1959

there were approximately 2,000. High schools decreased from 958 to less than 900, with schools having 12 or more teachers increasing from 136 to more than 300.

4. Provision for the employment of supervisors of instruction was made in 1949. Last year State funds were used to employ 232 persons in this field, and 56 others were employed and paid from local funds.

5. Beginning in 1949 by special appropriation, a school health program was inaugurated. Under this program thousands of chronic remedial defects of children have been found and remedied.

6. In. addition to supervisors, the instructional program has been strengthened at a number of other points:

a. Special education for the handicapped got under way in 1949 and is now an integral part of the school program with more than 14,000 children enrolled in special classes of speech, mentally retarded, crippled, visual defects and hard of hearing. The State is now paying the salaries of 206 teachers in these areas.

b. A new program of driver training and safety was authorized by the General Assembly of 1957. This program is now under way and reaching this year approximately 75 per cent of the eligible pupils. Progress in this area is greater than for any other state.

c. Last year the State Board of Education provided for the establishment of 18 Industrial Education Centers throughout the State. Eight of these Centers are in operation this year. New buildings for these centers represent an investment of nearly 8 million dollars.

d. An experimental program of television in the schools began two years ago with the help of Ford Foundation funds. This program was considered successful as an aid to classroom instruction, with the result that the General Assembly of 1959 made an appropriation of $25,000 for 1959-60 and $50,000 for 1960-61 toward the continuation of this activity.

e. The basic course of study has also been strengthened. Instruction in music and elementary science is markedly improved. Instruction in high school subjects—especially science, mathematics, and modern foreign languages—is expected to improve rapidly with the inception of the National Defense Education Program now getting under way in the schools. The use of library, audio-visual, testing and guidance personnel in the instructional process is taking on new life also this year. The number of persons devoting half-time or more to counseling and guidance increased from 35 last year to 171 this year. The number of full-time school librarians is now 469, having increased from 213 in 1948-49.

f. A part of this picture is the extended term provision of three days for which teachers will be paid in addition to the 180-day term for organization and planning before school opens and for making reports, etc. at the end of school. This provision has already proved its value, according to reports of school administrators.

7. The number of graduates from the public high schools increased from 30,485 in 1949-50 to more than 40,000 last year.

8. The General Assemblies of 1949 and 1953 each provided $50,000,000 for the construction of new school buildings throughout the State. This $100,000,000 in State money has been matched by local funds to the extent of $300,000,000, with the result that the value of school property increased from $231,000,000 in 1949 to more than $600,000,000 at present.

9. The General Assembly of 1949 authorized the State Board of Education to establish a Public School Insurance Fund. As of June 30, 1949, 97 of the 174 school administrative units were provided with an insurance coverage of $275,000,000.

10. Another area operated in connection with the public schools is the Lunch Program which began in 1943. This Program has grown annually until at present 92,000,000 lunches are being served 550,000 children from a total of 1,764 schools.—*North Carolina Public School Bulletin*, Vol. XXIV, No. 4, December, 1959, p. 1.

EXPENDITURES

TOTAL FUNDS

Expenditures for public education are divided into three parts in accordance with the purpose for which the funds are expended: (1) *current expense*, operation costs; (2) *capital outlay*, payments for buildings and other physical facilities; (3) *debt service*, repayment of principal and interest on bonds and notes.

Current expense for operation of the public schools is the largest portion of total annual school expenditures. The major portion of current expense comes from State funds, 78.4 per cent in 1963-64. Local funds provided 17.4 per cent, and only 4.2 per cent came from Federal funds.

	Current Expense			
Year	State Funds*	Local Funds	Federal Funds	Total
1934-35	$ 16,702,697.05	$ 2,099,538.73	$ 451,861.29	$ 19,254,098.07
1939-40	26,297,493.15	5,136,723.59	610,146.82	32,044,363.56

1944-45	39,465,521.35	7,265,140.48	3,357,469.23	50,088,131.06
1949-50	84,999,202.42	16,219,185.16	12,054,108.25	113,272,495.83
1954-55	122,998,428.30	25,027,038.50	7,051,801.48	155,077,268.28
1959-60	170,349,864.78	39,609,752.00	9,573,603.57	219,533,220.35
1960-61	179,747,463.64	43,923,830.49	10,059,973.97	233,731,268.10
1961-62	227,790,105.60	46,958,730.51	10,757,519.63	285,506,355.74
1962-63	230,278,820.34	51,068,671.09	12,419,636.01	293,767,127.44
1963-64**	248,318,900.00	52,000,000.00	14,000,000.00	314,318,900.00

Capital Outlay

1934-35	$	$ 2,890,317.99	$ 428,593.61	$ 3,318,911.60
1939-40	16,816.78	3,338,711.73	448,871.73	3,804,400.24
1944-45	48,538.96	1,774,531.97	3,778.17	1,826,849.10
1949-50	5,893,974.23	22,104,092.66	3,101.11	28,001,168.00
1954-55	9,194,988.86	34,449,132.59	671,151.51	44,315,272.96
1959-60	1,623,003.97	44,909,693.85	1,368,262.35	47,900,960.17
1960-61	950,070.34	50,500,816.89	2,152,606.46	53,603,493.69
1961-62	718,159.34	49,179,706.24	1,749,187.42	51,647,053.00
1962-63	182,249.94	43,954,164.19	1,823,297.28	45,959,711.41
1963-64**	162,083.75	47,987,916.25	1,850,000.00	50,000,000.00

* Includes Vocational, Textbook, and other State Funds.
** Estimated.

Per Pupil Expenditures

Year	Average Daily Attend.	Current Expense				Capital Outlay	Grand Total
		State	Local	Federal	Total		
1934-35	761,433	$ 21.94	$ 2.76	$ .59	$ 25.29	$ 4.36	$ 29.65
1939-40	790,003	33.29	6.50	.77	40.56	4.82	45.38
1944-45	713,146	55.34	10.19	4.71	70.24	2.56	72.80
1949-50	797,691	106.56	20.33	15.11	142.00	35.10	177.10
1954-55	904,029	136.06	27.68	7.80	171.54	49.02	220.56
1959-60	1,003,455	169.76	39.47	9.54	218.77	47.74	266.51
1960-61	1,024,943	175.37	42.85	9.82	228.04	52.30	280.34
1961-62	1,036,934	219.68	45.29	10.37	275.34	49.81	325.15
1962-63*	1,058,183	217.62	48.26	11.74	277.62	43.43	321.05
1963-64*	1,082,790	229.33	48.03	12.93	290.29	46.18	336.47

* Estimated.

Expenditures For Current Expense Per Pupil In ADA (Average Daily Attendance)

1934-35	$25.29
1939-40	$40.56
1944-45	$70.24
1949-50	$142.00
1954-55	$171.54
1959-60	$218.77
1961-62	$275.41
1963-64	$290.29

—*North Carolina Public Schools, Biennial Report of the Superintendent of Public Instruction, 1962-1964,* pp. 21-22.

NORTH CAROLINA RANKS

10th among the states in estimated public elementary and secondary school enrollment (1,183,430), 1963-64.

13th among the states in number (56) of school-age children (5-17) per 100 adults ages (21-64), 1961.

37th among the states in estimated average salaries ($5,050) of classroom teachers in public schools, 1963-64.

38th among the states in per capita expenditures of state and local governments for all education ($98.85), 1962.

41st among the states in estimated current expenditures ($320.00) for public elementary and secondary schools per pupil in average daily attendance, 1963-64.

43rd among the states in per capita personal income ($1,732), 1962.

43rd among the states in percent (4.0) of population 14 years old and older illiterate in 1960.

44th among the states in percent (34.1) of Selective Service registrants failing the preinduction mental test, 1962.

45th among the states in median school years (8.9) completed by persons 25 years old and older, 1960.

46th among the states in public high school graduates in 1962-63 as percent (60.0) of ninth grade in 1959-60.

46th among the states in pupils per classroom teachers (28.8) in public elementary and secondary schools, fall 1962.

—*Facts and Figures About The Public Schools,* North Carolina State Department of Public Instruction, Raleigh, May, 1964, p. 35.

180.   "A Challenge or a Curtain," 1946

The following document by Jonathan Daniels, author of several books about North Carolina and the South and now managing editor of the Raleigh *News and Observer,* is one of the most challenging statements by a North Carolinian about North Carolina in recent years. Mr. Daniels thinks that in some respects North Carolina "has been living on a reputation it made a dozen years ago. It has a choice before it now as to whether it will continue to lead the South, and it is a choice which cannot be delayed when there are already signs of slipping." He stresses the inadequacy of the school system, the health problem, the migration of North Carolinians to other states, and many other phases of modern North Carolina history.

There never was a better time to measure the progress of North Carolina than today, and few states serve better as a measure of the progress of the nation. We North Carolinians have been a proud people at home. If once we were proud only in our humility, in the years between the two world wars we became almost cockily conscious of our progress. We moved. Sometimes we boasted. We were the purest native American stock in the United States, and sometimes we had the feeling that our movement was a measure not only of ourselves but of the American himself. Unfortunately, the only way to count progress is to measure it.

Fortunately, there is present now in North Carolina the self-criticism which is always essential to progress at home. Our teachers are in revolt even against the proposals of their own leaders as to the pay they should receive. And sometimes the revolt is less disturbing than the withdrawal of the best teachers from a system which seems to promise even less to the child than to the teacher. That revolt comes at a time when the heads of our state colleges are reporting that from our school system graduates come inadequately equipped to cope with the national standards the colleges are expected to maintain. The chairman of our own State School Commission has announced that a study has shown that it would require $25,000,000 to bring the school buildings of the State up even to minimum standards of adequacy.

We have learned some other shocking things, also. We were brought face to face with the fact that in the Selective Service System no state had a higher percentage of men, both among the white men and Negroes, who were found on examination to be unfit for military service for their country in time of war. Undoubtedly education entered into that result, but among the men selected under the higher standards in the first year of the war, our educational weakness did not count for our leadership in unfitness. Indeed, ten states (all of them Southern) were ahead of North Carolina in rejections for educational deficiency. Seven states were ahead of us in the rejection of white boys for this cause. In rejections for the disease most closely related to ignorance, syphilis, 10 states led North Carolina in rejections. The physical failure of our men led in the total of all defects, many of them remedial. No wonder that we became aware of our lack of doctors and the fact that 34 of our counties lacked any hospital facilities at all.

These are facts important to North Carolina. They are the facts with which North Carolina must deal. We have not reached the limit of our powers. One of the most important things for us to remember is not that about 40 states have better schools for their children, but that in terms of their wealth and ability to provide, about 18 other states have made greater effort and sacrifice to provide good schools than North Carolina has. We would like to see North Carolina have schools as good as California's. But we know North Carolina, in terms of its wealth, can make just as much effort for its children as Mississippi can—and today it does not. The basic fact, however, is that the entire South spends a greater percentage of its state income on education than do the states outside the South which have much better schools. Yet, the average of white illiteracy is twice what it is in the rest of the United States. For those in school the South spends less than half the dollars of the national average.

The South has been in recent years almost the center of America's population increase. North Carolina has been a great producer of children. Until recent years we had the highest birthrate in the nation. We still have a very high percentage of children in our own population. But sometimes we—and the nation—miss the fact that we have been producing children for the export trade. That is important to both the nation and North Carolina.

In 1940 there were 611,000 native North Carolinians living in other states. More significantly, counting only civilians, a total of 307,000 North Carolinians left the state in the five-year period after 1940. That was nearly a tenth of the whole population of the state. Studies of this movement from the South indicate that it was more white than Negro. More important, if effective working North Carolinians are a North Carolina resource, nearly 70 per cent of those who left were between the ages of 14 and 44. That means the loss in five years of around 200,000 men and women in the most productive years of life—a number equal to the population of our two biggest cities—and it was offset by a much smaller number of people moving in.

Patriotic North Carolinians may well wonder why so many North Carolinians leave home. It hurts our home pride to think about so many people willingly departing. Their movement raises fundamental questions about the North Carolina economy, the North Carolina opportunity, the whole quality of North Carolina life. But it also emphasizes the fact that in this nation today the education of the child can no longer be a single state's concern. In the decade after the Gold Rush of '49 fewer people moved to California from a gold-hungry world than left North Carolina in the five years after 1940. And North Carolina was only one of the Southern states—all possessing the same problem of education and health—which poured more than a million and a half of their people into the rest of the nation in those five years—900,000 more than the number which came into the South in the same period.

North Carolina today is at one of the great times of choice in its history. In the years between the wars it chose to move. It did move, and in nothing did it advance so much as in its adoption of the understanding that the children in its poorest parts were entitled to an equal chance with those in its wealthiest counties and cities. But in the 1940's there are signs of creaking in its movement which should cause some crevices in its complacency. In some regards it has been living on a reputation made a dozen years ago. It has a choice before it now as to whether it will continue to lead the South. And it is a choice which cannot be delayed when there are already signs of slipping. Inadequate education gnaws from the bottom at the standards of the state's colleges. Inadequate teacher pay is draining the schools of the best brains in a process which would put our children in the hands of our incompetents. Poor health, which made North Carolina the least fit state in war, drags on our schools and our economy.

North Carolina must do its best or fall back. That best is not a choice between health or schools, but a choice for both or for backwardness. That best will not be enough. The North Carolina pattern of putting wealth wherever it is behind the education of its children wherever they are is a pattern which fits the problem of the nation as well as the state. We who were Americans in war have a right to insist that our children are Americans in peace also. We have no wish to loose the poorly educated and the physically unfit on other states. We have a right to ask that our people who remain in North Carolina have an actual equality of opportunity in America. Already, wisely, the Congress has authorized Federal support in the provision of facilities for health in America. That program must be maintained and North Carolina must move promptly to avail itself of all its aids. And now especially, thoughtful men and women must be aware of the needs for similar aids to public education in all the 48 states whose children will not stay put and separate, though they may be given at the beginning 40 varying qualities of opportunity.

It is time that we recognized that Federal aid to education in America is essential to collective security at home. There has been no mandate for backwardness in North Carolina or the United States. In great wars we showed both the world and ourselves that we could marshal all our resources, all our people, all our treasure in the defense of democracy on this earth. There remains now the cheaper, clearer, equally necessary demonstration that in the very basic things —in health and education—we can give some real meaning to equality of opportunity at home. This is the only firm foundation of democracy itself.—Jonathan Daniels, in The University of North Carolina *News Letter*, Vol. XXXII, No. 17, November 20, 1946.

181. REPORT OF THE STATE HOSPITAL AND MEDICAL CARE COMMISSION, OCTOBER 11, 1944

In February, 1944, Governor J. Melville Broughton appointed a commission to survey the hospital and medical care needs of North Carolina and to recommend a program to the people and the General Assembly. After many months of study and investigation, the full Hospital and Medical Care Commission, with Clarence Poe as chairman, adopted the following statement.

TO THE PEOPLE OF NORTH CAROLINA

On January 31, 1944, at a meeting of the Trustees of the University of North Carolina, Governor J. M. Broughton presented with strong approval a report from a committee of distinguished physicians . . . appealing for a great forward step in the life and progress of North Carolina.

These distinguished leaders of the state's medical profession pointed out that North Carolina is now the 11th most populous state in the Union but is 42nd in number of hospital beds per 1000 population . . . and 45th in number of doctors per 1000 population . . . and joined Governor Broughton in recommending two far-reaching remedies as follows:

1. *The Expansion of the Two-Year Medical School at the University into a Standard Four-Year Medical School with a Central Hospital of 600 beds or more;*
2. *A Hospital and Medical Care Program for the entire state with this noble objective as expressed by Governor Broughton: "The ultimate purpose of this program should be that no person in North Carolina shall lack hospital care or medical treatment by reason of poverty or low income."*

By unanimous action the Trustees of the Consolidated University approved this two-fold program. Almost immediately thereafter Governor Broughton named a "State Hospital and Medical Care

Commission" which has been busy ever since investigating conditions, scrutinizing defects, and weighing suggested remedies. . . .

After nearly eight months of investigation and study the State Hospital and Medical Care Commission now presents to the people of the state the following findings and recommendations:

1. Our basic and permanent aim should never be at any time less lofty and comprehensive than the Governor's declaration. . . .

2. In order both to remedy the most urgent needs of today and work toward the larger program of tomorrow, three things are supremely needed:

A. MORE DOCTORS
B. MORE HOSPITALS
C. MORE INSURANCE

These are the three mutually indispensable legs of our three-legged stool. We cannot have enough doctors without more hospitals . . . nor enough hospitals without greater popular ability to pay for hospital service . . . and such ability to pay on the part of the poorer half of our population is impossible without insurance.

3. In each area we must be especially diligent to serve where need is direct and most challenging. This direct need is:

Among economic groups, *the poor*
Among occupational groups, *tenant farmers*
Among races, *the Negro*
In the two major geographical areas of the state, *Eastern North Carolina and our mountain counties.*
Inside family groups, *mothers in childbirth and infants in the first months of existence.* . . .

Minimum approved number of doctors is 1 for each 1,000 people, but Rural North Carolina (1940) has only 1 doctor for each 3,613 people.

4. Our program is not one of communism. It is not one of "Socialized Medicine." . . .

5. The masses of the people are determined to find some way to work steadily toward the goal set forth by Governor Broughton. . . .

6. We fully realize that such a program cannot be achieved overnight or at one session of our General Assembly. . . .

For what we now face is the need for a normal two-year gain in a program already well advanced but the imperative need for a great advance in a highly important program 20 years overdue.

7. The poor of the state have indeed heard gladly of this program. Men and women of wealth, we rejoice to say, have been equally quick to proffer their support. Just as North Carolina in 1900-1920 spent larger sums than ever before for Better Schools but found it a good investment for all classes, and again in 1920-40 greatly increased its expenditures for Better Roads with similar benefits to rich and poor alike, so we may now greatly increase our expenditures for Better Health and find all classes of North Carolinians bettered as a result. . . .

The Commission recommends that the state encourage in every practicable way the development of group medical care plans which make it possible for people to insure themselves against expensive illness, expensive treatment by specialists, and extended hospitalization. The Blue Cross Plan of hospital and surgical service with some modifications, can meet the needs of that part of the state's population able to pay all their medical costs. It is recommended that these Blue Cross organizations be asked to expand their services to include the general practitioner and prescribed drugs. This is particularly important for rural people who depend so heavily on the general physician. The importance of insurance for hospital and medical care in a general program such as ours can hardly be overestimated. Every citizen needs to realize that it is just as important to have insurance against sickness-disasters as against fire-disasters.—Report of the North Carolina Hospital and Medical Care Commission.

182. THE EXPANSION AND RELOCATION OF WAKE FOREST COLLEGE

Three significant developments in higher education in North Carolina occurred between 1924 and 1946: the establishment of Duke University in 1924, the creation of the Consolidated University of North Carolina in 1931, and the 1946 decision of Wake Forest College to accept the "Reynolds grant" and remove to Winston-Salem.

Wake Forest College, under the leadership of Presidents W. L. Poteat, Thurman Kitchin, and Harold Tribble, has made steady and continuous progress in recent years. During the decade prior to moving to Winston-Salem it had more than 10,000 students, an endowment of over $3,000,000 and a physical plant worth about $2,000,000. The following statement was made by President Kitchin in 1947.

IN MARCH of 1946, trustees of the Smith Reynolds Foundation, Inc., offered to give to Wake Forest College in perpetuity the net income, up to $350,000 annually, of a trust fund valued at that time at about $10,500,000 on condition that the College be moved to Winston-Salem and on the further condition that the College and its friends provide funds for erecting suitable buildings in or near Winston-Salem for a college of not less than 2,000 students. Mr. and Mrs. Charles H. Babcock agreed to contribute to the College for its new campus an adequate tract of land lying within the bounds of their Reynolda estate. . . .

Approval of the conditions of the Reynolds offer was voted on April 11, 1946, by the Trustees of Wake Forest College, by the Baptist State Convention's Council on Christian Education, and by its General Board, subject to later action of the Baptist State Convention. A special session of the Convention was held in Greensboro on July 30, 1946, when an overwhelming majority of the members in attendance, about 2,500 in number, voted to comply with the conditions of the offer. . . .

Further approval of the transaction was given by the Baptist State Convention meeting in regular session in Asheville the following November. Besides voting its confirmation of the action taken by the special session in Greensboro, the Asheville Convention voted to set up an organization to enlist the Baptist churches of the State in giving $1,500,000 within three years to the Wake Forest College building program, and requested a continuation of the plans already in operation, under direction of the College Trustees, for securing gifts from individuals, corporations, foundations, and all other purposes.

On February 15, 1947, publicity was given to a movement to re-locate the Bowman Gray School of Medicine of Wake Forest College, already situated in Winston-Salem, and the North Carolina Baptist Hospital adjoining it, on the Graylyn estate, across the highway from Reynolda. The Board of Trustees of the Baptist Hospital and the advisory council to the Board of Trustees of the Medical School voted unanimously to recommend to the Baptist State Convention the sale of properties now occupied by the two institutions and the construction of new buildings, at a cost of approximately $6,000,000, on the Graylyn estate. The Graylyn property, including the mansion, was given to the Medical School some months earlier by Mr. and Mrs. Bernard.

If North Carolina Baptists comply with the conditions of the

Reynolds gift, and re-locate their Medical School and Hospital, as recommended above, they will own and operate in Winston-Salem an educational and medical center with an endowment and property worth more than $30,000,000.—Letter to the Editor from Thurman Kitchin, President of Wake Forest College, March 25, 1947.

183. A North Carolina Weekly Newspaper Editorial on the Ku Klux Klan

The following editorial was written by W. Horace Carter, editor of *The Tabor City Tribune.* It was the first of many editorials that appeared in this weekly newspaper over a three-year period and started the crusade against the Ku Klux Klan in North Carolina. It was written following the first parade of the Klan members in automobiles through a North Carolina community.

In 1952 the Pulitzer Prize for outstanding public service by an American newspaper was awarded to Mr. Carter and his newspaper. This was the first and only time a weekly newspaper ever received this award. The semi-weekly Whiteville *News Reporter* won a similar award the same year.

NO EXCUSE FOR KKK

In this democratic country there's no place for an organization of the calibre of the Ku Klux Klan which made a scheduled parade through our streets last Saturday night. Any organization that has to work outside the law is unfit for recognition in a country of free men. Saturday's episode, although without violence, is deplorable, a black eye to our area and an admission that our law enforcement is inadequate.

Sanctioning of their methods of operation is practically as bad as if you rode in their midst. It takes a united front to combat lawlessness. It takes all the law abiding people as a unit to discourage and combat a Ku Klux Klan that is totally without law. The Klan, despite its Americanism plea, is the personification of Fascism and Nazism. It is just such outside-the-law operations that lead to dictatorships through fear and insecurity.

The Klan bases its power on fear and hatred and not through love, understanding and the principles upon which God would have us live together. We have some racial problem in this country. That cannot be denied. However, we do not have open warfare which we will have if the primitive methods of the KKK are applied. In every sense of the word, they are endeavoring to force their domination upon those whom they consider deserving of punishment. It is not for a band of hoodlums to decide whether you or I need chastising. We grant you that there are cases in which it would seem individuals need punishment when none comes through the regular channels. In which case it is not up to a hooded gang to do the punishing. The cases must, like all others, keep within the bounds of the laws which you and I have made and have the power to enlarge upon should we deem the present ones inadequate.

The recent Democratic primaries in North and South Carolina did much to stir up trouble and build the KKK. Both States staged mudslinging and abominable campaigns based on racial hatred, perhaps the most un-Godly campaigns ever waged in the Carolinas.

The racial issue in the South has been overstressed. There is little tangible evidence of any struggle between races. A federal law forcing us to mingle together could not be enforced. Any non-segregation that comes about in the South will have to be a natural movement through generations and through education and the practice of God's teaching.

The Klan is a big talker for Protestantism, thereby being anti-Catholic and anti-Jewish. Yet, America was founded by persons seeking a country of religious freedom where they could worship God in their own way without fear. Would you have us resort to a nation of people wishing there was another America to discover so we could leave this one?

With the Klan's frequent reference to Jesus, God and religion they are the essence of sacreligion. Their very being is in contrast to God and the Bible. If you had the names of those persons appearing here Saturday night and if you had the church attendance slips for those persons, it's our opinion that not five percent entered any church of any denomination on Sunday morning.—*The Tabor City Tribune,* July 23, 1950.

184. MUSIC IN MODERN NORTH CAROLINA

The following account, written by the late William T. Polk, associate editor of the Greensboro *Daily News,* was printed in *The North Carolina Guide.*

THERE IS a good deal going on in music in North Carolina today. The foundations for this widespread and vigorous movement were laid by a number of Tar Heels including Mrs. Crosby Adams in the Mountains, Paul John Weaver at Chapel Hill, Dr. Wade R. Brown and

H. Hugh Altvater at Greensboro, and Hattie Parrott and the Pfohl family in Winston-Salem, much of it with the co-operation of the North Carolina Federation of Music Clubs.

Out of this interest has come music in many forms—symphony orchestras, choruses, opera, folk song festivals, and jazz bands.

One of the most important developments in recent years is the North Carolina Symphony Orchestra. Organized, directed and conducted by Dr. Benjamin Swalin of Chapel Hill, and supported largely by the State and partly by private subscription, this fine orchestra carries good music to all the people of the State, by bus, boat, and any other means of transportation that happens to be handy, from Hatteras to the Cherokee Reservation in the Great Smokies. In 1953 it traveled 10,000 miles to give 123 concerts. It devotes a good deal of its time and energy to bringing the appreciation of music to school children; this work is under the inspiring direction of Adeline McCall of Chapel Hill. In 1953, 140,000 school children heard concerts in which they had been given background information about the programs beforehand; to watch them responding to various kinds of music, from Beethoven and Mozart to *Sourwood Mountain* and *Gum Tree Canoe,* is a heart-warming experience.

Other symphony orchestras in the State are located in Greensboro, Charlotte and Winston-Salem.

The Grass Roots Opera Company, organized by Mr. and Mrs. A. J. Fletcher of Raleigh, takes both grand and light opera in English translation to North Carolinians in town and countryside, without benefit of any scenery or much costuming, for a guarantee of $60 for a small opera like Mozart's *Cosi fan Tutti* to $110 for a full-sized one like Bizet's *Carmen.*

The Transylvania Music Camp, which was started in 1936 by James Christian Pfohl, is primarily a summer school for musicians; each year, however, it puts on a music festival which attracts some of the best lecturers and performers in the country, such as Olin Downs, Joseph Szigeti and Eileen Farrell.

"About sundown the first week in August," Bascom Lamar Lunsford of South Turkey Creek not far from Asheville, who is known as "the Minstrel of the Appalachians," conducts a Mountain Dance and Folk Festival at Asheville. He also puts on a Carolina Folk Festival at Chapel Hill during the summer. . . .

North Carolina composers of ability include Lamar Stringfield who won a Pulitzer prize in 1928 with his suite *From the Southern Mountains,* Charles G. Vardell who composed *Carolina Symphony,* Hunter

Johnson who won the *Prix de Rome* in 1938, Lily Strickland of Hendersonville, Wilton Mason of Chapel Hill, William Klenz of Duke University, Rob Roy Perry of Salisbury, and Hermine W. Eichorn, Elliott Weisgarber, R. Nathaniel Dett and Herbert Hazelman of Greensboro. . . .—B. P. Robinson (ed.), *The North Carolina Guide* (Chapel Hill, 1955), 23-25.

185. ART MUSEUM MAKES HISTORY

The following article appeared in the May, 1956, issue of *The Wachovia*, a publication edited by James H. Newbury and issued by the Wachovia Bank and Trust Company. It was reprinted in *The State*, June 30, 1956.

THE RECENT opening of the North Carolina Museum of Art in Raleigh marked the first instance in the nation's history that a State has allocated $1 million in tax money for the purchase of art objects.

The Museum is housed in the former State Highway Commission Building which has been renovated and redecorated. There, are displayed more than 200 oil paintings and art objects representing the eight schools of Western culture. These are valued in excess of $2 million. And, the Samuel H. Kress Foundation has promised to add another $1 million in art to the collection.

This increase in North Carolina's art assets did not occur overnight. It might never have occurred but for the intense and enthusiastic interest of a Tar Heel who two decades ago privately dedicated himself to the achievement of this goal. He is Dr. Robert Lee Humber of Greenville, N. C., President of the State Art Society, and a former international lawyer who spent more than 20 years following his profession in Paris and other world capitals before returning to North Carolina. It was during Dr. Humber's work in Europe that he conceived the idea of a Museum of Art for his native State. Already a dedicated patron of the arts, he began to take particular note of the locations of the old world masterpieces. From these and other treasures he hoped that North Carolina would some day build a museum for her people.

The entire list of interesting events, legislative actions, occurrences and hard work behind the opening of the Museum are myriad. But here briefly are the accomplishments. In the early 1940's Dr. Humber proposed to the Kress Foundation that it pledge $1 million (later changed to $1 million in art) toward a museum for this State. The Foundation agreed to the suggestion provided that North Carolina would match this sum and produce a suitable home for the art. Following several years of work by Dr. Humber, members of the State Art Society and others interested in a Tar Heel art museum, in 1947 the General Assembly appropriated $1 million from tax funds to buy masterpieces in all art forms. Then in 1953, they added $200,000 to renovate Raleigh's State Highway Commission Building for the Museum's site, later adding $140,000 to finish the job. In the meantime, private donors both from this State and across the nation contributed to the Museum paintings, furniture, sculpture, porcelain and tapestries, valued at more than $1 million.

Today at the Raleigh gallery hang paintings by Rembrandt, Van Dyck, Gainsborough, Reni, Copley, Frans Hals, Rubens, and many other equally famous artists. With seven Rubens' paintings, the Museum is in the first rank of institutions owning works of that artist. . . .

The new Museum has been figuratively described as "an art company chartered by the State, with 4¼ million citizen-stockholders." And, from appraisals of the Museum's art by leading critics, it appears Tar Heel shareholders are in for rich dividends in enjoyment and education in future years.—*The Wachovia*, XLIX, May, 1956, No. 3, pp. 14-15. *The State*, XXIV, June 30, 1956, No. 3, p. 21.

186. NORTH CAROLINA EDITORIALS ON PUBLIC SCHOOL DESEGREGATION

The first editorial reprinted below is from the Greensboro *Daily News* and "represents the well-considered views of this newspaper." This carefully reasoned and well-written piece was the "composite view" of H. W. Kendall, the late William T. Polk, and William D. Snider.

The second editorial is from the pen of Jonathan Daniels, editor of the Raleigh *News and Observer* and author of many books relating to North Carolina and the South.

FACING THE SCHOOL ISSUE

THE PROBLEM for the leadership of both races in North Carolina is this: How can the state best and most surely maintain and preserve its public education system?

The common enemy of both races is ignorance. The common goal is education. Private schools are a useful supplement to public schools but they are no substitute for them. If the public schools are lost, we shall be integrated in ignorance and poverty.

The public schools are confronted with potential perils to their efficacy and even their existence. Both races bear a heavy responsibility to preserve the schools. How can this be done?

TO THE WHITES

The *Daily News* would say to the whites:

Preserve your public schools. State Superintendent of Public Instruction Charles F. Carroll, speaking in High Point recently, emphasized the indispensability of the public school system, as it affects the state's dearest, most precious and valuable resource, its children, and the kind of future which they are to build for themselves, their state, their nation and the Western civilization which is their blood-bought heritage of individual rights and undergoing institutions. The state's school head put it this way:

Meanwhile, it would be distressingly unfortunate if in the period required for solution of this major issue we should permit a condition to develop that would be used as justification or excuse for withholding essential moral and financial support from public schools.

Our one million children, in whose hearts, minds and hands rest much of the destiny of this state, are innocent parties to this segregation matter and they must not become its victims.

What Superintendent Carroll says simply means that the public school system is indispensable to our way of living and our future destiny, that the worst thing that could possibly happen to North Carolina would be abandonment or prejudicial curtailment of that system and that it is a time for rededication to education and not for undercutting it in the Old North State.

If there is any one thing that conscientious, sober-minded and responsible North Carolinians—white and Negro—should agree upon in this time of educational crisis it is that our public school system shall not be neglected or abandoned, that the educational foundations we have laid and the educational progress we have made over the years are not to be junked and that our children and their future are not to be sacrificed to bitterness, ill-will, prejudices or emotionalism. North Carolina has always been characterized by common sense; and we are confident that, as this saving quality once again triumphs, reason, judgment and the hard practicality of self-preservation and advancement will find a way in the area of maneuverability which the Supreme Court's desegregation decision leaves.

Whatever North Carolina does, amidst the emotionalism which threatens to take over, must be weighed in terms of educational worth and the opportunities which we have struggled all these years to assure for our children. We score and underscore Superintendent Carroll's grave declaration that our public school system is indispensable. Those who would wreck it are not merely myopic but blind.

The task of preserving the schools will be made easier if white leadership will allow experiments in mixed schools to be carried out in those communities where such experiments can apparently be conducted with some promise of success and without harming the schools, in reasonable compliance with the law and in that spirit of moderation which both races must manifest if the problem is to be worked out at all. The government doesn't mass-produce an entirely new type of bomber; it makes prototypes first. The same principle ought to apply to a most radical experiment in the public school system.

TO THE NEGROES

To the Negroes in North Carolina the *Daily News* would say this:

The problem for the leaders is how they can get the best education for the children of their race.

Through mixing them in the schools forthwith by force of law? Or through separate schools by choice?

If the decision is for integration by force of law nobody knows how much education the children of either race will get; it is an uncharted field in North Carolina. How good the schools would be or whether there would be any public schools are matters dependent on human reactions which no one can foretell with certainty.

If the choice is for separate education, the Negroes can count on getting at least as good education as they are getting now. It should become progressively better, as facilities are equalized and teaching improves. If the choice is for separation, the Negroes keep their powerful lever for equalization; once they choose integration, that lever is lost.

The question is whether Negro leadership in North Carolina will risk its vested interest in separate schools for a contingent and speculative interest in integrated schools. Will it shoot the works or pursue a conservative course?

Which is to the advantage of the Negroes in this state under all the circumstances?

The circumstances are important because the problem is not a theoretical but a practical one. Both races are confronted by a condition, not a theory. The problem will not be worked out in a vacuum but in a historic setting of emotions, values, customs, mores and traditions which—whether right or wrong—are genuine and powerful. Whether we call them prejudice or common sense is irrelevant, the solution or the problem; the point is that they exist, they are facts, and they must be taken into account as part of "the requirements of the problem."

Let us face the facts and try to analyze the problem in their light.

Suppose the Negroes choose integration on a broad scale by force of law, what is likely to happen?

Indications are that there will be scattered experiments with integration, some of which may be successful and form the basis for further developments. But the broad picture is that the whites at least for some time will resist integration strenuously, resourcefully, and perhaps bitterly.

This resistance is likely to take the form of delay or evasion as long as practicable. How long will that be? That depends on many factors, including the courts and the determination and resourcefulness of both sides. Our history shows how difficult it is to change long-established customs by court ruling. When the law runs up against the popular will, something has to give; not infrequently it is the law that is changed or modified, as in the experiment of prohibition.

If delay plays out and evasion fails, what then? What will happen if broad-scale integration is forced on the schools of this state?

Nobody knows for sure, but the danger is two-fold: That the public school system may be swiftly abolished or slowly abandoned. These are not fanciful perils but foreseeable contingencies which must be taken into account by those who would meet the problem realistically.

Abolition of the public schools and their replacement to a most uncertain extent with private ones is a last-ditch and double-edged weapon. Several Southern states have made preparations to use it by amending their constitutions. There is no way to prevent its use because there is no way to make people support or attend schools, if they have made up their minds not to. If it is used, the results will be appalling in ignorance, poverty and bitterness. Generations of both races will suffer incalculably by it, and it is likely that the Negroes will suffer most.

. . . North Carolina's public education system is the pride and prop of the state and it must be preserved if we want to continue to make progress. But it is founded on the faith and sacrifice and will of the people. If that foundation is weakened or shattered by changing the school system into something radically different from what it is now, nobody knows what will happen to it. What was built up so laboriously for half a century can be torn down in months or days.

It would be wise not to subject it to unbearable strains in the attempt to attain, by force of law, most uncertain benefits.

We want to make this clear. The *Daily News* expects to advocate preservation of the public schools under all foreseeable circumstances.

Abolition of the schools would be the worst and most costly thing that could happen to North Carolina and every possible effort should be made by responsible leadership to avoid it.

We believe the surest way to preserve them is for both races realistically to confront the dangers to the schools from both extremist Negro action and extremist white reaction. Moderation, forbearance and a certain amount of give-and-take must be exercised by both races if the problem is to be solved at all.

We have hope that it can and will be.—Greensboro *Daily News,* August 5, 1955.

IGNORANCE AS A POLICY FOR THE SOUTH

Certainly today, we seem to have only two things on our minds and in our mouths: the decentralization of American industry southward and the desegregation of the schools southward, too.

They are not regarded as identical twins. Eagerness attends one Indeed, we are credited with such eagerness to take our part of the pattern of industry from the North that we have been charged with a zeal in looting never before equalled except by Sherman's soldiers We were recently accused of robbing the industrial graves of devastated New England industrial towns. That was slander which will not stop the belated development of the South in terms of its neglected resources and the needs of its people. The building of new plants a a million-dollar-a-day rate in the Southeast will not slow soon.

The change in the people is more significant than the modern brick buildings which stand in the fields where the broom sedge was golden only in color. The Southern poor white, that creature deemed incapable of any but the dullest skills, seems to have disappeared every where except in Erskine Caldwell's novels. The tenant farmers o twenty years ago are imperceptible as the citizens of our bulging citie in a South in which urbanization is proceeding at a faster rate than the country as a whole—twice as fast in some sections. State the fac

implement the Court's decision through the Courts." The objectives of the NAACP, as stated in its Certificate of Incorporation, are given below.

THAT THE principal objects for which the corporation is formed are voluntarily to promote equality of rights and eradicate caste or race prejudice among the citizens of the United States, to advance the interest of colored citizens; to secure for them impartial suffrage; and to increase their opportunities for securing justice in the courts, education for their children, employment according to their ability, and complete equality before the law.

To ascertain and publish all facts bearing upon these subjects and to take any lawful action thereon; together with any and all things which may lawfully be done by a membership corporation organized under the laws of the State of New York for the further advancement of these objects.

To take, receive, hold, convey, mortgage or assign all such real estate and personal property as may be necessary for the purposes of the corporation.

The corporate name by which the corporation shall be known is NATIONAL ASSOCIATION FOR THE ADVANCEMENT OF COLORED PEOPLE.

The territory on which the operations of the corporation are principally to be conducted shall be the United States of America.

The principal office of the corporation and the center of its operations shall be in the City, County and State of New York, but the Directors may establish branch or auxiliary offices elsewhere in the United States for the purpose of carrying on the work of the corporation, each to be managed by its local organization under such powers as lawfully may be prescribed in the by-laws of the corporation.

The principal office of the corporation shall be in the Borough of Manhattan, in the City, County and State of New York. . . .

188. PATRIOTS OF NORTH CAROLINA, INC.

By unanimous vote the 1955 General Assembly resolved: "The mixing of the races in the public schools within the state cannot be accomplished and if attempted would alienate public support of the schools to such an extent that they could not be operated successfully." On August 8, Governor Hodges proposed to the people of the state to operate the public schools "in accordance with the policies set out by the General Assembly and at the same time avoid defiance or evasion of the United States Supreme Court" by having the children of both white and Negro races "voluntarily attend separate public schools." On August 22, the Patriots of North Carolina, an all-white organization aimed at maintaining the "purity of the white race and Anglo-Saxon institutions" was incorporated.

THE OBJECTS and purposes of PATRIOTS OF NORTH CAROLINA, INC., as set forth in its charter, are as follows:

(a) To maintain the purity and culture of the white race and Anglo-Saxon institutions.

(b) To promote the peace, domestic tranquility and the best interest and general welfare of all citizens.

(c) To encourage and promote friendly racial relations and racial peace and good will.

(d) To promote the value of maintaining the existing social structure in North Carolina in which two distinct races heretofore have lived as separate groups, and the value of educating the different races in separate schools.

(e) To promote loyalty to the traditions of the State and to appeal to all loyal and patriotic citizens for their wholehearted support in maintaining the integrity of those traditions.

(f) To promote the right of the State of North Carolina to regulate its own internal affairs in the manner it believes to be most conducive to the happiness and welfare of its citizens.

(g) To cooperate with and support our State and local civil authorities, agencies and committees, including State and local school boards and officials, to the extent that they are favorable to the objects and purposes herein set forth.

189. Report of the Commission on Higher Education, January, 1955

On April 30, 1953, the General Assembly adopted a joint resolution "providing for the appointment of a commission by the governor for the purpose of making a study of all institutions of higher education supported by state funds." This commission was authorized: (1) To make a comprehensive study of the purpose, organization, function, and operation of each of the institutions of higher education supported by state funds; (2) To determine the relationships between these institutions and to make recommendations deemed necessary to achieve maximum educational benefits for the people of the State; (3) To make a study of all the laws of the State pertaining to these institutions of higher learning and to make recommendations to the

1955 Session of the General Assembly as to any pertinent revision of said laws.

In the fall of 1953, Governor Umstead appointed a seven-member commission, which in accordance with the provisions of the legislative resolution, selected Victor Bryant of Durham as chairman. After a lengthy and careful study, the Commission on Higher Education, commonly called the "Bryant Committee," made its report to Governor Hodges, in January, 1955. The Commission made fifteen specific recommendations and concluded its report by recommending the passage by the General Assembly of "an act creating a State Board of Higher Education, and providing for its members, their qualifications, selection, appointment, powers, duties, and financing." Some of the "findings" of the Commission are reprinted below.

IN 1950, North Carolina ranked 47th among the 48 states as to the proportion of its population in college. Only 15.3 per cent of our college-age population group were in college. The national figure, by contrast, was 28.4 per cent. . . . North Carolina is "plowing under" much of its college-age population which could profit from higher education. . . .

North Carolina does not rank 47th in *support* of higher education. In 1950, North Carolina ranked 32nd among the states in the funds received by institutions of higher education from the State for operating purposes per capita. . . .

The Commission is deeply concerned with the fact that, although North Carolina is spending the money, it is apparently not educating its young people at the college level as is the rest of the nation. Why does a state which pays more get less in higher education? Is it possible that North Carolina is putting too much of its higher education money into "frills and furbelows" instead of into low-cost higher education at the undergraduate level? . . .

North Carolina is not getting the results in higher education which might be expected in view of the amount of money being spent. . . . In studying this problem, this Commission has discovered a number of situations which may account for it.

One is the unjustified duplication of programs and functions by the institutions. Such duplication in specialized areas of learning is expensive and wasteful. There is no provision for an effective allocation of functions at the present time.

Another situation lies in the present method of appropriating funds for the support of the institutions. Accurate analysis of financial requests from institutions requires that uniform systems of student and fiscal accounting be installed so that valid data on which to base decisions concerning the wise division of available funds may be secured. . . .

Among the State-supported institutions of higher learning there exist a number of divergent and, in some instances, conflicting educational policies concerning which the Commission feels that a measure of uniformity would be highly desirable. . . .

While this Commission has given careful consideration to the means whereby both economy and excellence might be achieved in the operation of the present system, it has nevertheless conceived that logical and sound planning for the future of higher education in the State of North Carolina is one of its more important concerns. Perhaps the situation which is most alarming in State-supported higher education in North Carolina is this lack of planning for the future. The many problems which the increased college enrollment in the next 15 years will precipitate furnish eloquent argument in support of the need for long-range planning. Plans for dealing with non-resident applicants and for stimulating the production of public school teachers should be made. Planning concerning the extent to which the State can afford to offer expensive graduate and professional programs for which there is little demand is essential. The recent decisions concerning segregation call for plans concerning the future of the Negro institutions. The separate institutions now independent and uncoordinated obviously cannot perform this planning function, for it requires some agency with a State-wide view and over-all jurisdiction.

190. The State Board of Higher Education

Following the recommendations of the "Bryant Committee," the General Assembly of 1955 passed AN ACT CREATING A STATE BOARD OF HIGHER EDUCATION AND PROVIDING FOR ITS MEMBERS, THEIR QUALIFICATIONS, SELECTION, APPOINTMENT, POWERS, DUTIES, AND FINANCING. The nine-member State Board of Higher Education, appointed by Governor Hodges, elected as its chairman D. Hiden Ramsey, retired Asheville newspaper executive and former member of the State Board of Education.

The most important provisions of this law are reprinted below.

SECTION 1. There is hereby created the North Carolina Board of Higher Education. The purpose of the Board shall be, through the exercise of the powers and performance of the duties set forth in this Act, to promote the development and operation of a sound, vigorous, progressive, and coordinated system of higher education in the State of North Carolina. . . .

Sec. 3. The Board shall consist of nine citizens of North Carolina, one of whom shall be a member of the State Board of Education but none of whom shall be officers or employees of the State nor officers, employees or trustees of such institutions. Members shall be appointed by the Governor for terms of eight years, except that of the first Board appointed, two members shall serve for two years, two shall serve for four years, and two shall serve for six years and three shall serve for eight years. Terms of all members of the first Board shall commence July 1, 1955. . . .

Appointees to the Board shall be selected for their interest in and ability to contribute to the fulfillment of the purpose of the Board. All members of the Board shall be deemed members at large charged with the responsibility of serving the best interests of the whole State. No member shall act as the representative of any particular region or of any particular institution of higher education. . . .

Sec. 5. The Board shall have the following specific powers and duties. . . .

(a) The Board shall determine the major functions and activities of each of such institutions, all such functions and activities remaining as they now are until changed with the approval or by order of the Board. In discharging this duty, the Board shall consider the purpose for which an institution was established, the provisions of its charter, its existing functions and activities, the need for the function or activity in question in that particular institution, and the extent to whch such need is already being met by other institutions. Further, the Board shall take into consideration the need to promote educational methods and standards for the training of persons for the teaching profession to the end that the entire field of public education will be best served.

(b) The Board shall determine the types of degrees which may be granted by each of such institutions.

(c) The Board shall inspect each such institution at least once biennially, and shall make or cause to be made such other inspections as it shall deem necessary.

(d) The Board shall prescribe uniform practices and policies to be followed by such institutions where it finds such uniformity will promote the purpose of the Board.

(e) The Board shall make plans for the development of a system of higher education and shall have the power to require such institutions to conform to such plans.

(f) The Board shall recommend to the Director of the Budget and the Advisory Budget Commission the biennial budget expenditures for each of such institutions. . . .

(g) The Board, in the event of a reduction of appropriations by the Director of the Budget in order to prevent an overdraft or deficit under the provisions of G.S. 143-25, shall, after consulting the officers of each institution for their recommendations, adopt a revised budget for each such institution. The total amount of the reduction for each institution shall be certified to the Board by the Director of the Budget. The revised budget shall be within the reduced appropriation for each such institution. Copies of the revised budgets shall be supplied to the Director of the Budget and such institutions.

(h) The Board shall have the power to make decisions concerning requests from each of such institutions for transfers and changes as between objects and items in the budget of the institution making the request, subject to the approval of the Director of the Budget as set forth in Section 6 of this Act. Copies of such requests and supporting data shall be furnished by such institutions to the Board as well as to the Director of the Budget. The Board shall promptly notify the Director of the Budget of decisions made under the authority of this subsection.

(i) The Board shall possess such powers as are necessary and proper for the exercise of the foregoing specific powers, including the power to make and enforce such rules and regulations as may be necessary for effectuating the provisions of this Act.

Sec. 6. In the exercise of the powers conferred on the Board, it is intended that its decisions on fiscal matters concerning such institutions shall be subject to the approval of the Director of the Budget, and its decisions of an educational nature shall be made by the Board within the limits of appropriated funds and fiscal availability.

Sec. 7. Before final action is taken by the Board in the exercise of powers conferred by subsections (a), (b), (d), and (e) of Section 5, the presidents and chancellors of such institutions to be affected, together with such other persons as they may desire, shall be granted an opportunity to be heard by the Board concerning the proposed action.

Sec. 8. All powers and functions of the State Board of Education concerning higher education and institutions of higher education, except for necessary collaboration with institutions of higher education in the training and certification of public school teachers and principals, shall be vested herewith in the North Carolina Board of Higher Education. . . .

Sec. 14 The various boards of trustees of the institutions of higher education shall continue to exercise such control over the institutions as is provided by law, subject only to the North Carolina Board of Higher Education within the limits of its jurisdiction as herein specified. It is not intended that the trustees of such institutions shall be divested of any powers or initiative now existing with reference to the internal affairs of such institutions, except to the extent that same are affected by the Board's exercise of the powers and performance of the duties specified in this Act. . . .—*1955 Session Laws,* Ch. 1186, pp. 1183-1186.

191. REPORT OF THE NORTH CAROLINA ADVISORY COMMITTEE ON EDUCATION, APRIL 5, 1956

After the State Board of Education voted, on June 3, 1954, to continue public school segregation for the 1954-55 school year, Lieutenant Governor Luther H. Hodges, as chairman of that board, appointed a committee to study the legal aspects of the problem, and on August 4, Governor William B. Umstead appointed a nineteen-member Committee, including three Negroes, to help work out "a policy and program which will preserve the state public school system by having the support of the people." This committee was headed by Thomas J. Pearsall of Rocky Mount. On November 15, Attorney-General Harry McMullan filed the State's brief with the United States Supreme Court, declaring that decrees calling for public school desegregation "forthwith" would be illegal and might lead to chaos.

The General Assembly of 1955 made the following basic changes in the North Carolina school laws: (1) elimination from the laws of any reference to race; (2) transfer of authority over enrollment and assignment of pupils from the State Board of Education to local boards —county and city; (3) transfer of ownership, operation, and control of the State's 7,200 school buses to local units; and (4) substitution of yearly contracts for teachers and principals in lieu of continuing continuous contracts. Resolution No. 29 of the 1955 General Assembly created a seven-member "Advisory Committee on Education," composed of Thomas Pearsall, Chairman, William T. Joyner, Vice-Chairman, Lunsford Crew, R. O. Huffman, William Medford, H. Cloyd Philpott, and Edward F. Yarborough.

On March 2, 1956, Governor Hodges declared that a special session of the General Assembly "doubtless will be required next summer" if the Pearsall Advisory Committee came up with specific recommendations for a declared purpose: . . . "To continue the education of our children, but, at the same time, insure that no child in North Carolina will have to attend a school in which the races are mixed." On April 5, 1956, the "Pearsall Committee" made its Report "to the Governor, the General Assembly, the State Board of Education, and the County and Local School Boards." About six weeks later Governor Hodges called a special session of the General Assembly to convene on July 23. After two days of televised public hearings, the "extraordinary session" of the legislature, with only a few dissenting votes, passed laws designed to carry out the recommendations of the "Pearsall Committee." Its most important action was the passage of a proposed constitutional amendment, which was approved in a popular referendum on September 8. A portion of the "Pearsall Committee's" report is given below.

IV. THE PROBLEM PRESENTED BY THE SUPREME COURT DECISIONS

At the very threshold of our tremendous problem there are some important conclusions which should be made clear. . . .

1. We are of the unanimous opinion that the people of North Carolina will not support mixed schools. This is to say that we believe if the schools were integrated in this State, the General Assembly, representing the people, would withhold support to a degree that the result would certainly be the ruin and eventual abandonment of the public schools. . . .

2. The second threshold conclusion of which we are quite sure is that the saving of our public schools requires action now. To do nothing would, we believe, destroy our public schools. Those who would insure the preservation of the public schools are those who would act. The United States Supreme Court has dealt our schools a near fatal blow and it now requires positive action to save them. . . .

3. In the past ninety years—1865-1955—the Negro race has made the most amazing progress which has ever been made in the history of man in any comparable period of time.

4. That progress has been helped, in fact has been made possible, by the cooperation and assistance of the white race.

5. The white race has been almost wholly responsible for the creation, development and support of an educational system which has been and is now educating the Negro children of the State, all of them. It was Aycock, Joyner and their followers who insisted in 1900 and thereafter that the Negro children of the State must be educated. And it was Aycock and his followers who insisted that there be no color line drawn between money expenditures for education, insisted that the Negro children be educated by the use of tax moneys paid largely by the whites.

6. The educational system of North Carolina has been built on the foundation stone of separation of the races in the schools. Our

State Constitution required that. Every particle of progress which has been made in education since 1900 has rested squarely on the principle of separation of the races compelled by State law. Such building on the foundation of law-compelled segregation met the approval of the Federal Courts for more than fifty years. Our system is a segregated system in its origin and in its growth. . . .

7. The decisions of the Supreme Court of the United States have destroyed our foundation of segregation required by law. The Supreme Court has declared that the principle upon which our system was built and upon which it has rested, is no longer valid. So, we do not have the problem of "preserving our school system." The Supreme Court of the United States destroyed the school system which we had developed—a segregated-by-law system. Our problem is, rather, to build a new system out of the Supreme Court's wreckage of the old. . . .

8. The decision of the Supreme Court of the United States, however much we dislike it, is the declared law and is binding upon us. We think that the decision was erroneous; that it was a reversal of established law upon an unprecedented base of psychology and sociology; that it could cause more harm within the United States than anything which has happened in fifty years. But we must in honesty recognize that, because the Supreme Court is the court of last resort in this country, what it has said must stand until there is a correcting constitutional amendment or until the Court corrects its own error. We must live and act now under the decision of that Court. We should not delude ourselves about that. . . .

10. Defiance of the Supreme Court would be foolhardy. Defiance would alienate those who may be won to our thinking, that separateness of the races is natural and best. Defiance would forfeit the consideration we must have from the Federal Judges if we are to educate our children now. Defiance of the Supreme Court of the United States and of the law as declared by that Court could mean the closing of the public schools very quickly. . . .

11. The Negro leaders from outside the State, and those who are now vocal within the State, appear to be totally indifferent to the fact that their belligerence, their attempt to use the threat of Federal punishment to achieve complete integration, will prevent Negro children from getting a public school education in North Carolina. They appear to be much more interested in assailing the whites with what they conceive to be a mandate of the Federal Supreme Court than in the education of their children. That attitude merely increases the

educational burden which the white man has borne for more than half a century, namely, the burden of educating the Negro children as well as the white children. If the Negro children in North Carolina are to continue receiving public education, it will be as the result of the work and effort of the people of the white race. But that burden must be borne and must include a willingness to provide, at whatever cost, fully adequate schools and facilities for the Negro children of our State. . . .

If the State of North Carolina is to go forward, if the white race in North Carolina is to go forward, the Negro must go forward also. The advancement of our economy and the preservation of our democracy depend in large part upon the education, the understanding, and the morality of the Negro as well as the white. If there prevails ignorance in either race, servitude in either race, hatred in either race, our economy will stall, our society will seethe, and our democracy will degenerate.

V. OUR SCHOOLS CAN BE REBUILT

We have pointed out that the Supreme Court has destroyed the school system which has existed in North Carolina—that is, a segregated-by-law system. Now, we must rebuild our school system. . . .

As we face the task of rebuilding, we are encouraged by the following facts:

1. No Federal Court has said that there must be mixing of the races—integration. No Federal Court has said that any child of any race must be compelled to go to school with a child or children of another race. This is of great importance. The precise Federal Court decision was that a law is invalid if it says that a child can be excluded from a school solely because of race. But no Court has said that a child must go to a school with children of another race.

2. The Supreme Court in May 1954 said that children have the right not to be barred from any public school by law because of color. In May 1955 that same Court indicated recognition of the gravity of the problem and the necessity of giving effect to local conditions in school admissions. To us the Supreme Court has said just this, a law barring a child from a public school because of color and nothing else is invalid; but an administrative body may well find, if it acts honestly and in the light of local conditions, that under existing local conditions it may not be feasible or best for a particular child to go to a particular school with children of another race. *A color bar by law is one thing. A factual local condition bar, even if color is one of the*

causes of the condition, is a different thing. An understanding and tolerant Court may well recognize that difference.

3. The United States Court of Appeals for the Fourth Circuit in a recent North Carolina case from McDowell County said that a child could not press his complaint in the Federal Courts for not being admitted to any particular school until after he had applied for admission to that school, had been denied, and had then exhausted his remedies in the State Courts, provided by the Assignment Statute enacted by the 1955 General Assembly. This decision recognized that each admission case must depend upon the individual facts of that case and that those facts should be completely adjudicated in the State Courts as required by State Statute.

4. We believe that members of each race prefer to associate with other members of their race *and that they will do so naturally unless they are prodded and inflamed and controlled by outside pressure.*

We think it is also true that children do best when in school with children of their own race. We think that in the course of time that will be plain to everyone. When the fires have subsided, when sanity returns, when the NAACP finds that it cannot use the Federal Courts as a club in a fight with the white people, and when the North Carolina Negro finds that his outside advisors are not his best or most reliable friends, then we can achieve the voluntary separation which our Governor and other State leaders have so wisely advocated. . . .

VI. WHAT THE COMMITTEE ADVISES FOR THE SUMMER AND FALL

At this time the people of North Carolina must think about what should be done this Summer and this Fall to meet the problems presented then. The first thing which we advise for each local school unit is to operate the assignment machinery provided by the 1955 Statute. . . .

Specifically, we recommend that all school units:

1. Recognize that there is no law compelling the mixing of the races.

2. Recognize that since the Supreme Court decision there can be no valid law compelling the separation of the races in public schools.

3. Declare that initial assignments to schools will be made in accordance with what the assigning unit (or officer) considers to be for the best interest of the child assigned, including in its consideration, residence, school attended during the preceding year, availability of facilities, and all other local conditions bearing upon the welfare of the child and the prospective effectiveness of his school.

4. After initial assignments are made, permit transfers only upon application and hearing in due course and in accordance with the provisions of the 1955 assignment law.

VII. INSURING A SAFETY VALVE

We think that what we are proposing is constructive; that it is affirmative. But it should be noted again that we are proposing the building of a new school system on a new foundation—a foundation of no racial segregation by law, but assignment according to natural racial preference and the administrative determination of what is best for the child. We know that this new program will present many problems, many difficulties and some controversies, but we think that it can be made to succeed to the satisfaction of the people of the State. . . .

We recommend that a special session of the General Assembly of North Carolina be called this summer to consider submitting to the people the question of changes in our State Constitution.

We recommend that this Legislature cause to be submitted to a vote of the people of North Carolina constitutional amendments, or a single amendment to achieve these desirable and, we think, necessary results:

1. Authority for the General Assembly to provide from public funds financial grants to be paid toward the education of any child assigned against the wishes of his parents to a school in which the races are mixed—such grants to be available for education only in non-sectarian schools and only when such child cannot be conveniently assigned to a non-mixed public school.

2. Authority for any local unit created pursuant to law and under conditions to be prescribed by the General Assembly, to suspend by majority vote the operation of the public schools in that unit, notwithstanding present constitutional provisions for public schools.

These proposed constitutional changes are recommended for consideration with the thought that such changes will give to the people of North Carolina the confidence and assurance which are necessary in order to aid the rebuilding of our school system. We do not think that these changes pose a threat to public education generally in the State. On the contrary, we believe that they will provide the necessary means to assure the support of the white people so badly needed to continue our public schools. If the white people support a public school system in North Carolina, public education will continue. If the white people do not support a public school system in North

Carolina, there will be no public education. To gain that support we believe it will be necessary to provide an available escape from a possibly unacceptable situation. . . .

192. A NORTH CAROLINA EDITORIAL OPINION OF THE "PEARSALL REPORT"

The following editorial was written by C. A. McKnight, editor of *The Charlotte Observer.*

DOES THE PATIENT REQUIRE SUCH A DRASTIC MEDICINE?

One of the best things that can be said about the Advisory Committee on Education report is that it is a *minimum* proposal.

The committee could have gone much further. It could have recommended some of the frenzied, cumbersome and implausible constitutional amendments adopted by other southern states. It could have suggested a variety of statutory changes in the school laws to be made by the legislature without recourse to the people.

Wisely, the committee avoided that temptation. Instead, it called for a special session of the General Assembly to propose a constitutional amendment or amendments to achieve these results:

1. Authority for the General Assembly to provide from public funds financial grants to be paid toward the education of any child assigned against the wishes of his parents to a school in which the races are mixed—such grants to be available for education only in non-sectarian schools and only when such child cannot be conveniently assigned to a non-mixed public school.

2. Authority for any local unit created pursuant to law and under conditions to be prescribed by the General Assembly, to suspend by majority vote the operation of the public schools in that unit, notwithstanding present constitutional provisions for public schools.

Such an amendment, or amendments, it should be noted, would have to be approved by the people of North Carolina in a statewide vote.

The recommendation is based on the assumption that "the saving of our public schools requires action now," as the committee phrased it.

We question that assumption.

The North Carolina scene is relatively quiet. In 1955, the legislature passed a pupil assignment law setting up local and state machinery for processing applications by Negro children for admission to white schools. In the only test case brought under the law, the U. S. Fourth Circuit Court of Appeals ruled that federal courts would not use their injunctive powers until the remedies provided by state law were exhausted. In the normal judicial process, there need be no mixing of the races for another year at least, if local school boards elect to deny such applications.

And it is entirely possible that the slow testing of the 1955 statute will establish a new legal principle which the committee report itself expounded in these words:

A color bar by law is one thing. A factual local condition bar, even if color is one of the conditions, is a different thing.

Why the urgency, then? Why the rush to put before the people two proposals which would seriously weaken the structure of public education in this state?

The first is of dubious constitutionality. Even if it were constitutional, it would introduce an entirely new set of problems. Who is to control the fly-by-night private schools that would surely be set up everywhere? Who is to set standards? What assurance would the people have that their public funds, so diverted, would be wisely used?

The second raises another point that needs a lot of thought. Suppose a majority in a given school district should vote to suspend public schools? What happens, then, to the right of the minority—the same right of the concurrent minority that is the very basis for the states rights doctrine? Would this minority be trampled upon?

In justifying its proposals, the committee calls them a "safety valve."

We rather suspect that they are a safety valve for office seekers, particularly candidates for the next General Assembly, who may be under pressure in some quarters to "do something." To that extent, the minimum program may have some merit.

Obviously, Gov. Hodges is going ahead with his plans for a special session. We hope that he and Committee Chairman Tom Pearsall have enough commitments from legislative leaders to assure that the General Assembly will adopt the minimum program and nothing else and then go home. Then the amendment or amendments can be debated on their merits prior to the statewide election.

If the people of the state finally decide, after hearing all of the facts, that such drastic medicine is needed now, it will be their decision, for better or worse. After all, the schools belong to the people.

—*The Charlotte Observer*, April 7, 1956.

193. WHAT'S RIGHT ABOUT NORTH CAROLINA

The entire contents of the December 31, 1955, edition of *The State*, published by Bill Sharpe and Carl Goerch, were devoted to telling the story of North Carolina's achievements and its prospects for the future. The following paragraphs are taken from this issue of one of North Carolina's most popular magazines.

NEW TRICKS FOR OLD DOGS

NORTH CAROLINA's dominant industrial specialization in tobacco, textiles, furniture and forest products has caused some persons to suspect that the state is not adapted to other types of processing. But the plain facts cut the ground right out from under that suspicion.

Within the framework of the textile industry alone you see many instances of rather radical diversification; the synthetic fibers produced by Enka and DuPont, the Cashmere sweater plant at Weaverville and the American Thread Plant near Marion are examples.

And there are many examples which step completely beyond the pattern of our traditional industry. The rubber plant at Hazelwood is one, and the vast Ecusta plant—*world's largest* producer of cigarette paper and one of the largest manufacturers of Cellophane—is another.

ELECTRONICS

But perhaps the best example of all is seen in this state's rapid rise as a producer of electrical and electronic equipment. Before World War II this industry was practically non-existent in North Carolina. (In 1939 there were three such plants and they employed only 66 people.) By 1947 there were 11 electronics plants and they employed 5,023 persons. Today, after an investment of approximately $42 million, there are at least 40 plants making electrical or electronic equipment and they employ some 22,000 persons.

WE CAN BUILD ANYTHING

Such a steadily growing state requires builders and capital. We have them.

The Carolina's Branch of the Associated General Contractors of America is the largest association of its kind in the United States with 363 regular members and 913 associate members.

These aren't local talent operators. One of them—the J. A. Jones Construction Co., of Charlotte—built the gigantic K-25 gaseous diffusion plant at Oak Ridge. *That was the largest construction contract granted a single company in the history of this nation. . . .*

FIRST IN TRUCKS

North Carolina *has more Class I motor carriers* domiciled within her boundaries than any other state. Charlotte is the trucking center of the South. In Winston-Salem the McLean Trucking Co.—one of the top ten in the nation—operates the *largest individually-owned* truck terminal in the world. . . .

CROPS LEAD

On 8.5 per cent of its cropland North Carolina grows more tobacco than any other state—flue-cured, burley and some Turkish. *Its tobacco crop is worth more than the cattle of Texas, the citrus crop in Florida, the wheat of Kansas or the potatoes of Maine.*

Livestock, once raised mostly for home use, ranks second [in agriculture] as an income producer. In 1939, livestock production in North Carolina was worth $90 million; in 1954, $217 million.

Forty years ago, North Carolina had only two small butter-making creameries, no pasteurization plants, no cheese or ice cream plants.

Today our farms carry about 411,000 dairy cows, and we sell some 700 million pounds of milk products annually. In the last few years the state shifted from a milk importer, to a milk exporter. . . .

We *lead the southeast* in ice cream production, and *rank 13th in the nation*. . . .

Farming is not a declining enterprise down home.

Only four states showed an increase in the number of farms in the 1940-50 decade and North Carolina was one of these, with a net gain of 10,000 farms, more than any other state. . . .

In 1954 total crop value was $160 million more than in 1949. (In 1954, North Carolina was *one of four states* to show an increase in farm income over 1953, rising 2½ per cent to total $927,823,000.)

POWER COMPANIES

The four large power companies serving North Carolina are in the midst of a program which will have cost over one billion dollars in the next few years.

Already, North Carolinians are using more electric power than the average American uses. In the case of Carolina Power & Light Company customers, the residential customer uses *42 per cent more electricity than the United States average*.

WHAT'S RIGHT ABOUT HIGHWAYS?

After pioneering in extensive and effective highway-building, North Carolina took a spectacular step, and *in five years paved 15,000 miles of secondary roads,* which apparently had been consigned forever to dust and mud. Within three years, the hard-surfaced mileage in our road system was tripled. . . .

From 1931 to 1954, over $600 million have been expended on this secondary road system.

Knitting together our 288,000 small farms and our 523 cities and towns, this secondary system now totals 56,902 miles, by far the largest such system under any state responsibility. . . .

WHAT'S RIGHT ABOUT MEDICAL CARE?

We don't hear so much criticism of medical care as we did a few years ago.

The *first* city hospital authorized by the legislature was created in 1881 at Wilmington.

Now we are "No. 1" in the nation in construction projects under the Hill-Burton Act. (As of October 1, 1955.)

We rank "seventh" in the nation in expenditures for these projects.

We rank "fourth" in the nation in new hospital beds. . . .

The Medical Care Commission, since July 1, 1947, has sponsored 216 construction projects, of which 100 were local general hospitals (44 new hospitals and 56 additions), 9 state-owned projects, 39 nurses residences to serve hospitals, 67 health centers, and one diagnostic and treatment center. (The figures are up to October, 1955.)

In all, 5,713 new patient beds have been provided or contracted for. The 216 projects in eight years have required the encumbrance of about $83 million, of which North Carolina local communities have put up 37½ million, the United States Government about 29½ million, and the state about $16 million. . . .

North Carolina has 100 counties, most of them rural, and yet *only 15 counties* are without hospital facilities now.

PUBLIC HEALTH

During the fiscal year 1953-54, North Carolina spent $1.97 per capita for public health, ranking us 13th among the states. In the entire nation, the figure is $1.62 per capita. But when it comes to expenditures in relation to ability to pay, we rank fourth. . . .

North Carolina is the *only* state in the union which has a full-fledged local public health department in each of its counties. When we consider that fully a third of the counties in the United States have no such service, the achievement is worth remarking.

In 1913 an act was passed requiring examination and registration of trained nurses—it was the *first* such act in the United States.

The first strictly rural county in the United States to install a county health department was Robeson. . . .

. . . Since 1947, the General Assembly has appropriated $44 million for hospitalization of mental patients, TB patients, orthopedic and cerebral palsy, and for medical teaching.

Medical men say that if the various expenditures were combined, North Carolina would rank near the top in outlay for medical care.

LIBRARY SERVICE

North Carolinians are not a particularly book-reading people, yet few states have a better record of making books available to all the population. . . .

Today just three of our 100 counties lack public library service. Fully 91 per cent of the population enjoys such a service, ranking North Carolina *9th* among all the states in library coverage.

North Carolina *leads the nation* in bookmobile service, with 101 vehicles serving the remotest rural areas.

RECREATION PROGRAM

North Carolina was the "first" to set up a recreation commission, and has more organized recreation for its size and population than any state in the nation. County-wide programs are being widely organized throughout the state.

There are over 30 full-time year-around industrial recreation programs. . . .

SECURITY PROGRAM

North Carolina's employment security program—now 20 years old —is one of the best-managed in the country.

Only *one* industrial state, New Jersey, has an unemployment fund reserve larger than North Carolina's, in relation to taxable wages. . . .

LABOR MANAGEMENT RELATIONS

North Carolinians have an impressive record of productive and peaceful labor-management relations. Our state has just over a million people working in all types of non-agricultural employment. Some 445,000 of these people work in manufacturing industries. . . .

North Carolina has *more than two per cent* of the nation's non-agricultural employees. Yet during most years, we have only a *small fraction of one per cent* of the nation's strike losses. . . .

RURAL STATE

Two-thirds of North Carolina's population is listed as rural, and a *third of its population makes its living from farming.* It has the *largest farm population* of any state in the union. It has the smallest average farms of any state in the union, which means a lot of subsistence farming.

According to the census, thousands of North Carolina farmers work 100 days or more off the farm, and many of these *report only the cash income received in that off-the-farm employment period.* . . .

We believe that if a properly weighted index were used, and the age factor and the subsistence farming factor were taken into consideration, the income of North Carolinians would rank much closer to the top than to the bottom of the list. To achieve such ranking in present statistics would require reported incomes in *every* economic group in North Carolina to be *higher than the income of the same people* in the nation as a whole.

It is only natural . . . that incomes and costs be higher in metropolitan than in rural centers. And yet, we continue to compare *rural* per capita income against *metropolitan* income as if they were comparable, and if the dollar had the same value in both areas.—*The State,* XXIII, December 31, 1955, No. 16, pp. 19-20, 25-27, 31-33, 53-55, 59-65, 69, 75, 83-84, 93-96.

194. SLEEPING "TAR HEELS"

In the spring of 1956, Roma S. Cheek, a member of the Department of Political Science at Duke University, published privately a ninety-five page booklet entitled *Sleeping "Tar-Heels."* In the preface to the challenging volume, she wrote: "It is not the intent of the author to overlook North Carolina's progress, but it is the conscientious feeling of the author that North Carolina has had more praise than we as citizens actually deserve." She points out the "inadequacy of North Carolina's governmental structure in meeting mid-twentieth century needs." She thinks that North Carolina officials and employees are "working within governmental machinery which seriously hinders them in the performance of their duties and prevents their maximum efficiency."

WHEN HISTORY is recorded for the mid-twentieth century, North Carolinians should realize that they may now be earning for themselves the title of "Sleeping Tar-Heels."

. . . Greatly needed constitutional and governmental reforms have been opposed throughout the first part of the twentieth century and are opposed today on the grounds that "everything is fine" and "North Carolina is a great leader among the states" and the "most progressive southern state," etc. Yet the over-all facts do not prove this. . . .

In 1954 North Carolina, for the first time, went to the bottom of all the states in earnings for its manufacturing employees. Not only was North Carolina forty-eighth in this important indices of economic well-being but "the rate of increase in average weekly earnings during the last five years has been lower in North Carolina than in any state."

During the year 1954 North Carolina was forty-third among the state in per capita income—moving up from forty-fourth to forty-third "by the slim margin of $4 per capita. . . ."

In bank deposits, which many people consider an important indicator of economic well-being, North Carolina ranks forty-fourth.

During the year 1954 North Carolina ranked "next to the bottom among states in the percentage of its college age population which actually attends college."

The average "Tar Heel" has less than eight years of schooling, making North Carolina forty-fourth among the states in this area. . . .

In the area of public service to its citizens, North Carolina is forty-sixth among the states in the large number of pupils per teacher in the classroom; forty-fifth in the percentage of its school age children actually in school; and eighth from the bottom in the average value of school property. In the latest year for which comparable figures are available, 1951-52, North Carolina spent $26.18 per person for its public schools and $37.41 per person for alcoholic beverages. . . .

During the first year of the Korean War, 34.6 per cent of North Carolina's young men who were given the Armed Forces Qualification tests failed them, making North Carolina forty-second among the states in rejectees. The average of rejectees for the nation as a whole was 16.4 per cent. . . .

Latest available statistics show that although one-fourth of North Carolina's gainfully employed citizens are engaged in farming the farm income is less than one-half of what it is for the average farmer across the nation. . . .

During the 1954 North Carolina's per capita retail sales placed the state forty-fifth in the nation. . . .

North Carolina ranks the lowest of all the forty-eight states in its public welfare expenditures. . . .

In the area of crime North Carolina is the highest of all the forty-eight states in aggravated assault crimes—its crime rate in this classification being 43.1 per cent greater than the average for the nation as a whole. . . .

In its over-all governmental patterns North Carolina is operating within antiquated, costly, and unduly complicated framework and procedures. . . . For example, most of the officials and agencies of the administrative branch of state government function without being directly responsible to the Governor, to the Legislature, or to the people but are responsible only to the pressure groups which created them. North Carolina now has in its administrative branch of government 178 governmental units having separate statutory status and set up in 49 different ways. Since no provision for removal of officials is provided by law for 138 of these governmental units they cannot be considered as being currently responsible to any higher authority for their actions and are without any over-all supervision.

There have been no basic revisions in North Carolina's tax structure since the depression year of 1932 and yet there have been great economic, social, and technological changes in the last twenty-four years. . . .

Instead of spending its time on the many complicated problems of state government which so badly need its attention the state Legislature appears more interested in its local political patronage, power, and interest and continues to make even minor governmental decisions in Raleigh. In the 1955 Legislature, for example, of the 1999 measures introduced 977 were local bills; eighty-eight per cent of all local bills introduced became law as against 54 per cent of the nonlocal measures. . . .

A state Constitution is supposed to contain only the basic framework and fundamental principles of government but the North Carolina Constitution now contains so much legislation that it can no longer properly be called a Constitution. It has become, in itself, a stumbling block to efficient, effective state and local government.

North Carolina's occupations and professions which constitute the source of livelihood, and the door of opportunity for the state's youth have largely become a monopoly of the vested interests. Each occupation or profession sets up its own special board to control its own particular field not only with the state's blessing, but endowed by the state with punitive powers to enforce its decisions. . . . Instead of correcting this situation each North Carolina legislature adds to it by creating additional licensing boards. . . .

Under the present system of licensing there is no central place to which an applicant can go or write for information on the requirements of the Boards. . . . There is at present no system for an impartial review of those applications denied or for a representative of the public on these boards. Also, there is at present considerable duplication in inspections—especially in the health field. . . .

Another area in which the public interest is neglected is in the handling of criminals. The North Carolina legislature refuses to relinquish the doubtful distinction of having this state the only one of the forty-eight with the prison system under its highway department. Even though some of the prisoners' repeated convictions go beyond the one hundred mark the legislature does not enact a "criminal repeater act" as many states have done so that upon a fourth conviction for a felony the criminal receives a life sentence. . . .

The recommendations that the prison system be separated from the Highway Department and that modern methods of handling criminals be set up have been repeatedly defeated in the legislature. Also, there has been no attempt by the legislature to set up a merit system for the employment of adequately trained personnel for the prison system and political considerations play a part in appointments at all levels. . . .

The 1941 Legislature provided for a merit system for state agencies that would be denied federal money if their personnel were not employed on a merit basis. Only six agencies are involved and there has been no real interest on the part of the legislature in extending the merit system to the great body of state employees. The 1949 Legislature set up a Department of Personnel but without a merit system. While this department has done a good job it has not been given the necessary funds and staff or the necessary authority by law for developing an over-all state personnel program based on merit. . . .

Another area in which the public interest has been neglected is in the failure of the legislature to enact the laws necessary to lessen and prevent much of the increasing death and injury on the public highways. Compulsory motor vehicle inspection laws have contributed greatly to accident reduction in other states. Laws providing for mandatory jail sentences for convicted drunken driving have been repeatedly rejected by the legislature. Also the legislature has failed to give the Department of Motor Vehicles adequate funds and staff for adequate highway safety education or for eliminating highway hazards and reducing the present legal loads. . . .

In the twentieth century every state except North Carolina, West Virginia and Wyoming have reorganized their state administration and in some instances their entire state government; or they are now officially considering Constitutional revision; or have had thorough official studies of state administrative reorganization during the current period 1950-1956. North Carolina has done none of these.

All too many Tar Heels in position of leadership have adopted the "ostrich policy" of sticking their heads in the sand and refusing to recognize the serious implications of North Carolina's manifold complex current problems. The philosophy of the "ostrich policy" is—if you don't recognize it, it doesn't exist or it will go away. . . .

Perhaps the most serious way in which North Carolina lags behind the other states is in the fact that no serious current efforts for effective governmental reorganization are being made in the state. Both the legislature and the citizens seem asleep to the needs and problems. . . .

If North Carolina is to fully develop its natural resources, its industry and commerce, and the potential abilities of its people it must set up without further delay a stable, healthy governmental structure. A competent and businesslike state governmental structure which concerns itself with the best interests of the total citizenship and gives the maximum in return for the tax dollars spent is the state's number 1 need. The greatest possible efficiency, economy and leadership in government has become a necessity in North Carolina. A state as rich in natural and human resources as North Carolina should not continue indefinitely to be a laggard among the 48 states. It should and can become a leader among the states if "Tar Heels" will awaken to their responsibilities and opportunities.—Roma S. Cheek, Sleeping "Tar-Heels" (printed privately, 1956), pp. 7-12, 43, 48, 51-52.

195. NORTH CAROLINA POPULATION TRENDS, 1950-1960

The two most notable trends of population in North Carolina since 1950 have been urbanization and migration. Within the state there has been a large migration from rural areas to towns and cities. There has also been a large out-of-state migration, particularly of nonwhites.

DURING THE 1950's the population of North Carolina underwent many changes. The outstanding theme of these changes was movement. Not only was there drastic redistribution of the population within the state but also a considerable loss of population by out-of-state movement. Population changes which took place within North Carolina during these ten years point out the following trends: (1) a low rate of total increase, (2) a relative loss of rural population, (3) the rapid growth of smaller cities and counties containing these cities, (4) the concentration of population in the large urban centers, (5) much movement of the population within the state and heavy loss by out-migration. These trends become evident when the data of the 1960 Census are compared with those of the 1950 Census for the state.

In 1960 North Carolina's population numbered slightly over four and one half million. This represented a gain of approximately one half million over the 1950 figure, a rate of increase of 12 per cent. This was the lowest rate of growth exhibited by North Carolina for any decade since the 1860's when the state sustained heavy losses during the Civil War. . . .

In 1950 North Carolina ranked first in the United States in non-white population, containing somewhat over one million. However, during the decade this sizable segment of the population increased by only 78,000, placing North Carolina fourth in nonwhite population. This gain of 7 per cent should be compared with a nonwhite increase of 27 per cent for the nation. As we shall see later the majority of persons leaving North Carolina during this period were nonwhite. The white population increased at a rate twice as great as that of the nonwhite but still was considerably lower than the national increase of 18 per cent.

According to the Census of 1950 two out of every three persons in North Carolina were classified as rural, that is, living on farms or in places of less than 2,500 inhabitants. This group, comprising over two and one half million persons in 1950, increased but 2 per cent during the decade compared with an increase in the urban population of 32 per cent. In fact, of those 35 counties which can be classified as rural in both 1950 and 1960—that is, containing no city as large as 2,500—24 lost population, one remained stable, and only 10 gained. . . .

When all counties are considered we find that 53 of the 100 counties lost rural population while in only 9 did the urban population de-crease. Of the 38 counties that sustained a loss in total population dur-ing the decade, 24 could be classified as rural. One of the main effects of the loss of rural population can be seen in the changing occupational composition of the state. In 1950 one out of every four workers was occupied in farming, either as a farm manager or farm laborer. How-ever, by 1960 this figure was cut in half, with only one out of eight engaged in farming.

We can divide the 38 counties which lost population into two distinct types, the counties in the eastern part of the state being very different from those of the west. Fourteen of the counties losing population were west of Mecklenburg county, and 24 were east of there. While the main cause of population loss of the counties in both areas was the decrease in rural population, there were different underlying factors. The western counties are characterized by small farms and scattered rural settlements. It is likely that a sizable number of the rural persons in this area work in furniture and paper factories and other industries, in some of the larger cities in neighboring counties. Judging from population shifts in the western part of the state many persons in rural areas moved into nearby counties with manufacturing and other industrial centers. For example, Haywood and Caldwell counties, containing large manufacturing centers, gained 10 and 64 per cent respectively in urban population.

The Piedmont and eastern counties have long been the cotton and tobacco centers of the state, having large farms and many tenant farmers. While it is possible that some of the migrants from the eastern counties moved into cities and urban centers within the area it is much more likely that a great number moved out of the the state. When we compare the color composition of the two areas this becomes evident. The average per cent nonwhite of the eastern counties losing population was 45 while the population of the western counties was only 33 per cent nonwhite. . . .

North Carolina had in 1950 thirty cities of 10,000 or more inhabitants located in 29 counties. These counties contained approximately 2.2 million persons or 55 per cent of the state's population. By 1960, however, nearly 6 out of every 10 North Carolinians lived in these 29 counties. These counties increased at a considerably higher rate than the state as a whole, 16 per cent compared with 12 per cent, while the 30 cities increased at an average of 25 per cent.

During the decade 5 additional cities passed the 10,000 mark bringing the total to 35 cities in 34 counties. By 1960 these 34 counties together contained two thirds of the state's entire population.

Together with the expanding growth of counties with large cities, the increasing concentration of the population in the large urban centers presents a picture of rapid urbanization. The Bureau of the Census has designated cities of 50,000 and over, together with their surrounding population, as urbanized areas. This was done to provide a better separation of urban and rural population in the vicinity of the larger cities. For example, most of our larger cities now have a sizable number of persons residing just outside the city limits in what is commonly called the suburbs or "urban fringe." Since most of these persons work in the city, shop and obtain other services in the city, they are in many ways actually part of the city. . . .

In 1950 North Carolina had 6 urbanized areas containing a total population of slightly over 500,000. These areas were centered around Asheville, Charlotte, Durham, Greensboro, Raleigh, and Winston-Salem. By 1960 these areas had a population of over 700,000, an increase of almost 50 per cent. During the decade High Point became an urbanized area bringing the total to seven areas containing three-fourths of a million persons. The rapid growth of these areas is emphasized when we point out the proportion of the state's population these areas contain. In 1950 approximately 13 per cent of North Carolina's population lived in urbanized areas; by 1960, 17 per cent of the population was contained within these areas.

The trends that have been pointed out so far—small rate of increase, relative loss of rural population, and the rapid growth of the urban population all result from one factor characteristic of North Carolina's population during the 1950's—movement. Although there was a great deal of movement within counties, and from one county to another, the more important fact is the great number lost by movement out of the state.

In 1960 only one-half of the population (5 years or older) was living in the same house in which they were living in 1955. However, the majority of the persons who had moved stayed within the same county and in many cases the same city. There were some 600,000 persons living in a different county in 1960. Of these slightly over one-half moved from one county to another within North Carolina while 270,000 had moved into North Carolina from another state. . . . It would be safe to assume that most of the persons who moved from one county to another and the great majority of those who moved in from another state settled in or near urban areas.

If we consider the number of persons moving into the state and the number of persons who moved out of the state, North Carolina lost approximately 330,000 by out-migration during the 1950's. . . .

Of the 330,000 loss to the state during the period, approximately two thirds were nonwhite. At the beginning of the decade North Carolina's population was 27 per cent nonwhite. But due to the loss of over 200,000 by migration the 1960 proportion was only 25 per cent. In fact, this loss by migration was nearly one-fifth of the nonwhite population in 1950. This number was approximately equal to the natural increase of the nonwhite population, that is, the difference between the number of births and the number of deaths.

In other words, the nonwhite population exported nearly as many persons as they produced during the decade.

While the loss of the white population was not nearly so large as the nonwhite loss, it was sufficient to lower the rate of increase much below that for the national white population. Between 1950 and 1960 the white population in North Carolina increased 14 per cent compared with a national increase of 18 per cent. Earlier we distinguished between the eastern and western counties which lost population and their differences in nonwhite population. Since the western counties contained such a small proportion of nonwhite, it is likely that they furnished many of the white migrants, moving into the adjoining states of Virginia, Tennessee, and Georgia. The eastern counties losing population were almost 50 per cent nonwhite and, no doubt, these counties lost much of their nonwhite population to larger urban centers along the Atlantic seaboard to the north.

The outstanding feature of North Carolina's population during the 1950's was *movement*. Not only did the state lose a great number of people by migration but there was much internal movement as well. The two aspects of these movements—internal and external—resulted in important changes for the state. The rapid growth of the urban counties and the concentration of the population in large urbanized areas was due mainly to internal movement in the state. This is shown in the decreases in the population of the rural and smaller counties. The other type of movement—out-of-state—is emphasized in the low rate of increase of the state for the decade.

We have no way of knowing what changes will take place among North Carolina's population during the present decade. If, as many suspect, the trends of the past decade continue, North Carolina will exhibit even greater changes in the future. We expect the rural and smaller counties to continue losing population or to increase only slightly, larger cities to increase rapidly, continued concentration of the population in large urbanized areas, and out-migration to continue, especially for nonwhites.—The University of North Carolina *News Letter*, Vol. XLVIII, No. 1, April, 1963.

196. TAR HEEL FARMING: A TIME OF SWEEPING CHANGE

Tar Heel farming is in the midst of revolution. In the following document, first printed in the University of North Carolina *News Letter* in 1961, S. H. Hobbs, Jr., a distinguished Chapel Hill rural

sociologist, analyzed the trends in the 1950's and made some interesting predictions about the future of North Carolina agriculture.

TRENDS IN AGRICULTURE in North Carolina during the last five years
or so have been more pronounced than during any period since the
Civil War.

If these trends continue for another 15 or 20 years at the pace
set in the last 5 or 10 years then agriculture in North Carolina and
in the United States will bear little resemblance to agriculture as we
have known it in the past.

The basic trends are: (1) A rapid decline in the number of farms;
(2) a large gain in the size of farms; (3) tremendous gains in mechanization and push-button farming; (4) rapid trends towards large-scale
agriculture with fewer farmers marketing larger per cents of farm
products; (5) rapid decline in farm tenancy; and (6) large increases
in the value of farms per farm and per acre, notwithstanding the
gradual decline in the net income of farmers.

In general, the five-year changes from 1954 through 1959 have been
the most pronounced of any period during the last 100 years, and
probably more pronounced than anyone had anticipated.

Every county in North Carolina lost farms from 1954 to 1959,
the losses ranging from 13.2 per cent in Washington County to
49.6 per cent in Cherokee and Polk Counties.

This is the first time in the history of the state that every county
in the state has lost farms. In fact, North Carolina farms tended to
hold up in numbers up to around 1950, being surpassed by only one
or two states in this respect.

There was a moderate decline in farms of some 20,000 from 1950
to 1954, while the decline from 1954 to 1959 was 77,339, or a loss of
28.9 per cent. Part of this loss, 16,671, was due to a change in the
census definition of what constitutes a farm. The current definition
is more realistic in that it eliminates quite a number of operations
classed as agricultural which more truly are simply residential
properties with a minimum of farming operations.

As a general rule, the lowest per cent declines in the number of
farms took place along the entire Virginia border, with slightly larger
decreases in the Eastern tobacco belt, or, to put it another way, the
more rural and tobacco counties of the state tended to decline less
than the more urban and industrial counties. The largest decreases
occurred in the Southwest quadrant of the state from Hoke through

Cabarrus, Caldwell and Avery, and practically all counties to the Southwest of the line connecting the above counties.

For the first time since the Civil War farms in North Carolina have increased in size.

The trend during the 100-year period following the Civil War was a steady decrease in the average size of farms.

From 1950 to 1954 the size of North Carolina farms increased approximately one acre upon an average. However, from 1954 to 1959 the size of farms increased from 68.2 acres to 83.4 acres with only 27 acres under cultivation.

While this is a sizable gain, in line with national trends, the increase in the size of North Carolina farms is far below the average for the United States. The increase for the United States was from 242.2 acres to 302.4 acres. North Carolina farms are still at the bottom in average size by a considerable acreage.

Practically every county in the state experienced a gain in the average size of farms. The main factor in the increased size of farms was the tremendous loss in the total number of farms. As a matter of fact, the amount of land classed as farm land declined from 18,260,346 acres to 15,885,724 acres. There is far less land in farms in North Carolina today than at any period since the Civil War.

There has been a steady decline in net farm income in North Carolina and in practically every state in the Union during the last decade or so. Notwithstanding this fact there has been a considerable increase in the value of farm real estate per acre throughout practically the entire nation.

Perhaps much of this is simply inflation. North Carolina farms in 1954 had an average value according to the census of $8,059, while the value in 1959 was $14,685. Much of the per value increase is due to fewer and larger farms. The per acre value increased from $128.10 in 1954 to $193.30 in 1959.

As a rule, the highest per acre values are in counties with large urban populations, plus the tobacco belt counties which have the highest values of the counties that are principally agricultural. As a matter of fact, the farm land values are much higher in some of the tobacco belt counties than in some of the highly urban counties. . . .

It is possible that change in the immediate future will be more substantial than it has been in the immediate past. This is true of agriculture in North Carolina and throughout the United States except that North Carolina has been reluctant to match the changes that have been taking place over much of the nation.

We are going to experience substantial gains in mechanization. There will be further consolidation of farms, and there will be more specialization in farm production. There will be considerable gains in integrated farming, such as has been developing in the Middle West in recent years.

The farmers who will stay in business will be more highly trained ones and farmers with initiative and imagination. Farmers will convert more of their edible crops into livestock and poultry products. Fewer and larger farm operations will be found in livestock, poultry and vegetable production.

Probably the best word to express successful farming in the future is agribusiness, which simply means applying business methods to the business of agriculture. We will always have family farmers and even a large number of subsistence and nondescript farmers but the market place is being and will be taken over by a smaller per cent of farmers who are businessmen as well as agriculturists.

This may not be what many people would like to see take place, but the trends of recent years definitely point in this direction.— Greensboro *Daily News*, July 2, 1961.

197. NORTH CAROLINA: AN ECONOMIC PROFILE

The best summary view of the state's economy in the early 1960's is contained in *North Carolina: An Economic Profile,* published by the Federal Reserve Bank of Richmond in 1963. Reprinted below are portions of this booklet relating to various aspects of the state's economic life.

Composition. The labor force of North Carolina numbers nearly 2 million persons. Manufacturing stands out as the major employer, providing jobs for more than a fourth of the total. In the South, North Carolina is the leading manufacturing employer and nationally it ranks tenth.

Agriculture follows manufacturing as a major employer. In 1961 only Texas had a larger agricultural work force.

Government—Federal, State, and local—ranks third in employment. More than half of all government employees work for the State and local units, a good portion of them as teachers. Federal civilian employees are relatively small in number, but this is not true for the military since the State ranks as one of the nation's leading defense areas. In 1961 only four states had larger military populations. The installations in North Carolina provide jobs for roughly 10,000 civilians and 80,000 officers and enlisted men.

PERSONAL INCOME

In 1961 per capita income was $1,642—an amount $621 below the national average and lower than in 41 other states. Compared with the adjoining states, North Carolina ranked above Tennessee and South Carolina but below Virginia and Georgia.

A number of factors contribute to the relatively low State figure. First, agriculture, in which a great many North Carolinians are employed, is not a source of large incomes. In 1961 net income per farm was just slightly over $3,000. Second, most of the manufacturing industries pay wages well below the national average for all manufacturing. In 1961 average weekly earnings were lower than in any other state except Mississippi. Third, because of the large number of children and the net out-migration of a substantial number of adults, the State has a smaller proportion of income earners than the national average. Fourth, most of the large nonwhite population hold unskilled jobs which pay poorly.

Although per capita income is well below the national average, it has risen considerably. In 1929, the first year for which estimates were made, the figure was less than half the national amount, whereas today it stands at nearly three-fourths. Also, the State has done well in comparison with adjoining states. From 1929 to 1961 only South Carolina bettered the State's five-fold increase.

MANUFACTURING

Probably the best dollar measure of manufacturing activity is the amount of value added by production. Its computation is fairly complex, but to simplify, value added is found by subtracting the cost of materials, supplies, and power from the value of shipments. Value added avoids the duplication in the value of shipments figure which results from the use of products of some firms as materials by others. Consequently, value added is a more accurate measure for comparing the relative economic importance of manufacturing among industries and geographic regions. In 1960 the $3.8 billion of value added by manufacturers in the State was highest in the South Atlantic Region and ranked fourteenth in the nation.

Another important dollar measure is the amount spent by manufacturers for plant and equipment. In 1960 it totaled $251 million

—more than in any other South Atlantic state. Nationally, North Carolina ranked twelfth.

In 1958, the year of the last comprehensive census of manufactures, there were 7,289 establishments, nearly half of which were small-scale operations with less than ten employees. Many of these small plants were saw mills, print shops, and food processors. At the opposite end of the scale there were 41 establishments with 1,000 or more employees, the majority of which manufactured textiles and tobacco products. The Piedmont is the leading manufacturing area. In 1961 nine of the top ten counties in manufacturing employment were located there.

Textiles. Textile production stands out as the leading type of manufacturing activity. In terms of value added, textile firms in the State make almost a fourth of all broad woven cotton goods made in America and more than a third of the man-made fiber fabrics. The State's spinning mills turn out nearly half of all cotton yarn produced for sale in this country and about the same proportion of the hosiery output.

Although textiles are manufactured in 78 of the 100 counties, the great majority of the firms are located along Interstate Highway 85—which could be called the "textile highway of the nation." Nearly one-fifth of the nation's textile employees work in North Carolina plants located within 40 miles of this highway which traverses the industrial Piedmont.

In 1960 the textile industry accounted for 44 per cent of the manufacturing employment and 33 per cent of the value added.

Furniture. Furniture and tobacco manufacturing follow textiles. Measured by employment, furniture ranks second; but in terms of value added this position is taken by tobacco. Basic differences in production processes account for the difference in rankings. Tobacco production is characterized by a high capital investment and a large amount of automation. Although the furniture industry is becoming increasingly automated as it adapts itself to assembly line methods, compared with tobacco it is a labor-intensive, low-capital industry.

The State is the nation's leading manufacturer of wood and wood upholstered furniture. Firms manufacturing these and other furniture products employ about 45,000 persons, nearly all in the Piedmont. Four counties in that region—Guilford, Catawba, Davidson, and Caldwell—account for over half of the furniture employment in the State. High Point, located in Guilford County, is the site of one of the nation's principal furniture markets. Four special showings are held each year in the mammoth Southern Furniture Exhibition Building which contains nearly a million square feet of showroom space.

During the 1950's employment in furniture grew above the State average for all manufacturing. The industry's growth also exceeded the national average for furniture, with the result that North Carolina increased its relative shares of national furniture employment and value added.

Tobacco. Tobacco, the State's principal farm crop, is of great significance to manufacturing. Employees of tobacco manufacturers represent about 7 per cent of the manufacturing total and in terms of its contribution to value added, the industry is even more important.

The manufacture of cigarettes and other tobacco products is concentrated in a rather small section of the Piedmont. Plants operated by four large firms in the cities of Winston-Salem, Durham, Reidsville, and Greensboro manufactured over 300 billion cigarettes in 1961, representing about three-fifths of the national total.

Between 1950 and 1961 production of cigarettes, the major product of the industry, increased by 53 per cent. Employment also increased but at a slower pace since firms used more efficient plant and equipment to increase production per employee. The employment gains were almost entirely confined to the cigarette manufacturing segment of the industry, while the number of persons working in tobacco stemming and redrying plants remained fairly constant.

PORT ACTIVITY AND FOREIGN TRADE

During 1960, 4.9 million short tons of freight traffic passed through North Carolina's two major ports located at Wilmington and Morehead City.

Wilmington, which is much the larger of the two, has a State-owned and -operated terminal with a wharf that can berth five 500-foot vessels simultaneously. It has three transit sheds, two warehouses, and ten acres of paved open storage. Most of Wilmington's trade is domestic (coastwise, internal, and local). In 1960 four-fifths of the 4.2 million short tons handled fell into this category.

The State-owned terminal at Morehead City has three transit sheds, five storage warehouses, and a wharf capable of berthing four 500-foot cargo ships and one petroleum tanker at one time. Domestic trade, which represented 57 per cent of the port's tonnage in 1960, is the major type handled.

Total foreign tonnage going through North Carolina ports more than tripled between 1950 and 1960, while domestic tonnage increased by only 8 per cent. Even with this marked increase in foreign trade, 78 per cent of 1960 tonnage was domestic. The major foreign domestic commodity was petroleum products. The major foreign exports were iron and steel scrap, wood pulp, and tobacco, while major foreign imports included petroleum products, fertilizer materials, molasses, and sugar.

A large portion of exports go through out-of-state ports. In 1960 the State generated more exports than either of the adjoining coastal states of Virginia or South Carolina. Yet, its ports handled less (measured by either tonnage or value) than either of those states. In 1960 total exports amounted to $604 million, but only $93 million was exported through Wilmington and Morehead City. Of the remainder, some was transported by rail, truck, and air, but a large amount left from ports of the adjoining coastal states.

AGRICULTURE

North Carolina has the largest farm population in the nation and ranks second in number of farms, but in terms of net farm income it ranks fourth. Tobacco is the most important crop, and for years North Carolina has towered above the other tobacco producing states. In 1961 the State's harvested acreage represented 40 per cent of the national total and was more than double that of Kentucky, the nearest competitor. The State also ranks high in the production of several other commodities, holding second place in peanuts and sweet potatoes, and fourth place in broilers.

Like other forms of business activity, agriculture is closely intertwined with the rest of the economy. For example, in 1958, 62 per cent of the State's retail stores sold goods related to agriculture and in the same year 73 per cent of the manufacturing firms used raw materials from the farm.

Measured by the value of principal crops in 1960, the most important agricultural counties are Pitt, Johnston, Robeson, and Nash. These counties, all of which are large tobacco producers, are located in the Coastal Plain.

Farm size and characteristics. The most significant feature of North Carolina farms is their small size and high value per acre. In 1959, the year of the latest census of agriculture, the average size was only 83 acres, and 91 per cent of the farms had gross sales under $10,000. The average acreage, at one-third of the national figure, was the smallest in the country. In contrast, value per acre was considerably higher than in most other states. Both of these conditions are primarily a result of the nature of the tobacco and cotton crops which require relatively large amounts of labor per acre, and which are subject to Government programs which have restricted acreage, maintained prices, and thus made land with allotments more valuable.

Because incomes from farming activities are generally low, many farmers spend a substantial portion of their working hours at off-farm jobs. The 1959 Census showed that more than one-fourth of the farmers spent 100 days or more at jobs away from the farms and that a third of the farm families received over half of their income from nonfarm sources. Part-time farming is most prevalent in the Mountain Region and the Piedmont.

Many of the farmers were not owners. In 1959, three out of every ten farmers were tenants and about half of these were sharecroppers. In sharecropping the landlord furnishes the tenant most of his basic equipment and all or part of his seed and fertilizer. In return for his labor, the tenant receives a share of the crop. Tenancy is most prevalent among nonwhites, who work on a majority of the tenant farms, yet represent less than one-fourth of the farm operators.

Major commodities. Crops are much more important than livestock, accounting for 71 per cent of the cash receipts in 1961. Over the years this distribution has been shifting in favor of livestock, but the imbalance is still pronounced. The big reason for this lopsided situation is the high-value tobacco crop. In 1961 it accounted for 70 per cent of the cash receipts from the sale of crops, yet it was grown on only 9 per cent of the harvested cropland.

BANKING

The structure of banking in North Carolina changed considerably in the last decade. In 1950 there were 225 banks with 218 branches; eleven years later there were 54 fewer banks but more than double the earlier number of branches. These shifts were primarily caused by mergers and extensions of customer service. The majority of mergers took place after 1955 with the greatest concentration between 1959 and 1961. The relative increase in total banking offices (banks plus branches) exceeded population growth with the result that at the end of the decade there were more offices to serve a given number of people than in 1950.

Changes took place in financial size as well as in structure. Resources increased from $2.1 billion in 1950 to $3.6 billion in 1961, a 77 per cent growth. This gain was greater than that of the nation, but less than that of the adjoining states, with the exception of South Carolina. Savings and loan associations grew at an even greater pace. Total assets increased by 317 per cent from $331 million in 1950 to $1.4 billion in 1960 while the number of such institutions increased by only eight (from 176 to 184).

In 1961 the two largest banks (which are among the 100 largest banks in the United States) accounted for 41 per cent of the State's total bank resources. In addition to being concentrated in a few banks, resources are also concentrated in the major cities. In 1960 the six standard metropolitan statistical areas of Charlotte, Raleigh, Greensboro-High Point, Winston-Salem, Asheville, and Durham, accounted for nearly one-half of total deposits, a slightly larger share than in 1950. Charlotte, alone, had 17 per cent.—John L. Knapp, *North Carolina: An Economic Profile* (Federal Reserve Bank of Richmond, 1964), pp. 1-3, 8, 12-13, 24-27, 31-32.

198. INDUSTRIAL GROWTH AND LABOR-MANAGEMENT RELATIONS IN NORTH CAROLINA IN RECENT YEARS

Expanded industrial payrolls and higher earnings of employees in non-manufacturing activities have figured strongly in causing the advances of recent years in North Carolina's per capita income. The state's per capita income, according to the U.S. Department of Commerce, has increased as follows: 1960, $1,562; 1961, $1,638; 1962, $1,732; 1963, $1,807.

The first document below gives a summary of the state's industrial growth for the decade after 1953; the second presents a brief statement about labor-management relations.

INDUSTRIAL GROWTH

BOTH TOTAL non-agricultural employment and factory wages have increased steadily in North Carolina during the past decade.

Non-farm employment expanded by 26 per cent between 1953 and 1963, rising from an annual average of 1,022,100 in 1953 to an average of 1,290,900 in 1963 for a net gain of 268,800 during the decade. An average of 26,880 new jobs per year were created during the ten-year period.

The manufacturing segment of total non-farm employment expanded by 20 per cent during the 1953-1963 decade, rising from an annual average of 448,700 in 1953 to 540,000 in 1963, for a net gain of 91,300 in the ten-year period. An average of 9,130 new jobs per year were created in manufacturing during the decade.

The over-all growth in the non-manufacturing segment of total non-farm employment was much higher than in manufacturing. Between 1953 and 1963, non-manufacturing employment increased 30 per cent for a net gain of 177,500 jobs, rising from 573,400 in 1953 to 750,900 in 1963. The yearly average of new jobs created in non-manufacturing occupations during the decade was 17,750.

NON-AGRICULTURAL EMPLOYMENT IN NORTH CAROLINA
(1953-1963)

Year	Total Non-Farm Employment	Factory Employment	Non-Manufacturing Employment
1953	1,022,100	448,700	573,400
1954	1,012,000	436,800	575,200
1955	1,059,400	460,400	599,000
1956	1,099,300	470,600	628,700
1957	1,101,300	470,300	631,000
1958	1,108,800	469,600	639,200
1959	1,163,700	496,900	666,800
1960	1,195,500	509,300	686,200
1961	1,209,100	509,000	700,100
1962	1,258,200	530,500	727,700
1963	1,290,900	540,000	750,900

An increase of 36.6 per cent in gross average hourly earnings of factory production workers took place in North Carolina between 1953 and 1963.

The "average" Tar Heel factory worker earned $1.23 an hour during 1953. By 1963 the average had climbed to $1.68.

Percentage gains of individual industries in average hourly earnings of employees during the ten years ranged from a high of 56.5 per cent in stone, clay and glass products to a low of 9.2 per cent in full fashioned hosiery.

Much larger percentage increases were recorded in several non-manufacturing industries, due principally to the influence of State and Federal minimum wage legislation upon these employment groups during the last four years of the 1953-1963 decade.—*Biennial Report of the Department of Labor, 1961-1963* (Raleigh, N. C., 1964), pp. 10-11, 16.

LABOR-MANAGEMENT RELATIONS

Labor-management relations have continued to be exceptionally peaceful and productive in North Carolina, with few interruptions of work and little time lost as a result of strikes. The great majority of cases involving negotiations between labor and management have been settled amicably without loss of production.

In the 23 years since the Conciliation Service was established in the Department of Labor, only six-tenths of one per cent of the national total of man-days lost from production as a result of strikes have been lost in North Carolina.

During the last four calendar years, 1960-1963, strikes came close to the vanishing point in North Carolina, totaling only seventeen-hundredths of one per cent of the national total of man-days lost during the period. This record is attributable to the peaceful climate of industrial relations which has long characterized North Carolina industry and to the effective work of our Conciliation and Arbitration services with management and labor.

In the vast majority of establishments in North Carolina, working relationships of employers and employees are orderly and cooperative. It is well known that for every critical labor-management dispute which develops into a work stoppage, many more negotiations are culminated by joint agreement between the parties without the need for outside assistance. This is a great tribute to the common sense of management and labor representatives in North Carolina.—*Biennial Report of the Department of Labor, 1961-1963* (Raleigh, N. C., 1964), p. 57.

199. "RISING INSURANCE FIRM: A SYMBOL OF ENTERPRISE"

At the invitation of *The Christian Science Monitor,* President Asa T. Spaulding wrote a long article, entitled "Rising Insurance Firm: A Symbol of Enterprise," which appeared in the September 16, 1960, edition. In 1964 this article was reprinted in an attractive booklet and circulated by the company which has been headed by Mr. Spaulding since 1959. Many illustrations, including one of the New Home Office Building, were added to this reprint.

THE NORTH CAROLINA Mutual Life Insurance Company of Durham, North Carolina, is more than a business institution—it is a Symbol: a symbol of Negro enterprise, faith, courage, initiative, industry, determination, perseverance and integrity. It is *the largest Negro owned and operated business in the world,* and is a shining example of what can happen in America. It ranks as Number 185 among all the life insurance companies operating in this Country, more than 1400 of them.

It is a far cry, however, from that day in 1899, when the presentation of the first death claim to the Company for payment in the amount of $40.00 created such a crisis that it necessitated calling a meeting of the Board of Directors to raise the money with which to pay it, to this day when a claim for a thousand times that amount can be paid without notice to or knowledge of the Board of Directors.

From an income of only $393.95, insurance in force of only $247.92, and assets of only $350.00 for the year 1899, the annual income now exceeds $19,000,000.00, the insurance in force is now more than $347,000,000.00, and the assets have passed $82,000,000.00. (Figures as of December 31, 1963.)

To appreciate fully what this means one must think back to the time and conditions surrounding the organization of the Company, October 20, 1898. The Negro in America was then less than forty years from slavery. The people upon whom the company was to be built were more or less poverty stricken, illiterate, superstitious, and suspicious. Their mortality rate was so high and they were dying so fast that many people were predicting that the "Negro Problem in America would soon solve itself by the Negro race dying out."

Need was in evidence everywhere. It was not unusual in those days, when a death occurred, to pass a hat at the cemetery for a collection to help the family of the deceased with the last illness and burial expenses. Furthermore, prominent citizens in the community were solicited also whether they were present at the funeral or not. Two people in Durham who were seldom missed were a Negro barber, John Merrick, who operated a barbershop for whites, and Dr. A. M. Moore, a young Negro physician. It was not long before they began to feel that something should be done in an organized and systematized way to alleviate this problem. Although they had no knowledge of nor experience in the life insurance business, they did have some familiarity with fraternal organizations.

Upon the call of John Merrick, a meeting with six other men (A. M. Moore, P. W. Dawkins, T. D. Watson, W. G. Pearson, E. A. Johnson, and J. E. Shepard) was held on October 20, 1898, and the North Carolina Mutual and Provident Association was organized as a mutual assessment association. It was incorporated February 28,

1899, by a special act of the legislature of North Carolina, with the Motto: "Merciful to All," written into the Charter.

The Association began business on April 1, 1899, in the office of Dr. Moore, with a carpenter-made desk, at a cost of four dollars, and four or five chairs constituting the office equipment, and the rental rate being two dollars per month, but it did not do so well. Its acceptance by the public was poor indeed. In 1900 a reorganization took place. All of the original organizers except John Merrick and Dr. A. M. Moore severed their connection with the Association. John Merrick continued as President and Dr. A. M. Moore as Secretary-Treasurer and Medical Director, and C. C. Spaulding was brought into the organization as General Manager (janitor, bookkeeper, salesman, and manager). For the next nineteen years, the management team of Merrick, Moore, and Spaulding directed the affairs of the Association with faith, courage, industry, determination, skill, and integrity. The experiences of these men in the early years of this business venture is a story within itself. John Merrick died in 1919 and Dr. A. M. Moore succeeded him as president. . . .

The story of the growth and development of North Carolina Mutual and Provident Association can very well be divided into three twenty-year periods. By the end of the first period (1899 through 1919) the premium income was $1,224,541.69, assets were $755,744.26, and insurance in force was $26,534,549.00. Also during 1919, the Charter of the Association was amended changing the name to "North Carolina Mutual Life Insurance Company."

Many were the disappointments and discouragements as well as the achievements during the first twenty years of North Carolina Mutual and Provident Association operations.

The late C. C. Spaulding described some of his early experiences as follows:

"I was manager, agent, clerk, and janitor and had to do local collecting as well as organize new fields in the adjacent counties. Mr. Merrick and Dr. Moore served without salaries . . . while I took to the field on a commission basis. . . . I learned to talk insurance on my first trip for I had to depend upon my success in selling insurance for my traveling expenses." He was stranded in Sanford on this trip. A white salesman recognized his embarrassment and gave him the additional 25 cents he needed to purchase his train ticket to Raleigh, his next stop.

Mr. Spaulding's success in Raleigh was no better than in Sanford. He said: "I tried to hustle insurance but everywhere met with discouragement. My friends, and others whom I tried to interest, were sympathetic and appreciative of the effort to establish an insurance company but they did not believe it could be done. They advised me on every hand not to waste my time. . . . Some flatly ridiculed the idea of a Negro insurance company. . . ."

The second twenty years, 1920-1939, included the eventful period between World War I and World War II. Unlike the beginning of the Association's first twenty years, many of the doubts, suspicions, and fears had now been proved unfounded. The demands on the treasury caused by the influenza epidemic of 1918, had been successfully met with more than $100,000 in influenza extra claims paid with dispatch. Consequently, despite the ravages of the depression during the second twenty-year period, the Company's growth was steady. In only one year in the midst of the depression of the 1930's did the Company show a decrease in assets.

The Company's reputation and prestige were now well established, and its future was vouchsafed.

For the year 1920, the Company's assets showed a substantial gain and reached and passed the one-million-dollar mark and was the first life insurance company managed by Negroes to reach that figure. . . .

The unusual growth of North Carolina Mutual during the last two decades has been due to several factors: (1) improved training of home office and field personnel; (2) expansion of territory to include Pennsylvania in 1938 and New Jersey in 1952; (3) addition of several new lines of insurance coverage; (4) improved economic status of the Negro and better job opportunities for him; and (5) increasing appreciation for the company by the public.

Next to his faith in God, the Negro's faith in his own life insurance companies has been one of the great contributing factors in his progress. These two great faiths are the foundation stones upon which are laid his spiritual financial security, and provide his closest unity and his greatest strength. . . .

The Company provides dignified employment to more than 1400 Negroes in more than fifty different job categories such as executives, technicians, lawyers, doctors, investment specialists, secretaries, stenographers, typists, clerks, salesmen, managers, and others. And it is serving nearly 800,000 policyholders in the District of Columbia and the States of Alabama, California, Georgia, Maryland, New Jersey, North Carolina, Pennsylvania, South Carolina, Tennessee, Illinois and Virginia. . . .

The larger significance of the North Carolina Mutual Life Insurance Company in the advancement of the Negro in America and in the life of the Twentieth Century of the world's progress cannot be measured in terms of money value. Its contributions have been inspirational and social as well as economic. And herein lies the quintessence of the merit which must be the basis for whatever value the future historian shall place upon it.

Any evaluation of the contribution of the North Carolina Mutual Life Insurance Company to the life of the Negro in the United States must be determined by the effect it has had upon the status of the Negro race, and in race relations and international relations.

At the time the Company was organized, a struggling people had received their physical emancipation but were poor and ill-prepared for the pursuit of life. Many charlatans preyed upon them with schemes and tricks to deceive them while enriching themselves. The establishment of the North Carolina Mutual meant that a new institution to promote thrift and saving had been opened to the Negroes of its section which was trustworthy and reliable. It stimulated deeper and wider faith in the honesty of Negro leaders on the part of the members of their race.

The "door of hope" to young Negro men and women of aspiration was opened and continued to swing wider and wider on its hinges as the surging stream of young humanity swept across its threshold.

Not only did this result in myriad commercial concerns springing into existence throughout the South, whose promoters were inspired and encouraged by the success of the Company, but also thousands of the young men and women of the race were uplifted because of its conspicuous achievement. . . .

To some the glass of freedom and equality for the Negro in America is "half empty"; to some it is "half full." Much depends upon the point of view. The most important thing, however, is that the glass is becoming "fuller" every day, and that is what the North Carolina Mutual story demonstrates.—*North Carolina Mutual Life Insurance Company, Durham, North Carolina . . . A Symbol* (Durham, N. C., 1964), pp. 3-4, 6, 8, 11, 16, 20, 22. First published in *The Christian Science Monitor*, September 16, 1960.

200. "BUSINESSMAN IN THE STATEHOUSE," 1954-1961

Luther H. Hodges was governor of North Carolina longer than any elective governor in the state's history. Elected Lieutenant-Governor in 1952, he became the state's Chief Executive in November 1954, upon the death of Governor William B. Umstead. In 1956, Hodges was elected "in his own right." Soon after the conclusion of his "second term," President John F. Kennedy appointed Hodges Secretary of Commerce. He held this national post throughout the Kennedy administration and during the Johnson administration until early 1965, when he resigned and returned to North Carolina, where he took over an important post in the Research Triangle. In 1962, he published an interesting book on his governorship, in which he dealt with such matters as race relations, labor problems, the Research Triangle, and the state's economic progress and problems. In the latter portion of this provocative book, Hodges made many suggestions for the improvement of state government.

SPEAKING DIRECTLY to the Negro citizens of North Carolina, I said:

"Any stigma you may have felt because of laws requiring segregation in our public schools has now been removed by the courts. No right-thinking man resents your desire for equality under the law. At the same time, no right-thinking man would advise you to destroy the hopes of your race and the white race by superficial and 'show-off' actions to demonstrate this equality. Only the person who feels he is inferior must resort to demonstrations to prove that he is not. . . .

"My earnest request of you Negro citizens of North Carolina is this: Do not allow any militant and selfish organization to stampede you into refusal to go along with this program I am proposing in the interest of our public schools; take pride in your race by attending your own schools; and make it clear that any among you who refuse to cooperate in this effort to save our public school system are not to be applauded but are to be considered as endangering the education of your children and as denying the integrity of the Negro race by refusing to remain in association with it.

"Let there be no mistake or misunderstanding about this thing. Those who would force this state to choose between integrated schools and abandonment of the public school system will be responsible if in the choice we lose the public school system for which North Carolinians of both races have fought so hard and find to our eternal sorrow the personal racial bitterness which North Carolinians of both races have avoided so successfully. We must as whites and Negroes work together to solve this problem. Men of both races of good will and faith will be needed and must be had! . . ."

In my State of the State biennial message to the General Assembly on February 11, 1957, I presented a proposed budget of over a billion dollars. It was the first in the history of North Carolina. I concluded that message with a description of a vision which I believe can be the North Carolina of the future. This "North Carolina dream" was and is:

"I see a land of thriving industry of many kinds—manufacturing, agricultural, research; with plants distributed throughout the state—east, west, north, and south, set well apart on our countryside and in well-planned small towns and medium-sized cities, drawing their workers from all the surrounding areas, without the slum conditions, the polluted air, the unmanageable congestion, and the other unwanted characteristics of the present typical American industrial center. This is a land where all workers are land owners and home owners, rather than modern-day cliff dwellers cramped in gloomy rented flats and furnished rooms; a land with prospering farms producing many different crops and no longer dependent for their existence on a one-or-two-crop market. I see in every community well constructed, modernly equipped and modernly run schools, staffed by adequately trained and adequately paid teachers, supported by an enthusiastic people who demand nothing less than the best for all children. This is a land where all citizens have sufficient economic opportunity, spare time, and education to enjoy the best there is in life through private pursuits supplemented by public cultural and recreational facilities. And in this land, looking out over all else, there are towers of colleges and universities—for it is an enlightened land—and the spires of many churches—for it is a moral land.

"This is the vision, the North Carolina dream. And it is not an unattainable thing. We have a great heritage, with past leaders who have shown us what courage and faith and hard work can do. We have the people, and the natural resources to turn this dream into eventual reality, if we but work and continue to have courage and faith in our own abilities. You and I, in the all too few years remaining to any of us, can do no more than lead our state a little of the way, but if we do this, and hand over to those who come after us the courage and the faith which were handed to us, then, God willing, this vision of North Carolina will become her destiny. . . ."

The heart and hope of North Carolina's industrial future is the Research Triangle. While it is actually a good deal more complex, the Research Triangle should be thought of as basically three things.

First, it is an actual tract of land—the five-thousand-acre Research Triangle Park spread over the beautiful central Carolina countryside, which a decade ago was empty pineland and where now a half-dozen laboratories and research buildings are a promise of even more to come. Second, the Research Triangle is the larger area surrounding the park, triangular in shape, with corners at Raleigh, Durham, and Chapel Hill—the homes of three of North Carolina's greatest institutions of higher education, North Carolina State College, Duke University, and the University of North Carolina. Finally and most important, the Research Triangle is an idea that has produced a reality—the idea that the scientific brains and research talents of the three institutions, and their life of research in many fields, could provide the background and stimulation of research for the benefit of the state and nation. In a way, the Research Triangle is the marriage of North Carolina's ideals for higher education and its hopes for material progress. . . .

In just five years the Research Triangle idea of using research facilities at universities in Chapel Hill, Durham, and Raleigh had developed into the Research Triangle Foundation, the Research Triangle Institute, and the Research Triangle Park. And they had developed into all of this. The future of the Research Triangle, with the continued support of North Carolinians, was and is unlimited. It will require more imagination, more dedication, more hard work, and more selling.

The result, however, will be worth it. It could mean, in twelve to fifteen years, a Research Triangle Institute with a staff of over a thousand. Many of these would probably come from out-of-state and would represent a payroll of several millions annually. They would buy homes and become an important part of our communities. But that would be but a small part if the Research Triangle Park develops at the same rate. Then, within twelve to fifteen years, there could be twenty industrial and governmental activities, averaging three hundred employees each, for a total of six thousand. This could represent up to $30 million in new home construction, up to $25 million in new office, laboratory, and industrial construction, up to $100 million in new income revenue and proportionate increases in every phase of business activity.

Even that is a small part of the total benefit the Research Triangle could mean for North Carolina. Where there is research, there is industry. And if the Research Triangle develops as fast as I imagine it will, then more cities, towns, and communities across North

Carolina will get their own industries, which in turn will supply more money locally. For the people of North Carolina, that means a better and a more enjoyable life. The poet Emerson once wrote, "Progress is the activity of today and the assurance of tomorrow." The Research Triangle offers North Carolina an assurance of tomorrow, but only if we remember that "progress is the activity of today". . . .

Serving as governor of North Carolina is a job for three men. One man is needed to answer the mail and to carry on the detailed work of the office. A second one is needed to get out, make speeches, and travel around the state. The third man is needed for work with special projects, such as the Research Triangle, and to plan many things necessary to insure a good future for our state. . . .

I have a strong feeling regarding the term a governor ought to be allowed to serve North Carolina. Under our state constitution, a governor can serve a four-year term and cannot succeed himself. . . . We had good reason at the time for putting this limitation of one four-year term in our constitution, but times have greatly changed since that was written nearly a hundred years ago, and today a governor should be allowed to succeed himself.

The governor usually comes into office after a hard campaign with its necessary compromises and a resulting need to proceed slowly. He simply does not have time in a single four-year period to get a full-fledged program more than just started. Seldom does he have the opportunity to complete his program or even a major part of it. When he comes into office, he has a legislature on his hands immediately, and he has numerous appointments to make as soon as his first legislature goes home. By that time, a new governor is completely embroiled in the day-to-day activities of the job, which is in itself too big for one man.

For these reasons, I suggest that the citizens of North Carolina allow their governors two successive terms of four years each. They do not have to elect him to the second term if he has not done well the first four years. But a governor ought to be given the privilege of running the second time and completing the program he has started. The people would back a governor if they believed in his program and felt he was doing an honest job. If they did not, then they would vote in a new man. . . .

The veto power should be given to North Carolina's governors. At present, our governor is the only one in the fifty states who does not have the veto power and the privilege and the responsibility of signing a bill into law. Under our present system, of course, we have generally had the kind of governors who by their influence have gotten a fairly good legislative program through the General Assembly. And, since our governors do not have the veto, we theoretically have had more responsible legislators in that they cannot pass the buck or the responsibility to the governor. I believe, however, it is getting more important day by day for the governor of North Carolina to have the authority to veto legislation he thinks bad or unnecessary.

The governor should also be given decent office quarters. I have visited many governors' offices and they are generally commodious, dignified, beautiful, and comfortable. The office of the governor of North Carolina is crowded, unattractive, and undignified. It does not even have a private wash room. If the office of our governor is to stay in the present beautiful old Capitol, then he ought to be given more room and great improvements ought to be made. I am very happy to see that the legislators have at last been given decent and dignified quarters. The new statehouse will be a magnificent edifice in keeping with North Carolina and her needs. Now something must be done for the governor's quarters.

The North Carolina General Assembly should, in a short time, consider meeting once a year instead of biennially. When I was sitting behind the governor's desk, I did not relish the idea of having to confront a legislature annually, but I realize that by doing so the legislators could tend to the state's business more efficiently and, overall, perhaps spend less time away from their homes and positions. One year, the legislature should meet to consider the budget and financial matters, and the next year it should consider other state business. . . .

Legislators should also be paid an annual salary that would be dignified and decent. The way that the pay for legislators is now handled in North Carolina is undignified and not conducive to good relations with the public. . . .

The General Assembly ought to have a continuing legislative committee to operate with specified authority during the period when the legislature is not in session. It could be called the Legislative Liaison or Legislative Reference Committee. . . .

The importance of the office of lieutenant governor should be emphasized more. . . .

A governor of North Carolina has tremendous responsibilities. And the job is getting more difficult all the time. He has large budgets to struggle with. He has a growing school system. He has the college situation to handle. He has a tremendous task, in highways, mental institutions, prisons, and many other things. And all of these things are becoming more complex and more difficult year after year. For this reason, a governor of North Carolina should have a team of his own that would carry out his program. We ought to have, in other words, a short ballot in North Carolina and let the governor appoint many of the officials now elected. We should not elect so many constitutional officers independent of the governor. . . .

There is a great need for planning on the part of the state. I said publicly on many occasions that North Carolina was far too conservative in its plans, especially for the comfort and convenience of its officials and its employees. . . .

The state has carried on some unusual experiments in approaching industrial prospects both here in the United States and abroad. Now and in the future, however, we cannot live on past momentum and we cannot take things for granted. North Carolina ought to continue aiming for national excellence by aggressive, but dignified, action. It should take part in trade fairs, not only its own but those in other parts of the country and other parts of the world. These trade fairs provide double-barreled action. They influence people from other states and they influence people inside our state.

We in North Carolina ought to take a long hard look at where our state is likely to be going in the next decade or so. We should decide now what industries North Carolina will need in the future to be a better balanced state as against the present predominance of textiles and furniture. We ought to decide soon whether or not we need steel mills, metal working, further development of electronics, or whether we should go in for some of the missiles and some of the components of satellite communications systems. The future will present many opportunities and many problems. North Carolina ought to plan ahead now to seek the opportunities it wants to solve the problems that concern it most.

The battle to raise the average per capita income of North Carolinians to or above the average per capita income of the nation is just beginning. I believe we made a successful start during my administration and that it is continuing. Before the goals can be accomplished many years will pass. More industry will have to develop here or move here. Agriculture must play an even larger part in the future. There, too, we must do forward planning and develop a long-range planning committee of leaders to project a program of agriculture for North Carolina. . . .

A great deal is right about our agricultural system in North Carolina, but some of it is not for the good of the state, and too many of us politicians have been afraid to speak out about this. I spoke out on our farm problems throughout my administration, and I was not the only one. People at the State College School of Agriculture and some of the people connected with the Extension Service did too. We preached diversification, food processing and industrialization, and pointed out that if we were not blessed with price controls, the North Carolina farmer would be in a desperate economic situation. I was criticized for my stand, particularly by the people in the eastern section. Landlords, who benefited greatly from the tenant tobacco system, were extremely critical and said I was interested only in industry. They were so wrong. . . .

Our schools in North Carolina probably give a better average or minimum instruction to our children than do the schools of most other states. But in our state the education is on the minimum side rather than the quality side. The system we have of letting the state pay practically all of the teachers' salaries and substantial parts of operating costs other than school buildings does guarantee a necessary minimum support for education, but it also tends to keep over-all support close to that minimum.

The fact we have followed the philosophy of protecting the local communities and the counties from paying more of the school expenses, particularly teachers' salaries, has hurt our school system a very great deal. It has given us what I would call a "minimum point of view." We think in terms of the over-all state system rather than in terms of quality education. There is no need in my recounting here the figures that show North Carolina is trailing badly below the average among the fifty states in the number of its students who go through high school and the number of those who finish college. It is pretty sad in comparison with other states. . . .

As we are looking ahead in North Carolina, we must also think in terms of our total population and its needs. More economic opportunities are needed for Negroes. Right now North Carolina is spending millions of dollars on our schools and colleges to train our Negro youth. When they get trained in the various professions, including engineering, for the most part they have to go out of the state and out of the South to find a job in keeping with their training and ability. This procedure ought to be changed. Perhaps the state in its various governmental agencies such as the Highway Department should set the example of furnishing employment to qualified Negroes. This would do much for the spirit of the state and for the economy and is the natural and correct thing to do. We will find that our Negro graduates as well as Negroes not so fortunate as to have college educations will do a better job if challenged and if given more equal opportunity for employment. . . .

North Carolina has been very fortunate in its highway system and its highway building program. Going back to the early 1920's, North Carolina was in the forefront of those states that looked ahead and saw the need for good roads to take care of a growing state. We were the first state in the nation to take over all of the roads on a state level, and since then we have improved far beyond what would have been done under the old system of one hundred different county road systems. We have made great progress, but now we again need to take a long look at where we are going and what our highway program is going to cost us. We should think in terms of a statewide system of roads, both primary and secondary, built entirely according to need and merit, and without any reference to political influence. . . .

We must also think more about the leisure hours of the people of North Carolina. The state has already done much in this field, but there is a need to revitalize our state parks system because it will have to accommodate increasingly large numbers of Tar Heels. We must also encourage cities and counties to do more along this line. We should set aside on a dedicated basis plots of ground in our communities, roadside parks throughout the state, and recreational centers in all the counties. This would not only take care of our own people, especially our young people who need attention, but it will take care of the tourists who are coming in by the hundreds of thousands. The tourist industry is one of North Carolina's largest.—Luther H. Hodges, *Businessman in the Statehouse* (Chapel Hill: The University of North Carolina Press, 1962), pp. 88-89, 155, 298-303, 305-8, 310-14, 316-17.

201. HIGHER EDUCATION IN NORTH CAROLINA IN RECENT YEARS

The General Assembly of 1955 established the North Carolina Board of Higher Education, a nine-member board appointed by the governor. The powers, duties, and general influence of this educational agency have been affected and modified by subsequent developments, particularly by later legislation. For instance, the General Assembly of 1963 passed, almost without fanfare, a bill revamp-

ing the entire higher education system in North Carolina. The three
major changes were: it placed the community college system under
the control of the State Board of Education and provided machinery
for the conversion of Industrial Education Centers into comprehensive
community colleges; it authorized the conversion of community colleges at Asheville, Charlotte, and Wilmington into four-year senior
institutions, and it solidified and clarified the position of the Consolidated University as the capstone of the state's system of higher
education. The General Assembly of 1965 made Charlotte College a
part of the University system. The following document is a portion
of the 1963 biennial report of the North Carolina Board of Higher
Education.

ONE OTHER FACT is notable. During the half century, 1875-1925, North
Carolina established five Negro institutions, and to this day has
more institutions than any other state. In 1962, to be specific, North
Carolina had more Negro colleges than our three neighboring states
taken together and whose plant value exceeded by more than three
million dollars the total value of the Negro colleges in these sister
states. These institutions have improved considerably in recent years
and meet a clear and demonstrable need. . . .

Graduate education has been an important part of our total efforts
in higher education from the middle of the 19th century. North
Carolina can be justly proud of its two distinguished graduate schools
of arts and sciences at the University (Chapel Hill) and at Duke
University. Similarly, we can be grateful for the sound development
of graduate work in our land-grant institutions, particularly North
Carolina State. The scope and depth of excellence that have been
achieved in its professional and graduate programs need to be better
understood by our people. In addition, graduate instruction through
the master's level is offered at a number of other institutions, private
and public.

The development of professional schools has been particularly
noteworthy: North Carolina has three medical schools (one tax-
supported, two private), four law schools (two tax-supported, two
private), three engineering schools (two tax-supported, one private),
six nursing schools (five tax-supported, one private), two agricultural
schools (tax-supported), two forestry schools (one tax-supported, the
other private), two theology schools (private), one school of design
(tax-supported), and others. Without these schools, the State would be
infinitely poorer.

Perhaps graduate and professional education are not sufficiently
understood and appreciated by the general public. This may be

true because people generally are unaware that the greatest single source of new knowledge stems from our graduate schools. Without these schools, the great advances in medicine, agriculture, science generally, and other fields could not have been made. No error could be more serious than a failure to support graduate education. Although it is expensive in dollars, time and energy, it must be done. North Carolina's graduate and professional schools must be in the mainstream of the continuing battle to add to knowledge and technology. . . .

The Governor's Commission on Education Beyond the High School has effectively, in its report, forecast the problems for the foreseeable future and made explicit a master plan. Obviously, this plan must be implemented lest we make a mockery of this excellent study.

The problems are qualitative and quantitative. The quantitative problem is easier to grasp and easier to utter. By 1970, there will be an additional 42,500 (and this figure could be higher) high school graduates clamoring for a collegiate education. Our private institutions, for understandable reasons, have indicated that they expect to be able only to provide for some 11,250 of this number. Thus, the State has no alternative to finding a way to provide for the remaining 31,250. How can this be done? The Board, in common with the Governor's Commission, believes that the problem can best be solved in the following three ways: (1) some expansion of our existing senior institutions; (2) conversion of three of our current community colleges into degree-granting institutions which are located in centers of high and expanding population; and (3) the establishment of a network of comprehensive community colleges to be located in those areas that can surely and successfully bring education to more of our people. An additional alternative is that the State find legal means of assisting financially the students who elect to attend private institutions. Only by extending education to more of our youth can we have *any* hope of lifting the economic, political and cultural conditions of our citizens. It is totally unacceptable that this good and beautiful State remain in the 46th position from the top among our fifty states in the ratio of our college age people who continue their education beyond the high school. It is no less bearable that we remain 42nd from the top in per capita income. Whatever sacrifices have to be made *must* be made.

The community college has proved itself on the national scene. It is our best and likely our only way to meet our educational obligations. This new venture speaks directly to the changing economy of our State. Within ten years, it is likely that thousands of our agricultural workers will have been supplanted by the revolutionary changes in farm technology. Tobacco, corn, cotton, and other crops are increasingly being handled by machines rather than hands. Such changes are also occurring in manufacturing and other industries. What will happen to these people? Chaos, rising juvenile delinquency, crime and empty lives can be the result. Our comprehensive community colleges, offering college parallel work, vocational and technical training and re-training, and many community services, cannot fail to ease the transition and reduce the dangers clearly inherent in the changes ahead.

Aside from the very real opportunity to attract more and more people into education and training, it is imperative that we be aware that these new senior institutions in Charlotte, Wilmington, and Asheville, and the community colleges will all be commuting institutions. Dormitory facilities will not be needed and the savings to the State and the people will run into millions of dollars. Somehow, someway, the expansion of our educational facilities must be effected. To do anything less would be economic and cultural suicide. . . .

The Commission recommended that the statutes be amended to include a definition of the purposes of the Consolidated University of North Carolina, in lieu of the particular statements now to be found there. The most significant element of this recommendation was to the effect that the University should be the only institution in the State's system of public higher education authorized to award the doctor's degree. We strongly endorse this recommendation and urge its implementation by the General Assembly. The following resolution, adopted by the Board on December 21, 1962, speaks to another important aspect of the University's development:

"The Board of Higher Education heartily agrees with the Governor's Commission on Education beyond the High School that the State can afford and adequately support only one tax-supported university, and reaffirms its confidence in the principle of consolidation of the University of North Carolina that has been in effect for more than three decades. The University, with multiple campuses, can and does give coherence, assurances of quality, and optimum use of resources within our University that are envied by other states.

"The systematic growth and strengthening of the three campuses of the University since consolidation have been significant; foreseeable demands on the University will call for even greater strength and unity if future accomplishments are to meet the requirements of the times. The Board therefore applauds the University Administration and Board of Trustees in their efforts to extend the usefulness of North Carolina State and Woman's College by creating on each of these campuses, as well as on the Chapel Hill campus, a true university environment to the end that we may have in our State one tax-supported University that ranks with the best in the land. . . ."

The Commission recommended that the community colleges in Charlotte and Wilmington be converted to four-year degree-granting institutions, and that to this end junior classes be admitted in Fall 1963. It also recommended that when Asheville-Biltmore College achieves an enrollment of 700 full-time equivalent students in college parallel programs that it also move to four-year status. We concur with these recommendations in general and originally favored the recommendation that would defer the transition of Asheville-Biltmore College. After additional study, however, we recommend that this college be permitted to plan for four-year status forthwith, with the intention of initiating the junior year in fall 1964. Recommendation of the Board concerning the financing of these institutions in the next biennium appear elsewhere in this Report.

The community colleges and the industrial education centers in North Carolina, both tax-supported institutions of post-high school grade, are completely separate systems at the present time. The community colleges are presently related to the Board of Higher Education and operate under the provisions of the Community College Act of 1957. The industrial education centers are operated under the State level supervision of the State Board of Education. Similarly, the methods of financing the two types of institutions are in no way related. The Governor's Commission recommended, consistent with the prevailing philosophy and on the advice of leaders in this field, that there be created a system of "comprehensive" community colleges having appropriate college parallel, technical-vocational, and adult education curricula responsive to the needs of the areas served by the colleges. An analysis of enrollment trends and a study of areas of the State with sufficient population density to assure the success of an institution for commuting students but lacking either public or private higher education facilities of any kind revealed the need for several additional community colleges. The Commission therefore recommended the establishment of fifteen comprehensive community colleges to be supervised by the State Board of Education. We endorse this recommendation in the realization that the community colleges and industrial education centers, which will tend to become more rather than less alike, should be brought together into one system of post-high school institutions of two-year grade. Further, it is entirely appropriate that these comprehensive two-year colleges, created to play and continue to play a versatile and flexible role between the high school and the four-year college, should be supervised by the State Board of Education. . . .

In accordance with the statutory purpose of the Board of Higher Education, and as noted in previous biennial reports, we envisage a system of higher education consisting of comprehensive community colleges, senior colleges and the University. This might be thought of as a tripartite system, all interrelated but each having responsibilities that differ in range and kind from each of the other parts. With the addition of our private institutions, junior and senior, which have played and do play a very important role, there emerges a solid educational pyramid comprised of community and junior colleges at its base, at the second level the senior colleges, and at the apex as centers of advanced study and research the universities of the State.

The Report of the Governor's Commission appropriately delineated the State's system of public higher education as consisting of the Board of Higher Education, the Consolidated University of North Carolina, the public senior colleges and the comprehensive community colleges, and reaffirmed the need for planning and coordination in higher education in these words: "The public system of post-high school education is going to grow. The times demand it. It is essential that such growth be well-planned and coordinated if the public's investment of money and energy is to produce maximum returns in terms of educational services to the people of the state. The state must have, in short, a functioning system of public higher education and not a mere aggregation of independent institutions, each pursuing its own conception of the public interest."

The Report also spoke to the responsibility of *all* for the successful functioning of the system of higher education: "constant attention must . . . be given to making our public institutions and programs function as a true system of post-high school education. This must be done . . . in order that the public funds devoted to that purpose may yield the maximum in terms of full and available educational opportunity for our people. The system . . . must be infused with a coherent sense of purpose and direction. Each element of the system must have a defined mission to serve within a framework of defined state educational policy. . . ."

Each institution has a significant role to play within the larger framework, and should aspire to excellence within its sphere of operation and work toward being the best institution of its kind to be found anywhere. The support of trustees, alumni, administrators, faculties, students and the public generally is imperative if a true system of higher education is to be developed in North Carolina. We all share this responsibility in the interests of our students, our institutions, and our State.

The State's ability to provide the facilities needed by the ever larger numbers of qualified students who will seek education beyond the high school cannot fail to be strained. Therefore, it is all the more urgent that all available facilities be used to optimum advantage. We urge therefore that each of our institutions prepare for year-round operation on academic calendars (i.e., trimesters, quarters, etc.) that will make for the most efficient use of available resources, and permit students systematically to accelerate their education.

The recommendations of the Governor's Commission concerning the University, senior colleges, and comprehensive community colleges, if enacted into law by the General Assembly, represent a significant step forward in the development of a State system of higher education and of public education in general. Public education through high school has for a number of years been available to all citizens of the State who are sufficiently motivated and capable of profiting from this opportunity. The proposal that public community colleges be established in a number of areas lacking higher educational facilities brings considerably closer the ideal of educational opportunity for all citizens who are interested in and qualified for additional education beyond high school. The individual and the State will share in the benefits to be derived from this extension of educational opportunity and, mutually, have large stakes in its development. The economic and cultural progress of society and of the individual depend upon education at ever more sophisticated levels. Occupational opportunities increasingly require education and training unheard of previously, and persons lacking appropriate vocational or professional skills in the future will increasingly and perpetually be disadvantaged in their efforts to live fruitful and satisfying lives. The challenge facing higher education is great. We have confidence that all of the people of North Carolina will accept this challenge, and that progress already achieved on a variety of fronts will continue at a quickened pace.—*1961-1963 Biennial Report, North Carolina Board of Higher Education* (Raleigh, 1964), pp. 3, 7-8, 26-27, 29, 30.

202. "A STATEMENT OF FAITH AND PURPOSE IN EDUCATION," BY GOVERNOR TERRY SANFORD

The following document is from an address at the Southern Conference on Education, University of North Carolina, Chapel Hill, November 21, 1960. James B. Conant, President Emeritus of Harvard University, said that "Sanford's program for education is far-sighted, intelligent, wonderful. It is a landmark in American education." The National Education Association declared: "Sanford's statement of faith and purpose has made many enviously wish that it could be a blueprint for governors across the country."

ON MANY OCCASIONS and in many ways I have tried to emphasize my conviction that North Carolina faces a New Day . . . bringing new opportunities, new responsibilities, an exciting future, and demanding that we be up and doing.

We North Carolinians have long understood that education is the means by which our State must reach its full potential in economic and human values.

We are justly proud of North Carolina's position. We came up the hard way, from ashes of the Reconstruction period. We have come a long route. We have no apologies. But too many of us are self-satisfied and complacent about our reputation as "first in the South," and too many think the job is finished.

The job is not finished. Whatever our success, it is not enough for the rapidly advancing, scientific, changing world we now enter. What we have really done is create new and unlimited opportunities. . . .

Quality education is the goal—and no mean goal. All others we seek for North Carolina can be measured by the quality, the scope, the reach of our efforts for better education. . . .

As Governor of North Carolina, I will work for a program which provides educational opportunity, appropriate and available, second to none in quality, for all the children of our State. I will work to obtain adequate support for that program.

The program is up to the State Board of Education, the Department of Public Instruction, the local school boards, the superintendents, the principals, the teachers and the parents.

The support is up to the General Assembly, the county and city officials, or, in other words, to the entire citizenry of North Carolina.

We have an excellent blueprint for the program. We have the people who have the ability to put it into effect.

I am confident that the people of North Carolina, believing that we can build a better state through quality education, will provide the support for this program.

In February, 1960, in Greensboro, I outlined our school needs and our State's potential, and called on the women of the State to lead a "Crusade for Education." I said then, and on numerous occasions since, that I value children more than money, and my position remains as I stated then: "I believe the people are eager to pay for quality education. They know this is the only basis for improvement. They know good men and women leave the teaching profession every month because they have to support families. They know that a disproportionately high percentage of college graduates, educated to a large degree at taxpayers' expense, leave this State to teach elsewhere because of our inadequate salaries. They know that ultimate salaries are extremely inadequate for career people. They know that to attract enough of the right quality teachers we cannot rely upon love of teaching alone, but must offer salaries commensurate with their training and education. I would not be honest if I did not promise that, if revenues are inadequate, I will have the courage to recommend to the General Assembly and the people the proper sources."

Our North Carolina plan for education might be called a "Four-star program." Its basic elements are these:

EDUCATION THAT IS APPROPRIATE

How Can We Do This?

1. Provide adequate guidance and counseling services.

2. Provide every child a sound basic education in English, mathematics, the humanities, elementary science, and the social sciences.

3. Provide education in depth in these subjects and in foreign languages for each student who can profit from such instruction.

4. Provide a sensible program of education in physical education and health.

5. In addition to the basic academic courses, provide courses in vocational and practical arts subjects.

This Should Be Provided For Every Child

The normal

The gifted

The handicapped

EDUCATION THAT IS AVAILABLE

Reach every child, no matter where he lives, with the kind of educational opportunity that will meet his needs, be adapted to his abilities, and challenge his best efforts.

How Can We Do This?

1. Provide as full a measure of state support as possible so that a sound minimum program will be in reach of every child, no matter where he lives.

2. Encourage consolidation of high schools wherever possible.

3. Provide within reach of every gifted and handicapped child special classes or boarding schools to challenge and develop his unique abilities.

4. Provide enough busses for each child to have safe transportation to and from school without undue crowding or excessively long travel time.

5. Provide as a county responsibility adequate school buildings, soundly and economically constructed, with a special state-aid bond issue to help out in this period of rapidly growing school population.

6. Expand the services of community colleges, industrial education centers, and of state-supported colleges and the university.

EDUCATION THAT IS EXCELLENT

See to it that the educational opportunity that is made appropriate and available is excellent in quality, both in terms of the opportunity itself, and in terms of the student's effort as he responds to the challenge placed before him.

How Can We Do This?

1. Insure full cooperation of all who are concerned with public education: the students, the parents, the teachers, the public.

2. Pay teachers salaries that are competitive with those in other states and in other professions.

3. Give strong support to teacher education, including scholarships for teachers.

4. Strengthen the program of up-grading the education of teachers now on the job.

5. Give teachers time to teach. This means that interruptions and non-teaching duties must be reduced to a minimum.

6. Give students time to learn. This means that conflicting demands on student time and effort would be eliminated.

7. Provide enough teachers so that students will not have to try to learn in crowded classes.

8. Provide all the libraries, shops, laboratories, textbooks, instruction by television, and other teaching aids that are needed.

9. Provide adequate support for enough non-instructional personnel work as janitors, maintenance people, and clerical employees to operate an efficient school.

10. Be sure that thoroughly trained guidance people are employed.

11. Insist on strong, well-prepared leadership on both the state and local level.

12. Encourage constant research to discover better ways of providing a good educational program.

EDUCATION THAT IS SUPPORTED

Support with money, with understanding, with encouragement, and determination the kind of program that will make appropriate and excellent educational opportunity available to every child in North Carolina, no matter who he is or where he lives.

How Can We Do This?

1. In 1960-61, North Carolina's average expenditure is estimated at $240 per child while the national average is $390. We can come closer to this national average if we are willing to try. In the next ten years, we can exceed the national average. Our children are worth it.

2. We must make teaching more attractive as a profession. Money is part of this but not all.

3. We must give more recognition to truly dedicated and excellent teachers.

4. Parents and other citizens must give strong support to local and state school authorities as they attempt to consolidate schools, eliminate waste in the school day, and develop a sounder and better financial school program.

5. Students must accept responsibility for learning.

—From a pamphlet printed and distributed by North Carolina Citizens Committee for Better Schools (Raleigh, 1961), pp. 1-12.

203. "THE GOOD NEIGHBOR PROGRAM" AND "THE GOOD NEIGHBOR COUNCIL"

North Carolina escaped many of the problems encountered by some Southern states in the matter of public school desegregation. By 1965 many of the state's public schools were desegregated. The state also made progress in "integration" at eating places, theaters, and the like—progress which was too slow for some of the state's citizenry and too rapid for others, but progress all the same. Governor Sanford received favorable national publicity for the role he played in the peaceful adjustment to "integration."

The first document below is Sanford's announcement of "The Good Neighbor Program" on January 18, 1963; the second is a statement by the governor at the first meeting of "The Good Neighbor Council."

"THE GOOD NEIGHBOR PROGRAM"

IN NORTH CAROLINA we will attempt to provide leadership for the kind of understanding America needs today.

To carry out these hopes we will do five things right now:

1. We have established the North Carolina Good Neighbor Council.

It will consist of 24 outstanding citizens of the State.

We will also name an additional advisory committee to reach more sections of the economy and the State.

The Council will have a two-fold mission (1) to encourage employment of qualified people without regard to race, and (2) to urge youth to become better trained and qualified for employment.

2. We are asking all Mayors and Chairmen of County Commissioners to establish local Good Neighbor Councils.

3. We have issued a memorandum to heads of State agencies, departments, and institutions, asking them, if they have not already done so, to examine and formulate policies which do not exclude from employment qualified people because of race.

4. Being aware that complete success cannot be achieved without wise and vigorous leadership from private business and industry, we will conduct a conference this spring, inviting leading industrialists and businessmen to participate.

5. We call on church leaders, pastors, civic organizations, to support the objectives of the Good Neighbor Councils in their own effective ways.

—Press Release, Governor's Office, January 18, 1963.

GOVERNOR SANFORD'S STATEMENT AT MEETING OF "THE
GOOD NEIGHBOR COUNCIL," RALEIGH, JULY 3, 1963

We are just going to have to open up jobs for all people on the basis of ability and training, and promotions on the basis of performance.

I believe this should be done, can be done and will be done by North Carolina people because it is right morally and because economically we cannot afford to do otherwise.

I do not intend to try to force anybody. I do not believe in force. I do believe the conscience of North Carolinians will get this done.

The Industrial Education Centers, training people in new skills, have the policy that there must be no racial discrimination in admissions to courses. We cannot have it any other way. These schools are supported by state, local and federal funds and they are open to anyone who can qualify. . . .

There will not be any discrimination in State jobs. Such discrimination is both unconstitutional and undemocratic. Negroes are invited to apply, just as all other citizens, to Walter Fuller, State Personnel Officer, and their applications will be judged solely on merit and ability.

I hope private employers will continue to examine their employment policies, and will join with other citizens of good will in wiping away the last remnants of economic discrimination. In North Carolina we will do this, not in token degree because it is forced by law, but in full and fair degree because it is the proper and decent thing to do. I am pleased with the initial voluntary reaction of North Carolina employers, and I am sure we will soon see the general end of policies which deny full economic opportunity to citizens who have the training and ability to do the job.

I also urge all leaders of the Negro communities to get across the message that jobs are being opened up, and that it is important, yes urgent, that young people take advantage of all training to earn the qualifications which will fit them for these jobs. This advice, of course, applies to all youth.—Press Release, Governor's Office, July 3, 1963.

204. NORTH CAROLINA FUND EXPERIMENT LAUNCHED, 1963

Governor Sanford called the North Carolina Fund "the first massive statewide effort in our country to break the cycle of poverty and dependency." By March, 1965, the Fund had undertaken these programs: a comprehensive school improvement program administered by the State Board of Education and financed by $2 million from the Fund and $2 million from the state; the North Carolina Volunteers, a type of Peace Corps experiment, with college students working during the summer in 11 project areas comprising 20 counties; "Community action technicians" to train for service in nonprofessional jobs in communities which have action programs against poverty; The Learning Institute of North Carolina (LINC), an agency working to promote learning techniques; and 25 community service consultants working under the State Department of Public Welfare.

GOVERNOR TERRY SANFORD on September 30 announced the launching of a privately financed five-year experiment in education and related research to combat poverty in the State. About $14 million in donations is expected under the North Carolina Fund, established in July. During the summer nearly $10 million was dedicated to the Fund. The Ford Foundation provided $7 million. The Mary Reynolds Babcock Foundation granted the Fund $875,000, payable over a five-year period. The Z. Smith Reynolds Foundation voted the Fund $325,000 a year for the first two years, and gave notice it would grant an equal amount in each of the following three years, for a total of $1,625,000.

About three-quarters of the funds will go into projects in about 10 representative communities, seeking to identify causes and remedies of school dropouts, poverty, and chronic welfare cases. Some of the communities to be named will be those in rural areas, and some will be in urban centers. Control will be local, with participation and commitment of governmental and community agencies concerned with the problems.

Administration of the Fund and its programs for a five-year period is to be financed within a $500,000 portion of the Ford Foundation grant. About $4.5 million from Ford will go to the projects in 10 or more communities of the State, and about $2 million will finance a special project requested by the State Board of Education to find ways to improve the learning of reading, writing and arithmetic in primary grades. Studies previously made in North Carolina indicate that inadequate achievement in these subjects produces dropouts in later years of school. Most of the funds committed from the Reynolds and Babcock foundations are to be used in the community projects.

Henry T. Heald, President of the Ford Foundation, released a statement calling the North Carolina Fund movement an imaginative effort "in city and rural areas." He said it is the first state-wide program to be assisted by a grant from the Ford Foundation. Heald stated, "It is of national significance that the full resources of a state, including local philanthropic foundations, are being applied to realistic plans for a coordinated effort to develop human resources to the fullest. In so doing, North Carolina leadership may well set a pace for other states."—*North Carolina Public School Bulletin,* Vol. XXVIII, No. 3, November, 1963.

205. "North Carolina: Dixie Dynamo"

One of the most interesting articles about modern North Carolina appeared in the *National Geographic* in February, 1962. Written by Malcolm Ross, a native of New Jersey and now living in Florida, this article referred to the state as the "Dixie Dynamo" and described most of the cities and many areas of the state. It was an impressionistic account and some newspaper editors thought it presented too rosy a picture of the state and its people. Only a small portion of the article is reprinted below. More factual details about the state's economy are to be found in other documents in this volume.

I traveled all over the State, everywhere asking people why North Carolina is changing so rapidly.

A Tar Heel electronics worker said the changes came with new black-top roads—which let a man work in town while still living on three-acres-and-a-cow up the hollow.

A college president said that the changes started about half a century ago with new schoolhouses for many a Tar Heel community.

An ex-paratrooper said it was a matter of spirit. "The spirit of North Carolinians is that they can do anything they want to do," he declared. "In education, industry, natural resources, agriculture —in all activities our goal is not to be the best in the South but the best in the Nation." The World War II combat veteran who uttered these confident words was Governor Terry Sanford. . . .

My tourist eyes saw the Shackleford Banks as tawny gold dunes speckled with the silver of sand-drowned cedars. To our Outer Banks skipper, however, the sand was a shroud, burying the village where his kinsfolk once lived so contentedly. . . .

Much depends on your point of view—and the weather. I have seen North Carolina's 6,684-foot Mount Mitchell, highest point east of the Mississippi, in all its solid superiority. I have also watched it melt into the impalpable mists and into obscurity. . . .

Driving through the State, I had been impressed with the large, unbroken tracts of forest. Timber seems abundant almost everywhere. Therefore I was astonished to learn that there are actually shortages among plenty. Certain valuable hardwood species are in greater demand than supply.

Resources may be limited, but is resourcefulness? Not in North Carolina! The large quantity of solid walnut that was made into great-grandmother's dresser is now stretched to cover some twenty items of furniture, in the form of carefully cut and matched veneer sheets of undiminished beauty. . . .

Among Tar Heels and outsiders, Chapel Hill means primarily one thing—the University of North Carolina. . . . The young university, born almost simultaneously with the Thirteen Original States, took its familiar name from a hill where New Hope Chapel stood. And almost at once Chapel Hill began weaving its academic way into the warp and woof of the State. The habit, I found, persists: Within minutes of my first Chapel Hill interview, the Research Triangle cropped up again.

Professor George L. Simpson of the Department of Sociology, the first director of the Research Triangle Committee, had just returned from New York, where he had explained to prominent industrialists the chief advantages of the Triangle area of North Carolina.

"Wooing them south?" I asked.

"Not wooing," Simpson smiled. "They will come only if it makes hard sense. We want them to think of the Triangle when they build a laboratory. Modern industry's biggest asset is its skilled researchers. Know any better way to keep them happy than by moving them to North Carolina?" . . .

We crossed the bridge from Roanoke Island to Nags Head, vacation center of that 300-mile-long wonder, the Outer Banks. . . . Summer on the Banks is gentle to the visitor, who, with the roads and ferries across the inlets, has at his command one of the world's great playgrounds—leagues of ocean beaches to seaward, and many gentler waters southward, lagoons and ponds with ducks and terns. There are the inlets, where fish pass from sea to sound, and then give the fisherman a second chance when they move with the tide back out to sea.

But below Whalebone for 80 miles to the tip of Ocracoke, [is] the first national seashore recreational area. . . . About midway in those

80 miles stands Cape Hatteras Light, aged guardian of North Carolina's dread hurricane-swept graveyard for ships.

The same sea winds that helped to pile up the Banks bore aloft in 1903 a wood-wire-and-canvas contraption near Kitty Hawk—and changed man's life forever. We visited the memorial honoring those two Dayton, Ohio, bicycle makers, Wilbur and Orville Wright, near their first test site at Kill Devil Hill.

It was the English who, founding their first permanent colony in the New World at Jamestown in 1607, gradually extended their exploration southward and established a foothold in North Carolina.

Following their route, we came to that outpost, North Carolina's first town—Bath, on the Pamlico River. Bath seems to sleep in the memory of past grandeur. No traffic moves on its shaded main street at noontime, and veranda-rocking occupies a good part of everyone's day. Silence wraps a river harbor once crowded with colonial shipping.

Bath eventually gave way to Edenton on Albemarle Sound as a colonial center. Nearer to Virginia, and blessed with rich bottomlands, Edenton put up fine houses with money from the export of great barrels of shad and herring and from the tobacco that flourished on the plantations of the sound.

Southward, at the junction of the Neuse and Trent Rivers, we toured New Bern, the last colonial capital of North Carolina before the Revolutionary buff uniform replaced the British red coat. Governor William Tryon's Palace—capitol as well as residence—has been restored at a cost of some $3,500,000. The story is one of the determination of indomitable women, liberally mixed with luck.

The idea of restoring the palace was gradually conceived some years ago in North Carolina. The only part surviving a 1798 fire and the years since was the west wing. Forty houses had been built over the original palace square. The architect's plans had disappeared. Governor Tryon had taken his furnishings to New York, where fire destroyed them in 1773 at his home at Fort George.

But that didn't stop Miss Gertrude S. Carraway. She discovered the detailed plans in the New York Historical Society library.

Mrs. Maude Moore Latham, of Greensboro, began collecting period pieces—to furnish a palace that wasn't there! She established trust funds of $350,000. When she died in 1951, the residue of her estate was bequeathed for the palace restoration. In 1952 Governor Tryon's inventory of his books and furniture came to light in England.

North Carolina appropriated $227,000 to buy about one-third of the property now included in the restoration area. Thanks to Mrs. Latham's generous bequest, the rest of the site was purchased and deeded by the Tryon Palace Commission to the State, which maintains and operates the restored building. . . .

From New Bern's quiet past we stepped into the supersonic future, by way of the United States Marines' 11,500-acre Cherry Point Air Station, down the Neuse River.

Another day we visited Fort Macon on Beaufort Inlet, whose protecting jetties were designed in 1840-41 by a young West Pointer, Lt. Robert E. Lee. Capt. Josiah Pender and 50 young Confederates seized it in 1861 and held it a year. Then, Union Gen. John G. Parke of Burnside's expedition took the fort and hauled down Pender's home-made Stars and Bars. Fort Macon never changed hands again in the war. . . .

Our last coastal stop was Wilmington, the Tar Heel State's largest port. Since earliest times, the stretch of the Cape Fear River where shallow-draft plantation boats met deepwater vessels was the logical place for a seaport. Wilmington it became.

The tar, pitch, and turpentine of the 1700's have given way to seed potatoes and tobacco leaf, bound for Pakistan or Hamburg, Germany. Heavy gantry cranes tower above the docks. They lift unprocessed New Zealand sheepskins, which a North Carolina firm processes and reships as chamois. They lower away 450-pound bales of a dried wild coastal plant called deer tongue, destined for the flavoring in European cigarettes. . . .

Leaving Raleigh, we headed for High Point, "Furniture Capital of the World." Here in the Piedmont is an industrial counterpart of the Research Triangle: High Point, Greensboro, and Winston-Salem. North Carolina makes half the bedroom furniture for the Nation and more than a third of its diningroom furniture. Wood furniture, that is. . . .

Even among the Piedmont's great textile firms, Burlington Industries, Inc., with headquarters in Greensboro, is a giant. It is the world's largest manufacturer of textiles—some 140 plants, 65,000 employees, and net sales of more than $866,000,000 a year.

From Burlington's diversified textile complex comes virtually every type of fabric and textile product. The company spins, knits, weaves, dyes, and finishes in modern plants located in 16 States and seven foreign countries—but almost half of its operations are located in North Carolina. . . .

Research is vital to the R. J. Reynolds Tobacco Company at Winston-Salem, which has 27 Ph.D.'s on its research staff. They live and think tobacco, whose flat green patches on the coastal plain and rolling fields in the highlands brighten the landscape along many North Carolina highways.

Tobacco is a crop with several costumes: a white patch of cloth over a spring seedbed; the green pyramids crowned in summer with pink bouquets; and at last the rows of brown tepees of cut leaf in the fields. . . .

If Winston-Salem's eye is on the tobacco crop, it is also on the stars. A few miles from R. J. Reynolds are three Western Electric Company plants that make guidance systems or component parts for the anti-missile missile Nike Zeus, a vital weapon in the Nation's future defense arsenal. How Western Electric does this is a very well kept secret. . . .

Five minutes' drive from Western Electric brought us to Salem— meaning "peace" in Biblical language—dedicated in 1766. The hyphen joined Winston to Salem in 1913. . . . Forty of Salem's sixty original buildings still stand on the quiet streets near the public square: some houses of log and white clapboard and many of rosy brick with hooded doorways and eyebrow-arched windows. More than twenty buildings have been restored, and six of them are open to visitors. . . .

Beyond Winston-Salem to the west lie North Carolina's mountains. A pale-blue silhouette takes shape as a solid range, the incomparable Blue Ridge. The sun scatters bright patches in the dense shade and highlights flashing mountain streams. Vine and wild flower, moss and fern, live in a manner of their own choosing. . . .

Every traveler to the mountains faces a painful decision—what special part to make his own. Will it be Boone, Chimney Rock, Highlands, Franklin, perhaps Cherokee? This choice of a favorite place, multiplied by tens of thousands of visitors each summer, is a most important happening in the mountains of North Carolina.

The western highlands were practically unknown to lowlanders before the 1920's. True, there were a few resorts. In the 1890's, for example, the summit of Roan Mountain reached by carriage from the valley railroad, had a wooden hotel from whose veranda spread out the world's most glorious display of rose-colored rhododendron.

The hunting set found the thermal belt around Tryon most agreeable. Here and there were pillared hotels with links for the itinerant golfer.

But America on wheels awaited the bulldozer to carve a road over the mile-high peaks of the Blue Ridge and make corkscrew ascents into sweeping curves.

This mile-high summit [Grandfather Mountain] commands a brilliant panorama. Hugh Morton inherited it together with the problem of what to do with 5,000 more-or-less perpendicular acres. His solution was to build a road to the top and string a bridge between Grandfather's nether and upper lips. So now you can stand dizzily on Grandfather's nose and see what appears to be the whole world beneath you.

"Tweetsie" at Blowing Rock is another attraction. . . . Retired steam locomotives are now collectors' items, but a Blowing Rock businessman rescued Tweetsie from an outlander and set her to hauling three diminutive cars packed with delighted passengers around and around Roundhouse Mountain.

The mountains were settled about the time of the Revolution by homestead seekers who came with their worldly goods on their backs. In the 1880's the railroad pushed through to Asheville, and a second Northern invasion came by Pullman and private car.

George Washington Vanderbilt liked everything he saw and bought it. His 125,000 acres reached from the edge of Asheville beyond Mount Pisgah. While a thousand workers were engaged five years in creating a French chateau of 250 rooms called Biltmore House, Vanderbilt toured Europe in search of treasures of ancient Rome and the Orient, the Renaissance and later European periods up to his own times.

For all that, Vanderbilt's contribution to the conservation of forest, field, and stream far outshines Biltmore's limestone walls and stately rooms. To plant, tend, and improve his huge private forest, Vanderbilt had the help of Gifford Pinchot, father of U. S. conservation, and Frederick Law Olmsted, one of the designers of New York's Central Park.

Today some of Vanderbilt's original acres form a generous section of Pisgah National Forest, the pride of every Tar Heel. In its 480,000 majestic acres wild animals have cover, trout swim in clear streams, and great trees stand guard.

Thanks to careful management, North Carolina's forest lands serve industry as well as wildlife. Take Champion Papers, Inc., at Canton.

Canton lies in a valley between the Blue Ridge and the Smokies. There a pungent smell emerges from Champion's huge stacks. From the company's loading platforms 900 tons of paper roll away each day for worldwide destinations.

Champion is a child of the forest. Twelve hundred cords of pine and 600 cords of hardwood are daily digested. But the company pays it back: Champion has planted 30 million seedlings on its 300,000-acre holdings in the Carolina area. . . .

All this we saw on our way to Fontana Dam, the highest dam in the eastern United States, whose 480 feet of concrete impound a 10,530-acre lake and produce electric power for cities far beyond North Carolina's borders.

The next morning we stood in Joyce Kilmer Memorial Forest, within a Tar Heel's wave of the Tennessee border—and our trip was done.

We had seen North Carolina from the sands of Hatteras to the lofty Smokies. We had talked, danced, eaten, and played with Tar Heels from Kitty Hawk to Cherokee—and loved every minute of it. Now it was time to go home and tell the story.

As we stood there, the cloud—or maybe it was mist—that blanketed our mountaintop drifted away, and the sun came out full and strong on the great trees, on the rocks, on the valley far below. North Carolina was bright with sun and promise.—"North Carolina: Dixie Dynamo," *National Geographic,* Vol. 121, No. 2, February, 1962, pp. 142-43, 146, 151-53, 157, 159, 161-64, 173-77, 179-83.

206. GOVERNOR DAN K. MOORE'S PROGRAM FOR A GREATER NORTH CAROLINA

Governor Moore's legislative message of February 4, 1965, presented a program that "will move North Carolina closer to the goal of a more abundant life for every citizen." Reprinted below are some of his most important recommendations.

PUBLIC EDUCATION

IF NORTH CAROLINA stands on the threshold of an era of unprecedented prosperity, as we have every reason to believe it does, then the path we must follow to achieve that goal is education. It is the first responsibility of State Government and it must be given attention commensurate with that responsibility by this General Assembly.

Much progress has been made in education in recent years. Even now plans are being made across the State to utilize fully the $100 million school bond issue for capital improvements which the General Assembly authorized, which I advocated and the people approved.

But, North Carolina is still behind in a great many areas of education, and now we must take specific steps to catch up.

I recommend that this General Assembly:

First, reduce class size by three in grades one through three, and by one in grades four through twelve.

Second, provide a salary increase of 5 per cent for public school instructional personnel for the first year of the biennium and 5 per cent for the second.

Third, provide additional guidance counsel and remedial teachers.

Fourth, restore the continuing contract for our teachers.

Fifth, extend the term of employment for public school principals.

Sixth, relieve students and parents of the burden of paying necessary school and book fees and initiate a study to find ways of eliminating unnecessary fees, and

Seventh, strengthen our school lunch program to insure that hunger is banished forever from the classrooms of North Carolina.

North Carolina should spare no effort to reduce the drop-out problem. We must expand the vocational training program for both young people and adults. Special classes must be provided for the emotionally ill and the retarded and for the gifted. The first responsibility, however, is to the average student; and the second is to the teacher on whom the success of any educational program rests.

We must appraise and reappraise the various experimental programs now being conducted in education. If in the judgment of our State education officials, these experiments show promise, they will be continued. If not, they should be discontinued, and new avenues sought to meet the growing challenge of education.

I strongly oppose any federal control in the North Carolina public schools system. In these changing times, however, we recognize that the federal government has involved itself in public education. There are now new laws and regulations which will change the way many of our schools are operated. As much as we dislike these changes, I remind you of our State's proud heritage as a peaceful and law-abiding people. The law must be obeyed.

HIGHER EDUCATION

North Carolina must act now to insure that its every son and daughter with a capacity for college work is given the incentive and the opportunity to attend a college of exceptional quality. This is a goal of my administration.

Our State-supported institutions of higher learning must be expanded physically and academically. I am deeply concerned about the capital improvement needs of our State colleges and the University. This is a matter which deserves your careful consideration, and I expect to speak directly to this problem in my budget message to follow at a later date.

Our facilities for vocational training, our Industrial Education Centers and our Technical Institutes, must continue to expand. Full support must be given to the community college. We must be concerned with and we must give every possible encouragement to the private and church-related institutions that have contributed so much to the well-being of North Carolina.

The University of North Carolina is today and will remain the single most important factor in higher education in our State. I am convinced of the value of the One University concept, and I will vigorously oppose any effort to deprive this State of the positive benefits of consolidation. We must strengthen rather than weaken the total University at Greensboro, at Raleigh and at Chapel Hill. In addition, I strongly recommend that the fourth campus of the University be located at Charlotte as proposed by the University Trustees and approved by the State Board of Higher Education. . . .

ROAD BONDS

To meet North Carolina's ever expanding road construction needs, I recommend that you authorize a $300 million road bond issue, subject to a vote of the people, to be spent over a five-year period. Of this $300 million, I recommend that $150 million be spent on the primary system, that $75 million be used for highways within our municipalities, and that $75 million be used for secondary roads. Where it would appear to be more economical, I urge that these roads be constructed by free enterprise upon the basis of competitive bids.

I recommend that this bond issue be financed within the present tax structure utilizing the 1 cent per gallon tax which has financed the secondary road bond issue of 1949. This tax can adequately provide for the $300 million bond issue after the 1949 bond issue is provided for in 1966. Until this is accomplished, I recommend that the debt service for the new bonds be derived from current revenues of the Highway Fund. . . .

INDUSTRIAL DEVELOPMENT

Industrial development is an important key to providing more jobs, more job opportunities and a better way of life for all our people. Creation of new local industries, expansion of existing industries and the location in North Carolina of new out-of-state industries will be major goals of my administration. The direct result will be a higher per capita income for our people. . . .

NATURAL RESOURCES

Our natural resources are a sacred trust passed from one generation to the next as a foundation upon which to build a better State. We are fortunate in the abundance of our resources. We have done well in beginning to conserve and develop these gifts of nature. The job is not completed, however, and our programs must be maintained or accelerated.

In forestry, we have set the pace in the Southeast but the job is far from finished. Our mineral resources must be more fully developed. Our park system is one of the finest in the country, but it has room for improvement. There is still work to be done to protect our Outer Banks and other Coastal areas. Our soils and our wildlife must be conserved. Our water resources are becoming more and more important. We must maintain our efforts to insure adequate supplies of clean, useable water for the future. . . .

HUMAN RELATIONS

Continued progress in human relations is essential. Substantial progress has been made in recent years. Some feel we have moved too fast; others, that we have moved too slowly.

I believe and sincerely hope that we in North Carolina have come to a time of calm and sensible reappraisal in this area. North Carolinians generally have become more rational and more tolerant of the views of others and they have a better understanding of the reasons for these views.

However, a time of reappraisal is not a time for complacency. The problems have not passed. They will require our constant and sincere attention in the days ahead. I am initiating a study of the role State Government is playing in this area through such agencies as the Good Neighbor Council. If these programs are meeting the need, they should be continued. If not, we will find new programs. . . .

AGRICULTURE

Agriculture has a time-honored place in the life and the economy of North Carolina. If our State is to move across the threshold of greatness where we now stand, our agriculture and related industry will have to provide much of the impetus. For this reason, my administration is going to give vigorous attention to all of the opportunities, as well as the problems, of agriculture.

Tobacco, our major crop, is being threatened as never before, both by over production and by a health scare. We are going to spare no effort to resolve the difficulties that confront our 165,000 tobacco farm families, and in turn, that large segment of our economy geared to tobacco. And, I include here the 40,000 North Carolinians who earn their livelihood from the manufacture of tobacco products.—*Legislative Message of Governor Dan K. Moore to the North Carolina General Assembly, February 4, 1965*, pp. 4-5, 7, 9, 11-12.

INDEX